INTERNATIONAL
INTERIORS

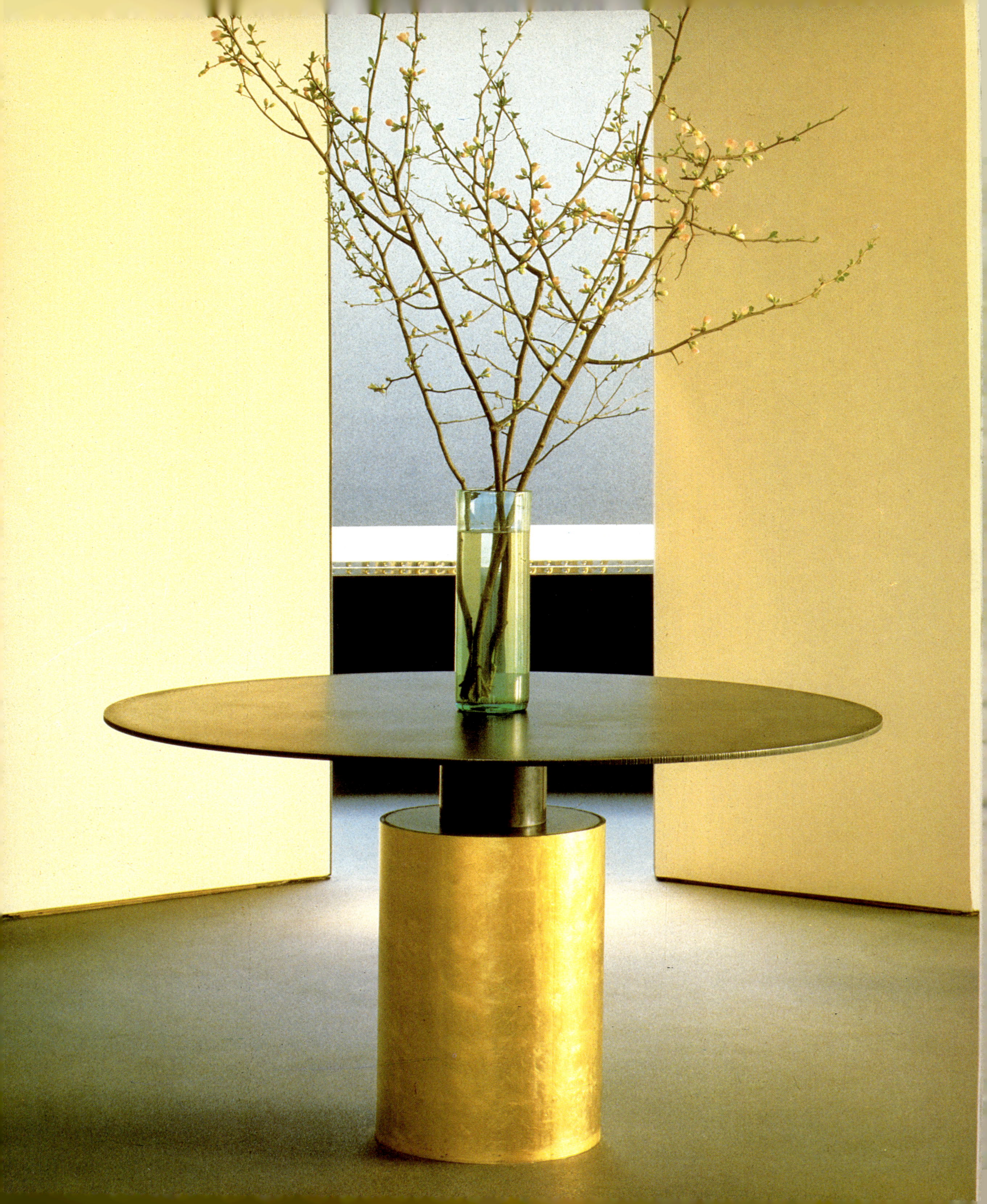

Offices · Restaurants · Bars · Clubs · Hotels · Shops · Cultural and Sports Buildings

INTERNATIONAL INTERIORS

LANCE KNOBEL

T & H

THAMES AND HUDSON

First published in Great Britain in 1988 by
Thames and Hudson Ltd, London

Assistant Editors
Helen Buttery and Jane Lamacraft

Front jacket illustration and frontispiece: Vignelli Associates, New York City, designed by Vignelli Associates (photographs by Luca Vignelli).
Back jacket illustration: The Gallery of Lanerossi, Tokyo, designed by Yasuo Kondo (photograph by Hiroyaki Hirai).

This book was designed and produced by
John Calmann and King Ltd, London
Designer Richard Foenander

Typeset by Black Box Ltd
Printed in Spain by Cayfosa

CONTENTS

INTRODUCTION

This volume is intended to be a unique selection of the most important commercial interior designs of the last two or three years from around the world. Attempts have been made to find worthy projects from as many countries as possible; there are exciting examples included from as far afield as the USA, Britain, Japan, France, Spain, West Germany, Austria, Finland, Italy and Australia. Thus the book provides a valuable international forum for different design ideas, allowing cross-fertilization between Japanese and American designers, Italian and British, Scandinavian and French; for this is a far wider survey than any offered by the few magazines (largely nationally focused) that feature contract design. In addition, many of the interiors are unpublished elsewhere, such as Ron Arad's The Bureau, or the somewhat bizarre designs of Finnish architect Leo Mitrunen. The selection has been made using the author's network of contacts in this field, by a process which has involved intensive research and several trips abroad over the last two years.

The offices, stores, restaurants, bars, galleries and other public buildings in the book exemplify both the most original and the most practical currents in modern design. Importantly, many also display an especially creative use of new techniques and new technology. Although the criteria for the inclusion of different projects vary, a number of considerations arose in most cases: first, aesthetic impact; second, the imaginative use of space, no matter how small or awkward; third, lasting style; fourth, innovation in finishes, materials and graphics; fifth, the thoughtful use of budget; and last, but especially important, functional success – did each interior enable the visitor to eat, drink, shop, work or enjoy himself in comfort? An office in which it was difficult to work, or which imposed an inappropriate system of management, would clearly be an unsatisfactory design, no matter how stunning initial visual impressions were. Apple's Advanced Computer Development Center (pp. 40–3) shows that providing a clearly functional environment is not incompatible with a strong design conveying an important message about corporate identity; and even Richard Rogers' Lloyd's Building (pp. 32–7), though unpopular with some of the more hidebound underwriters, has as its primary motivation the demands of a contemporary, information-led organization, not mere aesthetics.

The interior can have a far more profound effect on users than the exterior, however important a building may be in a cityscape. In the last decade, interior design, once the impoverished relation of architecture, has been transformed. In a number of crucial areas interiors have assumed an importance that on occasion transcends concern about exteriors. Office workers spend one-third of their lives in the office, and the shopping or eating 'experience' can be profoundly altered by the quality of the environment the designer provides (and hence the profits of the store or restaurant owner can also be affected). The revolution in information technology has dramatically increased the pace of change for commercial organizations, while in retailing and catering in particular the growing sophistication of the consumer has also altered the typical 'shelf-life' of an interior design. Thus, in the major cities of the Western world, the modern condition is for buildings – notably those that house offices and stores – to be standard shells (with perhaps a 'designed' external skin), within which the designer creates a relatively transient interior. Over the life of a building, its interior spaces may well be changed many times, adding up to a total cost far in excess of the building itself. The pressures of economics have placed interior design (as opposed to mere decorating) firmly at the centre of both architectural and commercial debate in today's world.

Thus interiors now have an even more vital role as a proving ground for new design ideas. While some of the projects included here may well cost a lot of money, on the whole this book shows that interiors can be designed and built in less time and on a smaller budget than any building; and, protected from the weather by the building shell, and often incorporating few specifically structural elements, interiors may show a disregard for many of the practical considerations forced on building design. Indeed, many of the examples in this book illustrate how a design in itself may be used as the primary lure for the customer. Nigel Coates and Shi Yu Chen's iconoclastic restaurants in Tokyo (pp. 54–9) are perhaps extreme instances of this, but others too, such as Jiricna Kerr's Legends in London (pp. 88–91), or the Sottsass-designed Esprit stores (pp. 194–207), are also inspired by the paramount need of the client to differentiate his business from that of a mass of competitors. Interior design can fulfil this basic commercial requirement.

All the projects in this volume satisfy both the client's and the user's functional demands; but they go beyond this achievement to explore new design ideas, to provoke a response, and sometimes even to amuse. The bewildering variety of styles reproduced here reflects the exciting range of ideas now current in design. From Tokyo minimalism to Los Angeles bizarre to Barcelona chic to London high-tech, an unprecedented array of talented interior designers are now exploring the limits of their art.

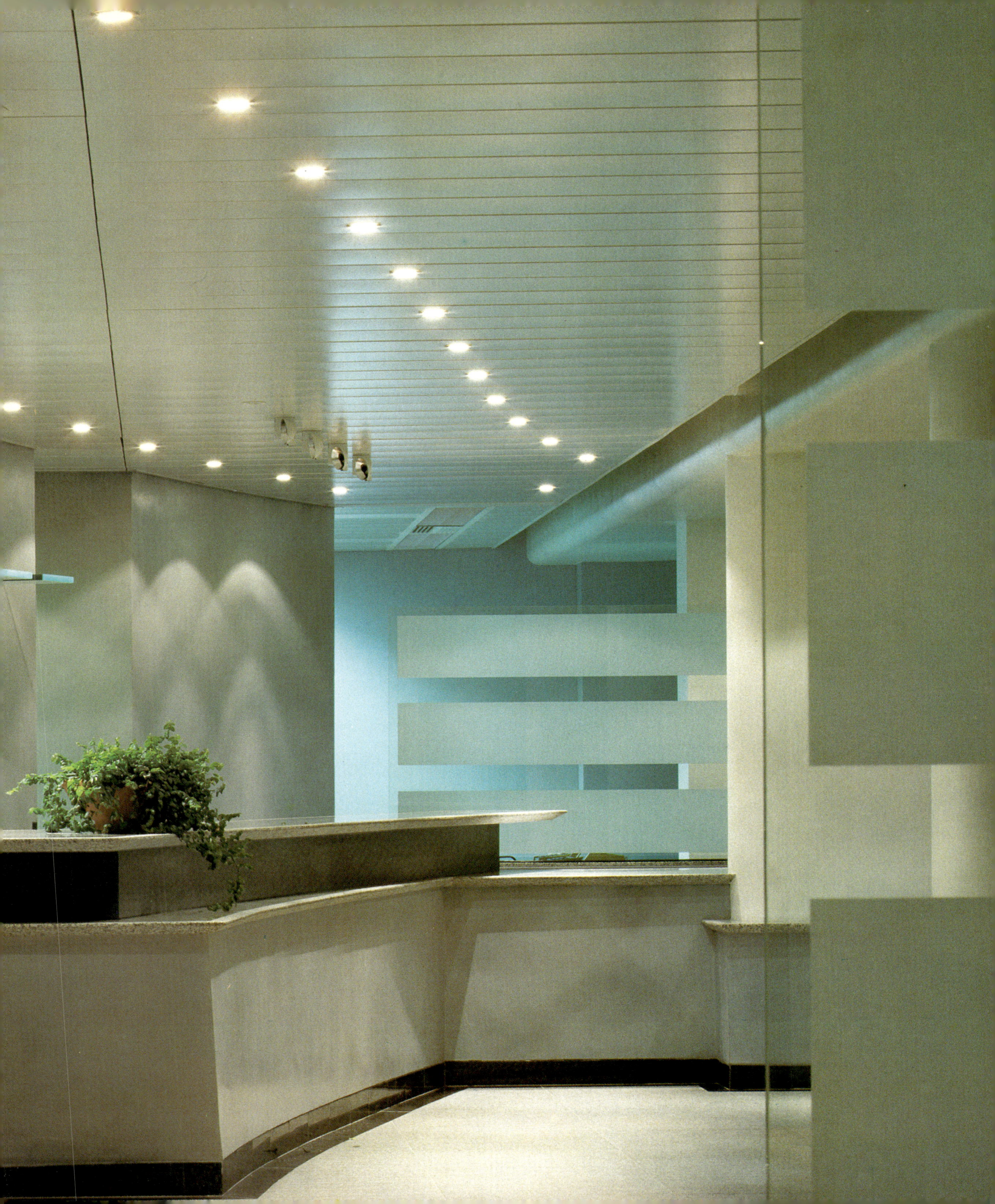

OFFICES

Note: Designers' or architects' names appear first, and are listed in alphabetical order.

William Adams Architects Pytka Film Studio, Venice, California, USA

Emilio Ambasz & Associates Financial Guaranty Insurance Company, New York City, USA

Ron Arad The Bureau, London, UK

DEGW Wang Laboratories, Brentford, UK

Coop Himmelblau Baumann Studio, Vienna, Austria

Coop Himmelblau Iso-Holding, Vienna, Austria

Leo Design Leo Design Studio, Helsinki, Finland

Mack Architects Mack Studio, San Francisco, California, USA

Richard Rogers Partnership Lloyd's, London, UK

Skidmore, Owings & Merrill The Boston Globe, Boston, Massachusetts, USA

STUDIOS San Francisco Advanced Computer Development Center, Apple Computer Inc., Cupertino, California, USA

Tilton + Lewis Associates Schwinn Bicycle Company, Chicago, Illinois, USA

Vignelli Associates Vignelli Associates, New York City, USA

The sleek efficiency of the modern high-technology company is communicated by the polished plaster walls, Sardinian granite and etched glass panels at Wang Laboratories, Brentford, UK, designed by DEGW.

PYTKA FILM STUDIO
VENICE, CALIFORNIA, USA

Designed by William Adams Architects

Film production companies are traditionally not keenly image-conscious, tending not to lavish time, thought and money on their environment. Pytka Film Studio is very different from this. In a standard warehouse building, William Adams has constructed a small office village, complete with 'buildings', 'streets' and 'landscaping'. Adams describes it as 'an abstract version of a traditional Venice walking street'. And since this is LA, there is nothing typical about any of these elements.

A broad 'street' of polished and sealed concrete runs down the centre of the building. Arranged irregularly along this internal boulevard are the 'buildings' that house the various office functions of the agency: meeting rooms, work spaces and even lavatories. The 'buildings' are a *mélange* of current architectural styles: an Oswald Matthias Ungers-like white pavilion topped by a barrel vault of square glazing, an Arata Isozaki-like curving white wall surmounted by a glazed cupola, and even a Mario Botta-like concrete and glass cubic composition (the affinity with Botta is somewhat strengthened by the use of his chairs for some reception areas). The designers were not responsible for choosing any of the other furniture used in the interior.

Pytka Film Studio might have been a strained architectural conceit but, throughout, the work has been immaculately detailed and carried through with conviction and flair. It would have been easy to descend into feeble pastiche, but Adams has built this office village with all the certitude of a grand town-planner, and some welcome humour as well.

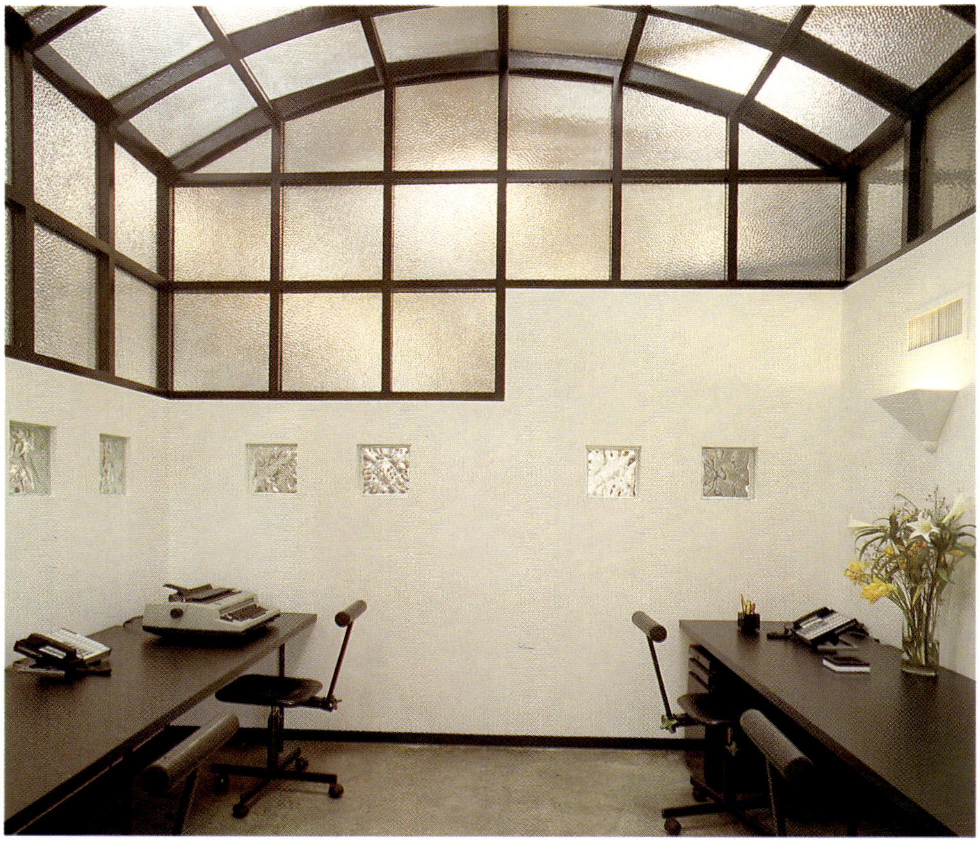

(left) Work spaces are housed in 'buildings', like this white pavilion topped by a barrel vault of square glazing. Furniture, chosen by the client, is minimalist in style rather than functional.

(right) Inside the standard warehouse building, the designers have created a small office 'village'. The Mario Botta chair from Alias is positioned for effect rather than visitor comfort.

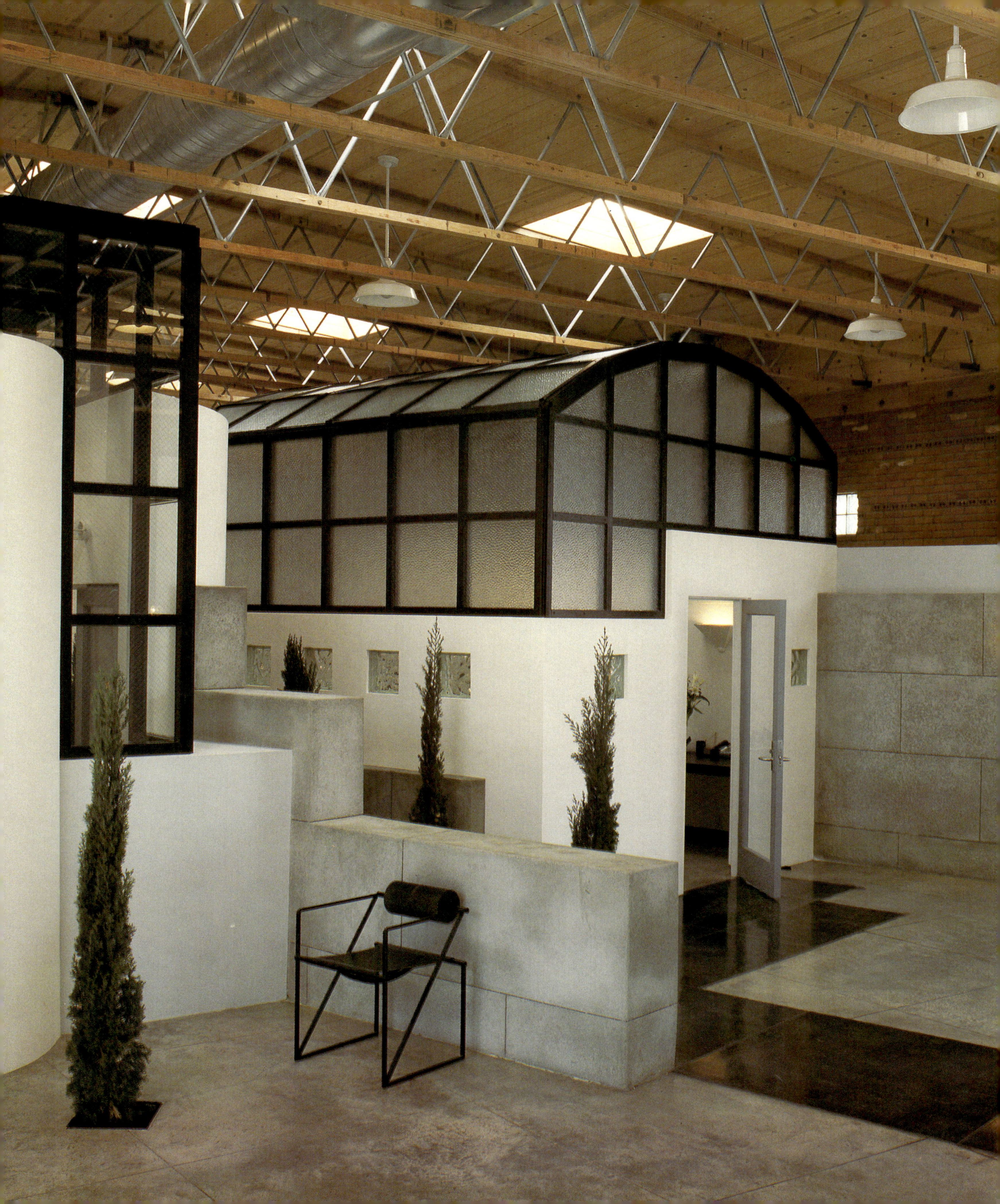

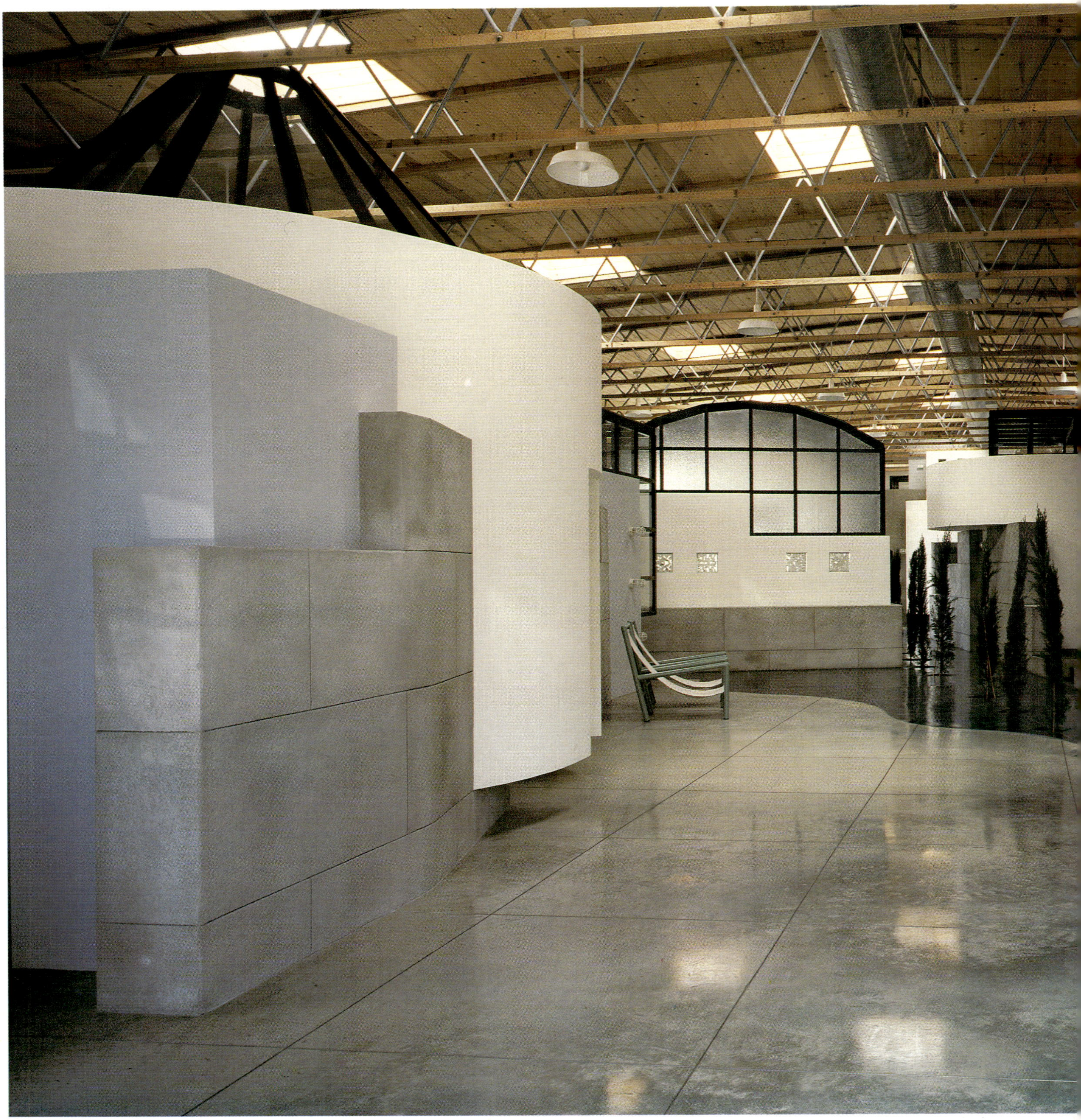

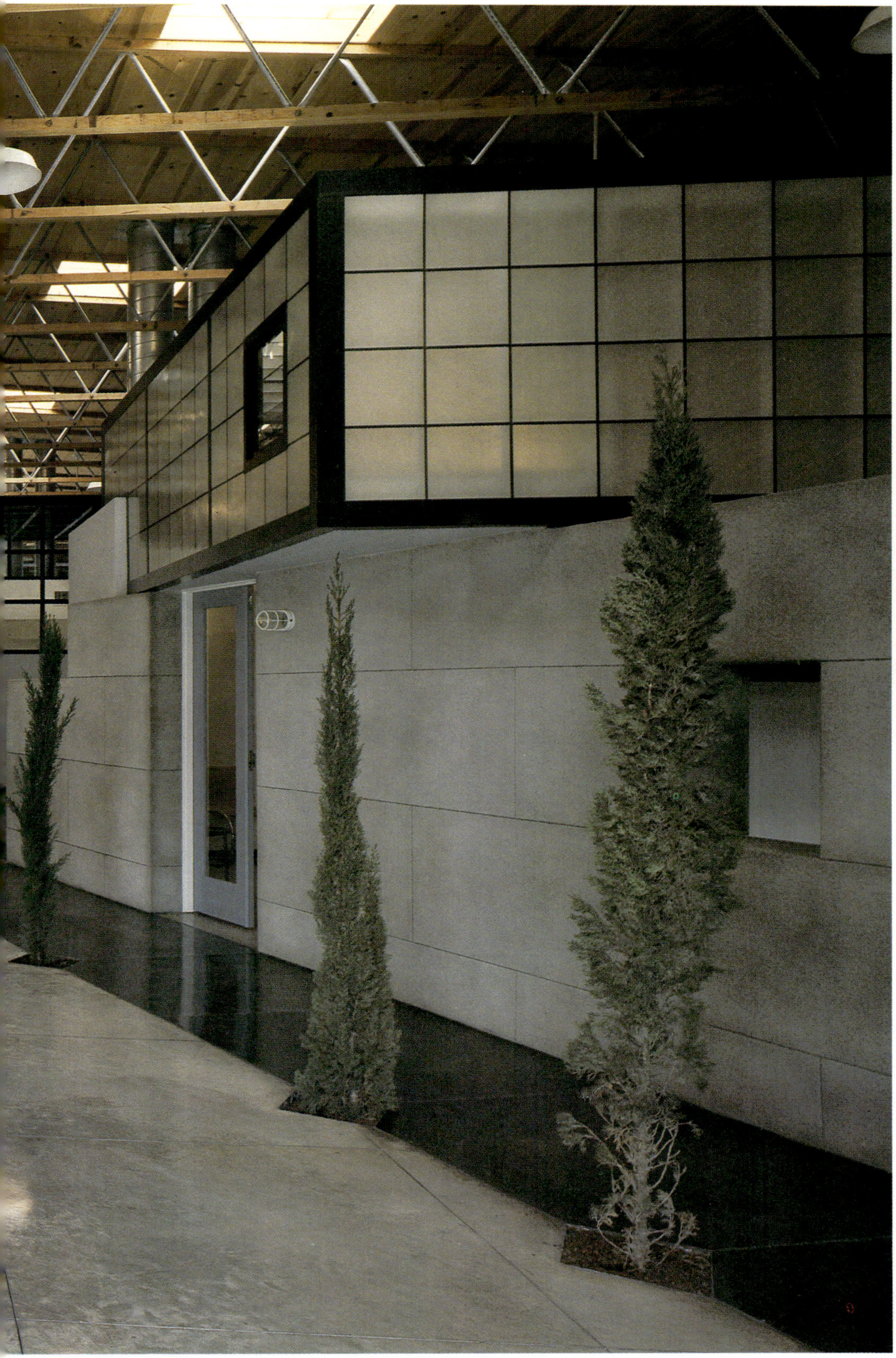

(left) Ranged along the wide central 'street' are the pavilions housing the main offices and production facilities.

(below) Even the lavatories are part of the design's grand conception: the walls beneath the glazed barrel vault are varnished plaster.

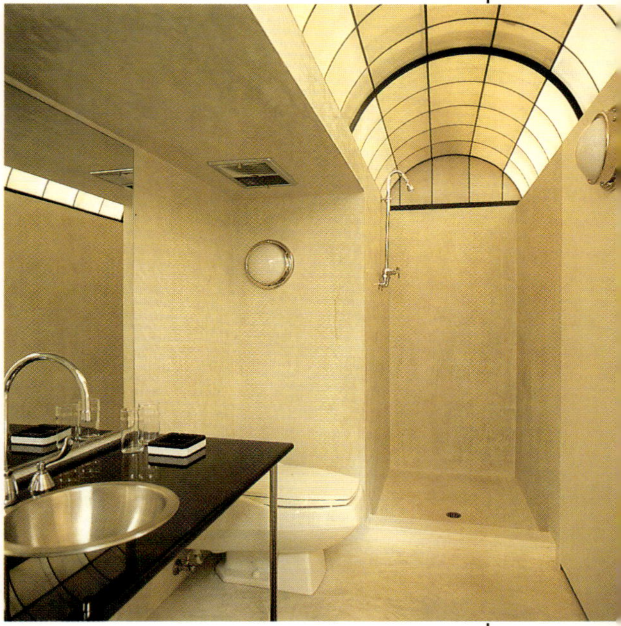

FINANCIAL GUARANTY INSURANCE COMPANY

NEW YORK CITY, USA

Designed by Emilio Ambasz & Associates

Emilio Ambasz's architectural projects are often fantasies that play on dream-like images, on illusion, on the intangible. So the dream world that strikes visitors to the offices designed by Ambasz for the Financial Guaranty Insurance Company is of a piece with his larger architectural projects. What is less apparent about the FGIC design is how practical and, in certain elements, innovative it is in terms of office needs.

The FGIC is a rapidly growing company which sells insurance for municipal bonds. The

(below) Ambasz's mysterious silk curtains separate the ranks of Knoll 'Hannah' desks and the Ambasz-designed 'Vertebra' chairs.

(right) Shimmering walls of light, created by curtains of gauzy silk strings which act like fibre optics, serve the functional purpose of dividing office areas.

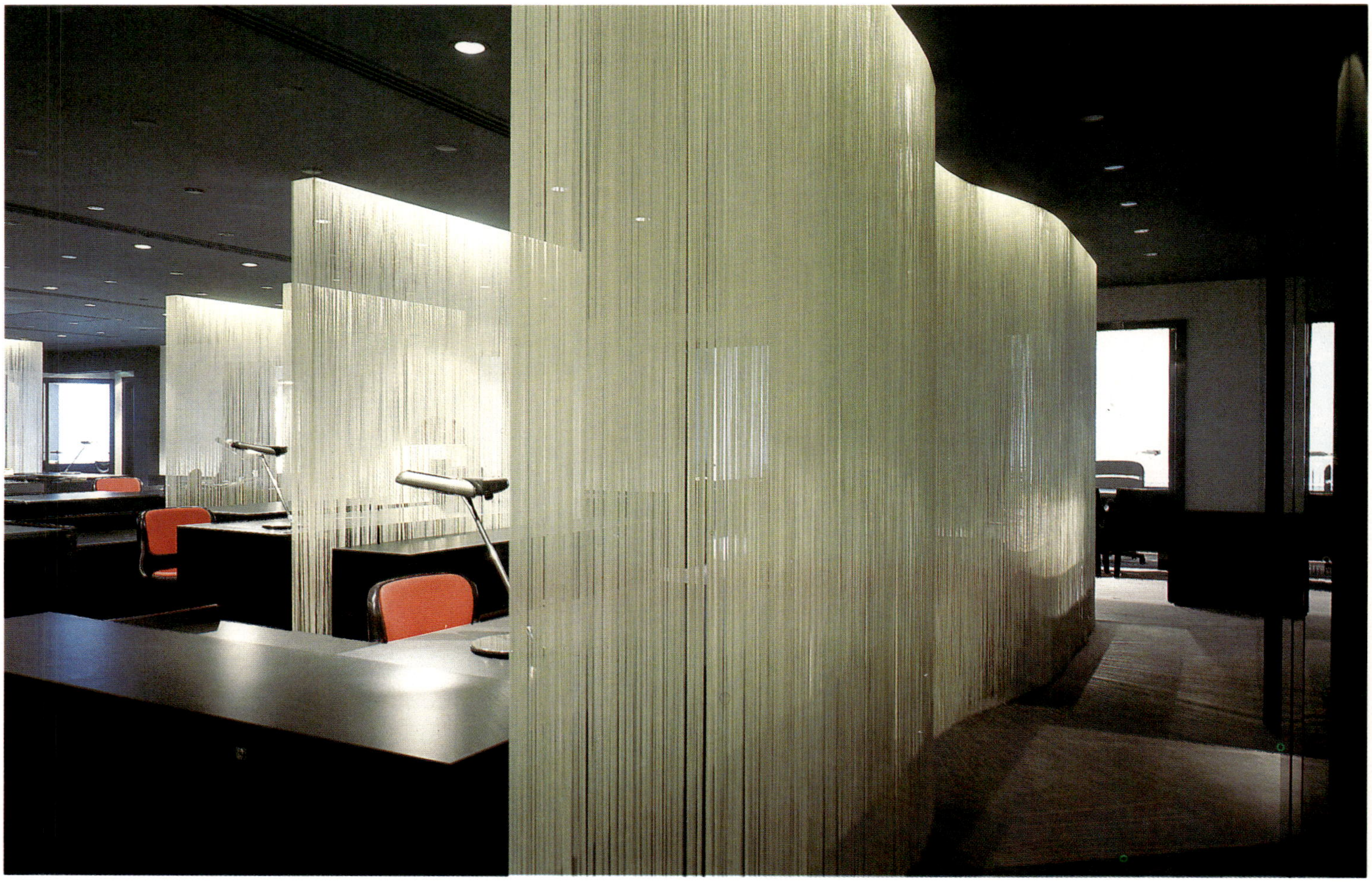

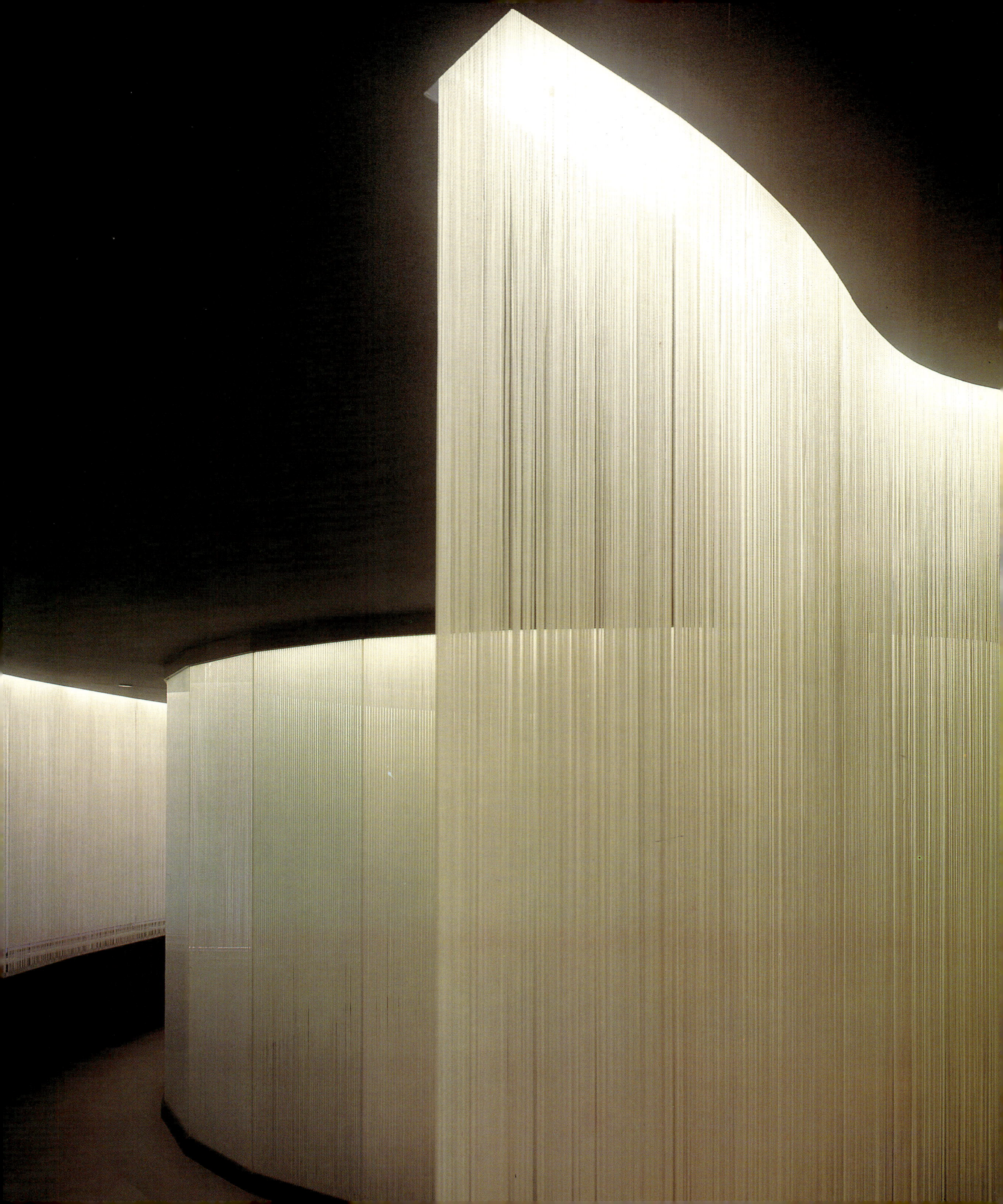

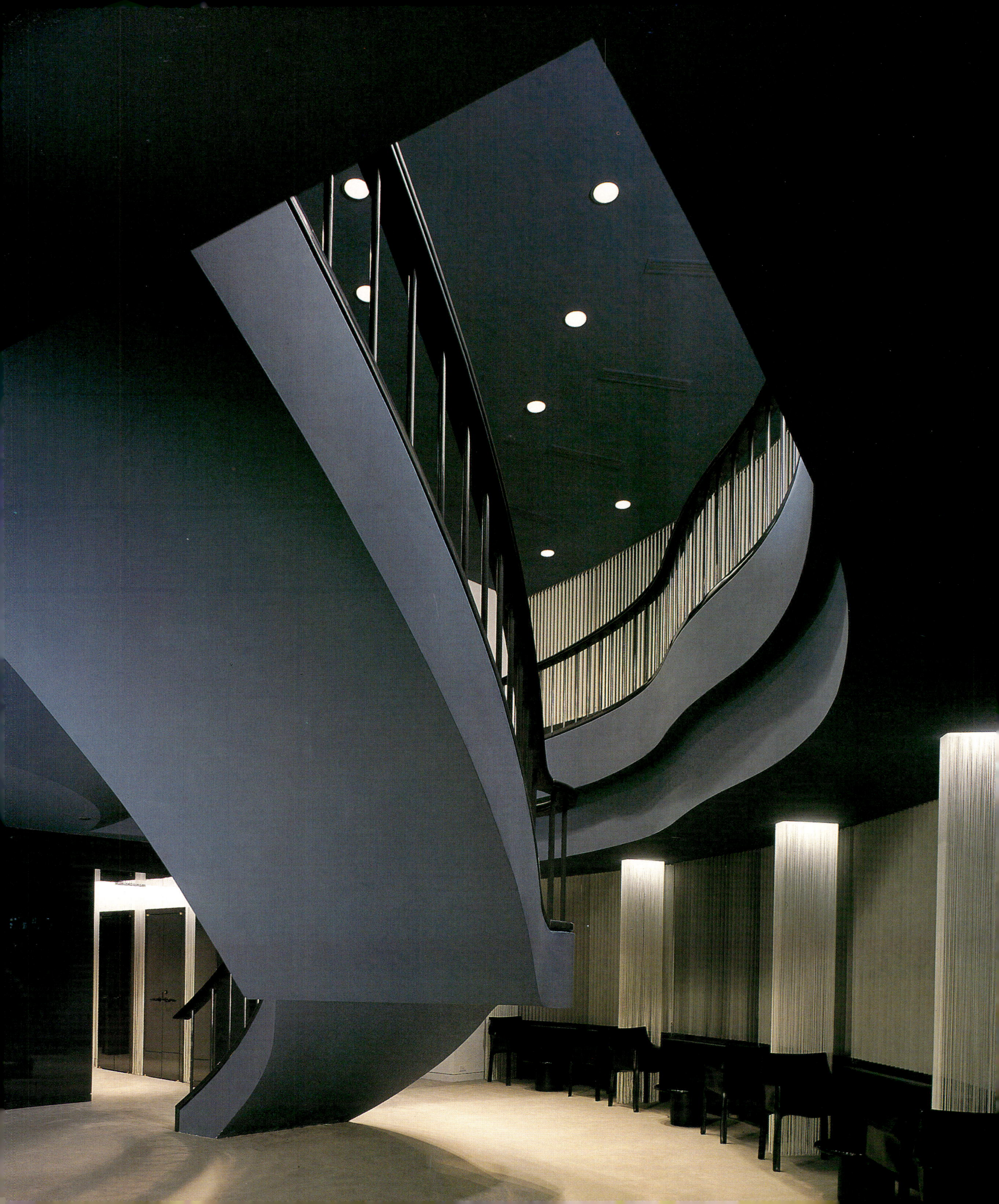

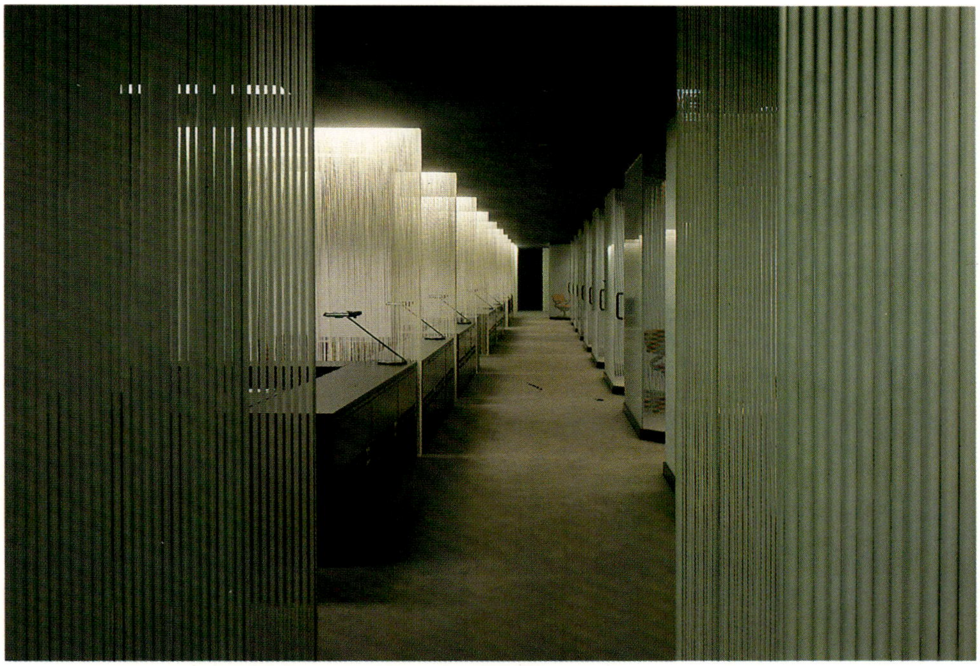

(left) The sense of movement implicit in the silk curtains is mimicked by the wilful curves of the grand staircase and balcony.

(right) Acid-etched glass partitions for the cellular offices echo the more ethereal walls of light that separate open-plan areas. The cellular offices, or 'Modular Self-contained Work Units', can be moved about with a small fork-lift.

16,146 square foot (1,500 square metre) space includes executive offices and conference rooms, working areas for analysts and traders, a legal staff, a sales and marketing department, a financial and administrative department, as well as support personnel and facilities. Because FGIC has no palpable product, Ambasz saw his task as projecting a strong and cohesive image for the company.

Ambasz chose as his 'themes' for the interior, richness of materials and mobility of form. These are expressed by a series of layers which shift with changing perspectives as one moves through the space. The layers are created by curtains of gauzy silk strings which transmit light like fibre optics. Each executive office and conference room is ringed with these curtains of light.

Behind the hangings, the walls are a blue which gradually intensifies from light at the bottom to dark at the top, like a twilight sky. The ceilings are gridded with a pattern of discs (actually sprinkler-head covers) with slightly reflective surfaces. The specially designed carpet has a pattern of hand-cut circles leading to an ever-changing vanishing point. The glass used for partitions, as well as the windows, is patterned with a grid of clear hemispheres: 'strengthening the ephemeral reality of its translucency', according to Ambasz.

Ambasz describes his design as 'a radically new synthesis of the conventional enclosed office and the open landscaped office'. The main device for this synthesis is a 6 foot by 8 foot (1.8 metre by 2.4 metre) 'Modular Self-contained Work Unit System' which can be moved about with a small fork-lift. Each of these work units is a complete and controlled environment with its own floor, roof and walls, furniture, equipment, light and air-circulation systems. The same pattern used on the glass partitions is used on the glass walls of the units and a partition of silk light-curtains between each unit adds another layer to the interior.

Within Ambasz's clear organization, the choice of furniture assumes less importance than in most office schemes. But his own 'Vertebra' chairs (designed with Giancarlo Piretti) combine with Knoll's desking system and 'Storwall' filing to create a subdued and distinguished counterpart to the innovative walls of light.

The use of these units retains the privacy of traditional enclosed offices, while their easy movement offers the flexibility of an open-plan environment. And Ambasz adds a note of mystery to this highly practical idea with his luminous, shimmering walls.

THE BUREAU

LONDON, UK

Designed by Ron Arad

Ron Arad is a designer who does not enjoy being put into categories. Looking at his work, however, it is not too difficult to see why he has been given labels such as 'high-tech ruinist' and 'neo-brutalist'. One has only to step inside One-Off, his shop in Covent Garden, London, and look at the furniture for which he is best known to understand why: materials are rough, rusted or jagged, often salvaged from the street; chairs are made out of car seats; clocks are huge metal horns; stereos are hewn from slabs of concrete. All of them have the power to surprise or shock.

Arad's designs for interiors have much the same quality. The offices he completed for clothing design company, The Bureau, at the beginning of 1987 provide one example. The Bureau had often bought Arad's furniture for their small offices in Farringdon, so when they moved into larger, riverside accommodation at Metropolitan Wharf, Wapping, it was a fairly logical step to ask him to design the whole interior for them.

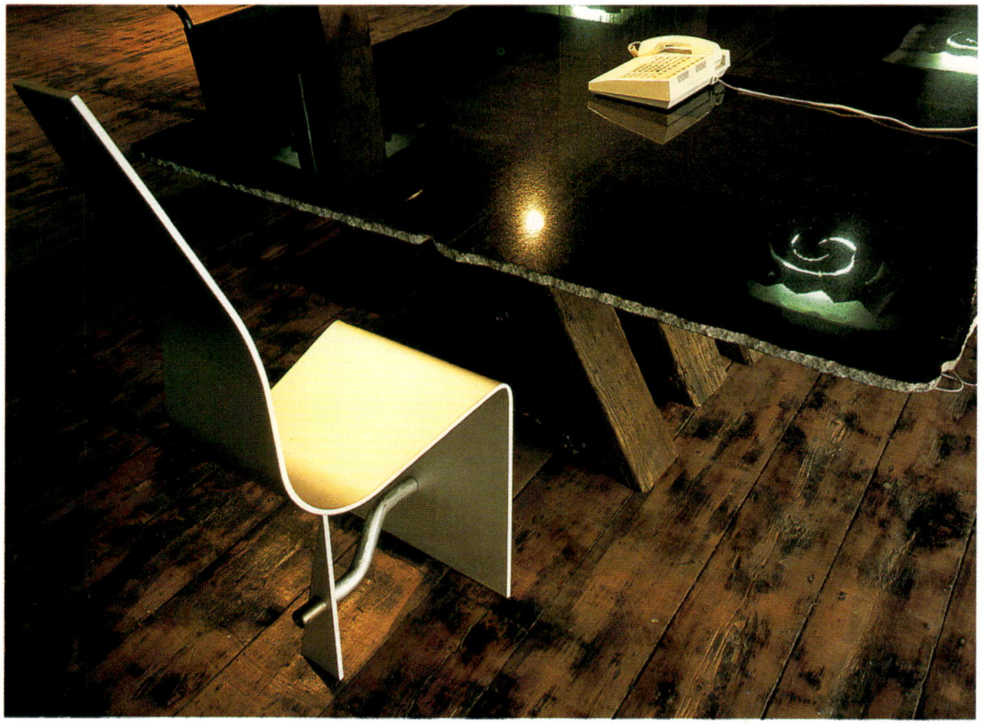

Surrounded by newly built riverfront apartment blocks, The Bureau's offices are in one of the surviving warehouse buildings, originally used to store sacks of coffee. The floor plan is common to each level, with a central staircase leading on to subdivided units at front and back. What Arad has done is to reshape that space within two storeys: a massive timber structure hidden by a brick façade has given him the opportunity to do this. By removing infill floors, he has opened out these two separate levels into one double-height space, thereby increasing the amount of daylight on the lower floor, and providing a welcome sense of spaciousness in what would otherwise be a low-ceilinged and oppressive environment.

A typical piece of Arad furniture – designed especially for this project – is the cantilevered work table which has been made from welded scaffolding and glass, and which actually incorporates part of the existing timber structure. The metal light fittings were also designed by Arad for this interior.

Among the rest of the furniture and fittings is Arad's earlier 'horn-chair', and there are also some chairs by Italian design group Zeus. But probably the most striking feature in a fairly sparse interior is the screen that serves to divide off a conference/meeting area. Designed by Danny Lane – a craftsman who has often collaborated with Arad – the screen is made of metal and several different thicknesses of toughened glass to create Arad's desired post-holocaust effect.

Lane was given total freedom in the design of the screen. Arad gave him the necessary measurements but then let him complete the work as he wished, so that the result was something fortuitous. But then, Arad is a designer for whom the expected and the ready-made are anathema.

(below left) A cantilevered work table, made from welded scaffolding and glass, incorporates part of the old warehouse's existing timber structure.

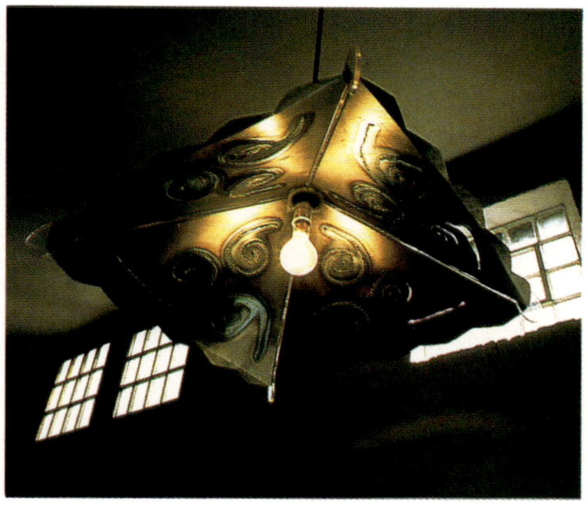

(right) Arad's light fitting combines the mundane – the standard light-bulb – with slightly bizarre and ornate metal decoration.

(below) The most striking feature of the interior is the screen which divides off a conference/meeting area. Using metal and several different thicknesses of toughened glass, the screen was made by artist/craftsman Danny Lane.

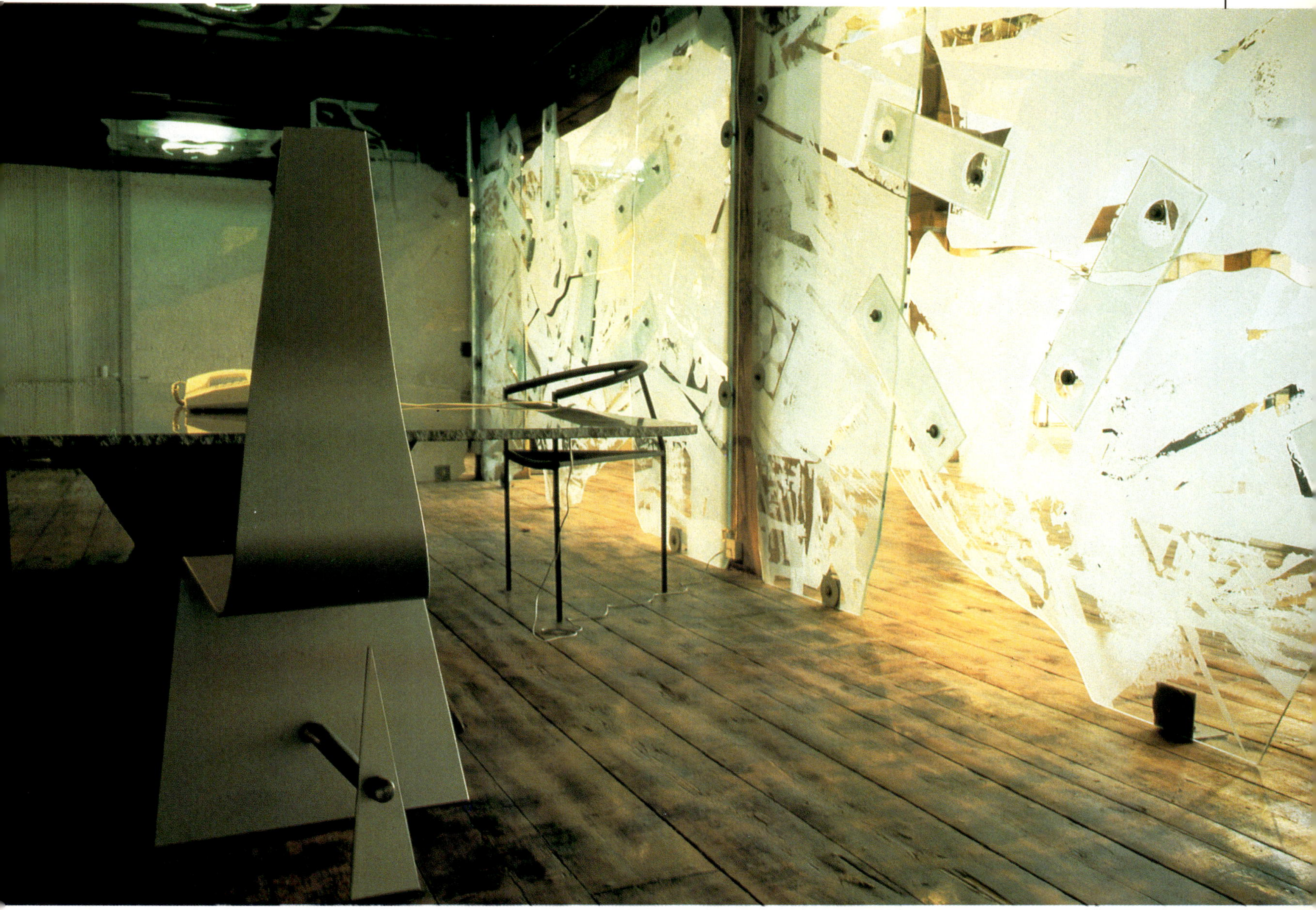

WANG LABORATORIES
BRENTFORD, UK

Designed by DEGW

Speculative offices seldom provide the kind of image that high-technology firms like to promote. This was certainly the case when Wang Laboratories chose a fairly typical 1960s block in West London for their new European and UK headquarters.

Although the building was being refurbished and reclad, the offices themselves were still not of the standard that Wang wanted. Therefore, they called in designers DEGW to alter extensively, update and upgrade the offices and bring them into line with a high-tech corporate image more appropriate to a major computer company.

Well over three hundred staff work for Wang in the Brentford office, and so creating a sense of identity on each of the various floors was important. To achieve this, the designers used different colours for the colonnades, which they established along the central axis of each floor. The axis is then slightly jarred by the addition of a central curved wall, which provides conference areas and a photocopying room. Deeper into the office floors, fin walls jut out to divide the space into individual working areas. Wang's existing Herman Miller 'Action Office' furniture has been used almost throughout, although new Ahrend Mehes furniture was specified for the executive secretaries. Each floor has low-energy fluorescent light fittings in a Gema suspended ceiling.

But, of course, few office buildings now are just offices: at Wang there is also a staff restaurant, a combined training/sales area, boardrooms and reception – and these have all received individual treatment from designers. The main reception, for instance, has been transformed into a double-height space so that visitors' first impressions are of a spacious, light building (the actual effect is almost that of an

(right) Curving walls, carefully selected artworks and a range of colour schemes create a distinctive identity for each office floor.

(below) Like a ship's prow, the sleek, polished plaster wall in the reception area at Wang Laboratories evokes an image of smooth efficiency.

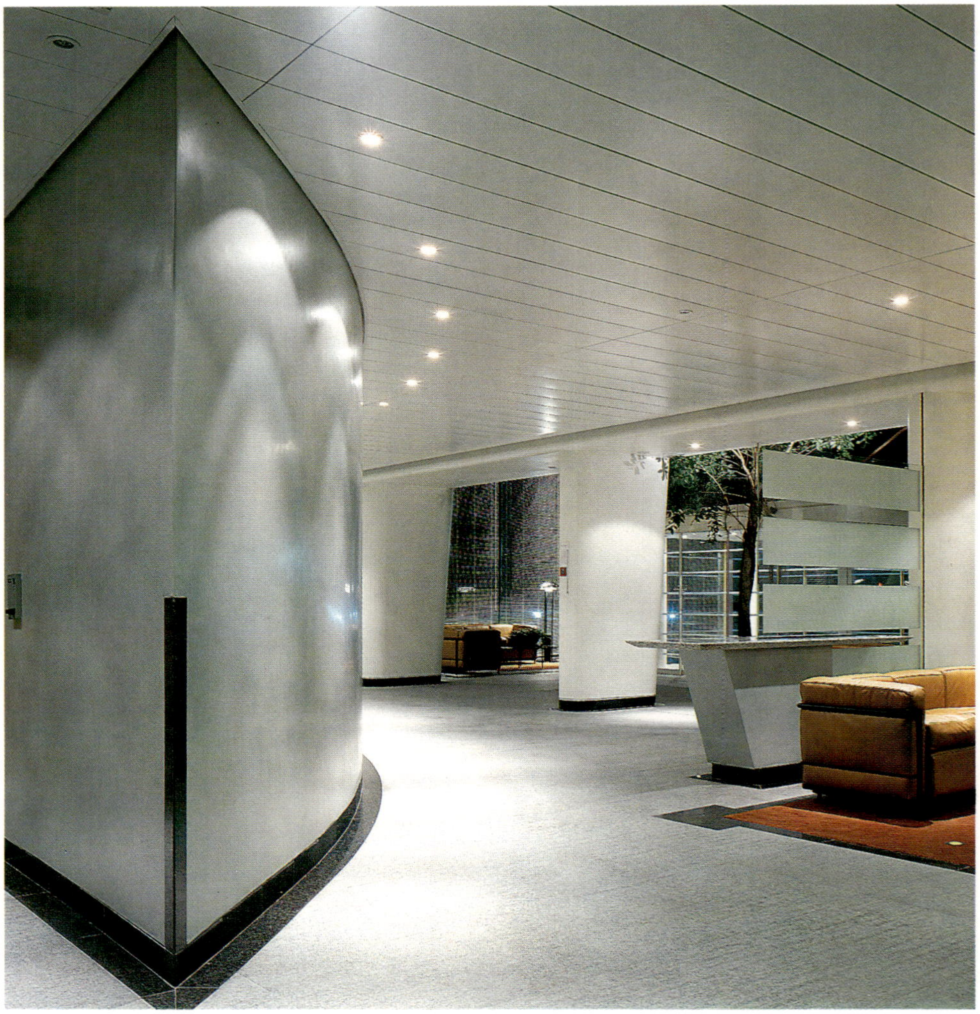

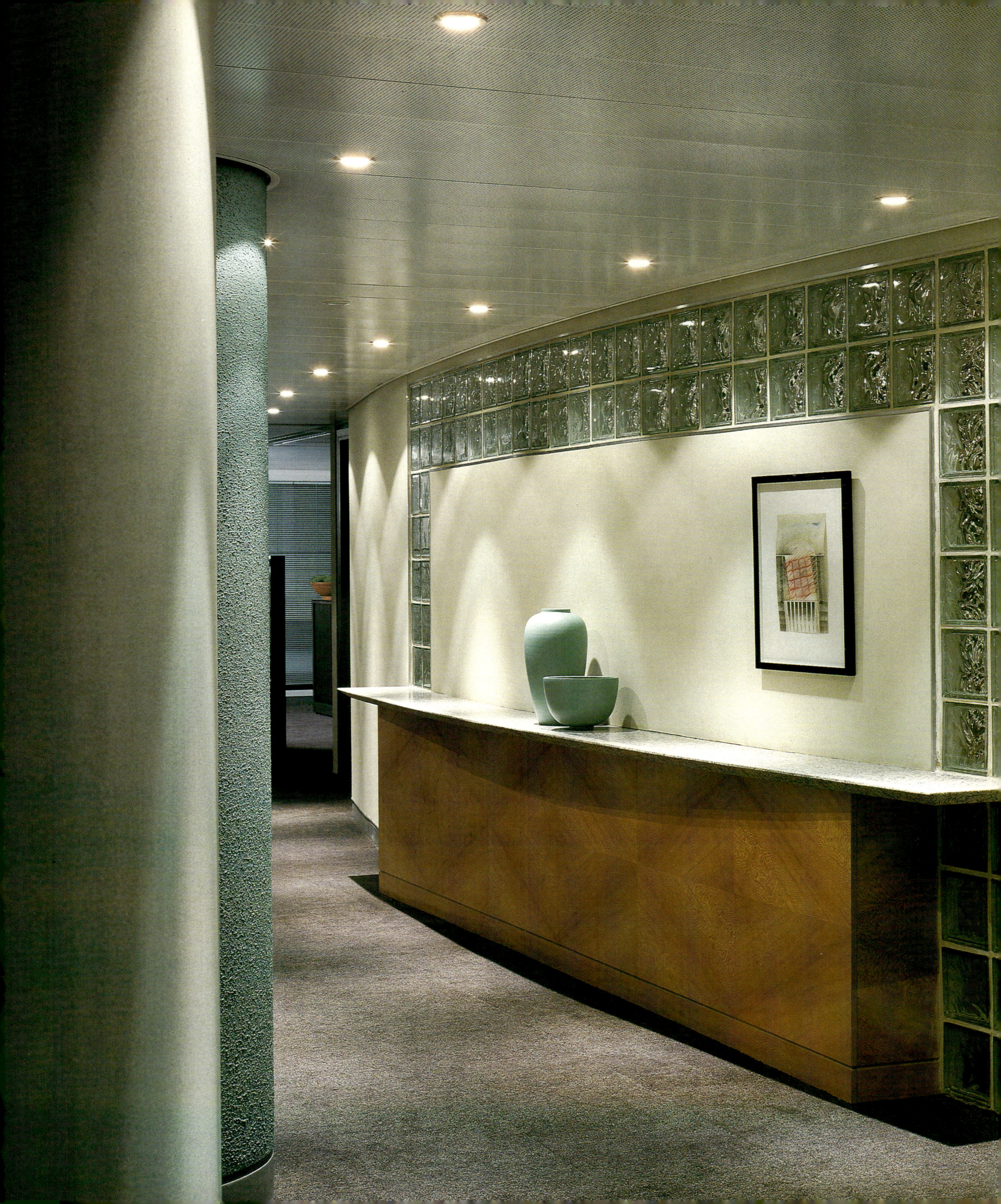

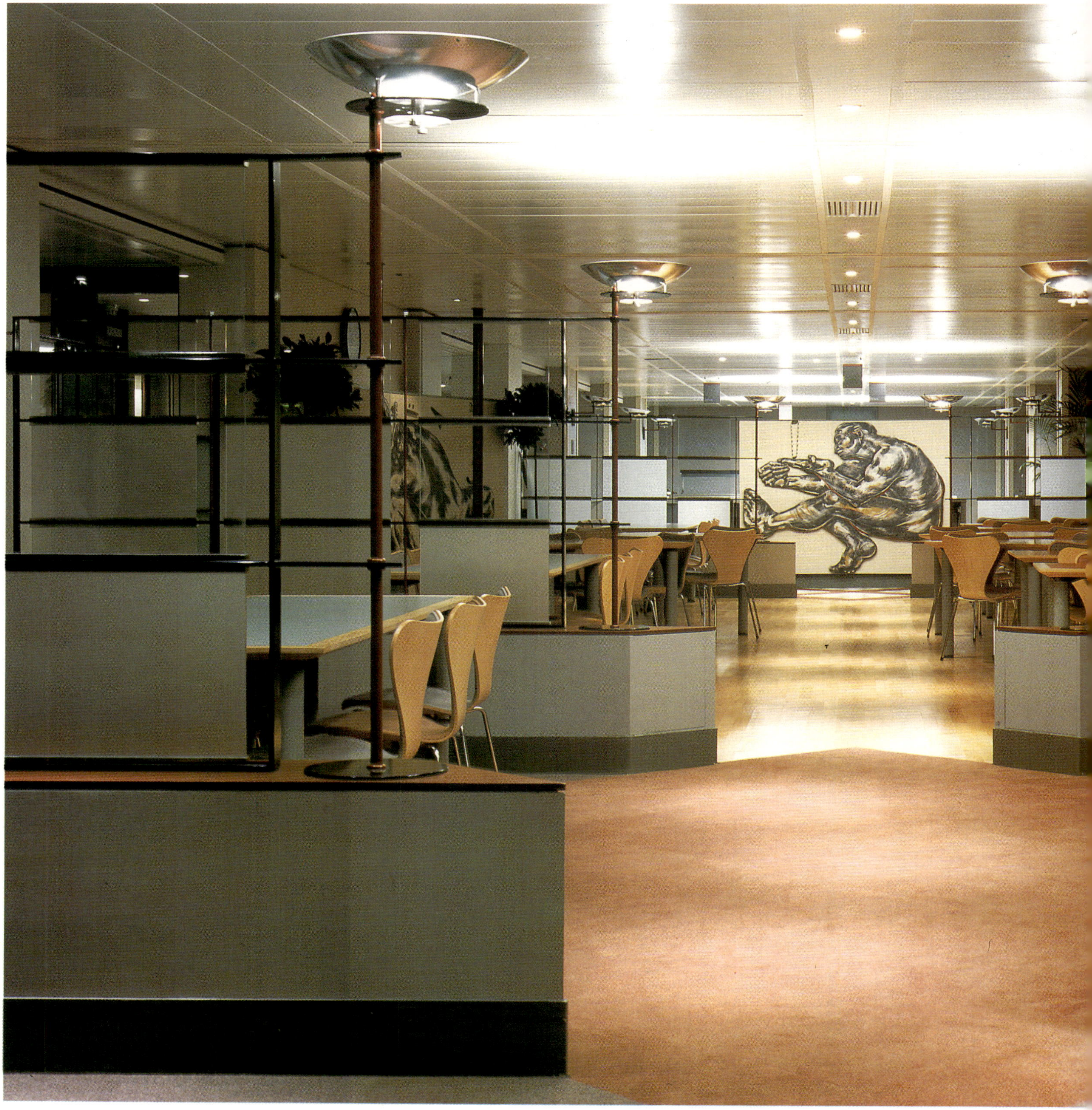

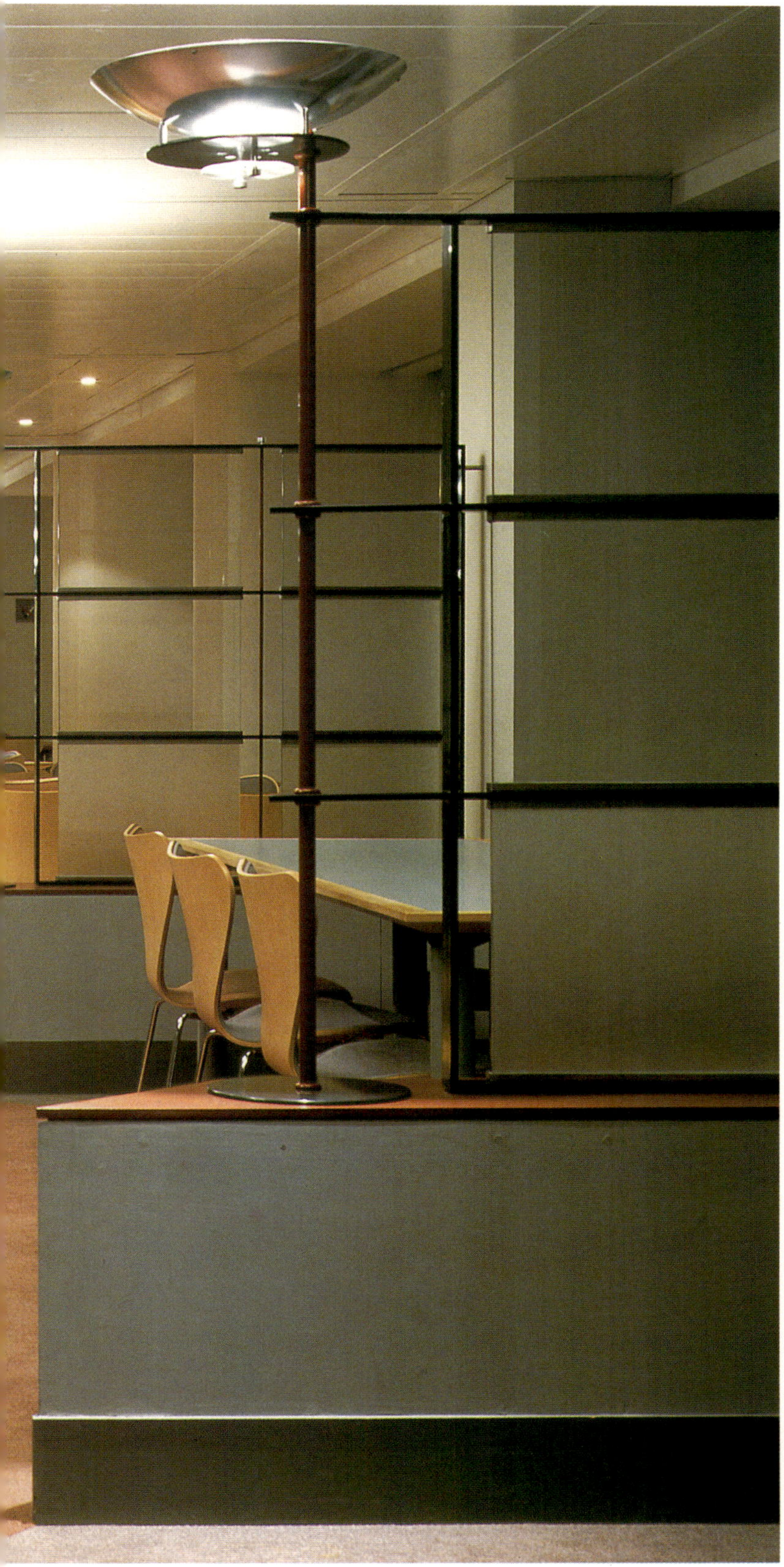

ocean liner). It is here, too, that the theme of curves is first introduced, both in the walls and in the reception desk of polished Sardinian grey granite.

The first-floor restaurant, another of the atypical areas, overlooks reception. It boasts bold, figurative murals painted by Tamara Capallaro and specially commissioned to give this communal space an interesting and, more importantly, informal feel. Uplighters by Gordon Burnett were also specially commissioned, and Fritz Hansen chairs in natural wood colours add to the relaxed atmosphere.

Since Wang is a high-technology firm, it is not surprising that servicing demands on the building are heavy. To deal with data cabling there are four large risers, and on each floor a 50 mm screed has been chased and 25 mm chipboard laid to provide six lengthwise channels. In both function and image, DEGW have provided Wang with a clear, appropriate identity.

(left) The clear, axial planning of the staff restaurant is emphasized by the specially designed uplighters and the central figurative mural by Tamara Capallaro.

(below) Each office floor is organized round a central space (marked by curved walls and glass blocks) that contains the principal meeting areas and other staff facilities.

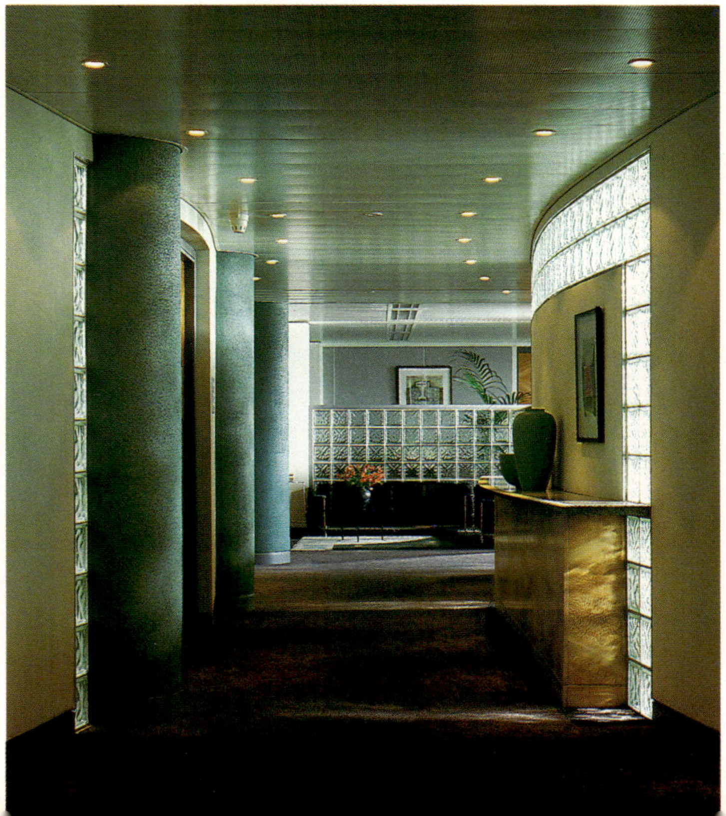

BAUMANN STUDIO
VIENNA, AUSTRIA

Designed by Coop Himmelblau

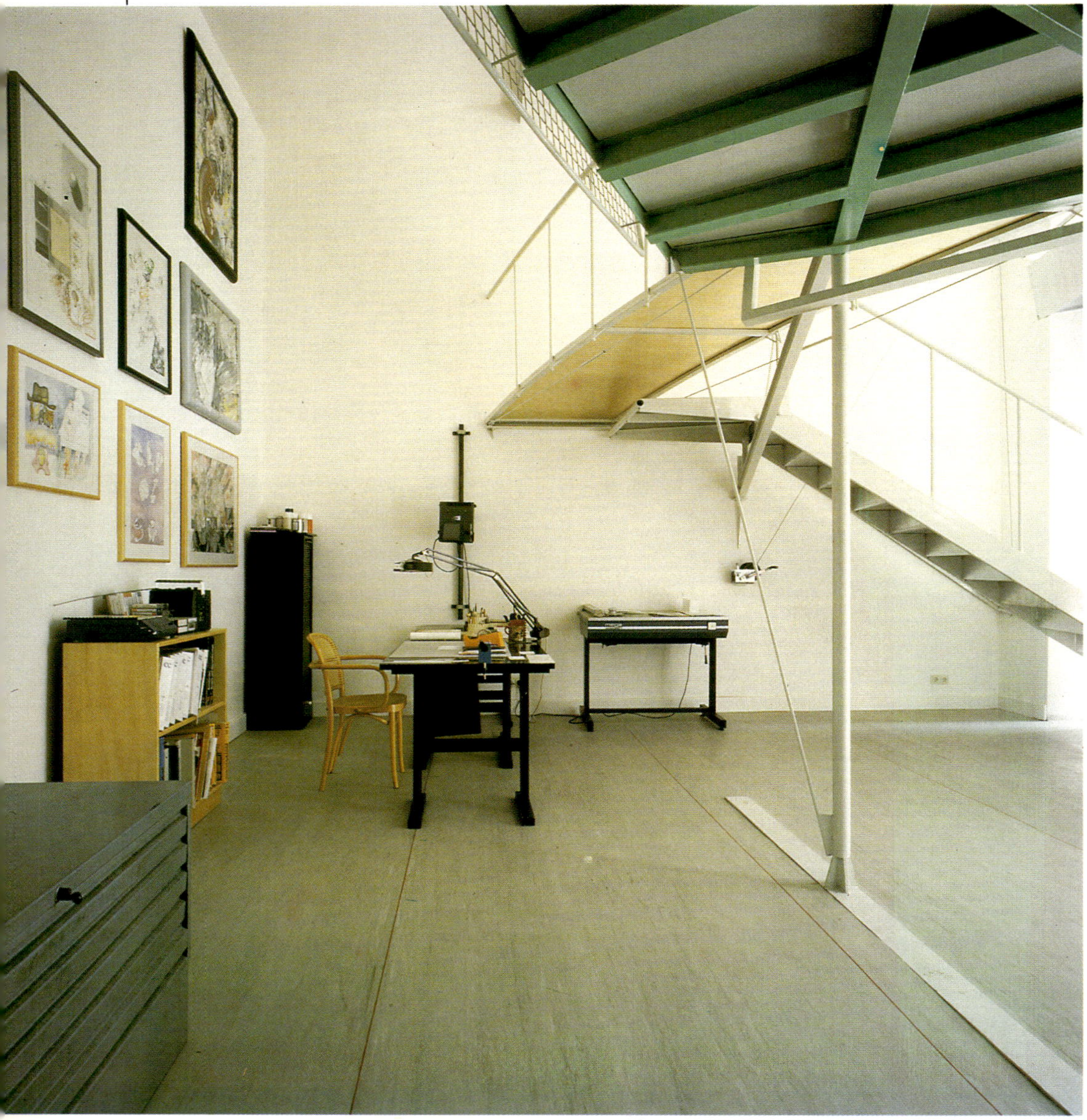

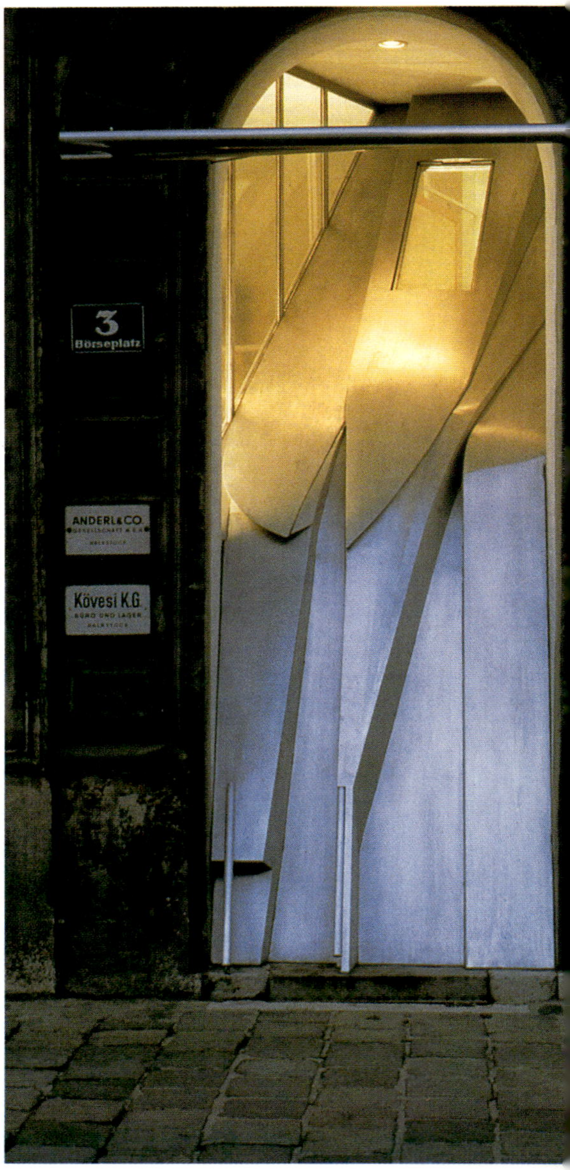

Erich Baumann gave Coop Himmelblau a simple brief for his studio: he wanted an atelier in which he could do his graphic work and in which his friends could 'live with the pictures'. And that was all. Fortunately, the raw material of the site had character: there were three arched doorways and noble proportions.

Coop Himmelblau's solution to this riddle of a brief was to insert an alien, almost insect-like piece of architectural sculpture into the building. The intervention is made clear from the outside: a steel 'wing' protrudes from the façade, while the two side portals have been filled with a giant steel overgrowth (the base of the internal bridge structure) and a gangplank-like steel staircase that can be raised and lowered from inside – fully lowered, it runs out on to the portal's threshold.

Inside, the complex structure dominates. There is a sense of impermanence, for the bridge has only a single connection to the ground, and that is merely an unfixed footing. The bewildering structural gymnastics of the bridge provide an additional 205 square feet (19 square metres) of space to the small studio. Baumann, by commissioning Coop Himmelblau's extraordinary fantasy, has collected an artwork in which to operate.

(left) The simply furnished studio is dominated by the zoomorphic bridge that provides a mezzanine level.

(middle) From the outside, a steel 'wing' protrudes from the façade and an arched opening is filled with a steel overgrowth.

(right) The delicate, intricate structure of the bridge serves as a foil to the spartan space below.

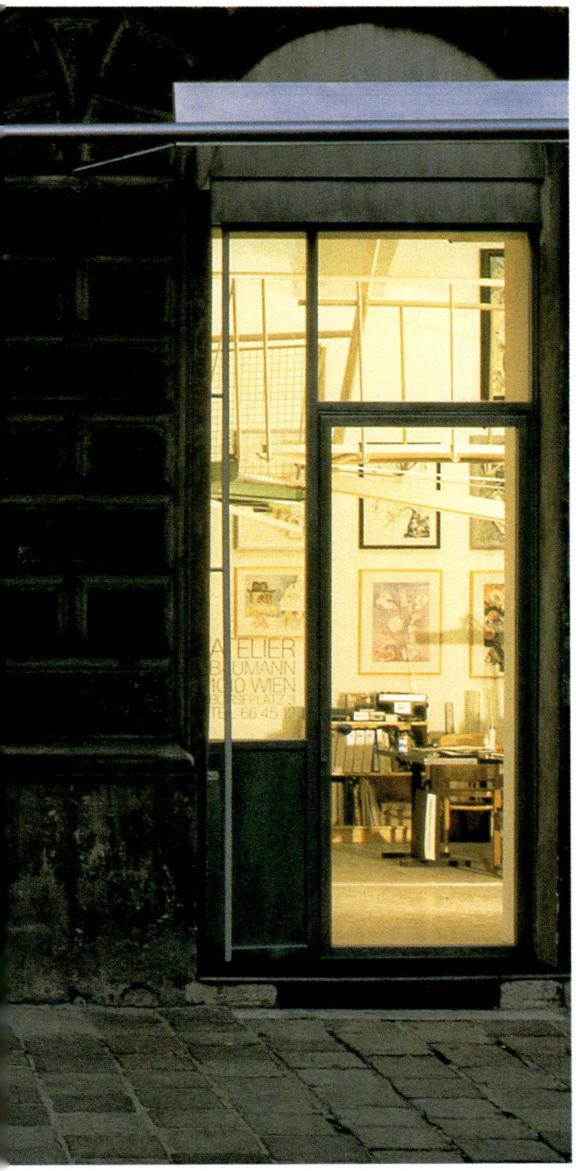

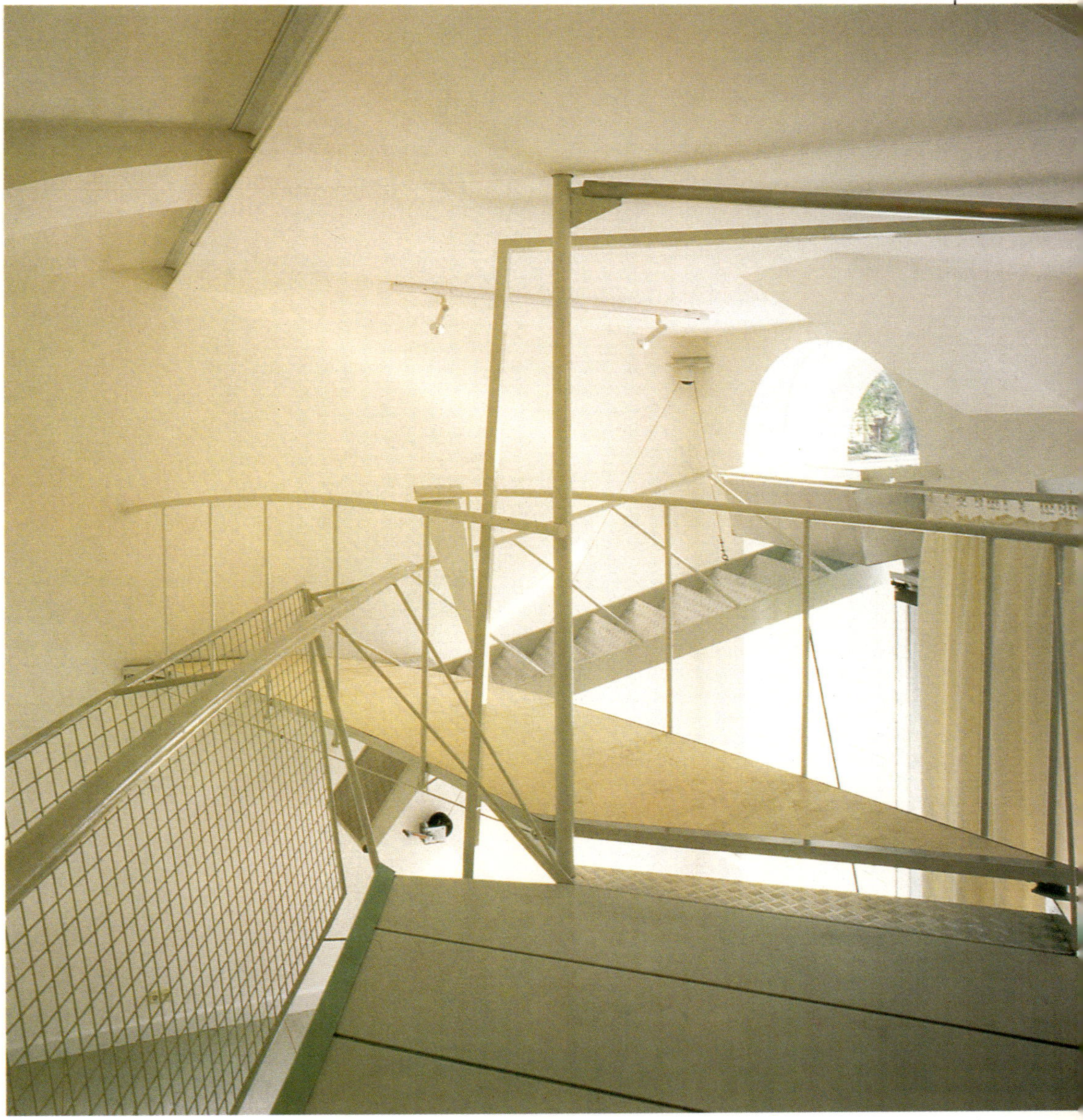

ISO-HOLDING

VIENNA, AUSTRIA

Designed by Coop Himmelblau

The occasionally bizarre exuberance that characterizes the work of Coop Himmelblau is perhaps to be expected with clients like art collector Erich Baumann (see pp. 24–5). But with their offices for Iso-Holding, Coop Himmelblau demonstrate how their geometric manipulations can be just as applicable to a standard office as to a shop or artist's studio.

Some parts of Iso-Holding are completely conventional, such as the offices with full-height glazed partitions and the safe, though classic, Eames Aluminium Group chairs. But even in some of these seemingly 'normal' rooms, there are some hints that a more anarchic design spirit may be at work: in the board-room, for example, a corner set of shelving features shelves that edge into the cabinet and disappear. Ceilings, too, occasionally erupt into a sea of white waves, intersected by metal poles that spear through the space.

These disjunctions encourage a closer look at what were once 'normal' offices: the metal poles crop up throughout the space, running into partitions, seemingly slicing an arc out of a doorway. In some corridors, the spearing poles become so prevalent as to suggest that the designers were attempting an obscure architectural allegory on the story of St Sebastian (Vienna's patron saint). Whatever the reason, the poles skewing through the offices add motion and a change of rhythm to enliven the space.

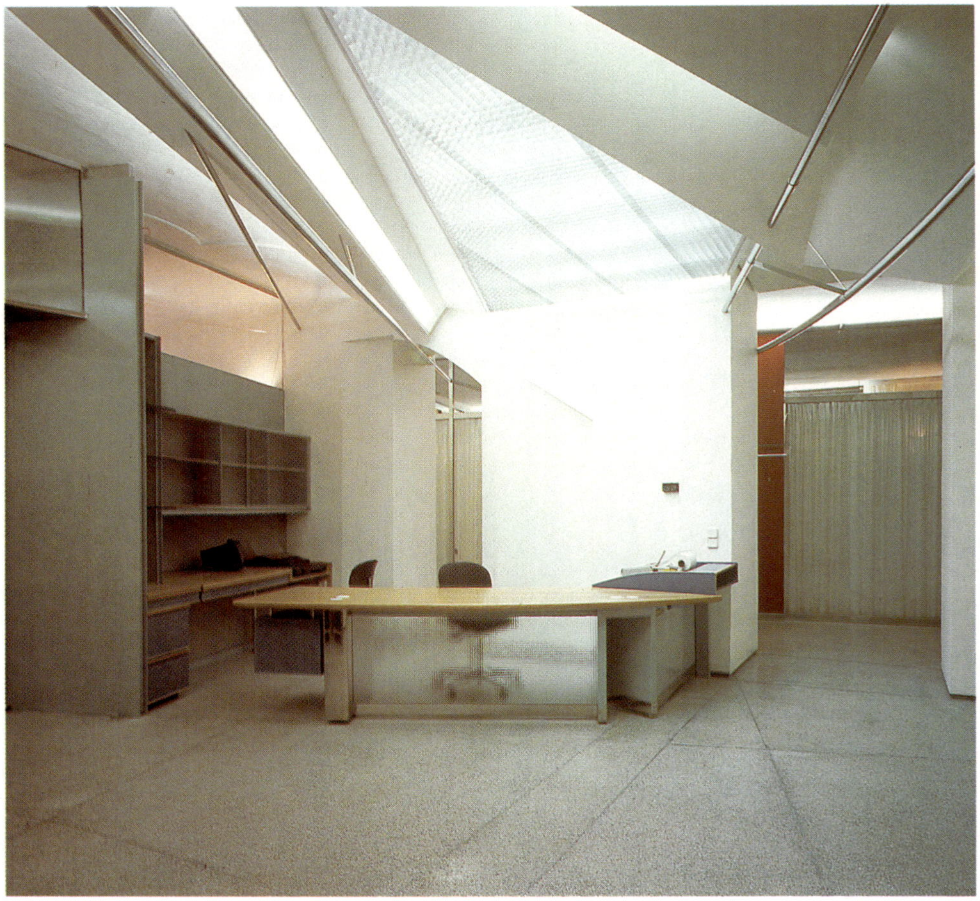

Ceilings at Iso-Holding occasionally erupt into a sea of white waves, intersected by the metal poles that spear throughout the office space.

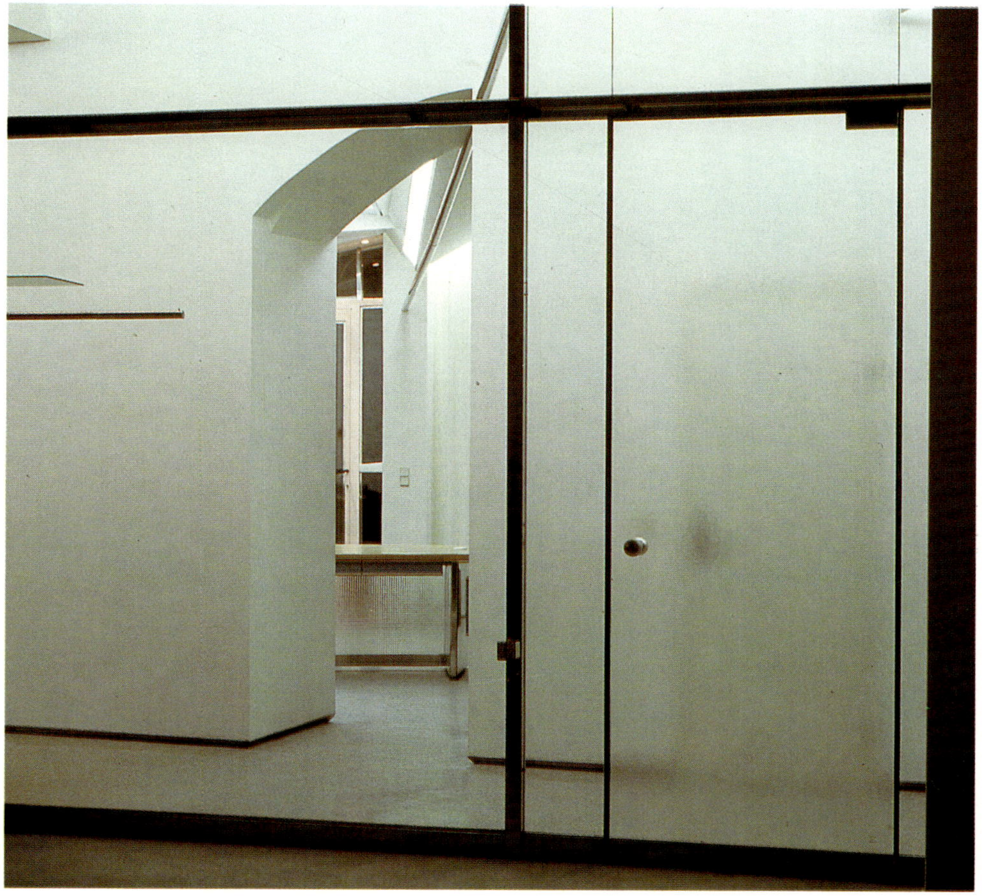

(left) The metal spears seem to have carved out the unusual doorways in the offices.

(below left) Most work spaces at Iso-Holding are quite conventional, with touches of Coop Himmelblau's design inspiration hidden in corners.

(below) The saintly allusion of the metal spears is emphasized by the arrowhead detail that secures the poles.

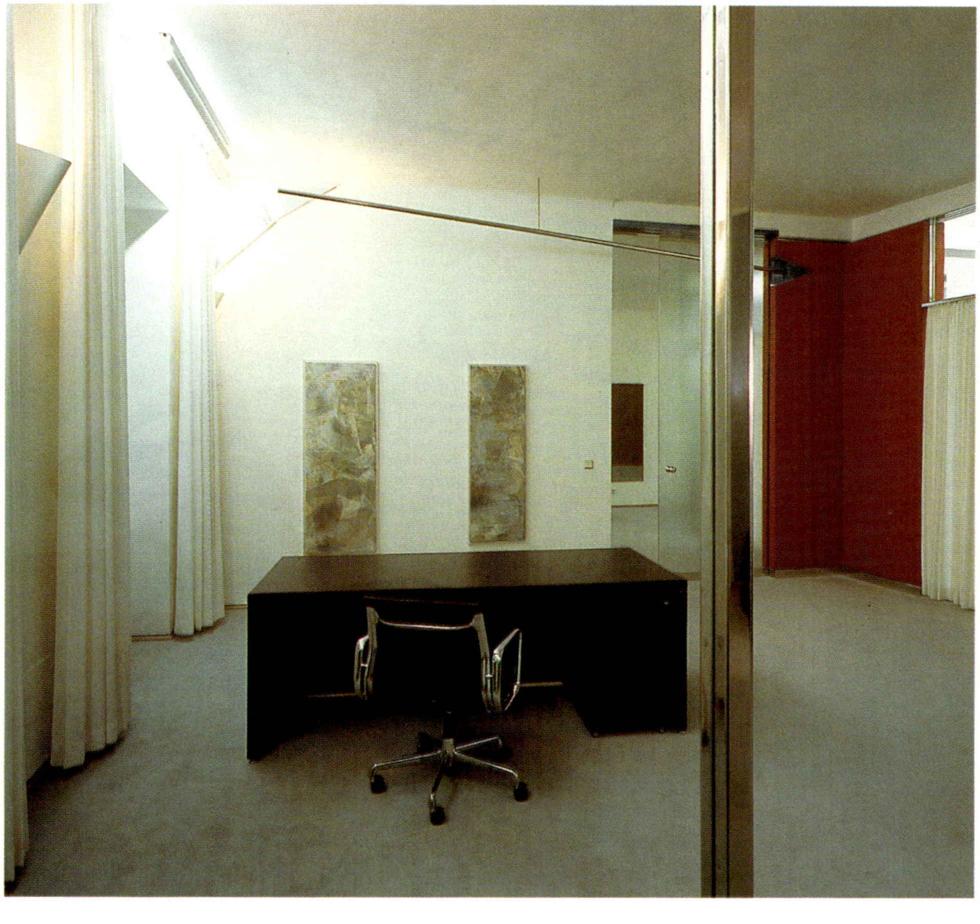

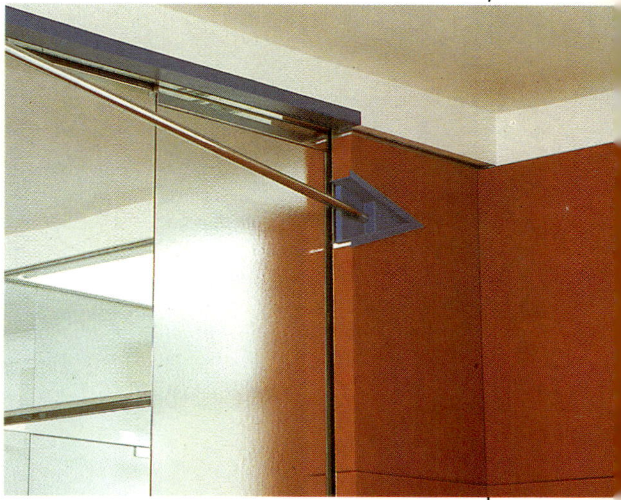

LEO DESIGN STUDIO
HELSINKI, FINLAND

Designed by Leo Design

Alone of the Scandinavian countries, in Finland a new mood has swept across design in recent years. The land of Alvar Aalto, where a humane approach to Modernism reached its apex, has seen its young designers swayed by the exuberant excesses of the Italian new wave, notably Memphis and Studio Alchymia. New furniture companies, such as Artzan and Avarte, have sprung up to market the designs of this Finnish new wave, and their best efforts easily rival the work of the Italians.

Leo Mitrunen, head of Leo Design, has not yet broken into the commercially successful ranks of Finnish designers. But his low-cost studio shows that he shares many of the preoccupations of the Italian-influenced new wave. At the entrance, a riot of mirrors and glass confronts visitors, perhaps causing slight disorientation.

This effect is only minimally dissipated in the actual working spaces of the studio. The designers have modified standard drawing-boards to display a subtle sense of humour: yellow ball feet and chrome trim give the impression that the drawing-boards are preparing to race around the studio. Such a race would be aided by the landscape the designers have created: the floor-coverings are varied using tiles, rubber-studded flooring and linoleum. Through such simple devices, Leo Design have created a lively and at times amusing showcase for their work.

(right) The entrance is a profusion of mirrors and triangular forms.

(below) Even functional furniture such as drawing-boards displays Mitrunen's playful oddities: yellow ball feet and 'go-faster' chrome trim.

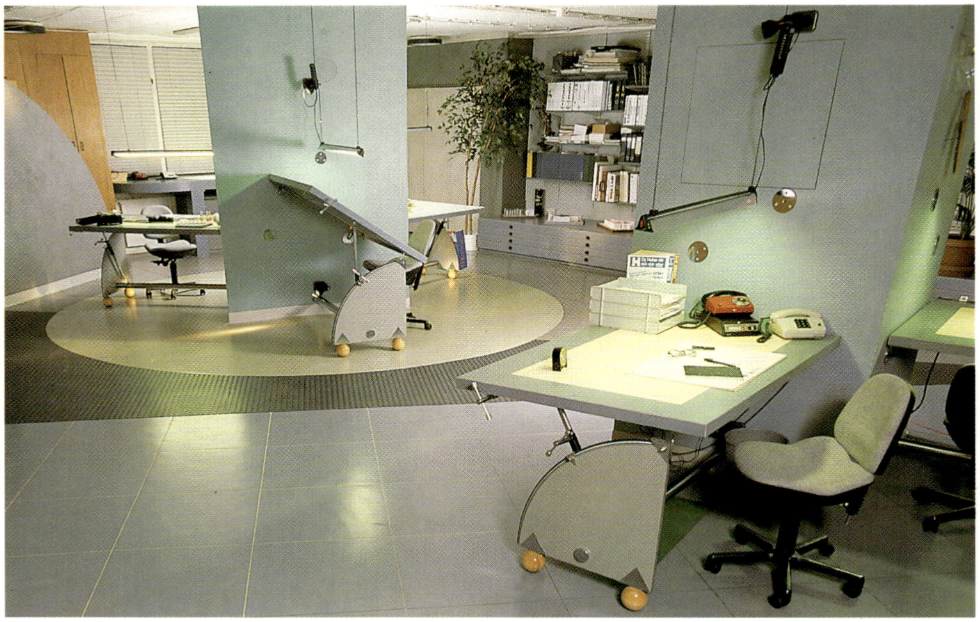

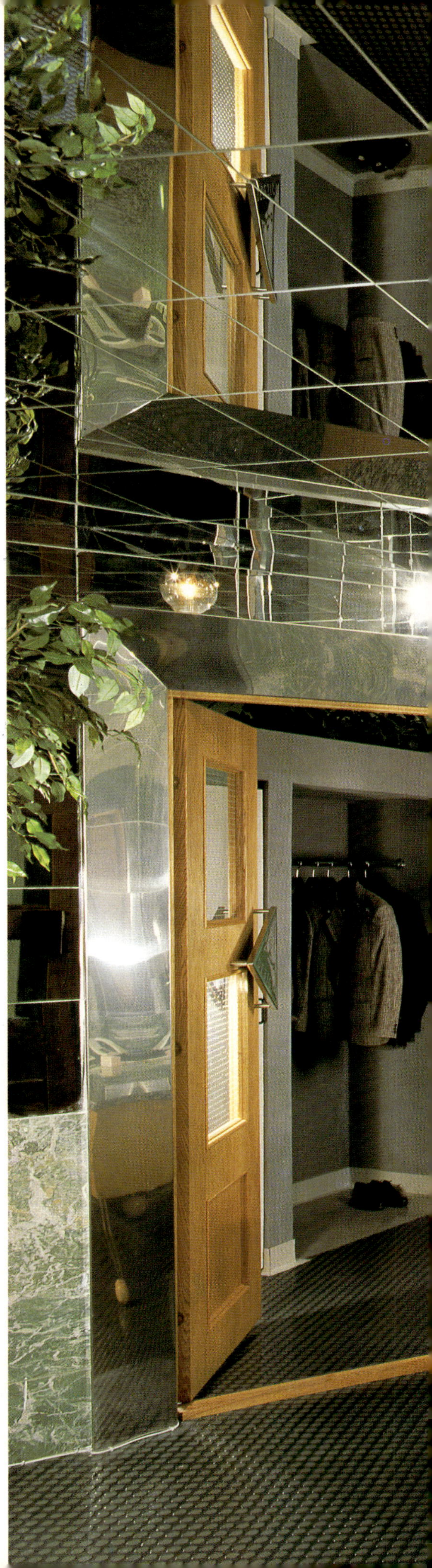

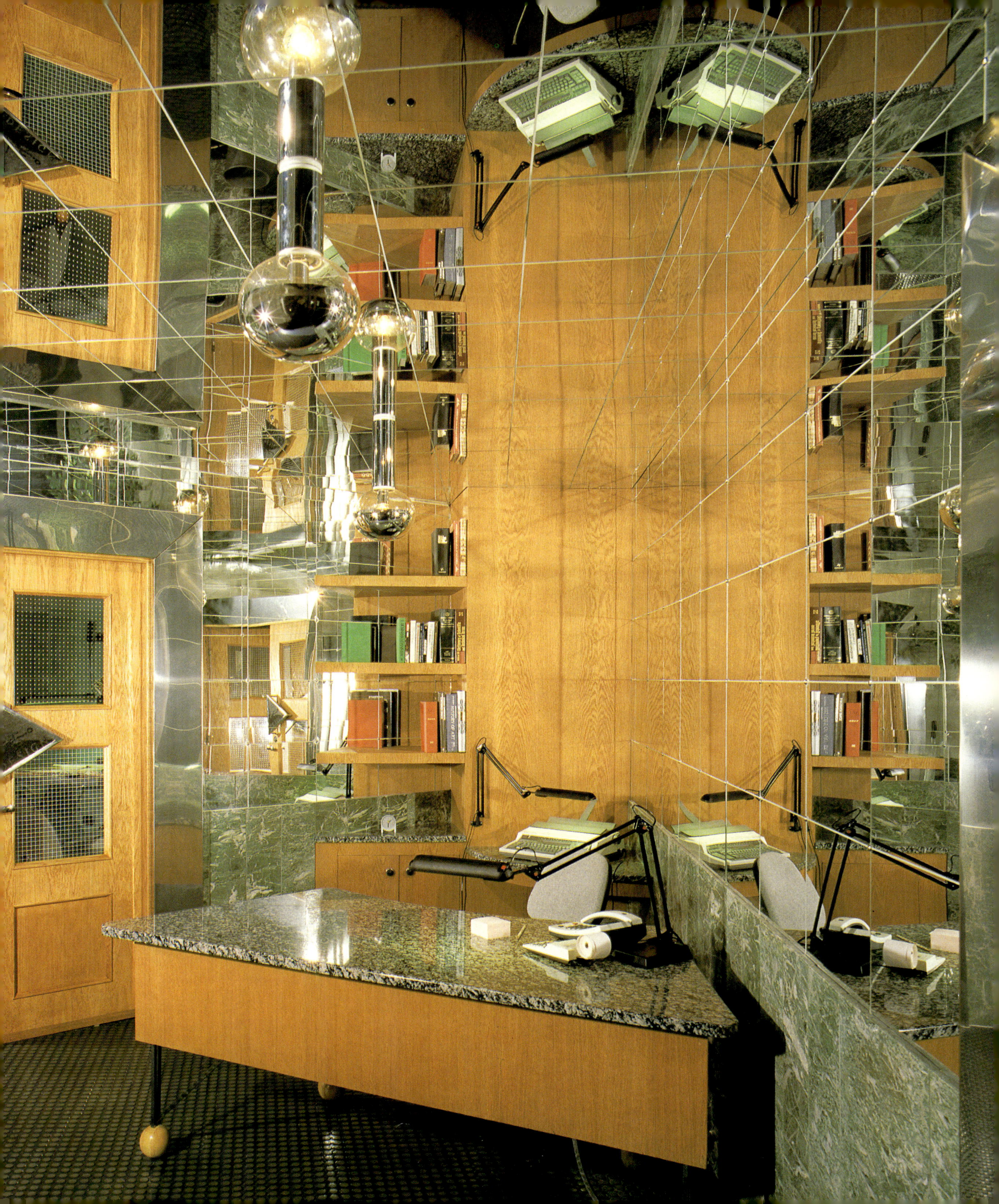
HISTORY OF ART

MACK STUDIO
SAN FRANCISCO, CALIFORNIA, USA

Designed by Mack Architects

Mark Mack is a particularly skilful practitioner of a characteristically California style of architecture: hints of a Mediterranean culture seep through in the bare, unfinished surfaces and strong, basic forms. Naturally, when he approached the task of designing his own studio he envisioned it as a representation of his architectural thinking.

In a former garage, Mack had built a small studio filled with tiny quirks and new ideas. The garage door has been replaced with a large window-wall, in one corner of which is the door. Inside, the rectangular room has exposed timber ceiling, whitewashed walls and a quarry tile floor. But Mack has enlivened this basic solution with concrete block partitions, ragged cutaway wall openings that expose the timber studs.

The furniture, all specially designed, also follows this pattern of simple shapes. Marble-topped tables sit on square timber bases, some with galumphing concrete feet. In such a small space, the solidity of furniture and architecture lends an air of permanence.

(below) A garage has been transformed by replacing the door with a large window-wall, and devising a design of clever simplicity for the inside.

(above right) The basic design of a quarry tile floor, whitewashed walls and an exposed timber ceiling is enlivened by small details, such as the ragged cutaway wall openings.

(below right) The furniture, too, has an aura of humorous austerity: a marble-topped table has a timber base with oversized concrete feet.

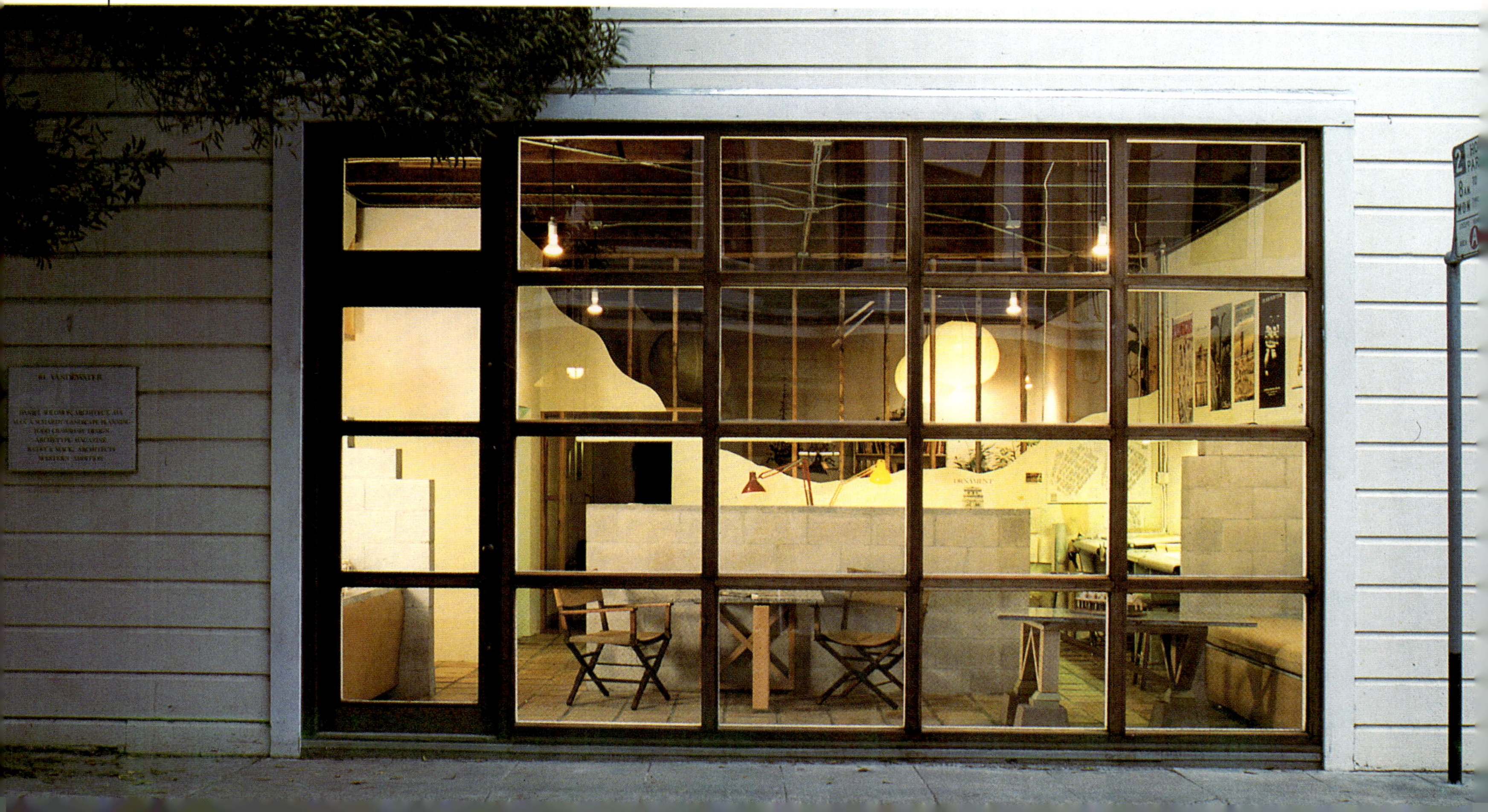

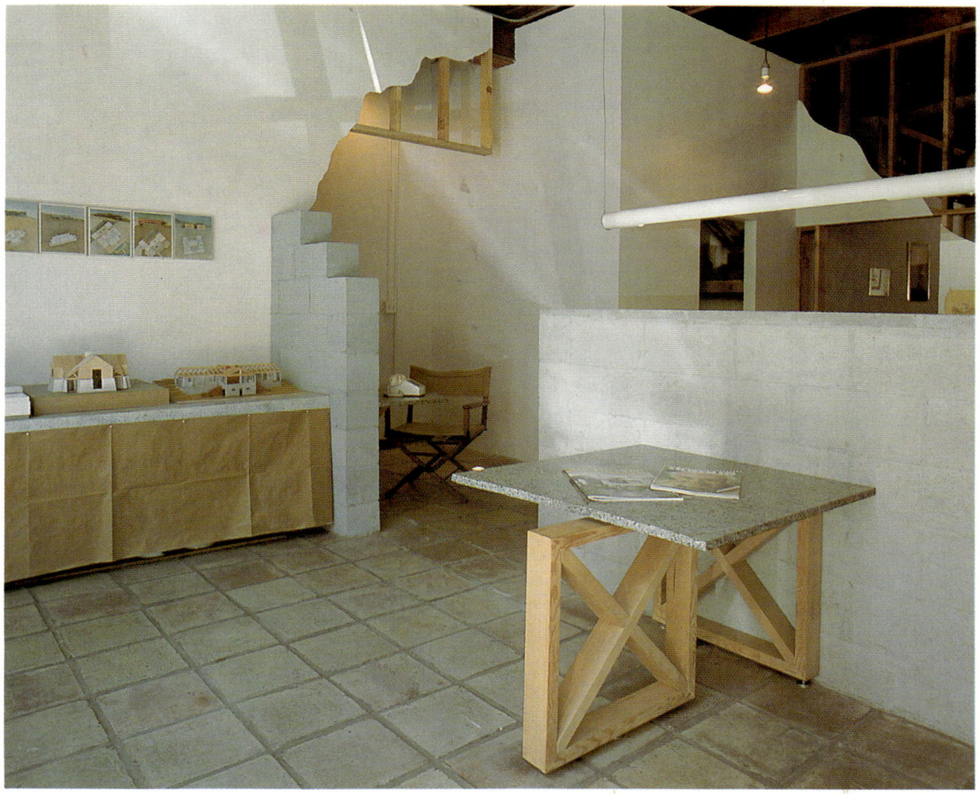

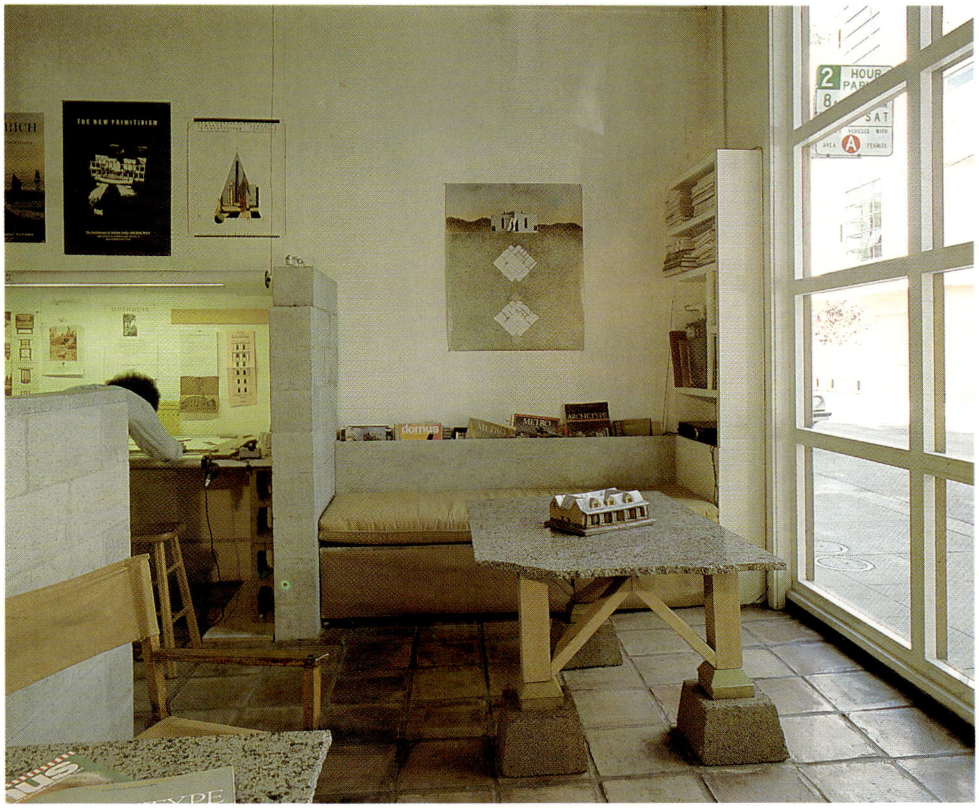
THE NEW PRIMITIVISM
domus
METRO
ARCHETYPE

LLOYD'S
LONDON, UK
Designed by Richard Rogers Partnership

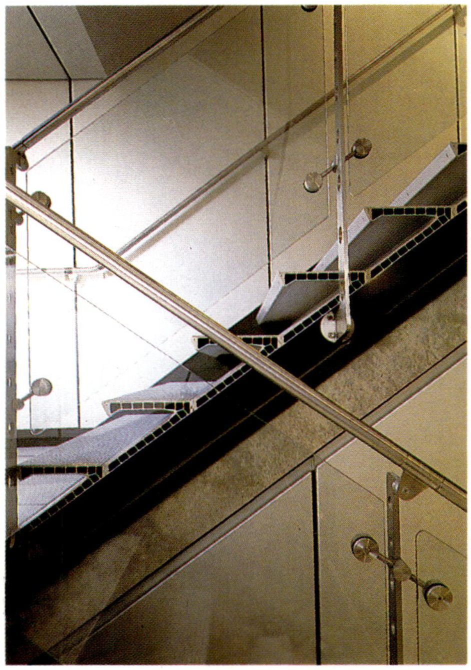

(above) The treads and risers of the escape stair are formed from a one-piece aluminium extrusion which is bolted to the stringer.

(right) In the cathedral-like space of The Room, the caller's rostrum sits on a marble plinth like some archeological relic.

To view a project as vast and all-encompassing as the Lloyd's building as interior design may seem perverse. Yet the building Richard Rogers designed to house the famous insurance underwriters of Lloyd's is as complex in its interior elements as in its controversial exterior. Partly this is because of Roger's belief in leaving little to chance – the haphazard situation of the standard speculative office building is one the practice has never encountered. But more than an exercise in one group's design philosophy, the immaculate interior design of Lloyd's is a response to the complexities of the underwriting task itself.

The centre of Lloyd's – both the building and the institution – is The Room, where hundreds of underwriters work amid mounds of paper (though the building is prepared for the gradual transition of all tasks to computers). In the grand double-height space, the designers have devised new 'boxes', the underwriting desks, and a sophisticated system of servicing to provide power, data and telecommunications, as well as fresh air, to all the workstations.

A 12 inch (30 centimetre) raised floor provides ample room for wires and cables and, an important innovation in the building, acts as a low-pressure plenum with air drawn by fans into flexible ducts connected to the boxes or to circular vents in the floors. As a result, each box is individually air-conditioned.

The two thousand boxes themselves were designed in association with Italian furniture manufacturer Tecno. The three thousand different organizations that make up Lloyd's all had individual requirements for their boxes, but the basic box has a veneered worktop with drawers, electrical data outlets and even ledger-wells. An additional kit of parts has a superstructure for storage, additional storage bins, footrests, leather lift-up desk tops and seats.

The veneers and leather of the boxes respect the traditions of Lloyd's, but most of the other interior elements have more in common with the building's high-tech pedigree. Perhaps most noticeable in The Room are the zoomorphic information stations, with their lunar module-like pod feet, perforated metal and a cluster of information screens with messages for underwriters.

Special areas are more typical examples of 'interior design' within the £160 million (259 million dollar) project. The Captain's Room, the main restaurant, is fashionably monochrome, with the exception of a few carefully chosen deep red objects. Lloyd's maritime heritage is reflected in the canvas sails which act as room dividers. Perhaps less sympathetic to the Rogers conception is the bizarre treatment of the executive offices on the eleventh and twelfth floors, where French decorator Jacques Granges was called in to execute an impoverished pastiche that lacks the quality of the rest of the building: unfortunately, the executives who originally commissioned Rogers in 1978 had moved on by the time the building was completed.

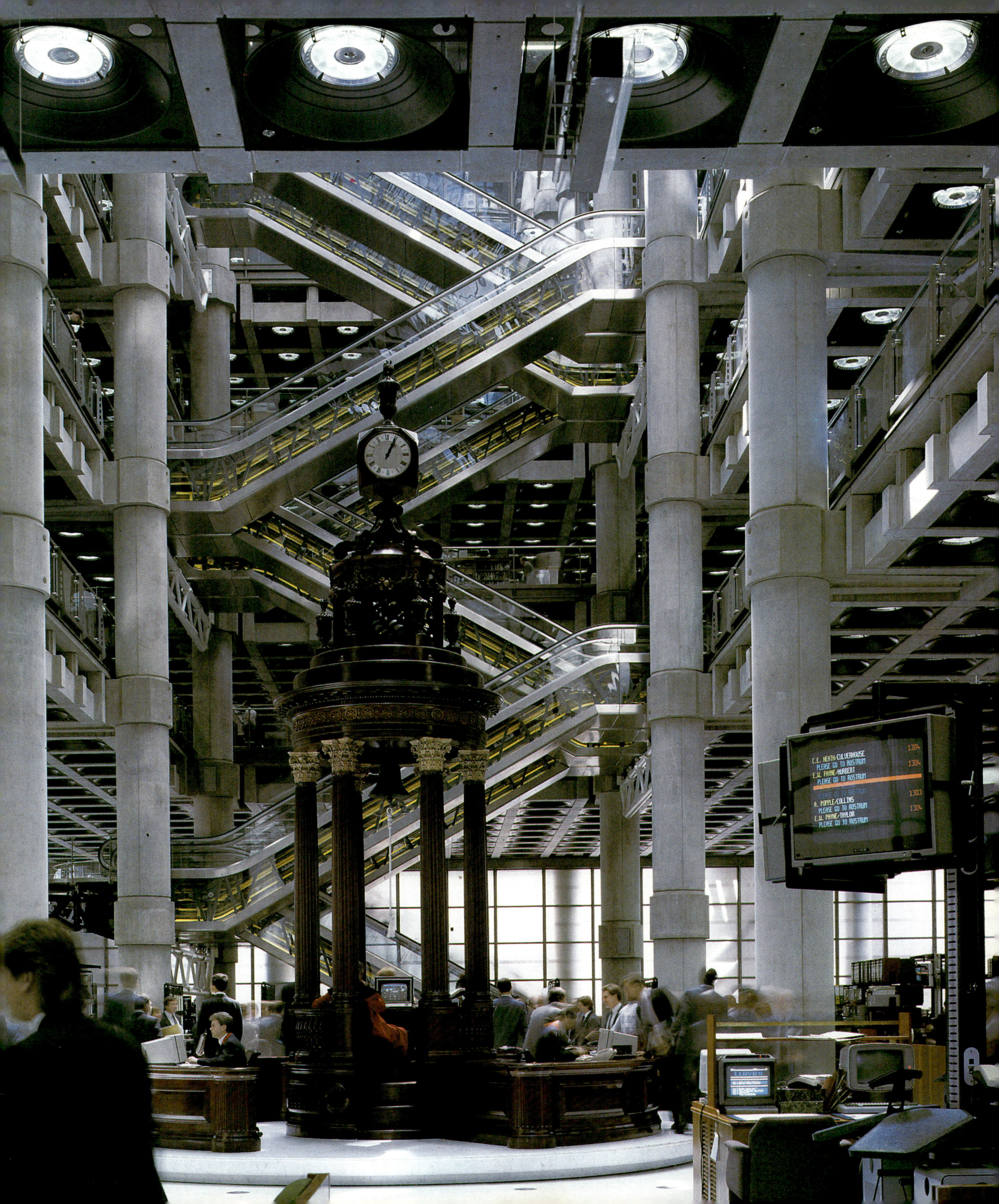
1304
C.E. HEATH/CULVERHOUSE
PLEASE GO TO ROSTRUM
1304
E.W. PAYNE/HUBBERT
PLEASE GO TO ROSTRUM
1303
A. POPPLE/COLLINS
PLEASE GO TO ROSTRUM
1304
E.W. PAYNE/TAYLOR
PLEASE GO TO ROSTRUM

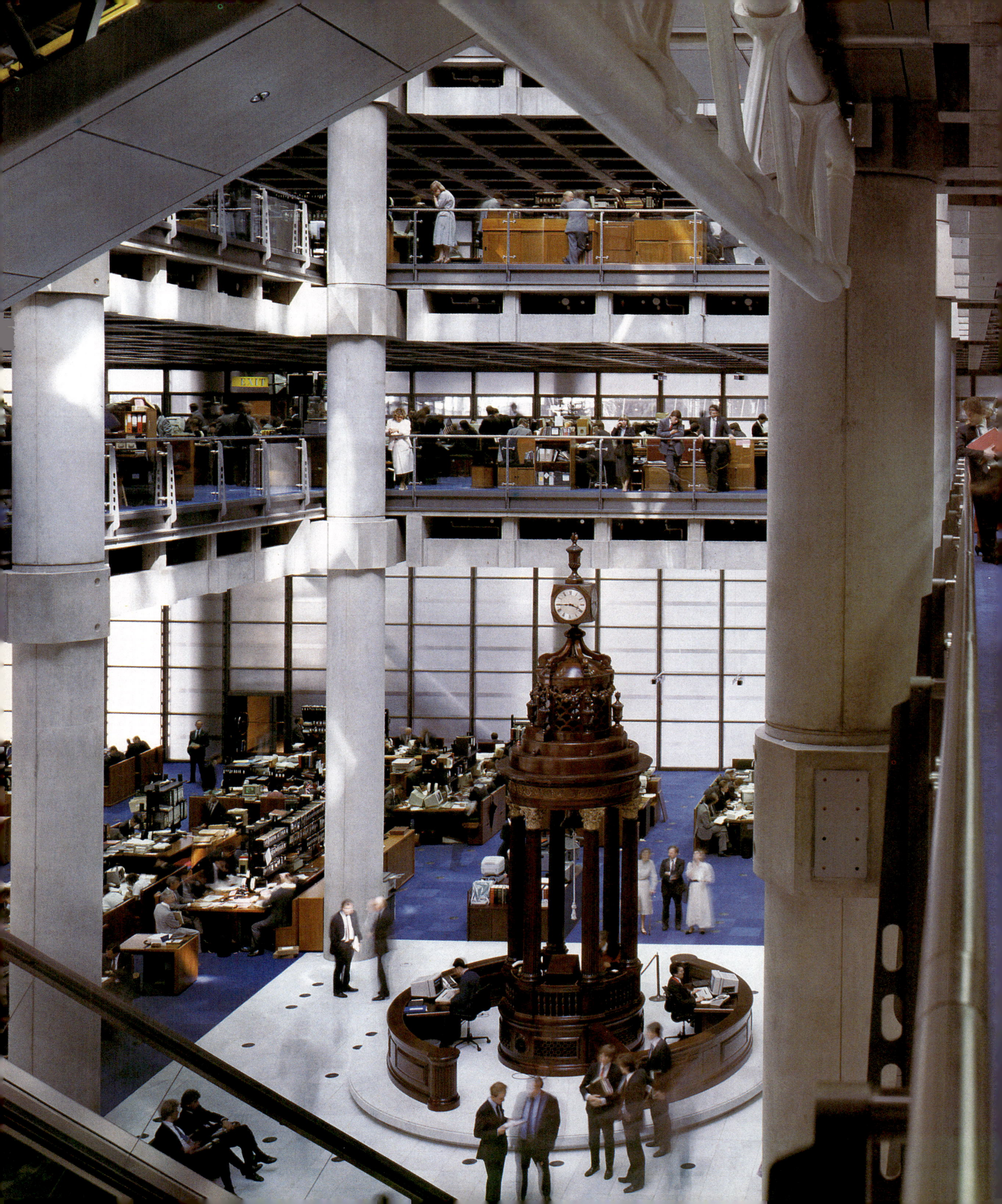
EXIT

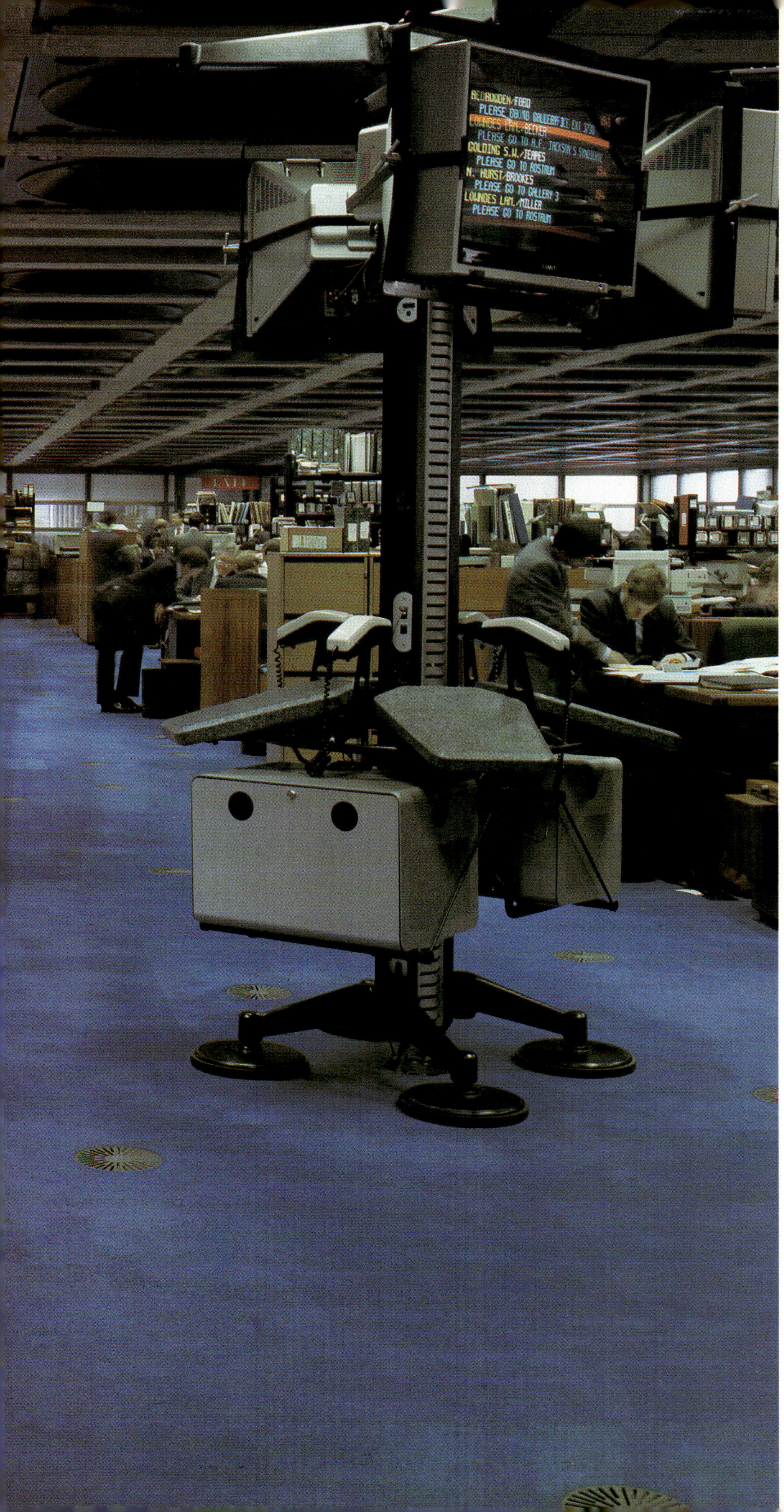

Underwriters' galleries overlook the turmoil of the double-height Room. Information towers, placed strategically throughout the space, display messages.

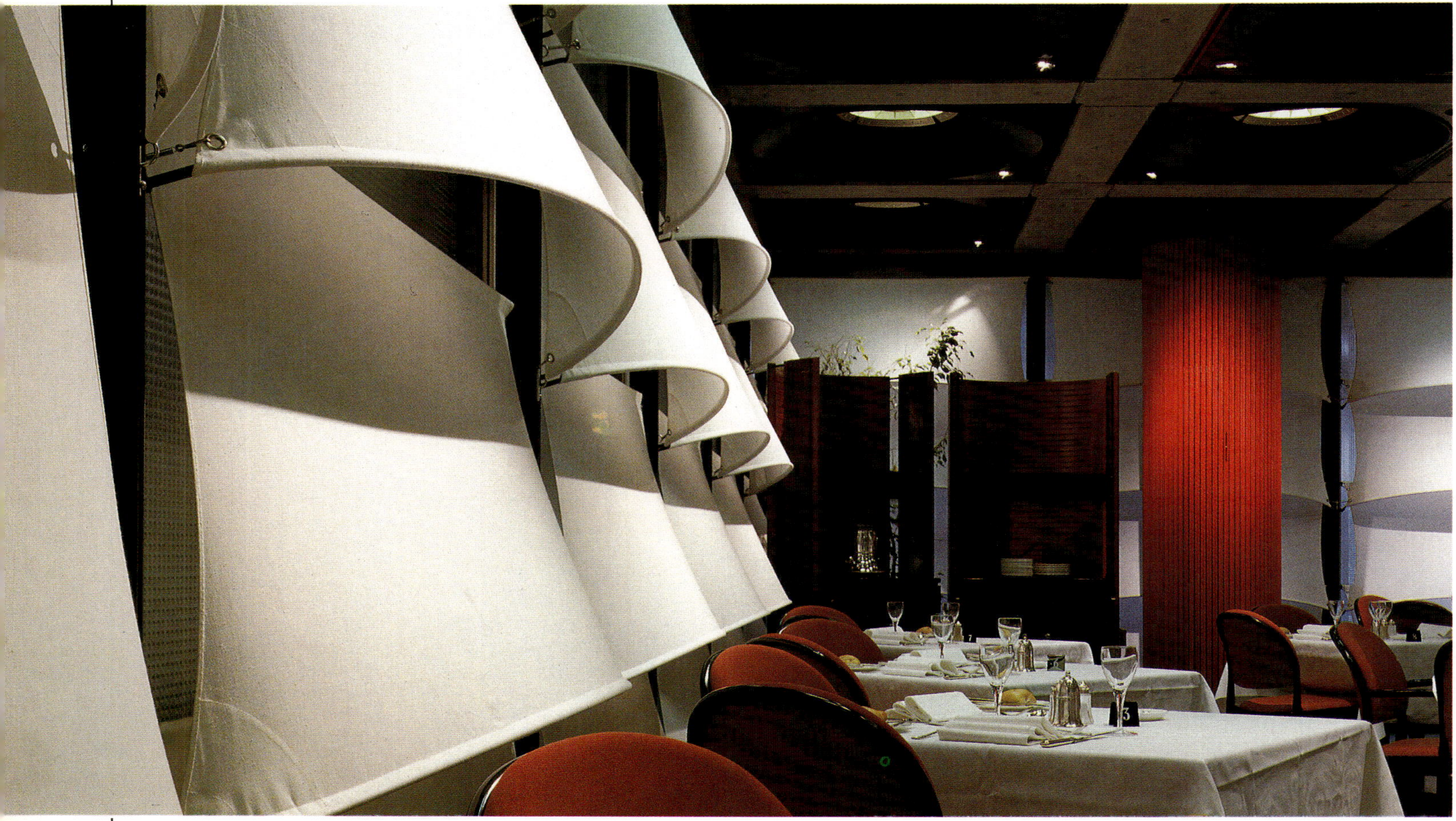

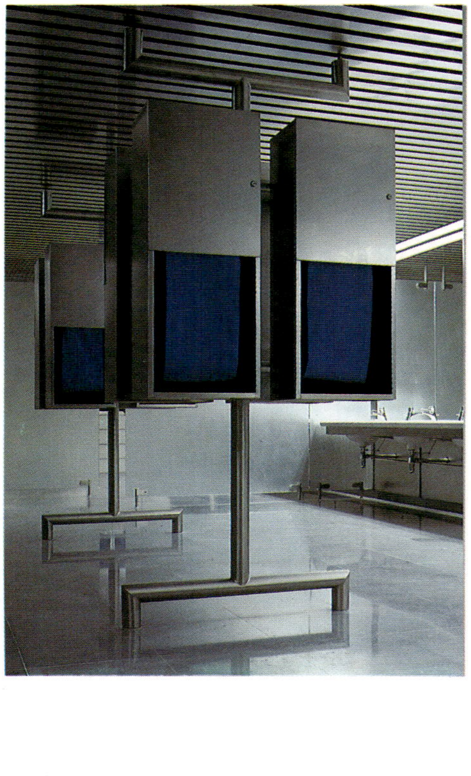

(above) In the Captain's Room restaurant, canvas sails act as room dividers and refer to Lloyd's nautical connections.

(right) Lavatories, designed in a style consistent with the rest of the project, are divided into separate areas for members, subscribers, associates and others.

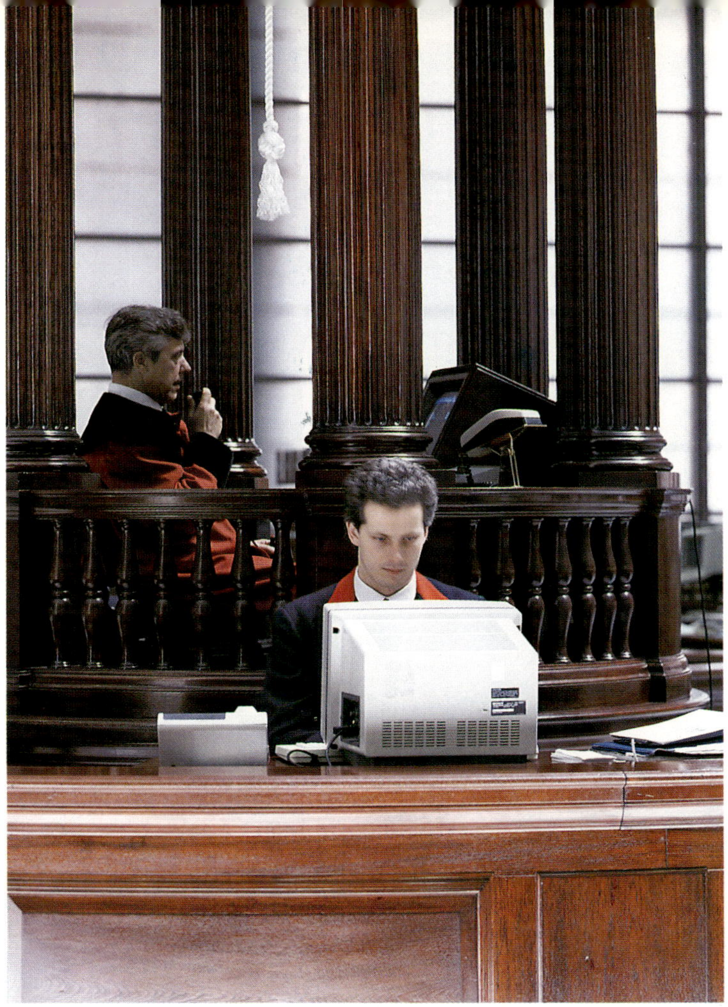

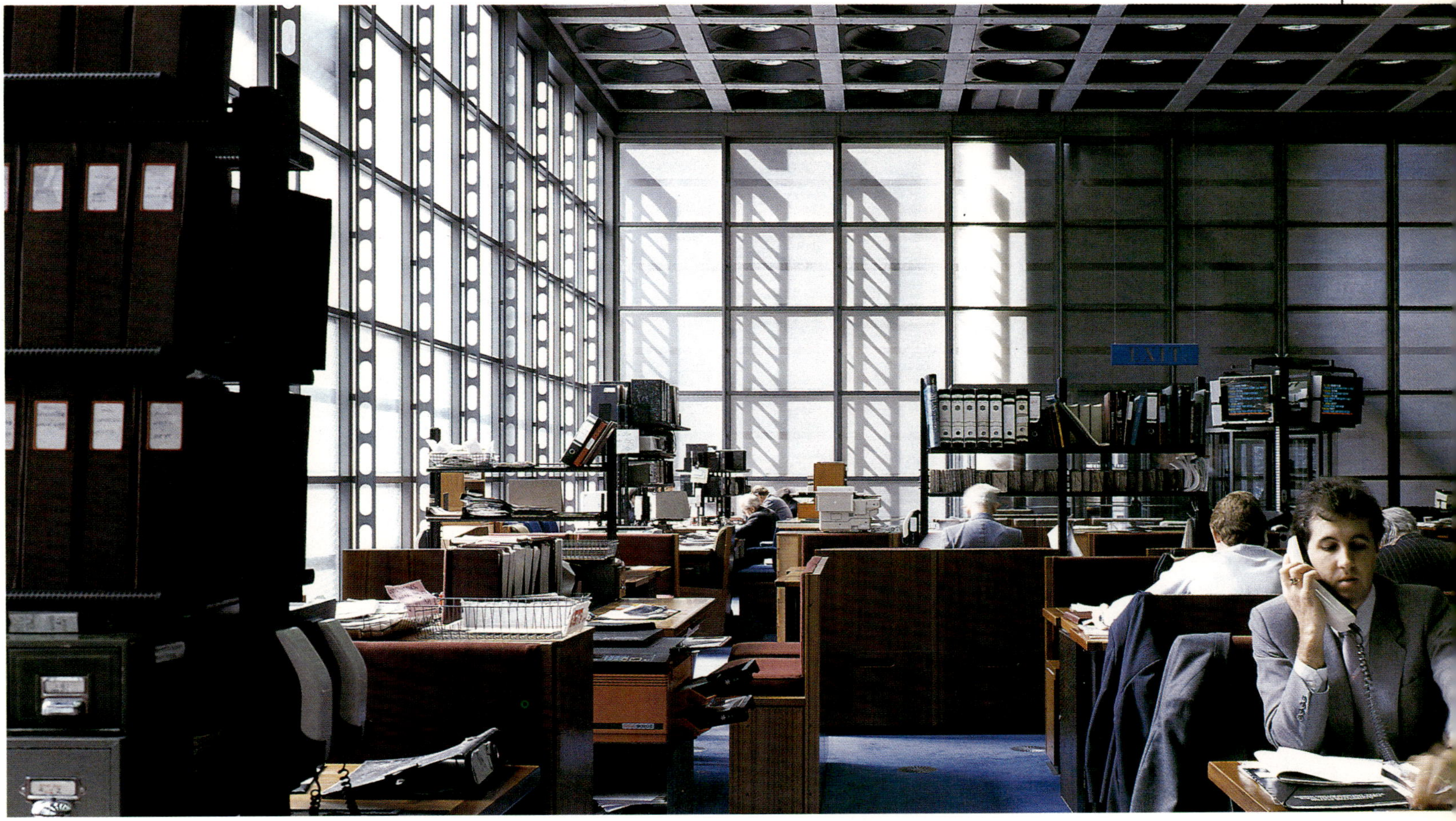

(left) Although the new building clearly signals Lloyd's modern status, old traditions continue to thrive.

(below) In The Room, underwriters are based at their 'boxes': Techno desks with power, data, telecommunications and fresh air, serviced from the raised floor.

THE BOSTON GLOBE
BOSTON, MASSACHUSETTS, USA

Designed by Skidmore, Owings & Merrill

In the popular imagination, newspaper offices are famously chaotic: filled with hard-bitten reporters with rolled-up shirtsleeves, overflowing with paper and throbbing with the tension of approaching deadlines. But newspapers are also big businesses, and their offices have many of the same requirements as any other organization. This addition to *The Boston Globe's* existing general office was designed to house the less dramatic areas of a newspaper: general offices, executive offices, a board-room and entertainment space.

The 49,000 square foot (4,552 square metre) addition is an extension of the existing building. An elliptical atrium acts as a hinge between the old and new buildings, and serves as the main entrance for the entire complex. To unify the interiors of the building, the designers developed a lattice screen motif that recurs throughout. First encountered in the entrance atrium, the lattice is expressed in 'window-walls' and doors of red-painted wood which act as transparent screens. The red screens are complemented by a blue carpet and yellow circular sofas which enliven the atrium, in contrast to the relatively sober adjacent executive office spaces.

Skidmore, Owings & Merrill's skill in providing American executives with 'traditional' offices that have the patina of modernism is well reflected in the executive areas. The screens of the atrium are repeated in stained oak. An English brown oak veneer in a white oak frame is used for panelling, storage walls and furnishing details. The choice of high-quality materials such as marbles, Italian oak burl, and English brown oak tops used for desks offers a mixture of textures and colours. Furniture comes from a wide range of sources, including Ward Bennett, Steelcase, Knoll and Sunar Hauserman.

On the third floor are the facilities for both

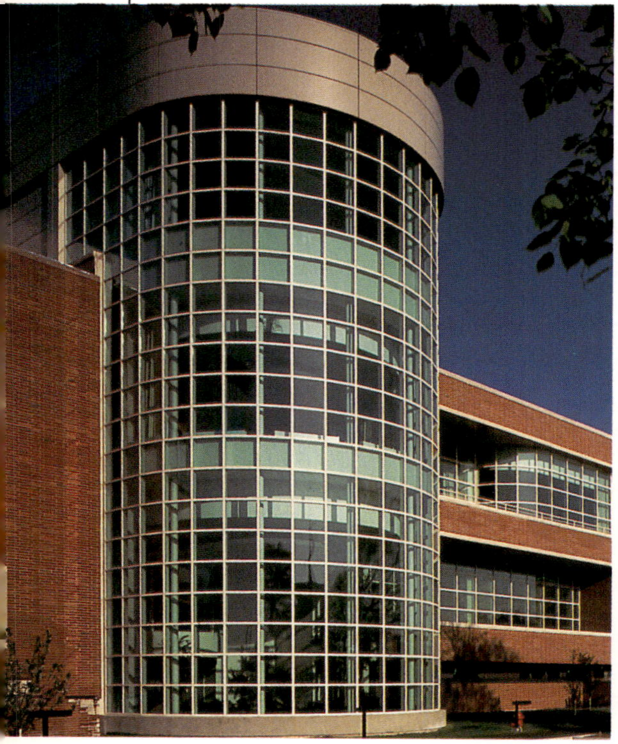

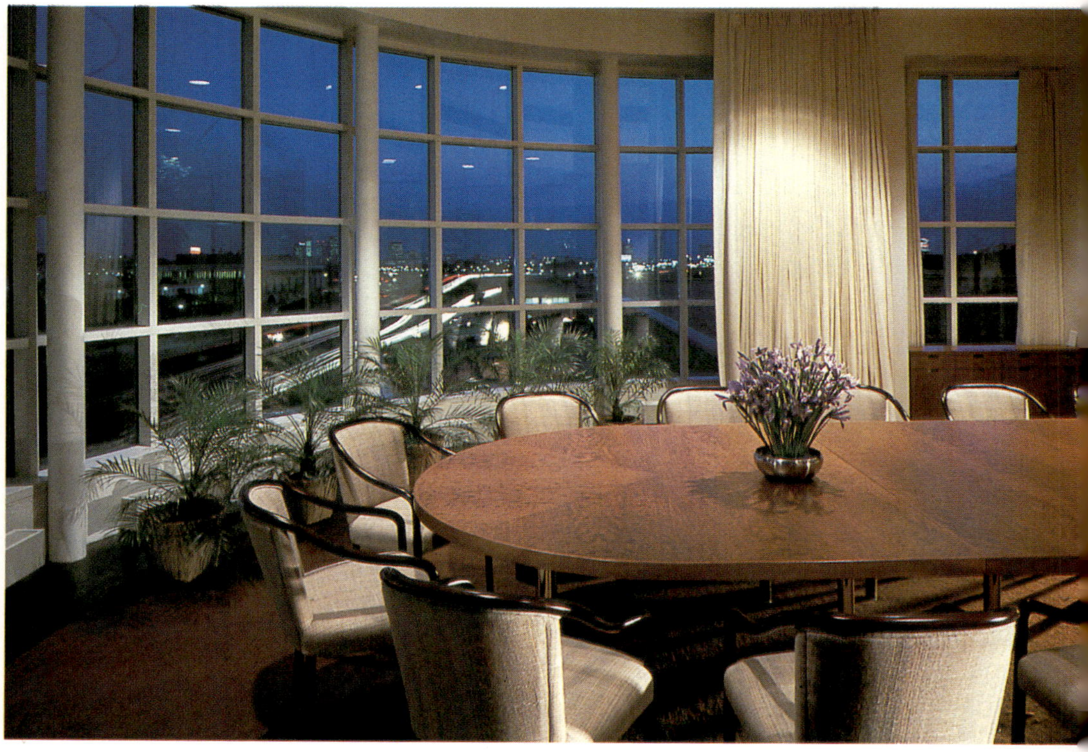

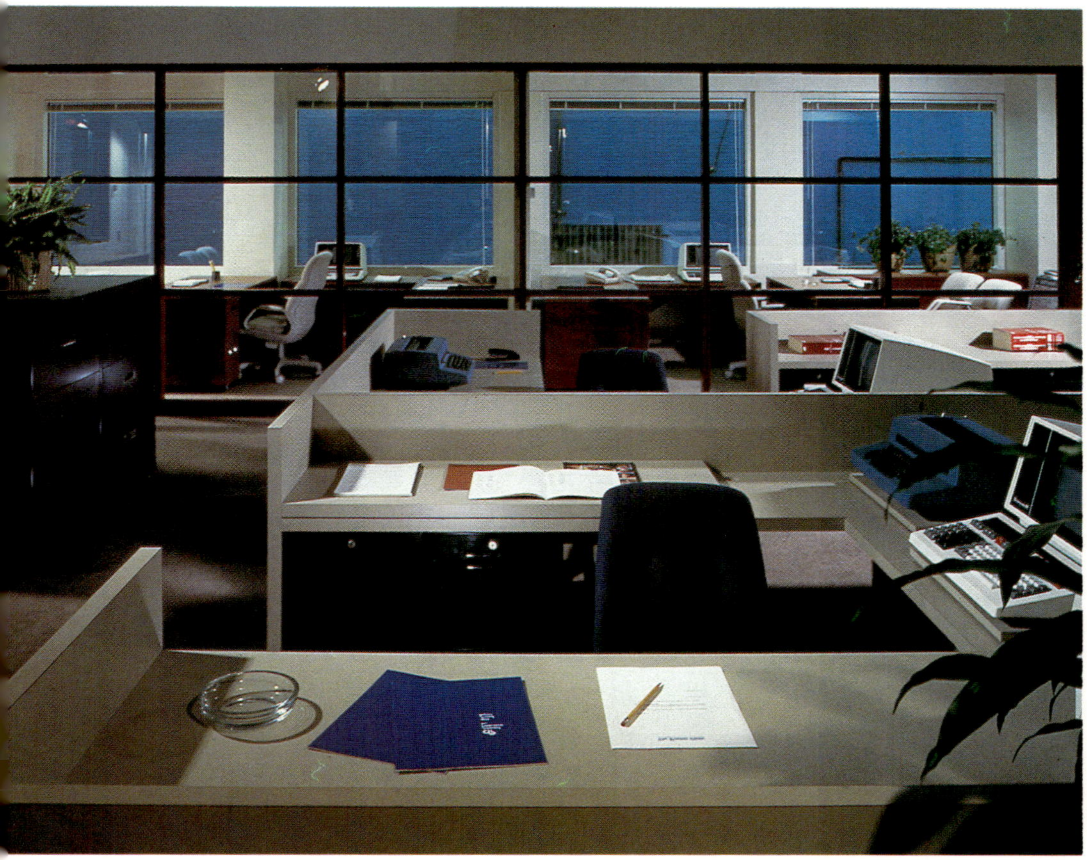

in-house and outside entertaining. Here, too, the lattice screens appear: this time as demountable wooden screens which can be used to redefine long, narrow corridors to create somewhat more intimate areas for parties and socializing.

The careful mixture of old and new, of the traditional and the modern (expressed not least in the seamless knitting of old and new buildings), is particularly appropriate to the leading paper of New England, an area of the USA famed for both its liberalism and its almost haughty pride in its relatively lengthy history.

(above) Work areas have a typical arrangement of open-plan space serving glazed cellular offices.

(right) The atrium contains the principal vertical circulation and communicates an atmosphere of well-ordered corporate calm. The lattice-screen motif is evident in the windows, doors and balustrades.

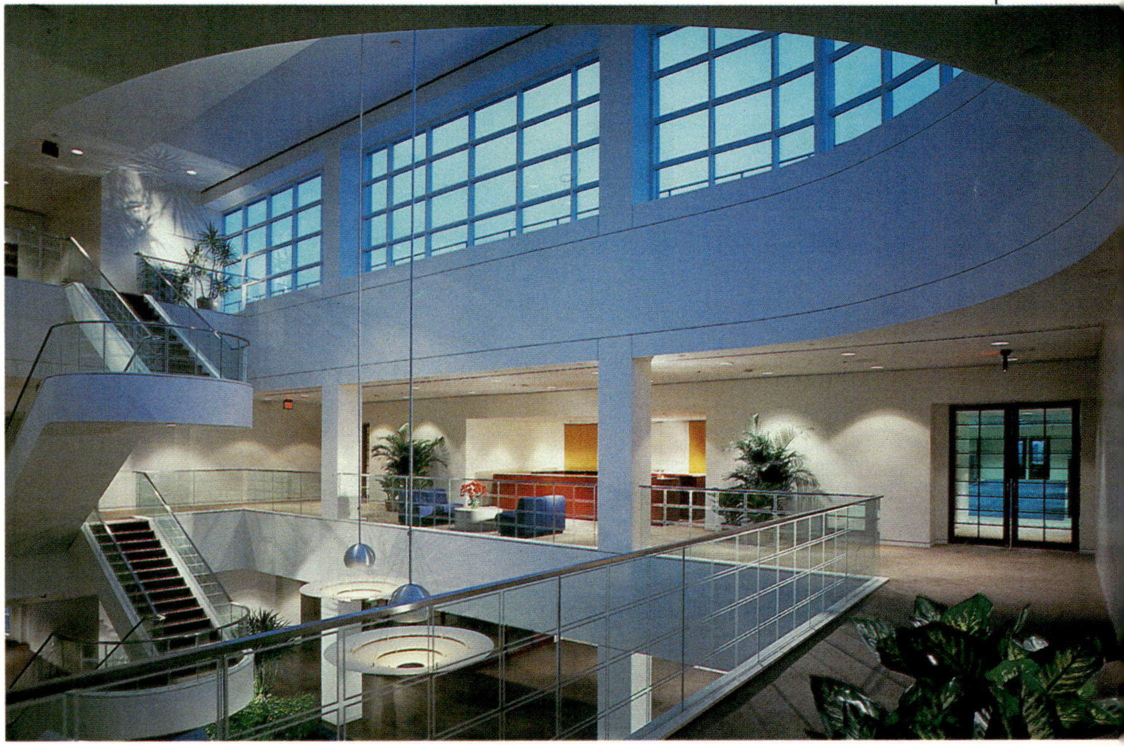

(far left) The elliptical atrium acts as the hinge between the old and new buildings, and also provides the main entrance for the entire complex.

(left) Entertainment areas have a more traditional atmosphere, partly created by the richly coloured oak table tops.

ADVANCED COMPUTER DEVELOPMENT CENTER

APPLE COMPUTER INC.

CUPERTINO, CALIFORNIA, USA

Designed by STUDIOS San Francisco

California's Silicon Valley is filled with anonymous speculative buildings, ideal for the fast-growing, high-risk companies that populate the area. The anonymity of these buildings generally extends inside, where obeisance to clean functionalism is only minimally mitigated by a sparse collection of Ficus Benjamina trees.

Apple Computer, however, have a reputation for doing things differently. When Apple purchased a 14 million dollar Cray supercomputer to help them develop the next generation of their products, it was clear that a special facility would be needed, both to flaunt their new toy, and to inspire the best work from the boffins who would use the Cray.

Designers STUDIOS stripped the 23,681 square foot (2,200 square metre) single-storey building to its architectural shell, exposing a 16 foot (4.9 metre) high plywood and heavy timber deck. The deck and rolled batt insulation, which was installed underneath, were painted white to reflect light into the space. Industrial lighting fixtures were installed upside down to provide indirect light; light fixtures and ducts were painted bright colours to draw attention away from the relatively uninspiring roof plane.

Piercing this simple space is a dramatic black and white striped tiled corridor. The corridor connects the entrance lobby to the viewing area, where visitors can see the custom-coloured purple Cray computer. Security and privacy are also provided by the corridor's segregation of visitors from the work spaces.

The strong colour contrasts of the public areas are replaced by muted, more soothing tones in the work areas along the building's perimeter. Office and research areas are tied back both graphically and physically to the Cray computer and to each other by a network of purple cable trays. This network reinforces primary circulation paths before it arches into cable tray spines which serve workstation clusters (the workstations themselves are specially made). The open cable trays carry the large quantities of constantly changing communication, data and electrical cabling and their very prominence and openness allow the engineers easy access to rewire as necessary. For a company that started in a garage little more than ten years ago, Apple's new home for its boffins is infused with the belief that a good environment inspires creativity.

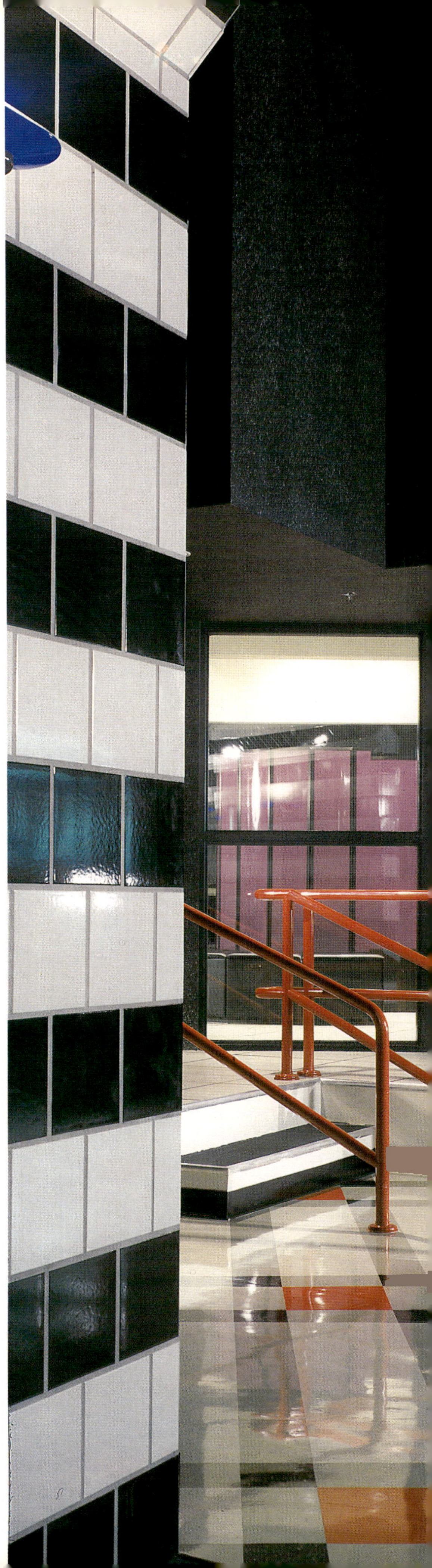

The dramatic central corridor allows visitors to view Apple's research centre, while at the same time ensuring the security of the work spaces. The black and white tiled corridor is lit with Atelier International's wall uplighters.

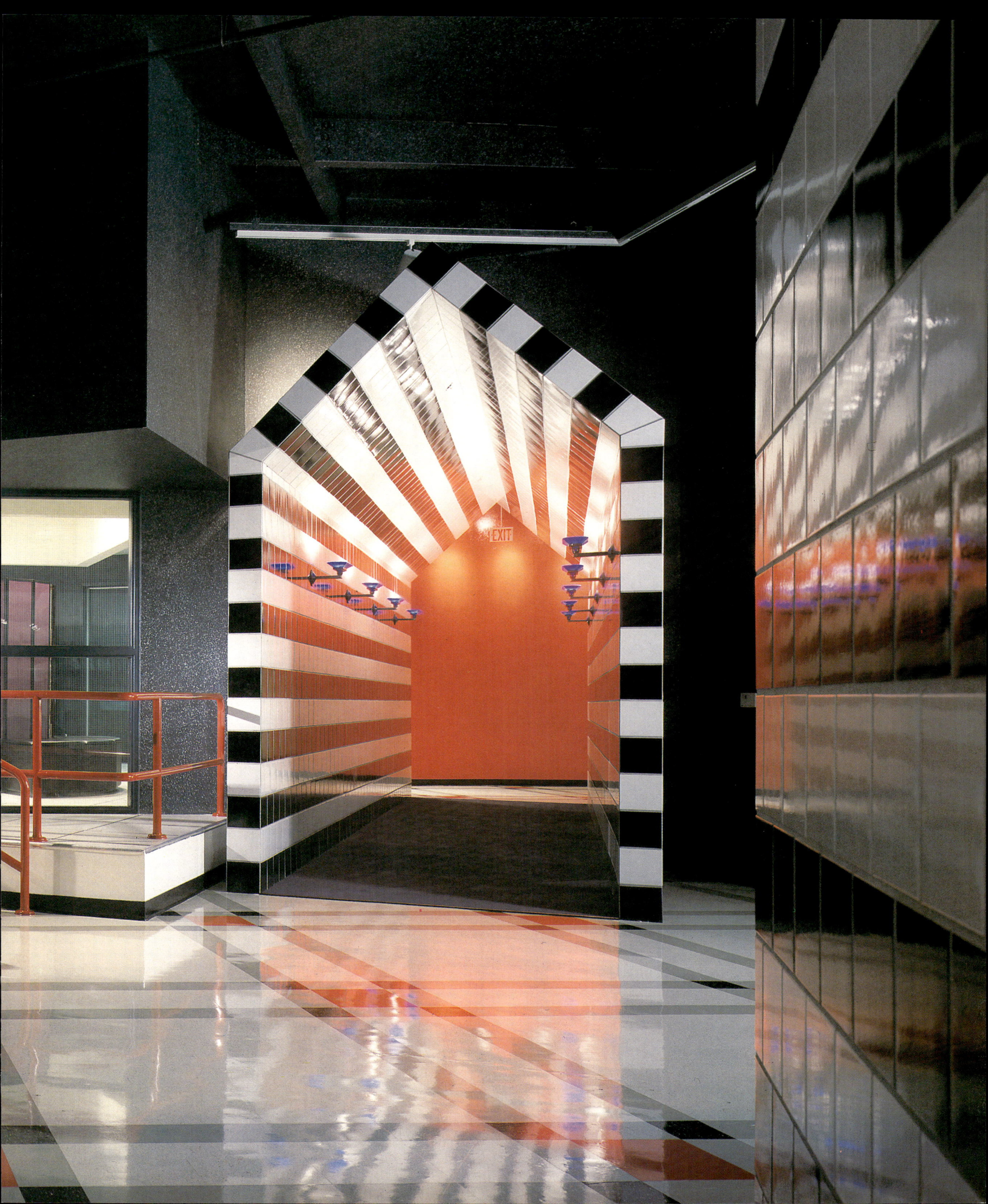
EXIT

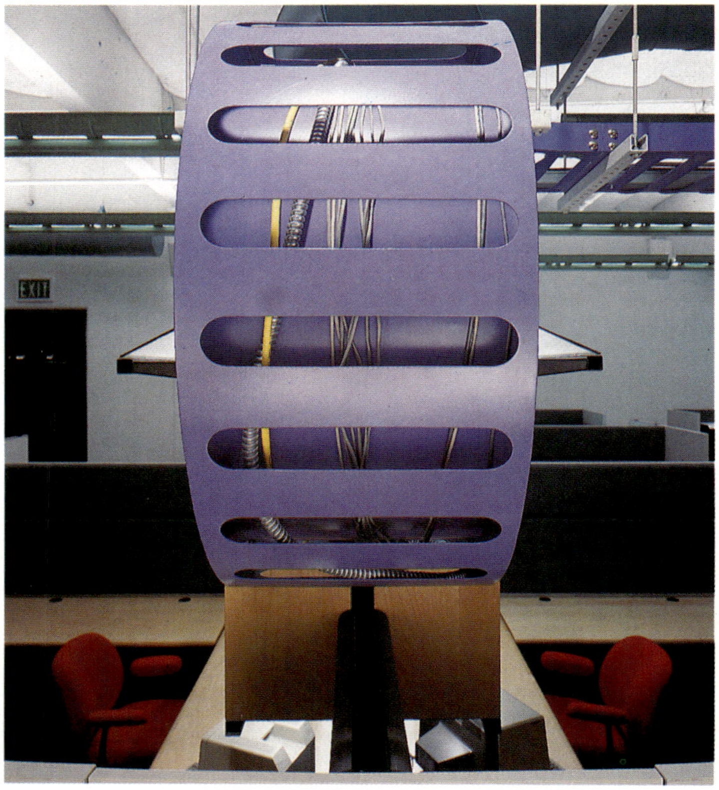

(left) Carrying the power of the Cray supercomputer to individual workstations, a network of purple cable trays allows access for simple and quick rewiring.

(below) Ground-floor plan.

(right) Specially made workstations are clustered round the cable trays that distribute the Cray's power throughout the building.

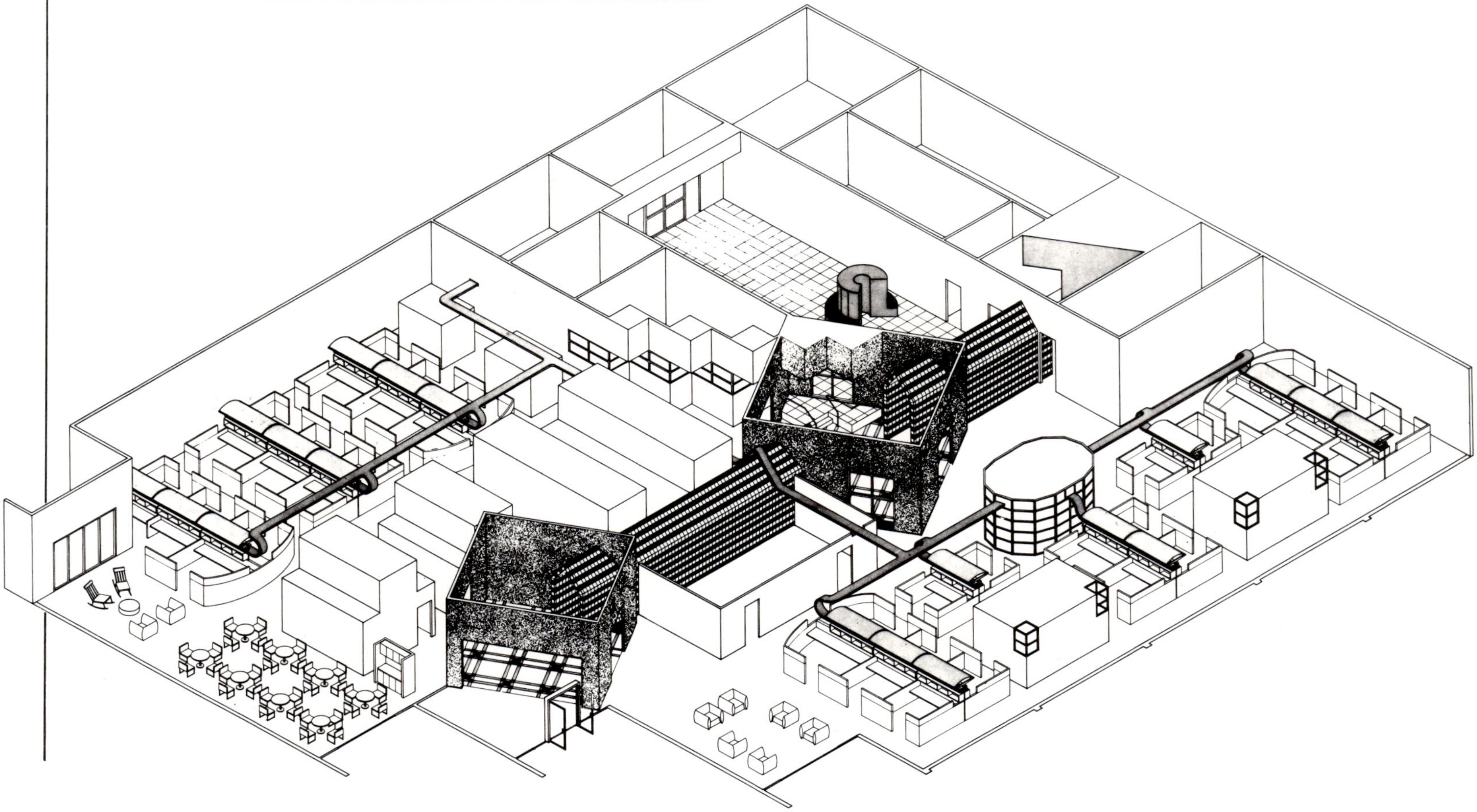

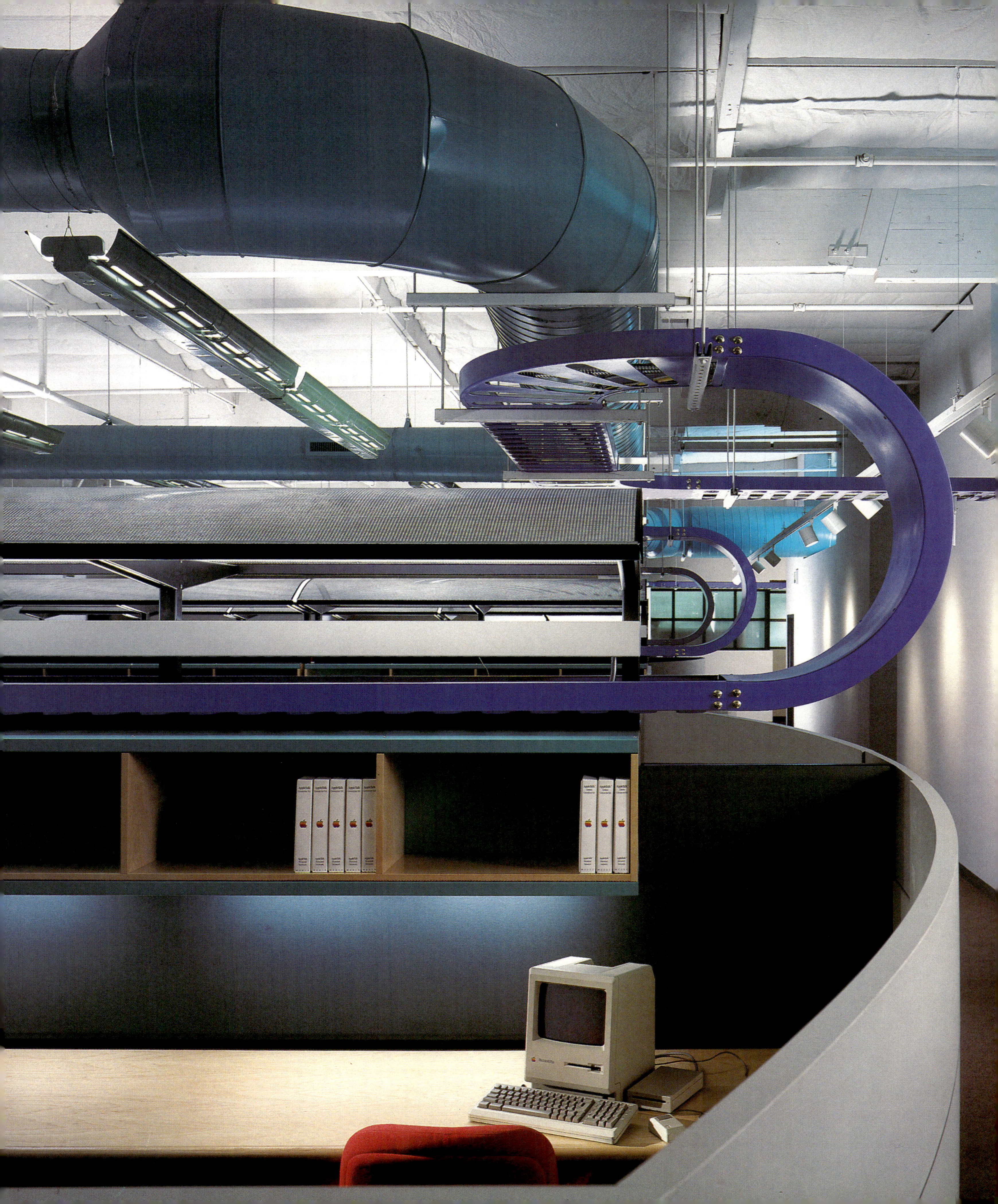

SCHWINN BICYCLE COMPANY

CHICAGO, ILLINOIS, USA

Designed by Tilton + Lewis Associates

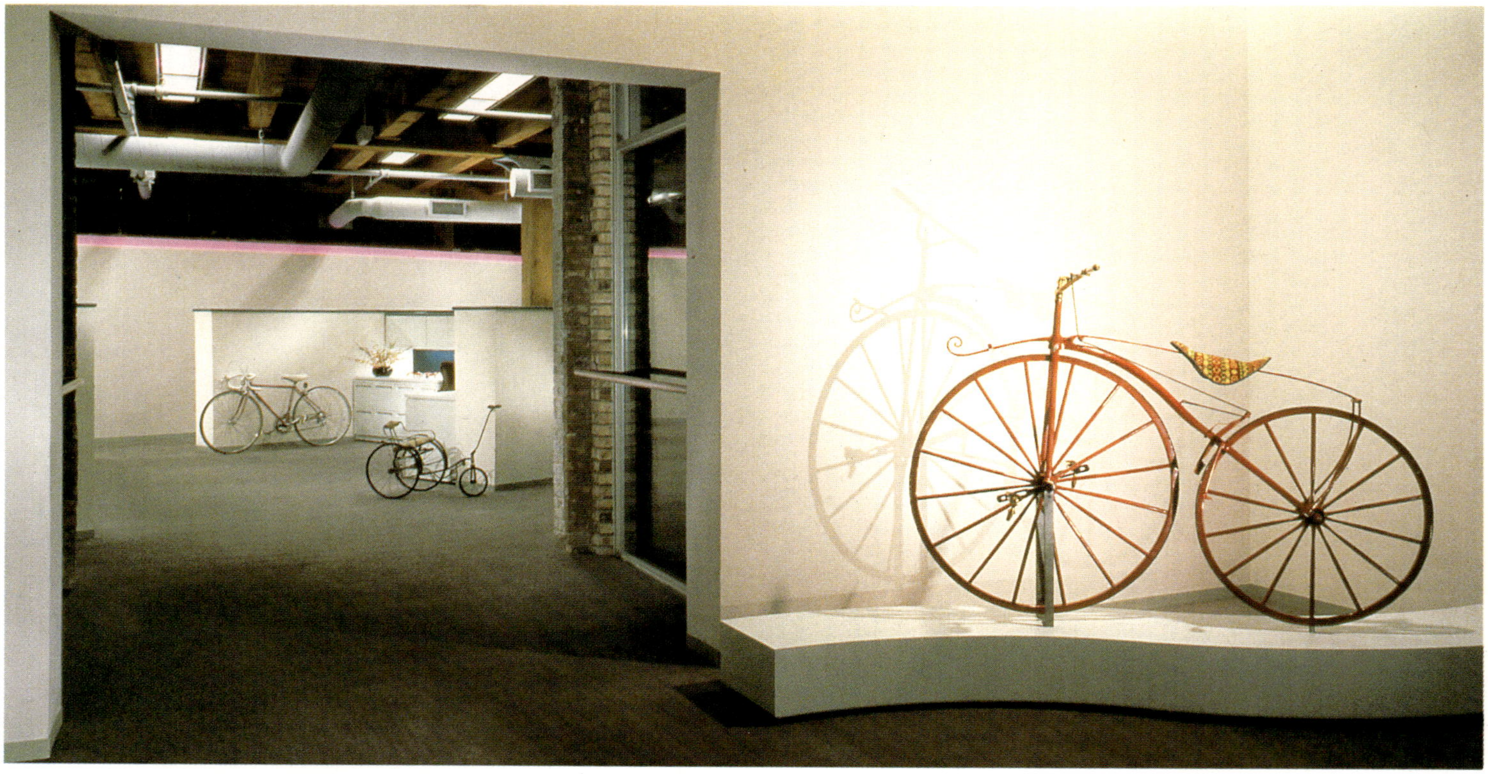

For most Americans of the post-war generations, the name Schwinn is virtually synonymous with bicycles. So it is perhaps not surprising that the design of their new corporate headquarters includes many elements to remind both visitors and staff of the company's tradition in their field.

Tilton + Lewis were commissioned to renovate completely the *circa* 1900 six-storey brick and timber loft building on Chicago's developing Near West Side. As part of the refurbishment project, a new free-standing elevator/stair tower and glass curtain wall was constructed on the site of an adjoining building which had previously been demolished.

Schwinn's management philosophy and style required an open-plan office environment to encourage internal communication and to provide a catalyst for better staff interaction. Since the existing building housed what the designers call 'a cacophony of architectural elements', the design uses a free-flowing floor plan which better fits the old building's character (thereby rejecting a more conventional grid furniture layout).

The open-plan workstation layout weaves

(above) The antique bicycle collection is displayed throughout the building to remind both visitors and staff of the company's history.

(right) The character of the renovated industrial building comes through strongly in the canteen, with the exposed ducts and timber ceilings.

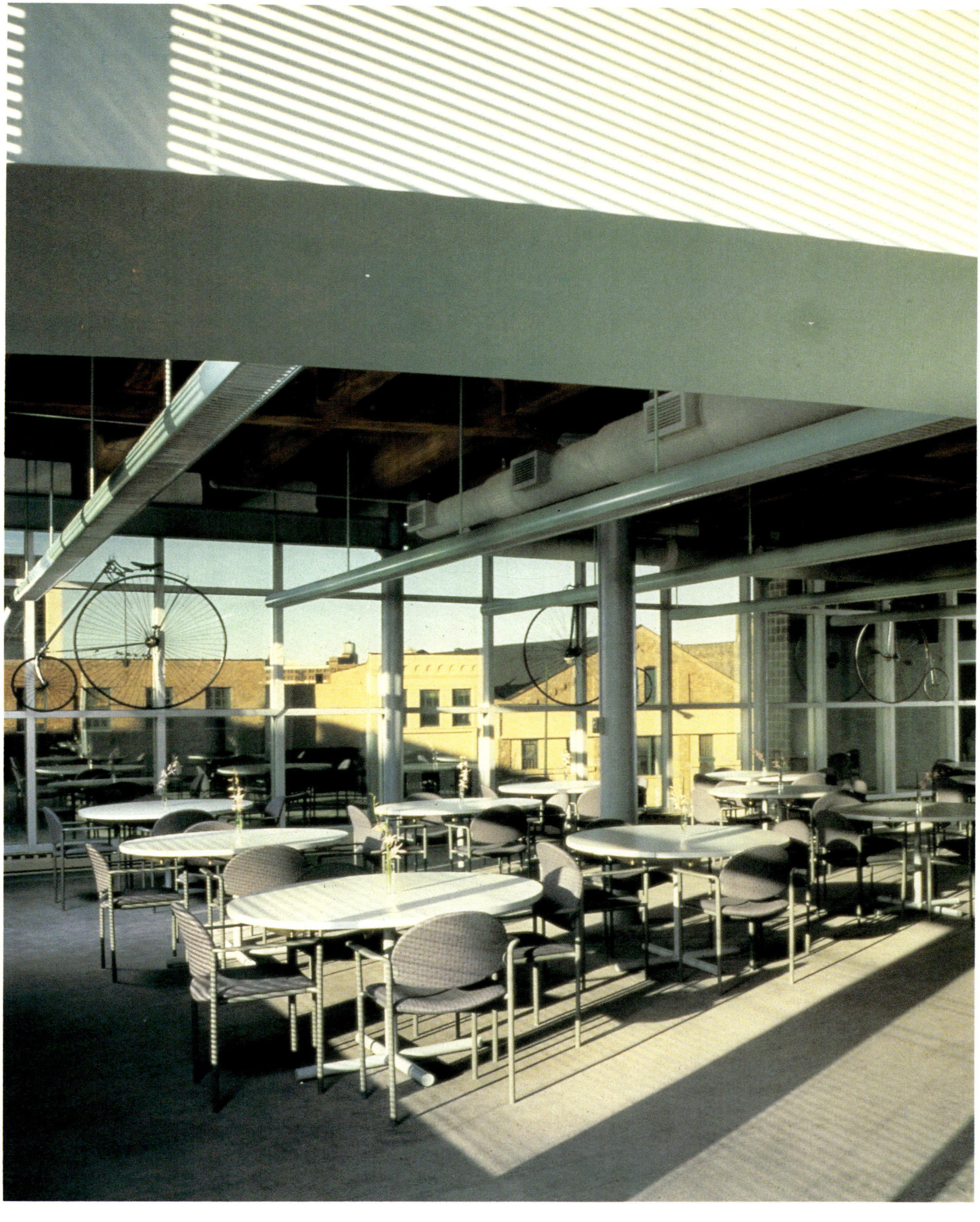

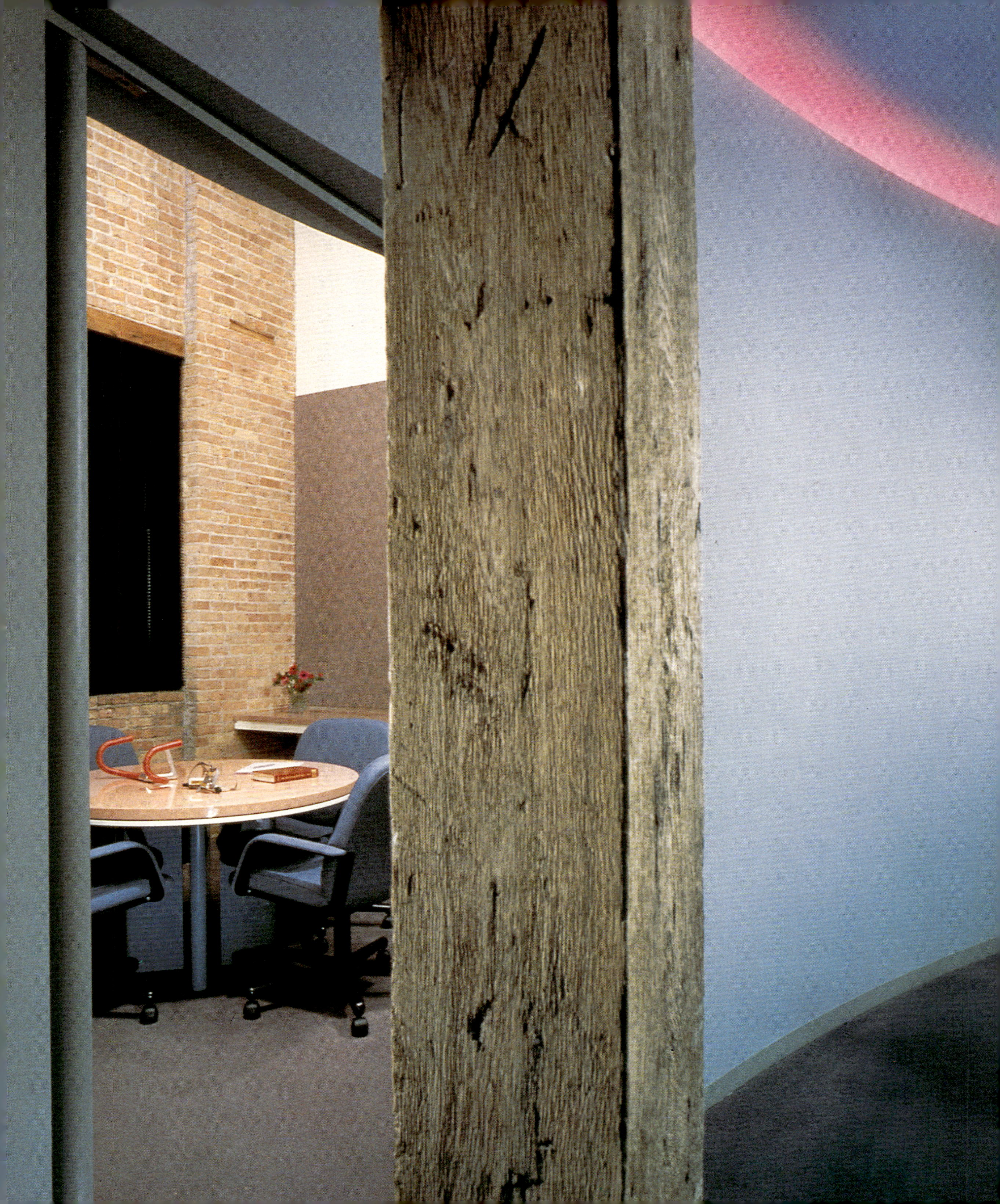

in and out of the irregularly spaced timber columns against the backdrop of a full-height curvilinear wall, which is accented by a continuous band of coloured neon light. The custom-designed office furniture incorporates both task and ambient lighting, which highlights the timber ceiling structure and the bicycles suspended above. According to the designers, 'The product has become the art' by displaying Schwinn's antique bicycle collection throughout the six floors.

The ground floor integrates the building's original cast-iron storefront with a prototype bicycle store which serves both as a display and as a dealer training area. Engineering labs, where new designs are fabricated and tested, are also on the ground floor. On the floor above are the staff restaurant, conference centre, personnel offices and computers. The top four floors house the corporate offices, in which all the staff, from the chairman down, sit at open-plan workstations. Enclosed rooms for special projects or meetings are located on each floor.

All too many companies pay lip-service to a democratic environment. It takes a manufacturer of bicycles – a truly populist product – actually to work in an office that ensures that everyone is treated alike in the workplace.

(left) Timber and brick, cleaned in the renovation, contrast with the continuous band of neon light that accentuates the curving walls.

(below) The open-plan workstation layout weaves seemingly informally in and out of the timber columns. The custom-designed furniture incorporates both task and ambient lighting.

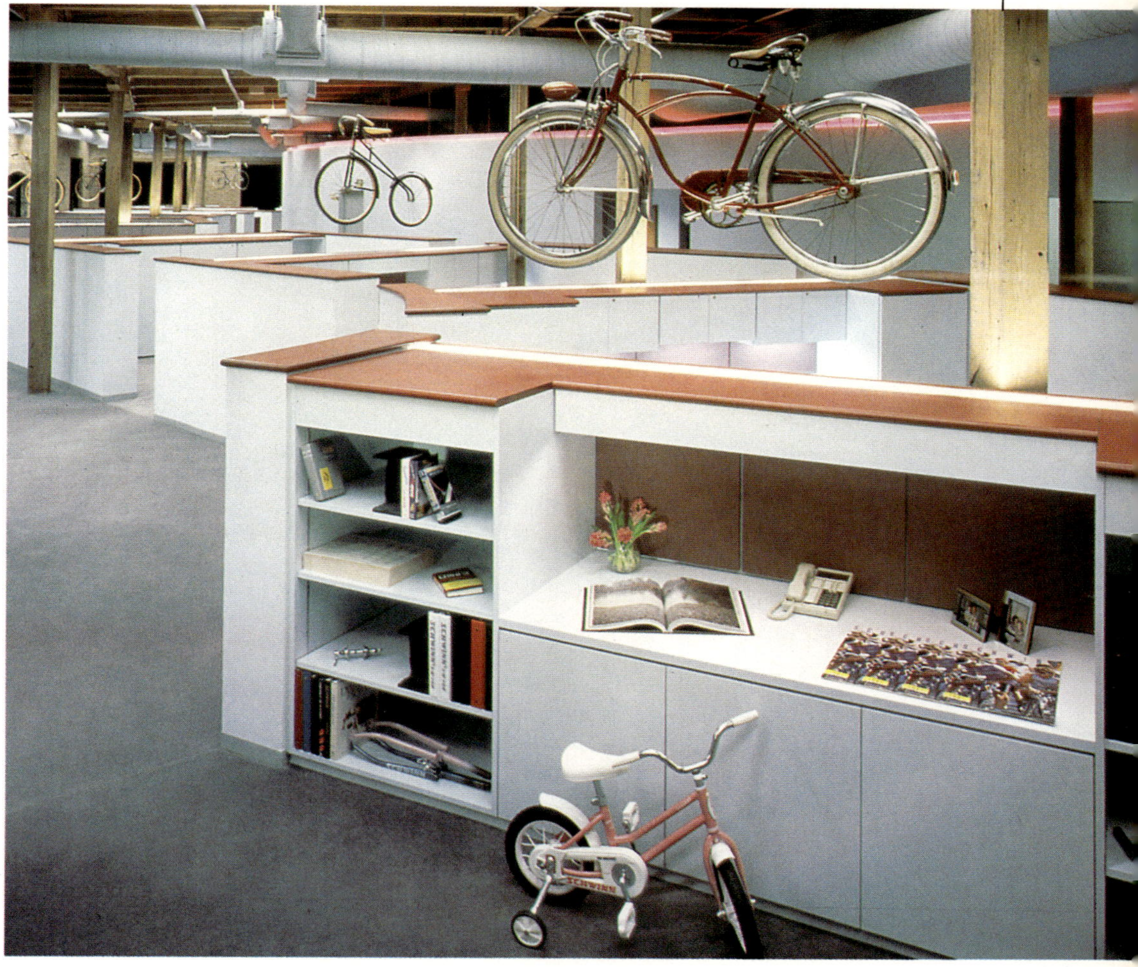

VIGNELLI ASSOCIATES

NEW YORK CITY, USA

Designed by Vignelli Associates

The new Manhattan studio of Vignelli Associates – 15,070 square feet (1,400 square metres) of office space in a converted factory building near the Hudson River – sums up the aesthetic of this leading design team. As both client and designer, the Vignellis' objective in moving from their old offices on East 62nd Street was not just to accommodate a staff of thirty-five, but also to express visually the firm's character and working philosophy.

Since the site on 10th Avenue was selected primarily for the stunning views it afforded of the city, it was natural for the designers to capitalize on this aspect. The plan therefore revolves round a central entrance gallery, from which two corridors branch off and lead to the design studio; here, workstations have been arranged to benefit as much as possible from some of the fifty-one wrap-round windows. Executive offices are also positioned to make the most of the skyline vista. Then, in the core between the corridors, are those areas – such as the photographic studio and conference rooms – where a view to the outside is not needed.

Crucial to the whole interior is the experimental use of materials: very ordinary

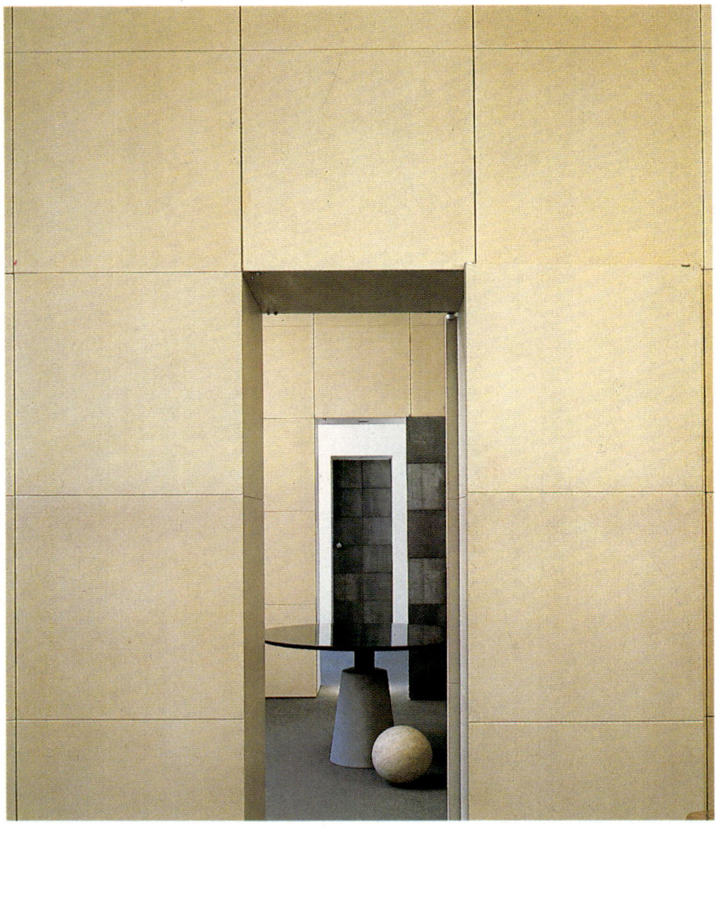

(left) Throughout the studios, views are carefully framed: visitors have the impression of a layer of rooms and materials.

(right) From the central entrance gallery two corridors branch off to the studio spaces. Crude sheets of steel, carefully polished, are used for the furniture.

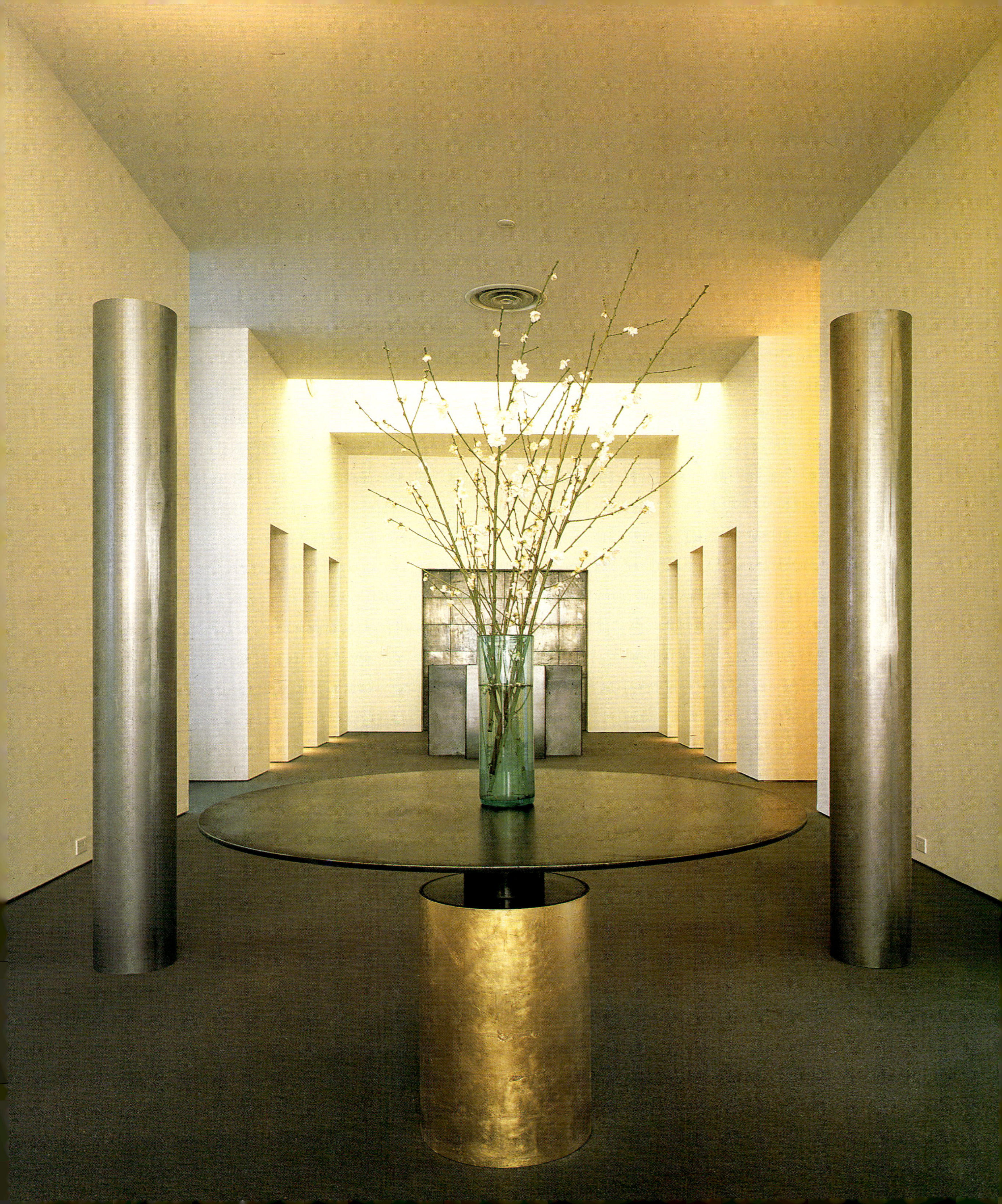

materials have been used in quite extraordinary ways. Some of the furniture, for example, is made of crude sheets of steel; walls and doors are covered with square sheets of lead (hand-waxed to protect them from oxidation and to prevent the escape of toxic fumes); and the flooring throughout is Dex-O-Tex, a composite of natural silicone more normally found in industrial or heavy commercial situations and here left unsealed. White lacquered particle board replaces the use of wood for the studio workstations. The dividing wall between service areas and the design studio is made of corrugated galvanized steel.

So that the carefully designed aesthetic of the offices is not marred by unsightly papers, the Vignellis have hidden all the usual office clutter in concealed closets that contain shelving for filing. In addition to the shelving, the smooth walls also hide the extensive range of audio-visual equipment that is stored in presentation rooms, as well as the projection screens themselves.

All furniture was especially developed for the project, and much of it is now in commercial production. The 'Handkerchief' chair seen

made of corrugated galvanized steel.

So that the carefully designed aesthetic of the offices is not marred by unsightly papers, the Vignellis have hidden all the usual office clutter in concealed closets that contain shelving for filing. In addition to the shelving, the smooth walls also hide the extensive range of audio-visual equipment that is stored in presentation rooms, as well as the projection screens themselves.

All furniture was especially developed for the project, and much of it is now in commercial production. The 'Handkerchief' chair seen

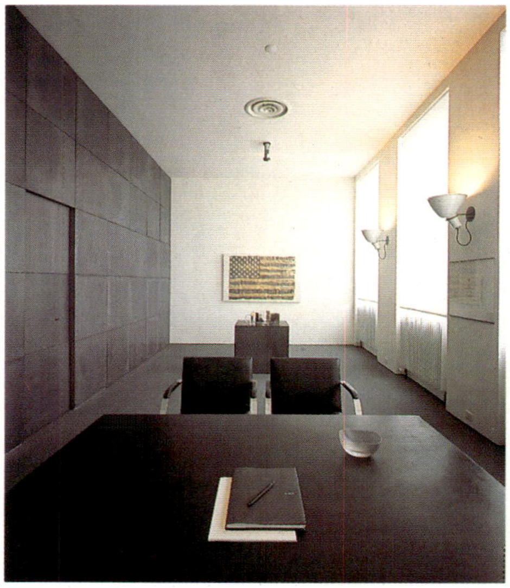

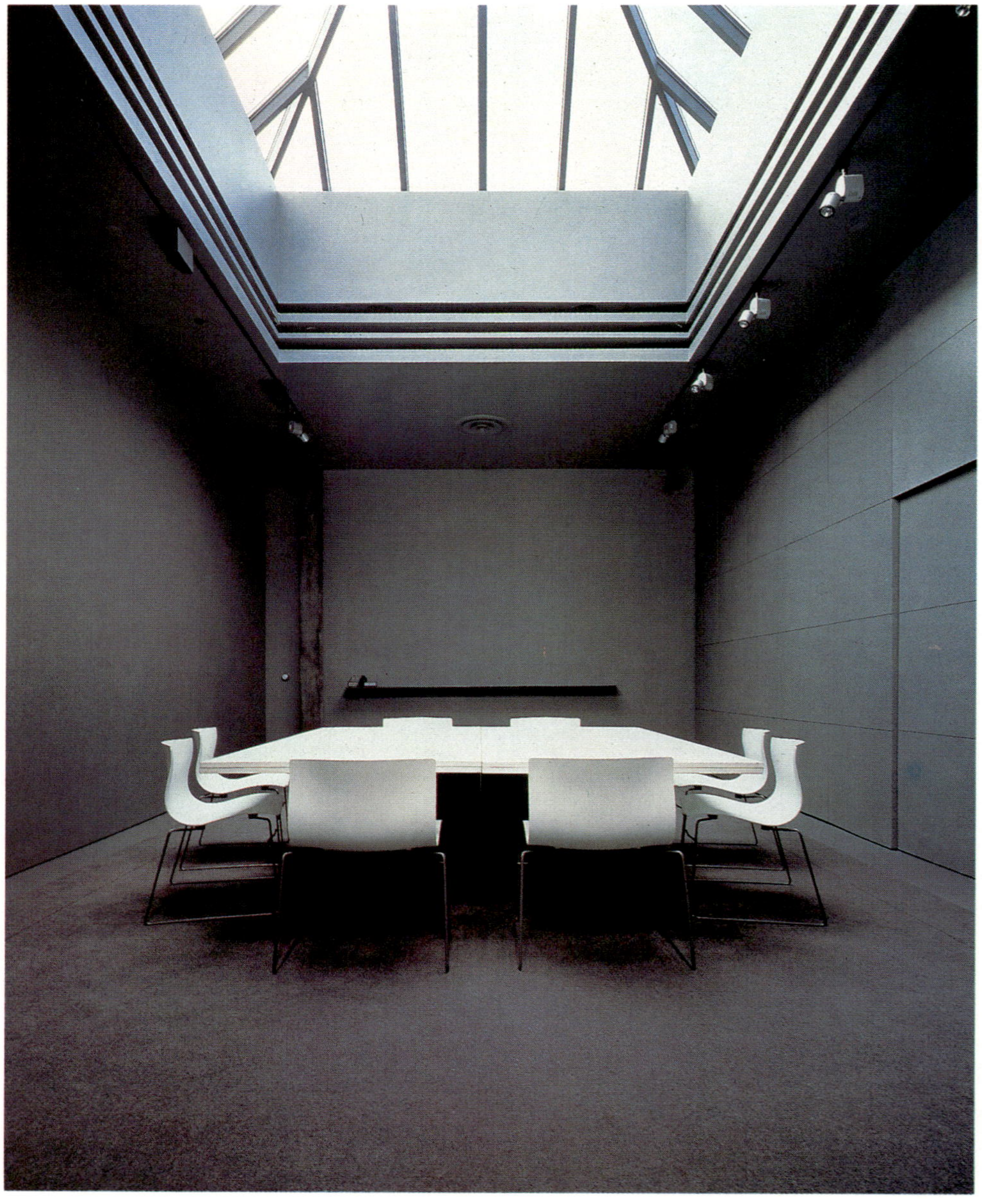

in the skylit conference room, for example, has a moulded plastic seat on a steel frame (now produced by Knoll); the 'Rotunda' armchair used in Lella Vignelli's anteroom is made by Sunar Hauserman, and the 'Ramino' wood library chair, by Italian manufacturer Driade.

The Vignellis do not describe their studio as minimalist, but they do admit an affinity for the work of minimalist sculptors such as Don Judd and Richard Serra. The final effect is serene, highly controlled and elegant, a distillation of their attitude to design over the last twenty-five years.

(far left) For the walls and doors, square lead sheets have been hand-waxed to protect them from oxidation and to prevent the escape of toxic fumes.

(left) In the presentation rooms, even projection screens are hidden in the walls, to be unveiled when necessary. For seating, the Vignellis' own 'Handkerchief' chairs from Knoll are used.

(below) Even in smaller rooms, great play is made of the clever use of materials.

(below right) To preserve visual order in the studios, the usual clutter is hidden in closets concealed in the walls.

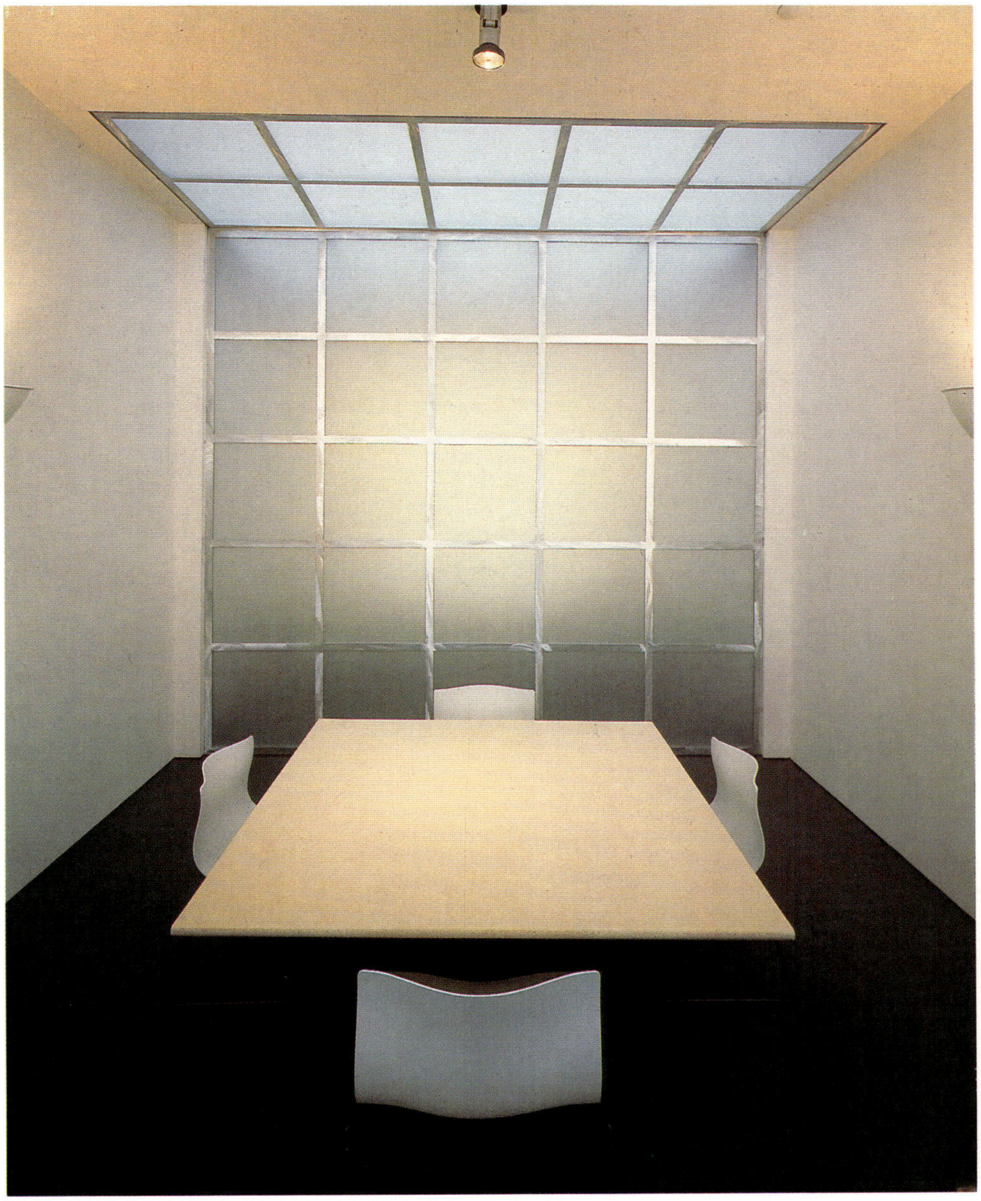

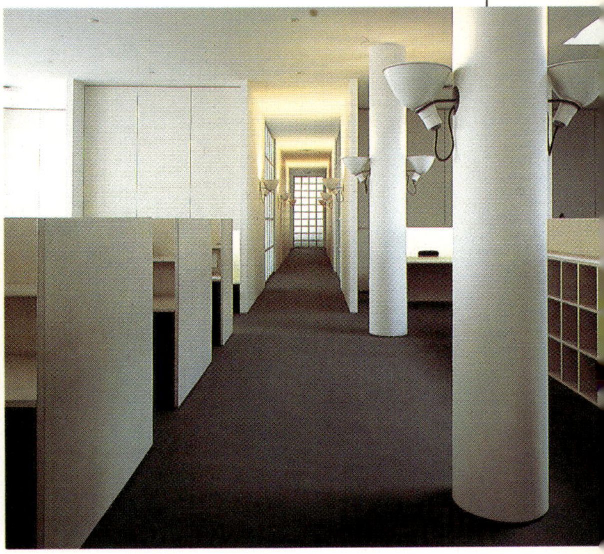

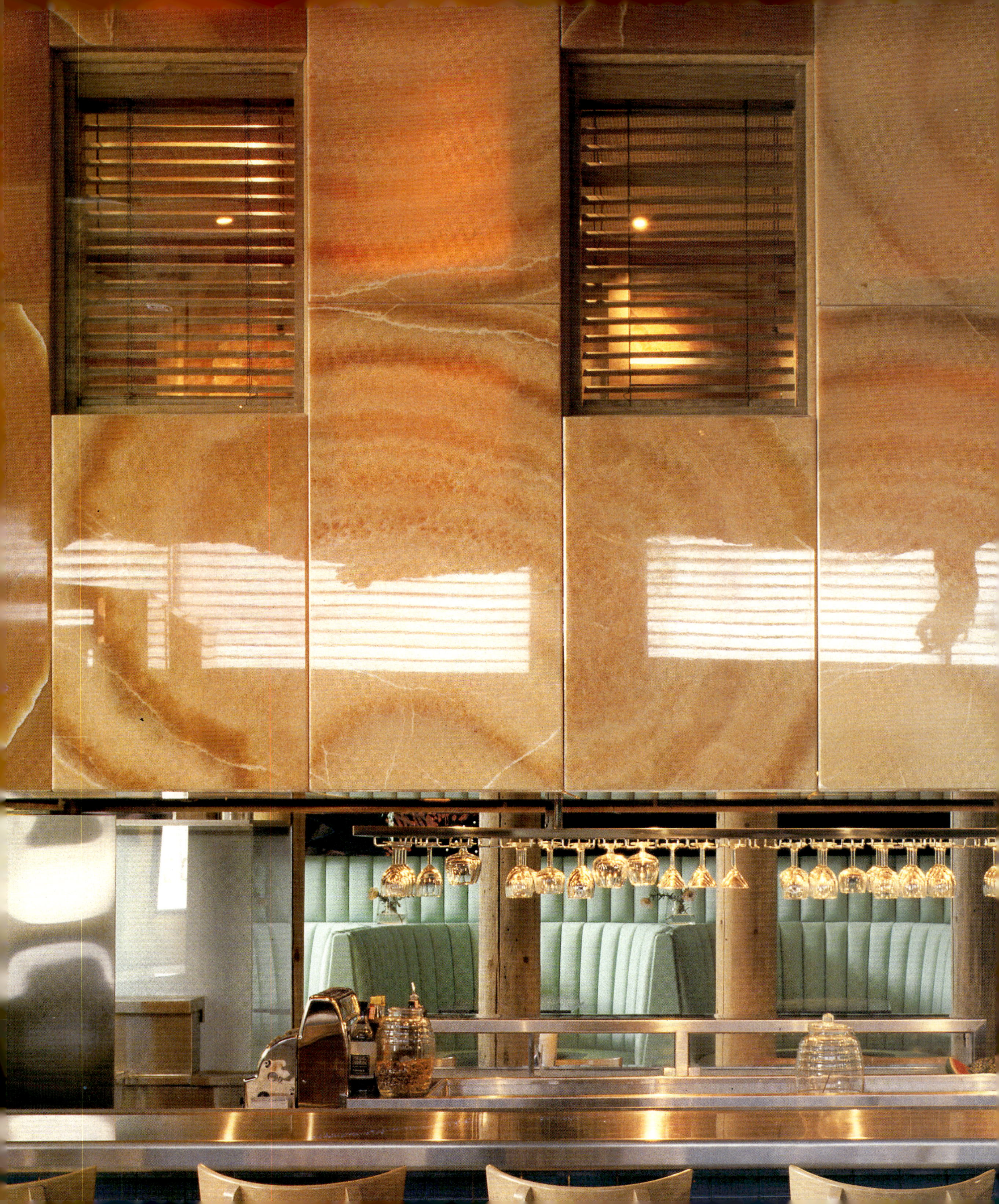

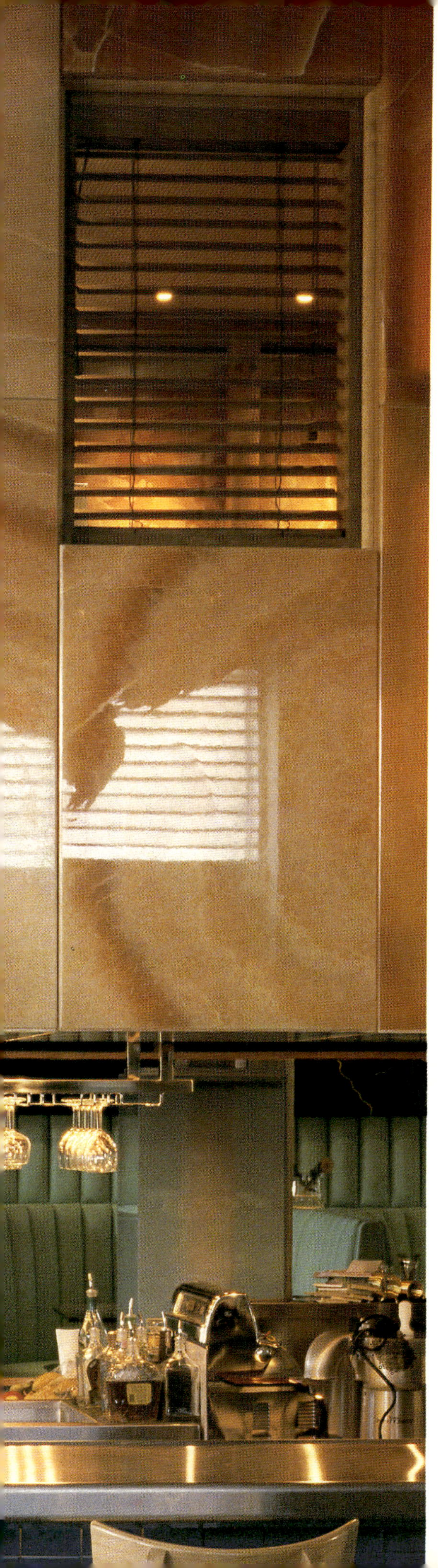

RESTAURANTS, BARS, CLUBS AND HOTELS

Nigel Coates and Shi Yu Chen Caffè Bongo, Tokyo, Japan

Nigel Coates and Shi Yu Chen Metropole, Tokyo, Japan

Max Dudler and Karl Dudler Café-Bar, Frankfurt-am-Main, West Germany

Dani Freixes and Vincente Miranda 33, Barcelona, Spain

Frank O. Gehry and Associates Rebecca's, Venice, California, USA

Milton Glaser with Tim Higgins Aurora, New York City, USA

Grondona/Architects Claudia's, Wonder Sushi Plus and Boardwalk Fries, San Diego, California, USA

Trix and Robert Haussmann Hotel Le Plaza, Basel, Switzerland

Naoki Iijima Arai, Tokyo, Japan

Toyo Ito Nomad, Tokyo, Japan

Jiricna Kerr Associates Legends, London, UK

McDonough Nouri Rainey & Associates The Casual Quilted Giraffe, New York City, USA

Morphosis Angeli, Los Angeles, California, USA

Morphosis 72 Market Street, Venice, California, USA

Gabriel Ordeig Bijou, Barcelona, Spain

Gabriel Ordeig Sisisi, Barcelona, Spain

Denis Santachiara L'Aquylone Restaurant, Reggio Emilia, Italy

Skidmore, Owings & Merrill The Palio, New York City, USA

Philippe Starck Manin, Tokyo, Japan

Superpotato Design Studio Bar Set/Off, Tokyo, Japan

Shin Takamatsu Dance Hall, Tokyo, Japan

Sue Timney and Grahame Fowler AD Coliseum, Tokyo, Japan

Svein Tønsager Café Paradis, Århus, Denmark

Shigeru Uchida and Studio 80 Le Club, Tokyo, Japan

CAFFÉ BONGO
TOKYO, JAPAN
Designed by Nigel Coates and Shi Yu Chen

(previous page) A prime example of the restaurant as visual and dramatic experience is Rebecca's in Venice, California, designed by Frank Gehry and Associates.

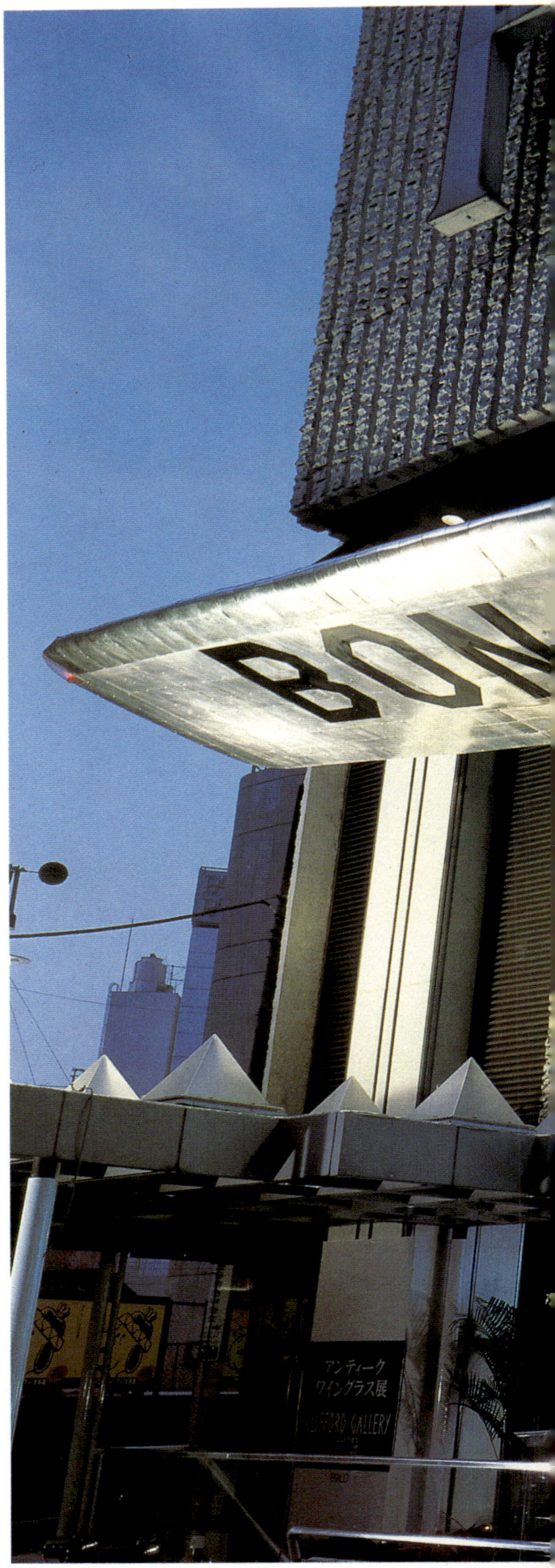

(right) Set inside one of Tokyo's leading department stores, the café presents a 'dynamic' image, with a giant aluminium aircraft wing crashing through the façade.

(below) The aircraft wing motif reappears within the space on the underside of the balcony.

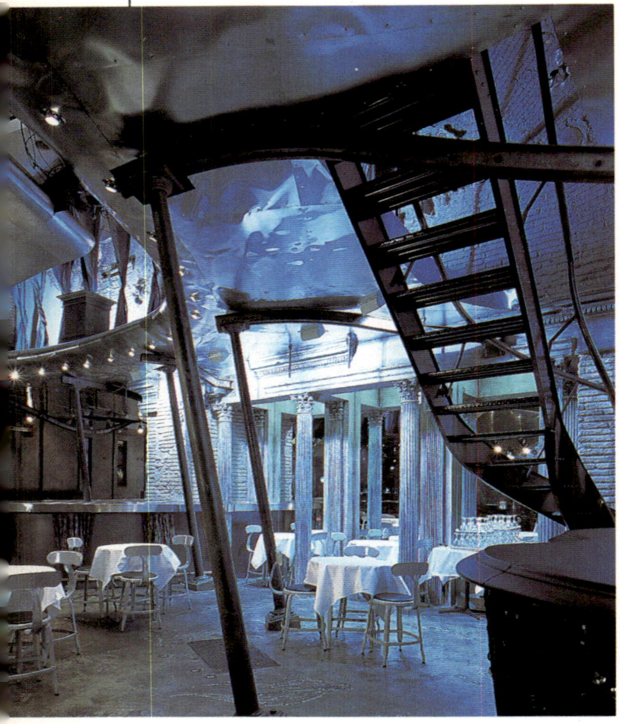

Department stores in Japan compete with each other on many levels, not just on price and merchandise. Art galleries, theatres, restaurants and numerous special events are all part of a campaign to draw consumers to Seibu rather than Marui or Parco. One of the most recent fusillades in this battle was the decision of Parco to renovate their existing café to present a more dynamic image.

Parco approached Shi Yu Chen and Nigel Coates (known for their Metropole restaurant in Tokyo, see pp. 58–9), who produced what they termed a 'theatrical image café'. According to the designers, Caffè Bongo incorporates 'narrative signs from Pompei, Rome, Italian '50s and modern Tokyo'. British designer Nigel Coates's reputation is based on his almost chaotic collaging of elements found in a disordered, slightly run-down urban environment. Curiously, it was in Tokyo that he had his first major opportunities actually to build his fantasies; in London, his work was confined to projects displayed on the walls of the Architectural Association.

Nothing is held back in Tokyo, however. A giant aircraft wing made out of aluminium sheet, seemingly crashed into the Caffè Bongo, announces the use of bizarre conceits in the design. The interior is more akin to a Fellini film set than to the work of Boeing. Coates gathered together a host of European artists to supply various elements of Caffè Bongo: a characteristic Keplerian chandelier by André Dubreuil, paintings by Adam Lowe, photographs by Ron O'Donnell and decorative

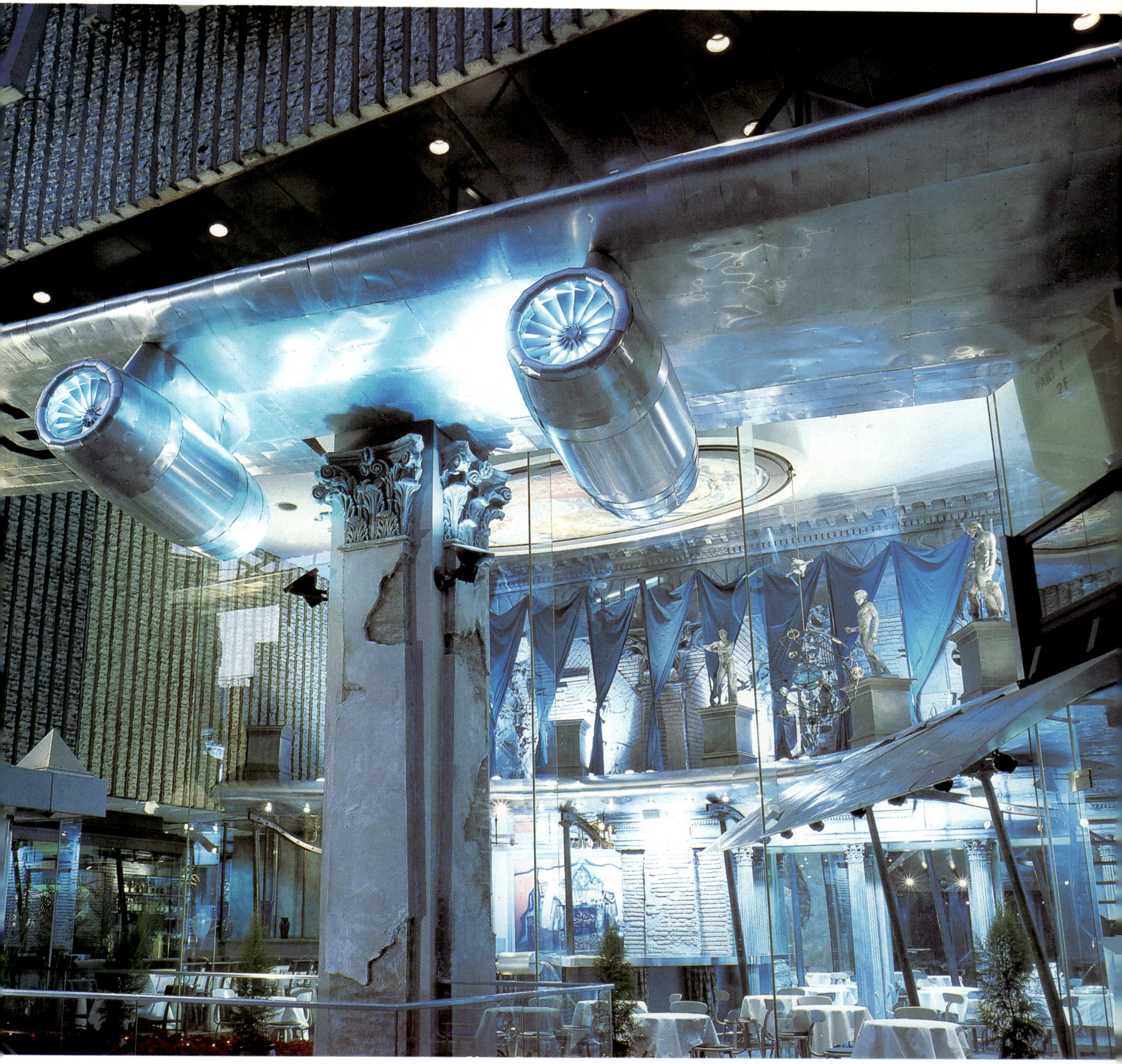
PART I
2F

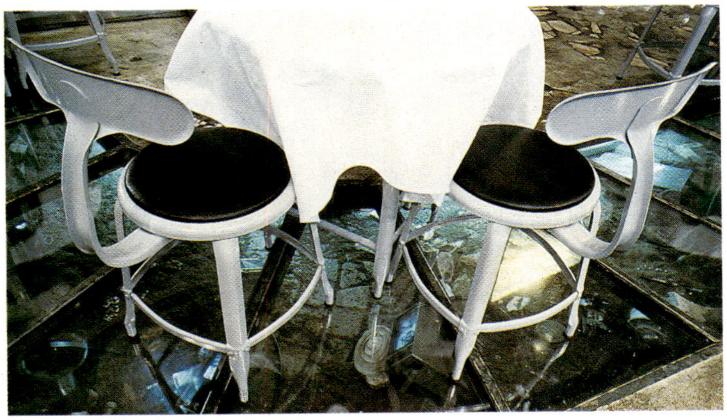

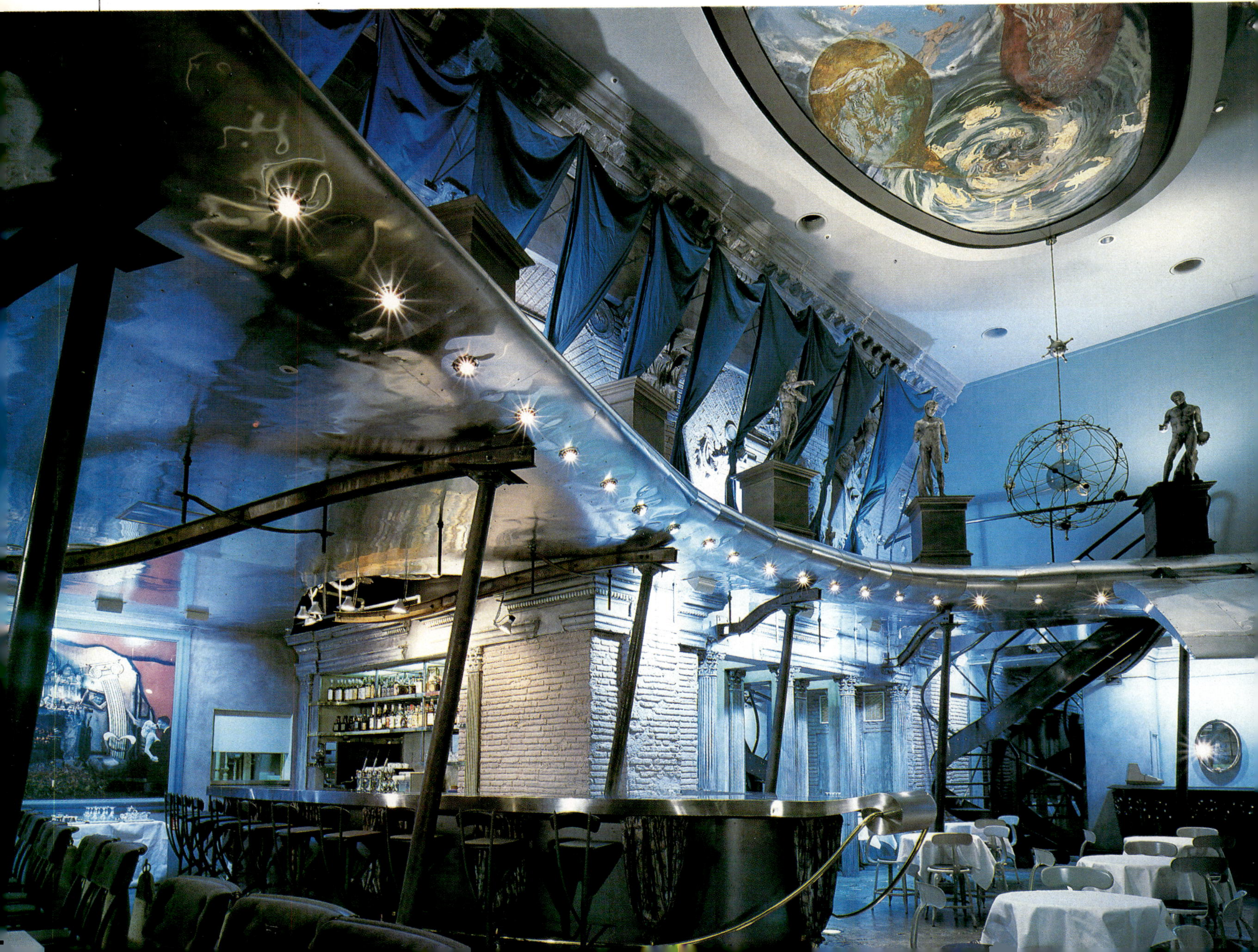

finishes by Zaza Wentworth Stanley. All the pieces for the project were purchased, imported, assembled and then finished in Tokyo, under the direction of Shi Yu Chen.

The furniture, all designed by Coates and manufactured in Japan by Rockstone Co., is consistent with the restaurant's aesthetic. Bar stools are in metal with black vinyl seats, while the dining-room chairs have a cracked paint finish on a metal frame. Café chairs have a grey paint finish with orange-brown vinyl seats.

The ancient look of the interior is carefully achieved, partly by 'distressing' the statues, cornice and capitals to make them look old (Zaza Wentworth Stanley was responsible for the distressing). The floor is mortar with a tile mosaic and urethane finish. Inset into the floor is tempered glass in a steel frame, offering glimpses of video screens and industrial detritus underneath. The exterior aircraft wing is echoed on the underside of the interior balcony, which is plywood faced with stainless steel. The total cost of Caffè Bongo's interior construction was 640,000 dollars. Perhaps the most extraordinary aspect of the project is that it is not an avant-garde enclave, but inside Tokyo's equivalent of one of the British Next stores.

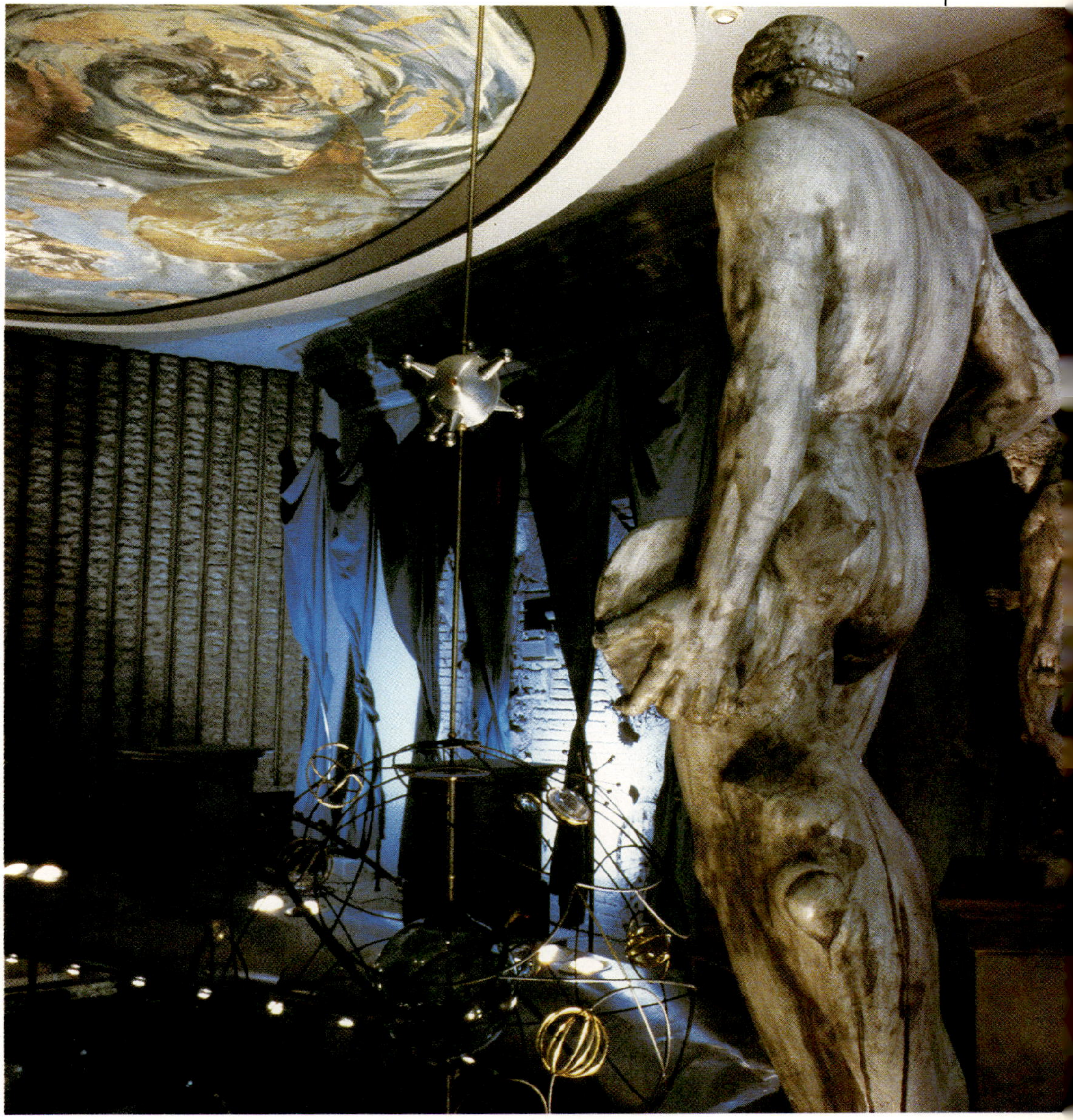

(left above) Furniture was all specially designed by Nigel Coates and made in Japan. Beneath the floor is a collection of débris and video screens, visible through insets of tempered glass.

(left) Objects, photographs and paintings by a number of European artists were assembled to form the interior collage, including a chandelier by André Dubreuil.

(right) Statues, cornices and capitals were 'distressed', to make them look old, using decorative paint finishes by Zaza Wentworth Stanley.

METROPOLE
TOKYO, JAPAN

Designed by Nigel Coates and Shi Yu Chen

Most designers work in a very conventional way: approached by clients with a brief, the designers devise a scheme to suit the requirements. With the Metropole restaurant, however, Chen and Coates invented a concept and then searched for the right client. Their idea was 'to create a space using a 1940s Shanghai atmosphere combined with the traditional English gentlemen's club'. The result might be described as slightly tamed decadence.

From the outside, store windows reveal the sizeable bar area of the Metropole. An ornate, reddish-brown pelmet hides a Renaissance-like 'fresco' with fragments of skies, legs and bodies. The dining-room itself is relatively straightforward (for Coates), with the exception of the frieze of Grecian sculptures peeking over the walls.

Materials are fairly simple, with the wood flooring and joinery enlivened by a few container-loads of salvaged materials shipped by Coates from London. Among the salvaged objects are an old hotel door, the working fireplace from London's old Central Post Office and upholstery from the London Underground (which is used for the velvet swagging on the ceiling). The Metropole was the first project where Coates and Chen originated the approach they have subsequently used in the Caffè Bongo (see pp. 54–7) and other schemes: Coates commissioned a variety of artists to execute the various elements (the furniture is Coates's own, however), while Chen acted as on-site co-ordinator.

In addition, Chen recruited the chef, head waiter and head bartender from Los Angeles and London; the international bravura is crucial, for Metropole is as much a production as any Hollywood blockbuster. And that is reflected in the budget – the interior construction cost 713,000 dollars but over two hundred thousand dollars was allotted to the opening.

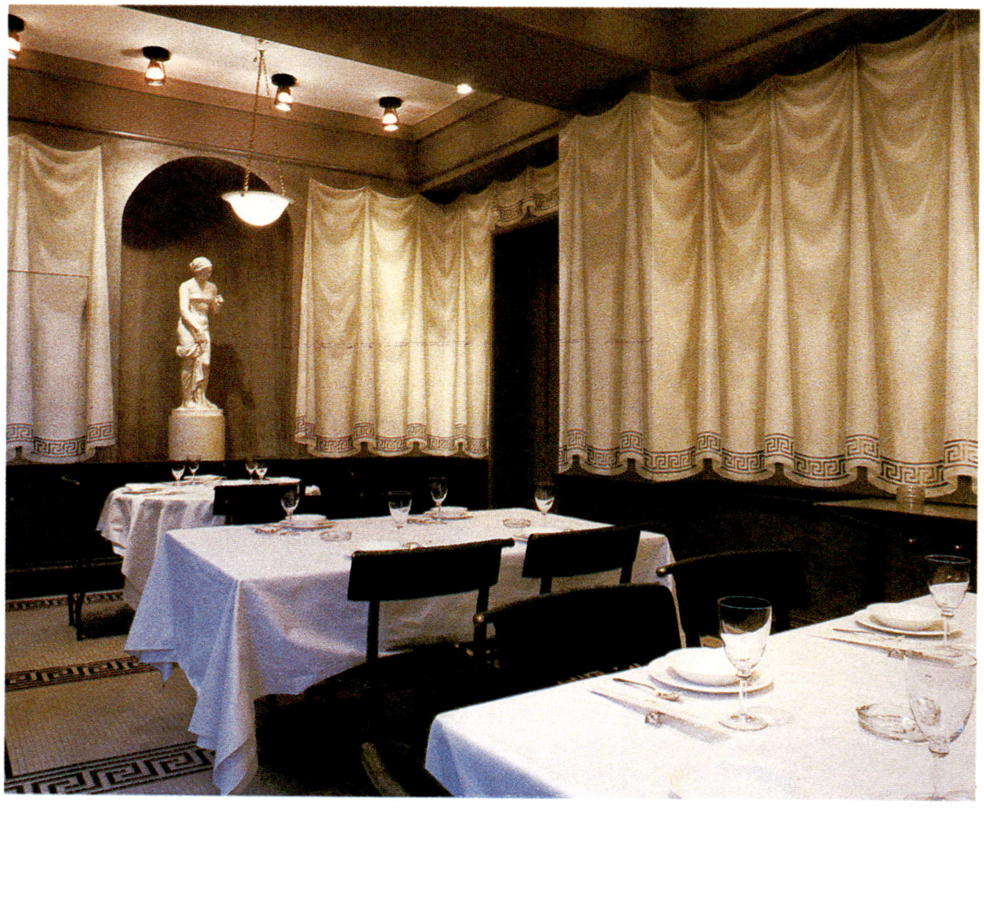

Grecian elements – statues and the traditional key pattern on floor mosaics and the painted hangings – combine with Coates's own furniture designs in the relatively restrained dining-room.

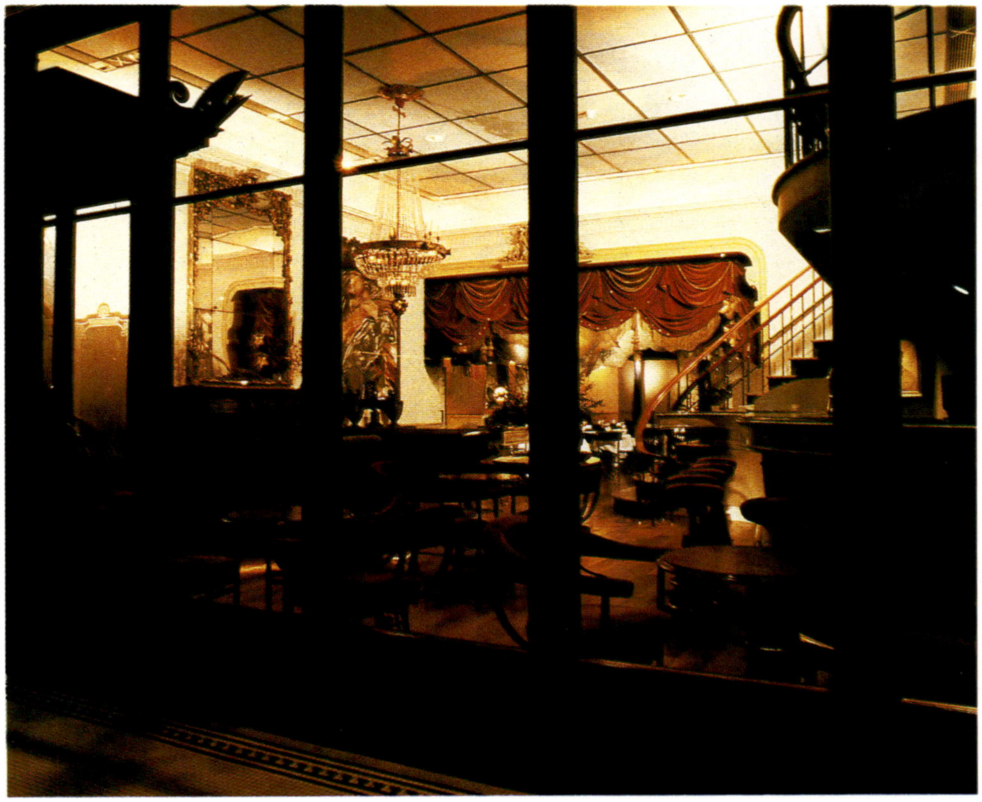

(left) A 1940s Shanghai atmosphere with the feel of the traditional English gentlemen's club was the brief the designers set for themselves. Here it is seen through the glass storefront of the exterior.

(below) Original salvaged materials add touches of fake authenticity. They include the fireplace from London's old Central Post Office and velvet upholstery from the London Underground, used as curtain swagging.

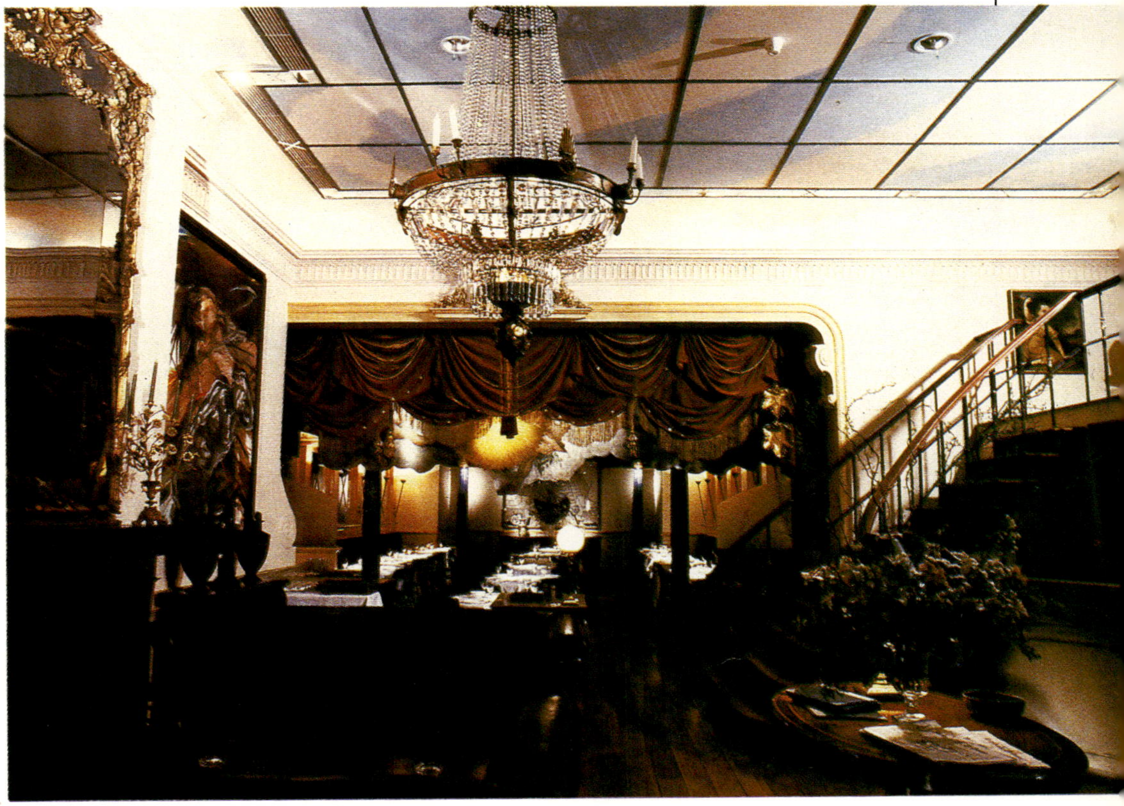

CAFÉ-BAR

FRANKFURT-AM-MAIN, WEST GERMANY

Designed by Max Dudler and Karl Dudler

Confronted with a long, rectangular room in which to site both a bar and a café, the Dudlers devised a novel solution that plays on notions of mirror-images, yet provides distinct identities for the two uses of the space. The entrance is centrally placed, and leads directly on to a 3½ feet (1.05 metre) wide, mysterious black element that runs down the centre of the space. This black wall, with its regular row of square lights forming a sort of cornice, has a dual function: it contains facilities such as the ladies' lavatories and a cloakroom, but it also divides the relatively small space into two quite separate areas.

On one side lies the café, with seating for thirty-two in its 564 square feet (52.4 square metres). Although the café is relatively informal, the march of the black walls down both sides creates a certain almost oppressive monumentality if the café is not filled with people. The bar side is virtually a mirror-image of the café, with the black walls echoed by the black bar (although the aluminium sinks and shelves add a sparkle to the generally dark interior). There are sixteen bar stools ranged evenly along the 33 foot (10 metre) length of the bar.

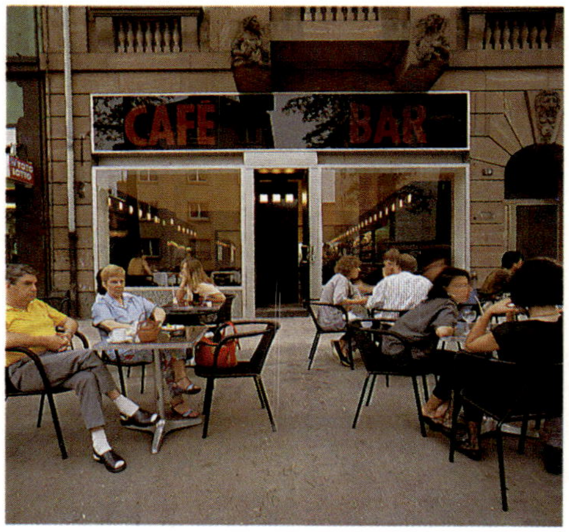

The Dudlers' café-bar is typical of an austere style that is especially prevalent in Germany today (the designers have, in fact, collaborated with this style's best-known exponent, Oswald Matthias Ungers). There is a certain pleasing logic to their scheme, with its classical ordering of elements and the carefully planned mirroring of these elements. It could be seen as an unusual choice of atmosphere for what is intended to be simply a casual, relaxed café.

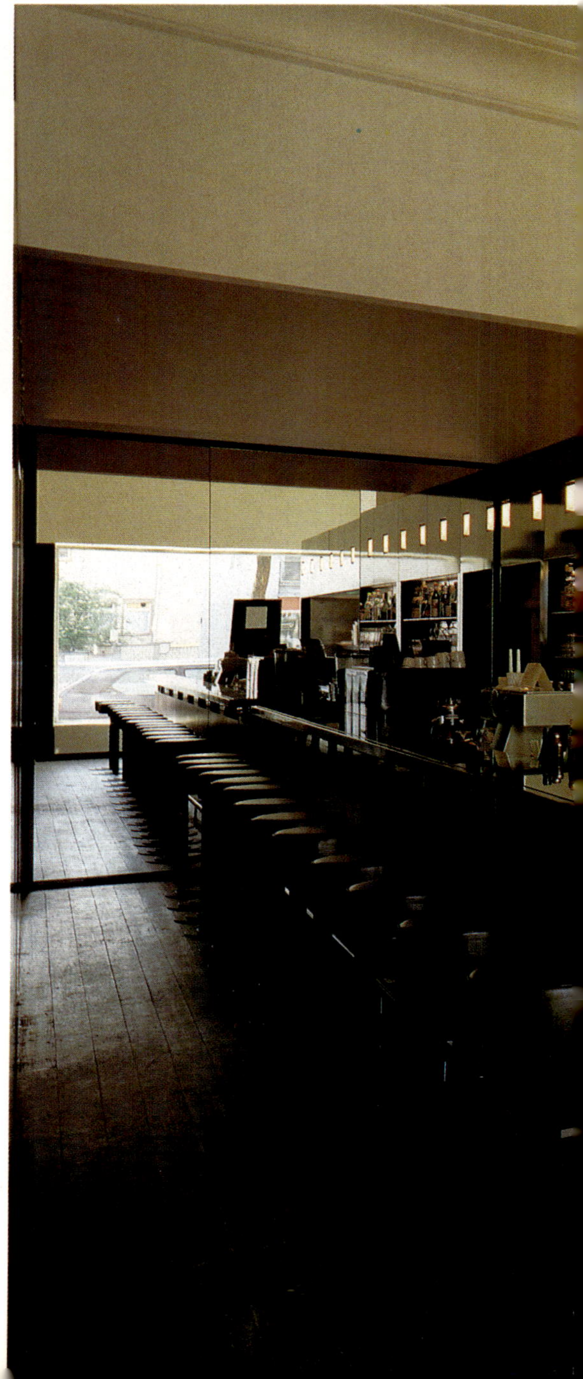

(above right) Glass and aluminium create the austerely symmetrical exterior, which fronts on to a wide pavement with room for tables and chairs in fine weather.

(above far right) Isometric projections show mirror-images: on one side is the restaurant, on the other the bar. The central wall conceals cloakrooms and lavatories.

(right) In a predominantly black and grey interior, the main design features are the receding lines of square lights, further elongating the long, narrow spaces.

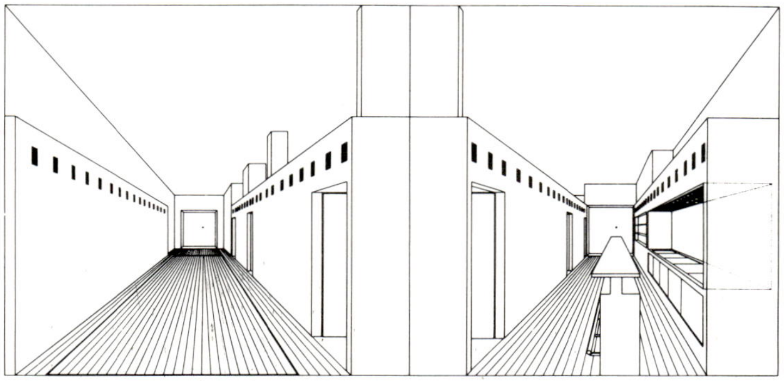

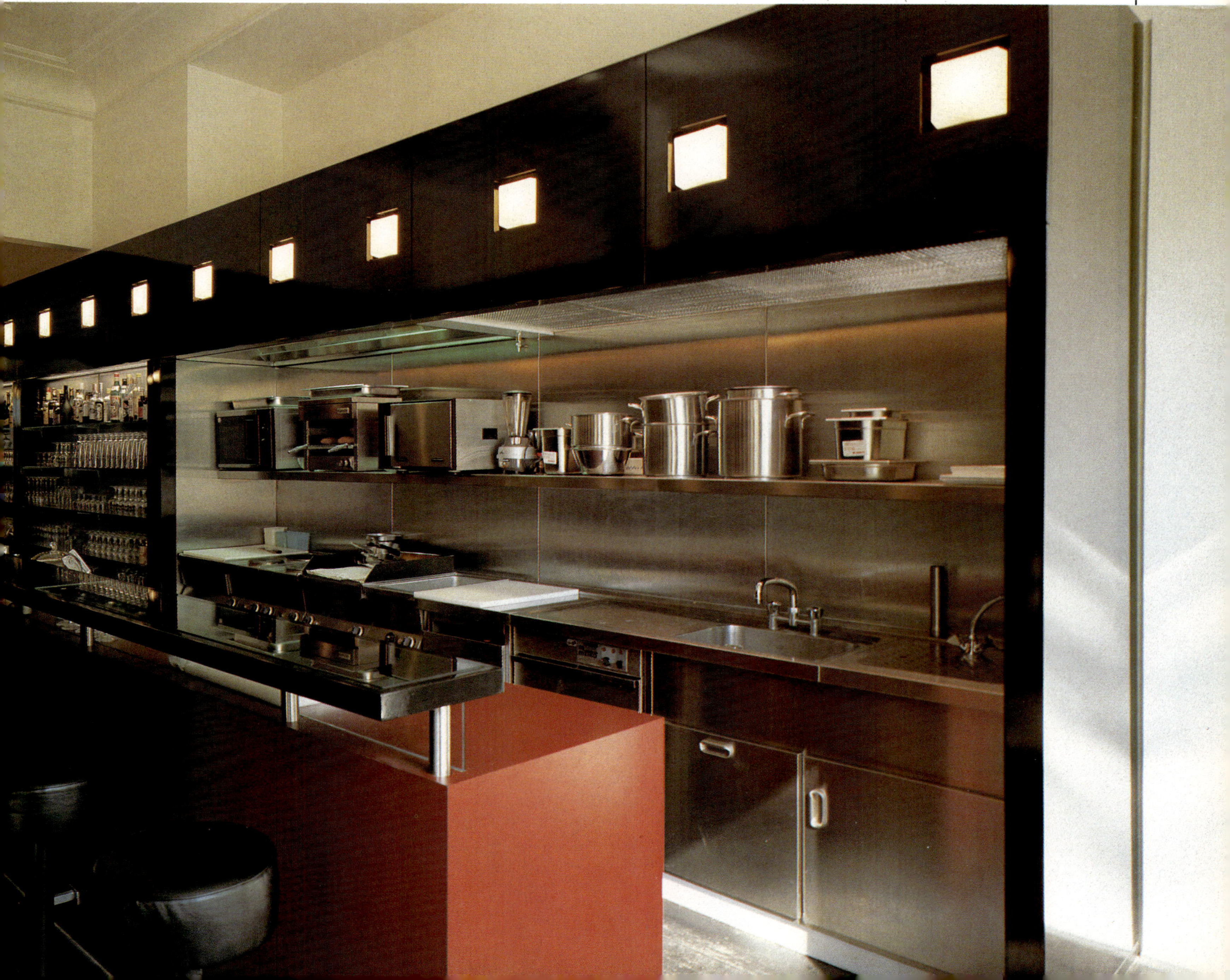

33
BARCELONA, SPAIN
Designed by Dani Freixes and Vincente Miranda

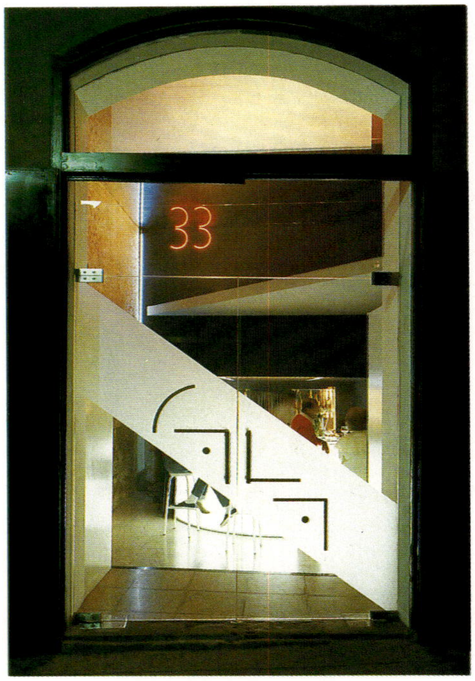

(above) First glimpse: apparently a very small space with a round bar.

(right) In fact, this is just one end of a much longer central bar. Internally lit, it is bright white with stools to match, to catch the attention of passers-by.

When Dani Freixes and Vincente Miranda began work on the 33 cocktail bar in Barcelona, they decided that – even in this small, narrow space – they wanted to create different areas with different atmospheres.

To do this they have deliberately exaggerated the size of the glass entrance doors so that, from the street, passers-by have a clear view into what initially appears to be a very small space with a round bar. In fact, what can be seen from the entrance is just the rounded end of a long, central bar. There were two reasons for positioning it in the middle: first, restrictions on space meant that separate tables were out of the question; secondly, in this way, only one waiter – or at most two – was needed to serve all customers. The rounded end of the bar, near the door, is white and internally lit, with white stools; further along, however, it becomes long and straight – more conventional in shape – and the stools are black.

The treatment of the ceilings also differs in the different areas: as customers go inside the ceiling above them is full height, but deeper inside the space it is lowered to give a more intimate effect. Visually and physically, it is the bar which links these two sections.

Finally, materials have been chosen to give contrasts: the exposed, textured stone of the walls, for instance, emphasizes the smooth, clear glass of the drinks shelves; the roughened metal sides of the bar bring into relief the bright white counter and the neon sign above it.

With the use of materials such as these – and much invention – Freixes and Miranda have succeeded in transforming a long, narrow and unpromising site into a cocktail bar that is imaginative as well as efficient: this is a small space that contains a lot of ideas.

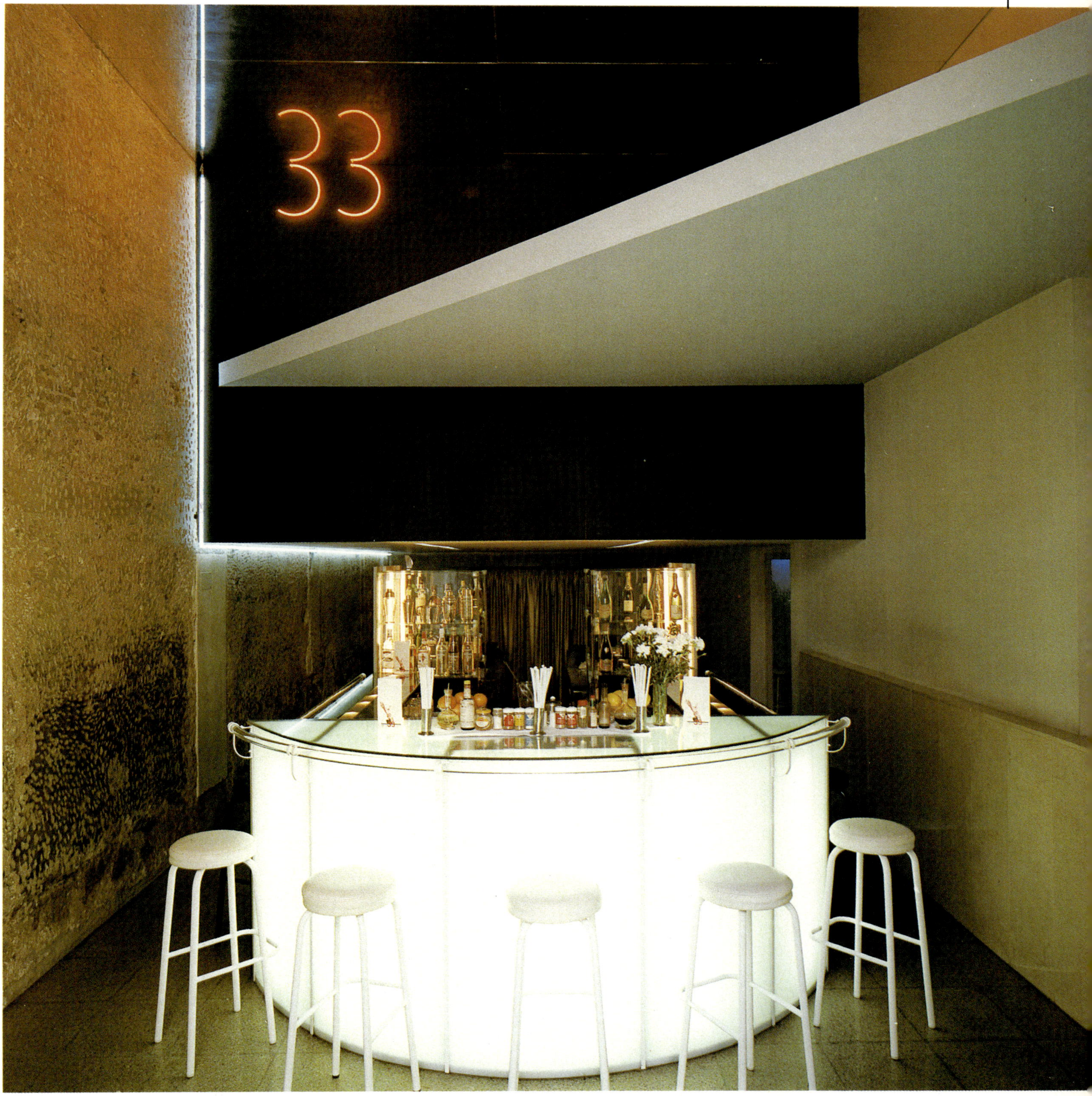
33

(right) Under a lowered ceiling, the rear of the café is more intimate, with subtle lighting behind the glass shelves and reflected in the mirrors.

(far right) At the far end of the narrow space, the bar straightens out. Here, finishes and furniture are black.

(below) Textural contrasts are used effectively, for example in the pitted stone walls and the smooth black bar counter.

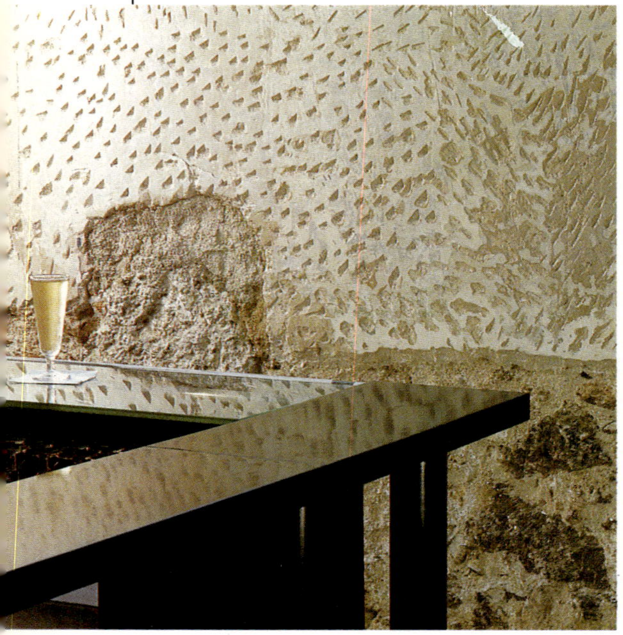

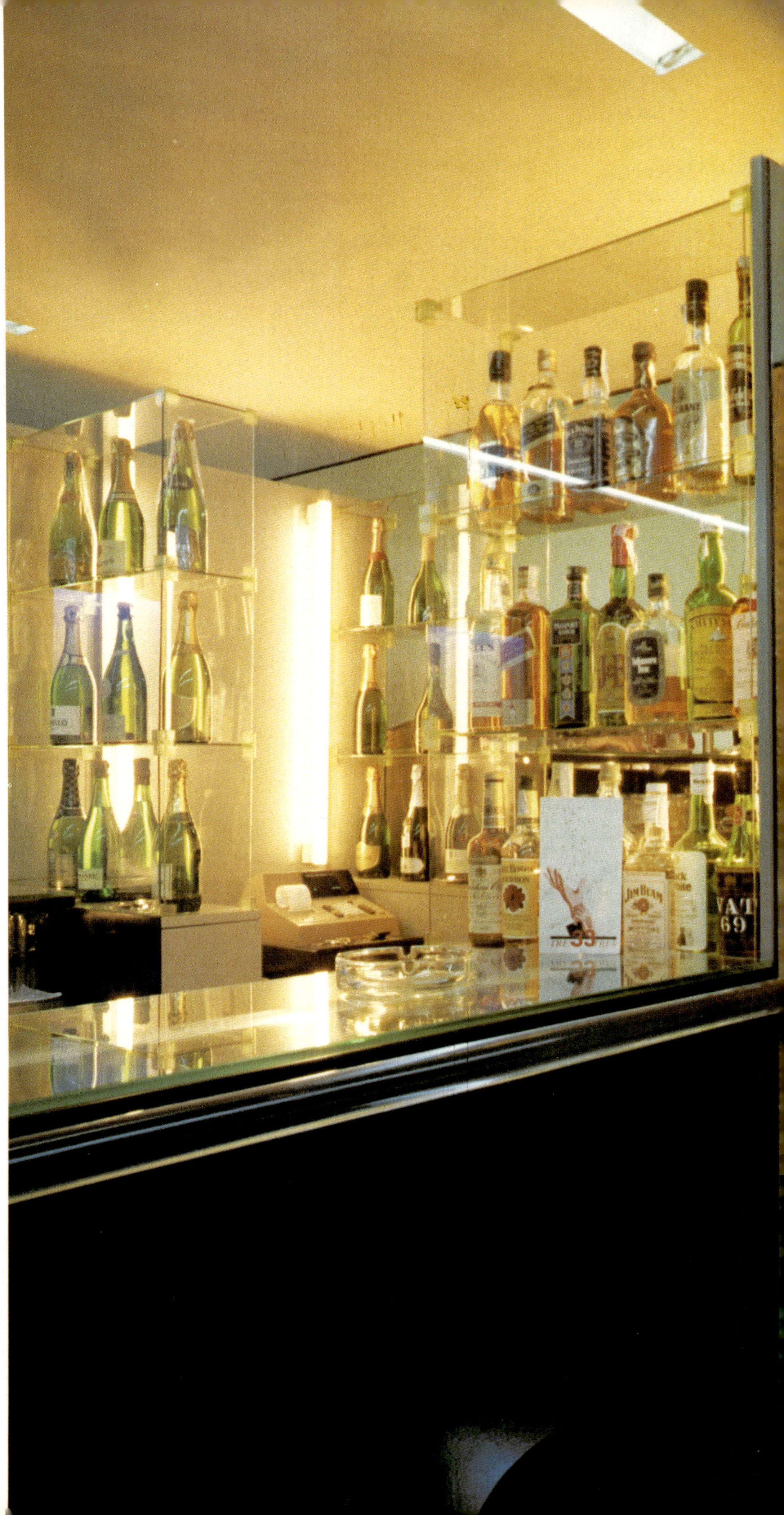

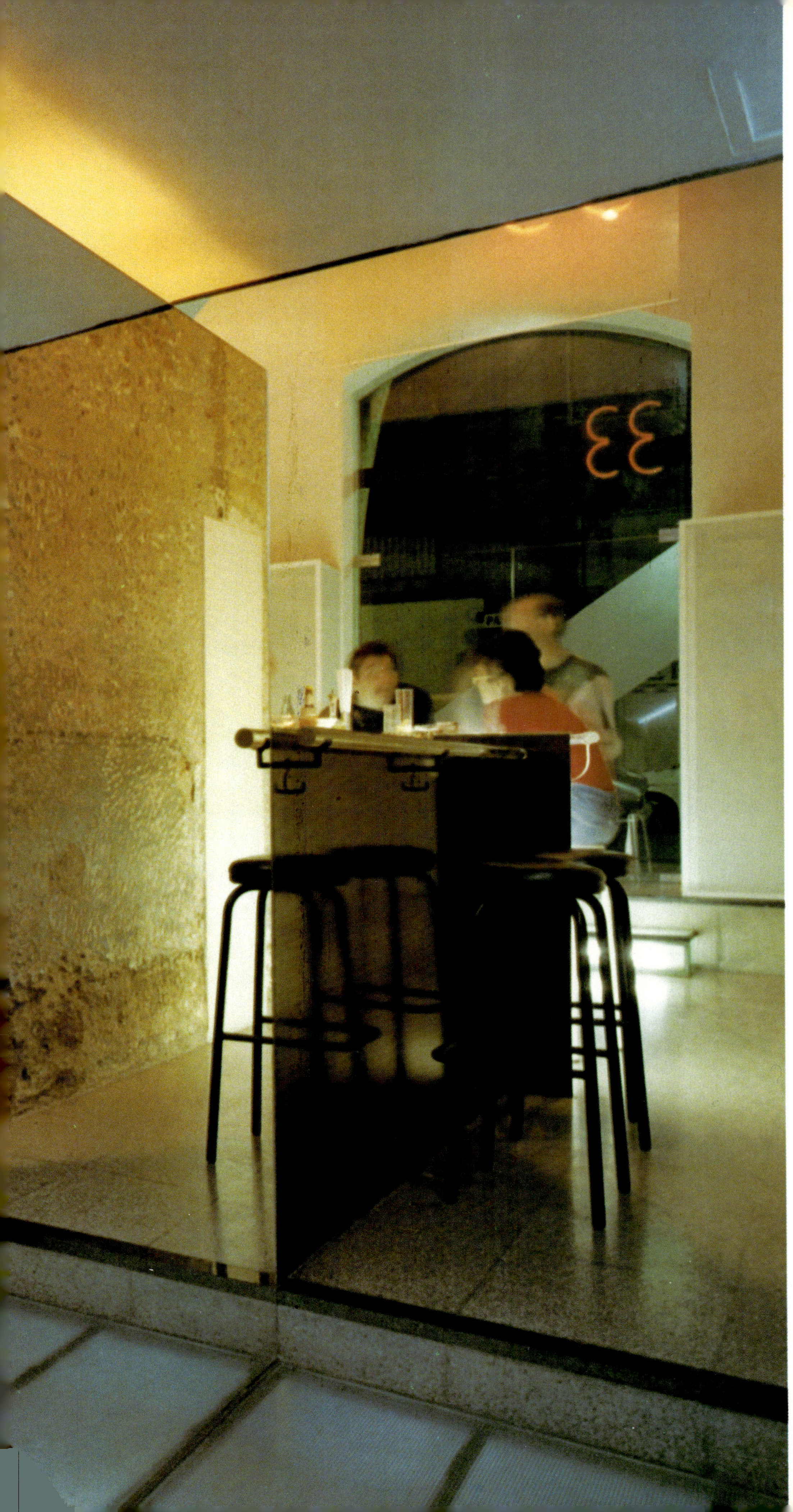

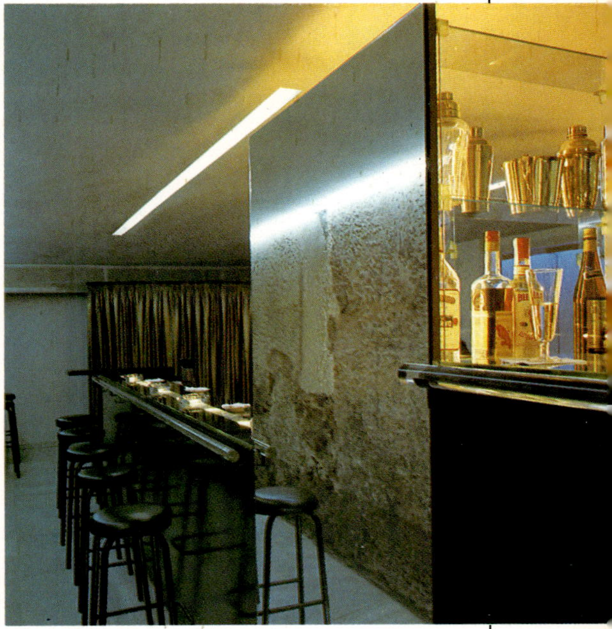

REBECCA'S
VENICE, CALIFORNIA, USA

Designed by Frank O. Gehry and Associates

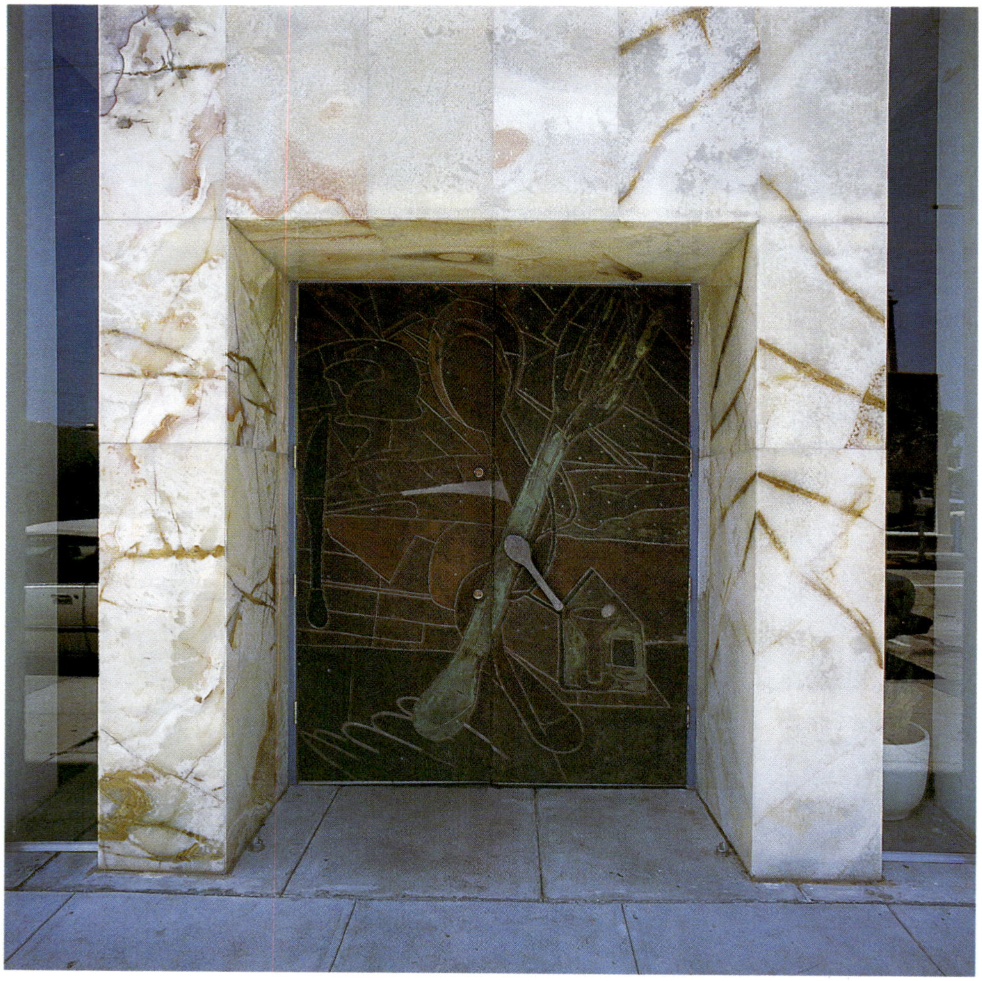

(left) Where it all starts – a white onyx entrance portal and doors decorated with a tin collage by Tony Berlant.

(right) In the open brasserie area, high tables and stools are custom-designed. Beyond the screen lies the dining area.

For a Frank Gehry project to be dubbed 'the most outrageous yet', it must be something truly special. For Gehry has made his reputation partly through projects intent on outrage: his house, which apparently transformed a quiet street into a traffic blackspot because of the number of sudden double-takes by passing drivers; the liberal use of chainlink fencing as a *brise-soleil* in sites such as the Cabrillo Marine Museum; the jet fighter seemingly crashing into the façade of his aviation museum.

So what makes Rebecca's seem Gehry's

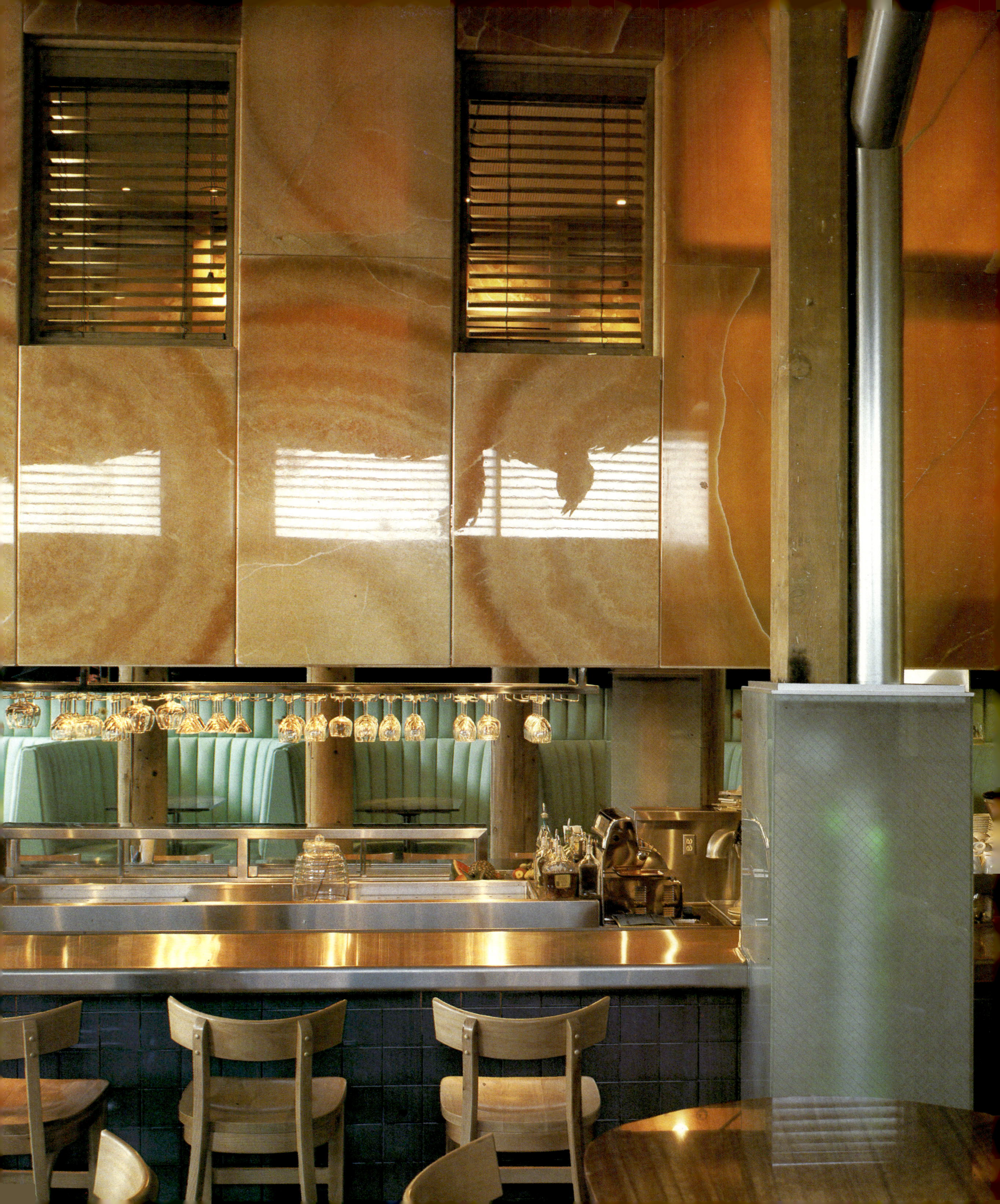

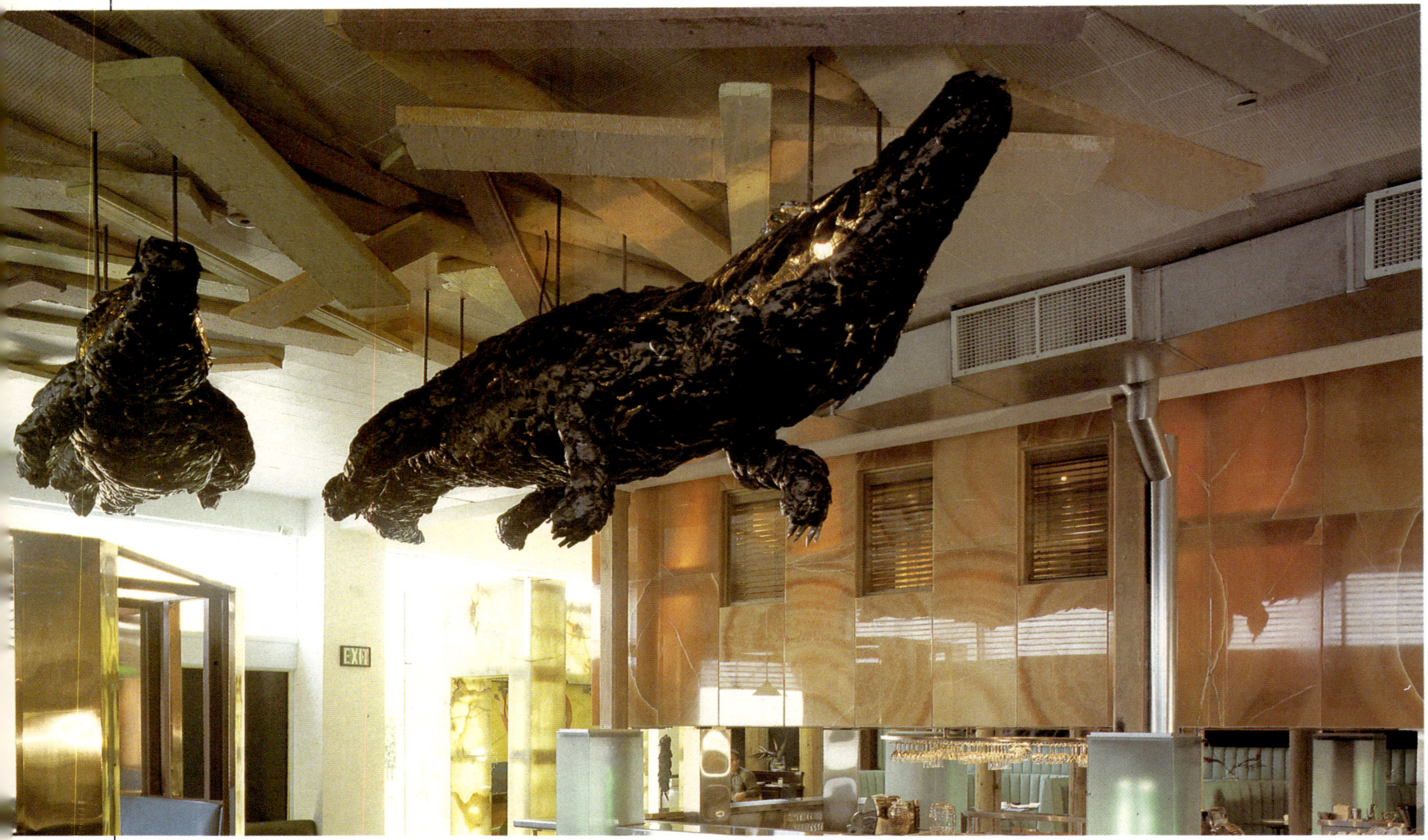

most outrageous project yet? It may be the two 16 foot (5 metre) long painted tin crocodiles suspended over the main dining-room, or perhaps the plate-glass murals of golden tarantulas or the red glass bead octopus, or possibly the 16 foot (5 metre) high timber 'trees' that march through the dining area. In Venice, where Gehry is based, the zoomorphic conceits of Rebecca's are the root attraction of the restaurant; if all the patrons wanted was Mexican food, they could find it somewhere else.

The surprises at Rebecca's start at the entrance, an illuminated portal of white onyx framing tin-collage doors by artist Tony Berlant. Inside, the organization of the restaurant is quite logical (many overlook the essential soundness of Gehry's designs, seduced by the shocking details). A long, narrow dining area runs from the left of the entrance with a series of aquamarine Naugahyde U-shaped banquettes. To the right of the entrance is a more open brasserie/bar; a U-shaped bar counter is directly in front of the entrance.

The brasserie has a central dining gazebo, a raised platform area and, on the raw cement floors, a collection of custom-designed high tables and stools. The long dining area is organized by the 'trees' and by the enforced regularity of the banquettes. Despite the logic, it is the 'art' that distinguishes the design. The tarantulas, which seem to be running across the plate glass, were created by painter Ed Moses. The crocodiles, which also serve as glowing lamps, were designed by Gehry and have a noble line of descent from smaller fish and snake lamps created over the years.

Gehry's design magic does not, however, come cheap. The 4,521 square foot (420 square metre) restaurant, with seating for eighty, and an additional eighty in the brasserie/bar, cost 1.5 million dollars. Fortunately, this artwork is also a highly successful restaurant that works.

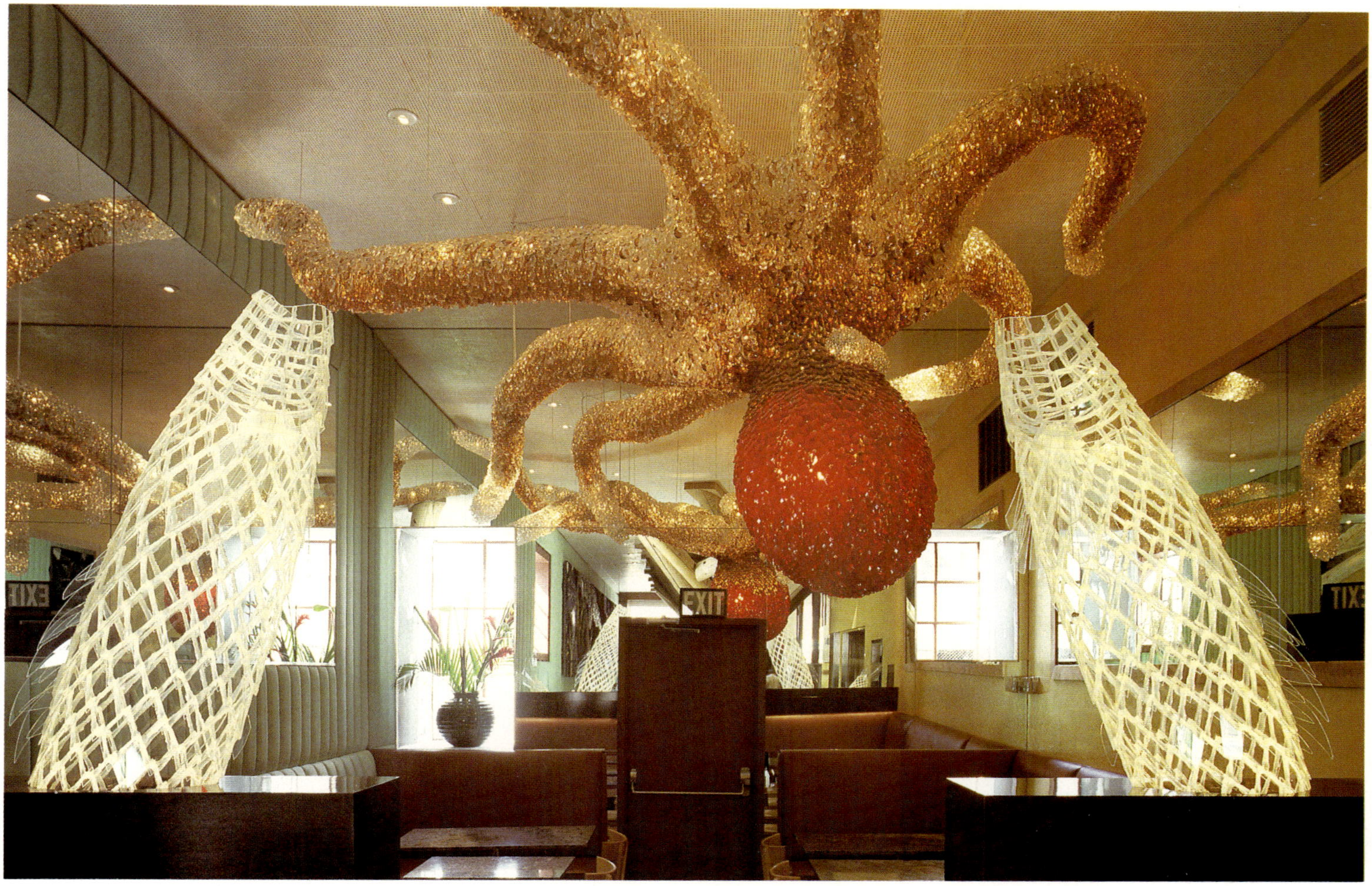

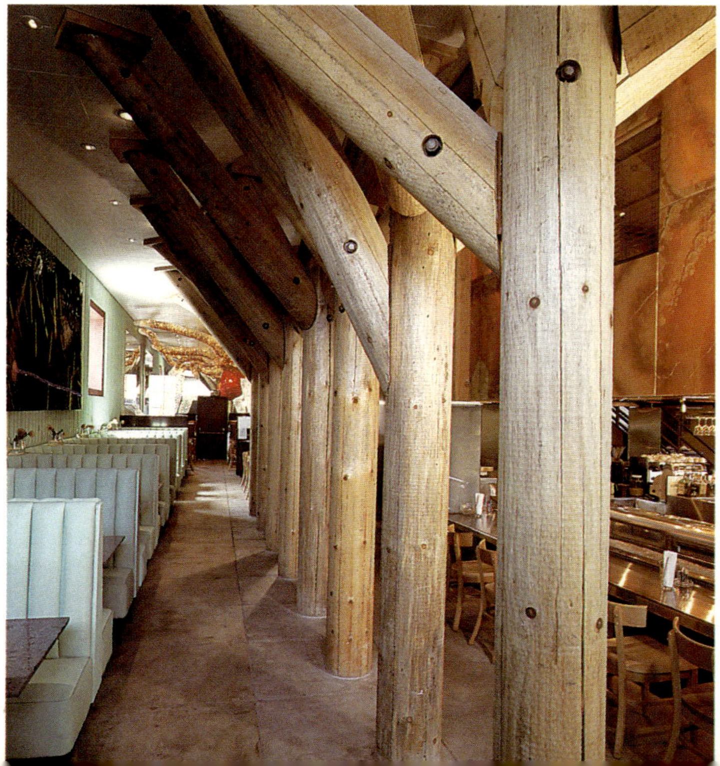

(above left) Calculated to outrage: 16 foot (5 metre) painted tin crocodiles hover menacingly over the bar. However, they also have a function – as glowing lamps.

(above) An outré octopus in glass with a glitter finish hangs from the ceiling.

(left) A long narrow space, the dining-room is flanked by brilliant turquoise Naugahyde banquettes on one side, and a row of timber 'trees' on the other.

AURORA

NEW YORK CITY, USA

Designed by Milton Glaser with Tom Higgins

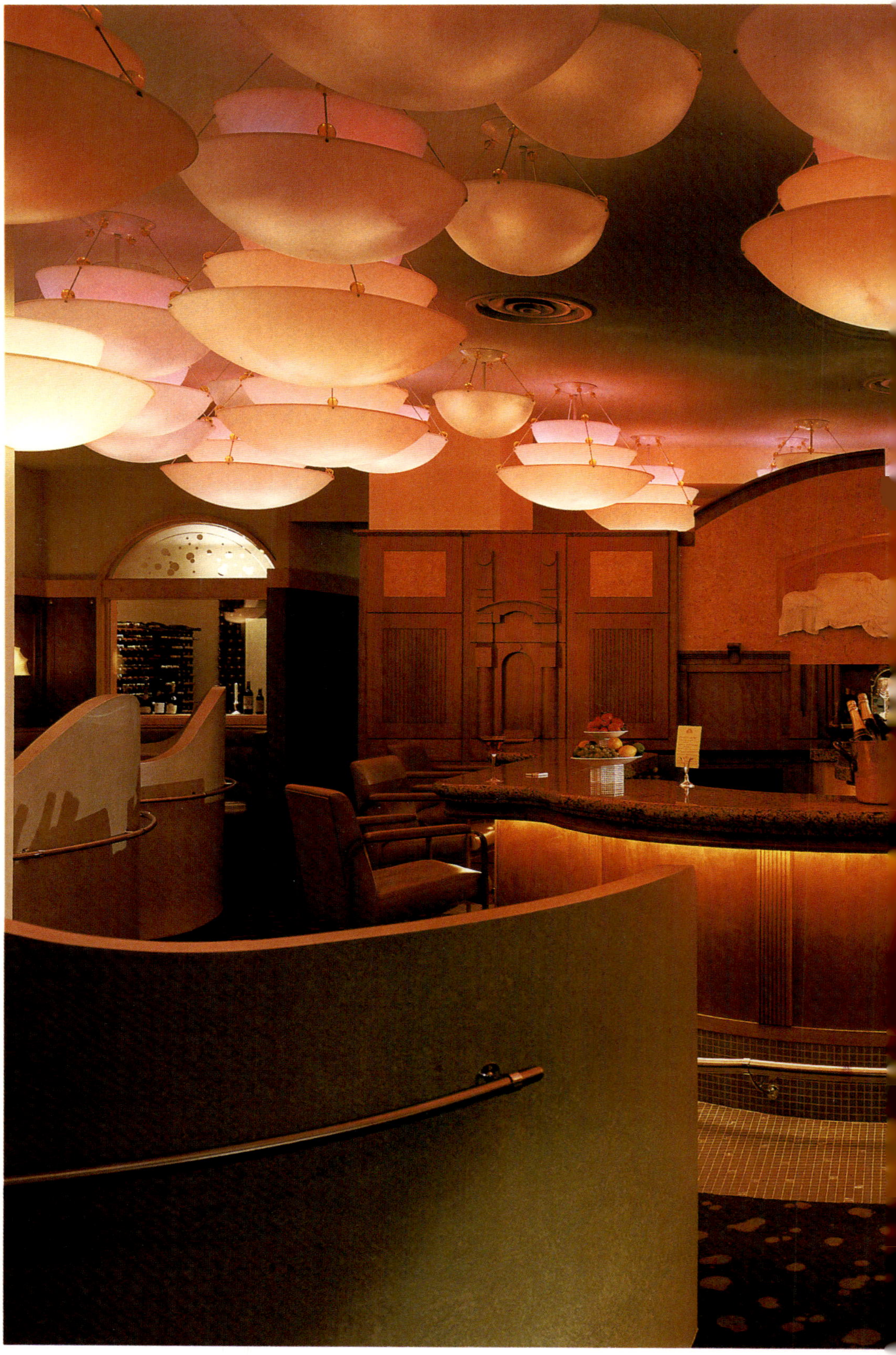

Anyone walking into the Aurora restaurant on East 49th Street could be forgiven for thinking for a moment that someone had just released dozen's of large pink balloons in the main bar area. In fact, these are specially designed multi-tiered light fittings which have been created – like everything else in the restaurant – by the designers at Milton Glaser.

One of the other immediately noticeable features in this 3,229 square foot (300 square metre) restaurant is the snaking central bar, which dominates the space. Its serpentine shape is echoed in the curves of the cherry-wood panelling near the door, the rounded banquettes, the pattern of the carpet and the light fittings.

Adjacent to the main bar there are two dining areas, together seating up to 125 people and surrounded by rich cherrywood panelling. Here, additional lighting comes from glass wall sconces. The carpet was designed so that its pattern reflects the shape of the pink, rounded light fittings. In fact, Glaser even designed the chinaware used by diners (as well as all the menu and other graphics, a field in which the practice is justly renowned).

With the use of traditional materials such as leather and cherrywood, and finishes such as faux marble, Aurora is an opulent environment, somewhat reminiscent at times of an English gentlemen's club. But, as one would expect from the perpetually grinning Glaser, touches of humour and oddity – those pink 'clouds' – ensure that Aurora is far from stuffy.

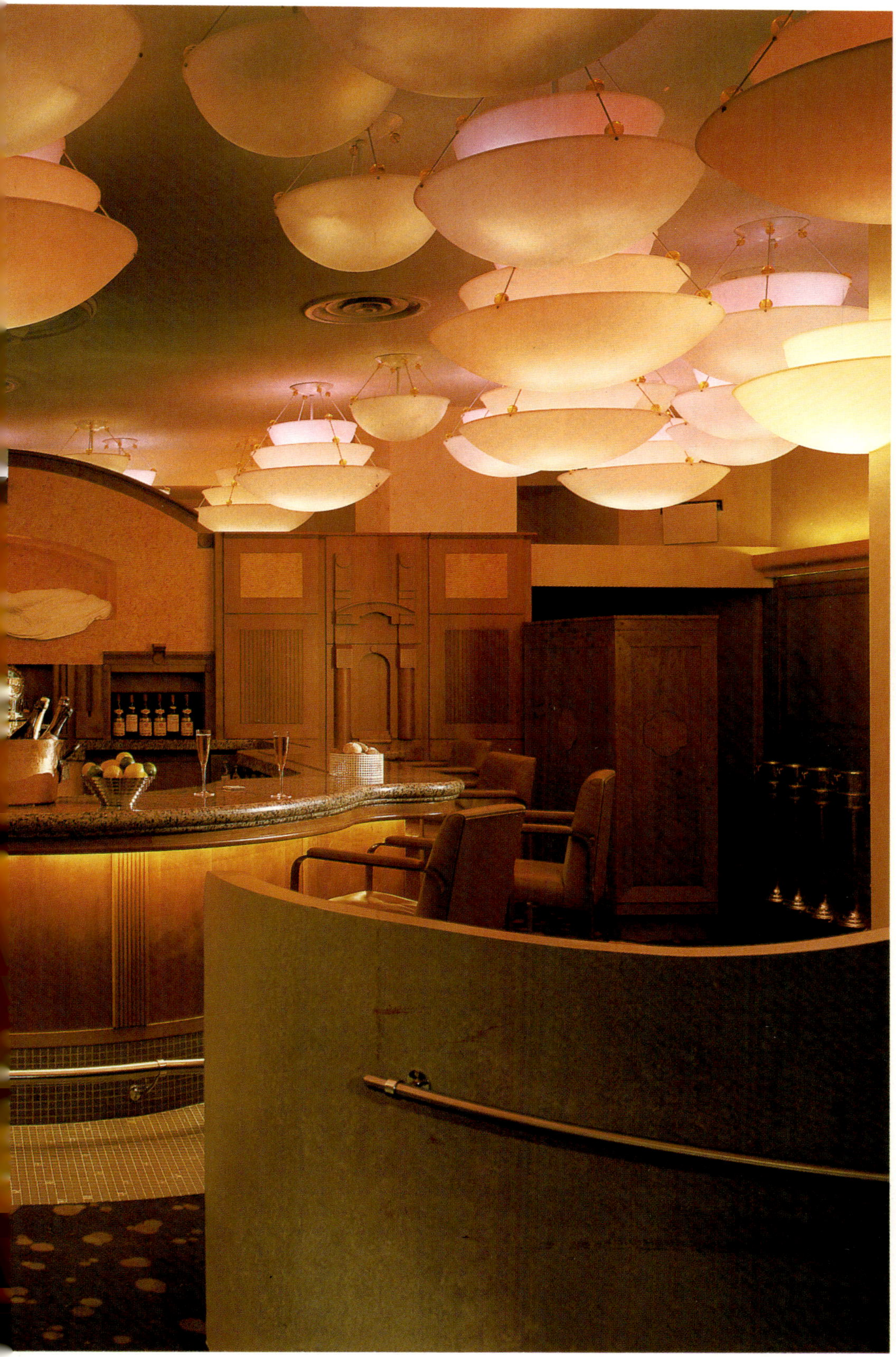

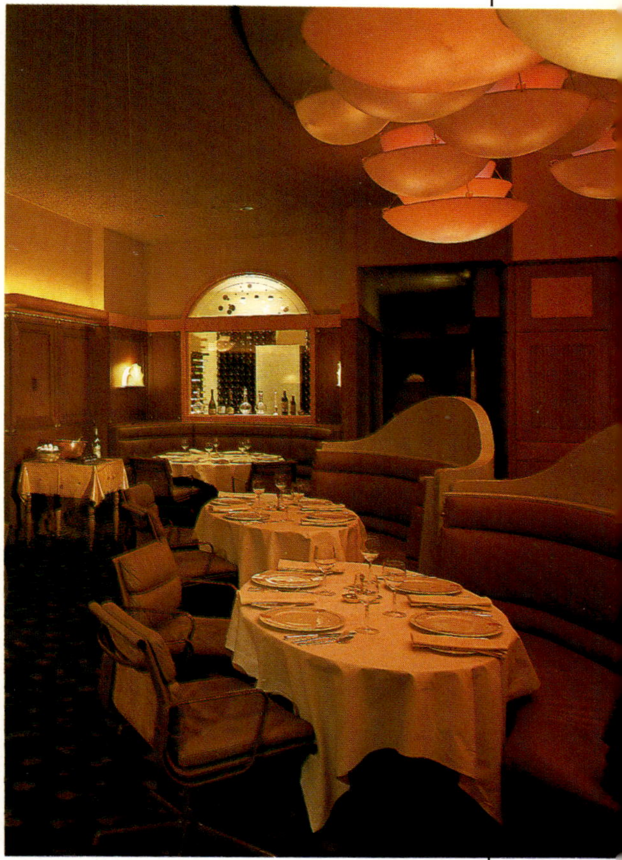

(above) Cherrywood panelling and padded leather chairs give the dining-room an opulent feel, but this is always tempered by the frivolity of the other elements.

(left) Curves abound in every detail, from the bar counter to the banquettes and, most noticeably, in the specially designed tiered light fittings. Their balloon-like shapes are echoed in the patterned carpet.

CLAUDIA'S, WONDER SUSHI PLUS AND BOARDWALK FRIES

SAN DIEGO, CALIFORNIA, USA

Designed by Grondona/Architects

San Diego's Horton Plaza shopping mall, designed by The Jerde Partnership, is justly famous among the retailing fraternity. Taking brilliant advantage of a warm climate, the design of Horton Plaza creates a fantastical outdoor shopping village that is popular with both customers and design critics.

But designers putting units into Horton Plaza face a difficult problem competing with the exuberant architecture. Guidelines and restraints, on features such as setbacks and awning projects, preserve the strong character of the mall, but designers understandably want to impose something of their own as well.

Grondona/Architects took a novel tack in their design for three fast-food outlets in the Plaza. Describing the mall as a 'Post-Modern battle zone', Grondona decided not to compete but to design art installations rather than pieces of architecture.

(right) Two of the three fast-food outlets exemplify the designers' approach. They make no attempt to rival the architecture but instead try to create three-dimensional art. Claudia's, a bakery, has a 'smell funnel' to waft the enticing scents of cooking to the outside. Next to it, the customers are confronted by huge styrofoam fries.

(left) Strong competition for any design comes from the existing building, an exuberant and colourful open-air shopping mall.

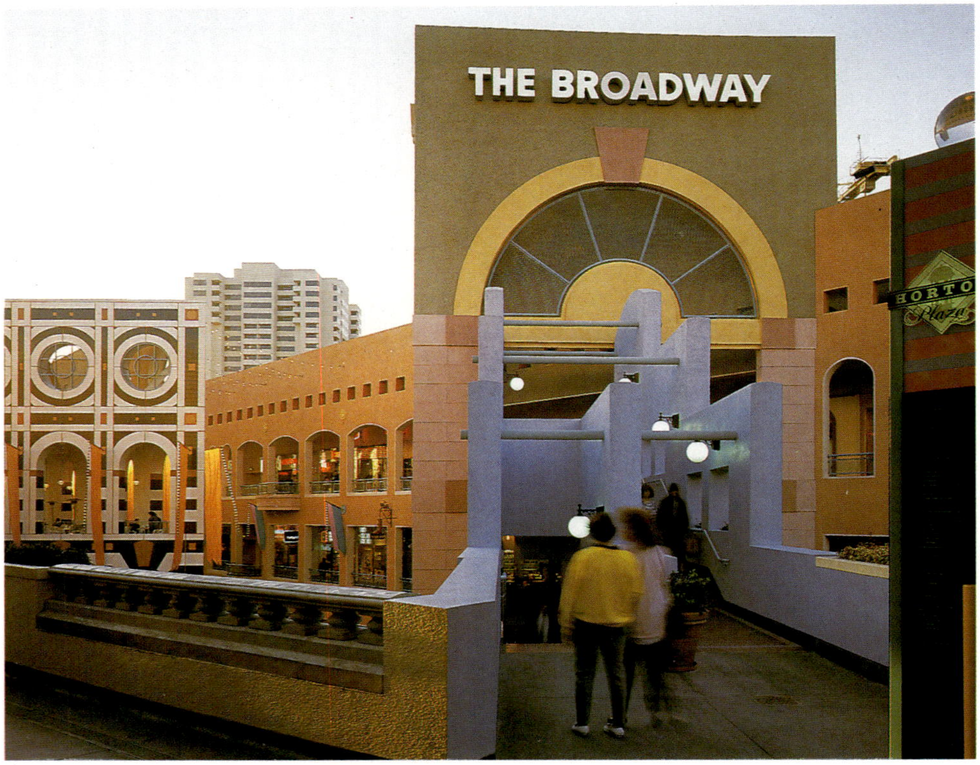

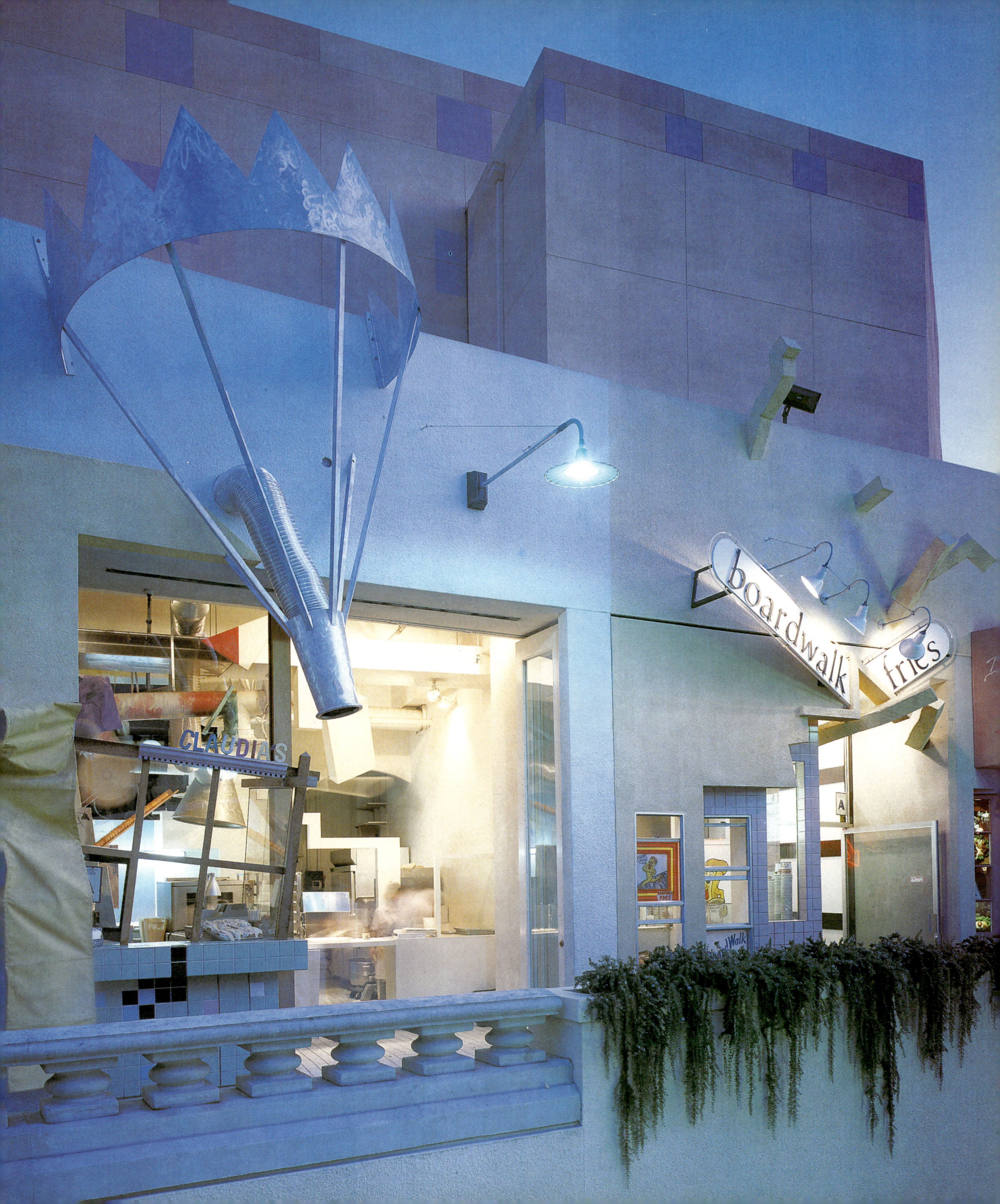
CLAUDIA'S
boardwalk
fries

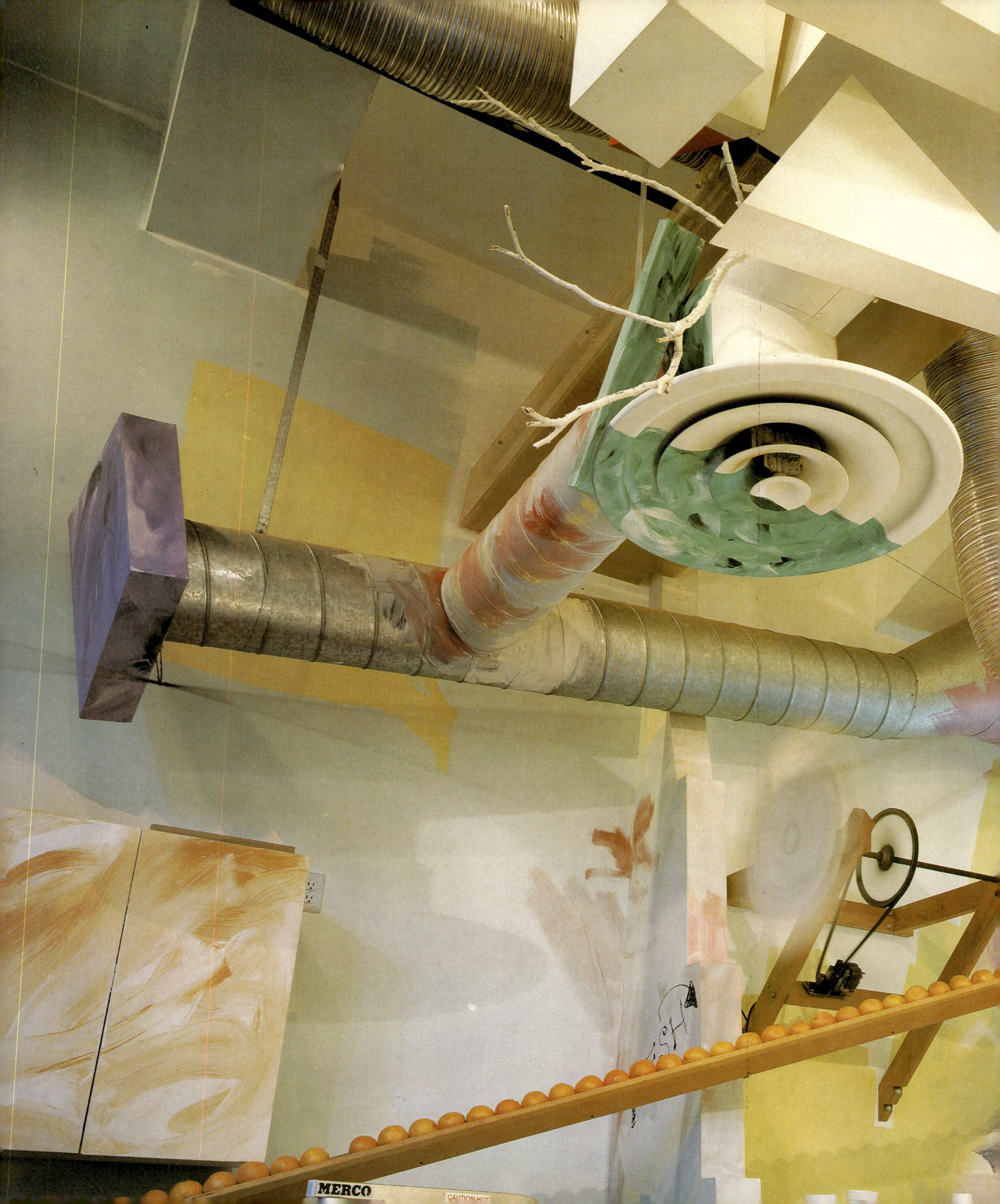
MERCO
CAUTION HOT

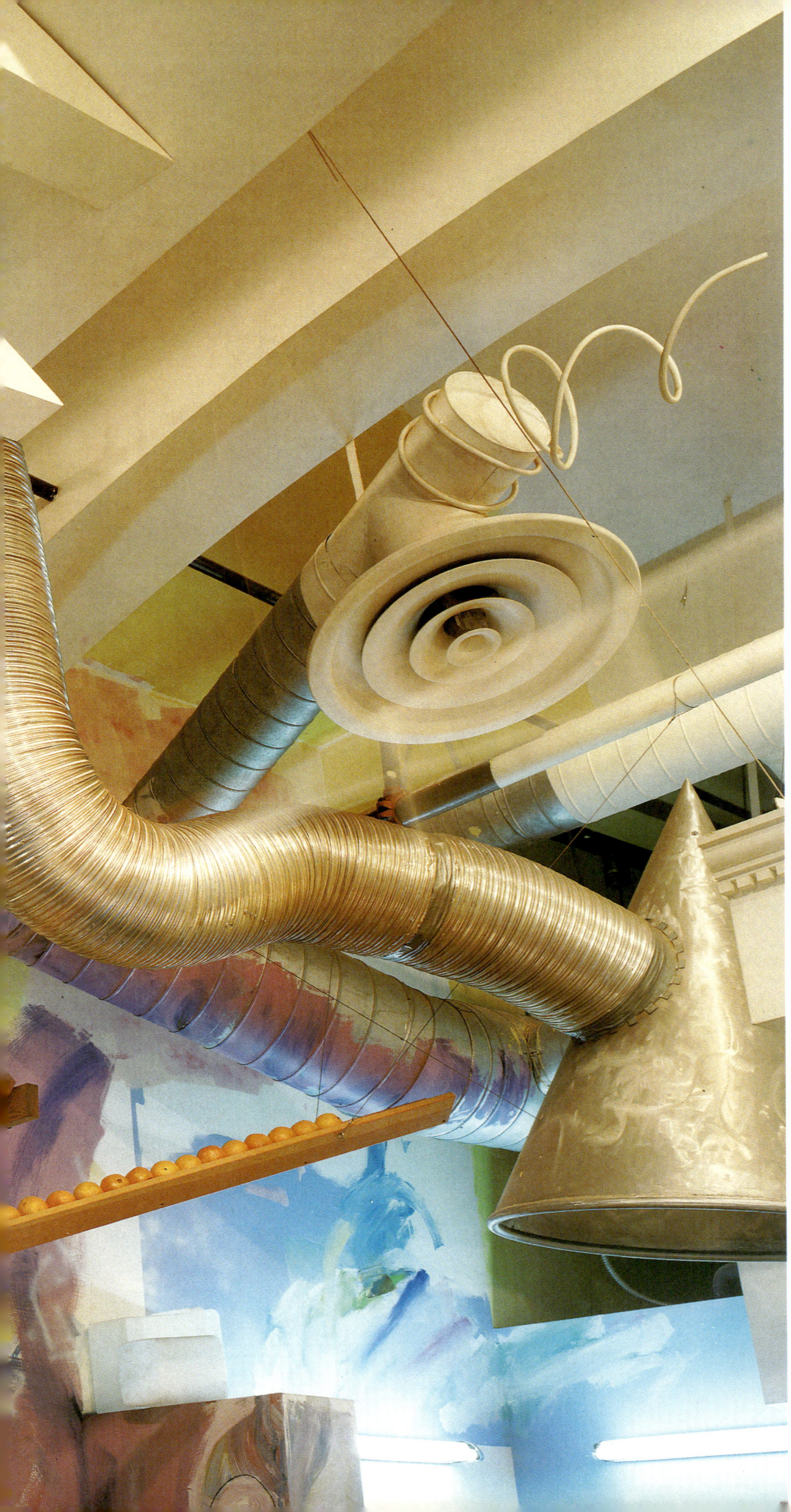

(left) Paint, marble, glue and tree branches form the interior of Claudia's, across which travels a chute of (real) oranges.

(below) In the sunny California climate, there is no ed for a closed store, so the bakery opens directly on to the mall.

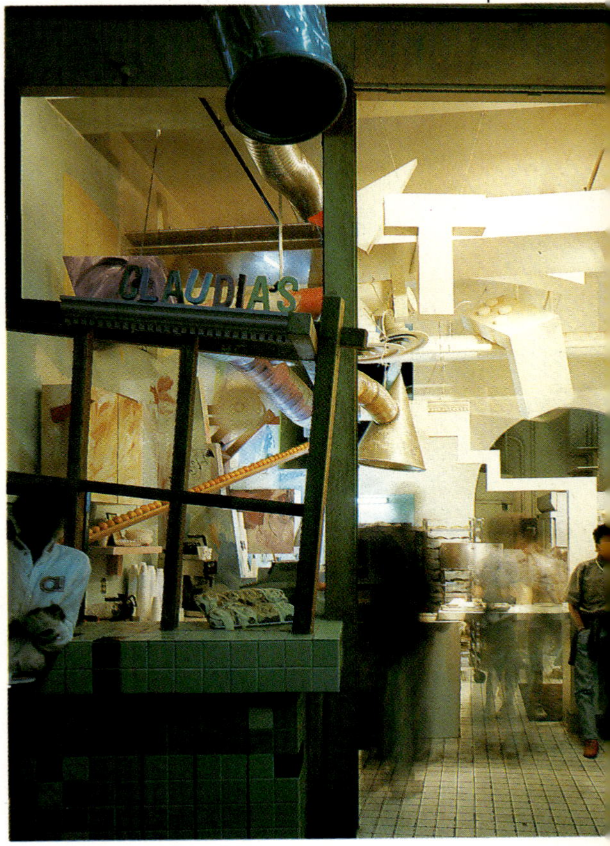

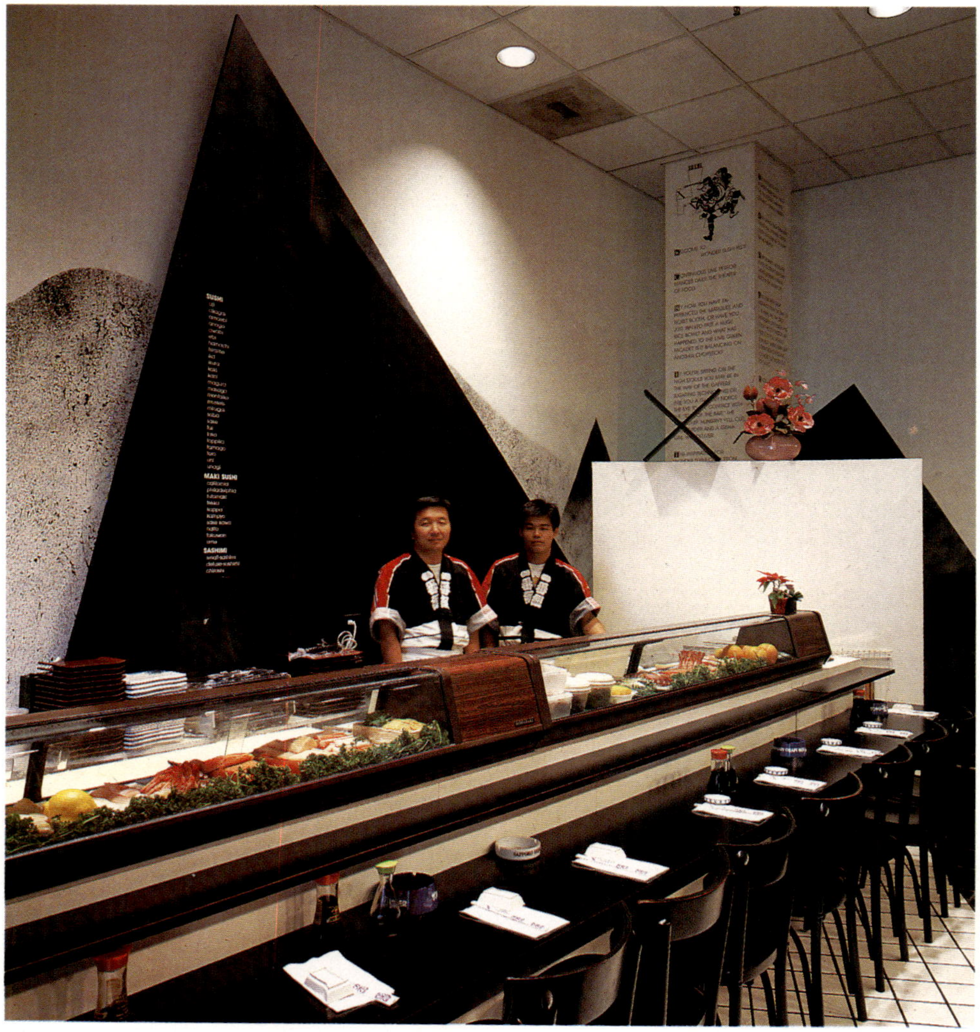

(below) On a larger scale than the other two is Wonder Sushi Plus. Materials are more conventional – slate, laminate and painted steel – and the treatment simpler.

(left) The real stars in a sushi bar, the sushi chefs themselves, backed by a display of their specialities.

(right) Cut-outs, bold graphics and three-dimensional sculptures of the products make this outlet instantly noticeable, despite the fact that it is little bigger than a kiosk.

A bakery, Claudia's boasts a 'smell funnel' at the base of a large crown, to vent the enticing smells of fresh baking to passers-by. Inside, a riotous assemblage of elements includes a long sloping chute of oranges tumbling through the shop. The cinnamon roll bakery and retail outlet is a tiny 538 square feet (50 square metres). An idea of the design's eclecticism can be glimpsed by the list of materials used: paint, tile, marble, sticks, glue, tree branches.

Wonder Sushi Plus treats the drama of the sushi-making process literally, announcing the specialities on a cinema marquee. Although the sushi chefs are the main performers, performance artists are invited to stage their works there, too. The take-out Japanese fast-food and sit-down sushi bar is larger than Claudia's at 969 square feet (90 square metres). The 'constructivist' design, less exuberant perhaps than the collagist bakery, uses a more conventional palette of materials: slate, drywall, plastic laminate and painted steel.

At Boardwalk Fries, the french fries explode from the façade. The seeming aggression of the painted styrofoam fries led one American critic to title his piece on the Grondona work 'Attack of the Killer Fries'. Boardwalk Fries is the smallest of the three units at 377 square feet (35 square metres). The rampaging french fries emphasize the three-dimensionality of Grondona's work at Horton Plaza, in distinct contrast to the applied decoration that prevails elsewhere.

Much of the 'art installation' aspect of the designs is done by Tom Grondona himself as part of 'The G-Force' art installation group.

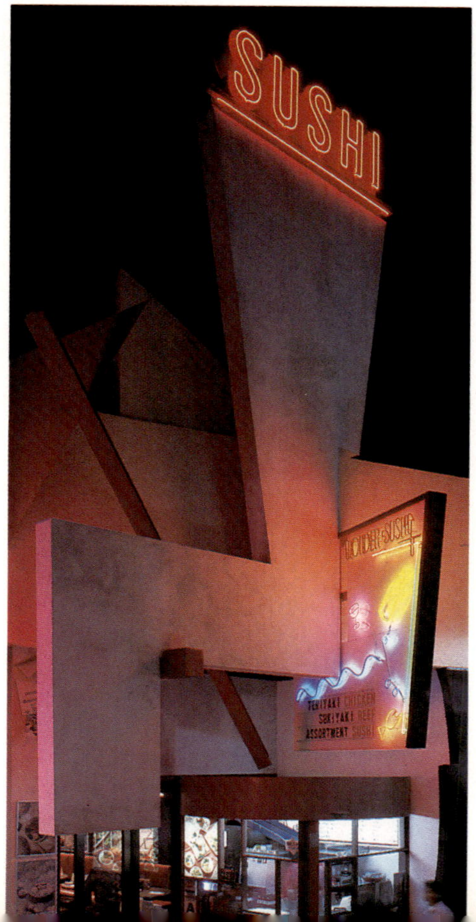

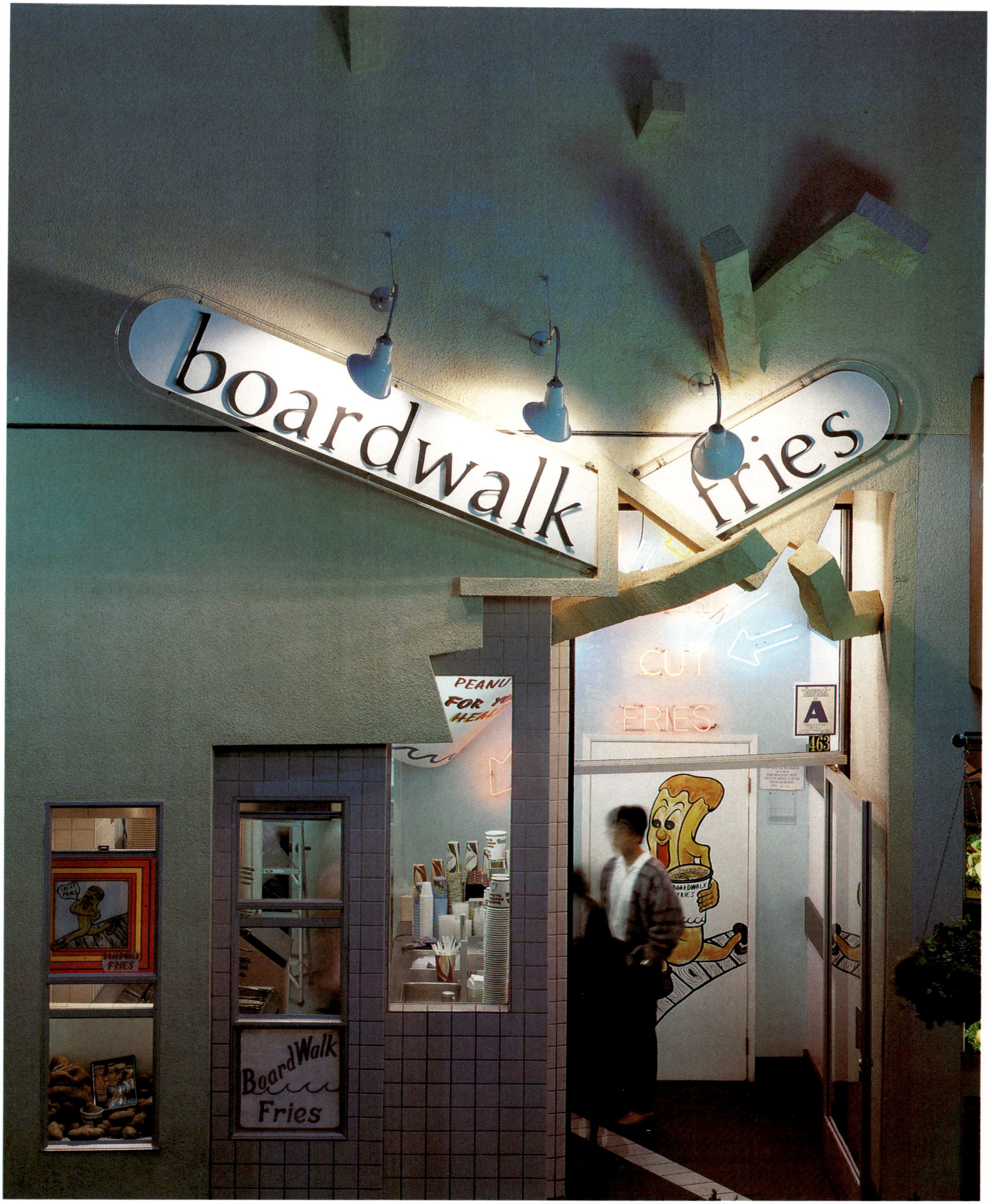
boardwalk
fries
CUT
FRIES
A
463
BoardWalk
Fries

HOTEL LE PLAZA
BASEL, SWITZERLAND

Trix and Robert Haussmann

Trix and Robert Haussmann, working in sober Zurich, have tended to ignore design trends and movements. Instead, the husband-and-wife design firm has been steadily refining its distinctive style, which relies on illusion and surprise for its effects. Mirrors, unexpected contrasts of materials and jarring changes of scale are characteristic of their projects.

When the Haussmanns were commissioned to design the interiors of Basel's Hotel Le Plaza, the construction plans were largely complete. For many, such a commission often proves impossibly restricting: the expense of changing building plans leaves the interior designers with a merely ameliorative role. The Haussmanns realized that they had to accept the given structure and the major part of the internal planning. With a relatively modest (though undisclosed) budget, their strategy was to concentrate on decorative, applied elements to create a design identity. The Haussmanns identify six techniques they employ in the Hotel Le Plaza: historical references, illusion, irony, parody, metaphor and poetry.

The meanings of these somewhat ambiguous terms is clarified when the design itself is revealed. The double-height entrance lobby has spike-like projections protruding menacingly from the walls (though in non-injurious positions), mocking the welcome most hotel designs attempt to convey. In the 'Black Horse Bar', a full-sized black horse stands imposingly on the bar counter, perhaps as a parody of the famous whisky brand. Mirror tiles are used on walls, making it difficult at times to tell what is wall and what is opening.

Most successfully, the Haussmanns have used fabric and paint effects to play with

(right) Illusion and parody in the entrance lobby: chairs are upholstered in a marble fabric made by Mira-X, matched by the decorative paint finish on walls and columns.

(below) Floor plan.

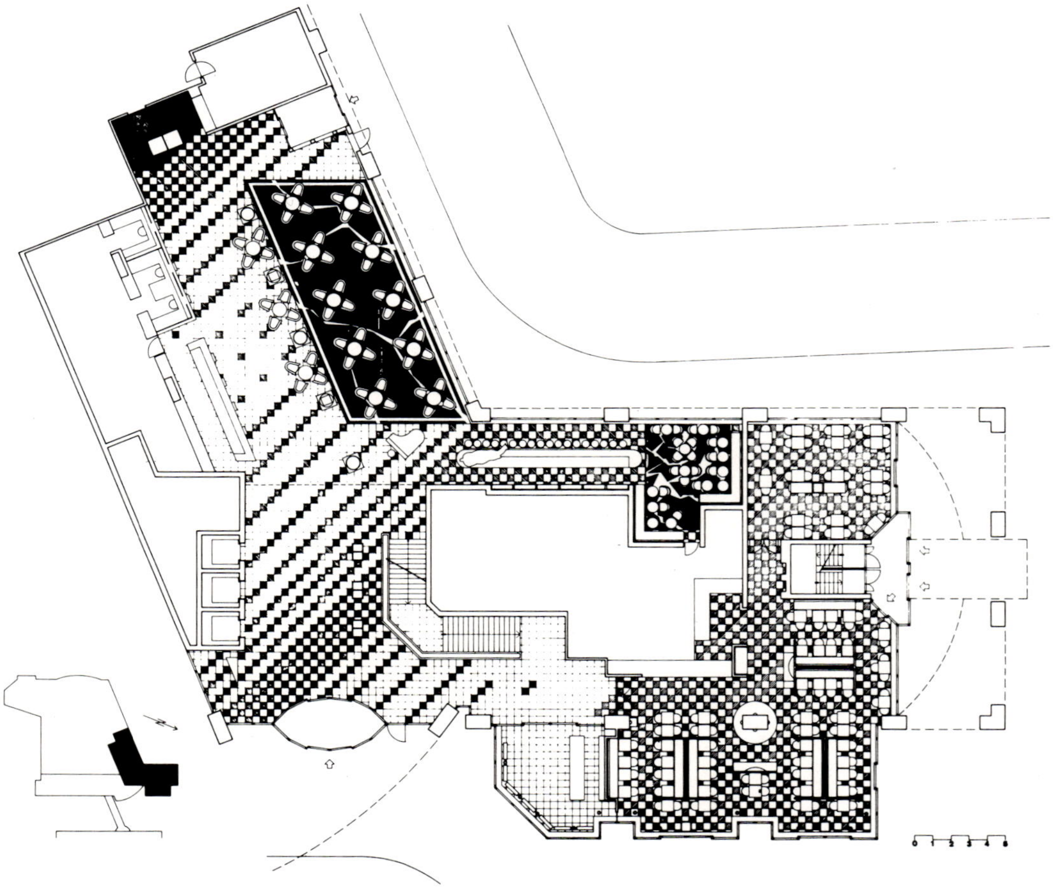

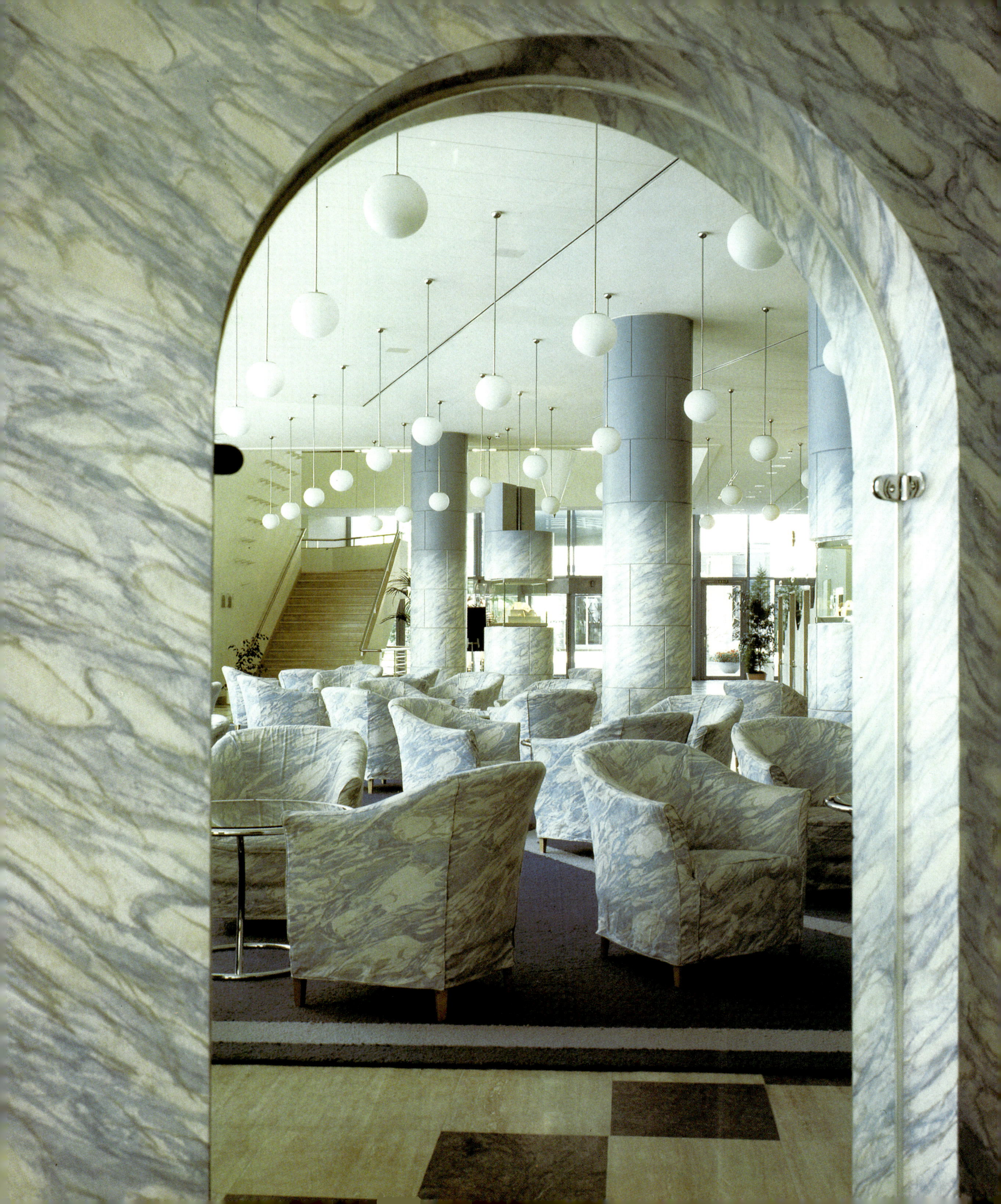

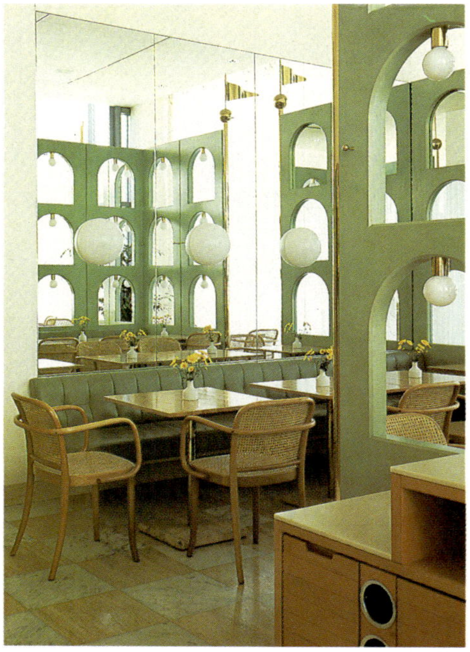

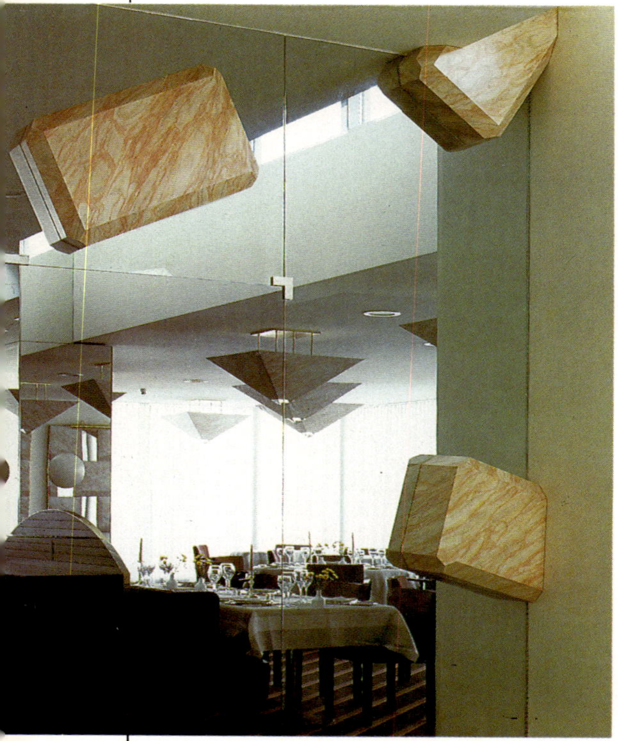

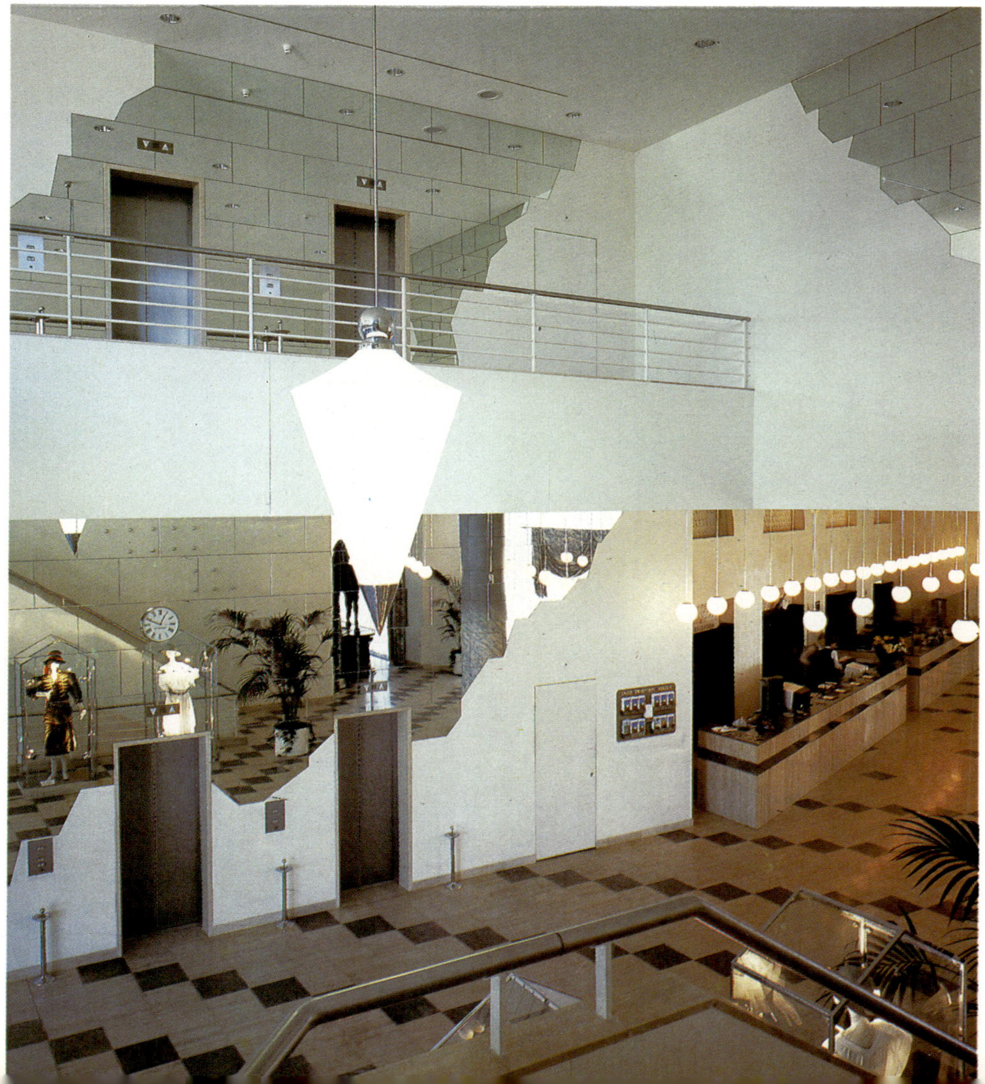

(below far left) historical references in the restaurant. The earthquake of tumbling marble blocks is apparently inspired by sixteenth-century Italian Mannerism.

(left) Arched walls in the ground-floor café are another architectural reference, to the Palazzo della Civiltá in Rome.

(below left) Poetry and illusion: contrasts of light and shade, space and solid mass are created by cutaway screens below, echoing the lines of the broken mirror tiles above.

(below) Each element is meticulously detailed and executed.

(below right) Parody, irony or metaphor? Or perhaps just to show that you can take a black horse anywhere.

expectations about materials. For example, in the entrance lobby, chairs are upholstered in a marble-like fabric (made by Mira-X and designed by the Haussmanns), while the walls and columns are painted to look like marble. Similarly, in the restaurant, 'marble' blocks seem to tumble down the mirrored walls, suggesting an earthquake-inspired destruction of the hotel. For the erudite Haussmanns, the implied reference is to the Italian Mannerists of the sixteenth century.

A more subtle reference still is the maze of round-arched walls in the ground-floor café – a direct borrowing from the Italian Rationalist Palazzo della Civiltá in Rome's EUR. The Haussmanns probably did not expect the users of the Hotel Le Plaza – largely business people – to recognize their allusions, but they have succeeded in creating a design to taunt and provoke in the gentlest of ways, and thus a hotel identity that is undoubtedly memorable.

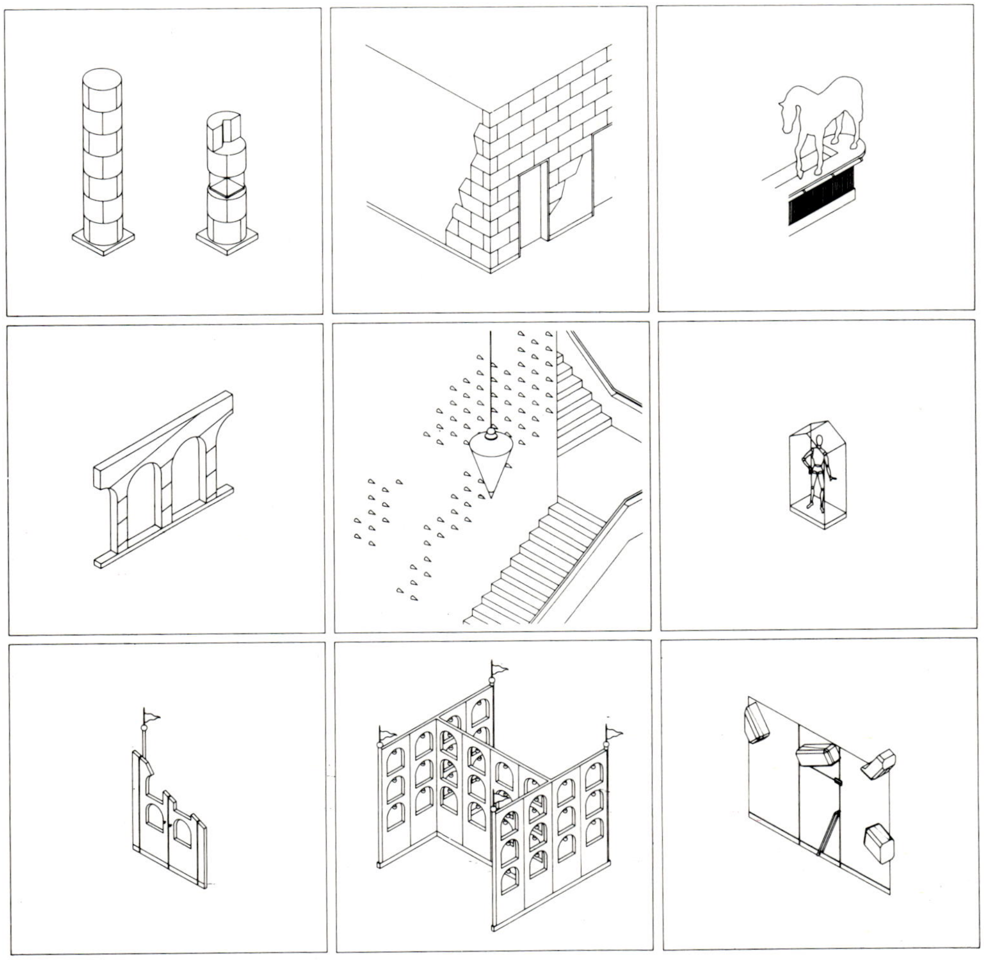

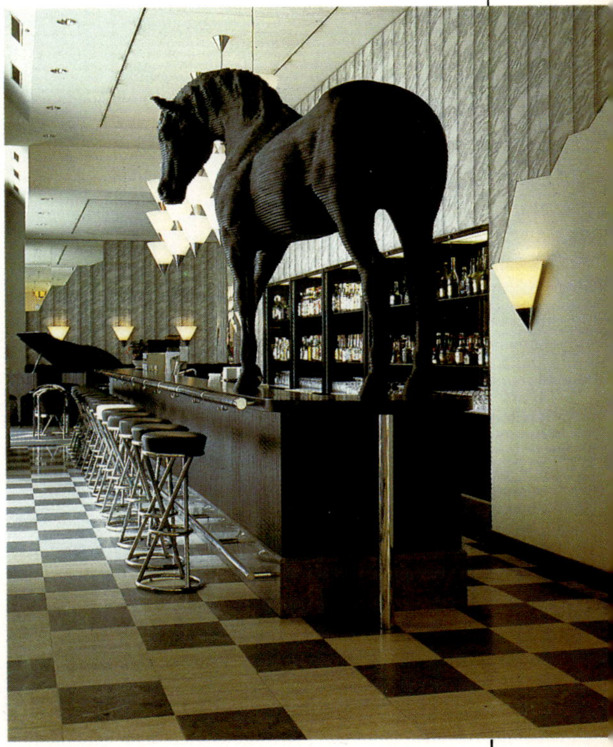

ARAI
TOKYO, JAPAN

Designed by Naoki Iijima

Much contemporary Japanese design rejects all but the most general notions of the rich architectural heritage of the country. In his work on the Arai restaurant, Naoki Iijima carefully intertwines the most modern of interiors with a distinctive sense of Japanese tradition.

Such a mixture is appropriate to a client who, although serving Japanese food, asked the designer for a 'contemporary interior design'. On one side, Arai is bordered by a brushed-steel screen, projected off the wall by steel pipes. A stepped pattern of pale wood tables and benches (made from the Japanese sen wood) leads the eye down the space to a huge brushed-steel disc. A spray of pipes seems to burst forth from the disc over the aluminium bar counter (bar stools are constructed from steel pipes with rubber seats). Where the pipes hit the opposite wall, they fan out into a striated shadow pattern. All is set against the bare concrete background. The total cost was 140,000 dollars. In such a space, the paraphernalia of dining – food, tableware, people – almost seems an incongruous intrusion.

(right) Minimalism with traditional and modern materials: the steel wall and stepped Japanese sen wood tables and benches form sculptural planes leading down to the huge steel disc at the far end.

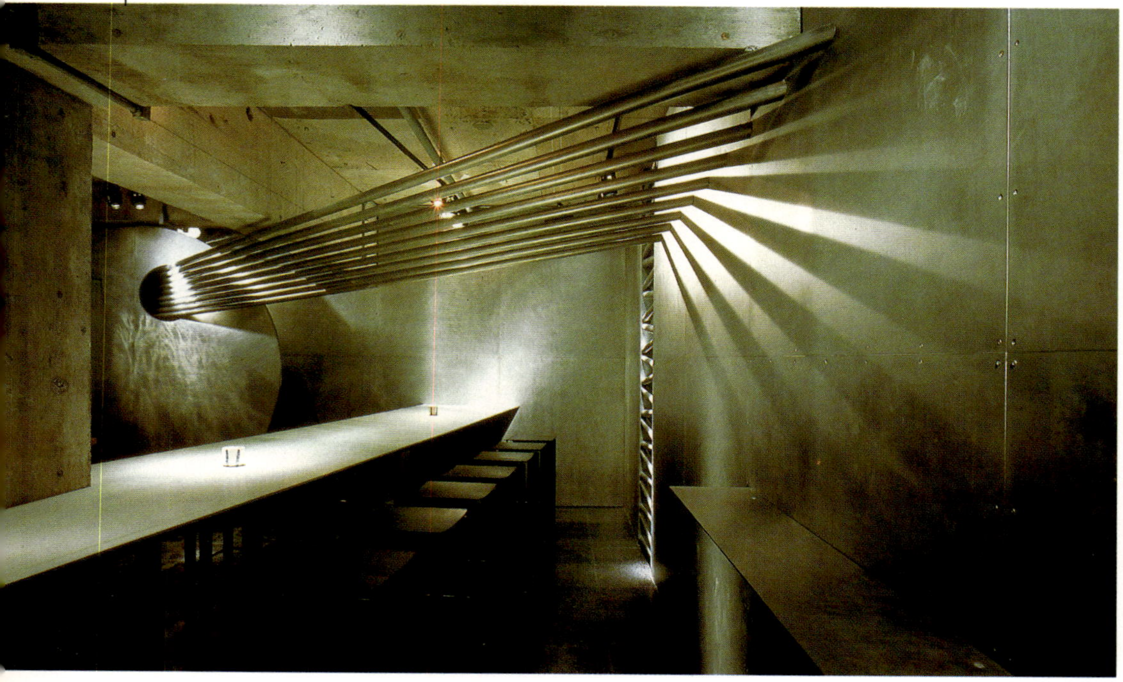

(below) Steel pipes spray forth over the counter, fanning out in a pattern of light and shade when they hit the bare concrete wall opposite.

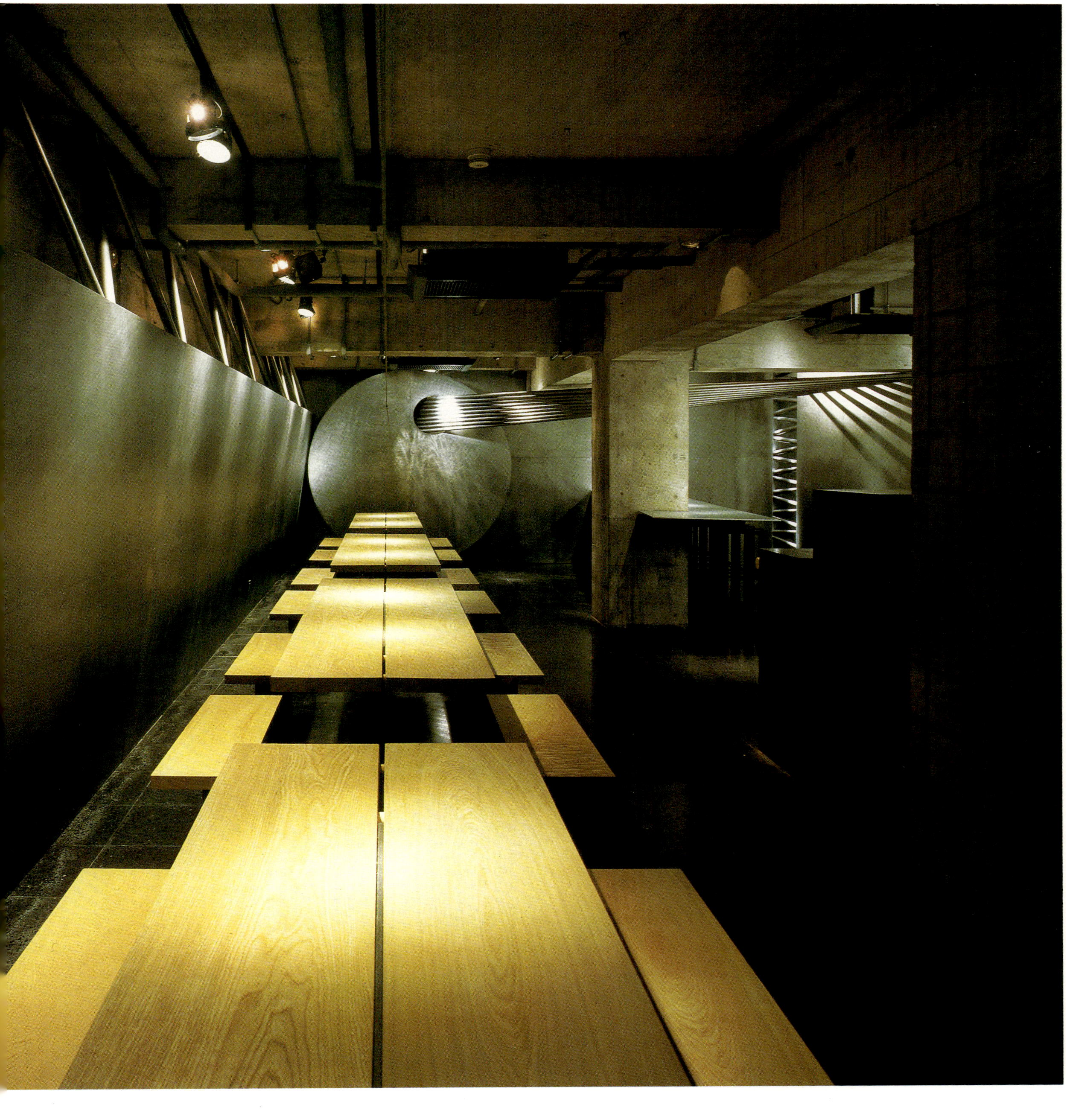

NOMAD
TOKYO, JAPAN

Designed by Toyo Ito

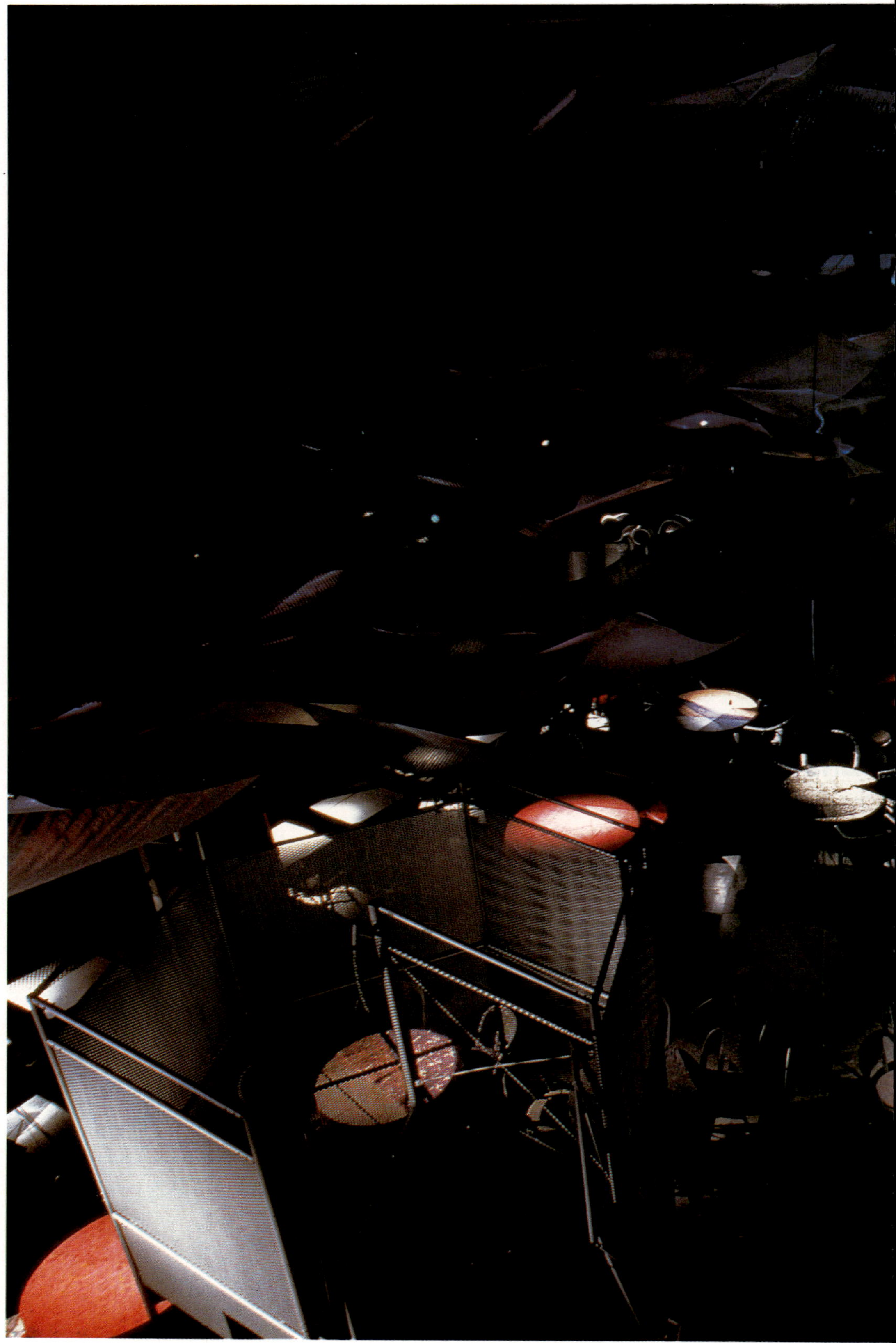

Toyo Ito's interior for the Nomad café-bar is designed not to last – not because it is shoddily constructed, but simply because the site is earmarked for another development in two or three years' time. The client, Makoto Sugasawara, had intended to build a small hotel on this and an adjoining site, but because the land purchase was delayed, he commissioned Ito to create a restaurant there as a temporary measure.

The space is a cavernous warehouse in a steel-framed industrial building. Because of the understandably low budget the existing steel structure is left exposed, apart from a sprayed fireproof finish, and becomes the dominant aesthetic. For example, the lower walls are clad with perforated aluminium sheets, and the benches and bar counter are in aluminium and galvanized iron.

To break up the vast open space, an upper-level terrace has been introduced around the perimeter, looking down on to the large central 'doma', or earth floor, a traditional Japanese space. Within this are crowded tables and chairs in a variety of sizes and finishes, from grey rattan to glazed batik fabric; a nice idea that just avoids being contrived and messy.

More effective is the use of metal and metallic fabric 'sails', lit from above and suspended from the 29½ foot (9 metre) high ceiling like colourful clouds. Seen from outside at night, through the hazy screen of perforated aluminium panels, they take on an ethereal quality that seems very much in keeping with the ephemeral nature of the building.

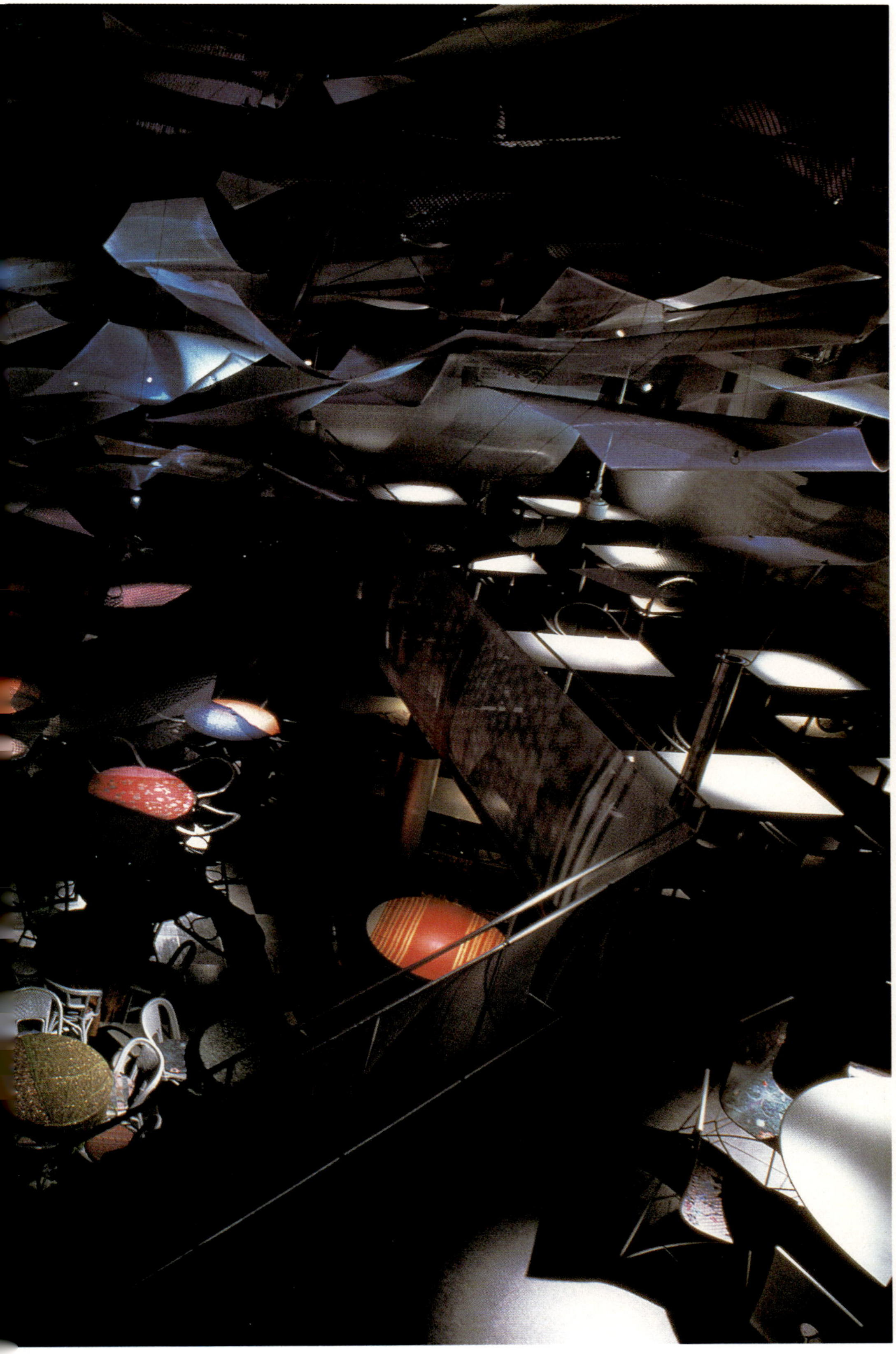

(left) Converted from an industrial warehouse, Nomad has a perimeter terrace overlooking the huge central earth floor, a traditional Japanese space.

(below) Inside and out the steel structure of the building is left exposed. Perforated aluminium panels reveal intriguing glimpses of the interior at night.

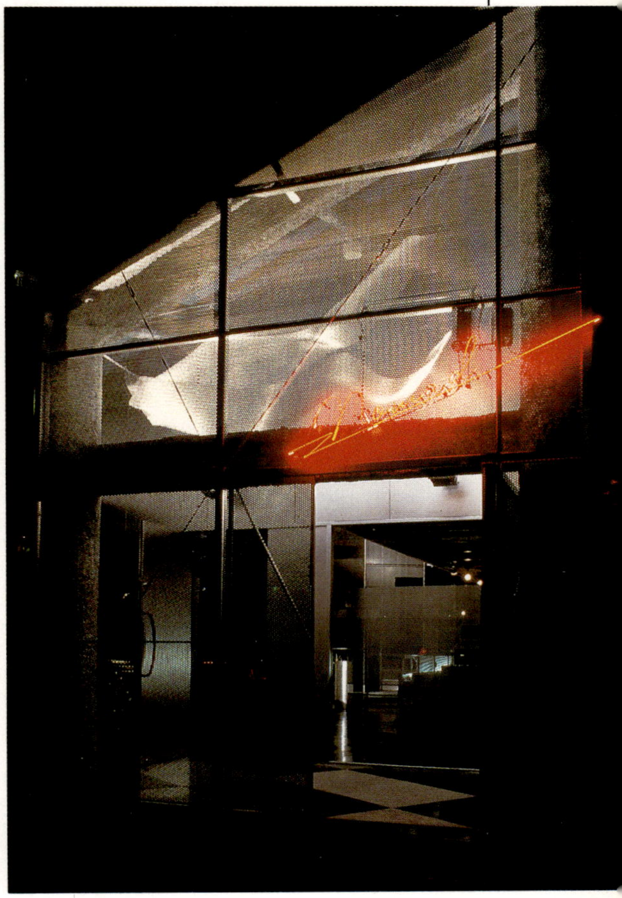

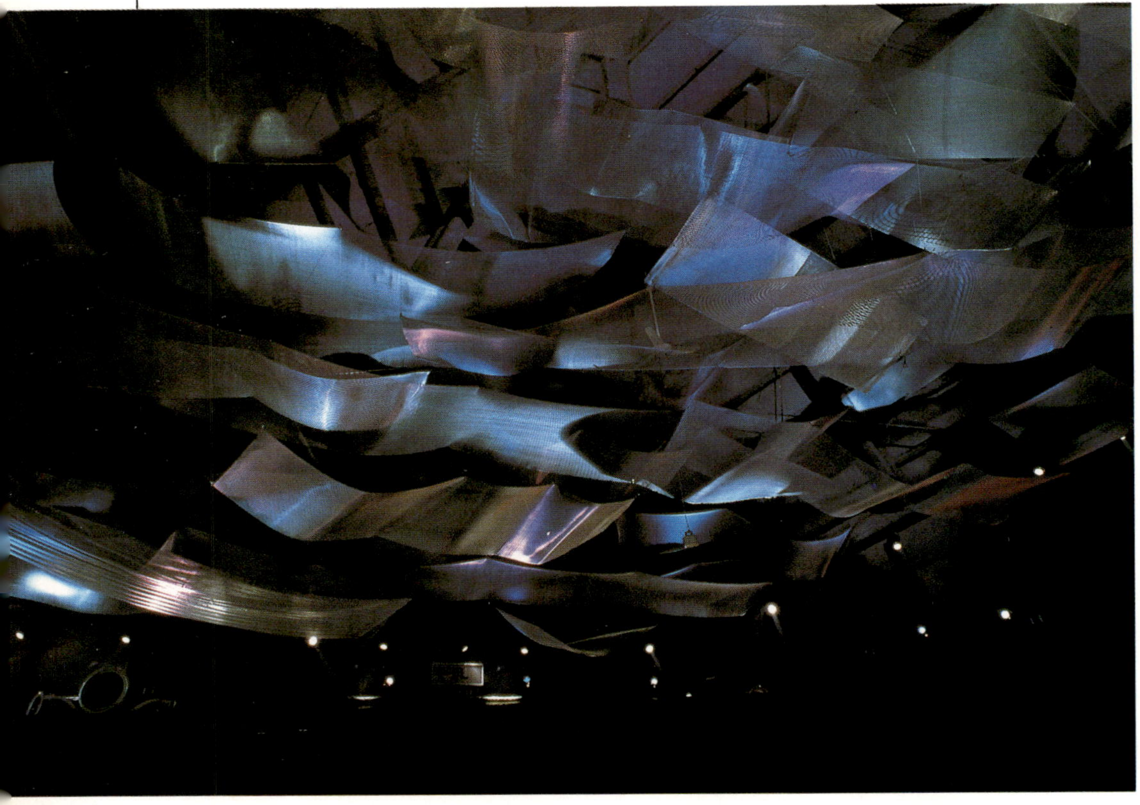

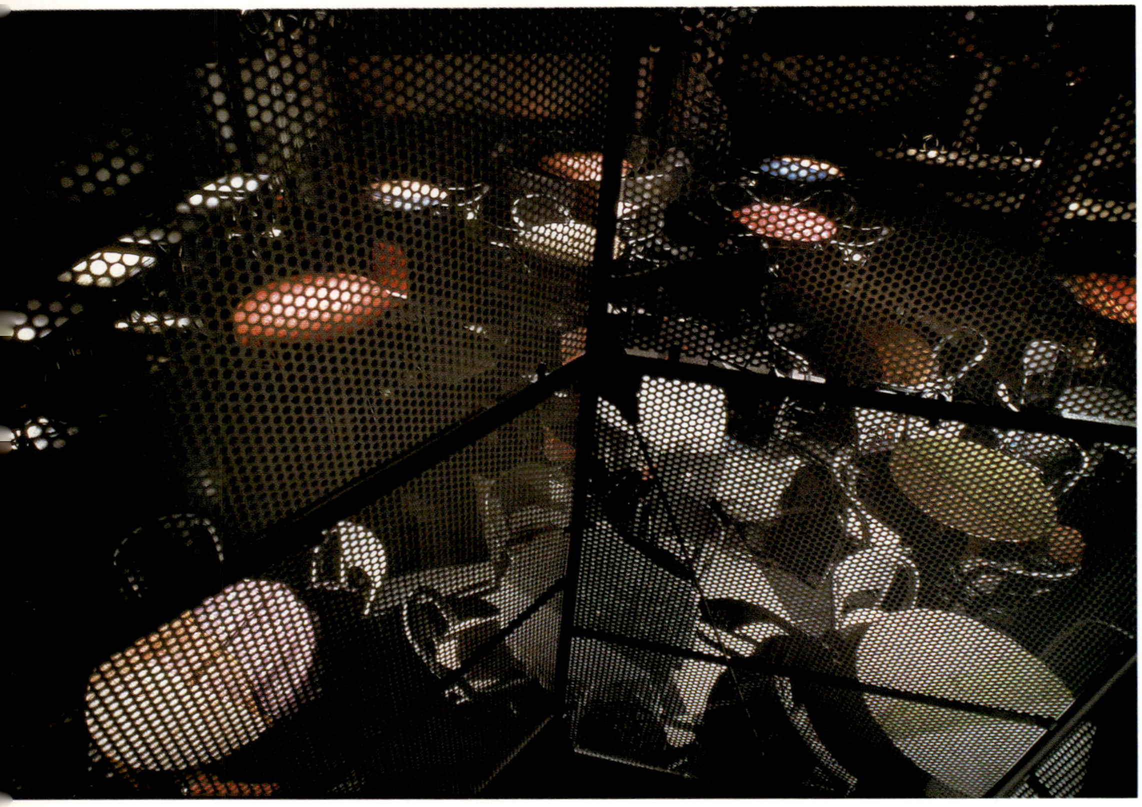

(left) Toplit metal and metallic fabric 'sails' are suspended from the high ceiling to break up the volume.

(left below) Tables and chairs in all styles and sizes crowd together on the central floor.

(right) Materials throughout echo the industrial aesthetic: perforated aluminium sheets line the walls, and the bar counter is in aluminium and galvanized iron.

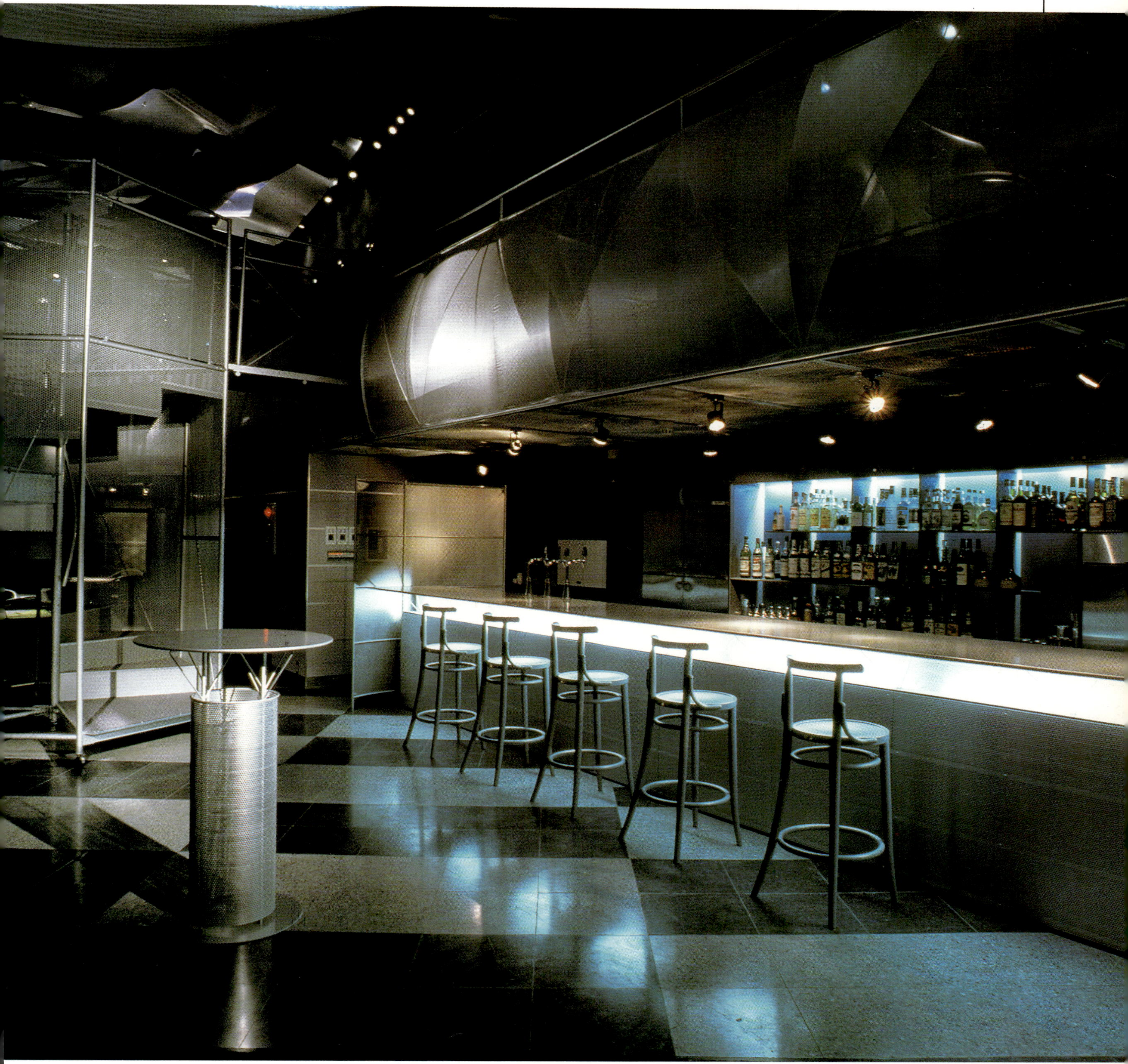

LEGENDS
LONDON, UK

Designed by Jiricna Kerr Associates

Jiricna Kerr Associates are well-known for their cool, elegant and immaculately detailed interiors – most notably in the Joseph fashion shops and in Way-In at Harrods.

The new look they have given to Legends, a nightclub just off Piccadilly in London's Mayfair, is no exception. The design is characteristically monochrome, with chromed metal and black leather throughout, but many previous ideas and methods have been distilled and developed. For example, the polished plaster walls are similar to those at Joe's Café (Joseph's restaurant in South Kensington), and the undulating ceiling defined by aluminium rods is a reminder of Way-In. The result is spectacular: Legends is less restrained and more glamorous than previous Jiricna Kerr interiors, and this seems entirely apt for its nightclub atmosphere.

To avoid unnecessary structural work,

(right) A specially designed staircase is the visual and physical link between ground floor and basement dance floor. Eames wire chairs complement the aesthetic.

(below) The ground-floor bar sets the tone: restrained monochrome finishes, marble, aluminium, stainless steel, but with extravagant detailing such as the undulating ceiling.

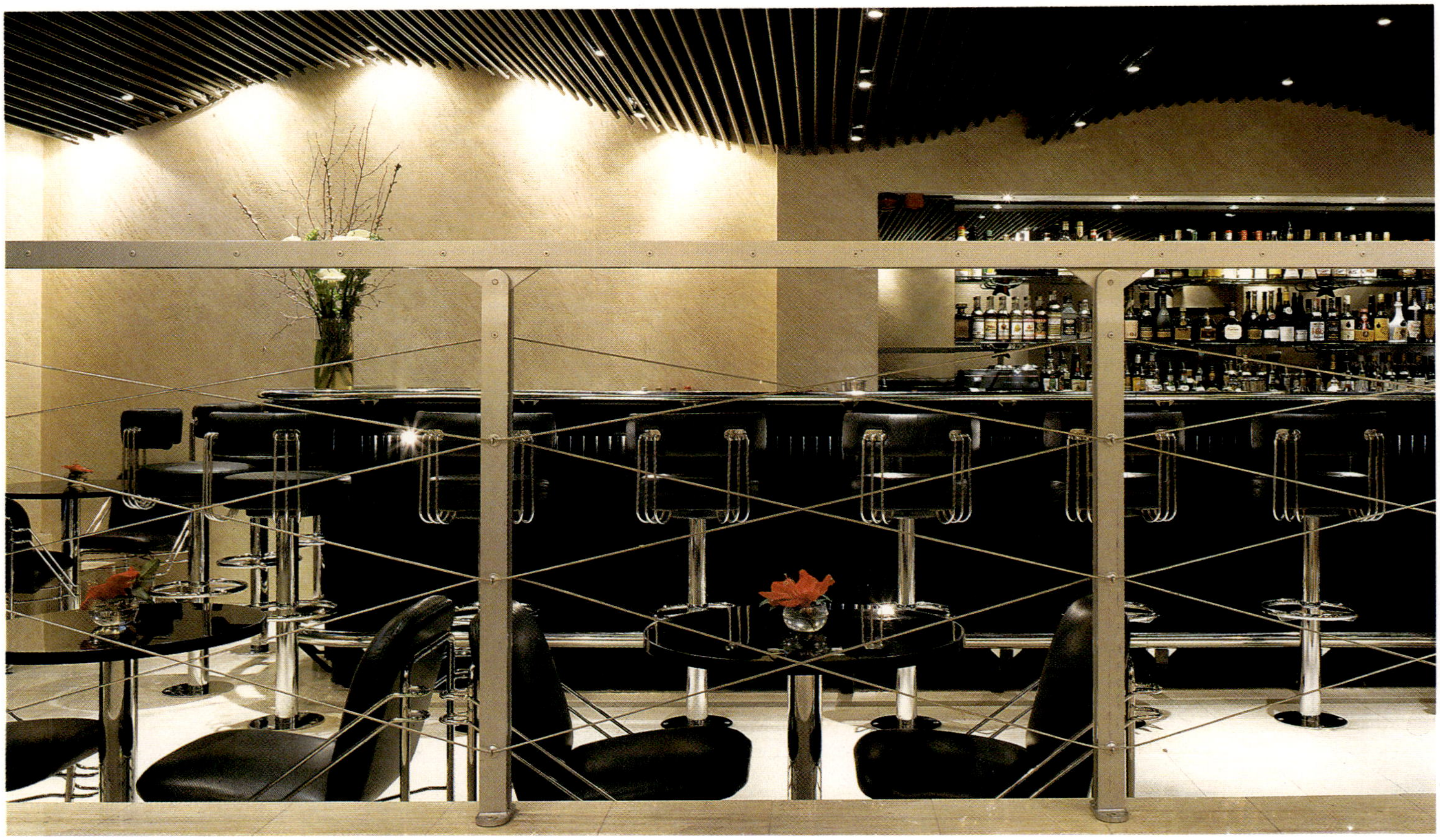

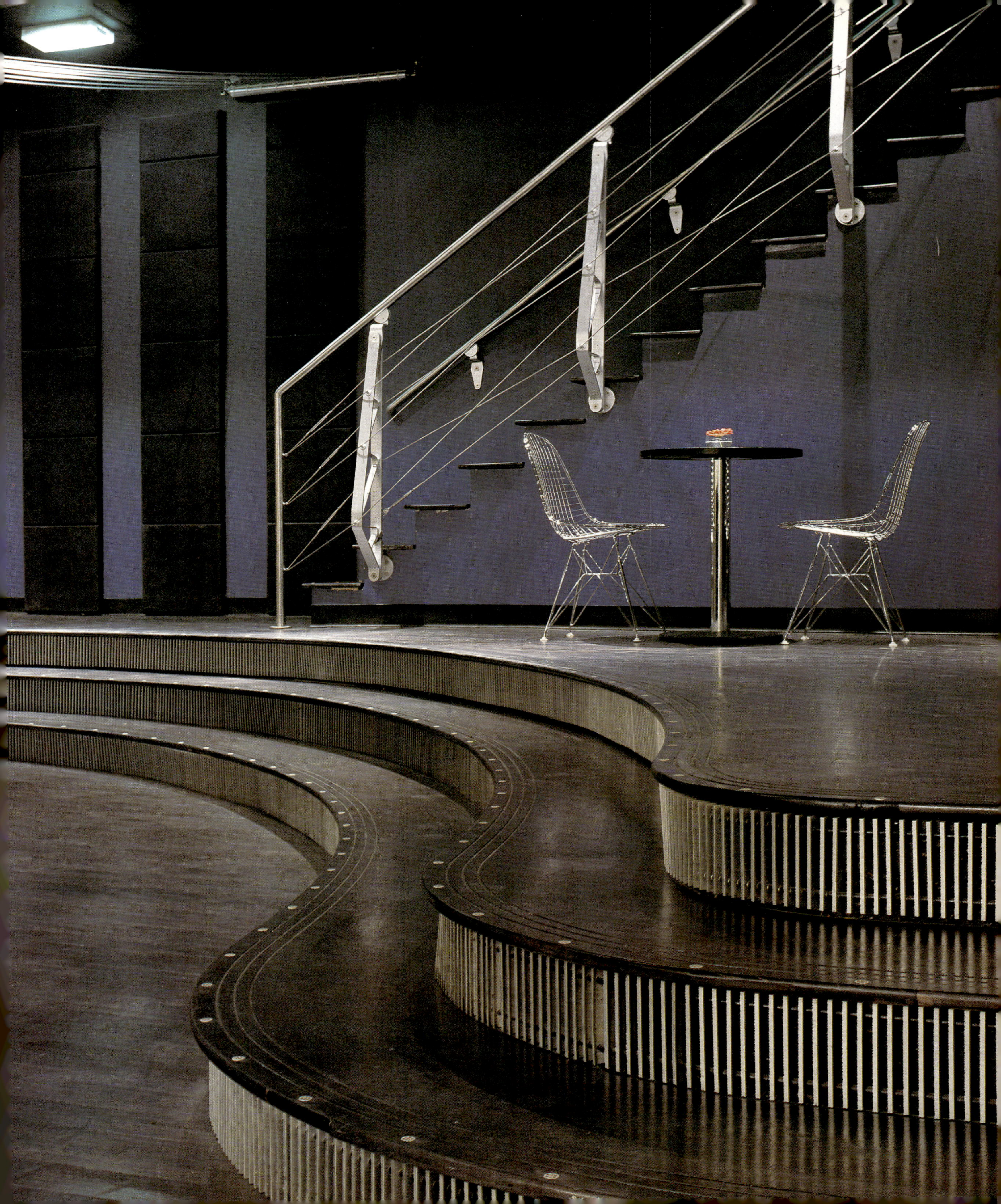

Jiricna Kerr have planned the new club around two floors, just like the old Legends. On the ground floor there are a bar and restaurant (which are open during the day), and in the basement are the dance floor, another bar and a sitting/conversation area. The two levels are joined – physically and visually – by the central staircase which curves gently down from the upper level to a mid-height mezzanine-cum-landing, and then sweeps down into the basement dance area. An important transitional element, joining relaxed restaurant with highly charged dance environment, the staircase is also the key feature and focal point of Jiricna Kerr's design. Not altogether surprisingly, it required several hundred hours of design time to perfect. The stairs themselves are spare, supported only by 200 by 20 mm steel stringers; the risers are two 27 mm diameter stainless-steel tubes. The handrail is also in stainless steel, and is supported by triangulated balusters of mild steel connected by tensioned stainless-steel cables to give a lightweight, filigree effect. Treads, on tubular steel trusses, are of polished, dimpled aluminium.

This same dimpled pattern reappears in the polished aluminium cladding of the large columns near the stairwell, and so gives just a touch of traditional nightlife sparkle.

The lighting at Legends reveals some carefully controlled small sources in the undulating ceiling and over the bar areas; low-voltage light sources give a starry effect in the black ceiling of the basement level, and warm light washes down the smooth plaster walls.

Most of the furniture – in the stainless steel and chrome that characterize the design – was specially designed for the project. However, the custom-built fittings are complemented by Eames wire chairs on the lower floor, which very effectively echo the light, skeletal look of the stairs and the balustrades.

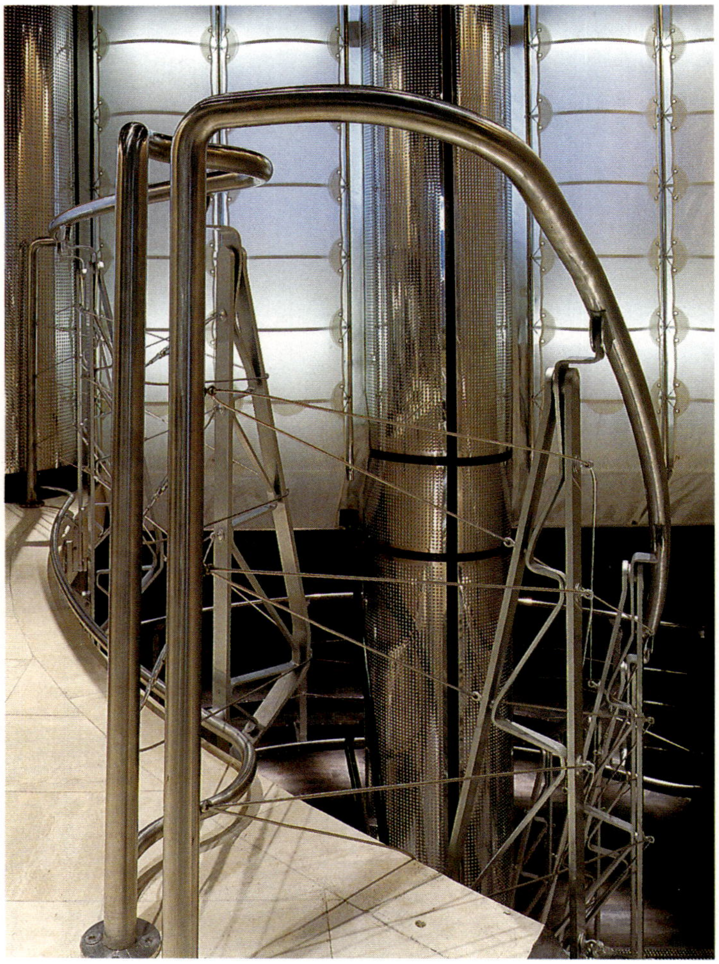

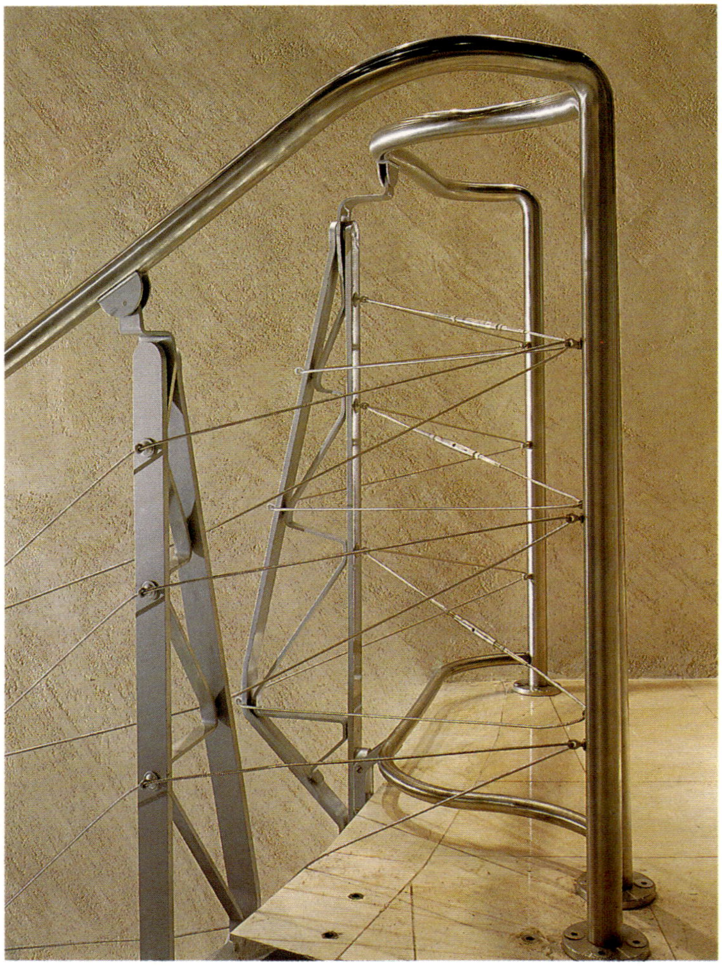

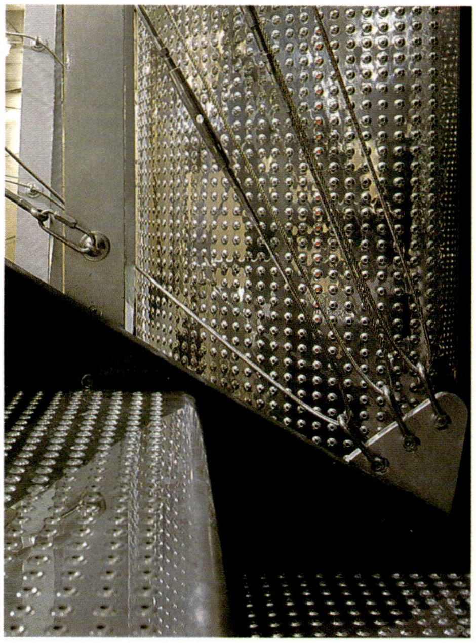

(above) Stair treads and columns are in polished, dimpled aluminium – a more subtle way to add sparkle than the usual faceted mirrors.

(right) With semi-open risers formed by steel tubes, the sweeping staircase looks light, almost insubstantial.

(left) Twisting stainless-steel handrails and a network of tensioned steel cables give the stairs a delicate, skeletal appearance.

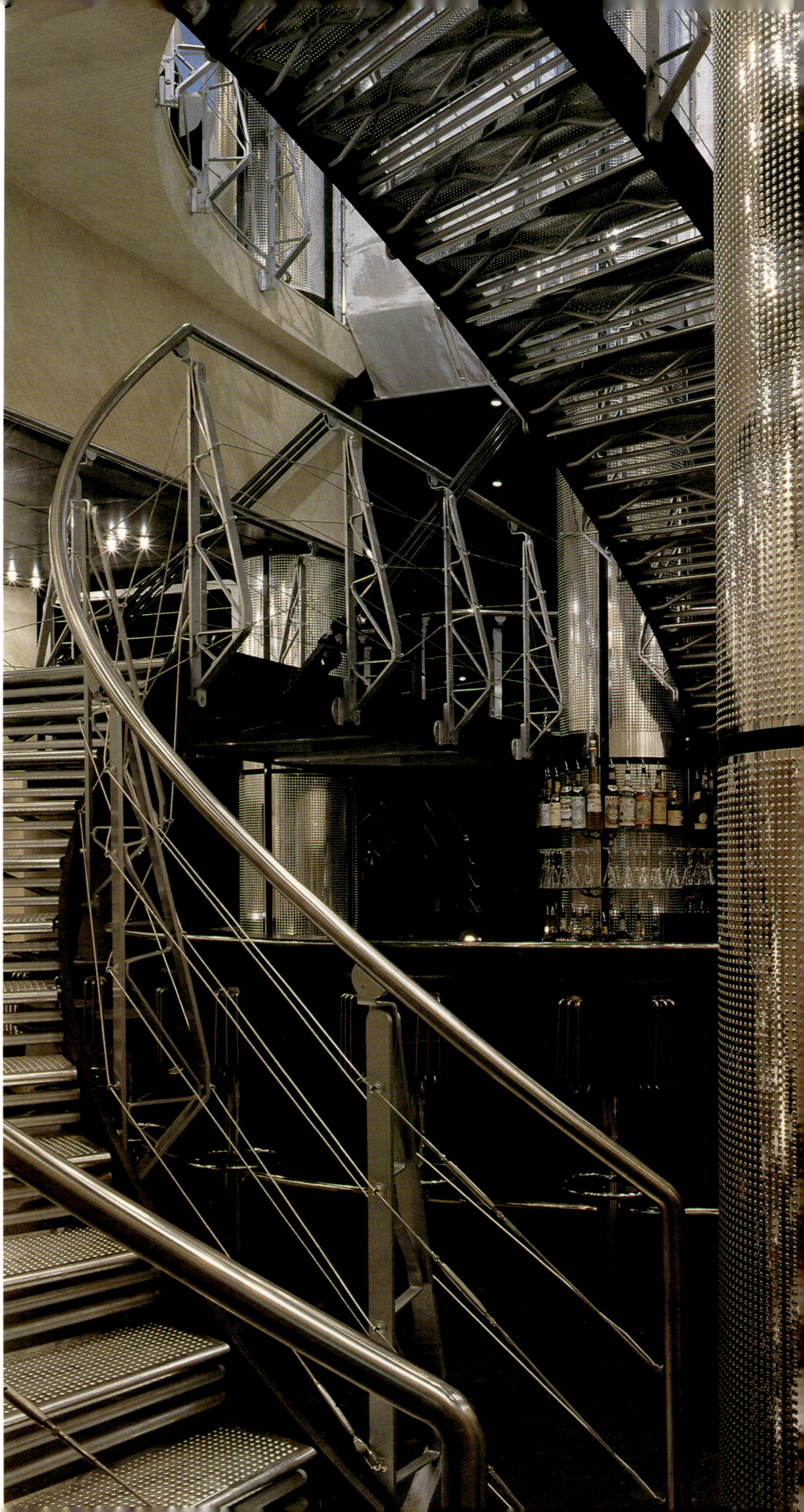

THE CASUAL QUILTED GIRAFFE

NEW YORK CITY, USA

Designed by McDonough Nouri Rainey & Associates

A name like The Casual Quilted Giraffe evokes images of those flash-in-the-pan brasseries and restaurants that litter most cities: a clever name, a good location, and unadventurous, well-priced food should be the rule. But The Casual Quilted Giraffe confounds these expectations. Built for Barry and Susan Wine, whose restaurant The Quilted Giraffe is one of New York's most lauded, CQG (as the designers conveniently call it) is located inside Philip Johnson's AT & T building on Madison Avenue. It is immaculate in its design and detailing, serves innovative food – and lunch for two diners will leave no change from a hundred dollars.

The form of the restaurant is a simple square with the entrance at one corner. The bar is to the right of the entrance, and the dining area fills the centre and extends to banquette seating on raised galleries on two sides. This basic plan is reinforced by pairs of stainless-steel and aluminium uplighters that anchor the corners of the central dining area.

But the real skill of The Casual Quilted Giraffe lies in the designers' immaculate detailing. Like the plan, the palette of materials is restrained, but used with panache: panels of perforated stainless steel clad the walls above the grey leather banquettes (the same panels are used in the vaulted ceiling), grey-black terrazzo is used for the floor, dividing walls and bar base, and black granite for the table and bar

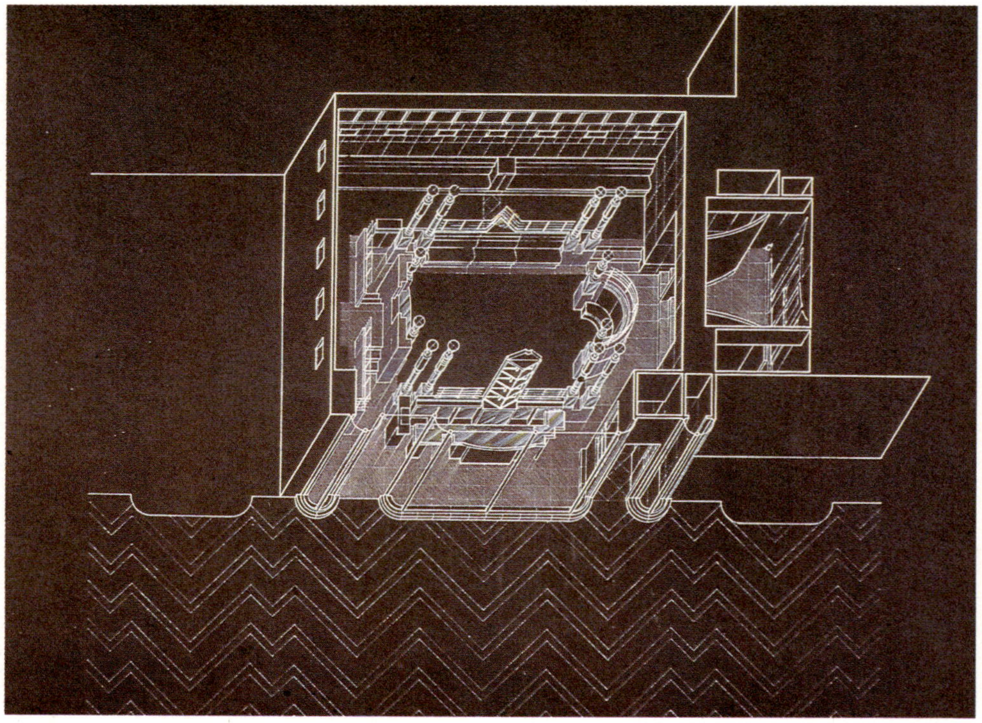

(right) Axonometric projection.

(far right) Perforated steel panels line the walls and the vaulted ceiling, complementing the grey-black terrazzo floors and dividing screens.
Both photographs © Nathaniel Lieberman.

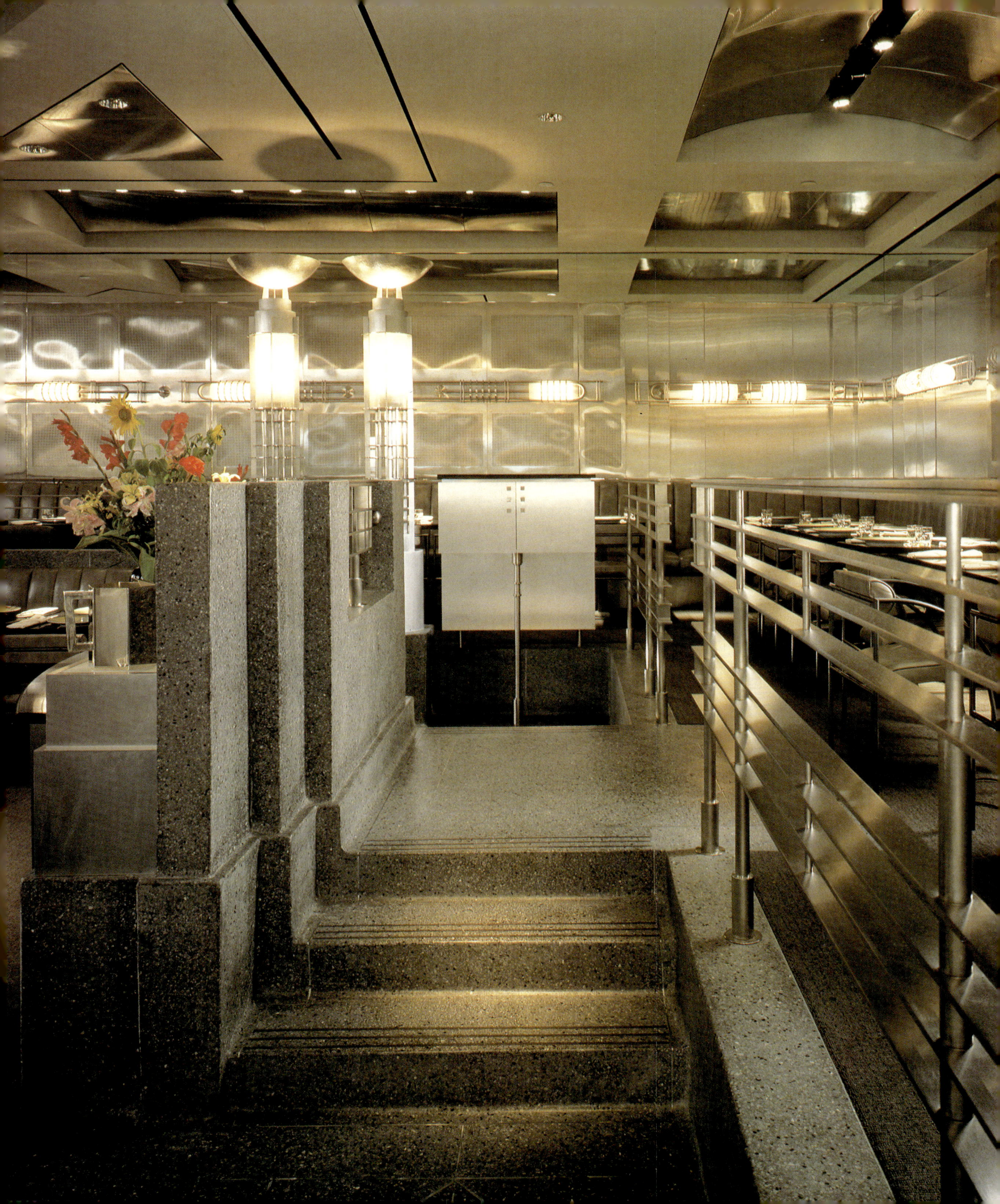

tops. The bar top has an inlaid plan of the restaurant (designers delight in self-referential details) in niobium and titanium, and the table tops have patterned inlays of the same materials. Etched glass is used for the kitchen's pass-through windows. Specially designed silver-plate wine buckets hang from the stainless-steel railings that contain the banquette galleries. Expansion joints in the terrazzo flooring vary in width to reflect the proportions of the room (just as the ceiling's geometry is a reflection of the dining-room's central square, rotated ninety degrees).

The cost of the project, excluding fees, was a decidedly non-casual 1.5 million dollars. The 5,500 square foot (511 square metre) space includes the 2,200 square foot (204 square metre) dining/bar area with seating for ninety, and a 3,300 square foot (307 square metre) kitchen. In the very corporate environment of the AT & T building, the design of CQG went almost too far: the owners have added bows to the uplighters and pink gels to the wall lights, as if with an eye to their less design-discerning customers.

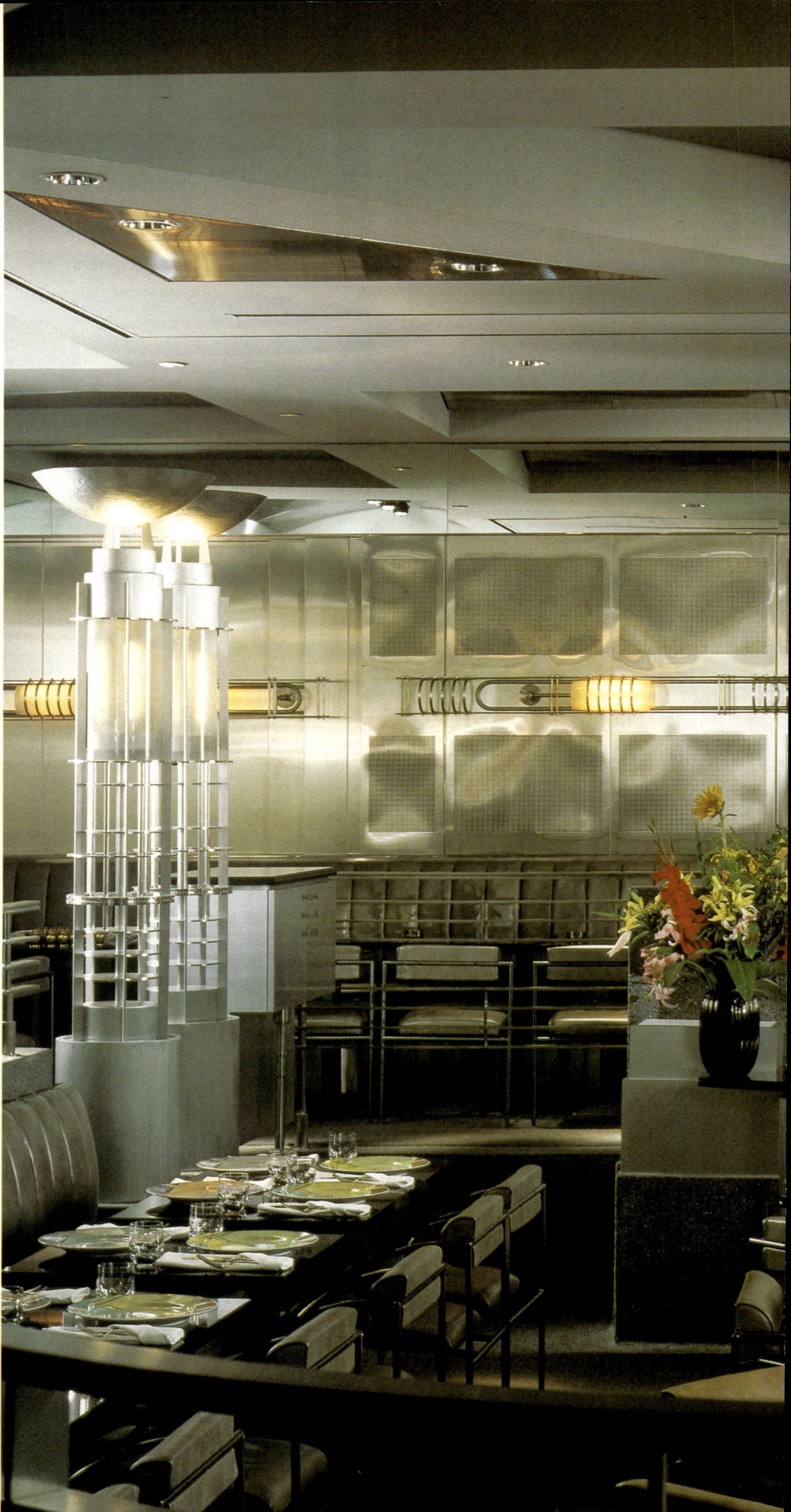

The geometry of the ceiling reflects the proportions of the central square, but rotated through ninety degrees. Pairs of specially designed uplighters mark the limits of the dining area.
Photograph © Nathaniel Lieberman.

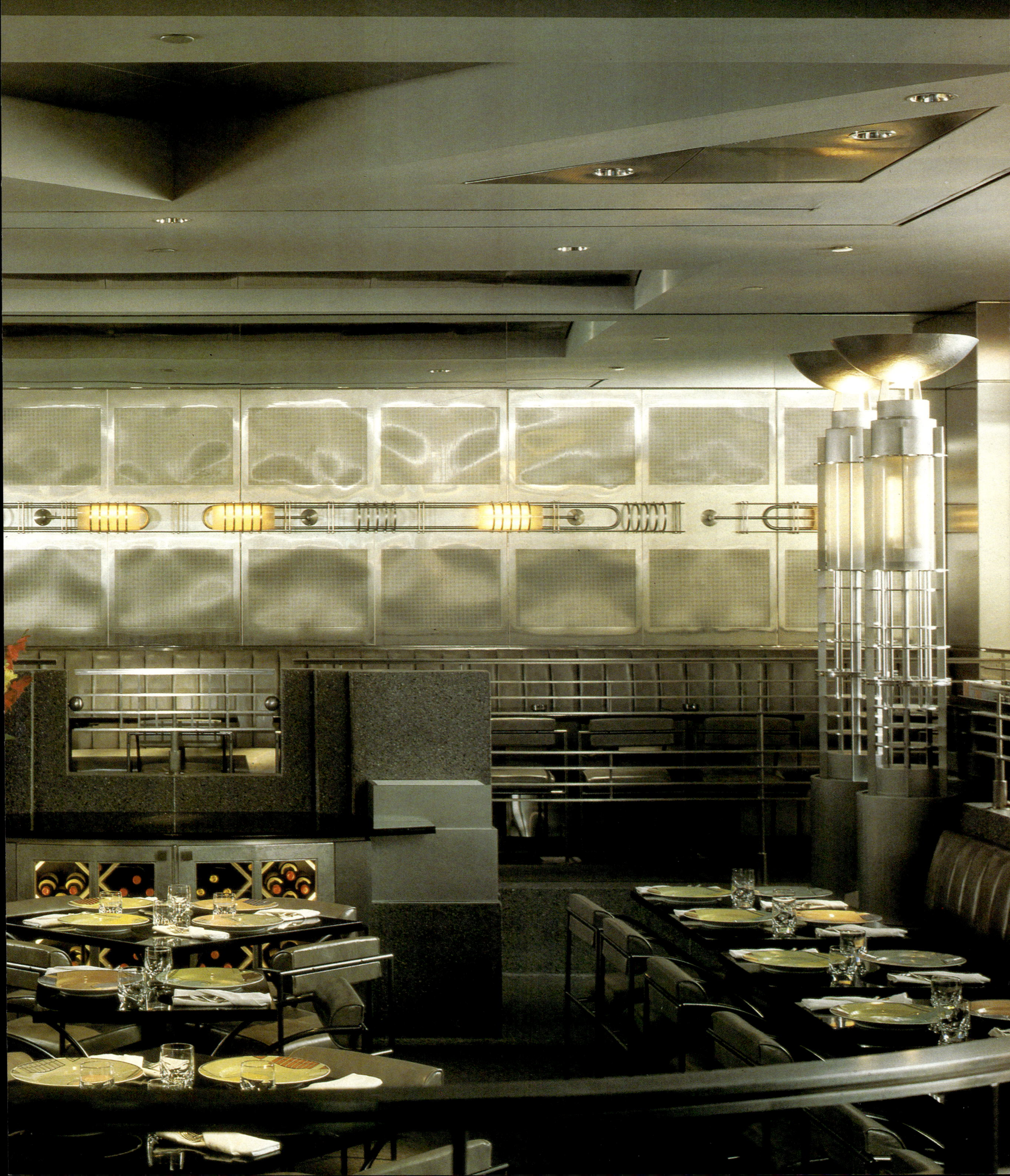

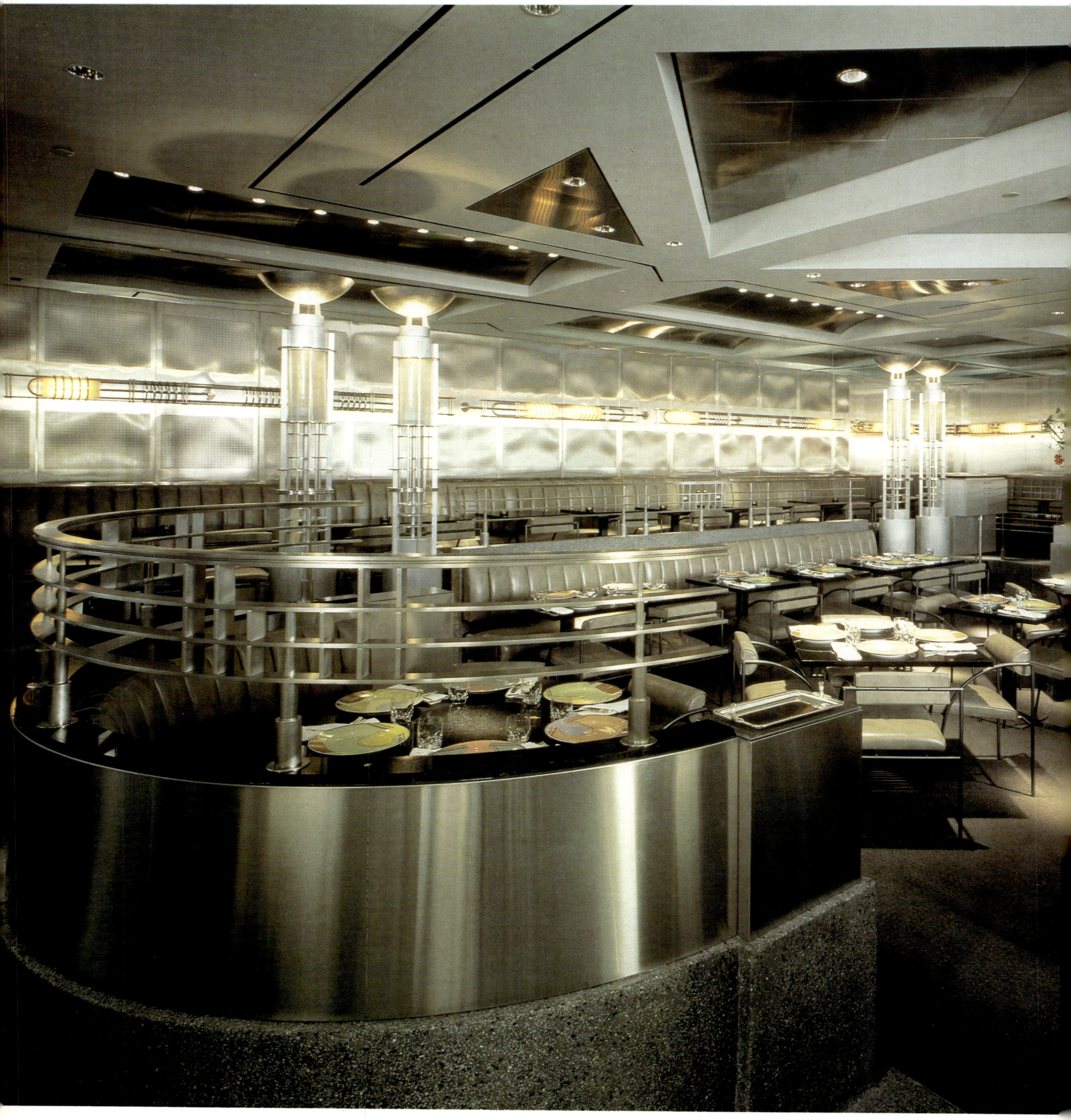

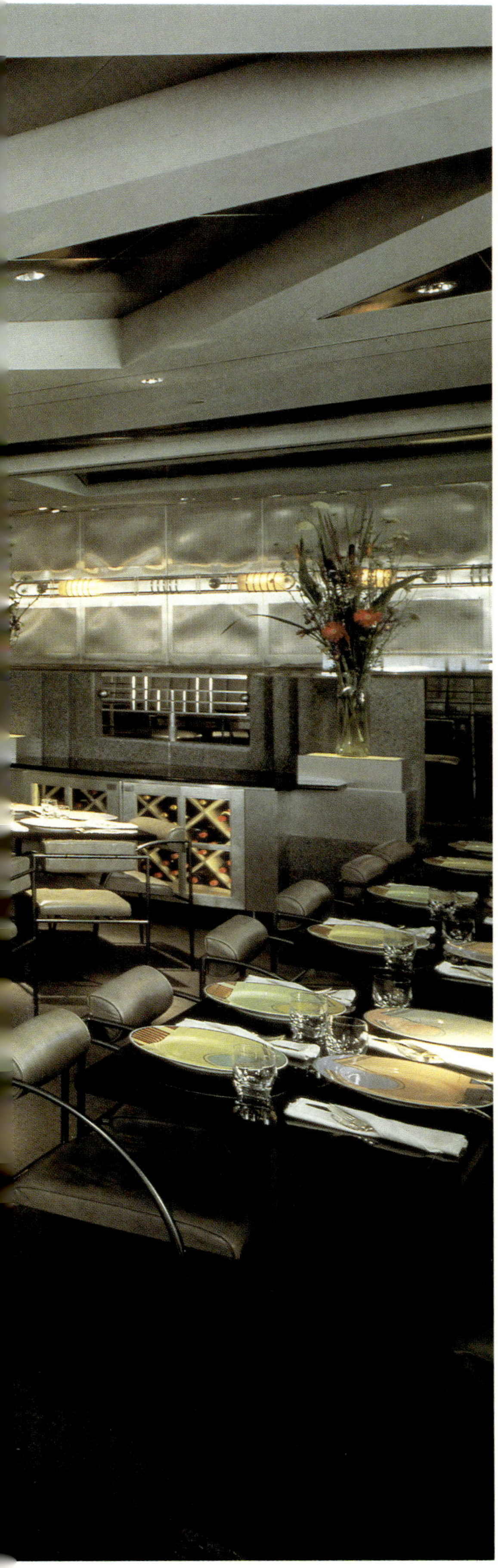

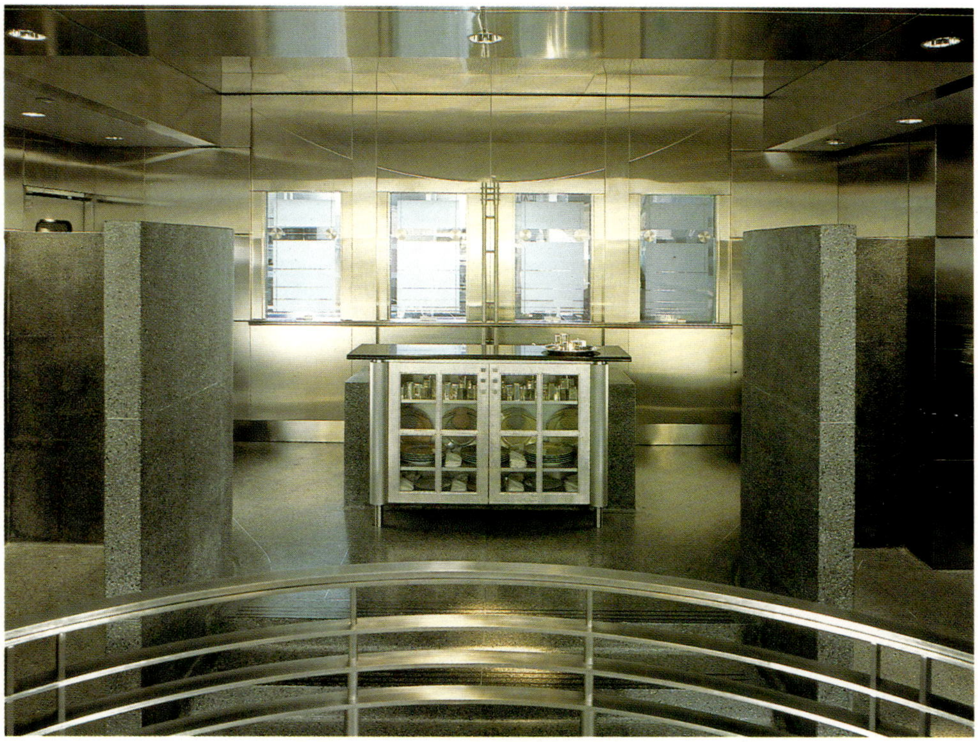

(above) Etched glass pass-through windows link directly with the kitchen.
Photograph © Nathaniel Lieberman.

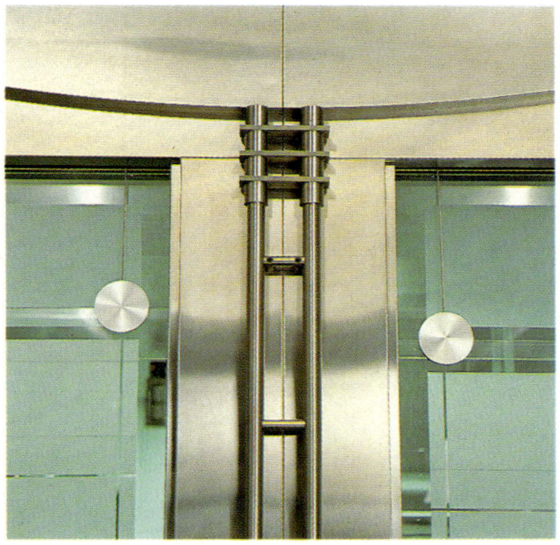

(right) Dishes from the kitchen are passed through an opening masked by acid-etched glass screens.
Photograph by Masao Ueda.

(left) Despite the luxurious grey leather banquette seating, the predominant finishes are hard, almost cold, with geometric stainless-steel railings and black granite table tops. Attempts have been made to soften the effect by using pink gels on lamps and bows on the uplighters.
Photograph © Nathaniel Lieberman.

ANGELI
LOS ANGELES, CALIFORNIA, USA

Designed by Morphosis

Morphosis describe their interior for Angeli's restaurant as 'a fragment of contemporary architecture...dead-tech'. From street level, you get some idea of what they mean: the Corten steel façade appears broken, asymmetrical, and the name 'Angeli' is disjointed so that the last two letters are over the shop next door. Above the glass-block doors, a timber beam crashes through and appears over the entrance.

Full-height glazing and glass blocks allow views from the street into the restaurant. Inside, the designers' approach has been much calmer: walls are painted white; the flooring is grey slate; the furniture consists of simple blue wooden tables, dining chairs and bar stools.

Here too, though, there are unconventional touches – most noticeably the glass-fronted display cases which are set into the walls. These contain objects that look like museum exhibits, or remains that have been unearthed during an archeological dig. Above them, tubular light fittings give an effect like ceremonial candles, throwing light up to wash the walls. Additional lighting comes from discreet spotlights recessed in the ceiling.

The feeling of ancient and modern elements being brought together has been emphasized by the designers' use of materials: natural timber contrasts with glass blocks; granite and slate with Corten steel. And, in a culinary milieu keenly aware of design (and other) trends, the 'dead-tech' of Angeli is essential to ensure success.

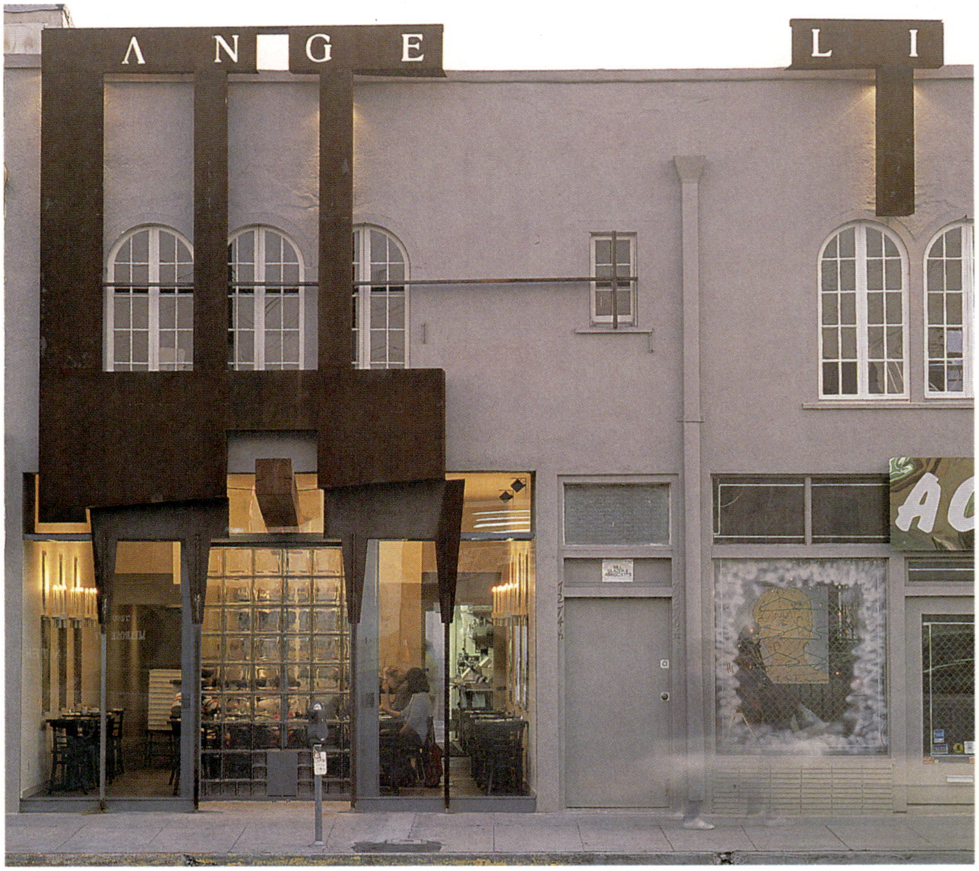

Designing in fragments: the asymmetrical Corten steel façade is broken through by a wooden beam; and the sign is split into two.

(right) Glass blocks and full-height glazing allow views in and out, and fill the space with natural light, supplemented by recessed spots in the ceiling.

(below) The cool, modern black and white interior contrasts with museum display cabinets, containing apparently ancient objects.

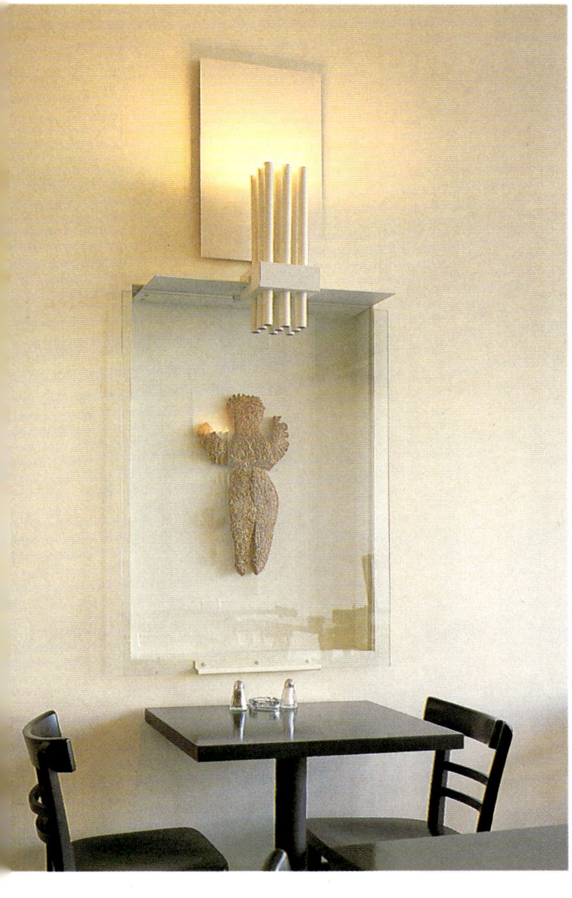

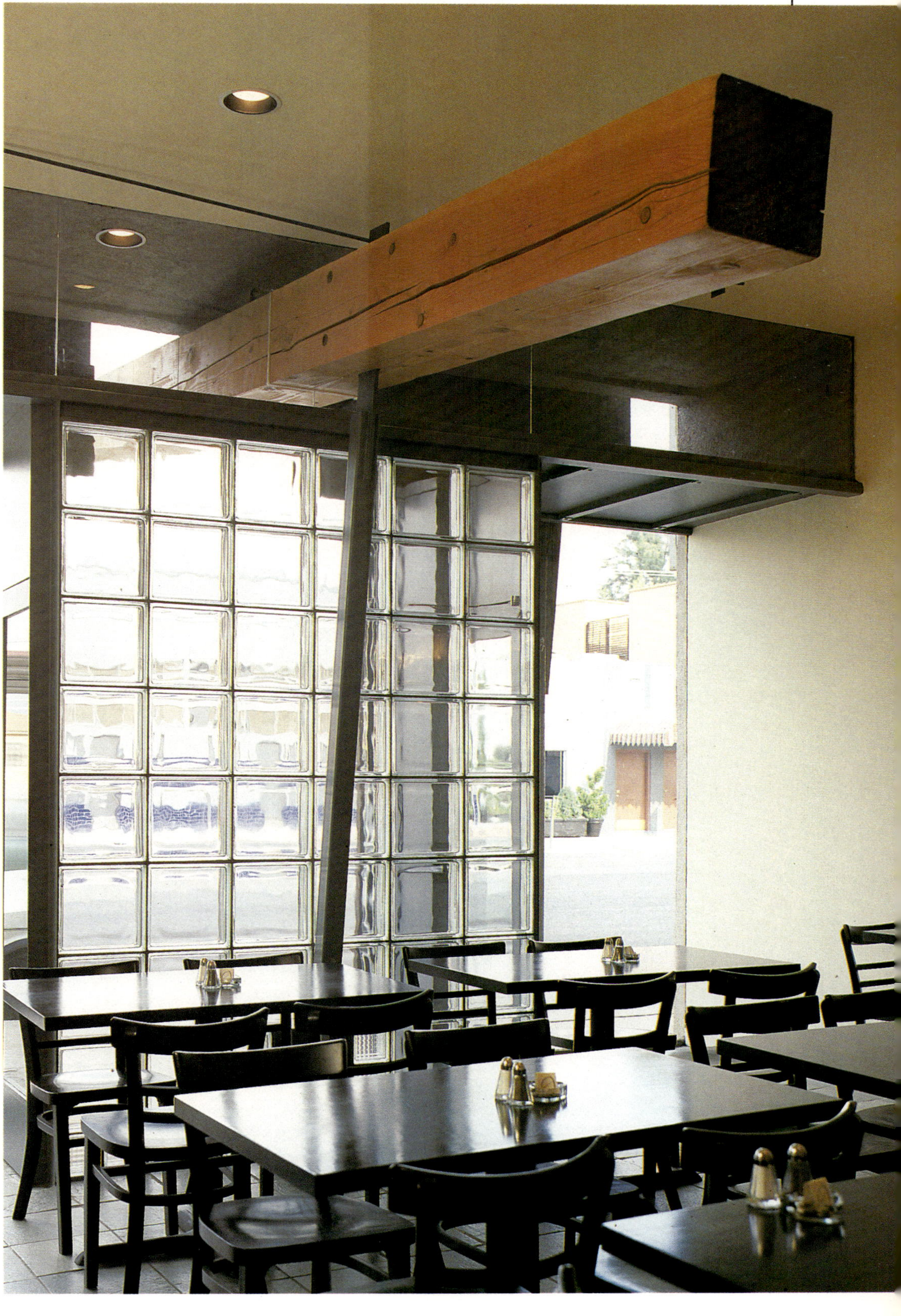

72 MARKET STREET
VENICE, CALIFORNIA, USA

Designed by Morphosis

From the outside, Morphosis's design for 72 Market Street is enigmatic: tarnished green copper cladding, a large window barred by a steel grid, and only the large number 72 to confirm that visitors have indeed found the restaurant. Inside, all is transformed. A soaring double-height space is revealed, with powerful concrete beams flung across the void. A central column in this main space acts as an anchor for steel braces that stretch up to a steel belt that girds the concrete atrium. Counterposed to these bold gestures are smooth walls clad in Douglas fir plywood, and exposed and sand-blasted bricks. The floor is of slate and granite, and the furniture is simple: rattan chairs and bar stools and basic tables covered with white tablecloths. The main dining area terminates in a glass-block wall which screens the less dramatic, single-height rear dining-room.

Morphosis seem to have a rare talent for creating truly inspiring, dramatic spaces.

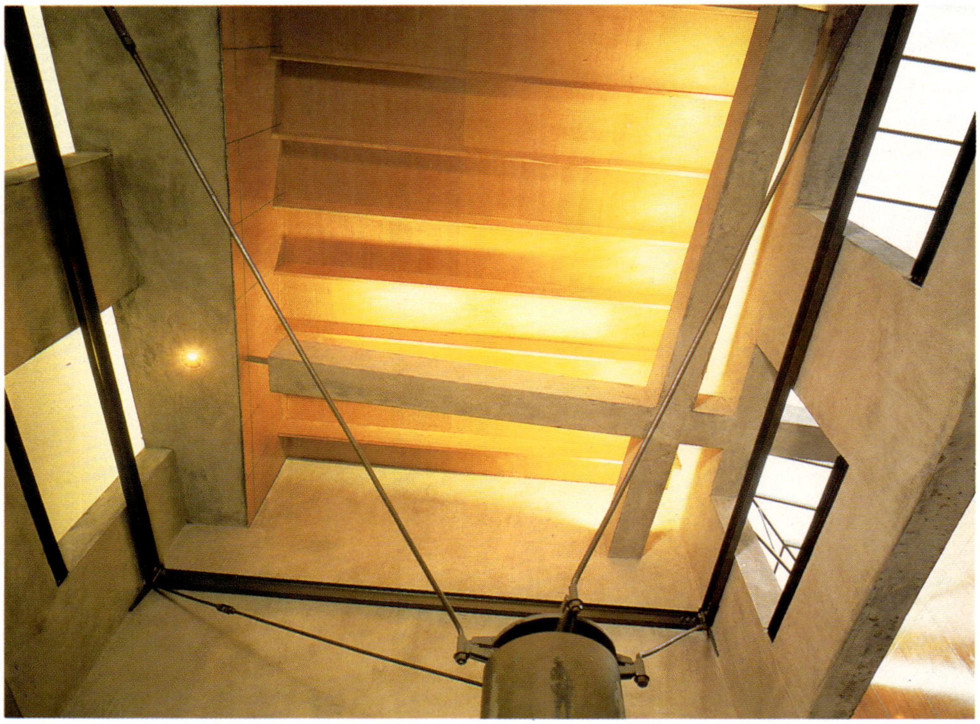

(above) Concrete beams crash across the dramatic double-height space, controlled by steel girders and braces linked to a central column.

(right) The oversized elements contrast with smooth finishes – Douglas fir plywood, concrete and exposed sand-blasted brick.

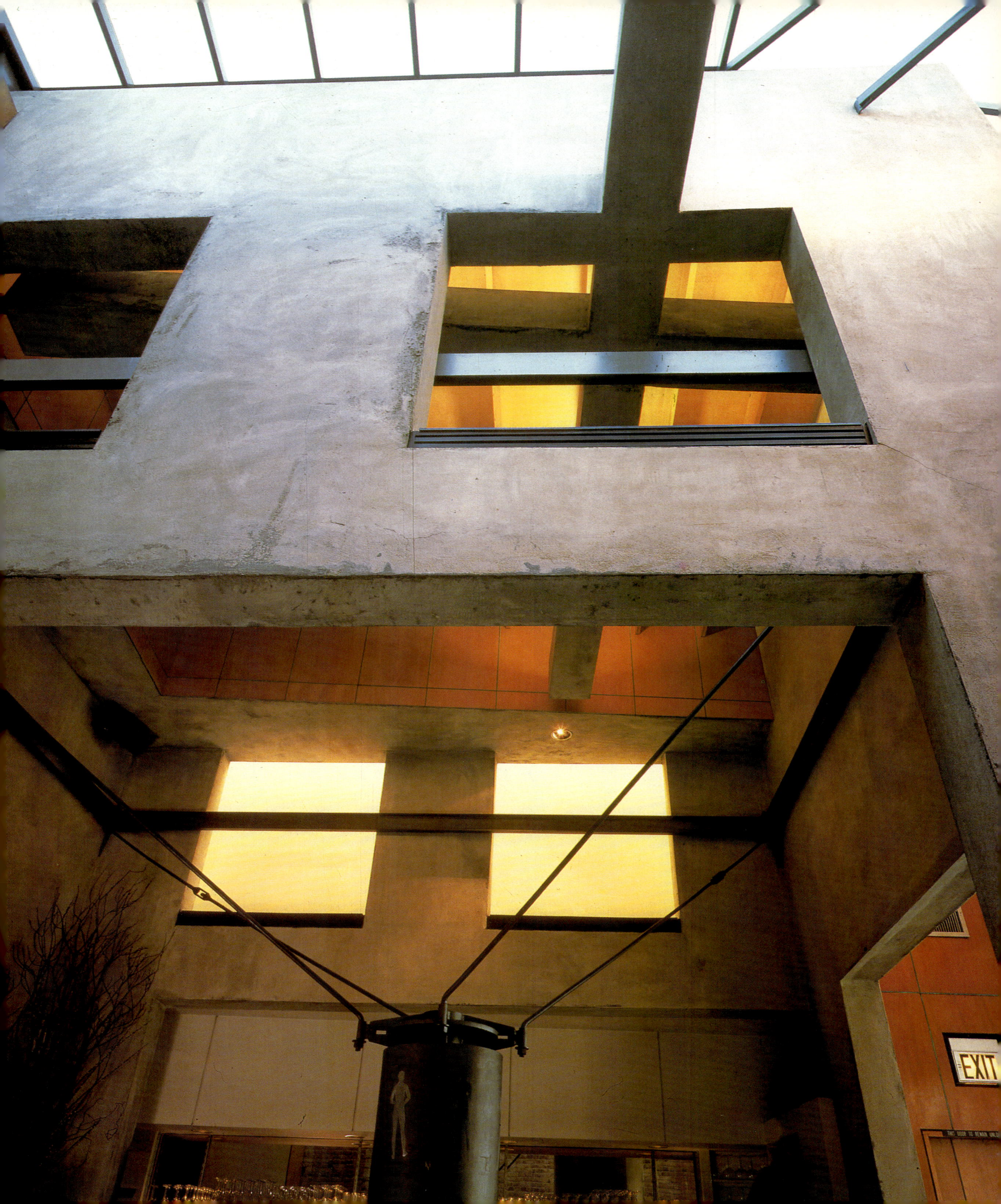
EXIT

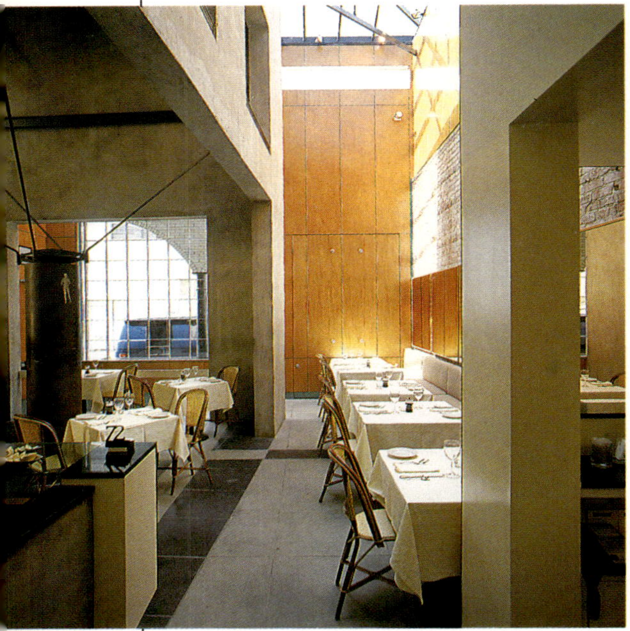

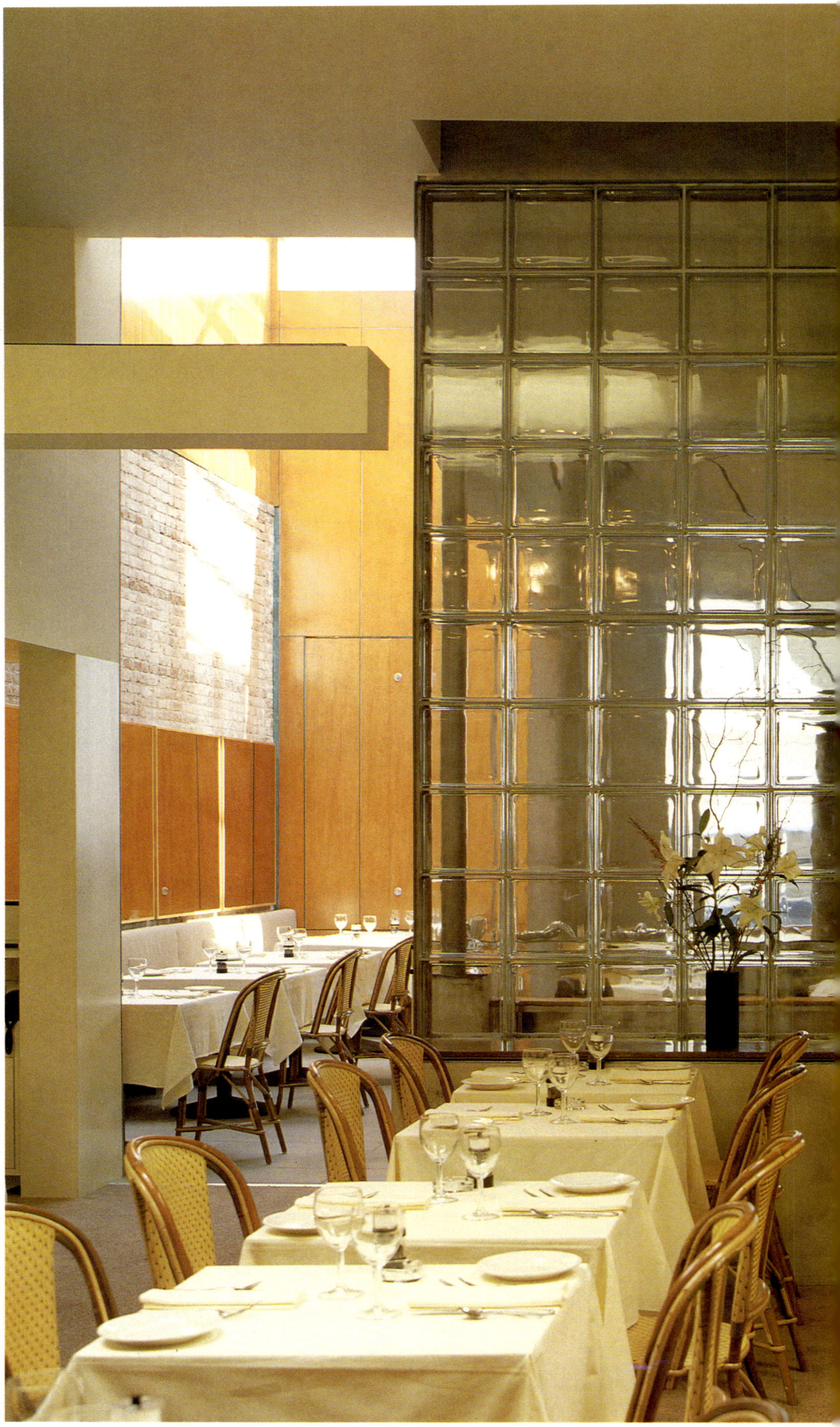

(above) Dining-room furniture is kept simple, with rattan chairs and white cloths covering the tables.

(right) A glass-block wall screens off and gives a focal point to the single-height dining area at the rear.

(far right) On the outside, a simple large street number and tarnished green copper cladding give little indication of the drama to come.

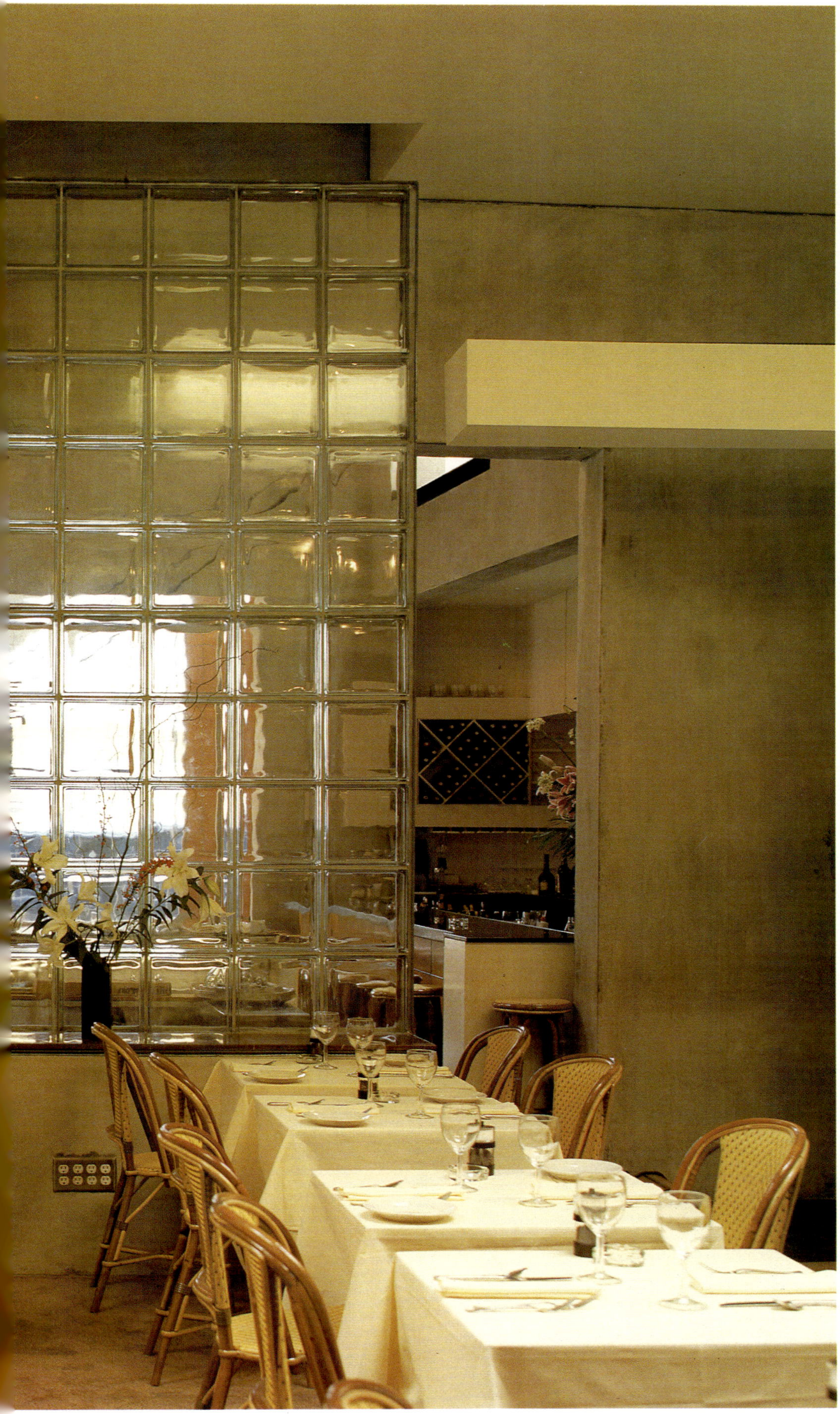

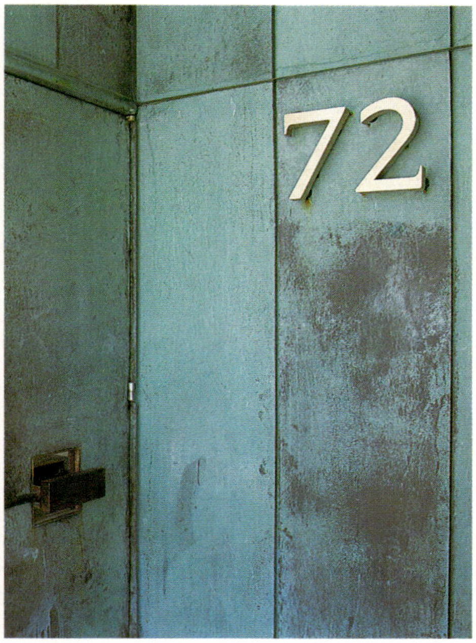
72

BIJOU
BARCELONA, SPAIN

Designed by Gabriel Ordeig

Barcelona has become a city of designer bars and nightclubs, where owners vie frenetically with one another to have the latest 'in' place. Bijou is like one of the cocktails that Barcelona's *jeunesse dorée* might imbibe: the ingredients are mixed with precision in exactly the right proportion for the needs of the place, with a few finishing touches which allow visitors to appreciate the taste to the full.

As its name implies, Bijou is very small, and the initial configuration caused the designers a few headaches: the tiny area was divided into two by a narrow door, and the dividing wall was structural, making removal expensive. So Ordeig merely widened the door and carved another hole in the wall, allowing the bar to be extended to the back area.

But it is in the details that the unusual mixture of Bijou becomes clear: an automatic door that opens by pressing a luminous button, the bar counter and floor made from a tropical wood, coraline, and the stuccoed walls, according to Ordeig, 'In the same colour as the wall in a painting by Alma Tadema'. Most startling are the stools upholstered with Indonesian goat-skins. Ordeig explains these, slightly tongue-in-cheek: 'Perhaps they will conjure up memories of the British colonial clubs, where gentlemen took refuge from a hostile environment to drink whisky and soda and discuss their hunting parties or the news that arrived from the heart of the empire.' In Bijou, visitors are more likely to encounter young, trendy Barcelonans discussing the latest design trends.

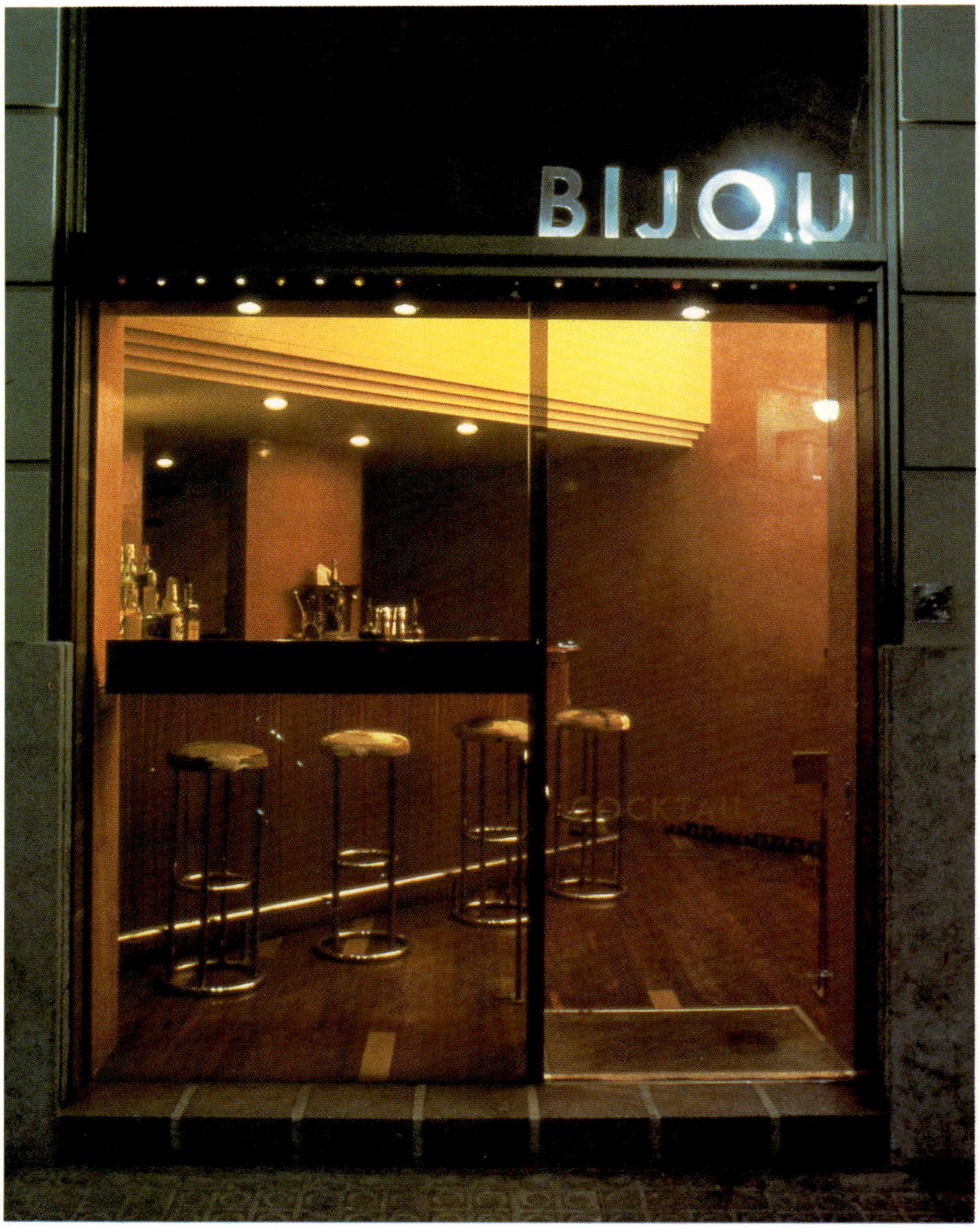

Entering the tiny bar through an automatic door, customers encounter an unusual array of finishes: tropical hardwood floors and bar counter, and stools upholstered in Indonesian goat-skin.

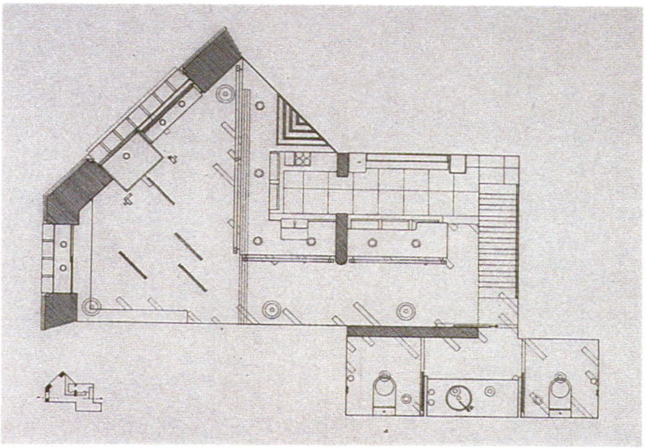

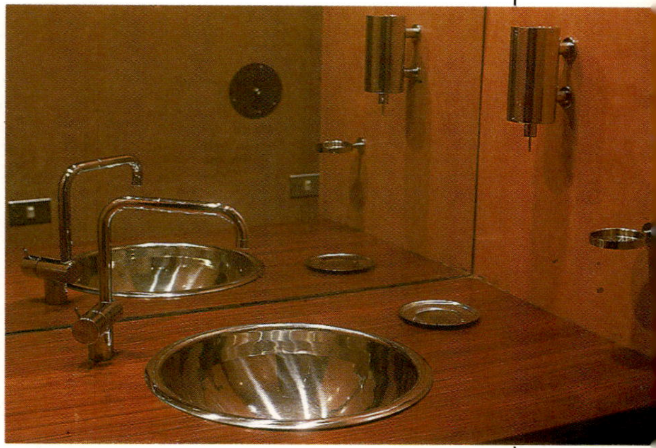

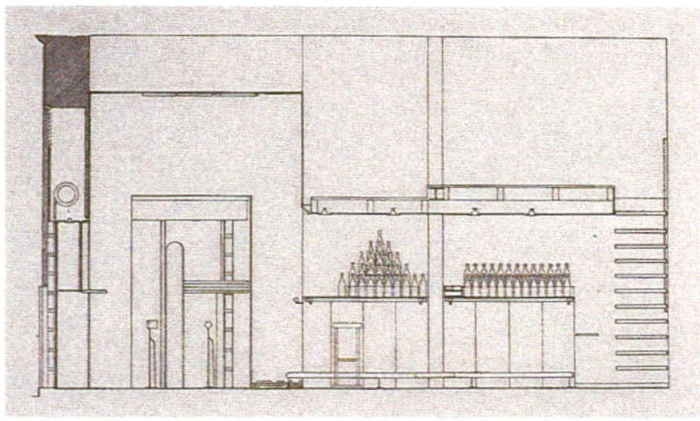

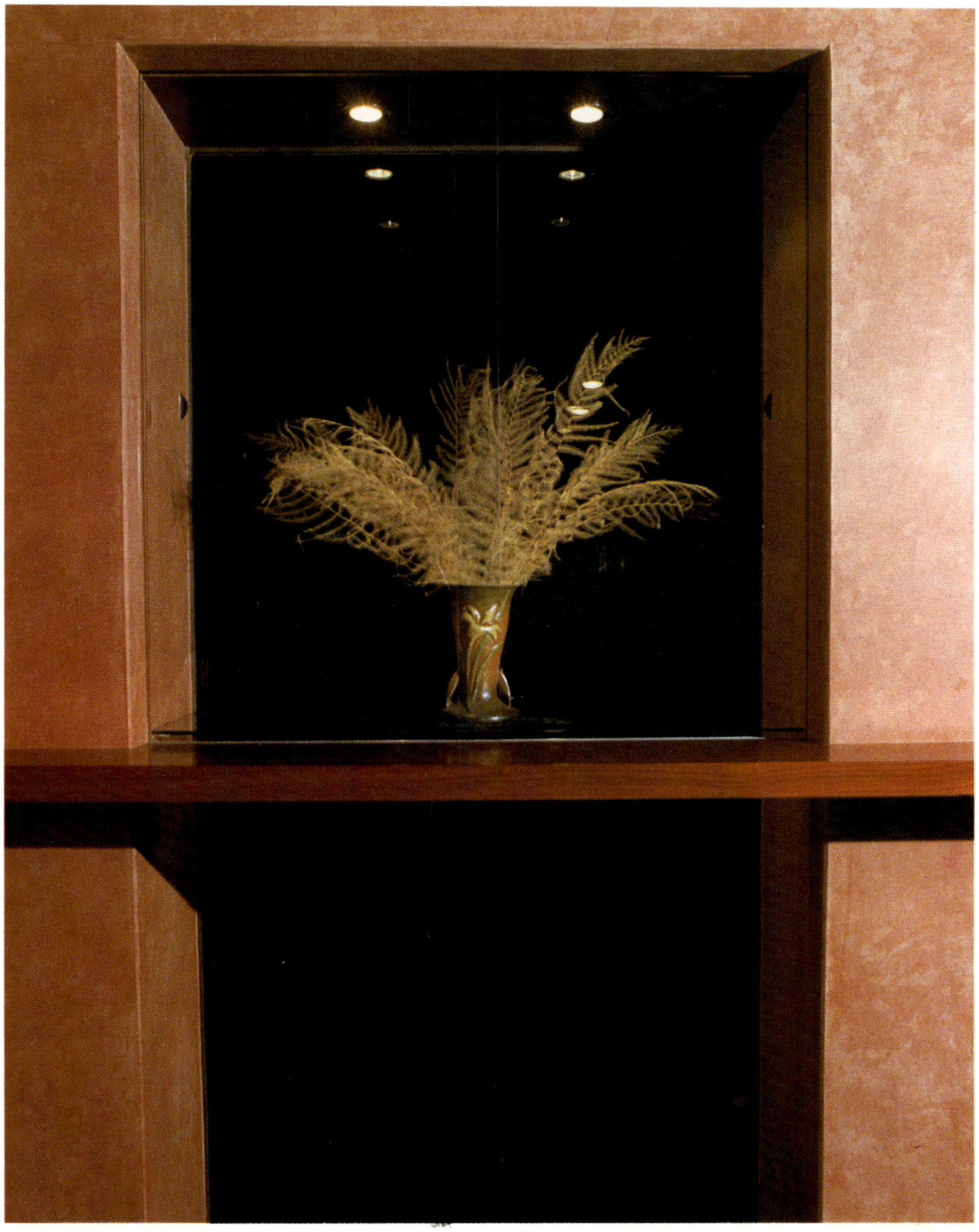

(top left) Floor plan.

(top) Careful detailing even extends to the built-in stainless-steel fittings in the lavatories.

(above) Longitudinal section.

(left) Stuccoed walls are a distinctive shade of pink, reportedly taken from a painting by Alma Tadema.

SISISI

BARCELONA, SPAIN

Designed by Gabriel Ordeig

Ordeig's Bijou (see pp. 104-5) was an exercise in compression; Sisisi gave him more room to experiment both with space and materials. Like so many of the new bars in Barcelona, the design was seen from the start as the key to Sisisi's chances of success. Ordeig had the advantage of a promising site: a long box of a room in a building by a minor practitioner of the Barcelona *modernisme* school. An entrance on the Diagonal, one of the main arteries of the city, provides exposure, while the wood and mosaic rear façade looking on to Calle Córcega provides the exterior with architectural character.

The planning of the long space is relatively simple. A bar stretches along most of the length of the left wall, and most of the seating is clustered in the larger room at the back. Sisisi looks in many ways like a relic of the 1950s because Ordeig sought out little-known materials and methods of construction that have largely fallen out of favour. The flooring is of 'hydraulic mosaic': coloured cements compressed by a hydraulic press in iron moulds (a method more usually used to produce slabs for street pavements). Because hydraulic mosaics require several months of drying after manufacture, few stocks are held, so the designers made do with what they could find in obscure material companies.

As a result, Ordeig made the best of necessity. Each colour of mosaic used corresponds to a size or shape; for example, black or white pieces are just under one foot square (30 by 30 centimetres), while red and yellow pieces are always rectangular. The design called for the same colour to touch only at the corners, creating the impression of a crazy quilt over the floor.

The same attention to detail applies elsewhere. Walls were stuccoed by a pair of Barcelona craftsmen, the Casadevall brothers. The wall behind the bar and the front of the bar counter are earthy yellow, and the ceiling and the right wall are ultramarine. The entrance area and the back seating area are stuccoed in turquoise. The lighting, too, is unusual: truncated conical parchment shades containing standard 100 watt bulbs hang over the bar, while a fan of strip fluorescent lighting illuminates the space devoted to seating.

The popularity of Sisisi led the designers to make some rapid modifications after the opening – four hundred people crammed into the bar late at night is not unusual. The capacity of the air-conditioning had to be quadrupled (which was accomplished without changing the visible parts of the air-handling system) and, perhaps the best testament to Sisisi's success, the skirting boards had to be replaced with Travertine marble to protect them from the indiscriminate scuffing of hundreds of shoes each night.

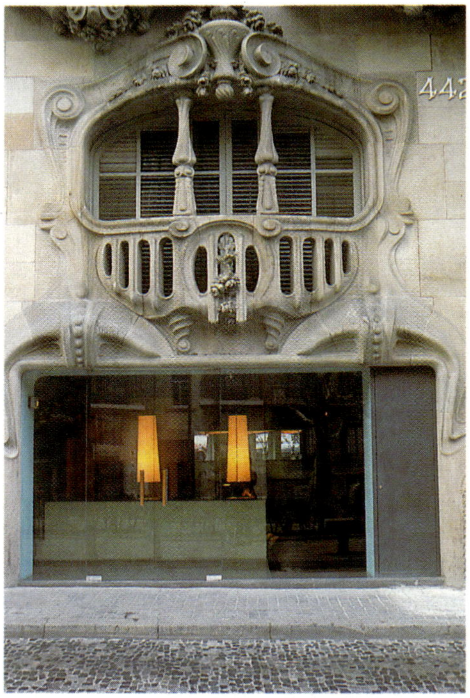

(above) Ready-made architectural character: the original building which houses the bar was designed by a member of the Barcelona *modernisme* school.

(below) Floor plan and longitudinal section.

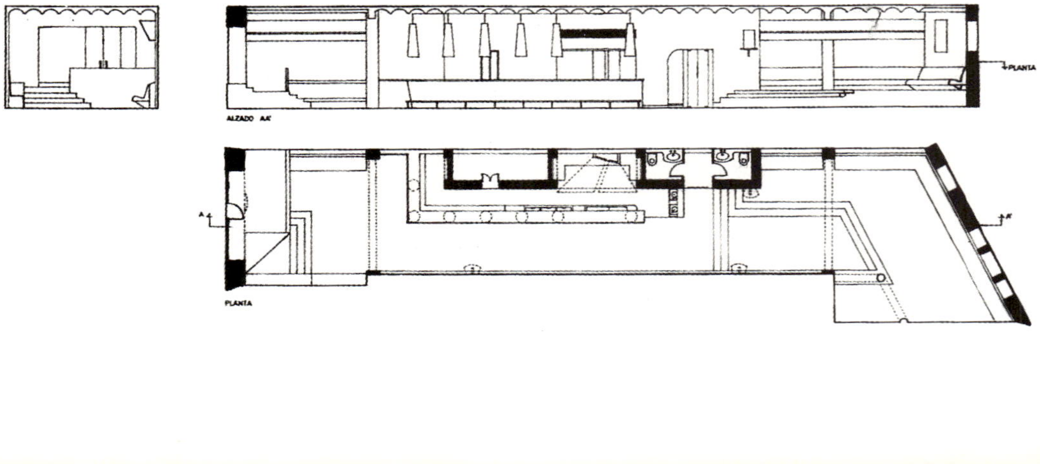

(top left) The design has proved so popular that as many as four hundred people have been crammed into the bar, necessitating a radical upgrading of the air-conditioning soon after opening.

(top right) Whimsical touches include black palmprints up the wall, stuccoed by Barcelona craftsmen.

(below left) Reminiscent of the 1950s, the earthy yellow and bright blue colour scheme is complemented by parchment lampshades over the bar, and the complex quilt of hydraulic mosaic floor tiles.

(below right) Air-conditioning ducting is discreetly hidden in the beams.

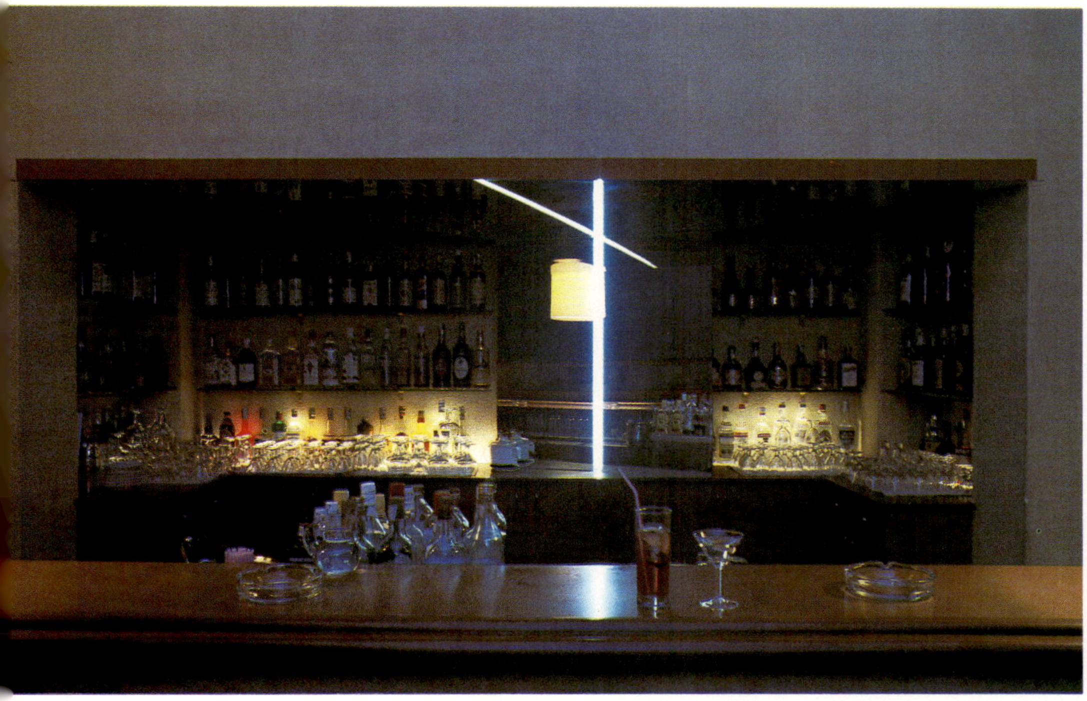

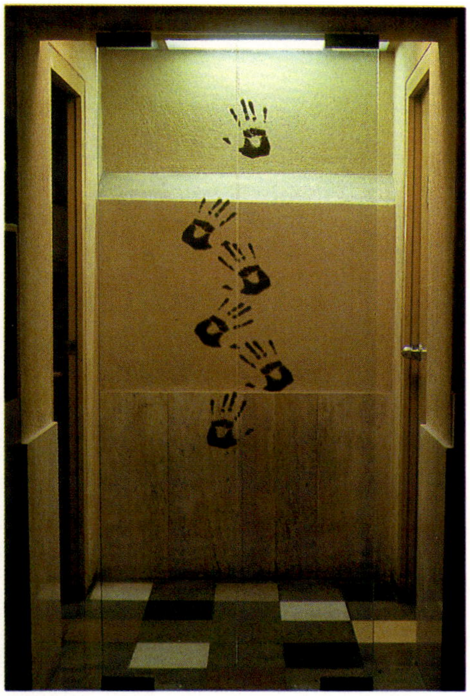

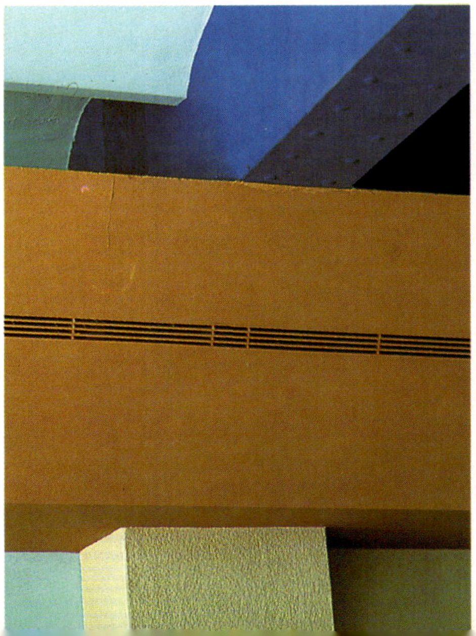

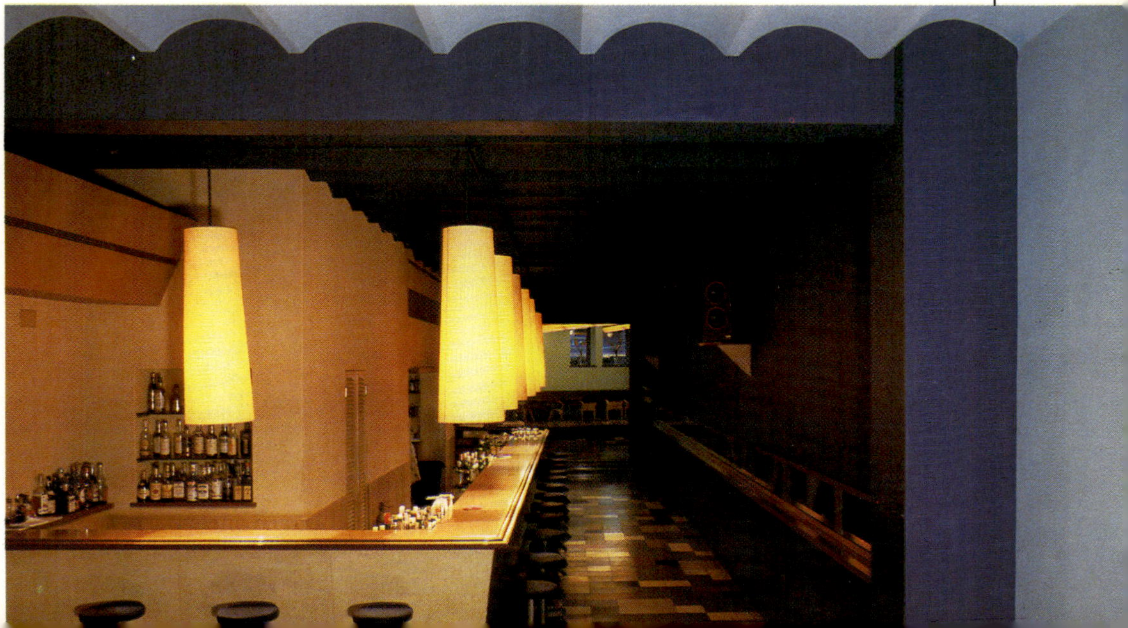

L'AQUYLONE RESTAURANT
REGGIO EMILIA, ITALY
Designed by Denis Santachiara

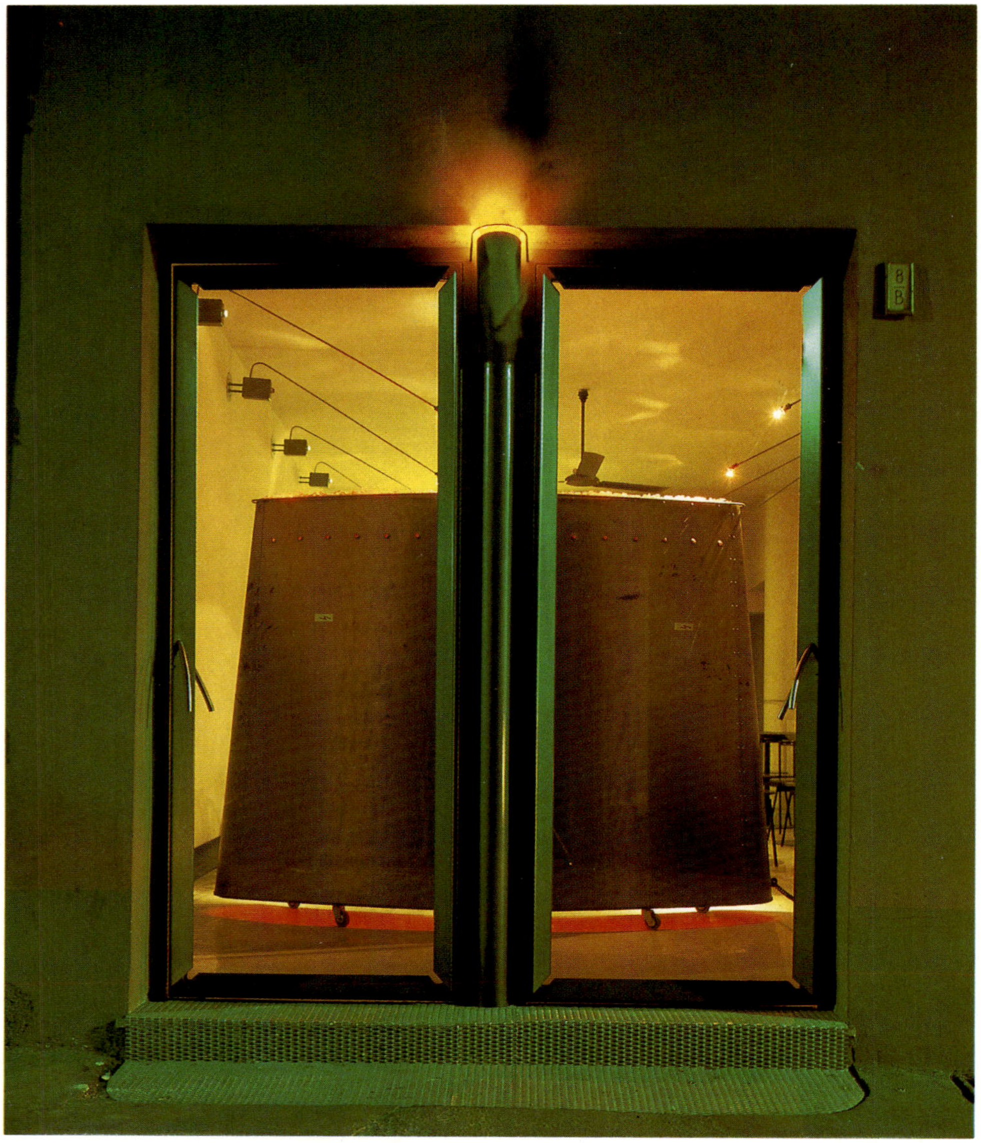

The words 'fast-food restaurant' usually conjure up an image of plastic chairs, wipe-down tables and jazzed-up graphics. The idea seems to be, if you want a quick turnover, not to make the interior too inviting. However, from the moment customers step inside L'Aquylone they are aware that this interior, designed by Denis Santachiara, is an exception to that rule.

Santachiara wanted, he explains, to introduce a sense of movement and animation into his design, and so has looked to the world of television, video and cinema for his inspiration. The first evidence of this is in the waiting area where customers can sit on a sofa until a table becomes available, and where a television screen has been built into the floor. The inflatable plastic sofa itself changes shape as air is puffed into it from time to time.

The next surprise for customers eating at L'Aquylone is the trail of luminous 'crumbs' that leads them from the first dining area, past the drinks bar, to the second dining-room. It is an effect that has been achieved with fibre optics which are set into the resin floor, and which can be programmed to give a variety of different effects. For Santachiara, clever visual jokes like these are a way in which to counterbalance the otherwise high-tech treatment of the interior.

Santachiara has also introduced what he calls 'events'. The first of these is in the restaurant room nearest the entrance, an area

(left) Glass doors with a screened view of the interior confound the conventional 'pull them in and get them out quick' strategy of fast-food restaurants.

(right) Axonometric projection.

(below) In the restaurant area nearest the entrance, diners hear the sounds of a subway train, which give the atmosphere of a bustling metropolis.

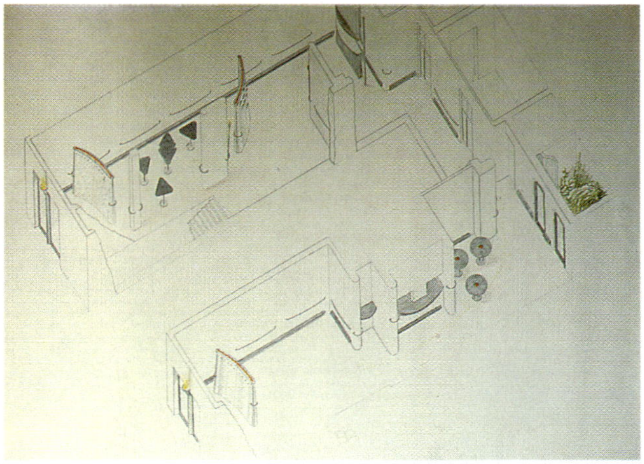

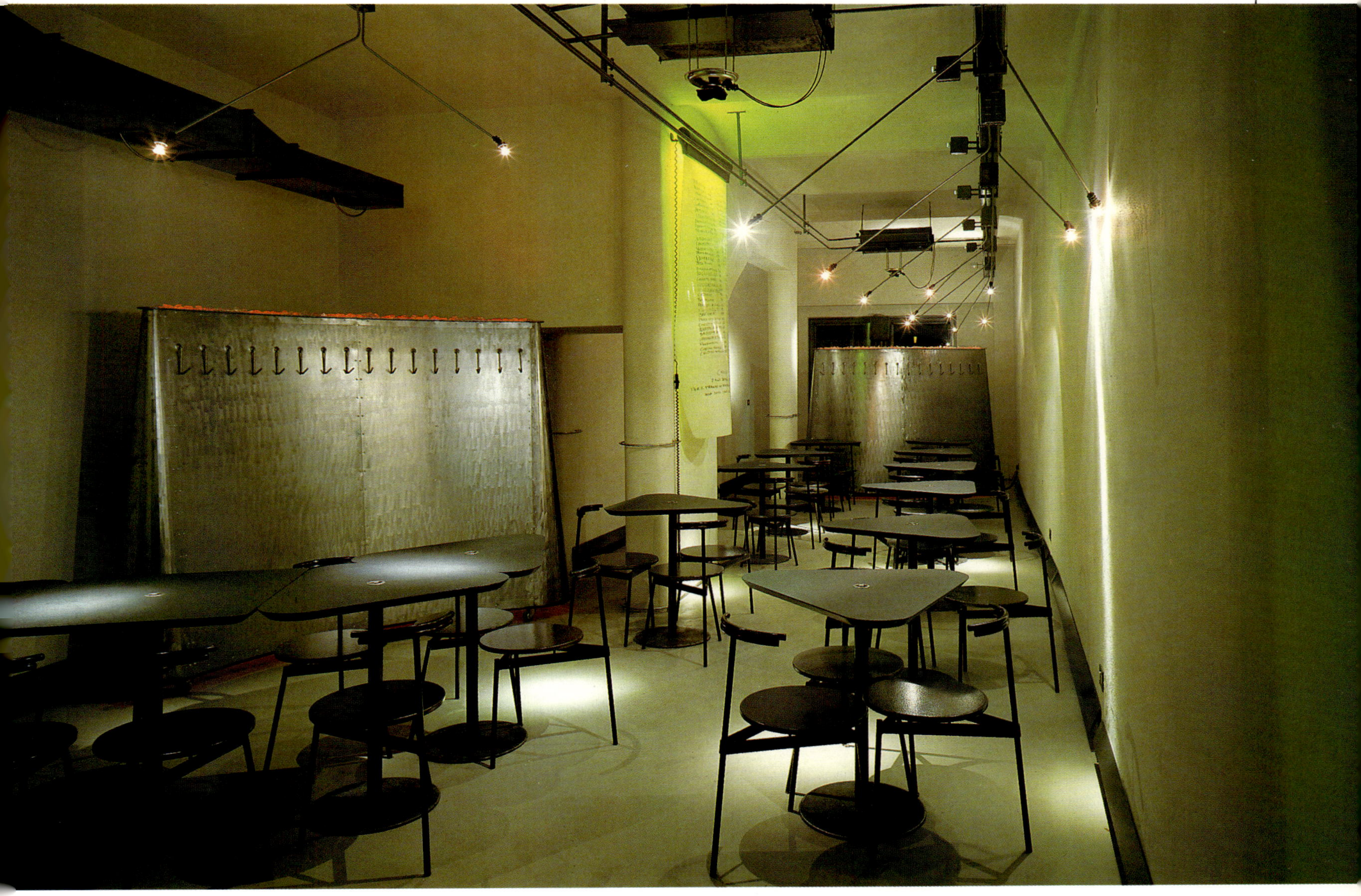

where young people tend to meet for a quick meal before or after going to the local cinema. Here, the designer has provided recordings of a train passing underground, in order to re-create the noise and excitement of a big city.

The second 'event' can be witnessed in the other dining-room where the four round tables have centres of glowing blue or red fake coals. Set in the walls are two large glass panels through which a garden of real and artificial flowers can be seen. As diners begin to eat, a stage-set thunderstorm – complete with wind, rain, lightning and thunder – starts to rage behind the glass, followed after six or seven minutes by sun and the sound of birds singing.

If there is any criticism to be made of Santachiara's design for L'Aquylone, it can only be that it will slow the turnover of business. With so much going on and so much to see, customers will be tempted to stay much longer than it takes them to eat their fast food. Santachiara clearly had a fairly indulgent client in Reggio Emilia.

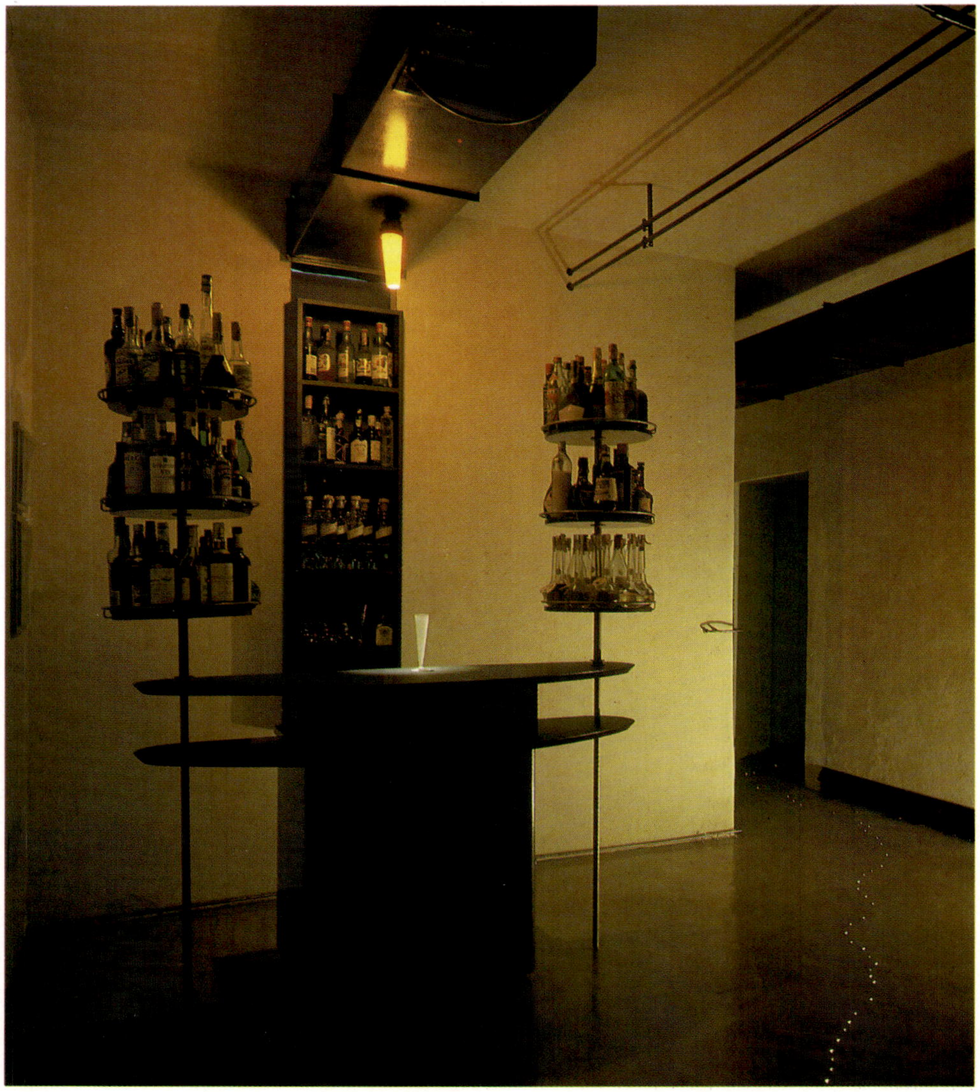

(right) Inspired by the dynamic arts of film and television, the interior contains a series of visual and aural jokes. First is the trail of fibre-optic 'crumbs' leading through the dining-rooms and past the bar.

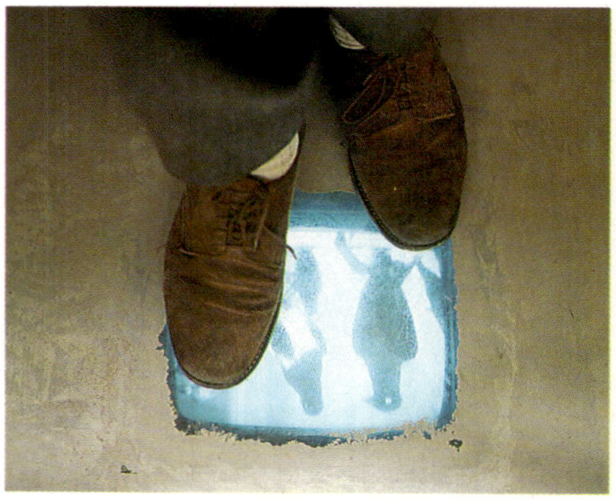

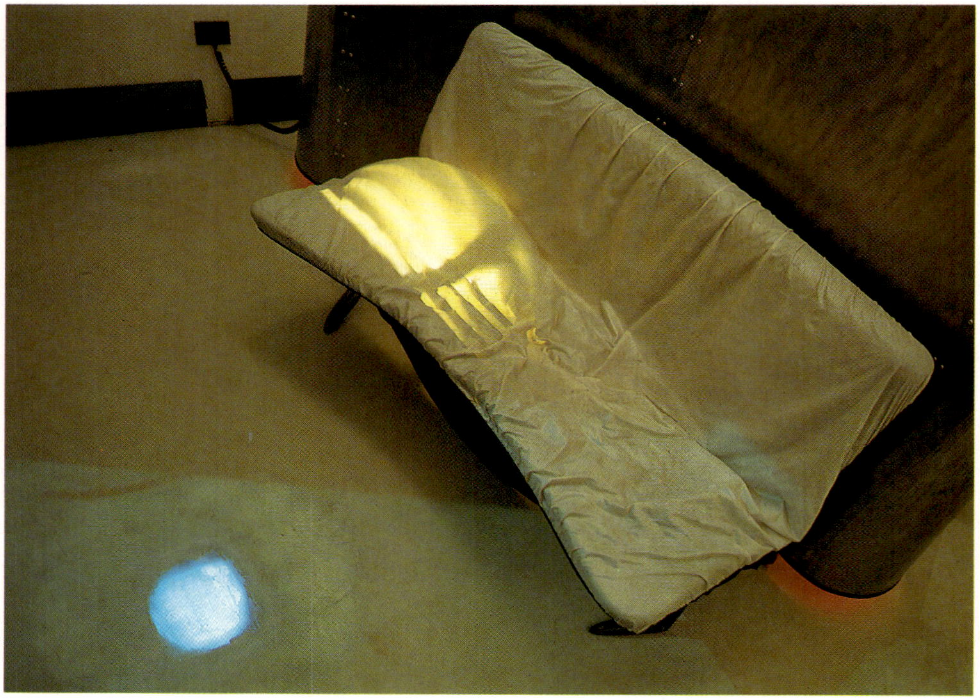

(above and right) More visual jokes in the waiting area: a television screen is built into the floor, and the plastic sofa changes shape as it is automatically inflated.

(far right) Visual events in the second dining-room include a staged thunderstorm in the garden behind glass panels, and glowing fake coals in the middle of the tables.

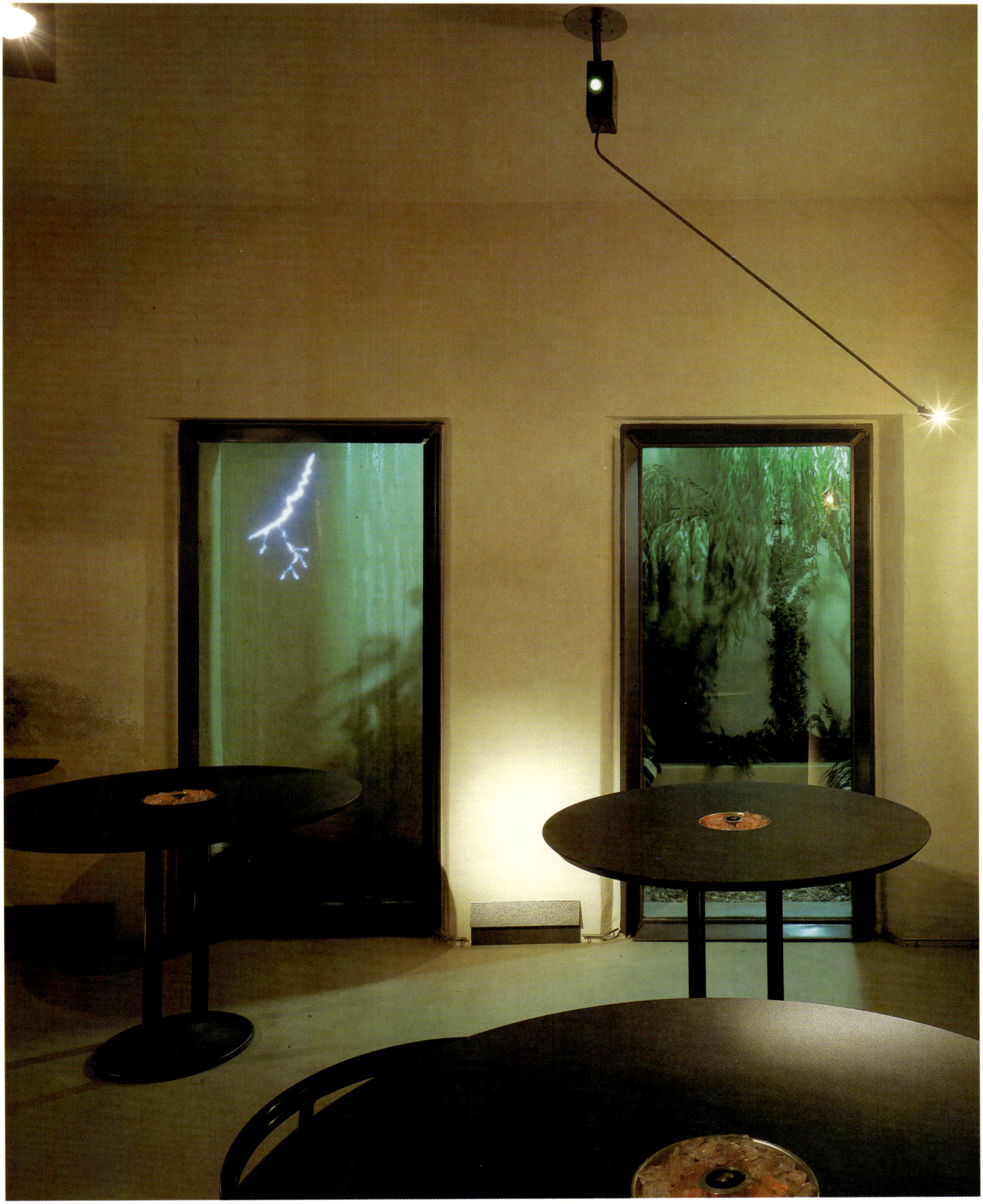

THE PALIO

NEW YORK CITY, USA

Designed by Skidmore, Owings & Merrill

American designers have perfected a certain style of interior often found in restaurants or bars: it is redolent of the lushness of an earlier era, using fine materials, but is discernibly modern. The Palio, a large Italian restaurant in the Equitable Center office building, is a particularly well-fashioned example of this genre.

Skidmore, Owings & Merrill are better known for their large office buildings than for relatively small projects like The Palio. But the same thoroughness of execution that marks their skyscrapers, corporate headquarters and public buildings can be glimpsed here: it is clear that SOM have a deep understanding of the corporate style and way of life.

The brief to the designers was to build a first-class Italian restaurant with seating for 175, with a bar/café on the ground floor and the main dining-room and two private dining-rooms on the first floor. The ground-floor bar is the most evidently 'Italian' element in the project, with its black and white chequerboard marble floor and marble-topped bar counter. Dominating the bar is a four-wall mural by Sandro Chia, based on the Palio, Siena's annual equestrian competition.

On the floor above, the restaurant is more subdued. Screens and panels, as well as the ceiling grid, are of a rich brown bog oak, conveying some of the aura of a stately gentlemen's club. Ceiling-mounted downlights provide a comfortable overall level of illumination (none of the gloomy darkness favoured by some upmarket restaurants), while brass wall sources add a touch of warmth. Leather-upholstered banquettes along one wall are surmounted by a series of banners, made by Cesare Olmastroni, displaying the symbols of the Sienese *contrade* or families. Modern corporate *contrade*, dining in The Palio, may well feel a common cause with these centuries-old bands of fierce Tuscan rivals.

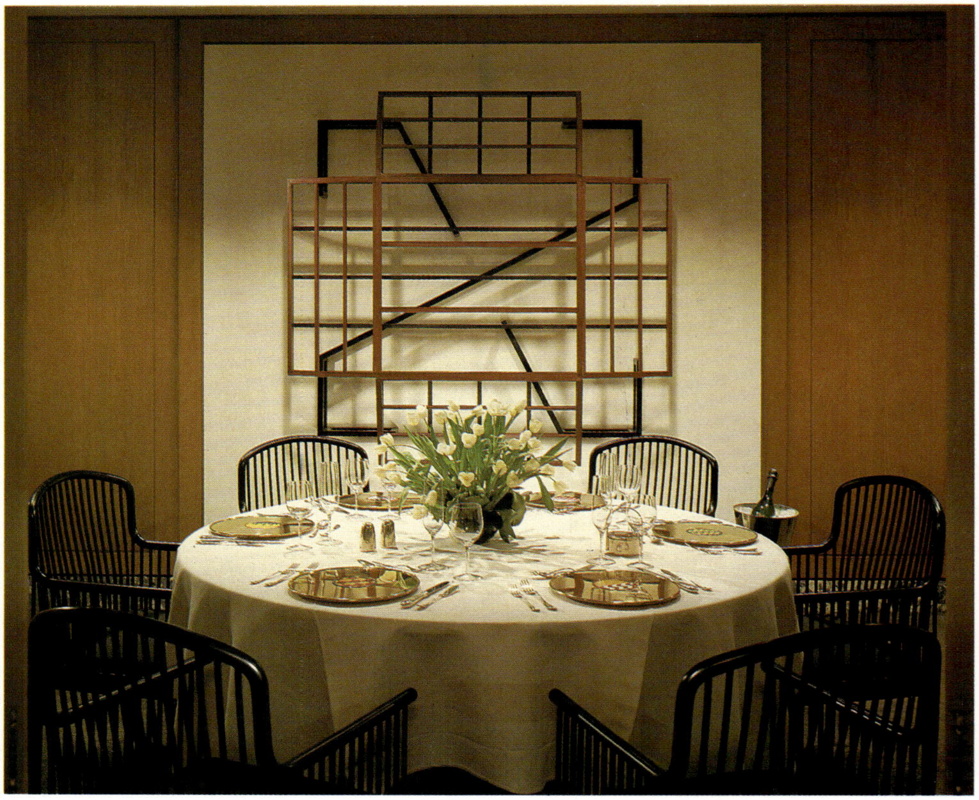

(right) An Italian restaurant in the American corporate style – light, spacious and well executed.

(far right) Warm brown bog oak is used for the screens, panelling and the ceiling grid. Together with lighting from wall sconces and glowing, internally lit panels, it creates a solid, reassuring atmosphere.

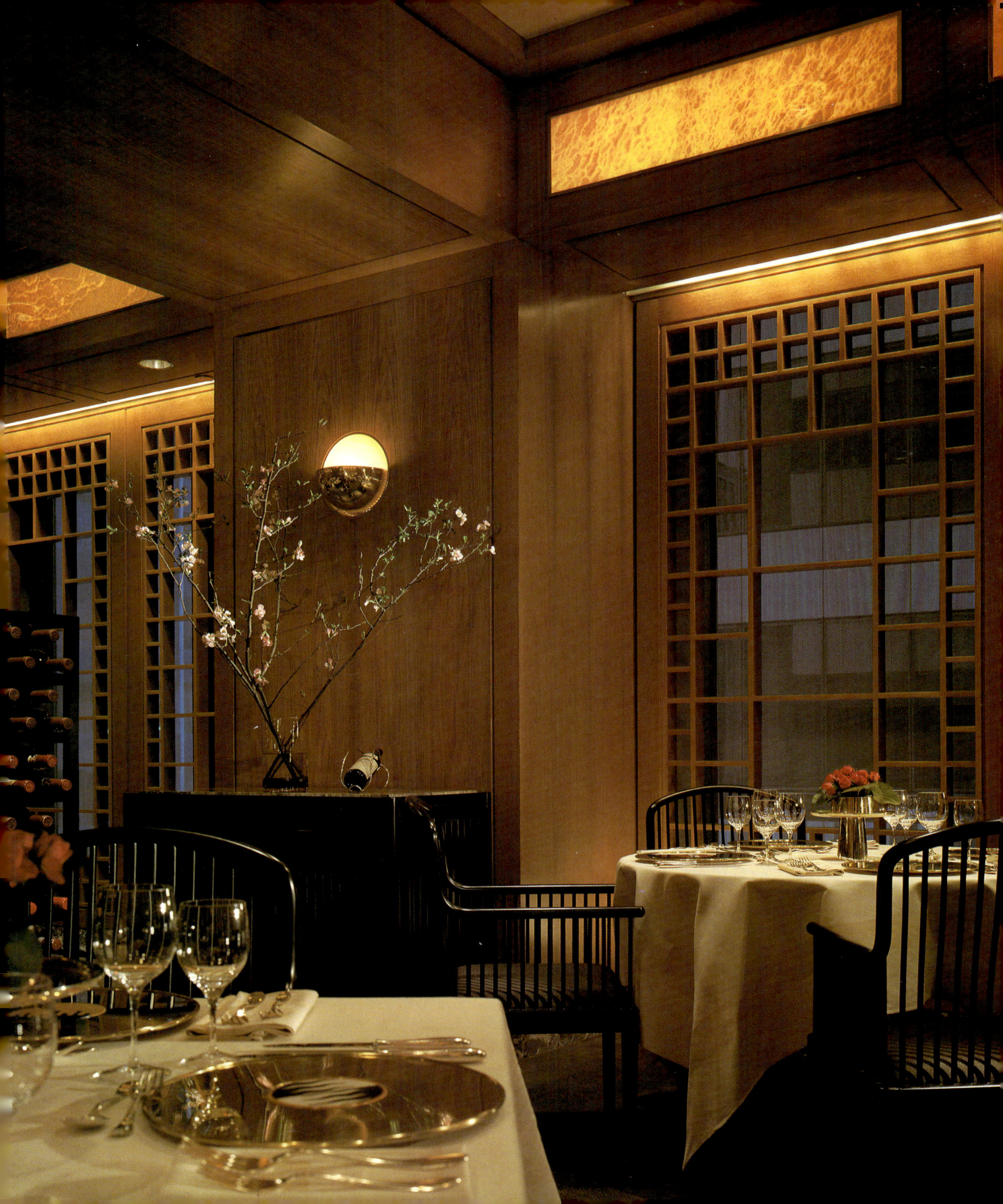

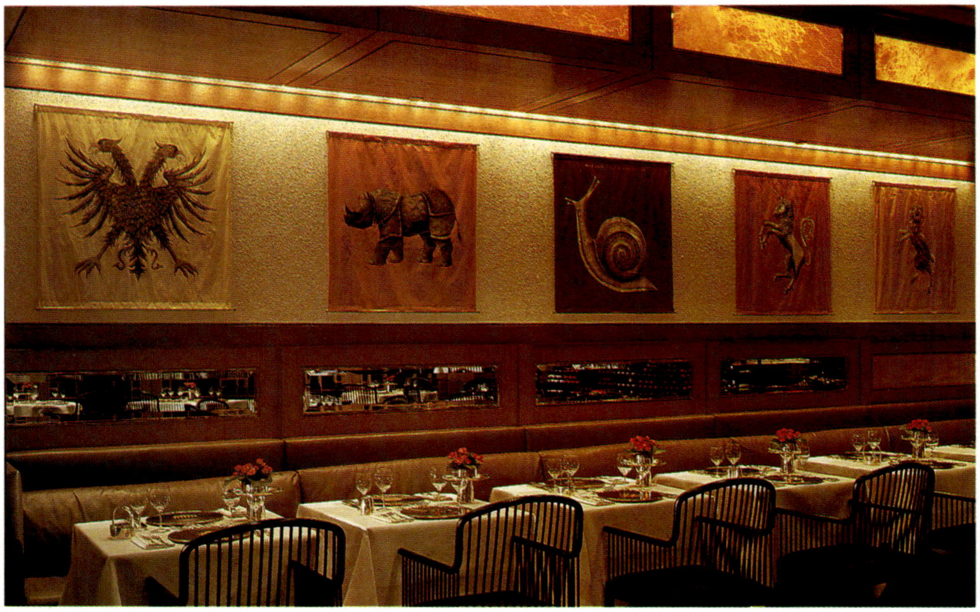

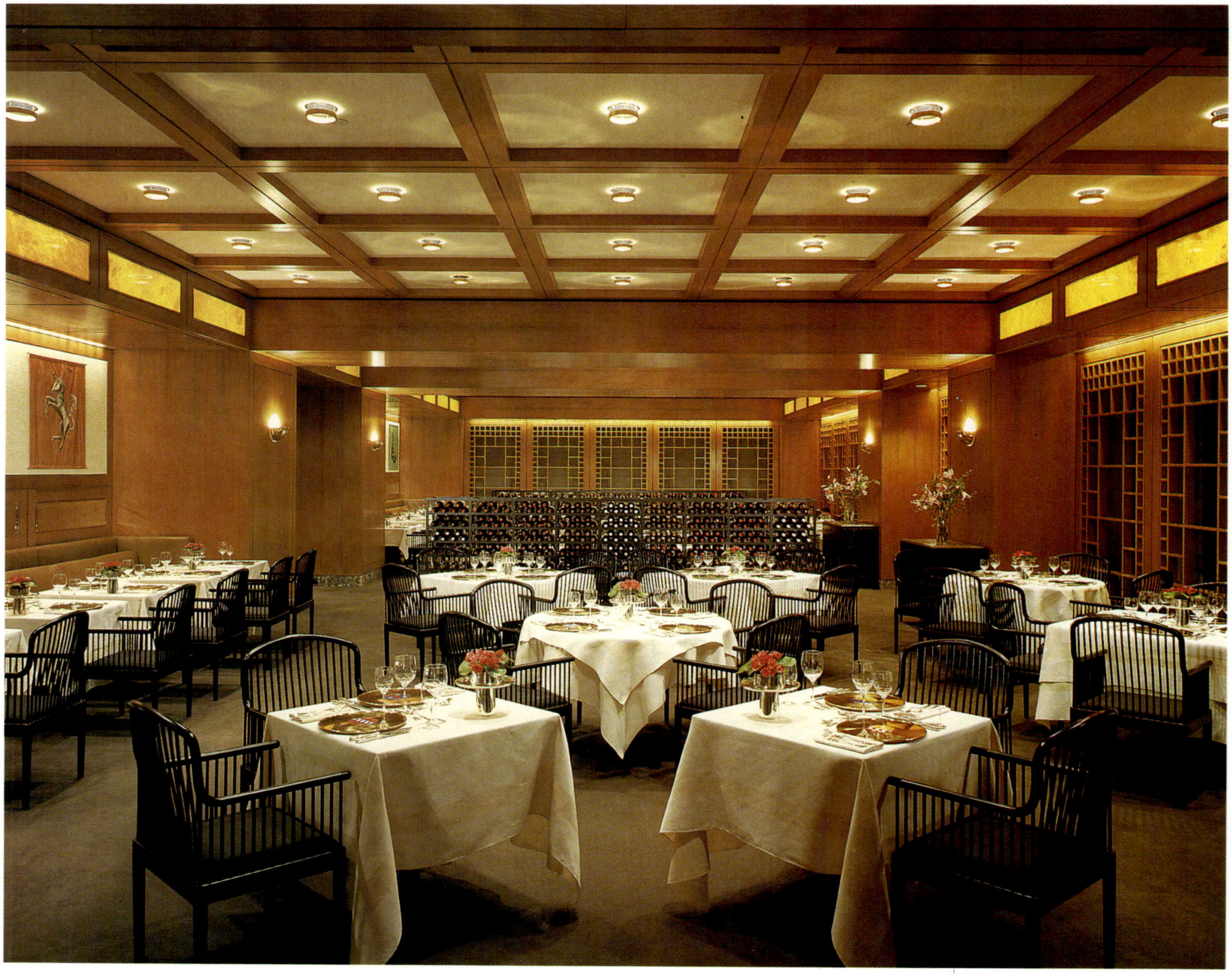

(left) Banners by Cesare Olmastroni, again in warm earthy colours, show the symbols of various Sienese families.

(below left) Dining in style: no references to the familiar trattoria here.

(below) Perhaps the most recognizably Italian element is the marble-topped bar with its chequered floor. Above it is a mural by Sandro Chia, based on the Palio, an annual horse race held in Siena, after which the restaurant is named.

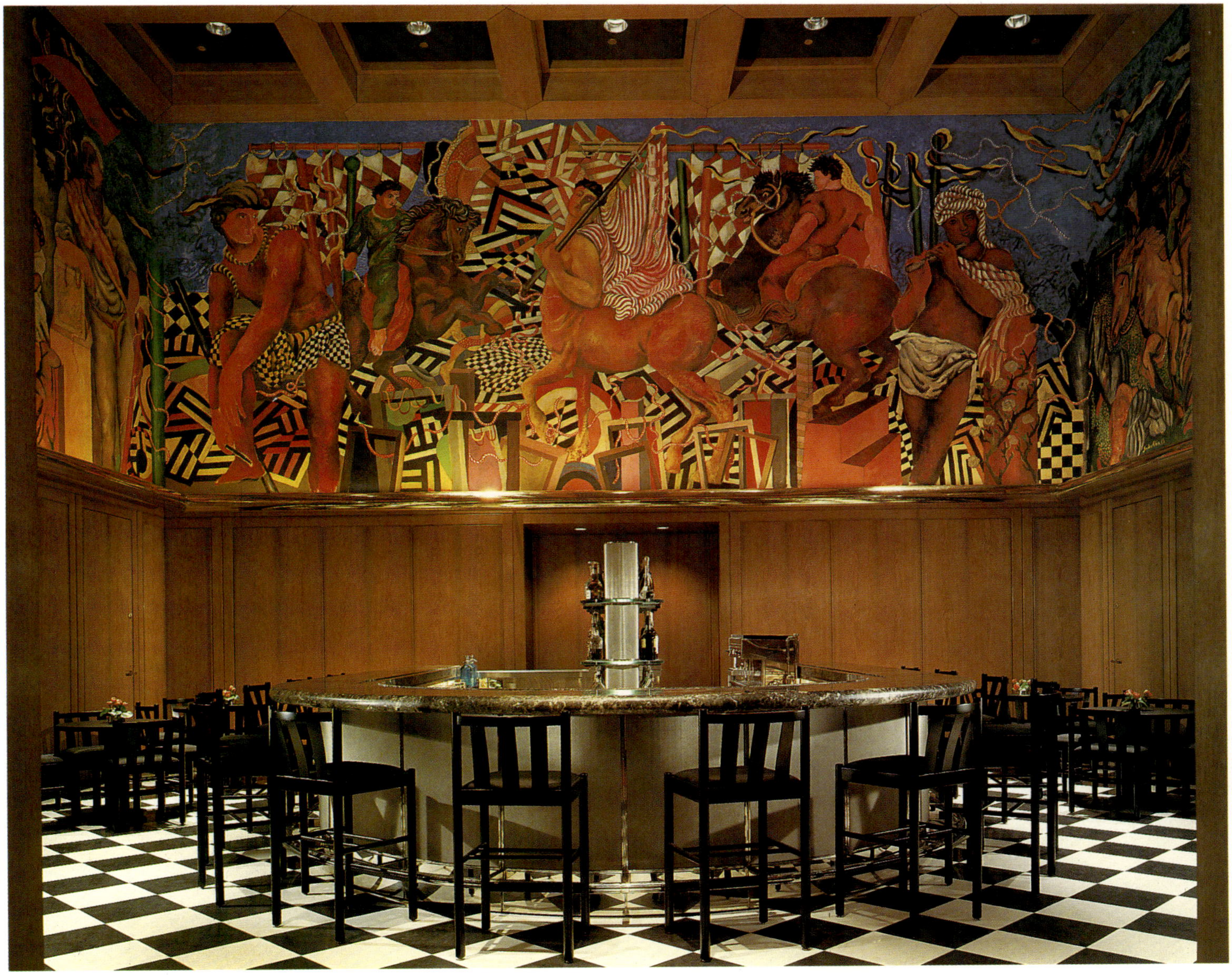

MANIN
TOKYO, JAPAN
Designed by Philippe Starck

Philippe Starck is the most conspicuous of a growing band of Western designers who are working in Japan. Born in France, he established an international reputation with his interiors for nightclubs and restaurants in Paris, notably the Café Costes, in which a main feature was Starck's own steel and glass furniture designs. Here, too, with a generous budget of 855,000 dollars and a brief to create an upmarket, elegant Italian restaurant, Starck has produced a giant showcase for his work.

Commissioned by Person's, a Japanese fashion company, the restaurant, called Manin, is in a large double-height space. It is as if the intervening floor has been removed, leaving the steel beams as a kind of overlaid sculptural grid.

This grid imposes order on the void and becomes a design motif. The square, black terrazzo floor tiles, and the square panels of polished mahogany that line the walls all have aluminium joints, emphasizing the chequerboard pattern. The short end wall is panelled too, though in a rather lurid red velvet, a strange choice in an otherwise strong, hard environment. Furniture, designed by Starck, is fairly simple: three-legged aluminium chairs covered in leather, and white wood tables with cast aluminium feet (mostly hidden under the tablecloths). It is an impressive setting, but one that rather dwarfs the furniture and the diners, who none the less flock to pay outrageous prices to eat in a Starck creation.

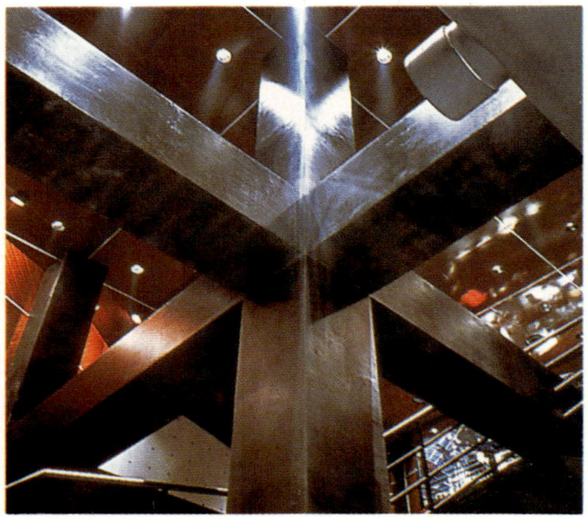

(above) A key element is the exposed structural steel grid, imposing order on the double-height space and providing a design motif.

(right) The chequerboard pattern of the grid is repeated throughout. Floor tiles are squares of black terrazzo; polished mahogany wall panels are divided into squares by aluminium joints, and the end wall is also panelled, in bright red velvet.

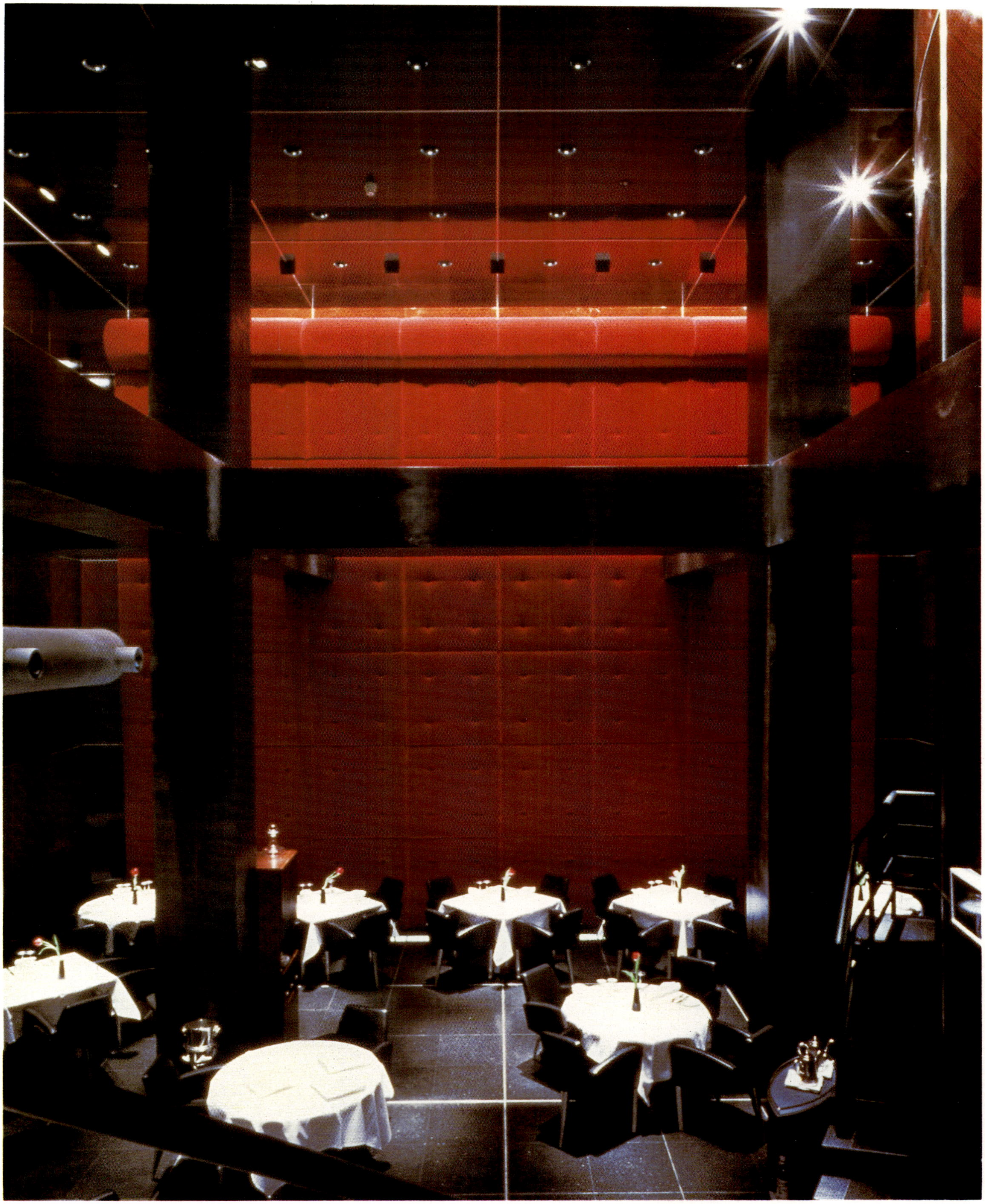

(right) Following the trend for subdued lighting in restaurants, light sources are confined to ceiling- and wall-mounted spots.

(below) Huge sculptural elements like this metal bridge are in keeping with the scale of the space.

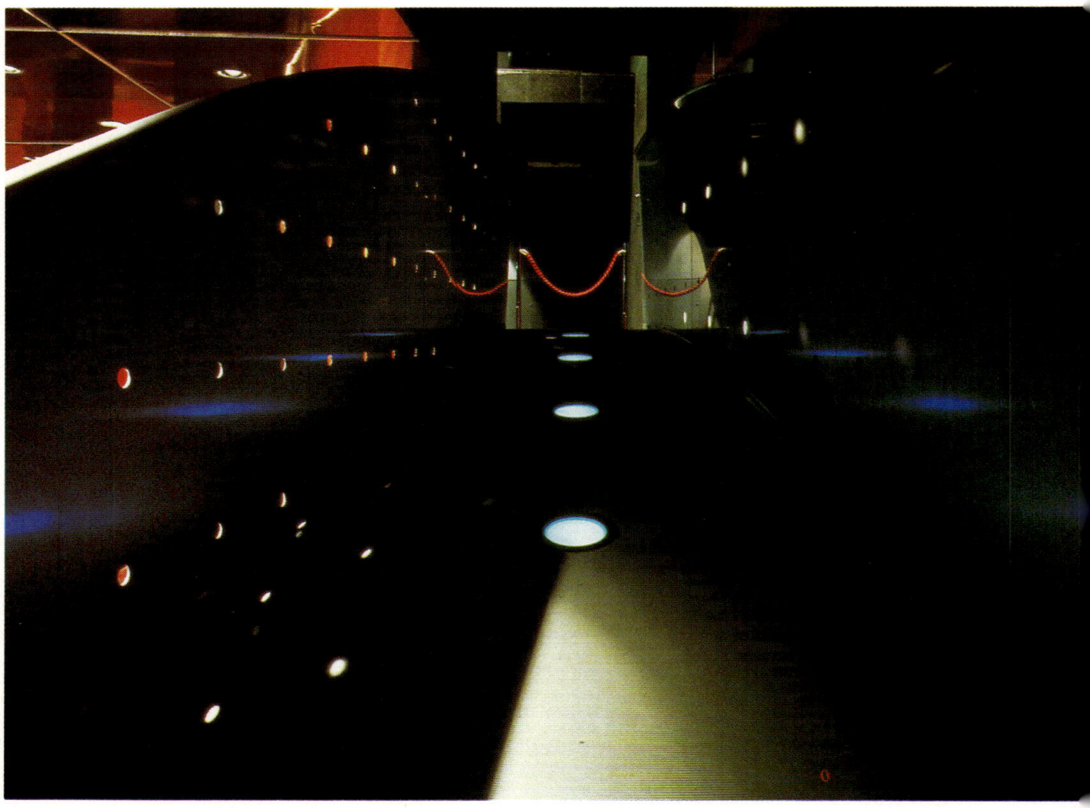

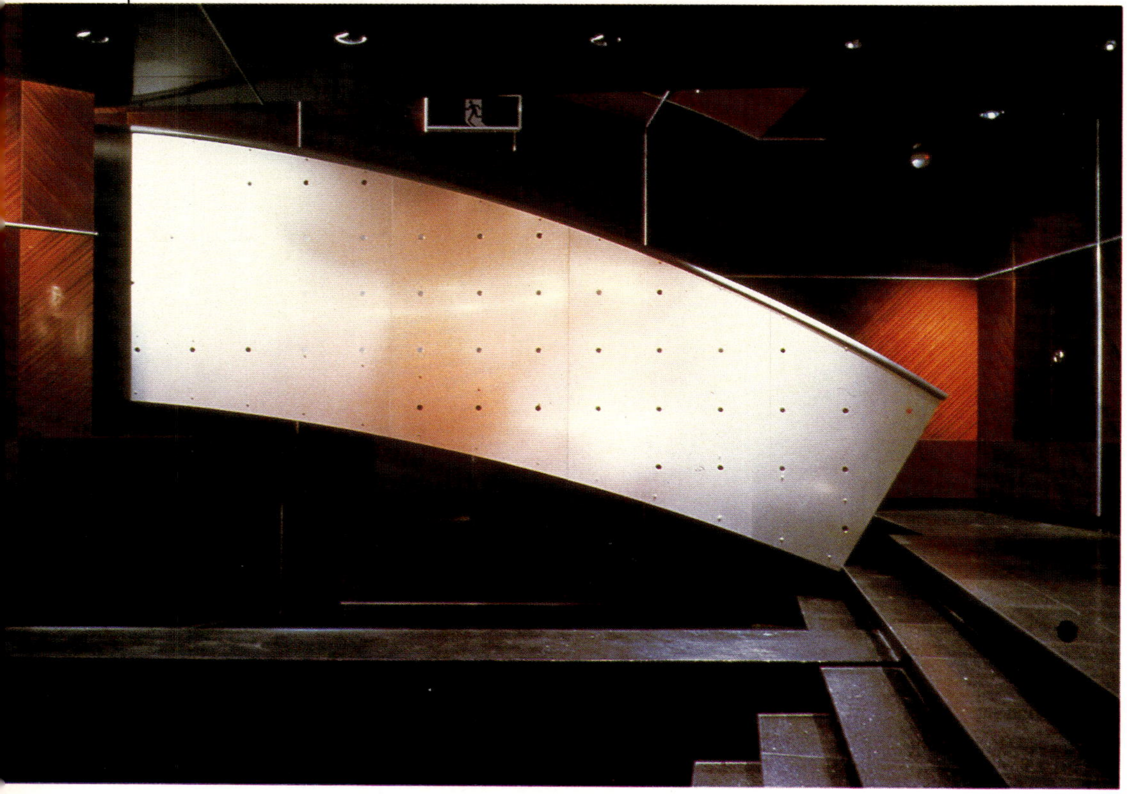

(below) A mysterious translucent blue table provides a resting place near the bar counter.

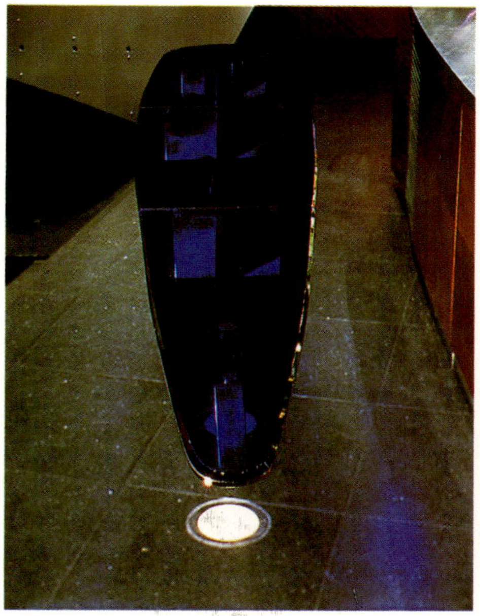

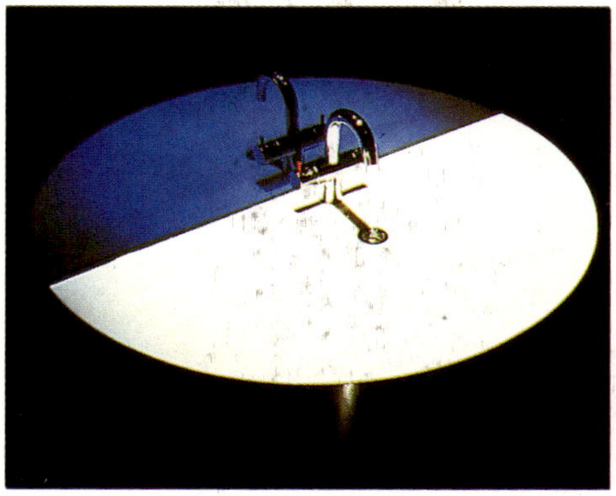

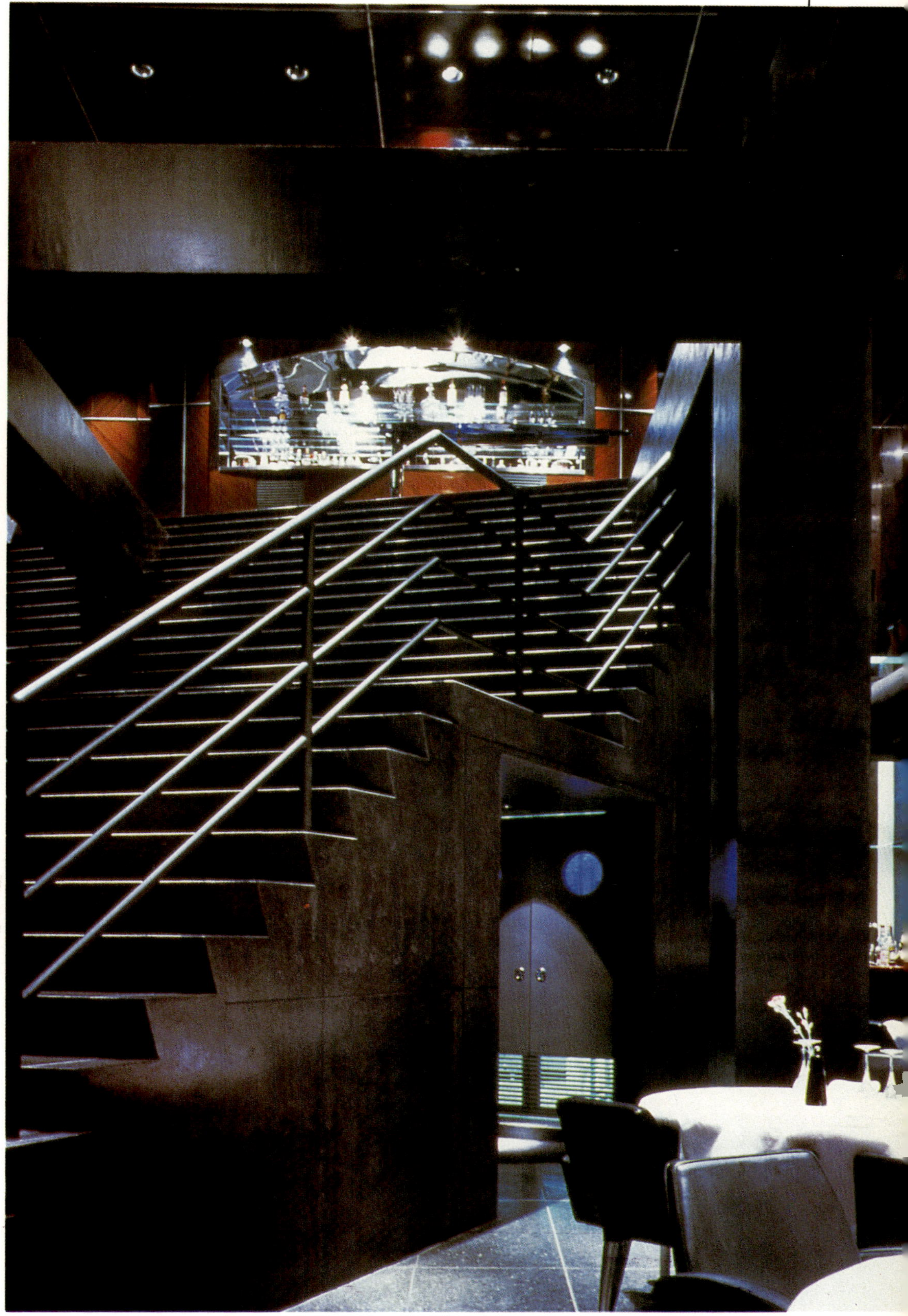

(above) Even the humblest details repay attention, including the taps – a work of sculpture in their own right.

(right) The monumental staircase would be suitable for a medieval castle. Unfortunately, the specially designed furniture, usually a main feature of Starck's interiors, is dwarfed by it.

BAR SET/OFF

TOKYO, JAPAN

Designed by Superpotato Design Studio

The bustling Shinjuku area of Tokyo is the setting for the Set/Off restaurant and bar designed by Takashi Sugimoto, head of the bizarrely named Superpotato Design Studio, in collaboration with Inoue Satomi. With accommodation on two floors, the brief was for two separate areas: a singles bar on the ground floor, with a restaurant above.

Of the two, the restaurant is more typical of Sugimoto's work – dark and dramatic with the emphasis on natural materials and chiaroscuro lighting effects. Lining the walls are layered steel plates studded with a grid that is repeated in the perforated glass screens. Concealed lights throw up the shadows and make the holes in the glass screen seem like a hundred pinpoint light sources. Direct lighting is confined to the downlights over tables, which are black-stained ash, matching the marble floor.

With a budget of 214,000 dollars, the materials and detailing are immaculate. The result is highly dramatic, almost to the point of claustrophobia.

Downstairs, the atmosphere is much cosier and more welcoming. Here, the use of walnut furniture and fittings and warm light sources makes it easier to accept Sugimoto's assertion that he is influenced by traditional Japanese farmhouses.

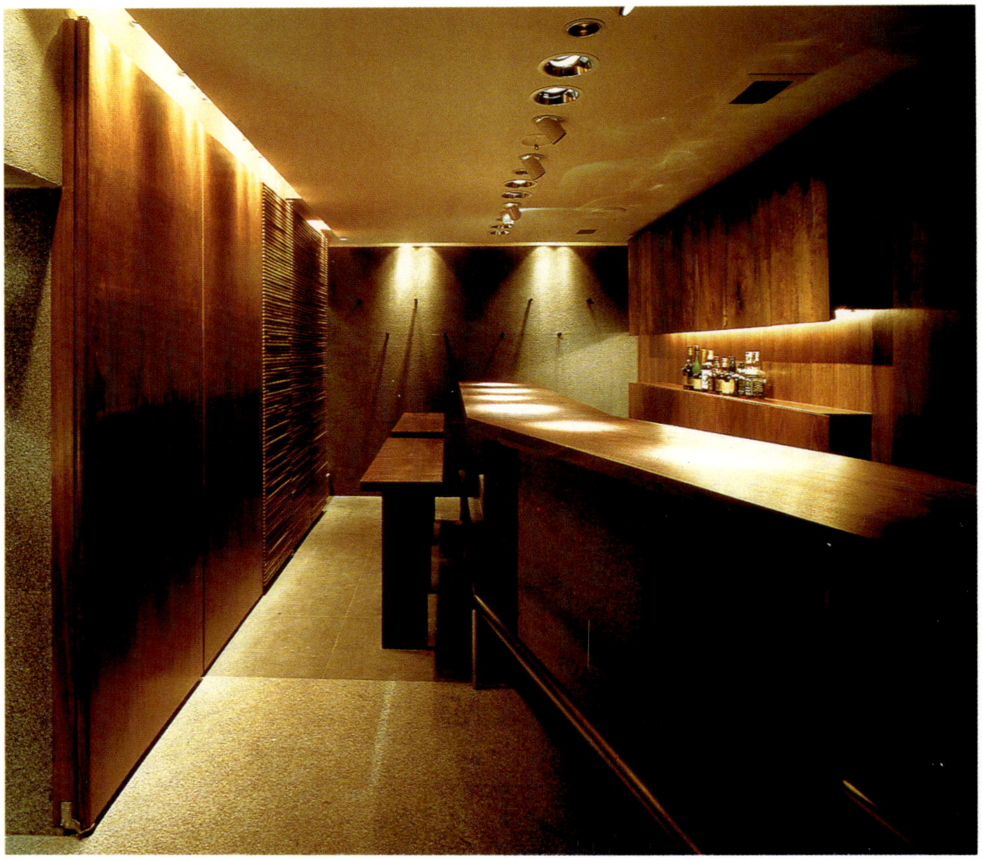

(above) Walnut furniture and fittings and warm lights, supposedly influenced by Japanese farmhouses, create a cosy atmosphere for the downstairs singles bar.

(right) Marble stairs and a steel-clad wall set a very different tone for the upstairs restaurant.

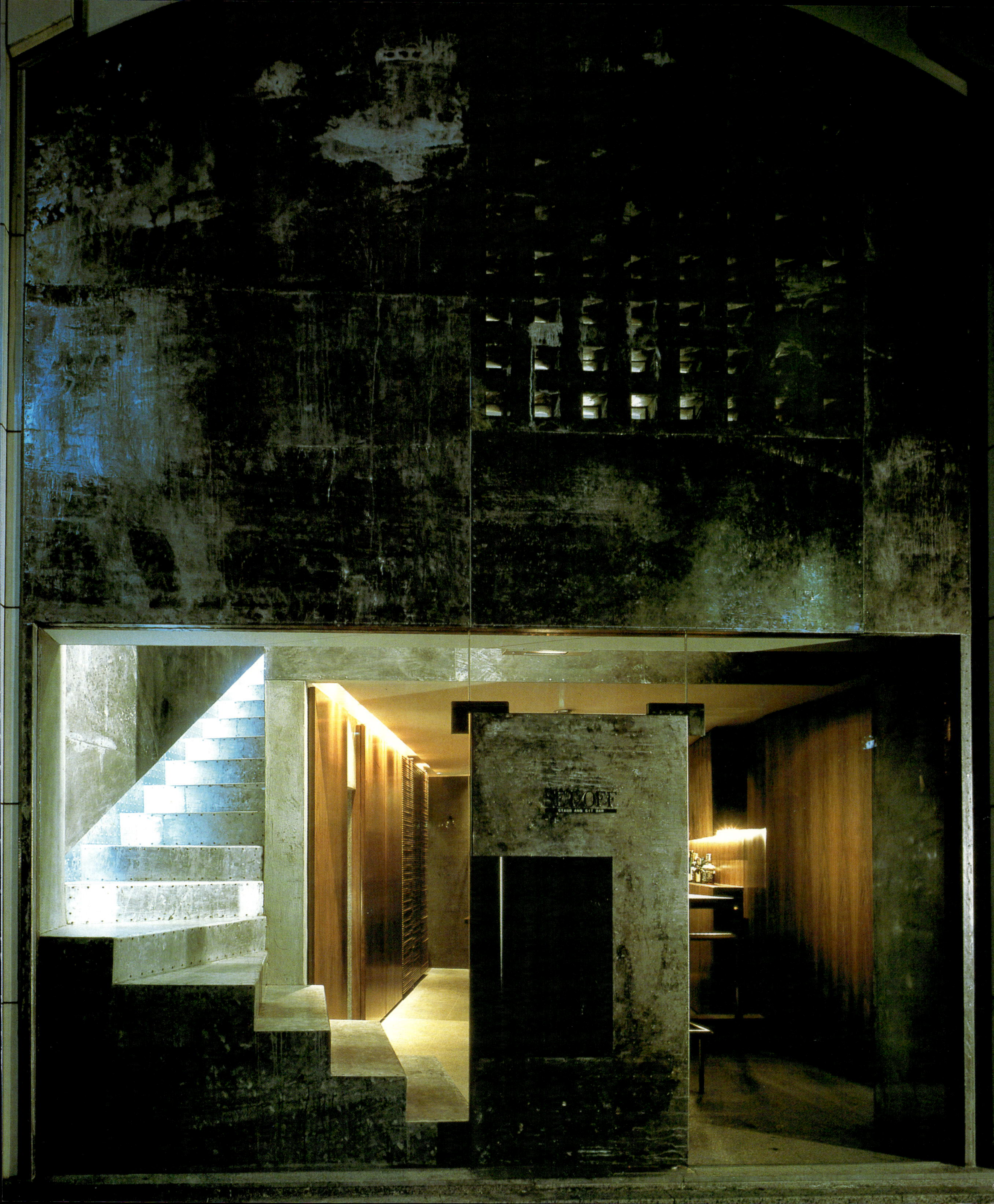
STAND AND SIT BAR

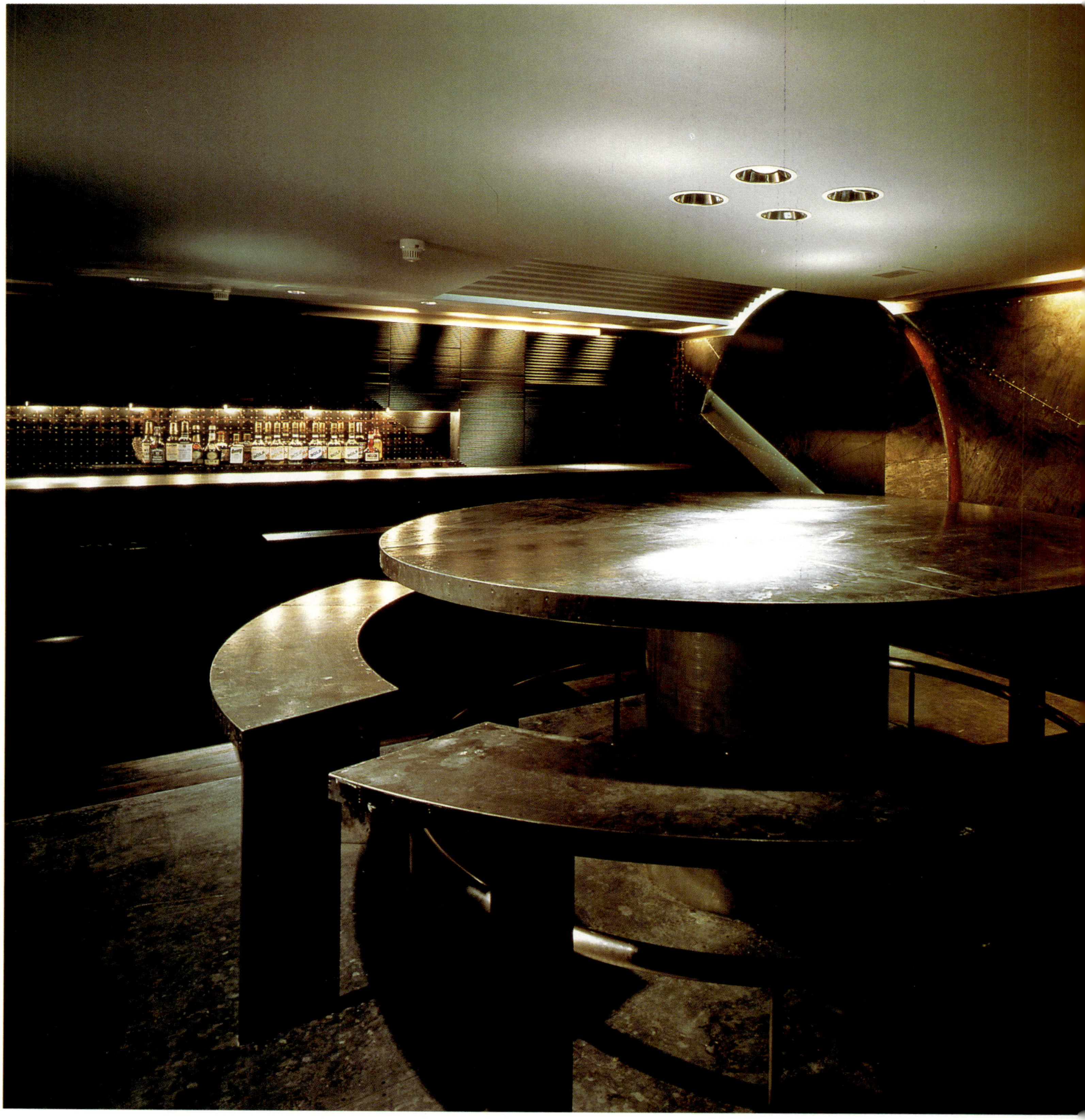

(left) Upstairs, smooth, hard materials – marble, steel and black-stained ash – are used in large sculptural planes to dramatic effect.

(below) Chiaroscuro lighting, here with perforated glass screens and concealed sources behind the overlapping studded wall plates, are a hallmark of Sugimoto's work.

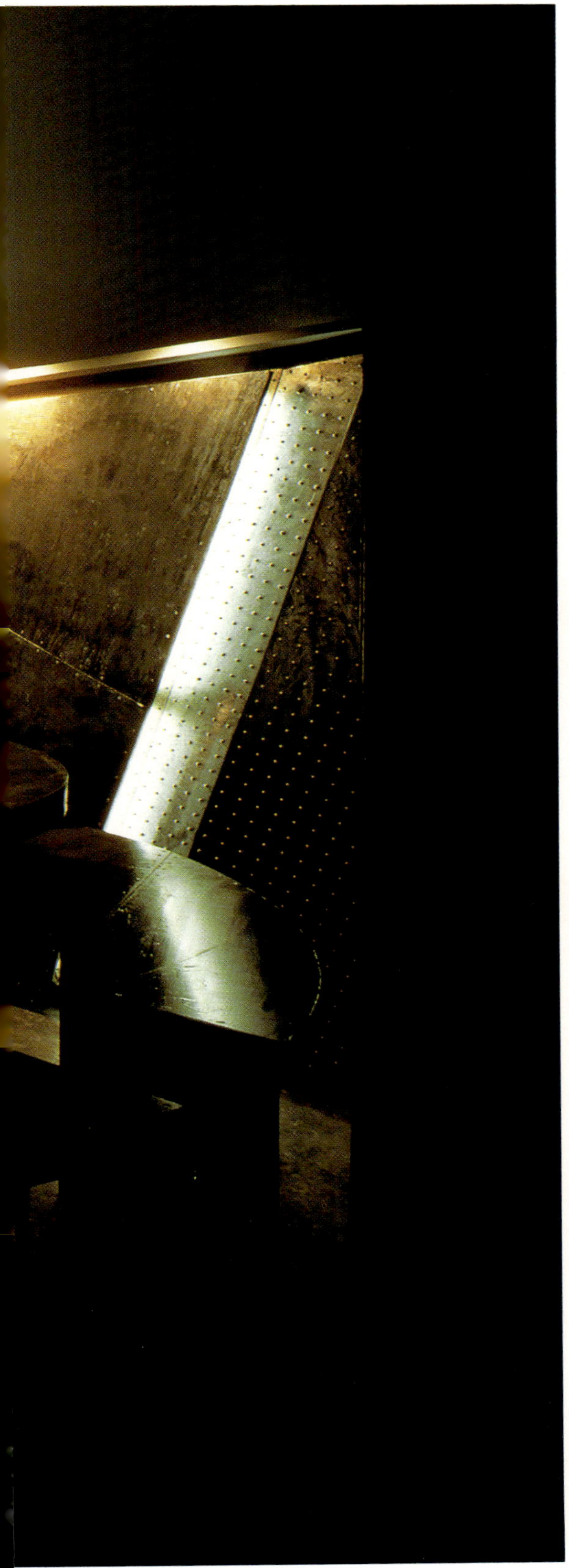

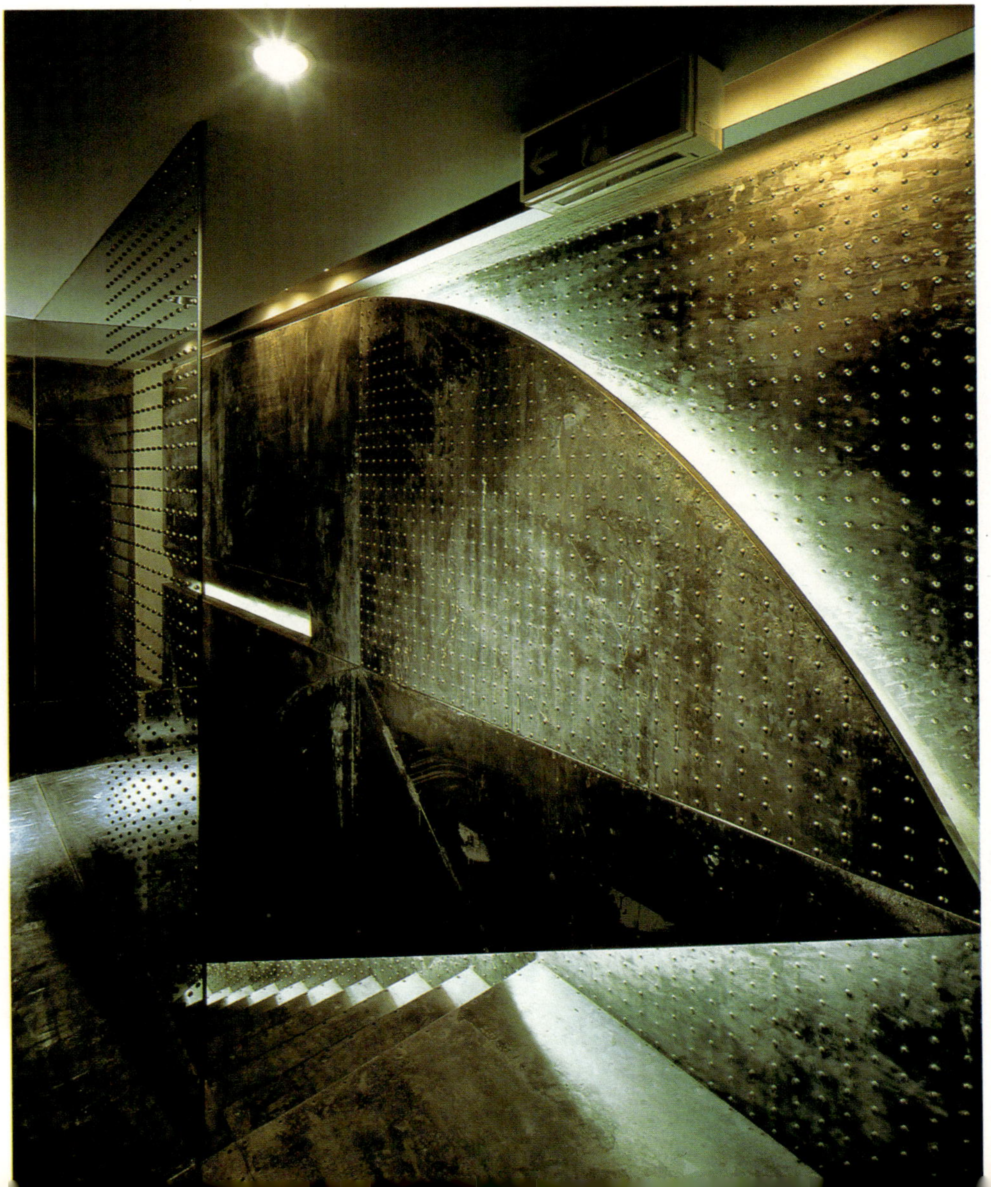

DANCE HALL
TOKYO, JAPAN

Designed by Shin Takamatsu

Few designers ever get the opportunity to produce anything as outrageous as Shin Takamatsu's nightclub called Dance Hall. It was commissioned by IDX Co., whose only stipulation was that it should symbolize the company's change of policy, from steady to enterprising, and create a new style of amusement.

From the start it is clear that this is no ordinary interior. There is no sign, only a jagged steel beam jutting out over a doorway between two bolted, rusted pillars. Once inside, visitors confront the distorted perspective of the corridor, an effect achieved by cutting a series of asymmetrical slits in the steel plates of walls, floor and ceiling, and backlighting them with fluorescent lamps.

At the end of this space, past the reception desk, is a silver door into the main dance hall – which is reminiscent of a set for a big-budget science fiction movie (in fact, the budget was

(below) Rusted steel girders and a jagged projecting beam form the low-key entrance.

(below left) Inside it looks more like a set from a science fiction movie than a disco. The 'lighting machine' moves up and down over a tempered glass floor.

(right) Along the entrance corridor the perspective is distorted by a series of asymmetrical slits cut in the steel plates of walls, floor and ceiling, and lit from behind.

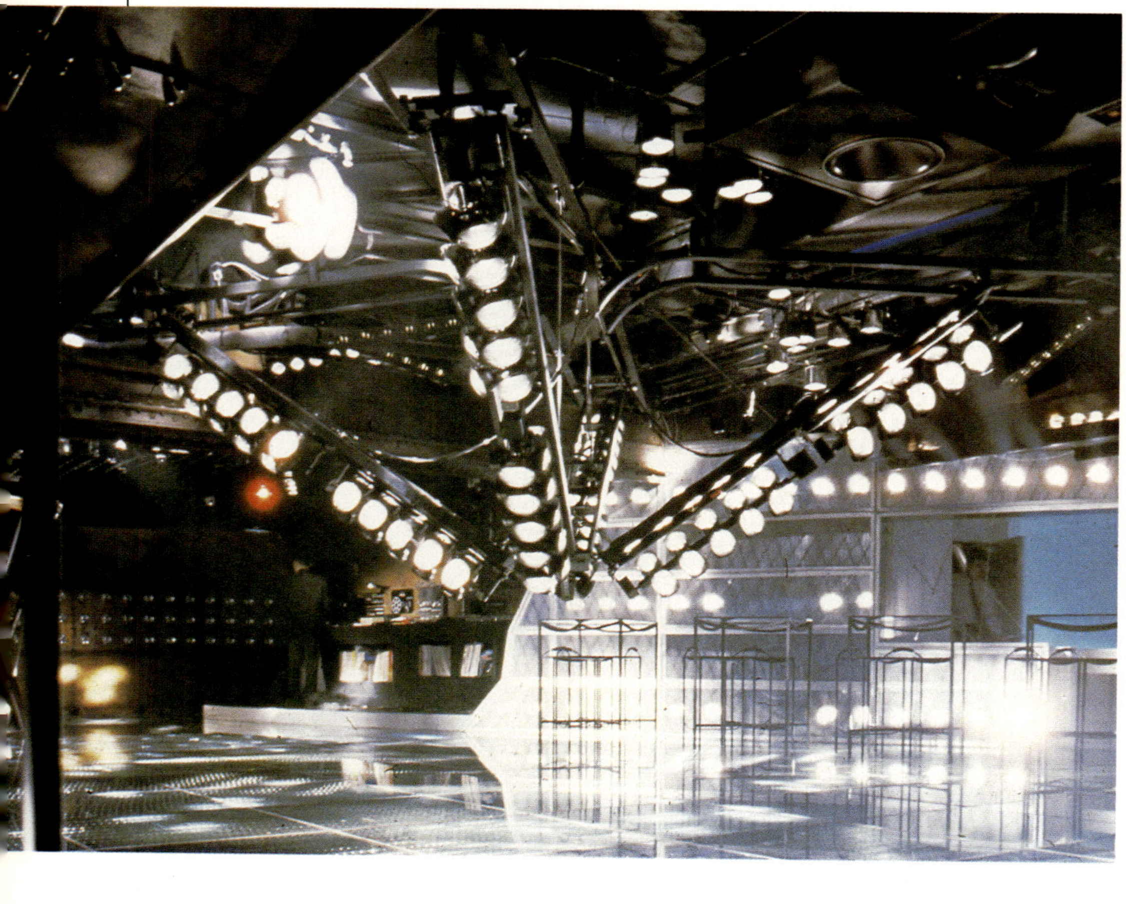

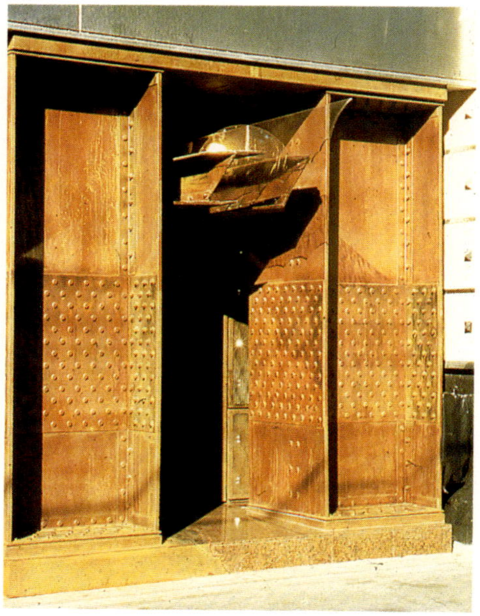

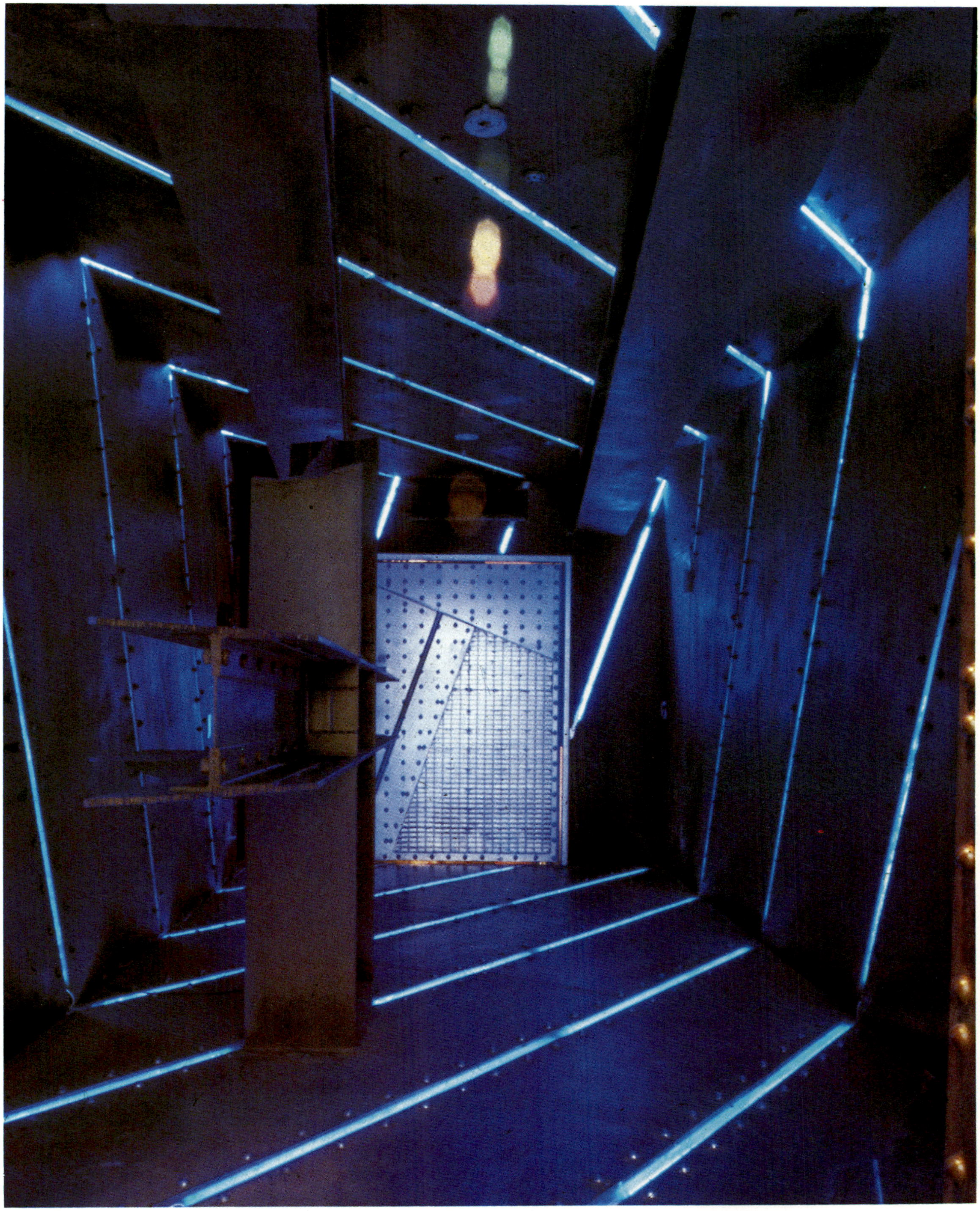

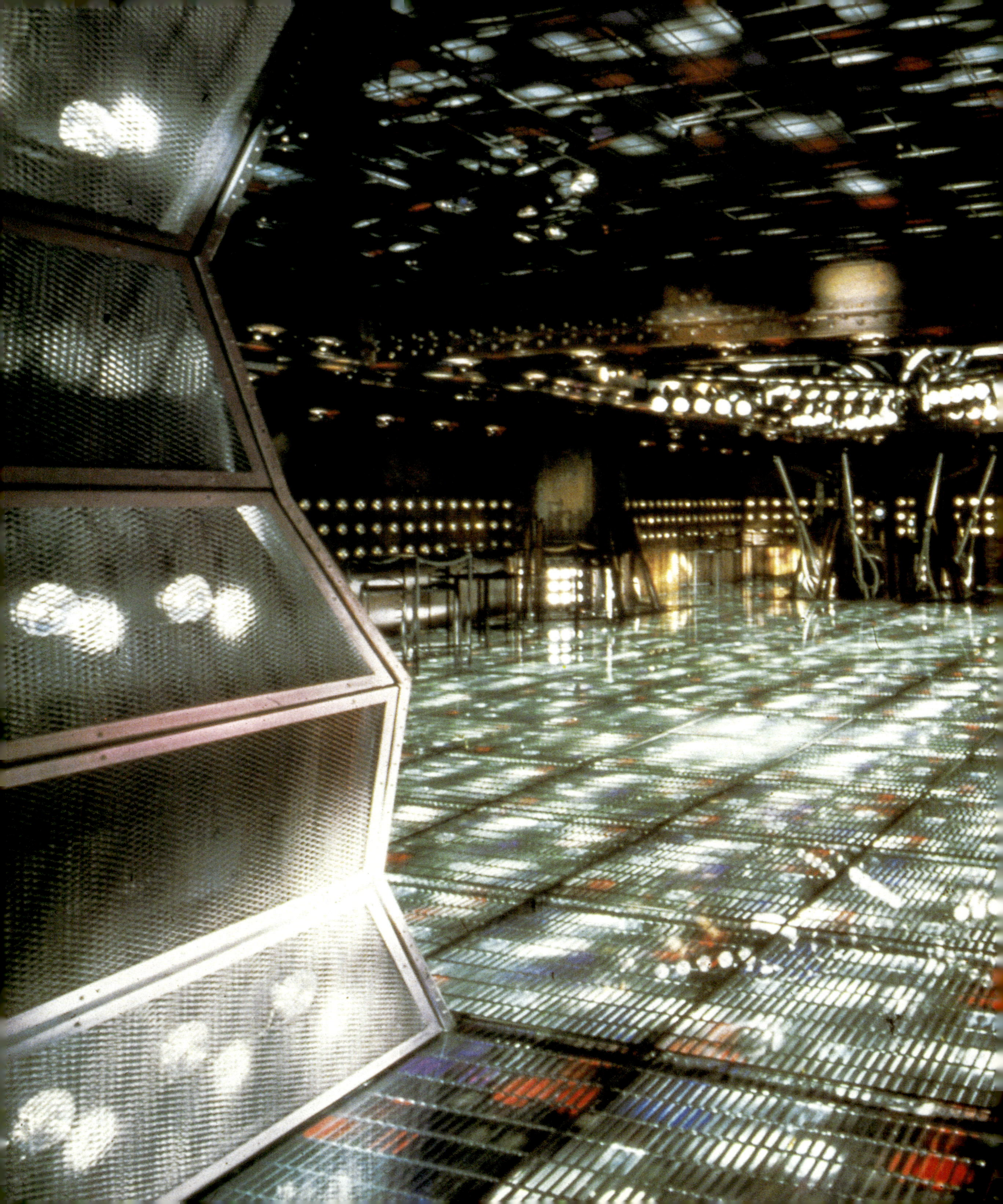

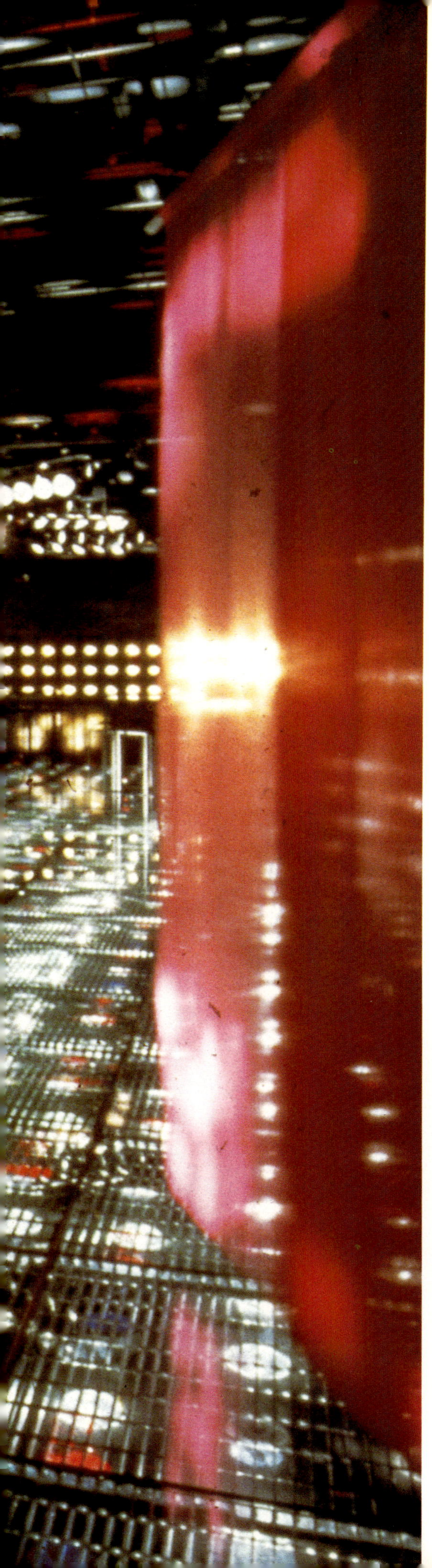

784,000 dollars). A vast but apparently insubstantial floor stretches out into the distance. Made of tempered glass on a steel supporting grid, it is lit from beneath by white and coloured beam lamps. Walls and ceiling have the same rusted finish as the entrance, and again contain a maze of lights: over two thousand are used in the whole project.

As if that were not enough, there are two sinister-looking 'lighting machines': one which moves up and down, suspended from the ceiling; the other, which opens and closes, on the floor. And by discharging clouds of dry ice into the space, beams of light can be made to look like solid columns. Saturday night at Dance Hall is an occasion that has to be experienced in order to be believed.

(left) A galaxy of beam lamps mounted on walls and ceiling and under the glass floor illuminates the space.

(below) Another lighting machine, which opens and closes, adds to the surreal atmosphere.

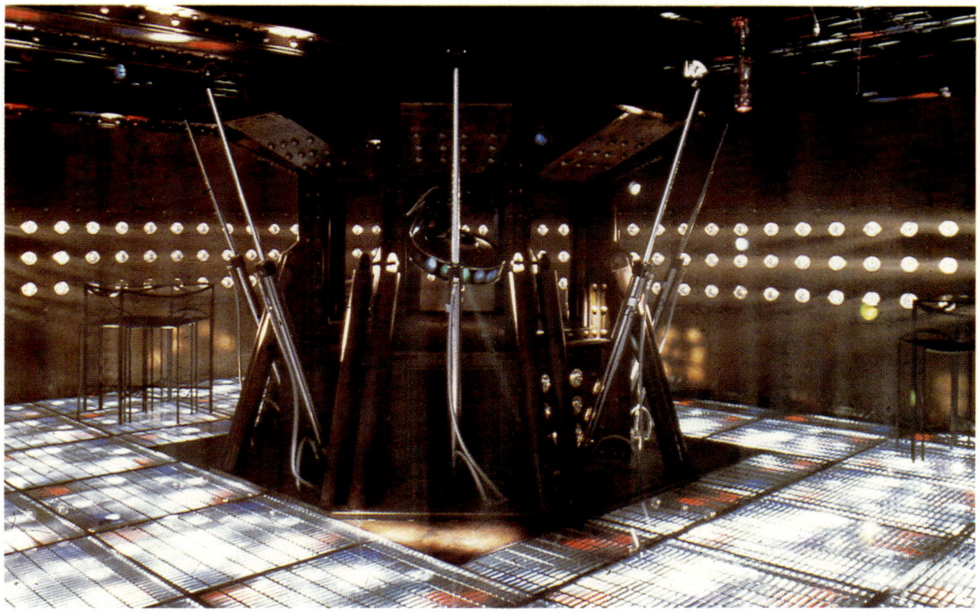

A D COLISEUM

TOKYO, JAPAN

Designed by Sue Timney and Grahame Fowler

Most contemporary Japanese design is bold and direct; the designer may feel that the work is invested with deep symbolism, but to the uninitiated the appeal is in the subtle play of shapes and materials. When British fabric designers Sue Timney and Grahame Fowler were commissioned to design a restaurant in Tokyo, the result was bound to be different.

Timney and Fowler had made a name for themselves in Japan through sales of their fabrics, often printed in black and white, to several top Japanese fashion designers. Their interior for A D Coliseum reflects their work.

A D Coliseum is a Vietnamese restaurant which also has cosmopolitan roots in Paris. The interior was therefore designed to be sophisticated and urban, and anything but ethnic.

Timney and Fowler were responsible for virtually every element in the restaurant (except the furniture, which they chose). Like

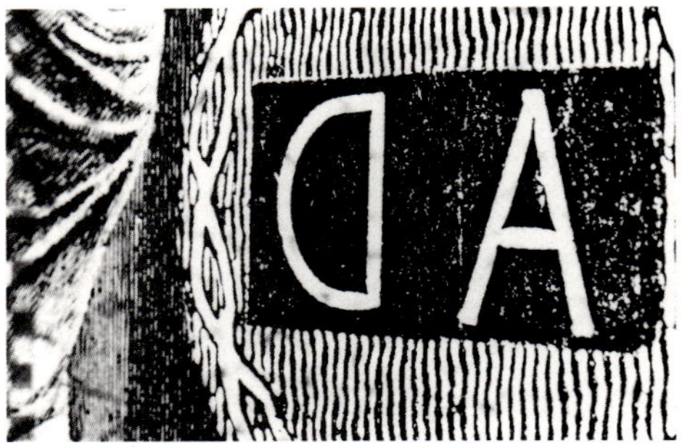

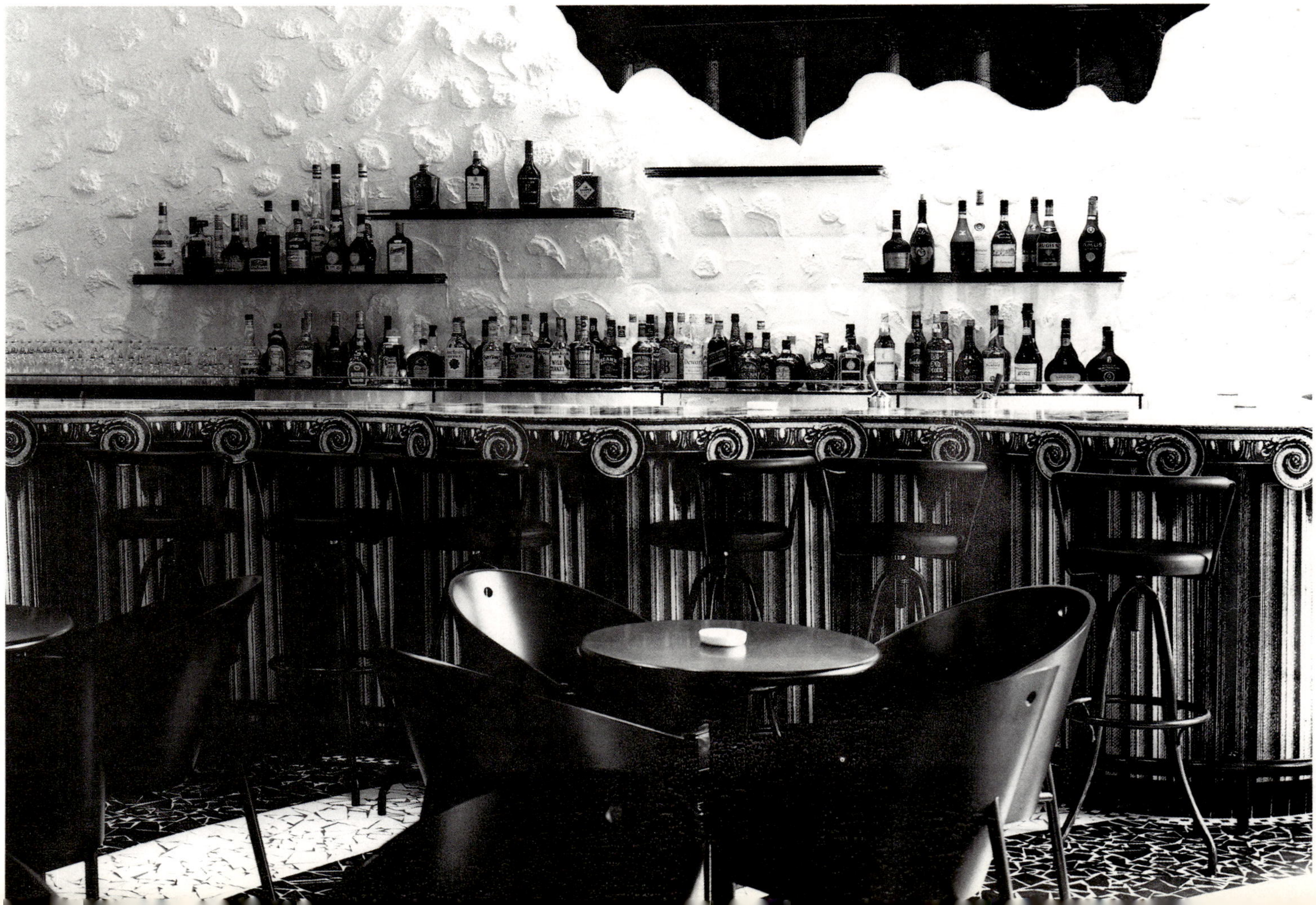

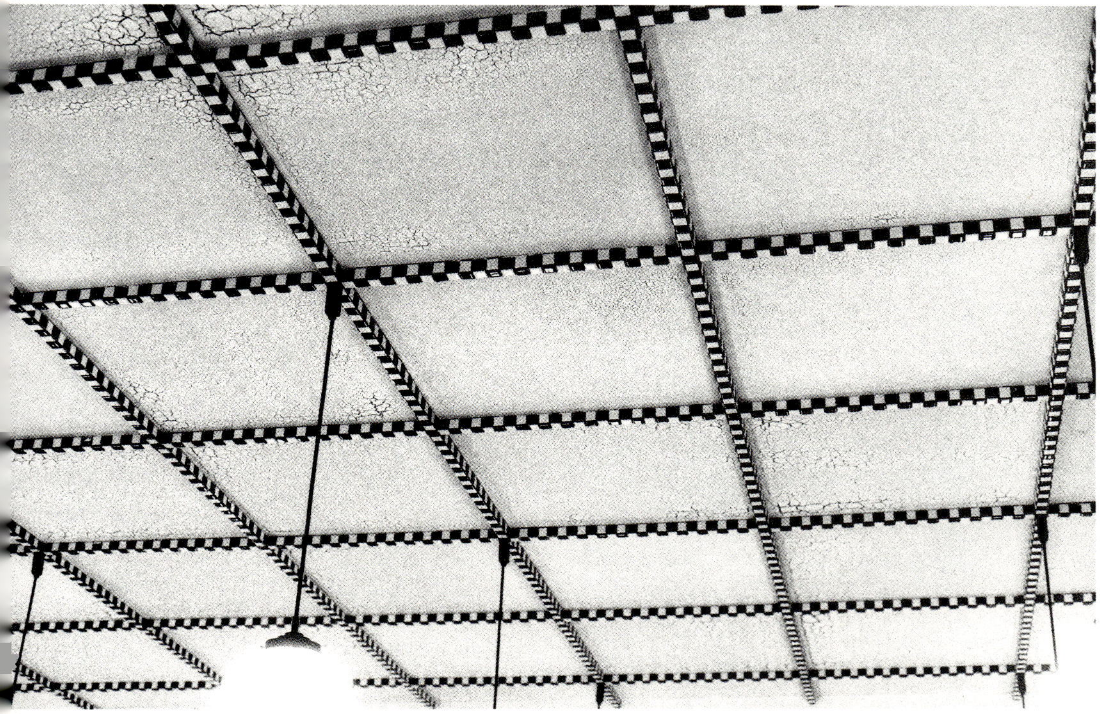

many of their fabrics, the interior is wholly in black and white. As the name implies, a strong classical theme runs throughout, unifying the L-shaped space. Classical fragments – caryatids, heads, pediments – are offered in repetition on the wallpaper; trompe-l'œil caryatids and pilasters seem to prop up the walls; overlapping Ionic columns support the bar counter.

The ceramic tile floor (again in black and white) initiates a cracked pattern and suggests the mosaics of Pompeii, an impression heightened by the inlaid mosaic 'medallions'. Above, a sense of aging (classical buildings, after all, should be old) is conveyed by a cracked paint effect in a seemingly incongruous Mackintoshian grid, again using ceramic tiles.

In the frenzy of some foreign-designed restaurants in Tokyo – such as Caffè Bongo, Manin and the Metropole (see pp. 54–7, 116–19 and 58–9) – the cool, black and white simplicity of A D Coliseum comes as a relief. And the skilful use of trompe-l'œil ensures that the project never sinks to restrained boredom.

(above) Despite the carefully aged look of the cracked ceiling, achieved by paint, and the consistent use of black and white, the chequered grid seems rather incongruous – more Mackintosh than Marcus Aurelius.

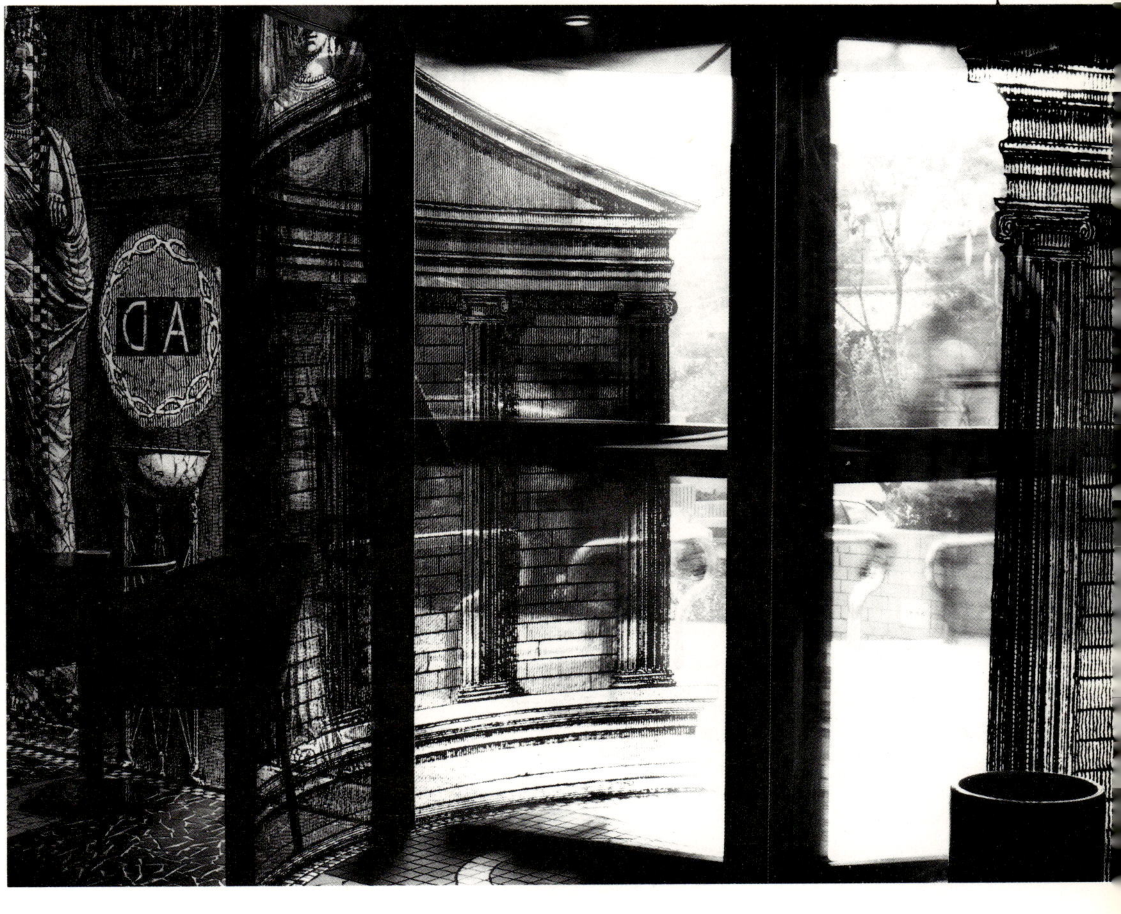

(left) Like many of their fabric designs, Timney Fowler's restaurant interior is entirely black and white and incorporates classical themes. Overlapping Ionic columns appear to support the bar, and an ancient cracked mosaic in alternate black and white bands forms the floor.

(right) Most intricate is the wallpaper, a complex layering of statues, pediments and classical fragments in the style of an old engraving.

CAFÉ PARADIS

ÅRHUS, DENMARK

Designed by Svein Tønsager

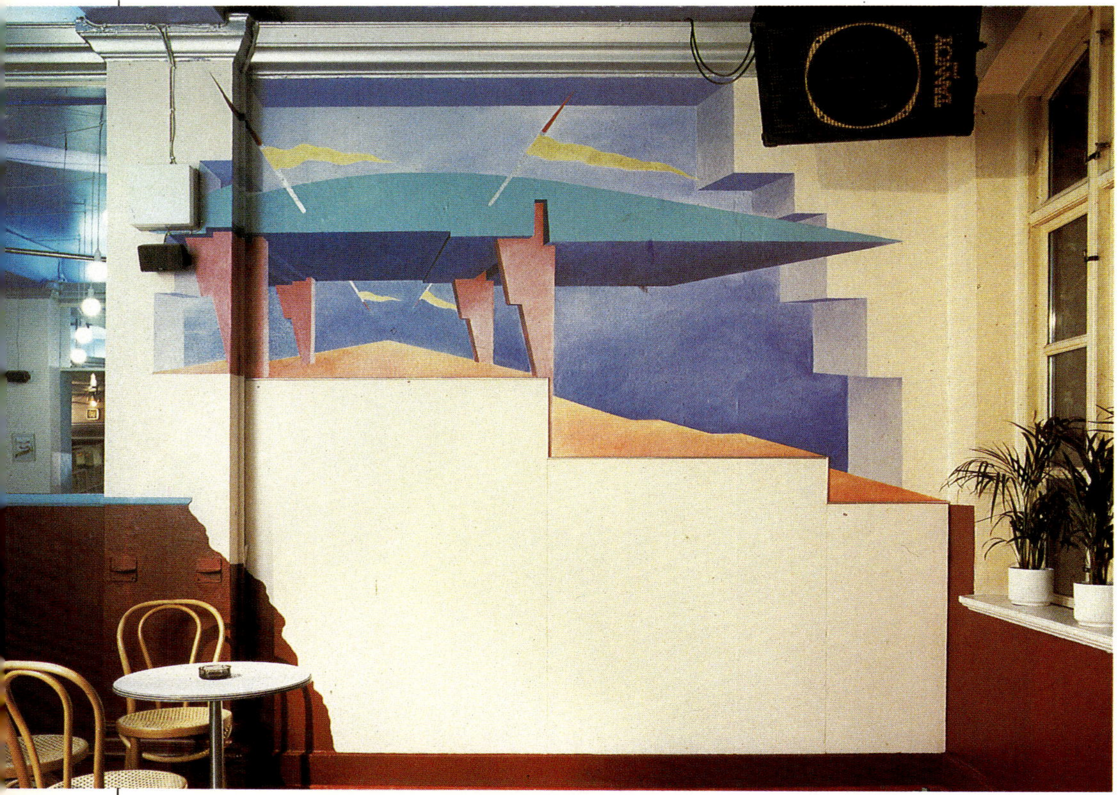

Contemporary Danish designers labour under a heavy burden. Classic 'Scandinavian Modern' design had Denmark as its heartland, and the image of pale, blond wood, and clean, uncluttered interiors is a strong one in the country. But the Danish young are just as likely to have succumbed to the more riotous influences of Italy, Britain or the United States as any other, so that Scandinavian Modern tends to be distinctly out of sync with today's trans-European youth culture.

Café Paradis, which has the subtitle 'The Last Café', is on the second floor of a building that also contains a cinema complex. Architect Svein Tønsager designed Café Paradis for the new youth, and although some of the Scandinavian heritage may be dimly visible in its wood floors, the project owes more to the designer's own inspiration than anything else. The bar is in the middle of the room, acting as a focus for the design and is, in the words of the designer, 'an eyecatcher from all angles'. A series of tilted elements – a shelving unit with a goldfish bowl, a wing-like mirror – and the

(above) Breaking away from 'Scandinavian Modern' with fresh colours and trompe-l'œil painting – only the wooden floors are a reminder of the Danish heritage.

(right) Paint finishes have a lightly brushed top layer which adds texture and can easily be patched if isolated areas become chipped or scuffed.

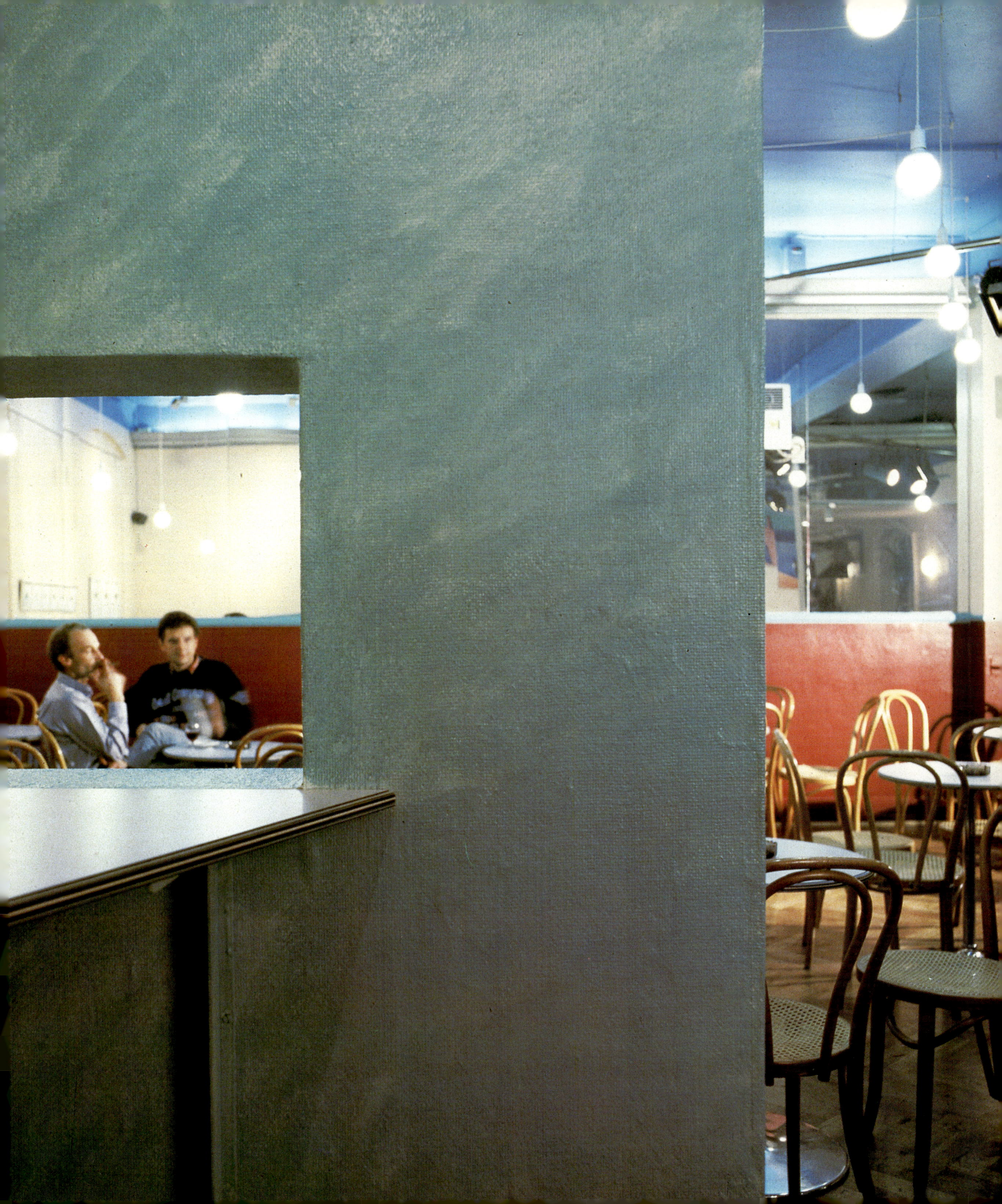

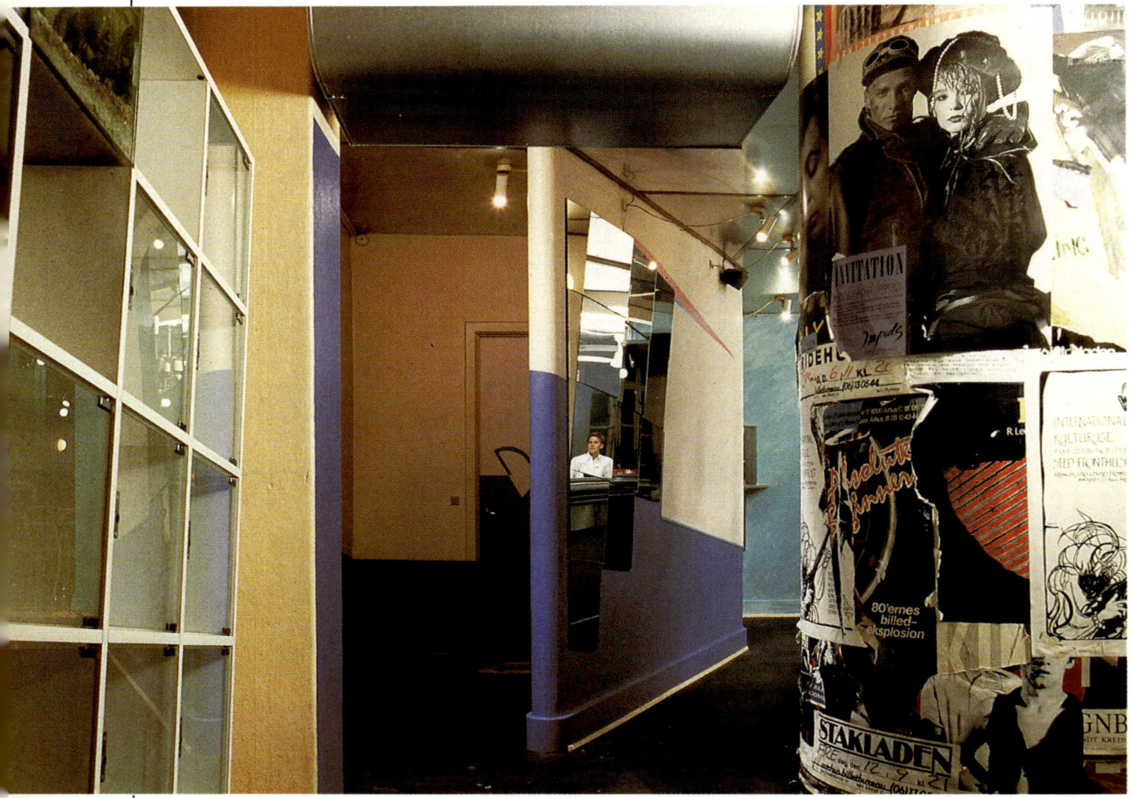

(left) Angled elements such as the mirror and the shelving unit, complete with goldfish in one glass compartment, define the circulation route.

positioning of both tables and lamps in the main room determine the circulation around the café. This path also leads visitors to the small triangular dance floor.

Tønsager carefully co-ordinated the colours throughout the café to reinforce the route of circulation. The walls are mainly yellow and pink, but an ultramarine blue is intended to lead visitors around the bar to a light green wall, which marks the end of the path. A painting technique has been used in which the upper layer is applied with light brush strokes then rubbed out or spread with the brush. Since the wear and tear on the café is enormous (with up to 350 people crowding into the small space on a busy night), this technique enables easy renewal of worn areas.

The ceiling in the bar is made from an old aluminium ceiling, with some bits cut out and a new profile of aluminium to describe the area of the bar. Chairs are classic wood café chairs, and the tables are made with Perstorp laminate. Café Paradis, with its designed suggestions of the unexpected, the slightly anarchic, provides an ideal escape from the order and reserve often found in Denmark.

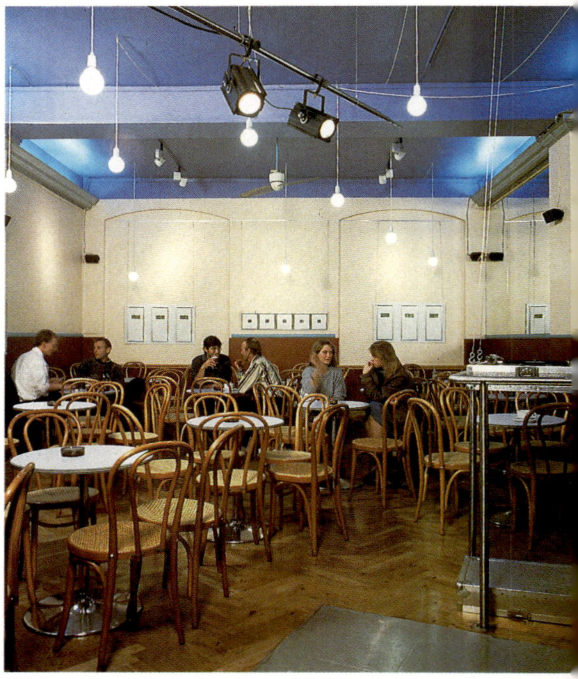

Tables and chairs are classic café furniture, arranged to leave space for a tiny triangular dance floor.

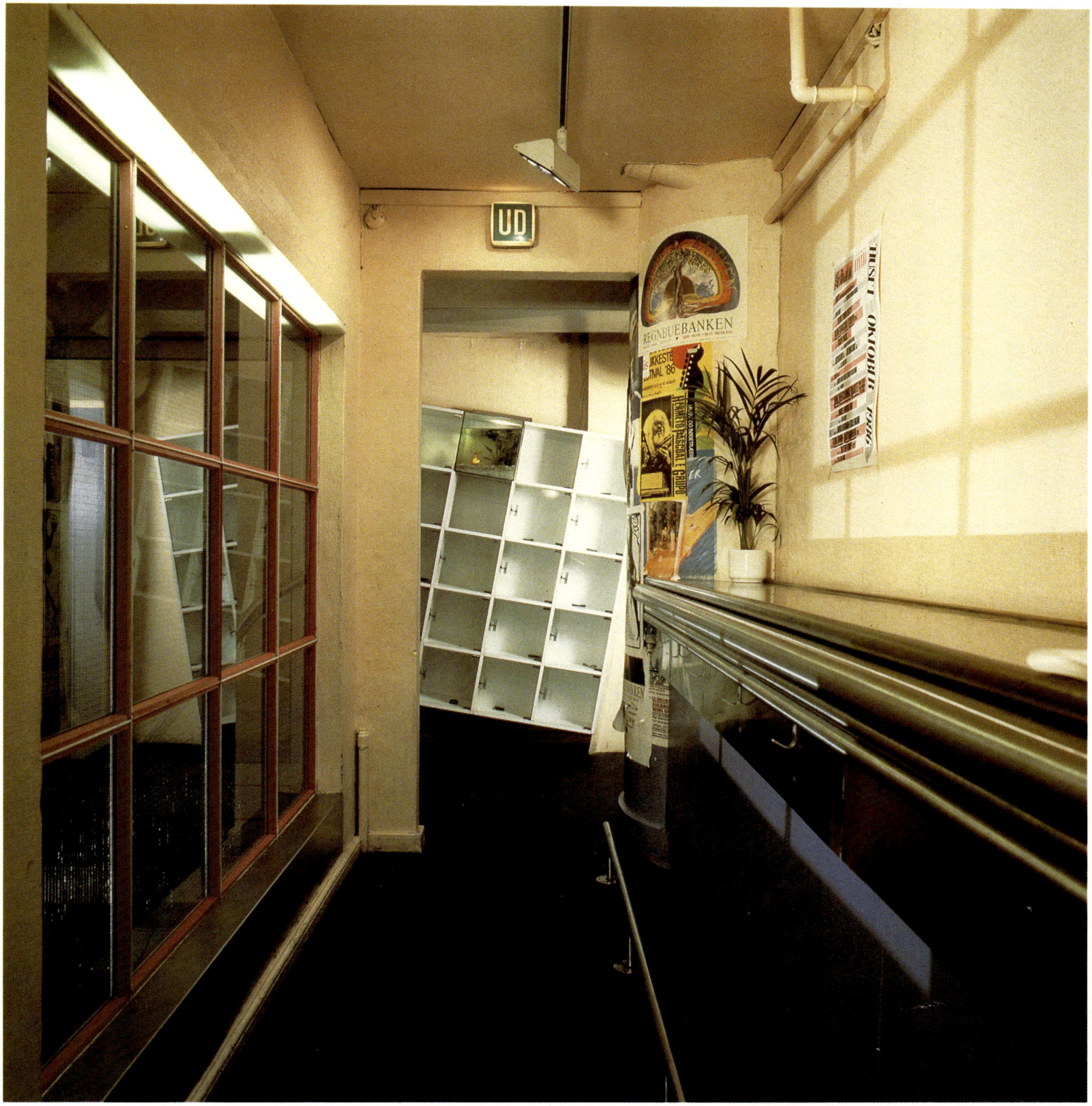

The centrepiece of the design, the aluminium profiled bar, is intended to be 'an eyecatcher from all angles'.

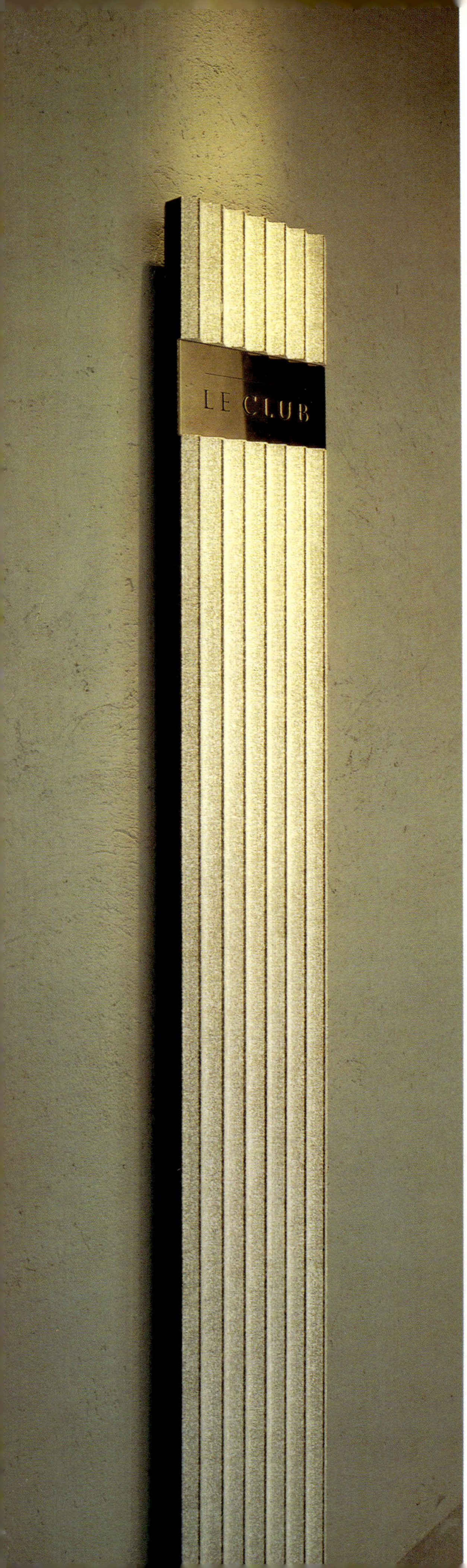

LE CLUB
TOKYO, JAPAN

Designed by Shigeru Uchida and Studio 80

It is difficult to imagine the following brief being given in any country but Japan: a bar counter with a shelf to stock three hundred bottles, and spaces for flower arrangements. That was the starting point for Shigeru Uchida's Le Club, a Tokyo bar.

The bottles are an impressive sight, illuminated by spotlights and stretching along a whole wall. Facing it, a row of columns form little alcoves for the flowers. These two elements, bottles and flowers, provide the only sources of colour in an otherwise monochromatic interior, although there are contrasts of texture. The black table tops and bar counter, for example, have a glossy polyurethane finish, while the walls are clad in grey granite, either simply polished smooth or ribbed, horizontally and vertically. Spotlights on the vertical ribs create the illusion of another row of columns made of light and shade.

As might be expected from Uchida, a furniture designer with his own showroom called Chairs, the tubular steel bar stools were specially designed. Combined with the complex lines and imaginative use of materials, they make this an interior of classical elegance.

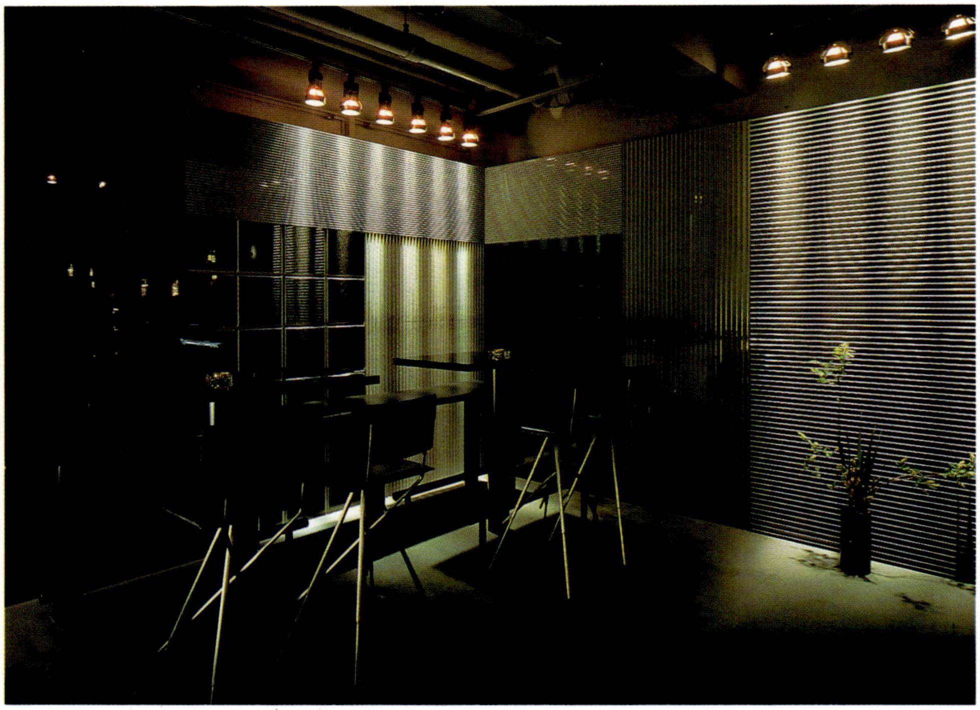

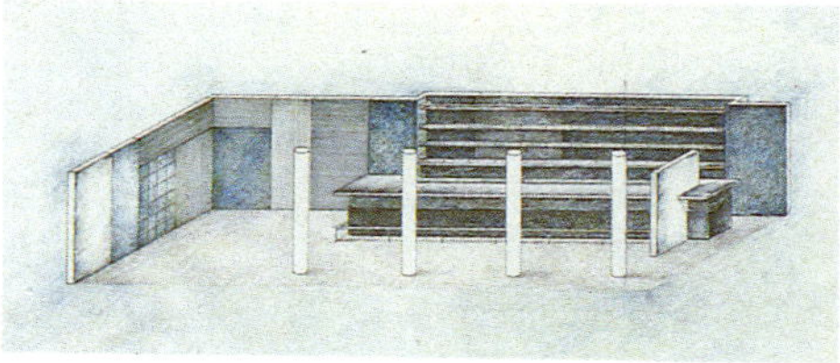

(above) The plan is straightforward and uncluttered, leaving the long bar as the main element.

(far left) A flattened ribbed column and minimal graphics announce the elegant interior.

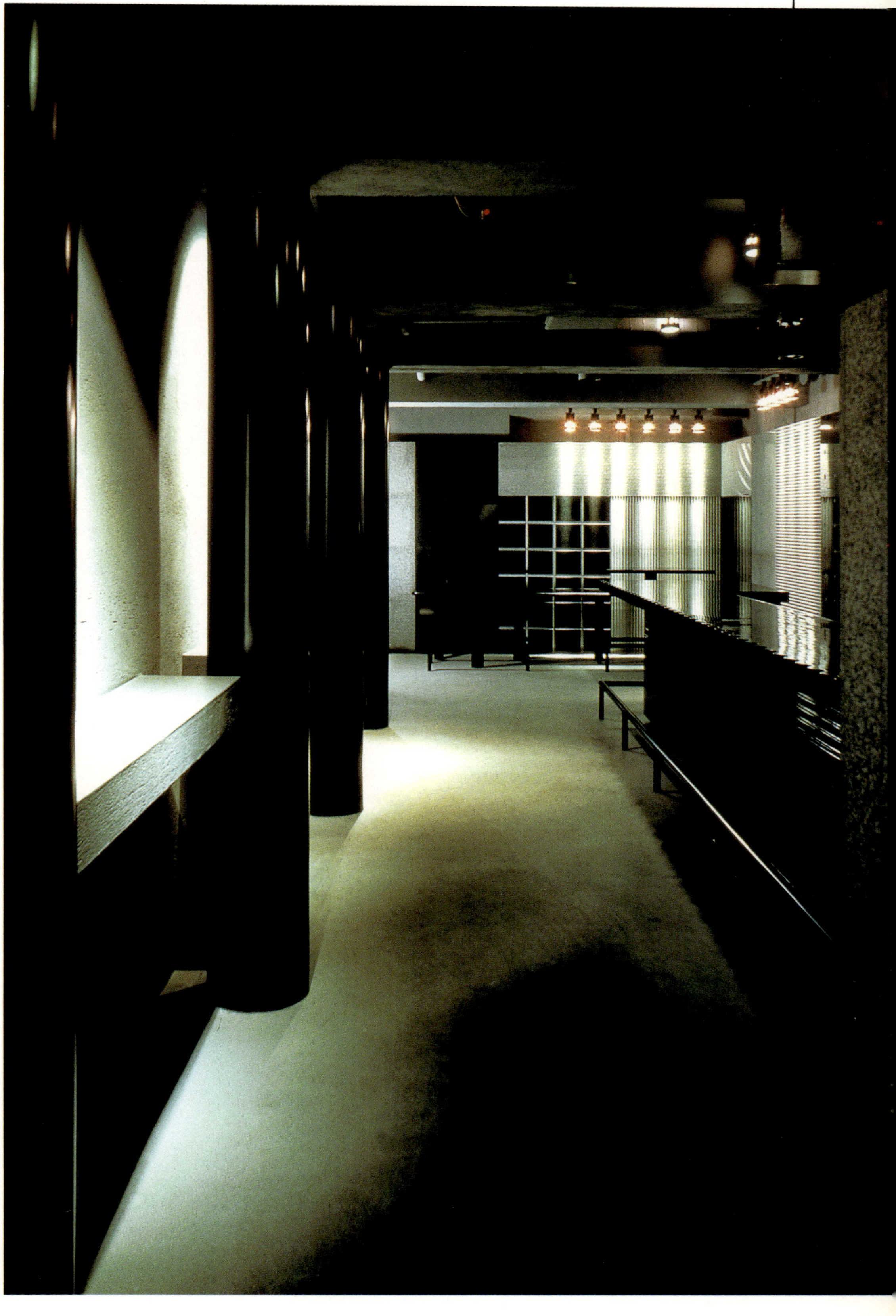

(left) Materials are used imaginatively to provide contrasts of texture, with ribbed grey granite walls and smooth black surfaces for the bar and table tops. Spotlights add further contrasts with alternating bands of light and shade.

(right) Opposite the bar, black columns provide niches for flower arrangements. Apart from the bottles, they are the only source of colour in a monochrome interior.

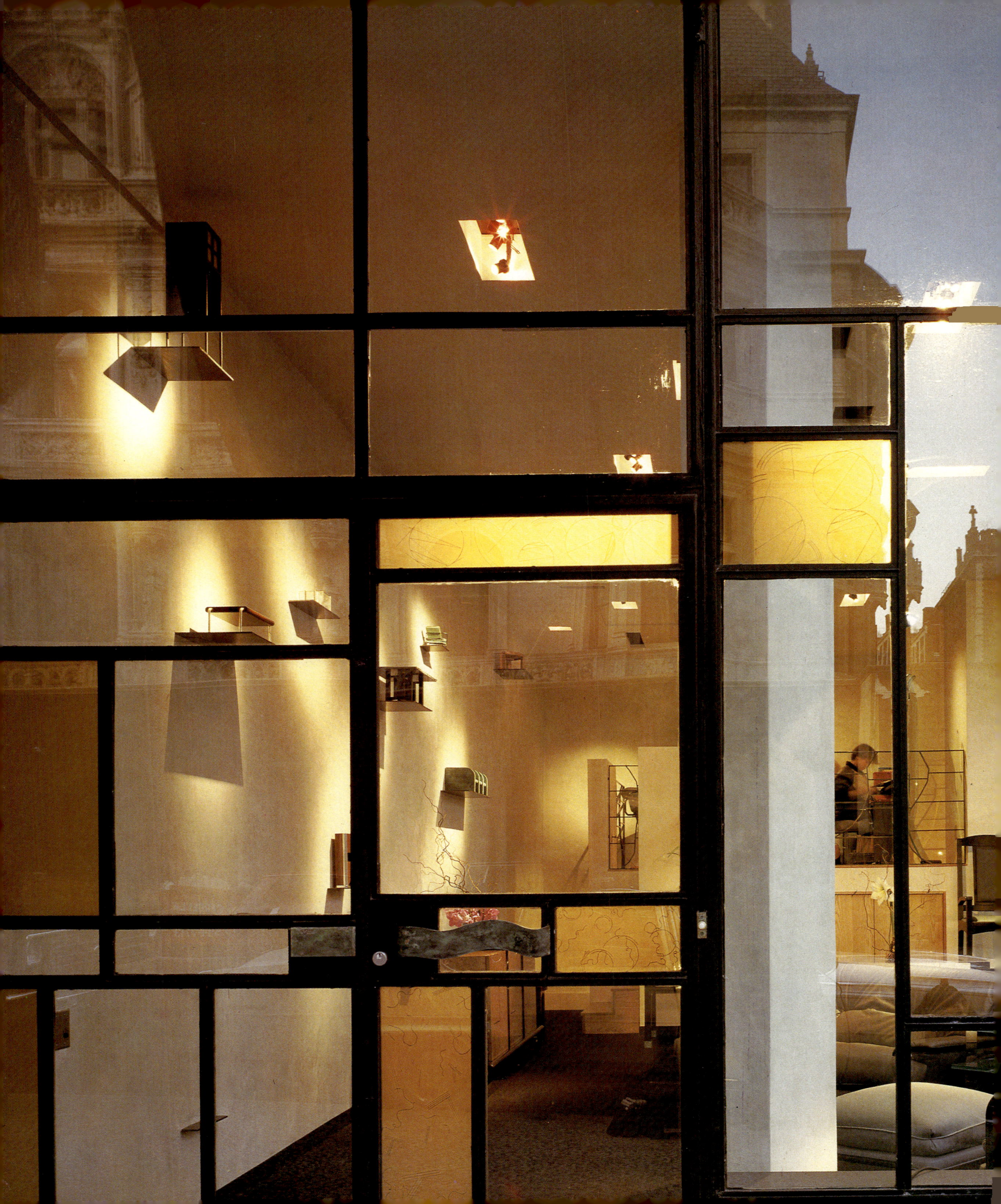

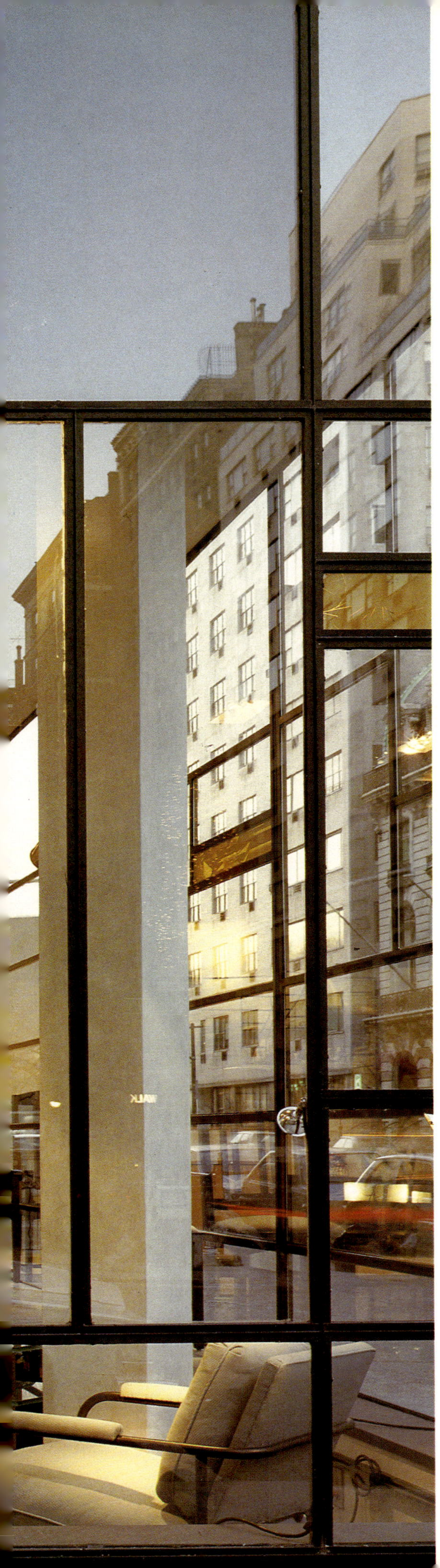

STORES

Armstrong Chipperfield Issey Miyake, London, UK

Chipperfield Associates Equipment, Paris, France

Coop Himmelblau Passage Wahliss, Vienna, Austria

Max Dudler and Karl Dudler Menswear, West Berlin, West Germany

Joseph Paul D'Urso with Bentley LaRosa Salasky Gullans International, Long Island City, USA

Fitch & Co. Esprit du Vin, London, UK

Fitch & Co. Midland Bank, Bristol, UK

Foster Associates Katharine Hamnett, London, UK

Gregotti Associati Cashmere Cotton & Silk, Milan, Italy

Steven Holl Architects The Pace Collection, New York City, USA

Naoki Iijima Ex Jun Boutique, Kôbe, Japan

Setsuo Kitaoka Takeo Kikuchi, Tokyo, Japan

Yasuo Kondo The Gallery of Lanerossi, Tokyo, Japan

Shiro Kuramata Issey Miyake, Kôbe, Japan

Leo Design Rahikainen Furs, Helsinki, Finland

Peter Leonard Associates W H Smith, Southampton, UK

Masaki Morita Eight Star Diamond, Tokyo, Japan

Schwartz/Silver Architects Domain, Chestnut Mill, Massachusetts, USA

Sottsass Associati Esprit de Corp, Düsseldorf, Cologne, Berlin, Melbourne

Tigerman Fugman McCurry Formica Corporation Showroom, Chicago, Illinois, USA

Masanori Umeda Yamato, Tokyo, Japan

More and more, clients are recognizing that the design of their stores or showrooms can be a competitive tool. Space at The Pace Collection on Madison Avenue, New York, is so limited that only a few items of furniture can be displayed, but Steven Holl's amber-set window-walls ensure maximum visibility and effect.

ISSEY MIYAKE
LONDON, UK

Designed by Armstrong Chipperfield

When Armstrong Chipperfield were asked to design a store in Sloane Street, London, for fashion designer Issey Miyake, they had the task of creating an environment that would show off the clothes to their best advantage without distracting the customer; at the same time it was to be in no way anonymous.

The designer's solution was one that concentrated on the store's most important elements: that is, the clothes rails and other display areas, the changing-rooms and the seating. To do this, they conceived two axes emanating from the existing street façade – the shorter of these ending at the side of the dressing-rooms, the longer raised above sidewalk level by two steps near the entrance, extending along the store's entire 52½ foot (16 metre) depth. The result is that, from street level – with nothing to obscure the view inside except for the words 'Issey Miyake' turned on their side on the glass door – the most noticeable feature of the interior is the single metal hanging rail which stretches along one inside wall. The wide-open spaces of the store are unashamedly intimidatory for the less fashionable shopper.

Throughout the store, the materials used are mostly natural – wood, stone and marble – and colours are predominantly pale and neutral – grey and white – though with touches of dark blue. The flooring, for example, is Portland stone or, in places, sycamore; a bench for visitors is also in sycamore; the buffer wall between the main retail area and the changing cubicles is in grey-white marble; and a ripple-effect table top made by John Harwood has been carved from a single piece of wood. The suspended ceiling is in fibrous plaster.

At the far right end of the store, interlocking partitions of painted timber provide six changing-rooms. The designers' treatment of this area contrasts sharply with that given to the rest of the interior: in each compartment, dark blue canvas is stretched and held in tension to form a seat. The walls here were painted by artist Sally Greaves-Lord in a rich dark blue. Sand-blasted glass panels ensure privacy, and a section of the canvas can be pulled down to act as a curtain. The atmosphere is intentionally far more intimate and intense than in the open, light and spacious environment of the store proper.

What unifies the different aspects of this interior is the quality of the materials and of the specially commissioned fixtures and fittings. Miyake does not design middle-of-the-road, high-street clothes, and Armstrong Chipperfield have ensured that his store leaves no one in any doubt about that.

(below) Almost all the clothes are displayed on a single hanging rail which stretches along the shop's entire 52½ foot (16 metre) depth.

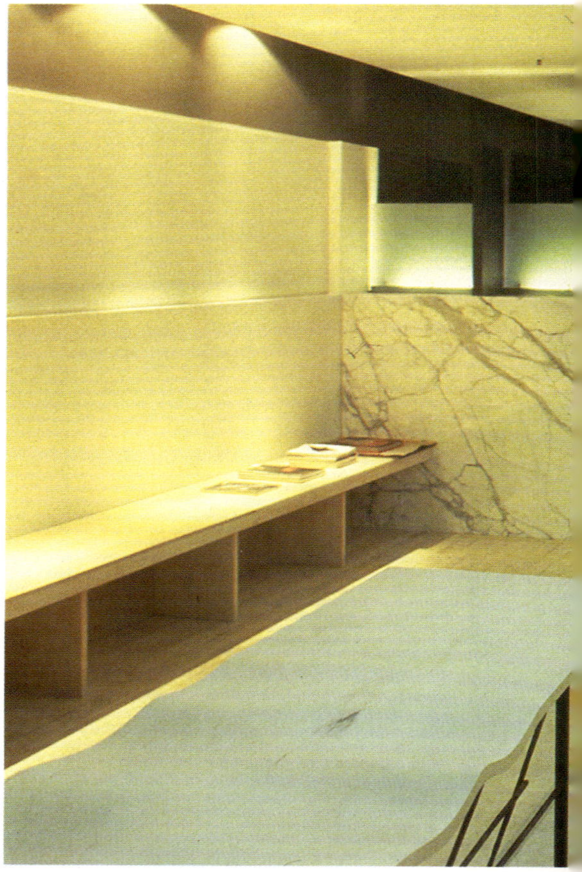

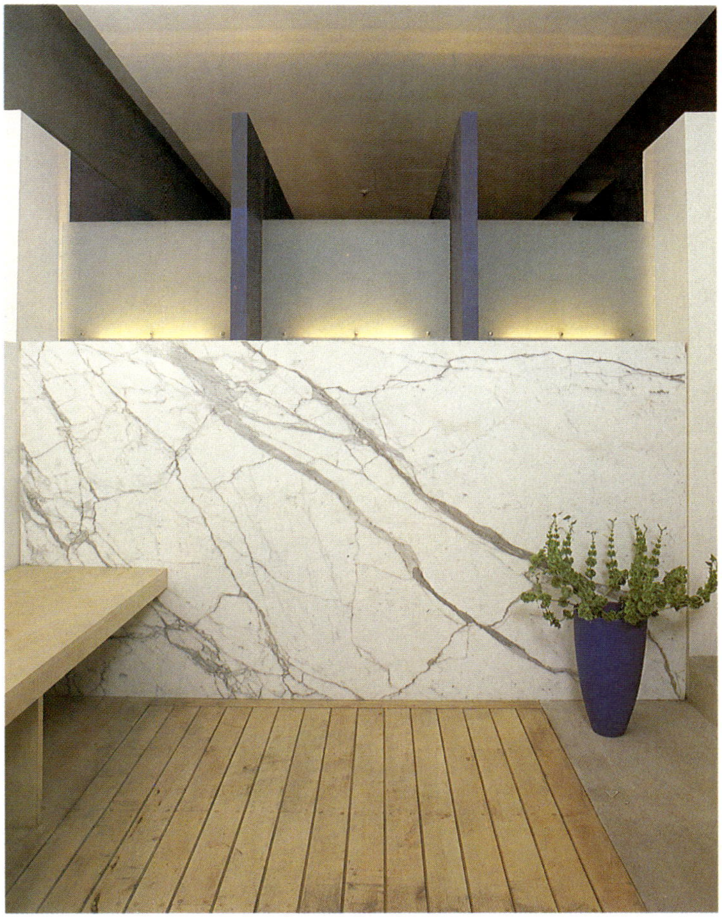

(left) In the main sales area, materials are predominantly natural and neutral in colour: a buffer wall is in grey-white granite, while the flooring is either in Portland stone or sycamore.

(below) Painted deep purplish-blue, with blue stretched canvas seats, the changing-rooms introduce a rare splash of colour.

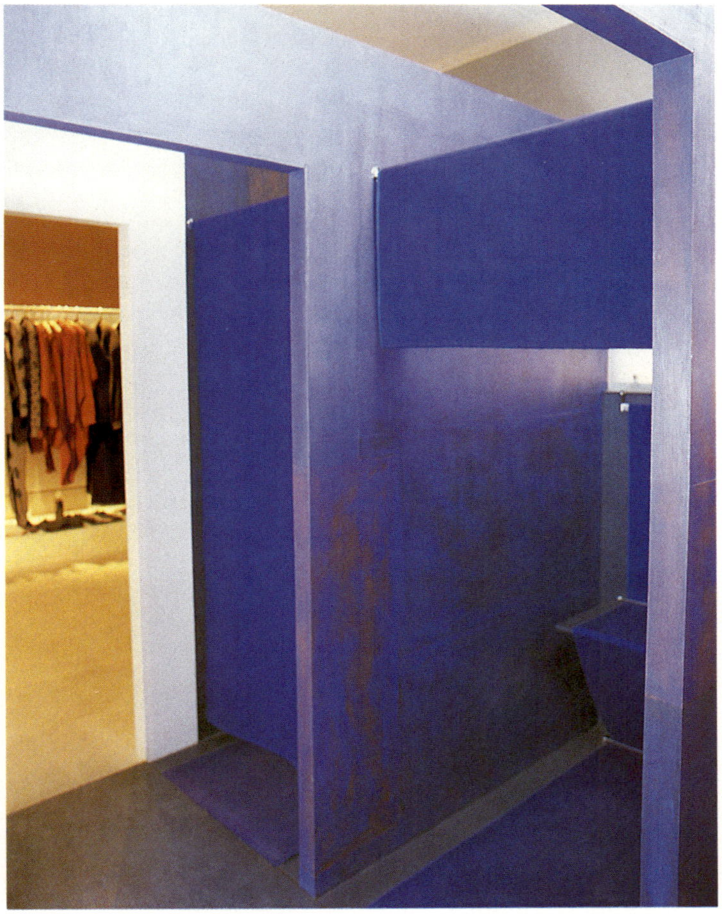

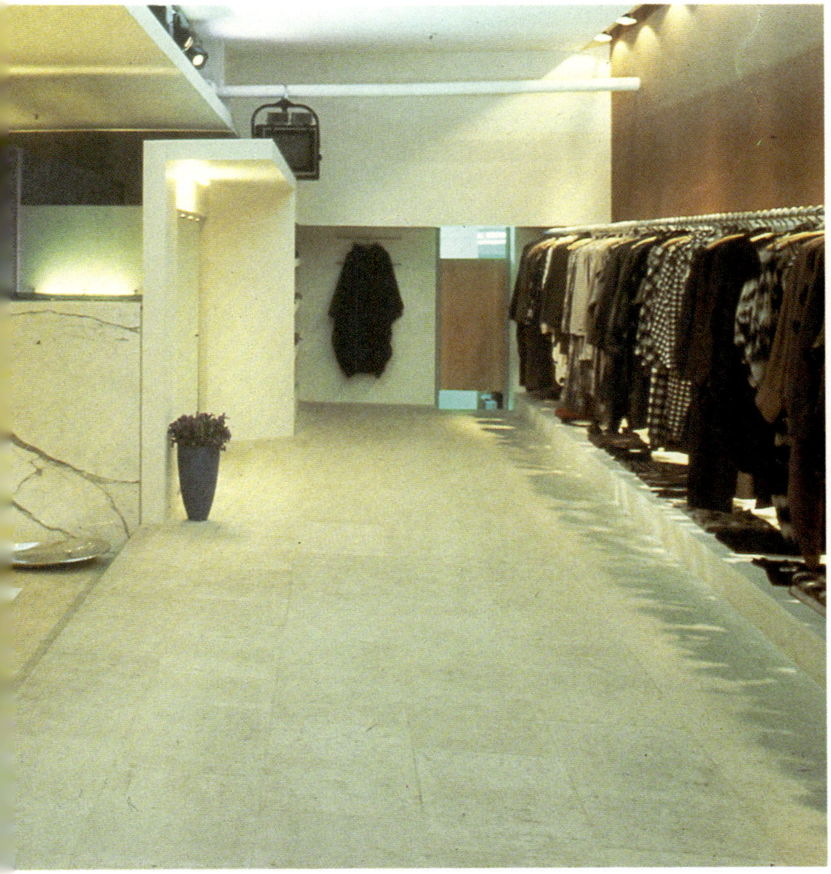

EQUIPMENT

PARIS, FRANCE

Designed by Chipperfield Associates

When Equipment wanted to transform a brasserie on Paris's fashionable rue Etienne Marcel into their new one-item store, they turned – despite cross-Channel distances – to the British practice Chipperfield Associates.

On a corner, the site was small, boasting only one window looking on to the street, and only one door. However, since Equipment sell nothing but shirts, there was no call for the usual hanging rails, bulky gondolas or any other cumbersome item of display. What was needed above all was an effective and practical shelving system; this was therefore specially designed by Chipperfield, made in prototype in London, and shipped over to Paris. In fact, the shelving system has become a major feature of the interior. A timber 'wall' supports three shelves which run the whole length of the unit; beneath are drawers for the storage of additional merchandise. Each shelf is made up of two thin aluminium slats, with a small air-gap behind to allow light to penetrate. Only the very minimum of stock – three or four shirts to a pile at most – is on show, and any of the sense of overcrowding that might have been expected in so restricted a space has therefore been studiously avoided.

Other than the shelving system, the designers' major invention at Equipment is the partitioning wall. About 6½ feet (2 metres) high, it curves from the changing-rooms at the back of the store, extends behind the shelving and then curls round the cash-desk. (This desk, like everything else at Equipment, was specially designed and made for the project; it has an extension flap which gives staff the room to wrap or re-fold shirts with ease.) Above the desk, the soffit of the suspended ceiling conceals downlights, which wash the wall and accentuate its curve. Additional lighting comes from a row of uplighters positioned behind the single display window. Flooring, like the shelf unit, is in pale sycamore, and the walls are painted white.

Finally, the changing-rooms have been designed very simply: placed behind the shelf unit, they consist of nothing but a mirror on one wall and a red drape that serves as a curtain. Chipperfield seem content, as in their work for Issey Miyake (see pp. 138–9), to allow simplicity and small details to make a design statement.

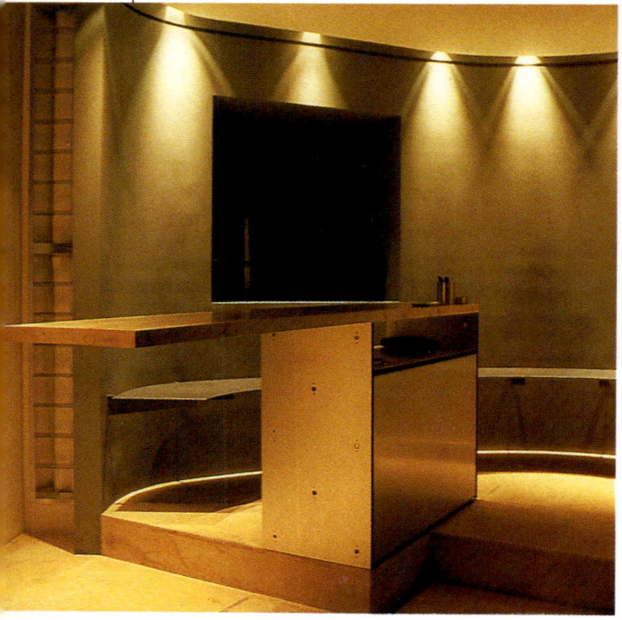

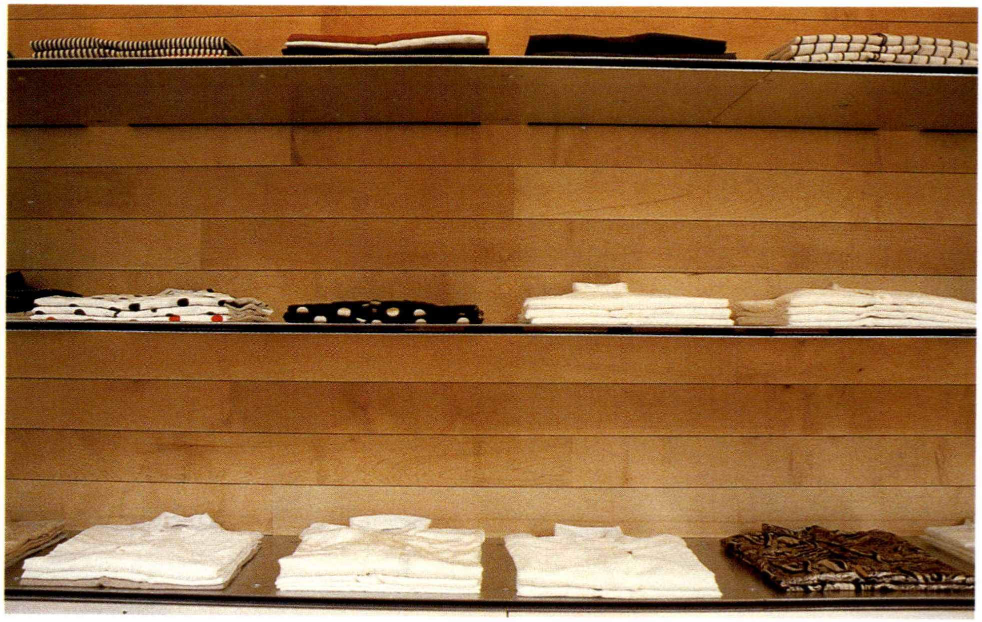

(below far left) Lighting is cleverly used to accentuate the curved timber wall behind the cash-desk which is the main feature of the interior.

(below left) Each shelf is made up of two aluminium slats; a small air-gap allows light to penetrate.

(right) Working with such a limited amount of space, the designers had to reject conventional means of displaying the clothes.

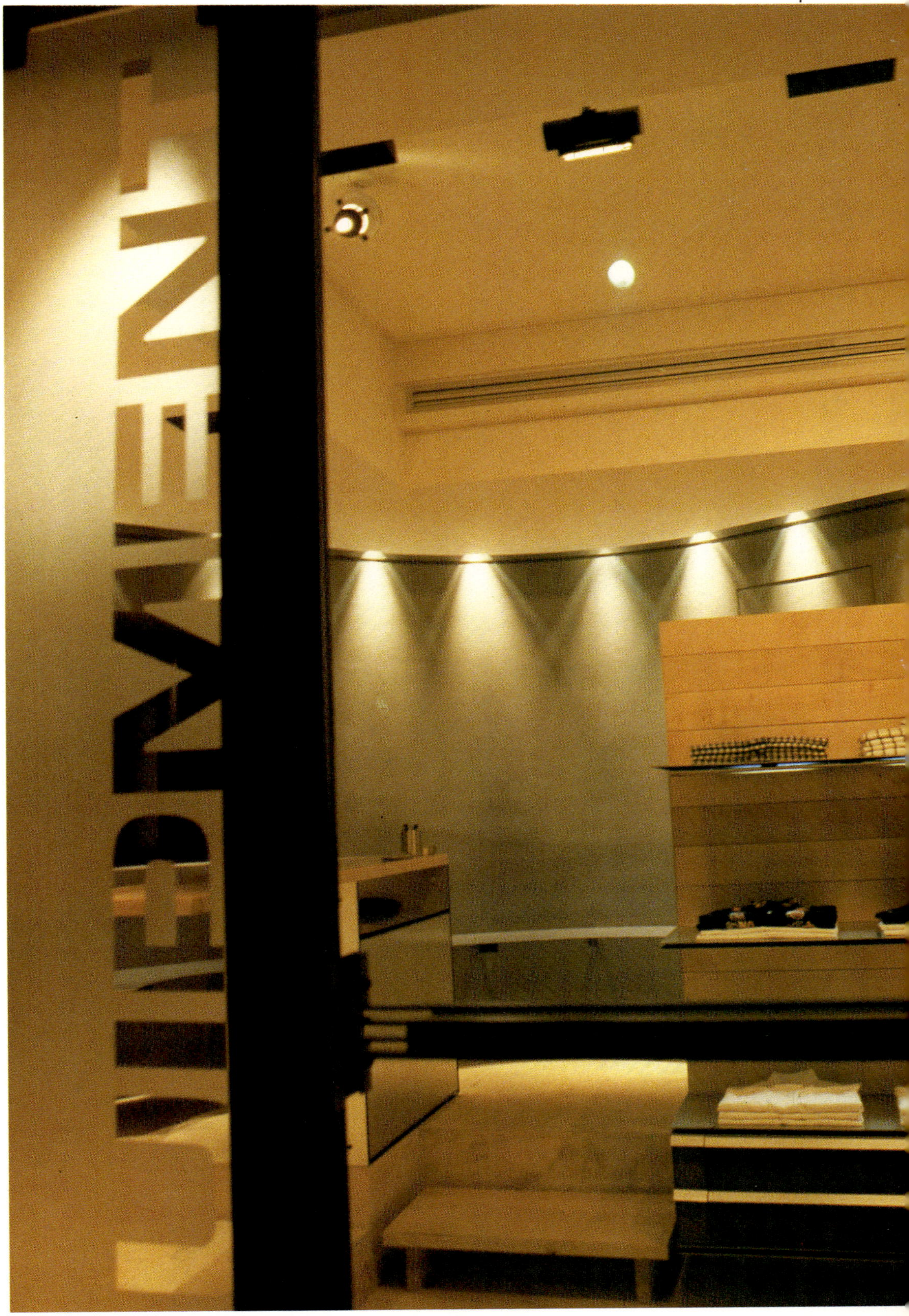

PASSAGE WAHLISS
VIENNA, AUSTRIA

Designed by Coop Himmelblau

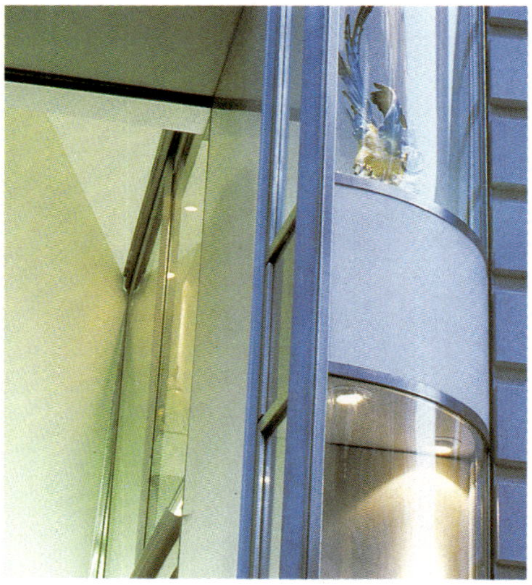

Coop Himmelblau is one of a small band of designers in Vienna who continue to extend the bounds of convention in a very hide-bound city. Their projects are highly abstract and rely on complex, sometimes seemingly random, geometric elements for their effect.

Passage Wahliss is a scheme that involved the reordering of the entrance passage to the Wahliss porcelain store on the Kartnerstrasse, Vienna's main shopping street. Wahliss seems an unlikely client for Coop Himmelblau; it was established in 1879, and the products of the company are still very traditional. But the commission was given to Coop Himmelblau in the hope that a new design would draw customers down the passage off the street and provide a new store window for the company.

The passage is 49 feet (15 metres) long and 13 feet (4 metres) wide, but the parallel display windows gradually expand from an initial 6½ foot (2 metre) depth to a full 13 feet (4 metres) by the time the entrance has been reached. The store is announced by a wing that has apparently crashed through the façade and carried on into the passageway at an angle. In this designed collision, chunks of the entrance to the passage seem to have been sliced away.

Geometry is everything in this design, for the materials are unexceptional: sand-blasted aluminium profiles, steel, marble for the floor and Corian for the façade elements. But it will have to be a very incurious pedestrian who walks by Wahliss without wanting to look at what Coop Himmelblau's design conceals.

(right) A wing has apparently crashed through the façade, while chunks of the passage have been sliced away.

(above) A column of glass, lit from inside, allows for display in a small space.

(below) Floor plan.

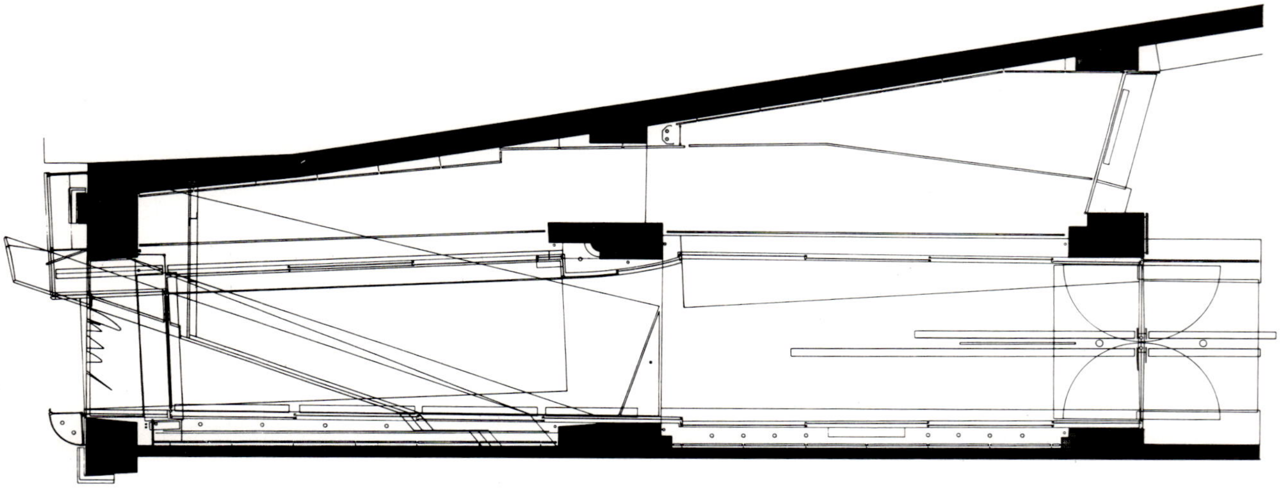

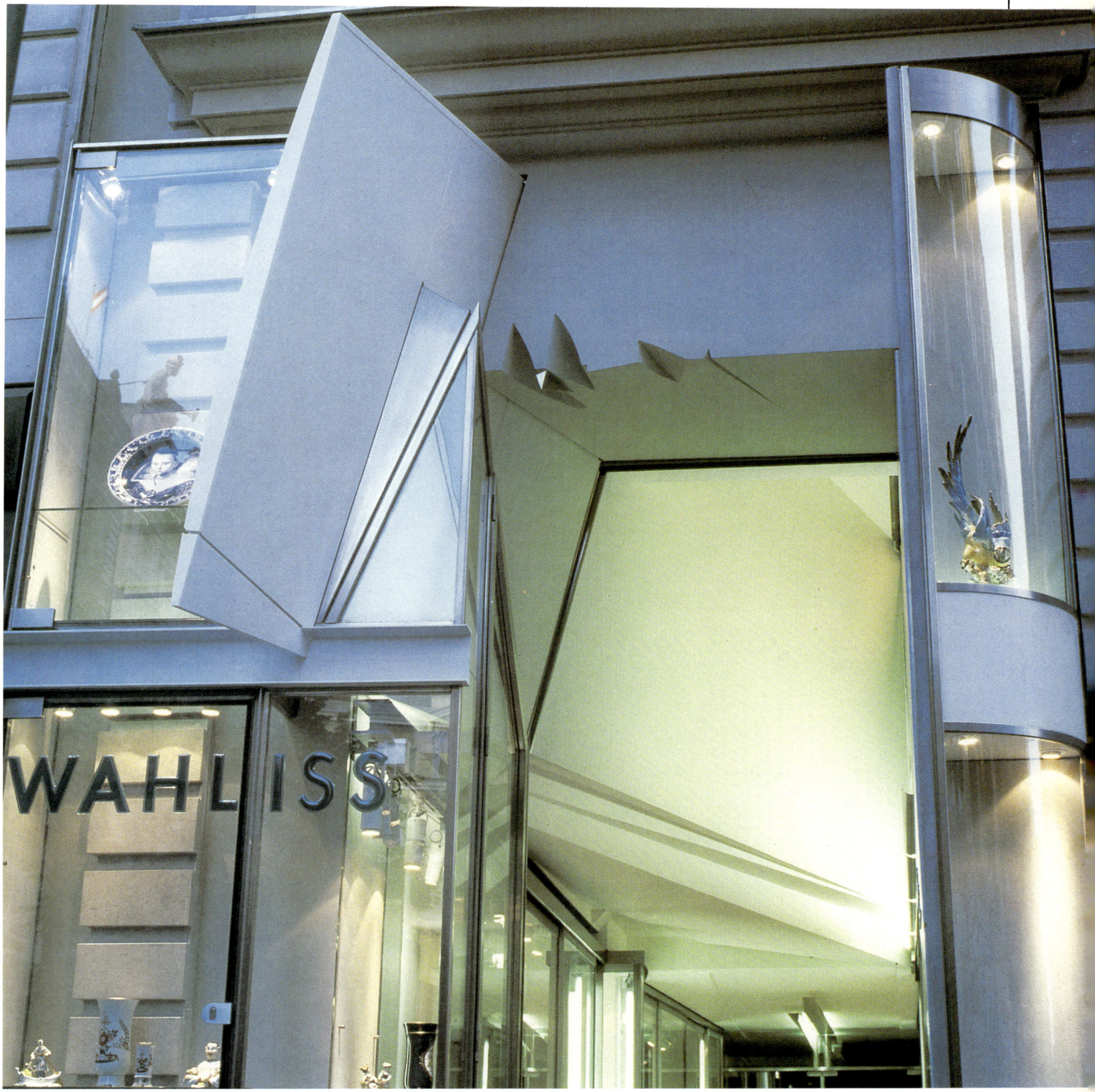
WAHLISS

MENSWEAR
WEST BERLIN, WEST GERMANY

Designed by Max Dudler and Karl Dudler

In all of their work, the Dudlers strive for some sense of order, preferring the rectilinear over the curved, the axial path over the meandering one. In this Berlin clothes store, their preference has been exploited with complete conviction and attention to detail to create an elegant interior.

The store is organized around a series of set-piece rooms, but with views through the *en filade* arrangement of arched openings. In these vistas, a change of mood – and of merchandise – is signalled by small touches: the floor shifts from timber to marble, lighting moves from ceiling-mounted recessed downlighters to a flood of natural light in the rear *sanctum sanctorum*. Here, the regular grid of the marble floor is reflected in the ceiling grid, which carries the spotlights. Above, a long skylight provides the flood of natural light that entices customers through to this back room.

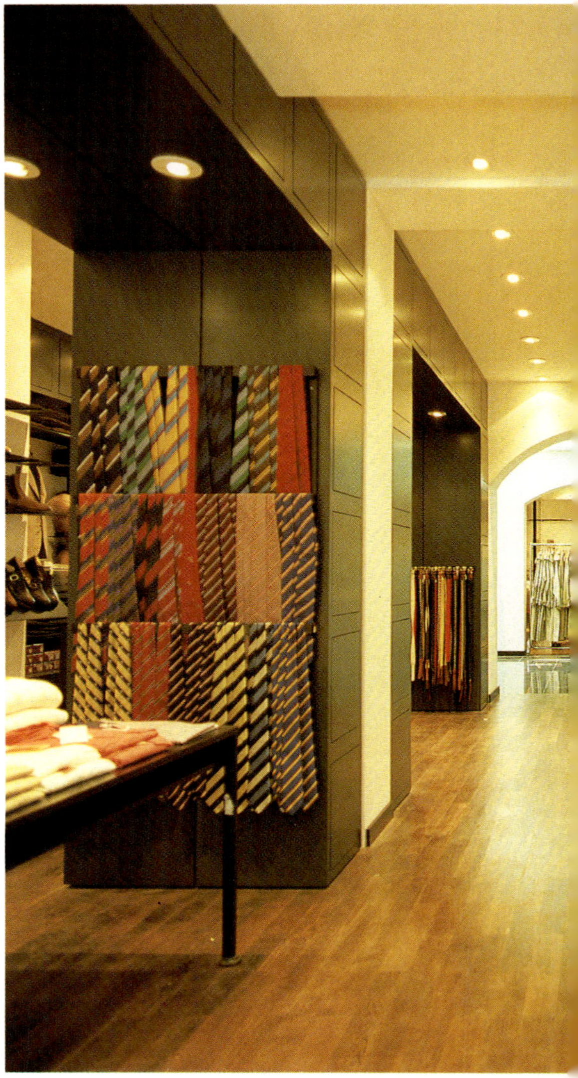

(right) Various sales areas are set off a central thoroughfare.

(far right) Lighting comes from discreet spotlights recessed in the ceiling.

(right above) A change of flooring – in this case from timber to marble – indicates a change of mood and of merchandise.

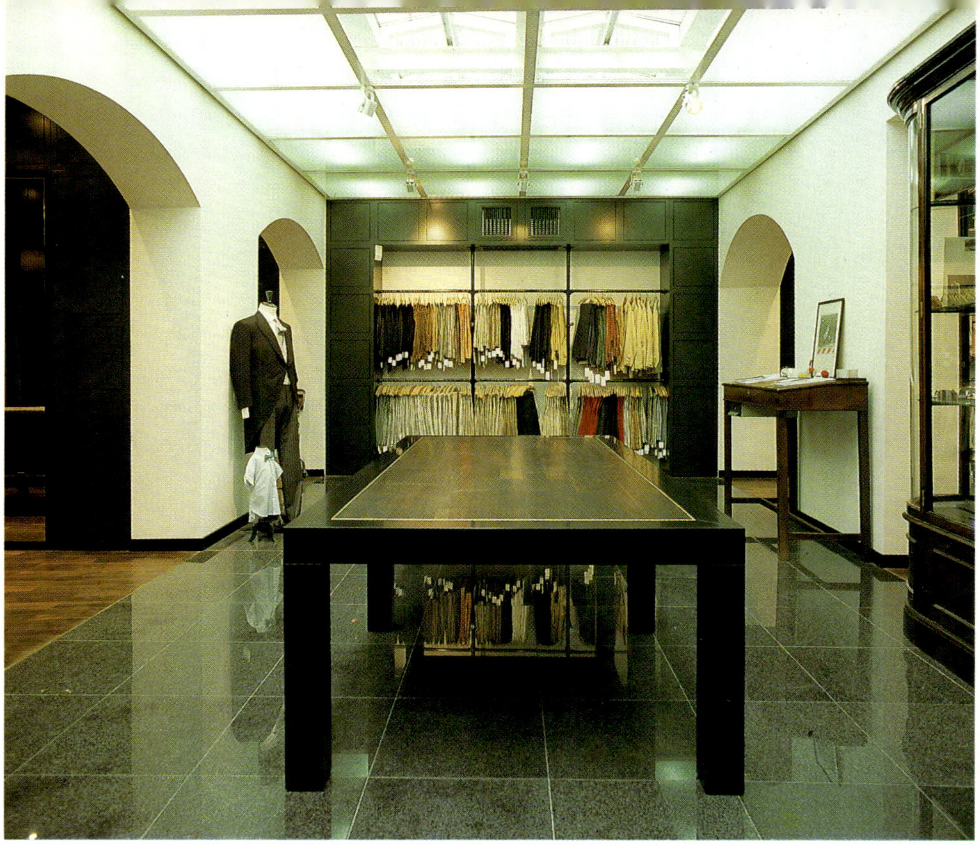

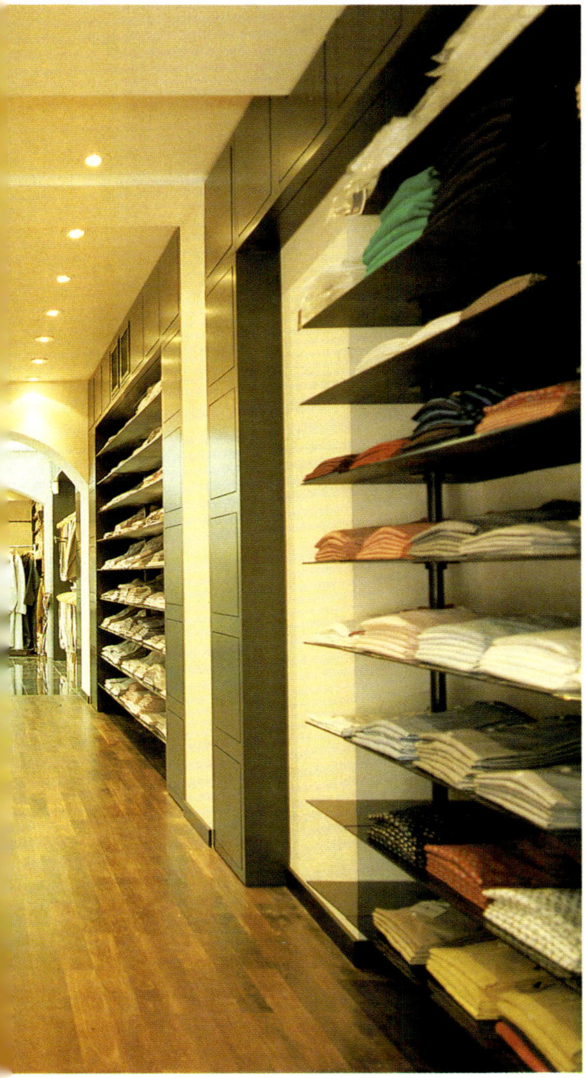

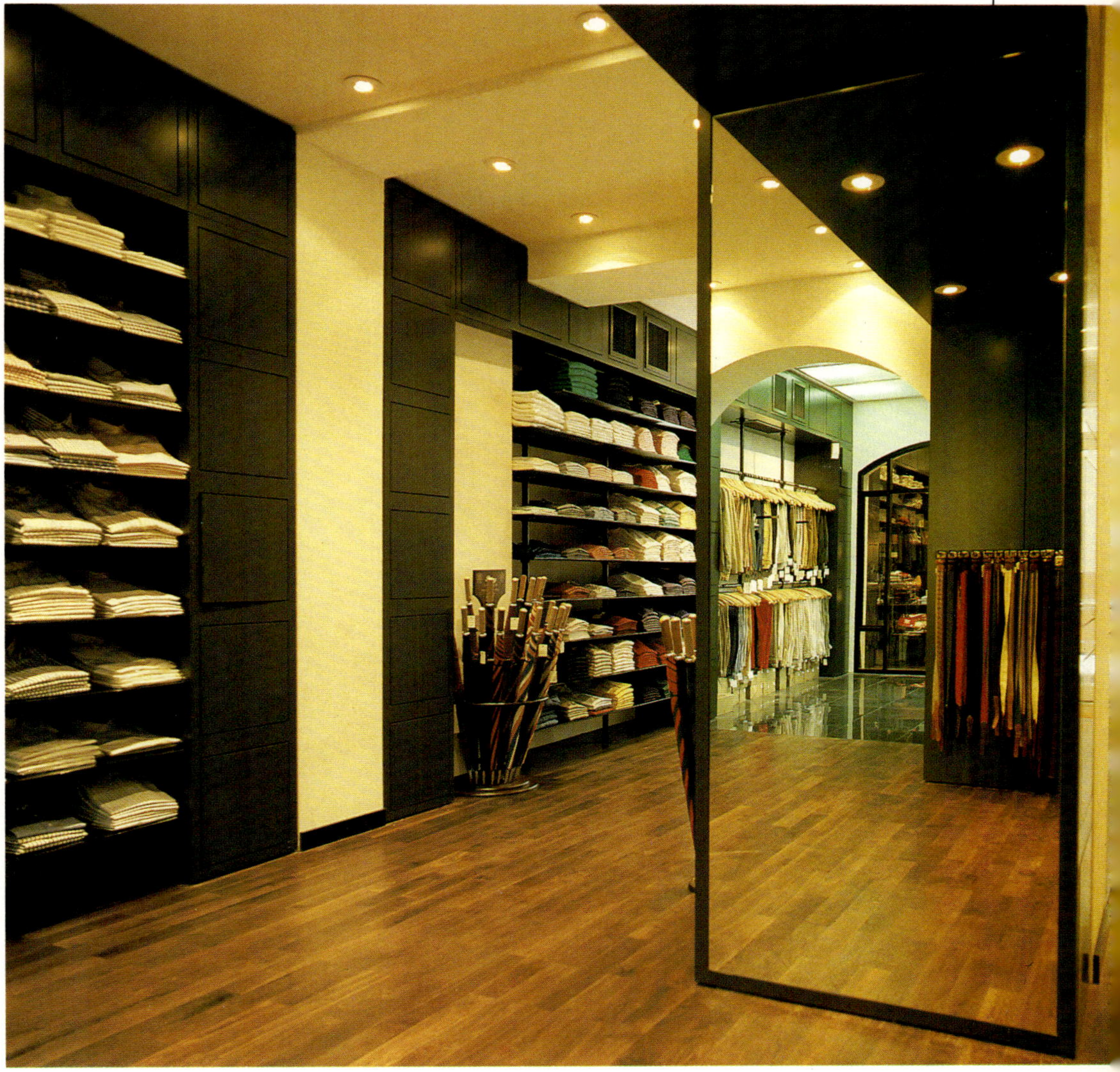

GULLANS INTERNATIONAL

LONG ISLAND CITY, USA

Designed by Joseph Paul D'Urso with Bentley LaRosa Salasky

Gullans International is in one of the designer trade marts that are springing up in cities across America (and in Europe). Filled with showrooms that mostly look alike, selling fairly similar furniture, trade marts allow designers to stick their necks out in the hope that their client will be noticed in the mob.

At the International Design Center, the designers had the advantage of a strong, existing industrial character, which, unlike many of the neighbouring showrooms, they elected to exploit. But in keeping with the smooth lines of the Italien Bieffeplast furniture that Gullans sell, the industrial aesthetic was tamed: concrete columns were sand-blasted and the concrete slab floor was filled, ground and waxed.

The 2,400 square foot (223 square metre) box of a space is animated by a large rectilinear enclosure for receptionist and staff and a bold, curving wall for the owner. Above, diagonal lighting tracks form an 'implied' ceiling 2 feet (0.6 metres) below the 12 foot (3.6 metre) ceiling slab. In the space between the tracks and the ceilings, the designers borrowed from the high-tech brigade to create an assemblage of ducts and red pipes.

Since the drama of the interior is meant to surprise visitors, a small display window looks on to the public corridor, allowing only a glimpse of what lies beyond. Designer Salvatore LaRosa explains this lure: 'Sometimes an ankle is sexier than a leg.'

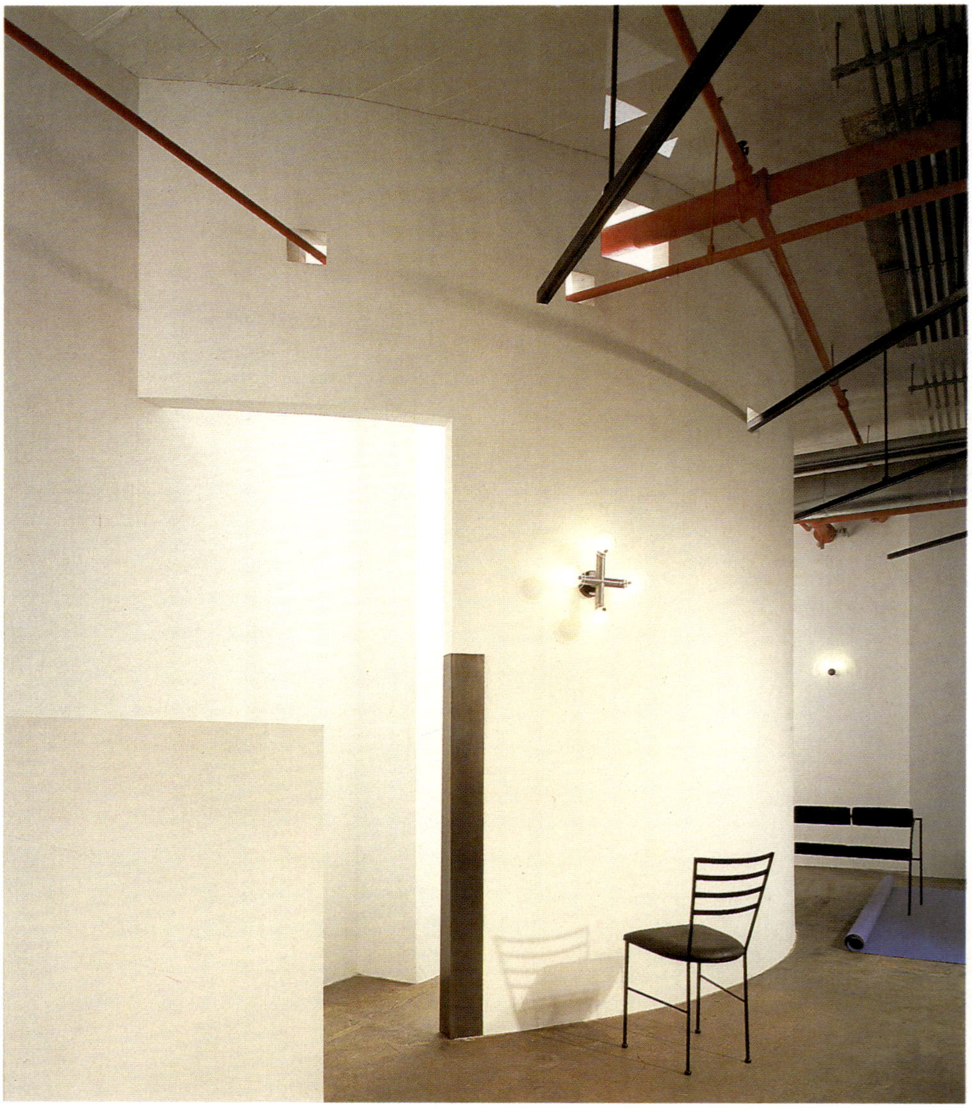

A curved wall has been introduced to bring animation into an otherwise box-shaped space.

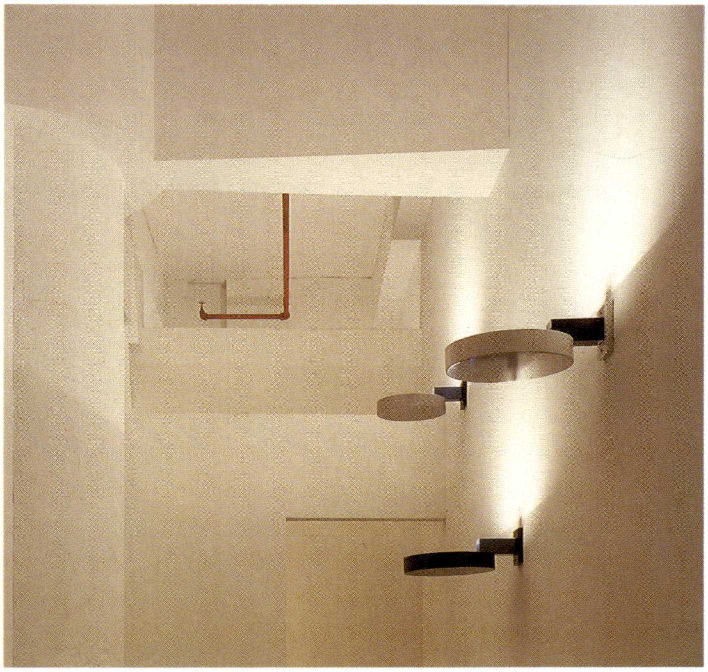

(left) Light is washed up on to the white walls of the corridor which leads into the showroom.

(below) To complement the sleek Italian furniture on sale, the somewhat rugged character of the building has been smoothed: concrete has been sand-blasted or waxed.

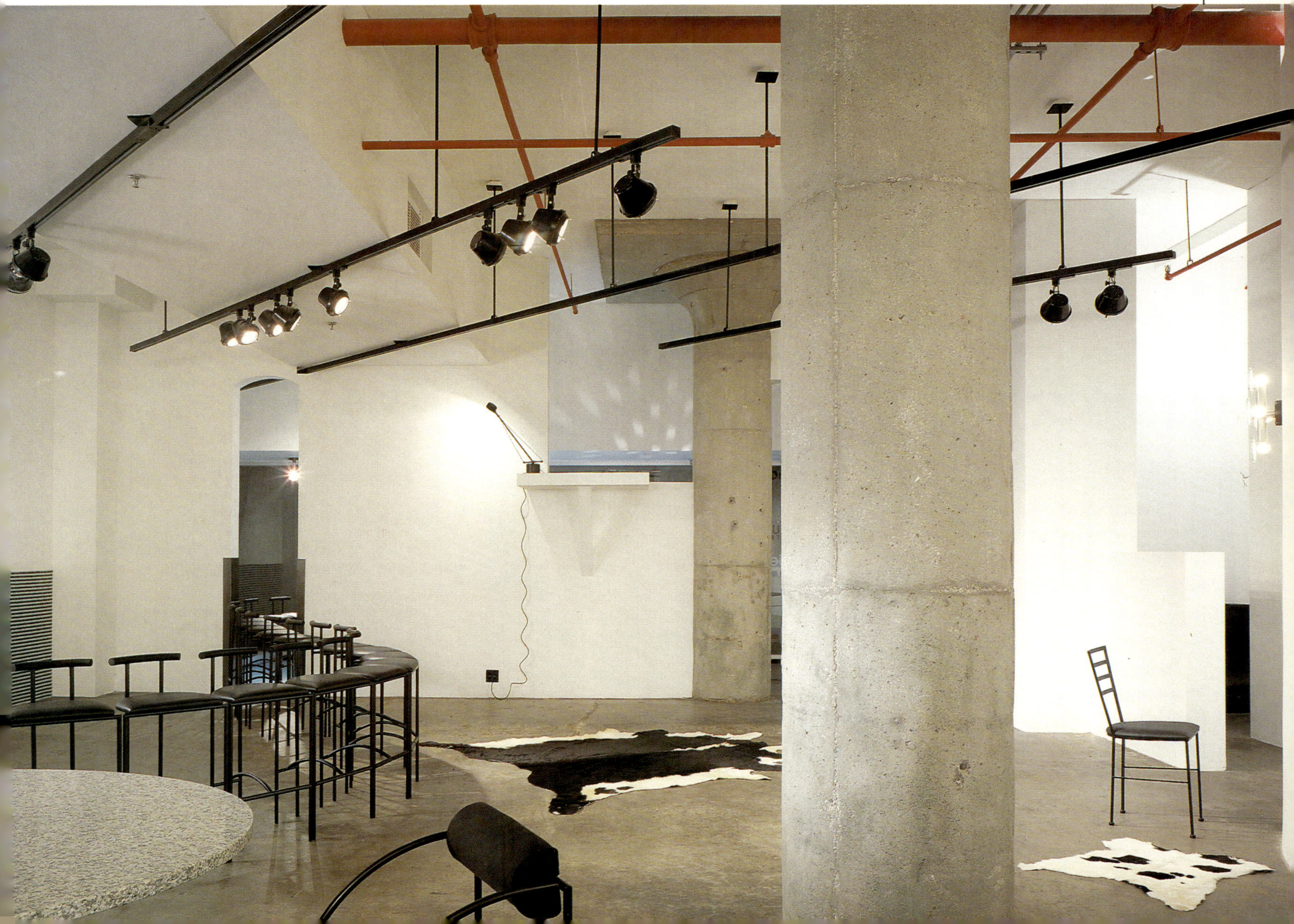

ESPRIT DU VIN
LONDON, UK

Designed by Fitch & Co.

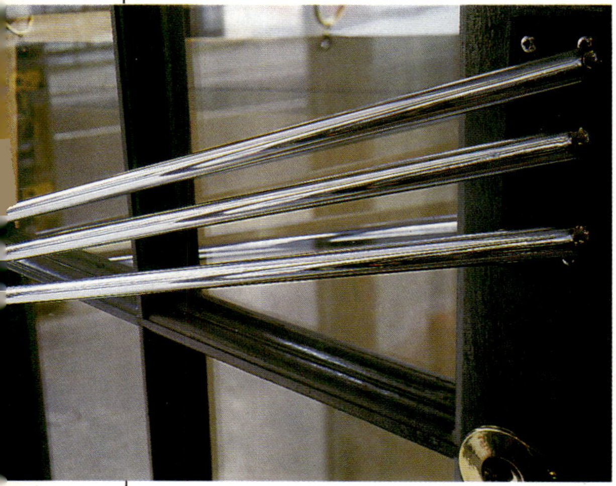

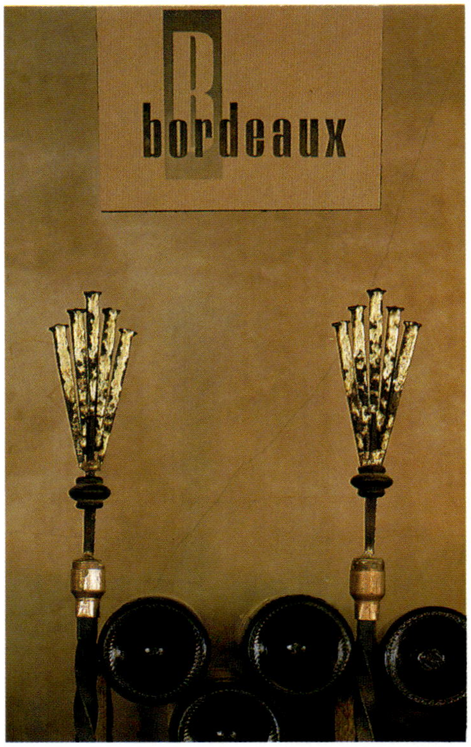

There has always been a yawning chasm between wine merchants and mass-market off-licence chains in Britain. The merchants offer fine wines in an atmosphere reeking of tradition, and usually not a little genteel decay. The chains, in contrast, are brash retailers, some perhaps with a reputation for well-chosen wines but all competing on price.

The giant brewery group Whitbread are owners of one of the largest off-licence chains, Threshers. Early in 1986, Whitbread approached Fitch & Co. with the idea that there was room in the market for something midway between the chain and the merchant. The design of Esprit du Vin, the upmarket chain that has resulted, owes little to either tradition. Bare floorboards may be reminiscent of some merchants, but the exposed plaster walls signal something else.

Even more surprising are the extraordinary metalworks by artist Tom Dixon. Described by some as a practitioner of 'post-holocaust baroque', Dixon produced three free-standing window display 'sculptures', each designed to hold twelve wine bottles. Bronze, steel, iron, masonry nails, Chinese ladles and a wok or two have been welded into a fantastical whole. Dixon was also responsible for the ornamental finials that top the interior shelves, as well as the 'jousting spears' from which hang details of the wine regions.

But the Dixon artworks are not incongruous bits of metal overlaid on a bland design. His finials sit atop twisted reinforcing rods that serve as the shelving structure (all this metal led the designers to use a blacksmith rather than a store-fitter for the shelving). A black tubular light fitting runs down the centre of the store, with bare bulbs hanging from the middle and low-voltage fittings shining against the walls, creating eerie shadows against the bare plaster.

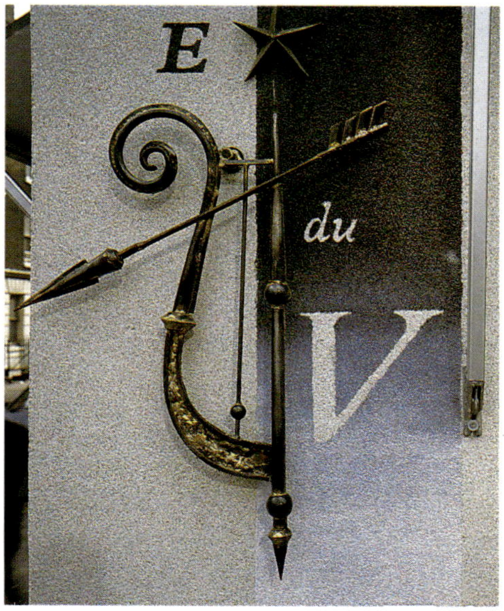

Wine bottles are stored both end-on and, for display, at 45 degrees to the vertical. Although the effect looks fairly uncluttered, between three and four hundred wines are housed in the store. Champagne is displayed on terrazzo-topped stands in the middle of the store, a prominent position which has had a consequent impact on sales. Despite some initial client reservations about the innovative design, the first Esprit du Vin in London's Marylebone has been so successful that Whitbread have commissioned a series of the stores for sites around the country.

(top left) At Esprit du Vin, attention to detail goes as far as the specially designed door furniture.

(left) The exterior graphics are the first indication that this is no neon-lit, supermarket-style off-licence chain.

(above) Most unexpected is the 'post-holocaust baroque' metalwork which was commissioned from Tom Dixon.

(right) Exposed wall surfaces, floorboards and bare light-bulbs give an earthy feel, rather reminiscent of a wine cellar or a cave.

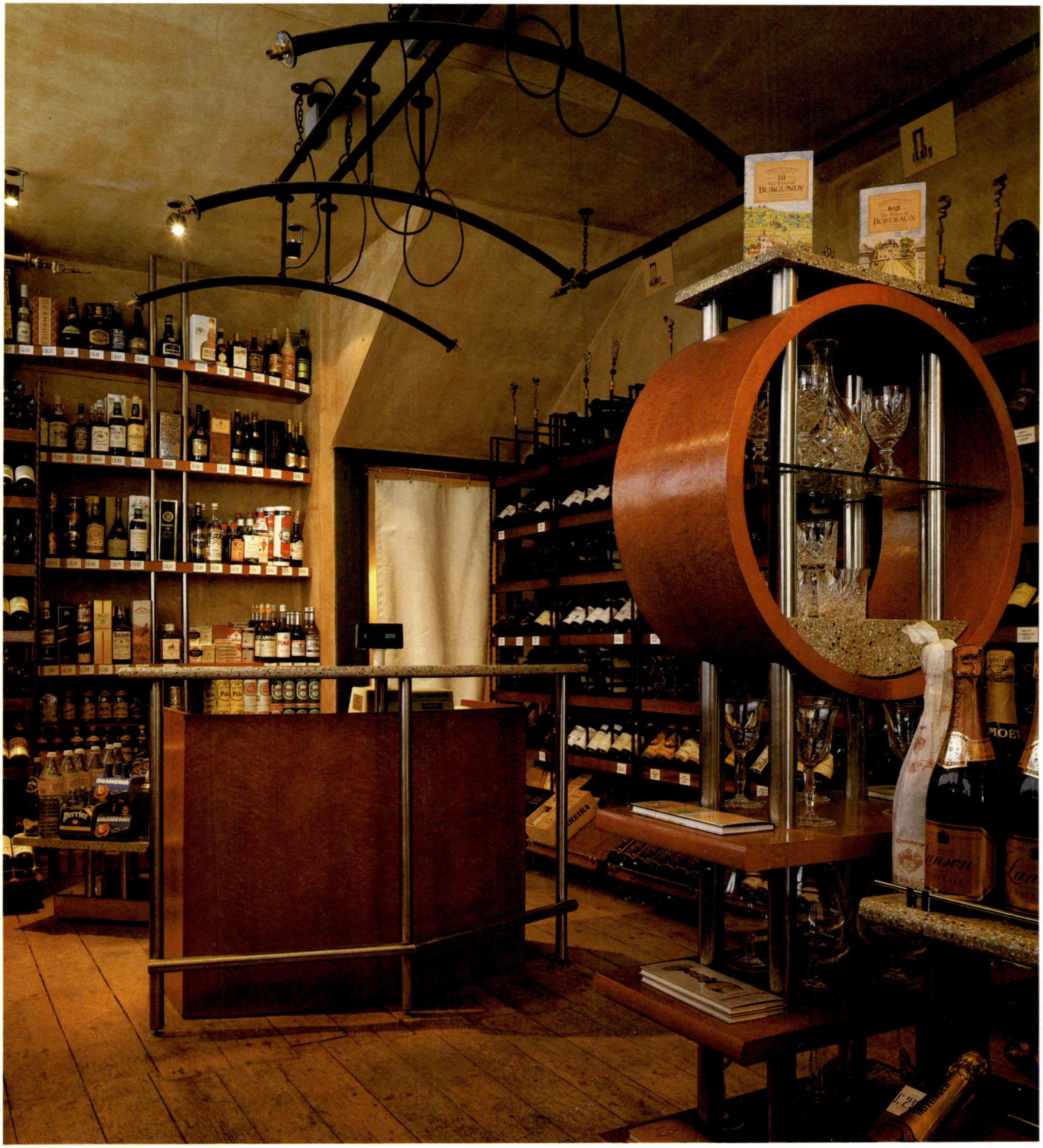
The Wines of BURGUNDY
The Wines of BORDEAUX
MOËT

MIDLAND BANK
BRISTOL, UK
Designed by Fitch & Co.

Banks have never enjoyed the liveliest of images – at best they are formal and unwelcoming, at worst downright stuffy and intimidating. Certainly, they are rarely thought of as light, open and inviting places. However, those adjectives could well describe Midland Bank's first high-street 'money store', which was designed for them by Fitch & Co. after some three years' collaboration with the bank's own branch development department.

The increased competition between banks, and also now building societies, added to the way in which new technology has affected the movement of money, prompted Midland Bank to open this test store in Broadmead (at the same time, Fitch also redesigned two existing Bristol branches using similar elements). Its purpose is, basically, to sell the bank's financial services by presenting customers with clear information about them: in short, to transform a bank into a retailer. For Fitch, this necessitated the design of several special items such as signs directing people to the services, interest rate and foreign exchange boards, queue organizers, housings for automated teller machines, and so on. Of course, the designers also had to come up with an interior which would still express the bank's traditional image of trustworthiness and permanence.

Fitch have therefore specially designed every item in the customer areas, and none of the usual posters or unco-ordinated promo-

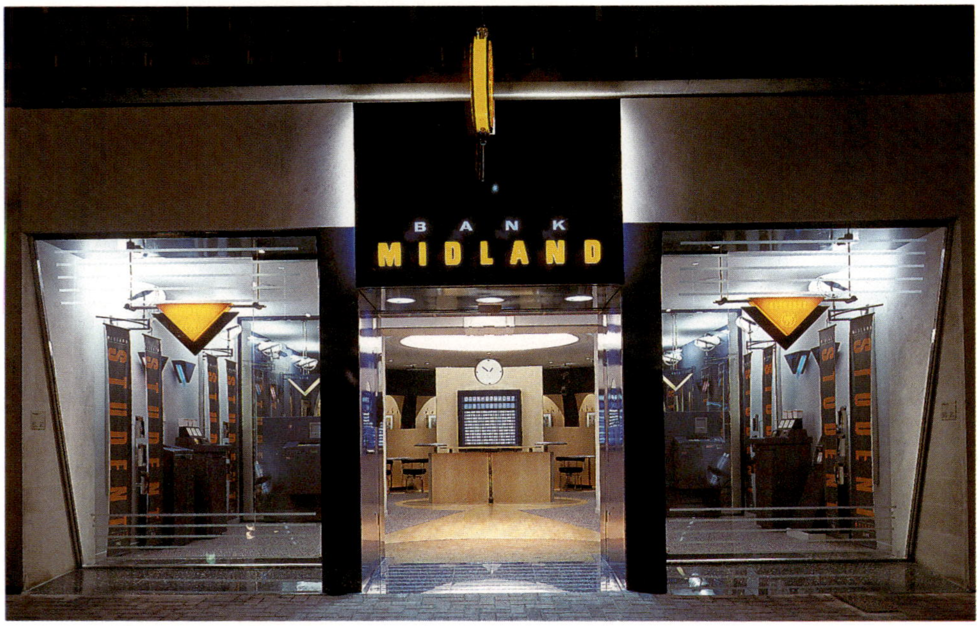

(left) Even from street level, the new shop projects an image that is far from the reliably boring one more often associated with banks.

(right) Neon signs clearly indicate the role of the various teller machines, and introduce a young, bright approach.

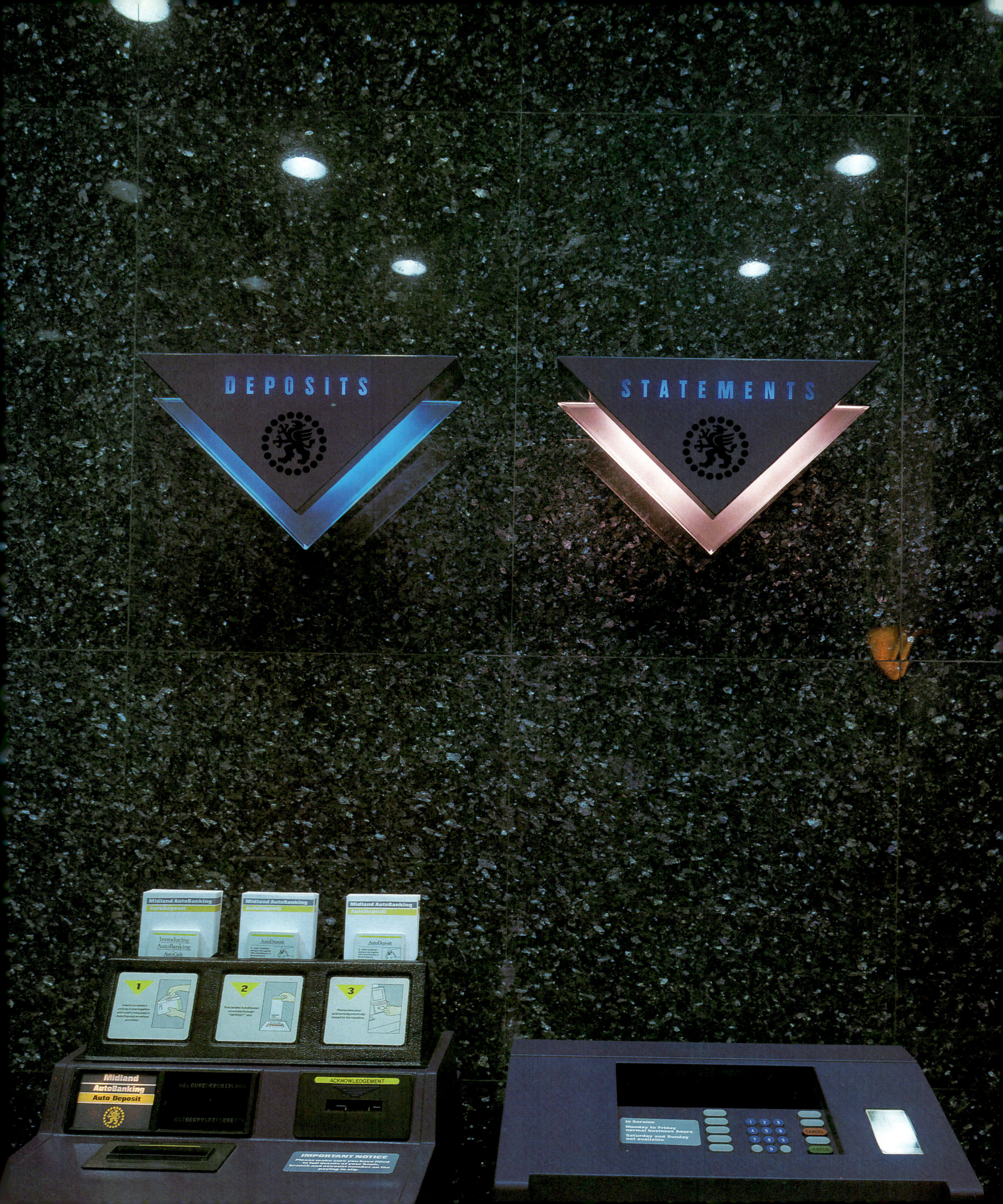
DEPOSITS
STATEMENTS
Midland AutoBanking
Auto Deposit
ACKNOWLEDGEMENT
IMPORTANT NOTICE

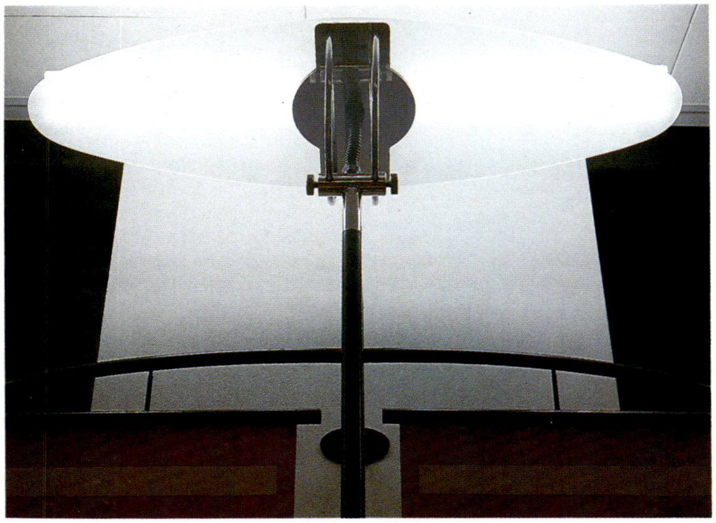

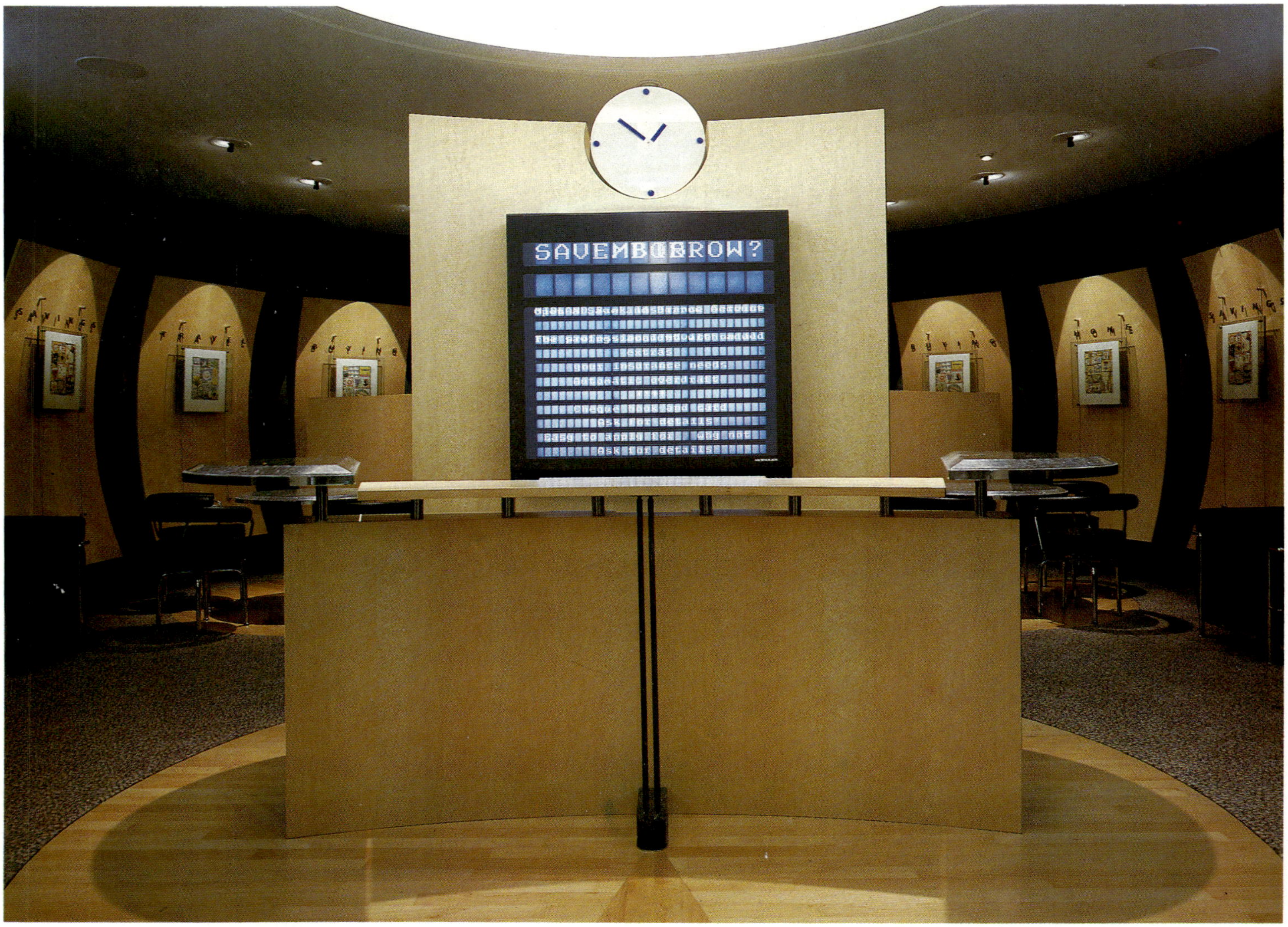

tion material is allowed to intrude. From the automatic glass doors at street level, the customers progress through the lobby (where cash machines are situated), to a reception desk and then to a screened area with chairs and tables for more detailed advice or discussion. Beyond that is a meetings room, access to back offices and the cash counters.

One-word signs, internally lit, mark out the different functions of the various machines; in other sections, the design of the furniture alone is enough to make their purpose clear. The reception desks, for example, have standing-height writing ledges, and the area used for customer advice has comfortable leather chairs and a curved plywood screen so that clients have a feeling of quiet privacy.

The effect given by the materials that Fitch have used at Midland Bank is one of warmth and quality: furniture, screens and parts of the floor are wooden; customer writing surfaces are made of Italian granite; and the specially made carpet is an imitation of a slightly pinker granite (its colour chosen to withstand soiling as much as for aesthetic reasons). With this combination of high-quality materials and custom-made fittings, Fitch have struck the right balance between tradition and up-to-the-minute technology, between the permanence of the bank and the rapidly changing financial world in which it operates. The proof is that, since the branch opened at the end of 1986, business at the Midland Bank Broadmead has been buzzing.

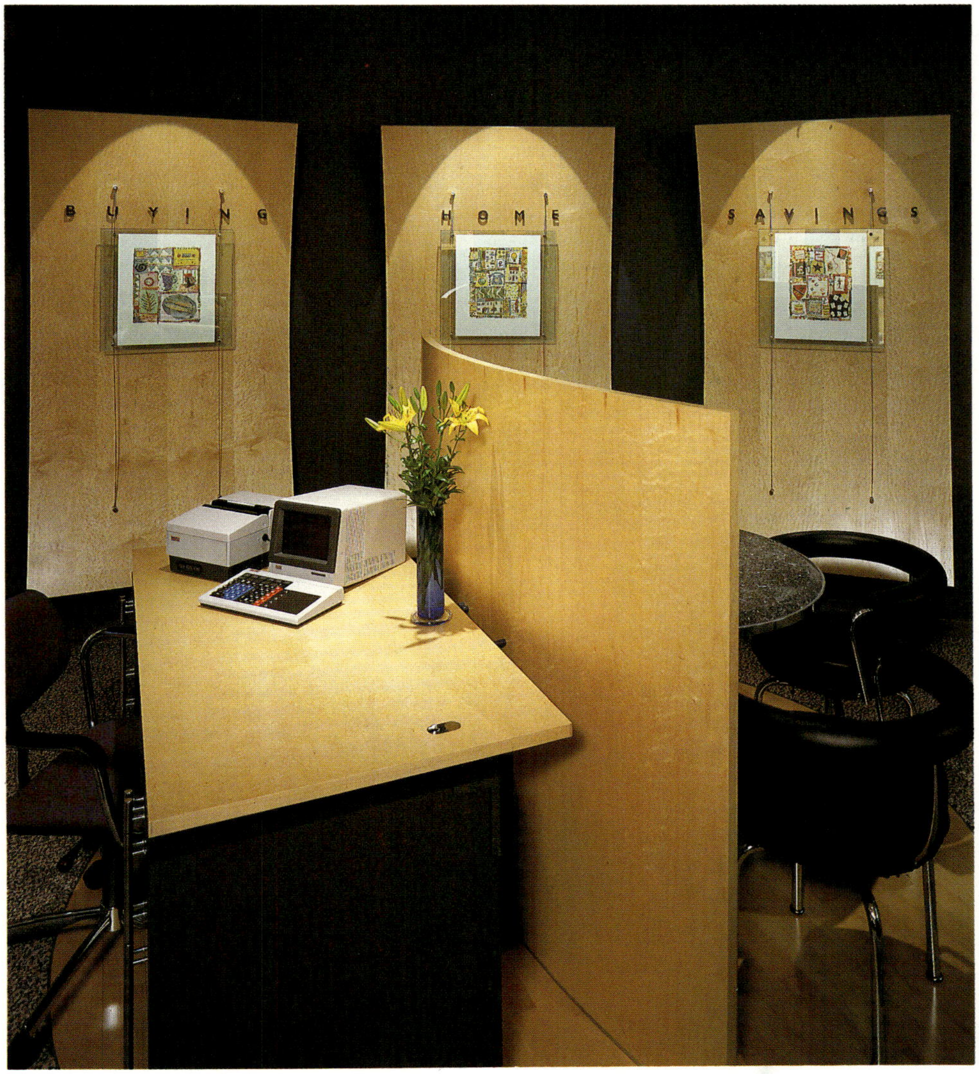

(far left above) Everything – including these light fittings above the information panels – was specially made for the project.

(far left) Essential to Fitch's design was an inviting atmosphere with accessible, easy-to-understand information.

(left) Screens provide privacy for customers wishing to discuss loans or savings. The natural wood hints at the bank's traditional strength and stability.

KATHARINE HAMNETT
LONDON, UK

Designed by Foster Associates

Shortly after the opening of the 1,008 million dollar headquarters of the Hongkong and Shanghai Banking Corporation, Foster Associates finished another immaculate project. But the Katharine Hamnett store in London's South Kensington is minimal, pared down and, of course, Lilliputian compared with the giant bank building.

The site for the store was in fact a garage – 'a two-storey industrial slum', according to Norman Foster – with only the barest hints of a more graceful past: a fragment of cast-iron column, a blocked-in circular window, industrial glazing. But the designers preferred the existing 'slum' to standard store sites which they condemned as 'pedestrian'.

What Foster Associates did with this seemingly unpromising raw material was to strip away the tatty accretions of the garage to reveal a large, studio-like double-height space. The minimalism of the project is clear from the

(far right) Lit from below, a dramatic glass bridge leads the way along a long corridor and into the store proper.

(right) Axonometric projection.

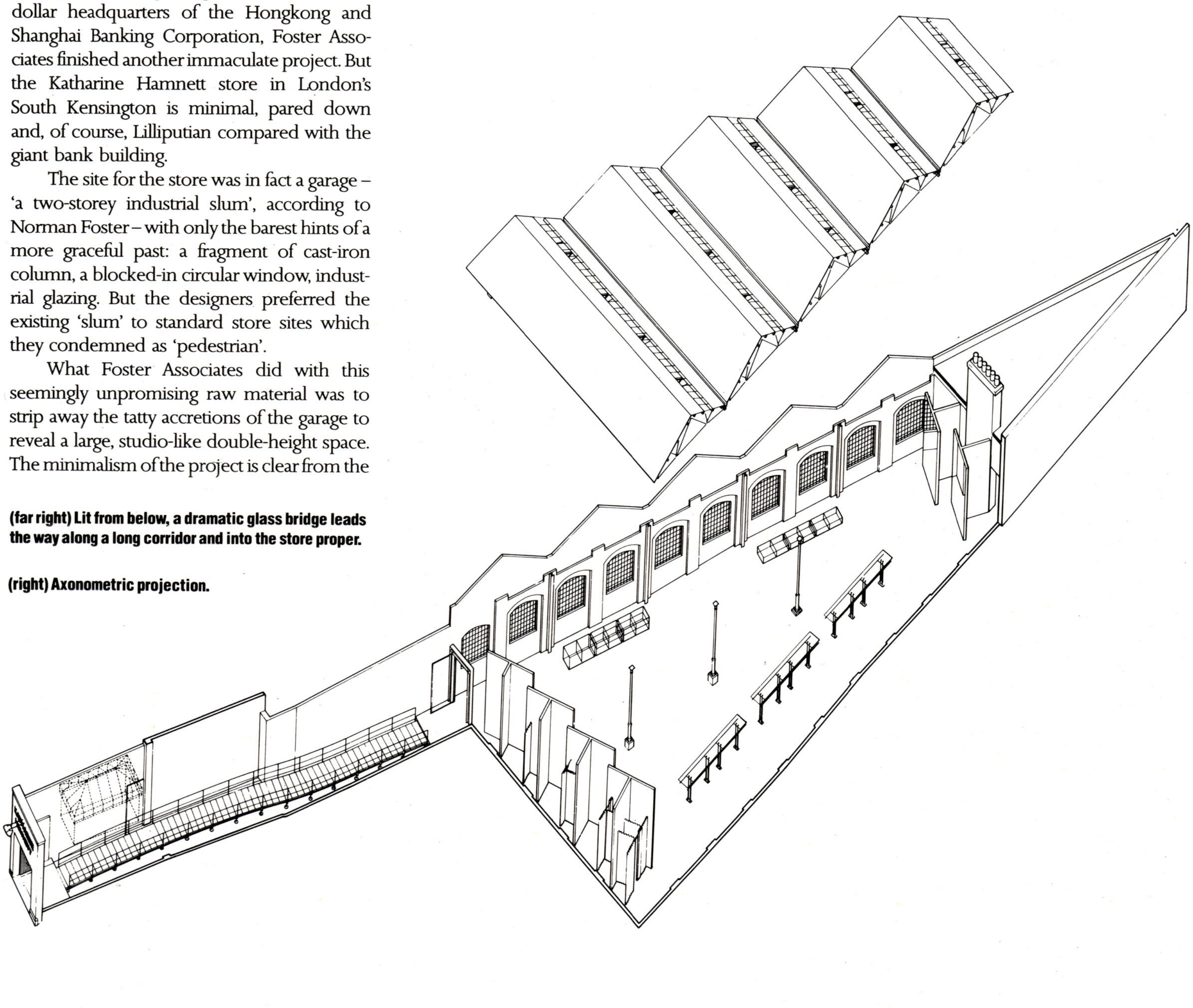

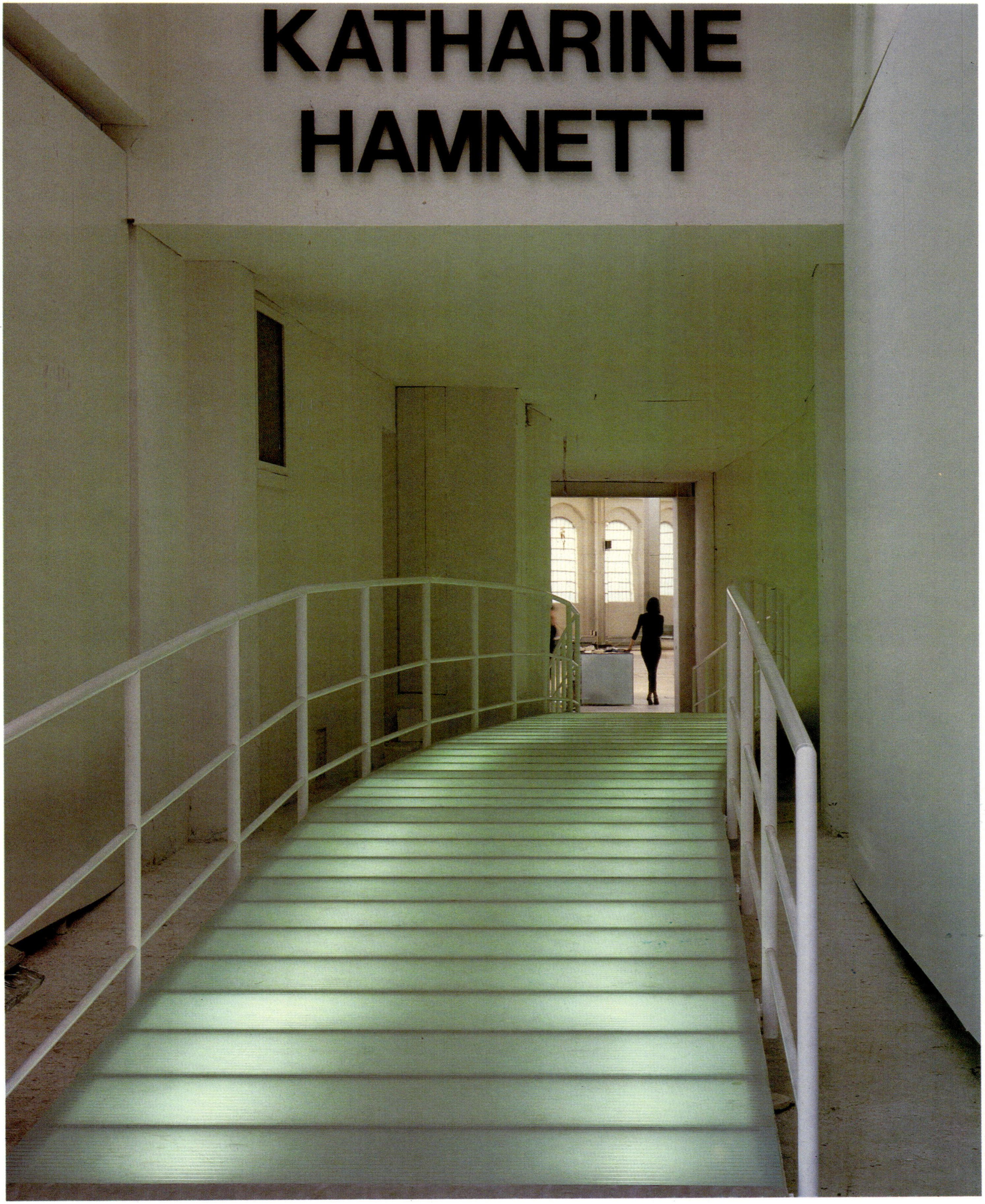
KATHARINE
HAMNETT

outset: no store window entices passers-by, only the bare words 'Katharine Hamnett' and a mysterious glass bridge leading down an enigmatic tunnel. The bridge meanders through the entrance tunnel, lit from below to heighten the mystery.

Past the bridge, the central space of the store seems almost subdued. The simple white space is lined with full-height mirrors on two sides, with a row of large windows providing a flood of natural light. But the store is almost devoid of clothes. Simple steel hanging rails are clustered along one wall on the polished concrete floor, while glass display cases line the other wall. Immaculately clothed store assistants pose within this pristine space, presenting a challenging front to the more timid shoppers who manage to summon the courage to brave the entrance bridge.

(right) Foster has transformed a 'two-storey industrial slum' into a double-height studio-like space.

(below) This is no place for the unfashionable or timid shopper, but beautiful people can admire themselves in the vast mirrors that line the space.

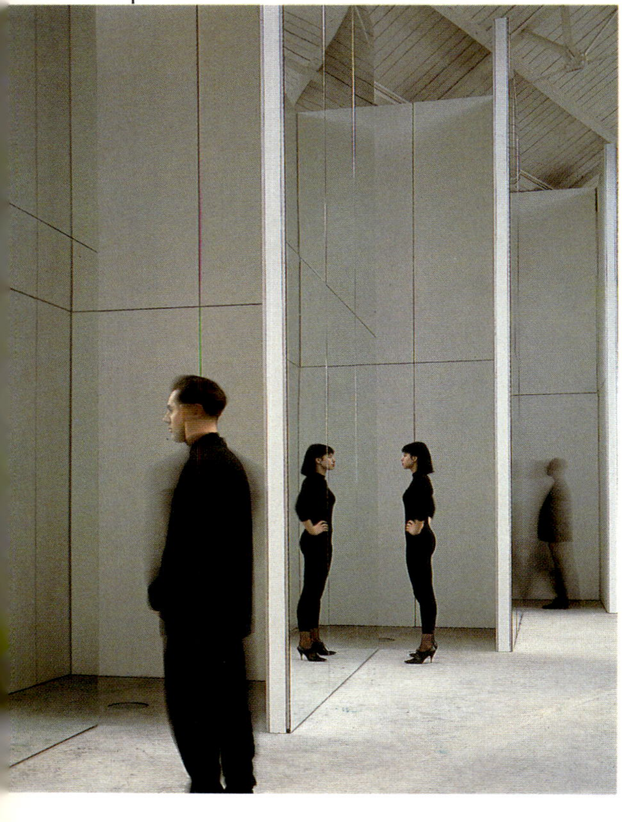

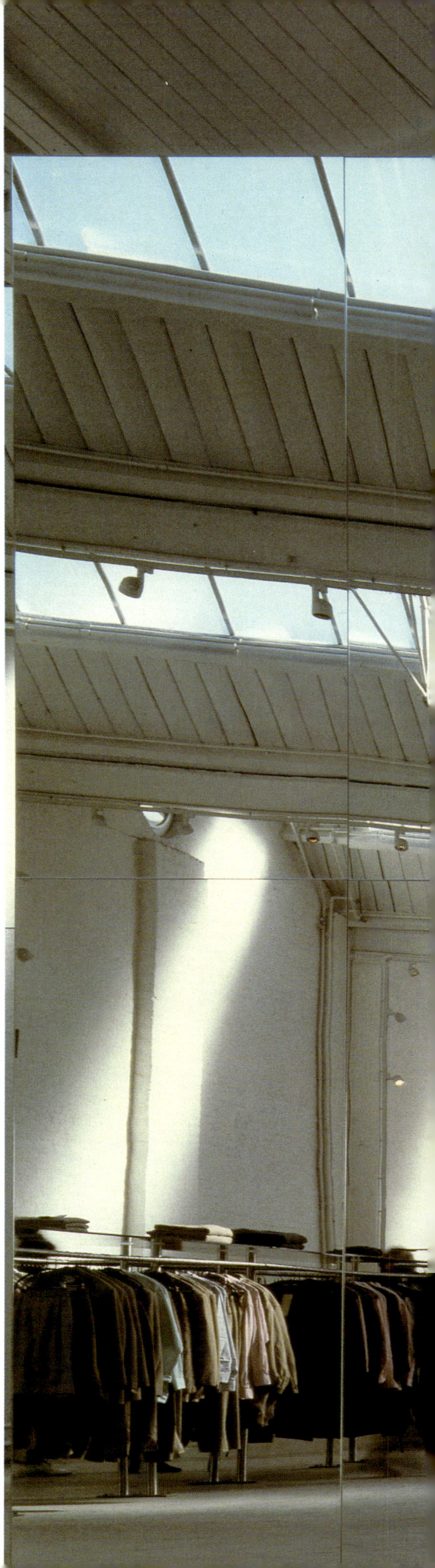

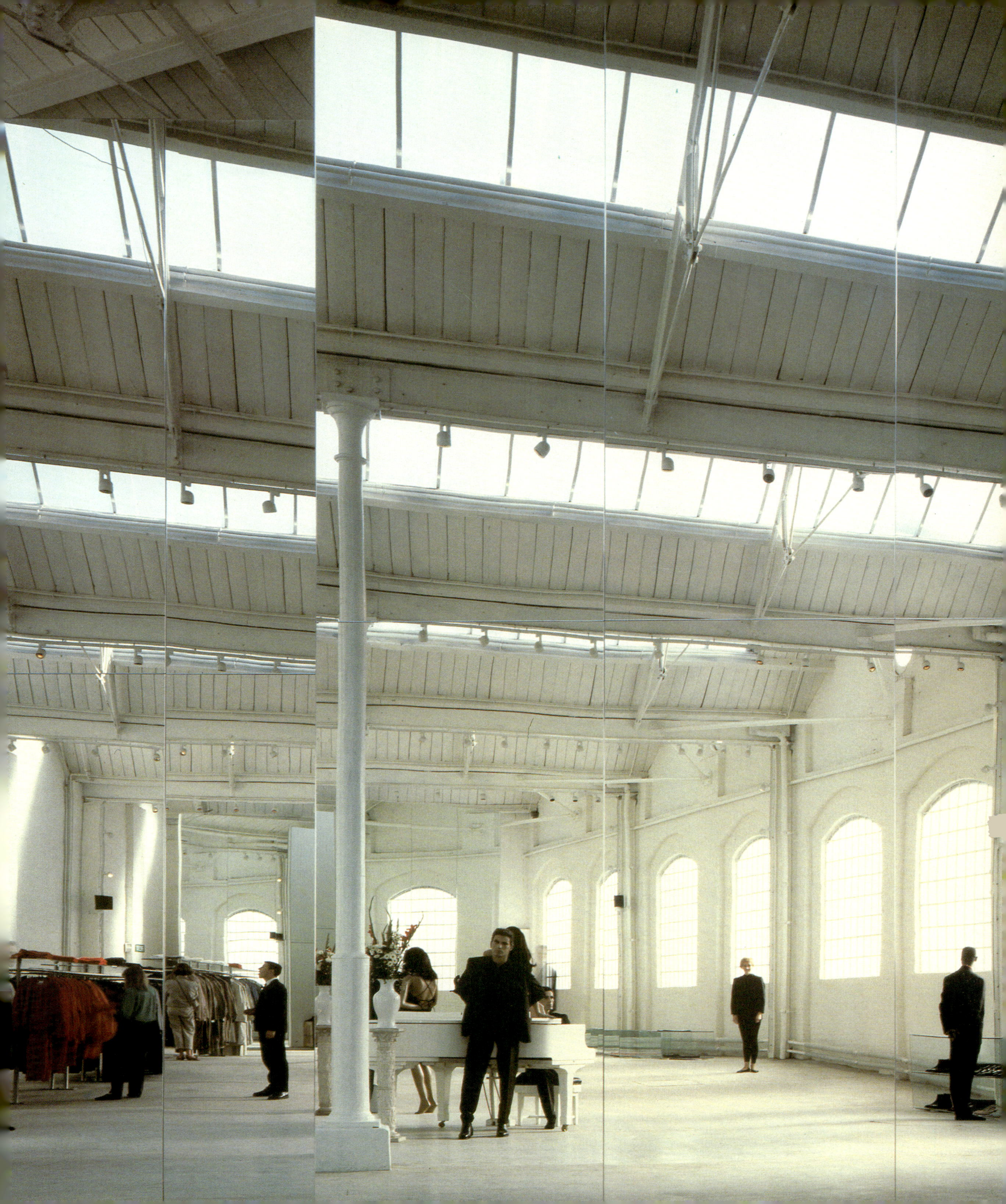

CASHMERE COTTON & SILK

MILAN, ITALY

Designed by Gregotti Associati

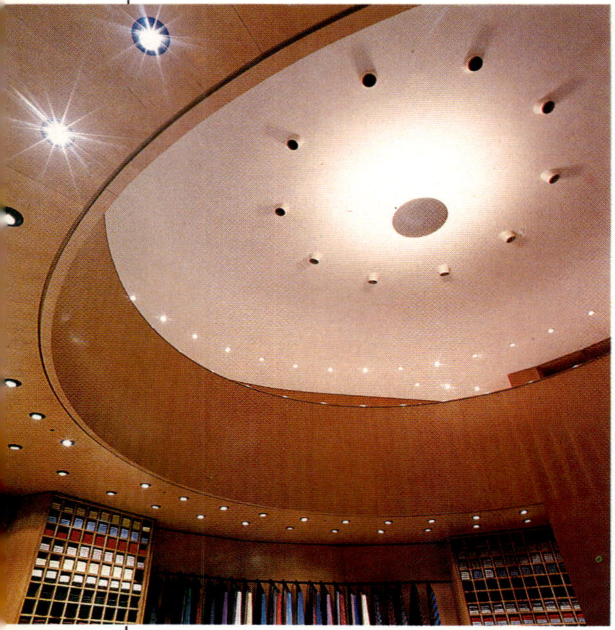

(above) An awkwardly shaped area gave the designers the opportunity to play some clever spatial games, extending up to the ceiling space.

Most store interiors rely on clever manipulation of materials and textures to enliven the essentially boring box; opportunities for designers to play spatial games are strictly limited. So Gregotti Associati were fortunate to have what might seem an awkward, difficult space for their men's fashion store, Cashmere Cotton & Silk. The store's site was spread over several different levels and reached down a long corridor.

The long corridor has been transformed into an interior street with a line of store windows. Conceived as a continuous polygonal 'store-front', the windows are painted dark green and lit by a system of remote-controlled spotlights. The passage invites strollers to window-shop, and offers a friendly invitation to explore, rather than the mystery of the similarly long corridor in Norman Foster's Katharine Hamnett store in London. (see pp.154–7)

Beyond the corridor, access to the store is through a cash-desk area which leads to the two sales floors. At the lower level, the space is defined by the sweeping array of display cases and storage units. Projecting over these is a circular balcony reached by a staircase built into the thickness of the walls.

The richness of the clothes' fabrics is echoed by the designers' palette of materials. The entire display area is built of pink pearwood, and is wedged between walls and floors of grey trachyte slabs. Nothing in this carefully controlled design has been overlooked. According to designer Pierluigi Cerri, 'Ornament may be a crime, but a rational distribution of the air-conditioning vents has described a vaguely Asplundian decor on the ceiling' (a reference to Swedish architect Eric Gunnar Asplund).

The publicity talents of Memphis and its followers have led many to believe that traditional Italian design has vanished. But the rich, elegant detailing of Cashmere Cotton & Silk, and the preference for 'real' materials as opposed to the plastics and synthetics favoured by Sottsass and his band, show that the old Italian current runs deep.

(right) Materials, such as pink pearwood, are rich and natural, and they hint at the old-fashioned outfitters or the gentlemen's club.

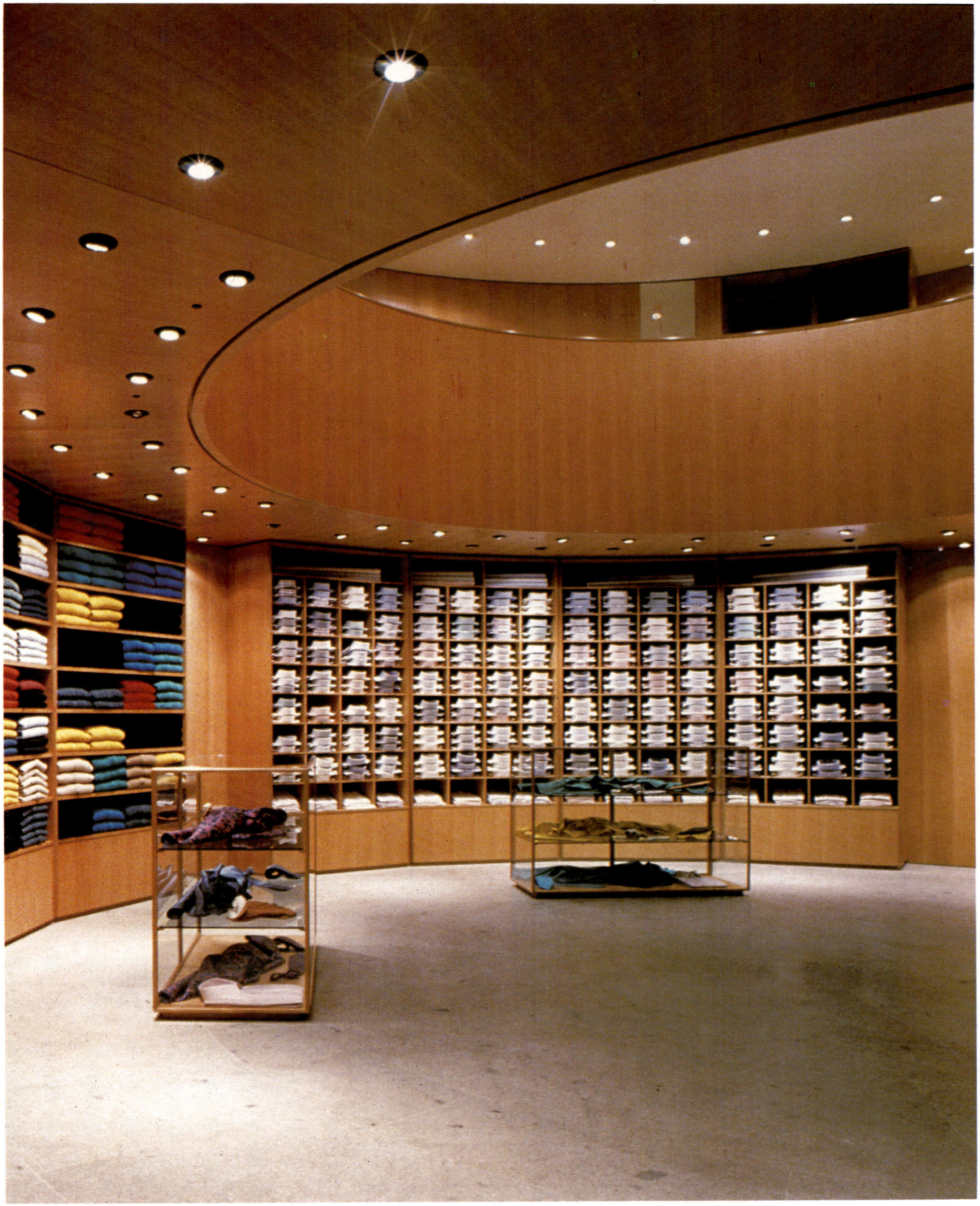

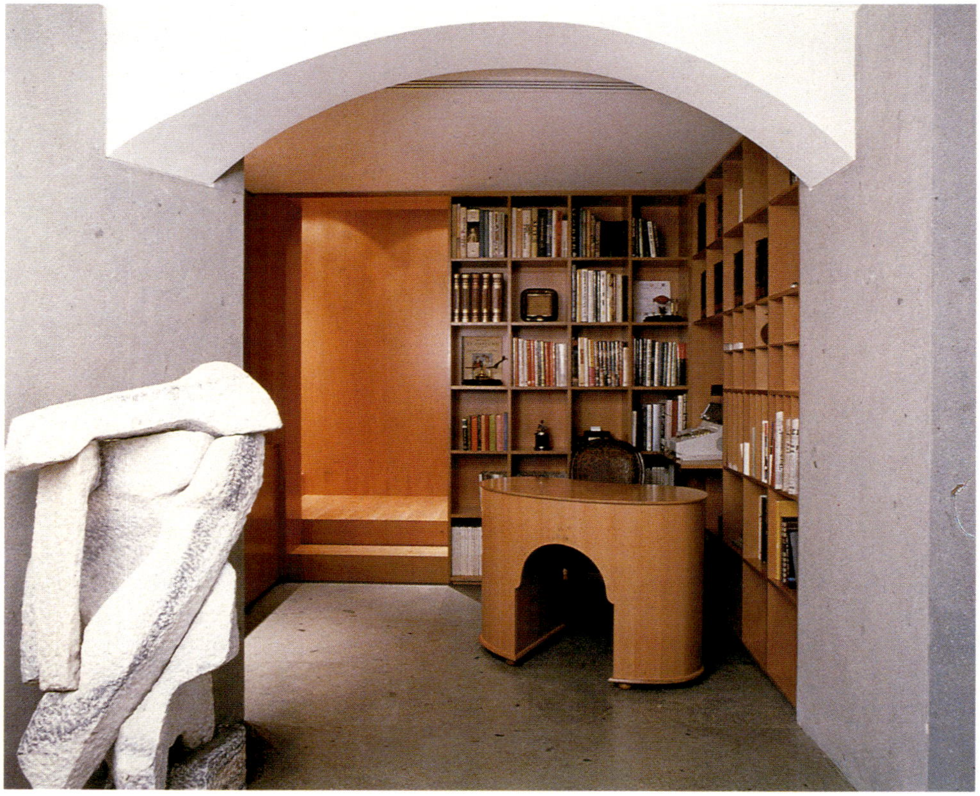

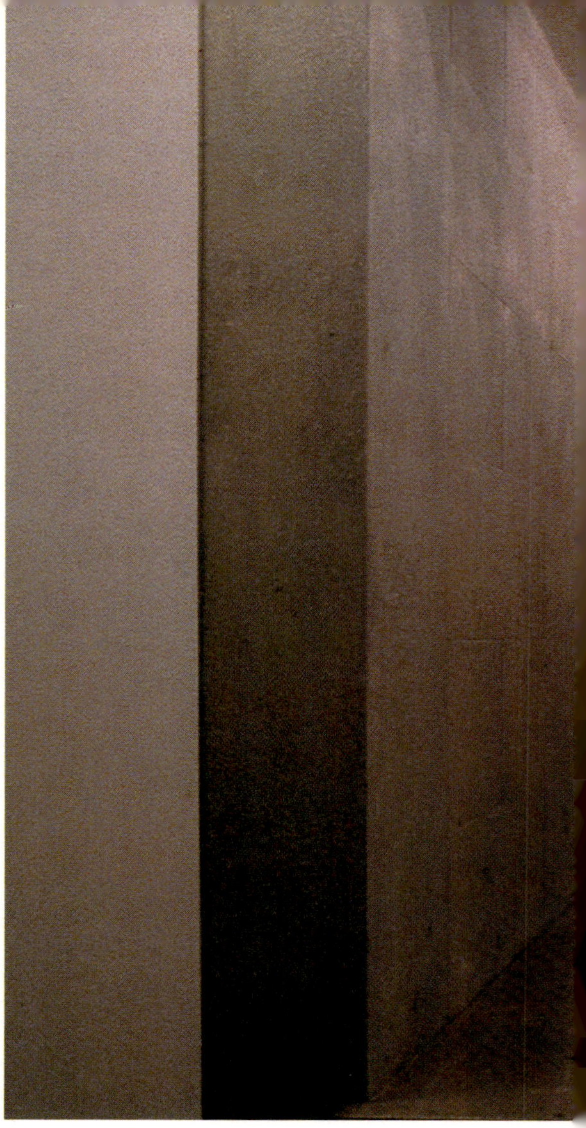

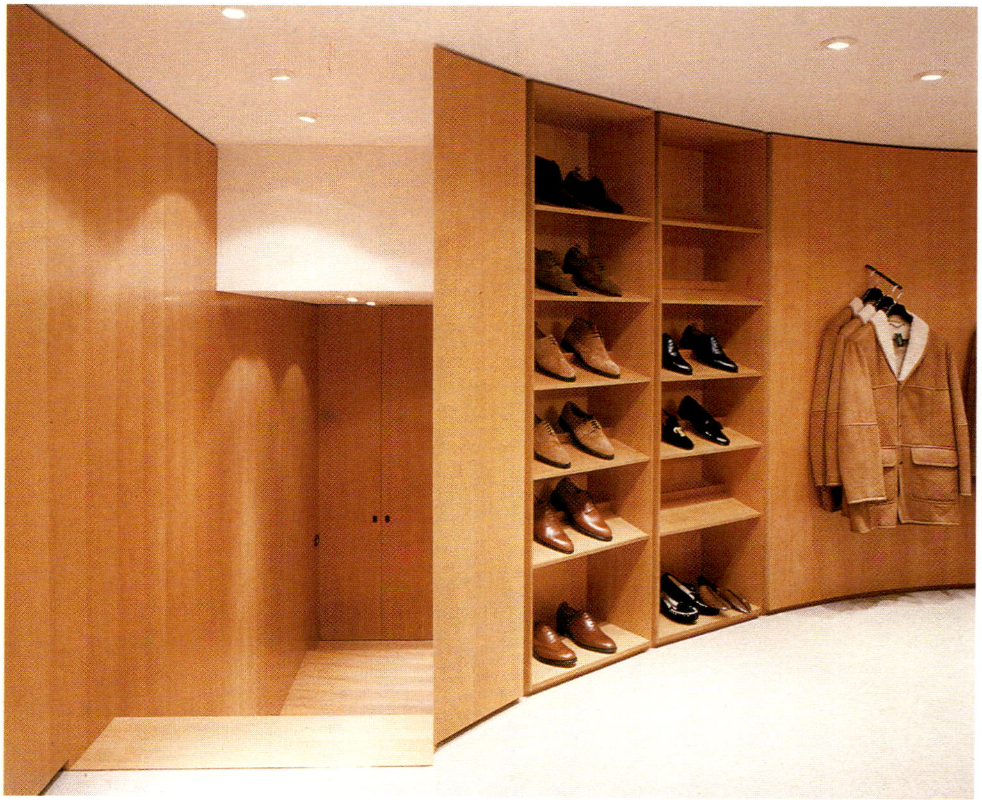

(above) Customers pass the cash-desk before arriving at the main sales floor.

(right) Curves characterize the sales area: a sweeping array of storage and shelving units contains the clothes.

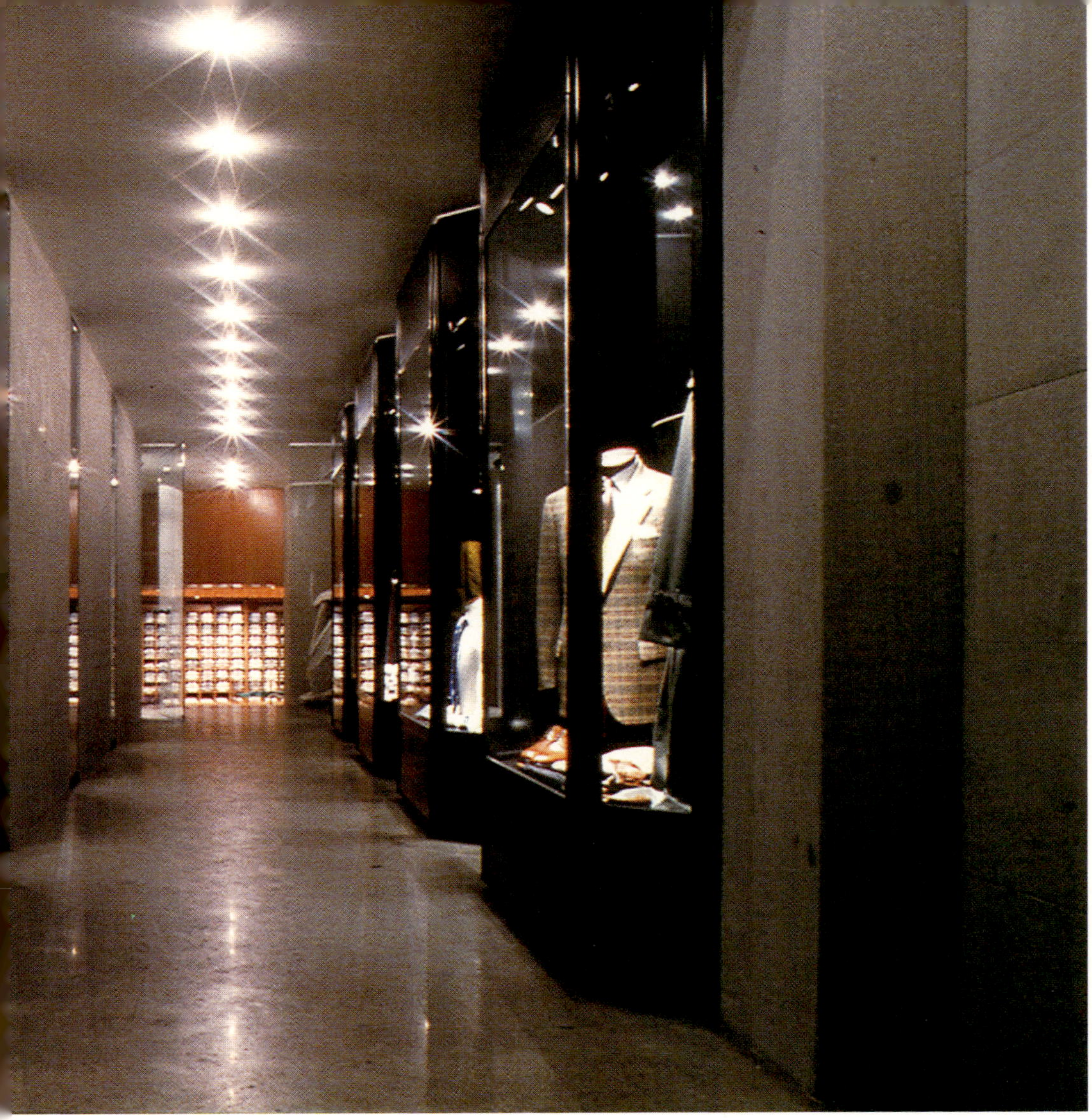

(left) The long corridor which leads into the store has been treated as an interior 'street' containing windows which invite customers inside.

(below) The designers have made the most of the available space with a balcony which curves above the retail area.

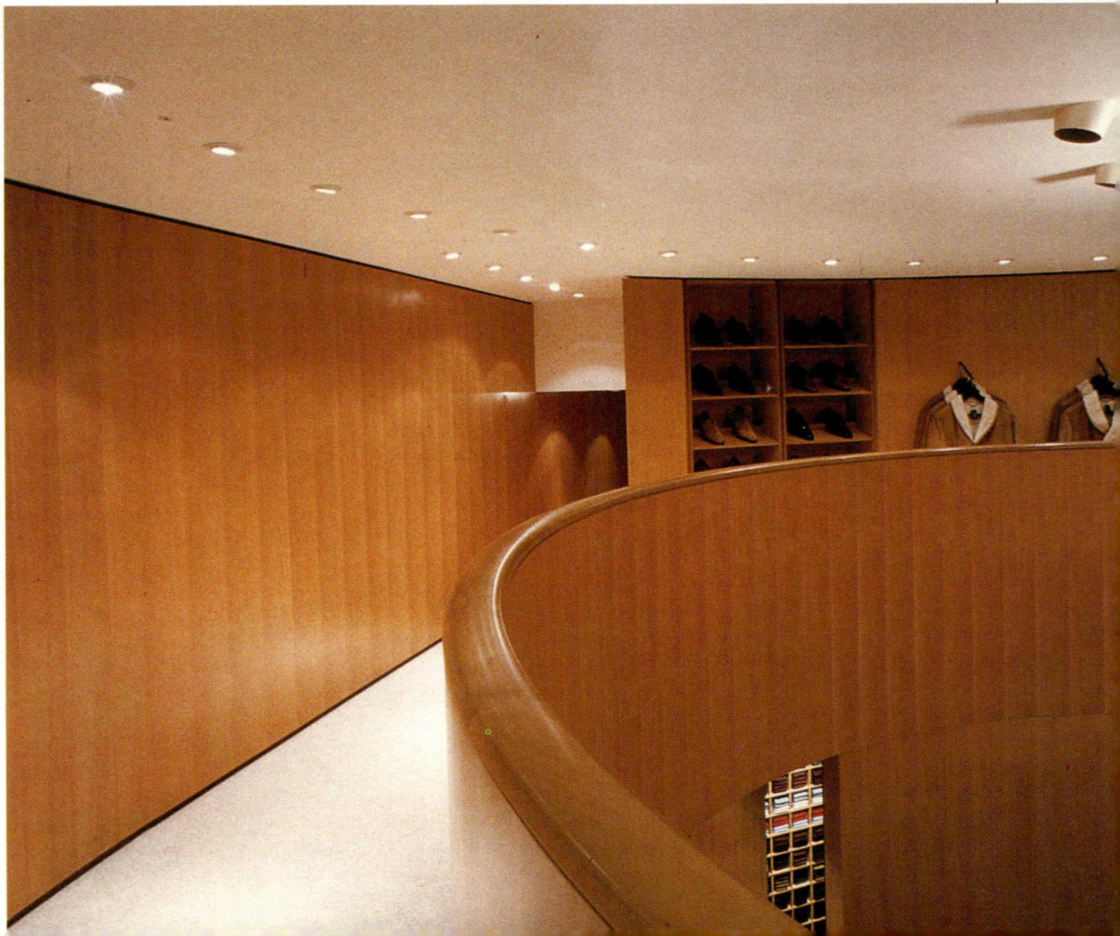

THE PACE COLLECTION

NEW YORK CITY, USA

Designed by Steven Holl Architects

The work on the showroom for The Pace Collection on Madison Avenue was originally described in the most mundane terms: 'In the base of the small limestone commercial building on the southwest corner of Madison Avenue and 72nd Street in New York City, a small furniture showroom is inserted. The maximum glass exposure on Madison and on 72nd was requested by the client. A close spacing of window mullions eliminated the need for typical roll-down security gates.' These grey phrases sound more like a police report than the appropriate words for a tiny, unhyped gem on a most visible site in New York.

Like Stanley Tigerman's showroom for Formica (see pp. 208–11), Holl's design takes its inspiration from the grid of the city. But his design is much more understated than Tigerman's work. The Pace Collection is tiny – only 377 square feet (35 square metres) – and Holl has played a delicate architectural fugue using a complex counterpointing of elements. The 'maximum glass exposure' is provided by Mondrian-like window-walls, with amber glass elements set against the horizontal steel bars of the main mullions. Along 72nd Street the bars are predominantly horizontal while along Madison they are vertical. Sand-blasted glass drawings in the 'contrapuntal' panels carry the idea on a smaller scale. An additional subtlety: along Madison these drawings 'show the equivalent of an end grain (lines) while along 72nd Street they show an edge grain (planes)'.

Inside, this contrapuntal theme is picked up with painted steel shelves cantilevered from integral colour plaster walls. Curvy blue steel handrails extend the concept. The steel shelves hold maquettes of The Pace Collection's furniture. Such a carefully detailed design relies on immaculate realization, and Holl estimates he spent half of his working week on site during construction. This enabled him to make a number of crucial on-the-spot decisions as well

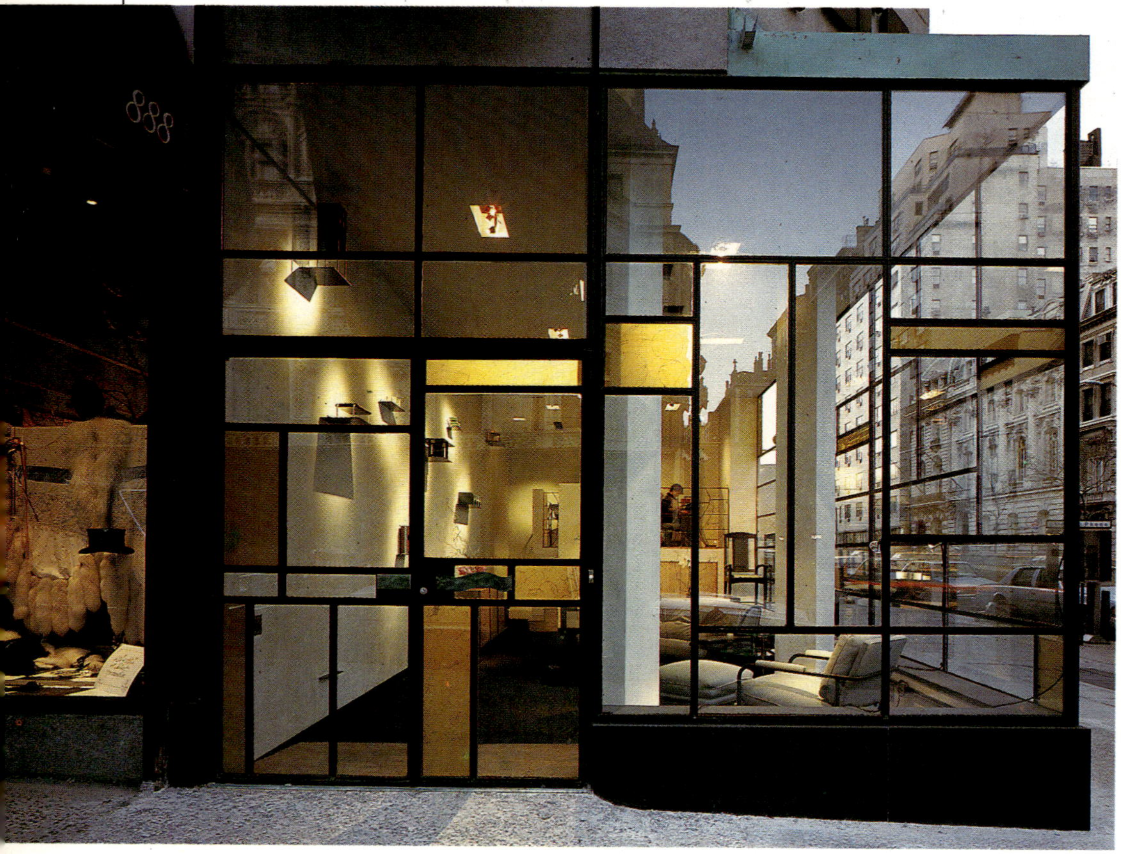

(left) Steven Holl's Mondrian-like window-walls ensure maximum visibility and effect.

(right) The client wanted maximum visibility from street level; window-walls are set with small panels of amber-coloured glass.

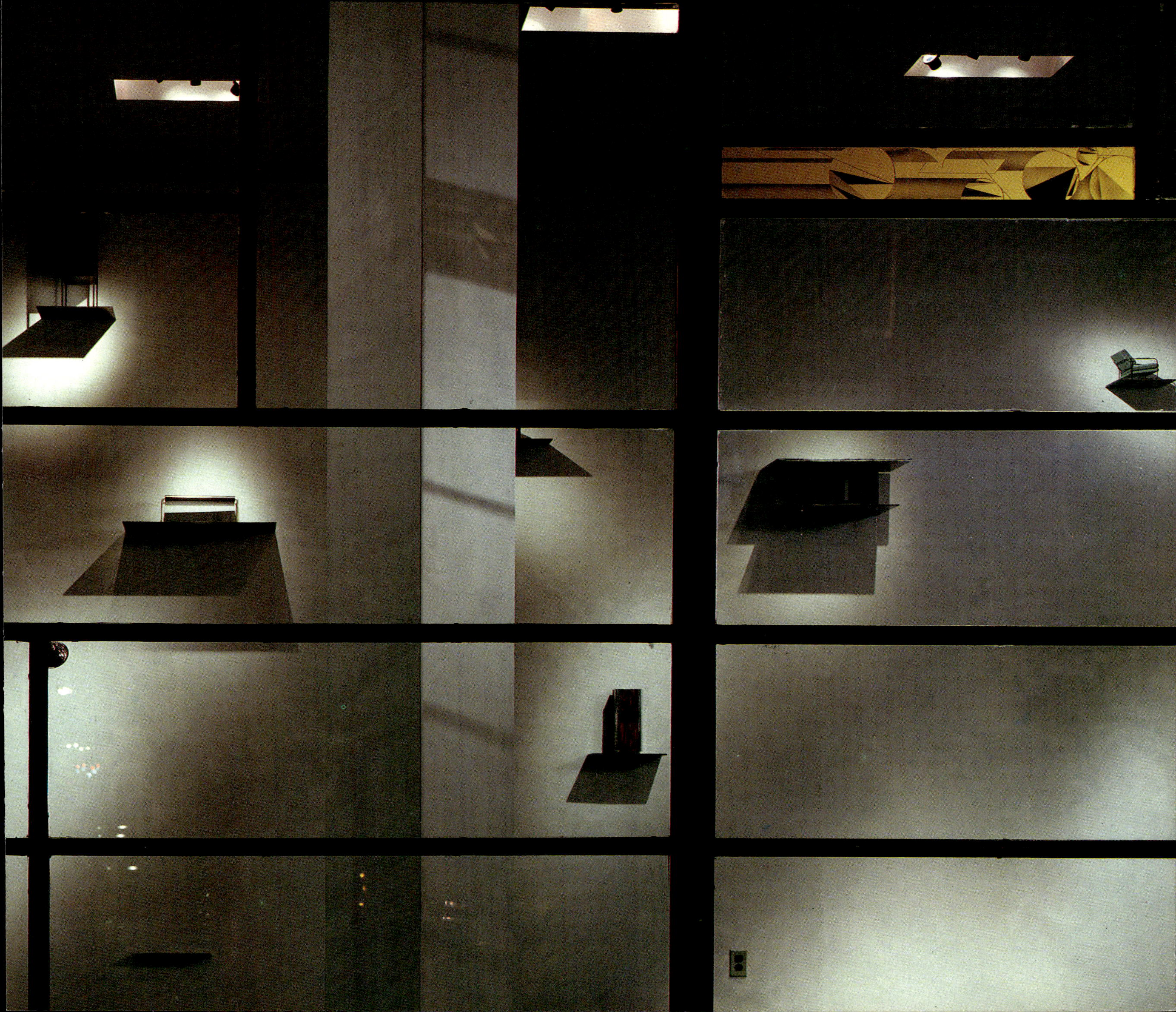

as to work closely with the craftsmen involved in the project: the glassworker who sandblasted and etched the amber panels, the plasterer who made the stairwell fresco, and the steelworker who balanced the window mullions' structural role with the thinness that was required for aesthetic reasons.

Although a few full-sized pieces of furniture are artfully displayed in the showroom, the company relies on their 10,000 square foot (929 square metre) showroom fifteen blocks away to show the full range. Holl's artwork is intended to attract attention more than to display furniture, and since the opening the showroom has been drawing a crowd of one thousand people a week. For the 190,000 dollars that the project cost, The Pace Collection has built a beautiful marketing tool that should outlive the vagaries of fashion.

(below) The clear view from Madison Avenue into the shop is perhaps at its most striking at night.

(right) Inside, small steel shelves of different shapes and sizes are cantilevered from plaster walls, and display small-scale models of the furniture. A few (full-scale) items of furniture are artfully displayed.

(far right) Fresco plaster softens the look of the stairwell walls.

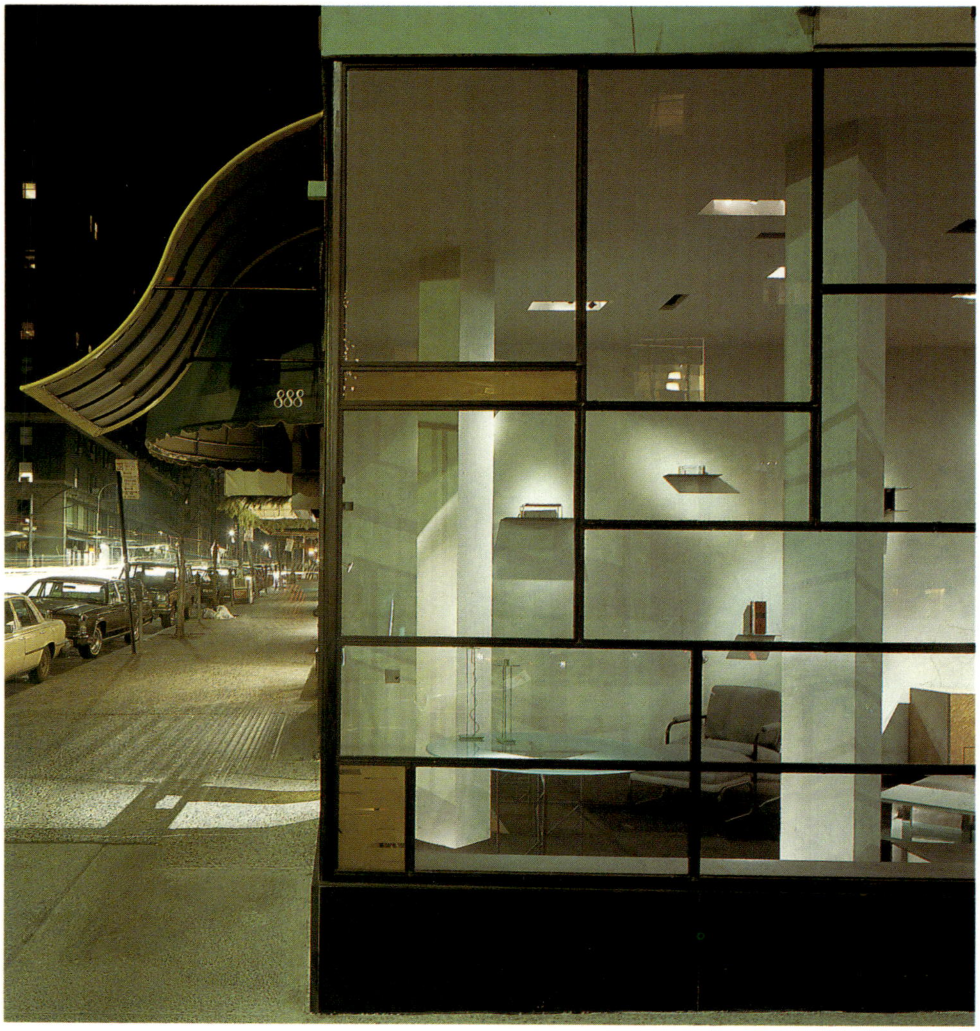

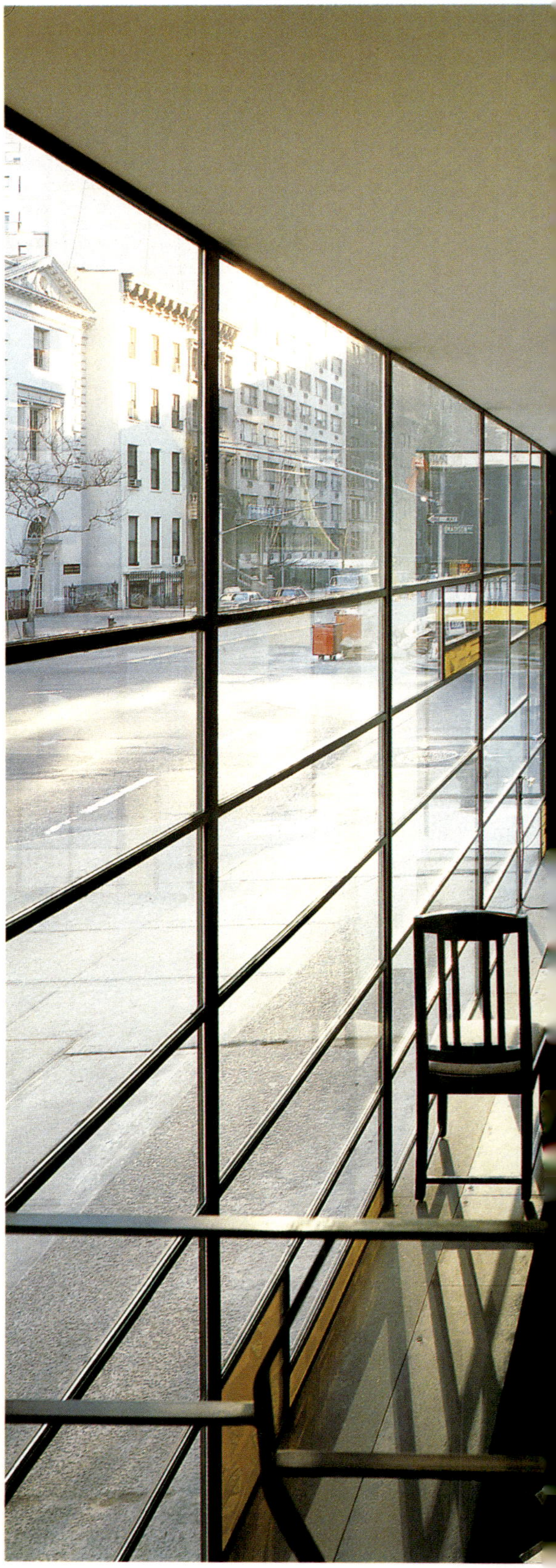

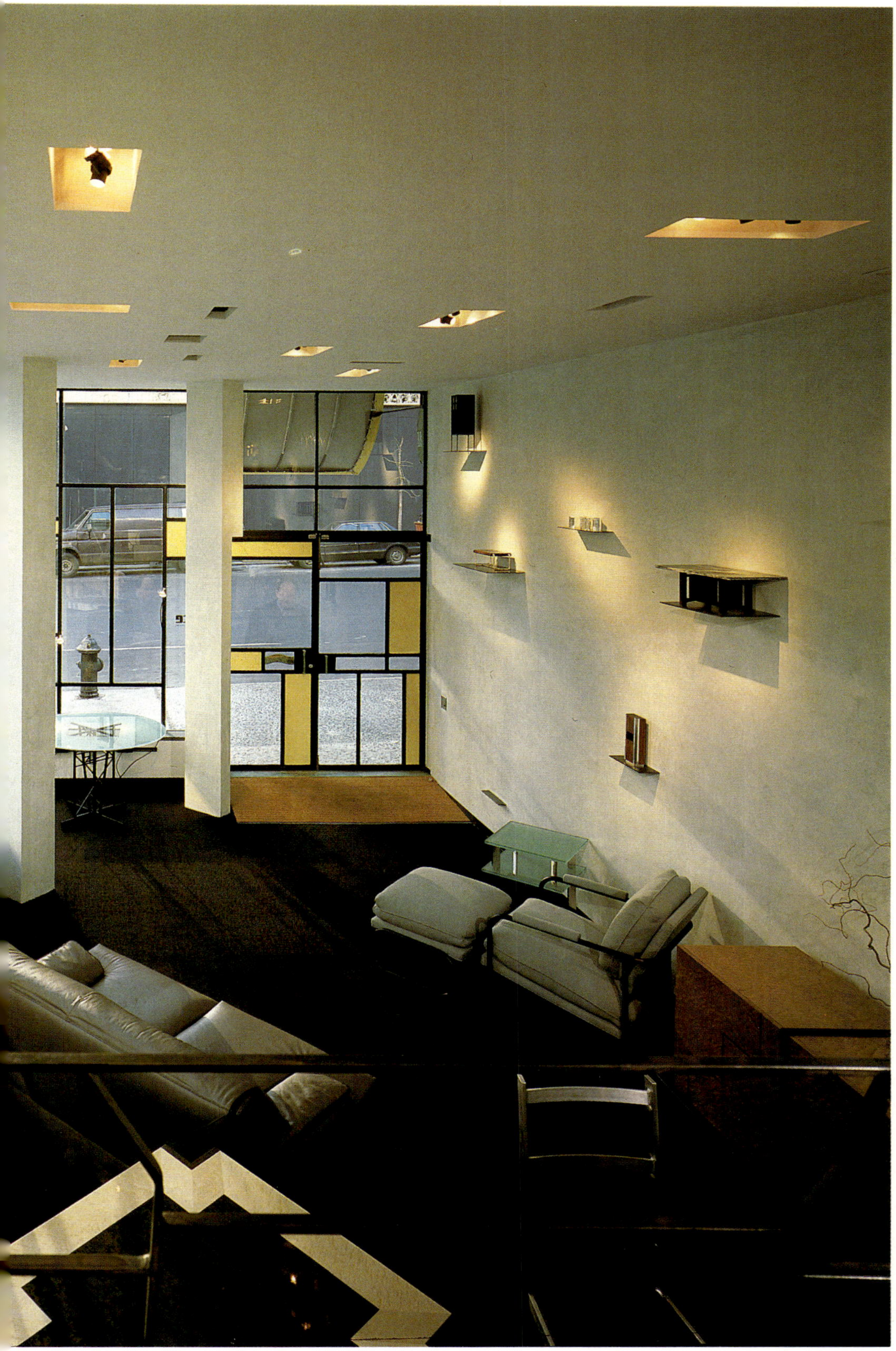

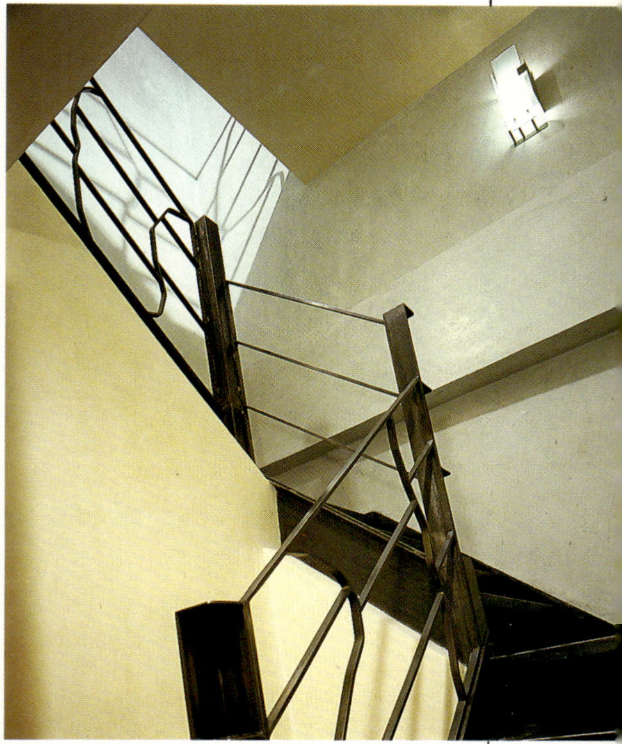

EX JUN BOUTIQUE
KÔBE, JAPAN

Designed by Naoki Iijima

The contemporary Japanese penchant for minimalism has transferred somewhat uneasily to the West. The quality of finish, the perfect arrangement of objects, the very severity implied by the most minimalist interiors somehow seem more appropriate to Japan than to London or New York. Few designers have exploited the potential of minimalism more successfully than Naoki Iijima.

The Ex Jun store, in Kôbe, is classically minimalist. According to Iijima, the client for the store is a great fan of Marcel Duchamp. Whether Duchamp would have understood the professed homage to him is a moot point, for the brushed-steel cabinets and arched ceiling of Ex Jun seem to have little to do with the French artist. The architecture of the store makes clear that the design has been inserted into some anonymous shell: steel cabinets stand proud of the walls, while the ceiling arches are segmented, as if to exhibit their non-structural nature.

The basic materials are rigorously consistent. Brushed steel is also used for the hanging rails and shelving structure, with wire-reinforced glass for the shelves. The floor is sandstone, providing a natural contrast to the fabrication of the remainder.

One of the attractions of minimalism to clients, aside from the effortless style it conveys, is its relative cheapness. Iijima's immaculate store cost only 83,000 dollars.

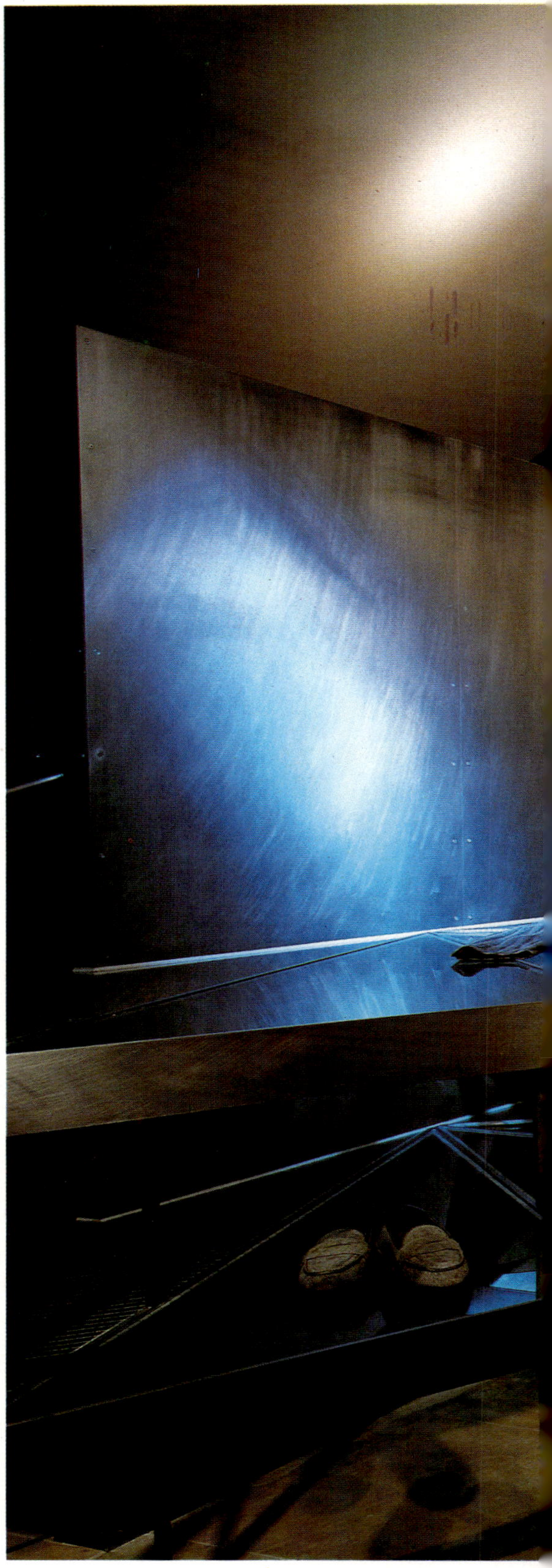

Beneath an arched ceiling, industrial materials such as steel, sandstone and reinforced glass make up Iijima's immaculate minimalist interior.

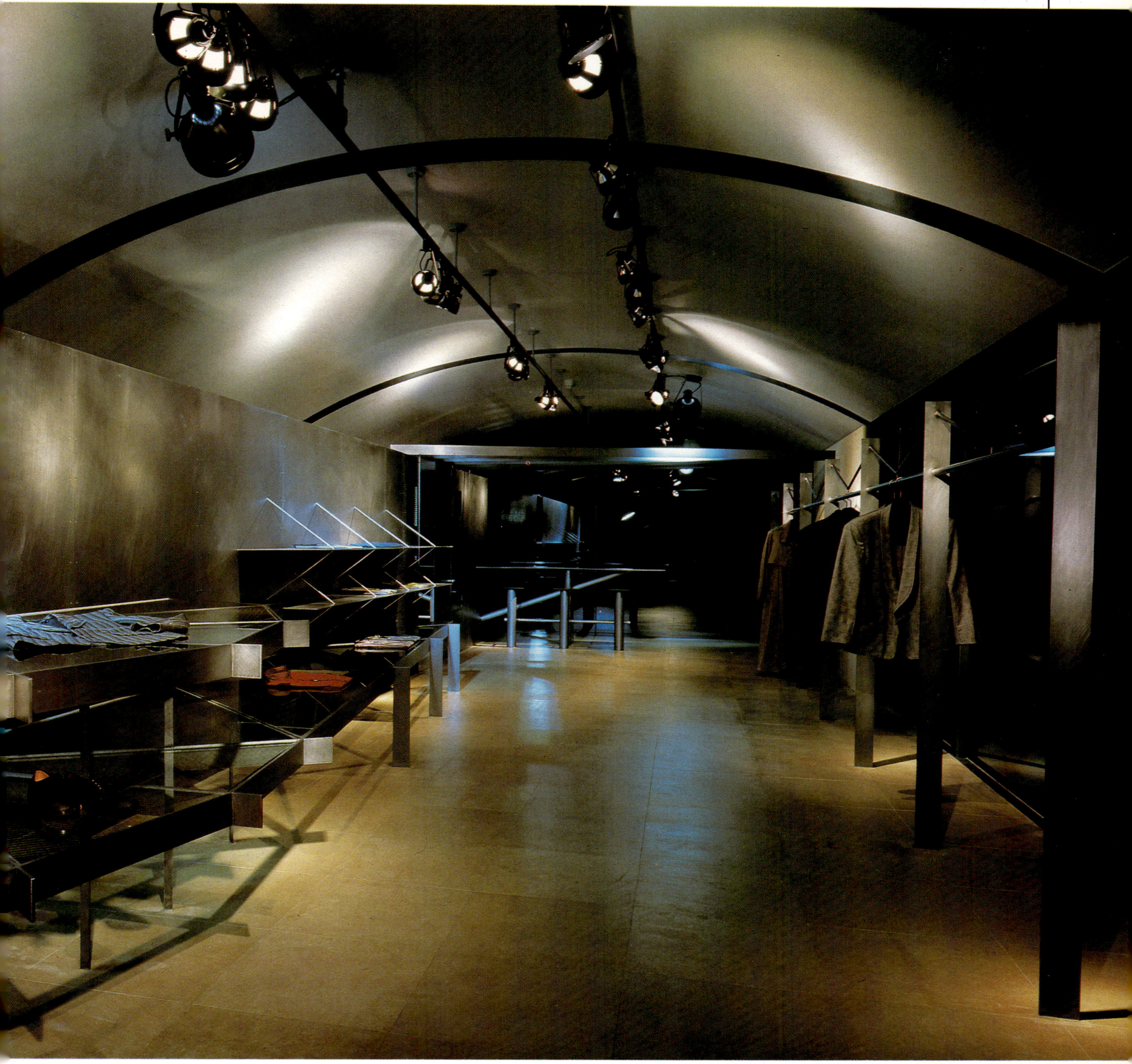

TAKEO KIKUCHI

TOKYO, JAPAN

Designed by Setsuo Kitaoka

The current preoccupation with structure and with engineering, evident in the work of internationally acclaimed architects such as Richard Rogers (at the Pompidou Centre, Paris, and the Lloyd's headquarters in London) and Norman Foster (notably at the Hongkong and Shanghai Banking Corporation headquarters), is also a feature of Japanese retail design. When seen on a smaller scale, as in the Takeo Kikuchi clothes store designed by Setsuo Kitaoka, it also evokes the muscular engineering of Victorian industrial buildings.

One-half of the space is like an arched Victorian railway station, or perhaps a hangar, albeit constructed in honeycomb aluminium rather than iron and steel. At first it appears to be supported by giant crossbows, blue steel columns which form the frame for hanging rails. In fact the columns stop short of the ceiling topped by black cinema spotlights.

At the opposite end, clothes are laid on a large glass table with metal supports intended to look like plant stems. Above, a suspended honeycomb aluminium ceiling canopy diffuses the light into muted starbursts. Below, there is a punched aluminium industrial floor.

Amid all this hard tech, the one soft element is the changing-room or, rather, changing-box, for it is a steel-framed box covered with yellow fabric, but even that is heavy-duty canvas. It is difficult to avoid the feeling that the only clothes one can buy here are overalls and flying suits.

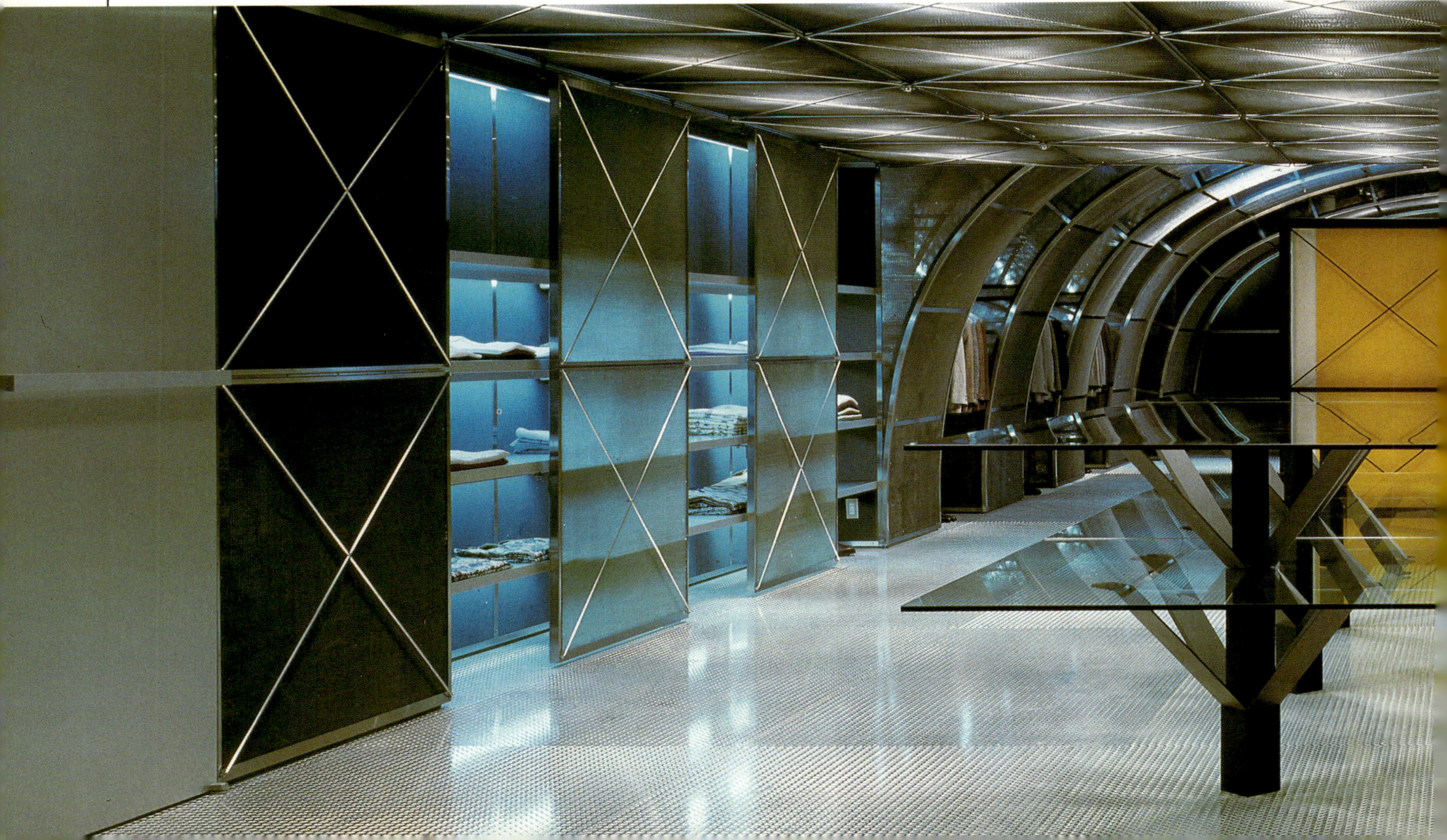

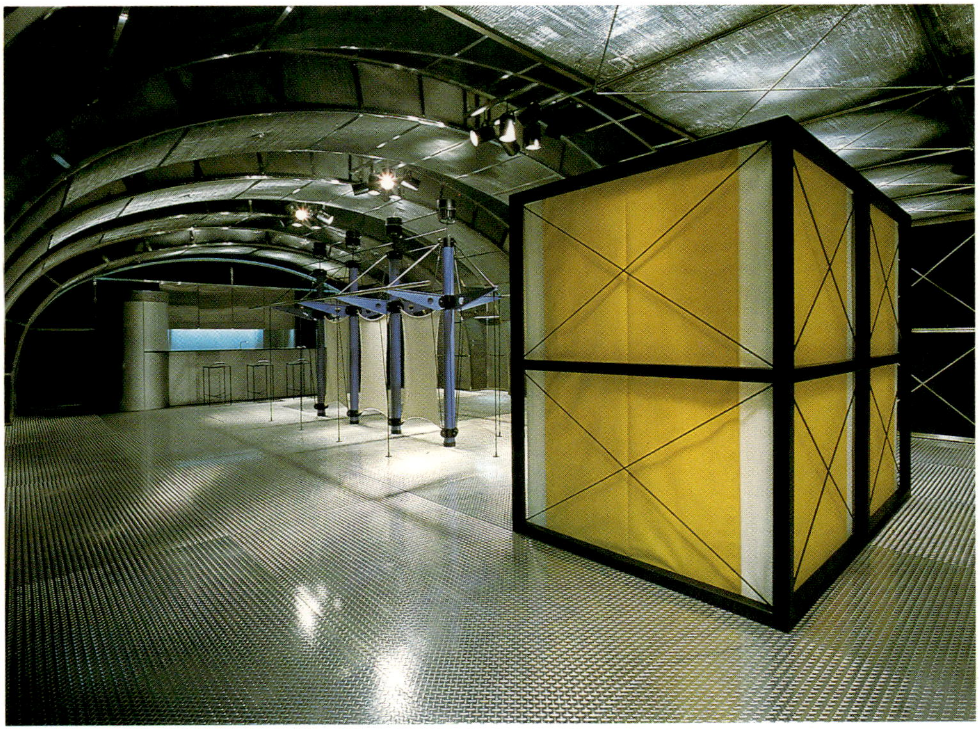

(right) The changing-room is more of a changing-box; its yellow fabric introduces a rare element of bright colour.

(below) Structure and shapes are all-important in Kitaoka's tunnel-like design.

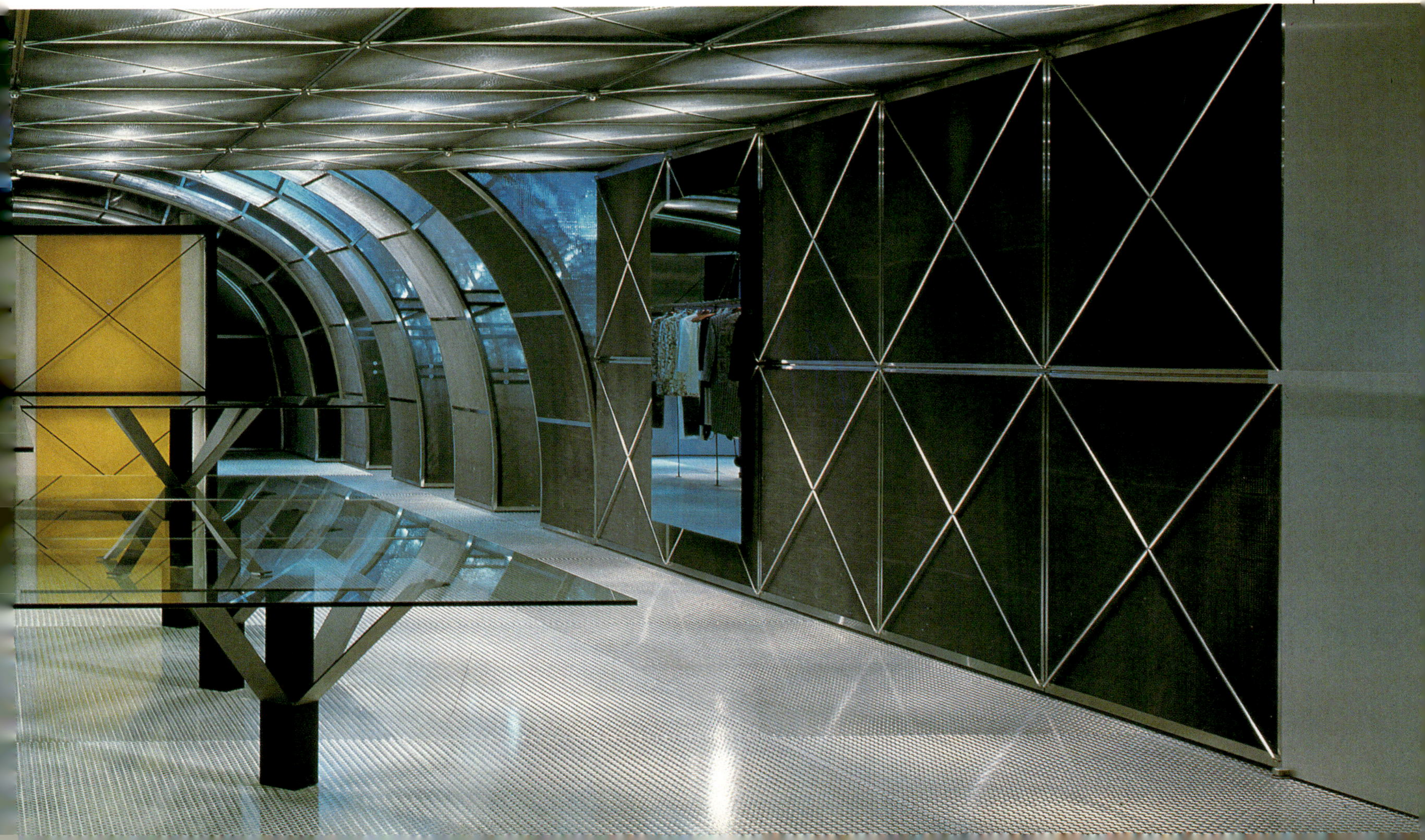

(right) A large glass table, sometimes used to display the clothes, reflects the honeycomb aluminium of the suspended ceiling.

(below) Made of punched aluminium, the floor has the hard, industrial feel that characterizes the design.

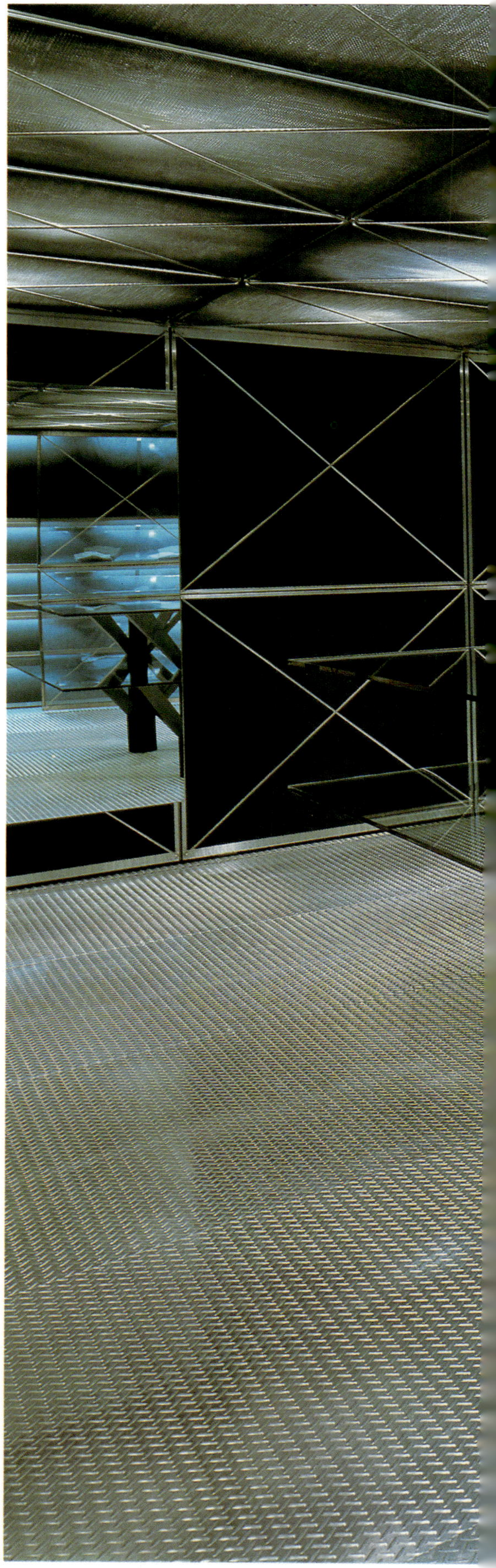

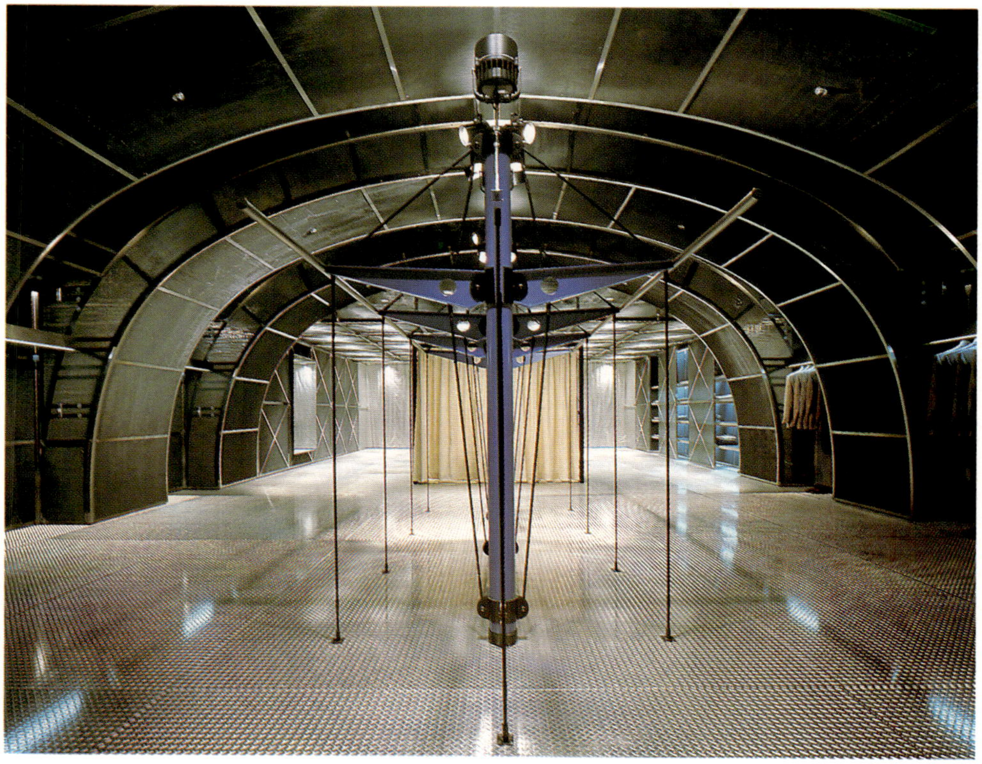

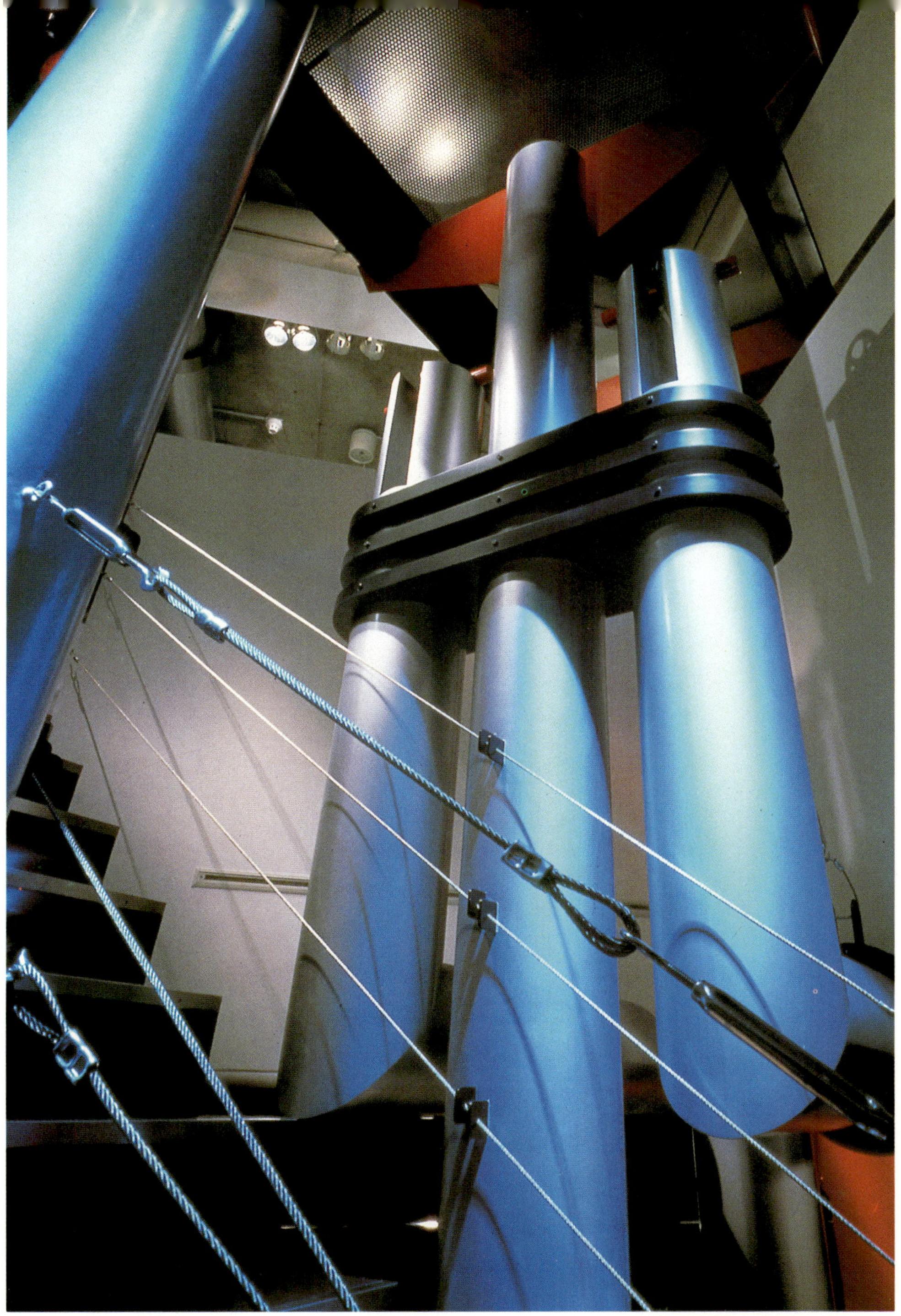

(far left) Huge, colourful steel pipes stretch up into the full height of the interior.

(middle) A steel staircase links the two levels of the gallery.

(left) Inside, steel tension balustrades add to the overall industrial aesthetic; the effect is almost like the boiler-room of a factory or a ship.

ISSEY MIYAKE

KÔBE, JAPAN

Designed by Shiro Kuramata

Few projects can boast such an illustrious collection of names as this high-fashion store: in a building designed by Japanese architect Tadao Ando, designer Shiro Kuramata is working for fashion designer Issey Miyake. All are members of that select group of Japanese names who have achieved international acclaim.

With a brief to provide space for both men's and women's clothes in two separate but linked areas, Kuramata has retained the existing walls and sweeping arches of the building, installed a plain terrazzo floor, and concentrated on a few large-scale elements within.

Chief of these is a huge glass screen, crazed with a random pattern that evokes trees and rivers. It is made by sandwiching together three panes of glass, the middle one of which is tempered so that it can become a maze of hairline cracks without actually breaking. The back pane is frosted to make the screen translucent but not transparent. An impressive piece of engineering as well as design, the screen accounted for much of the budget of 146,800 dollars.

On the women's side, clothes are displayed an a steel slab, lit from above by spotlights. All other lighting in the store is indirect, using eighty low-wattage lamps under the shelves to illuminate the screen, and as many more powerful ones to wash the ceiling and walls.

Black and white steel posts provide hanging space for clothes on the men's side, where there is only one other item of furniture, a monumental piece of sculpture, in plywood covered with aluminium with an etched finish, that turns out to be a cash-desk. It typifies the overall effect of the interior, which, apart from the beautiful glass screen, seems deliberately over-scaled – perhaps even more suitable as a setting for painting or sculpture rather than clothes.

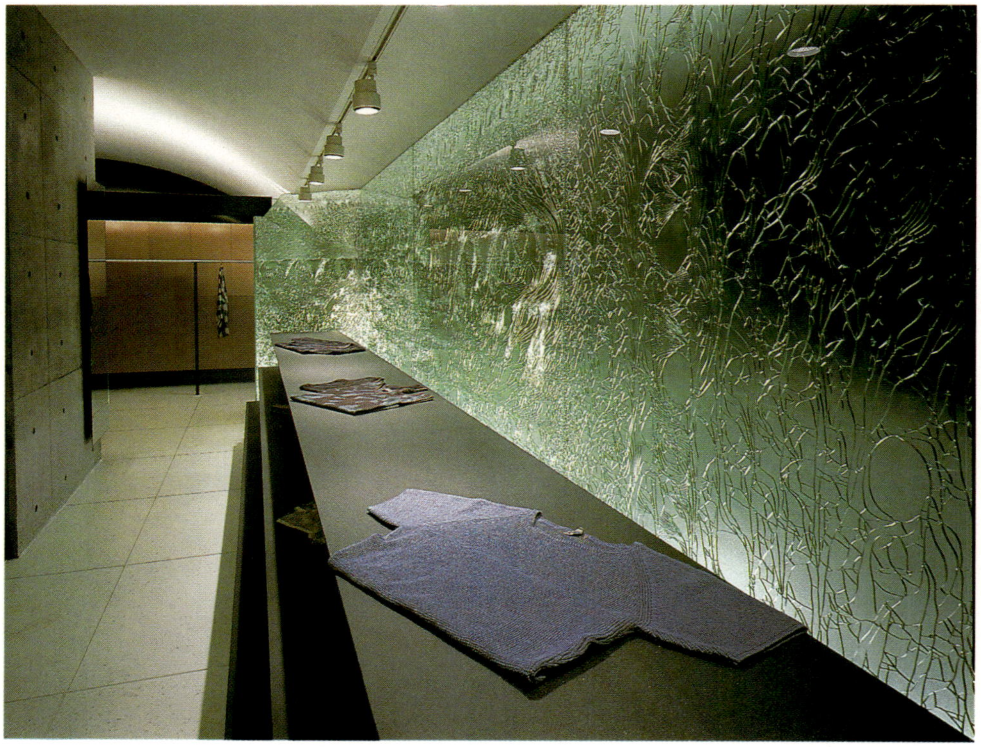

(right) Concentrating on strong architectural lines, Kuramata has introduced only a few large-scale elements.

(far right) Possibly the most sriking feature in the interior: the crazed-glass screen which took up a substantial portion of the budget.

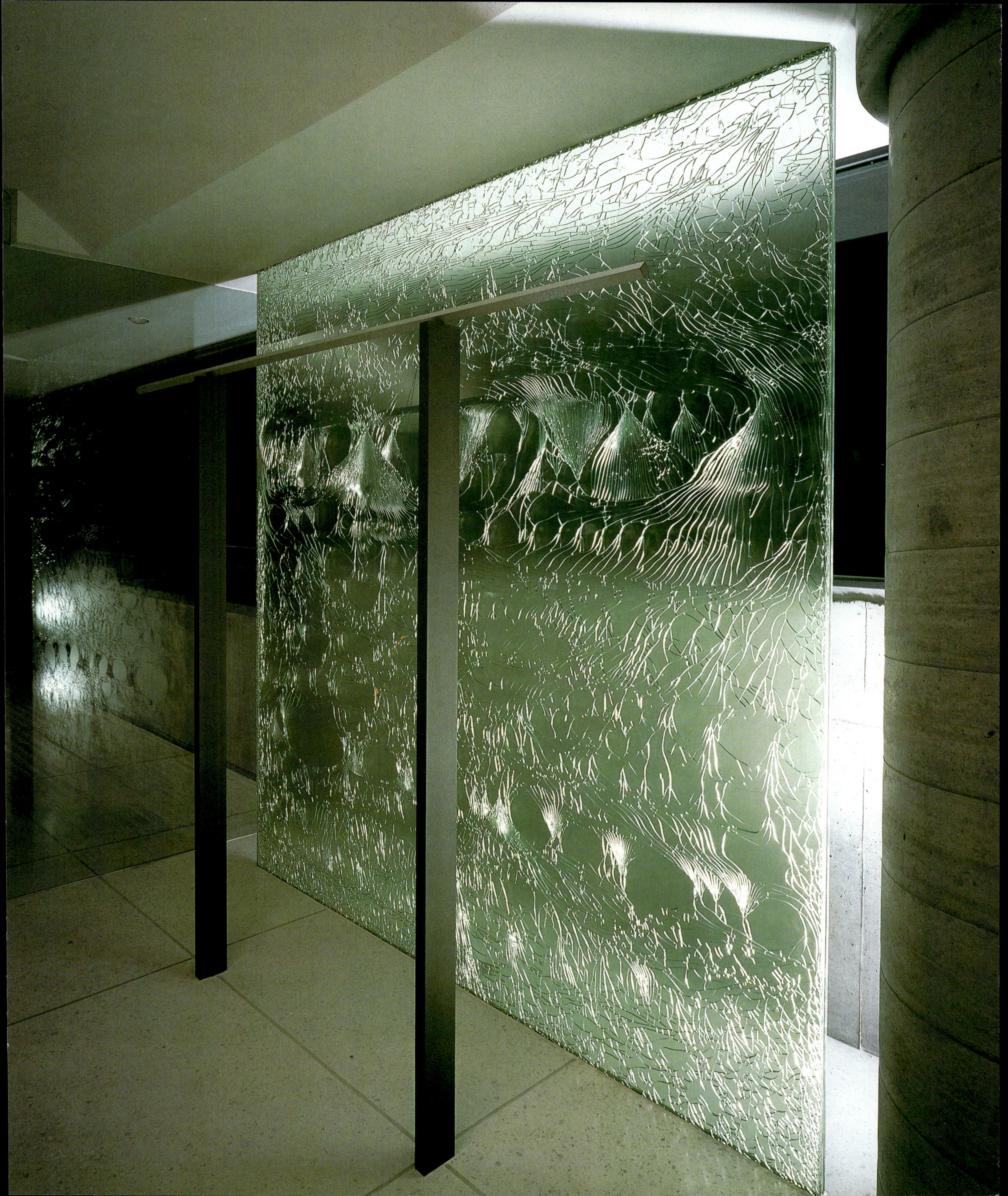

The cash-desk has been designed to look more like a monumental piece of sculpture.

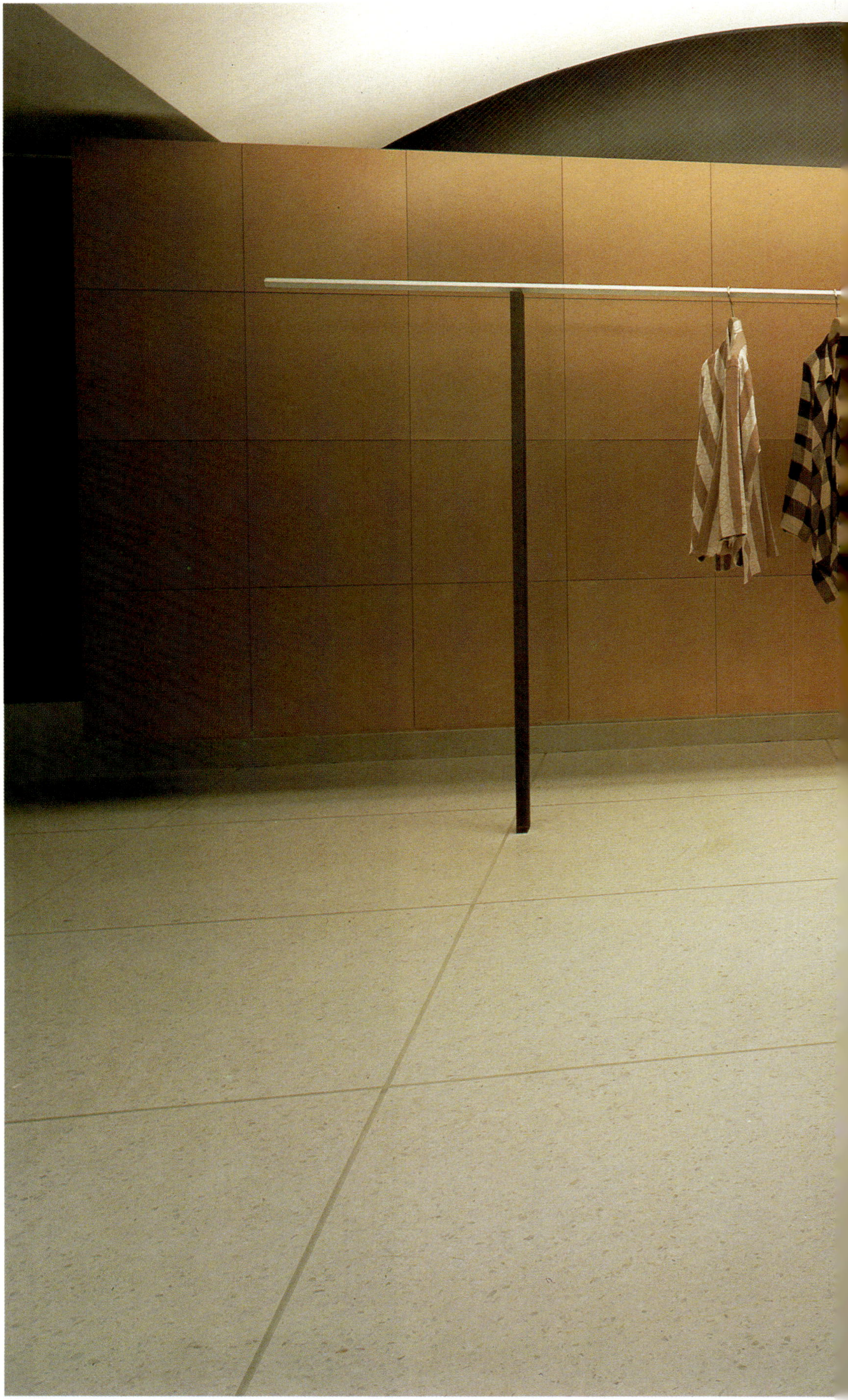

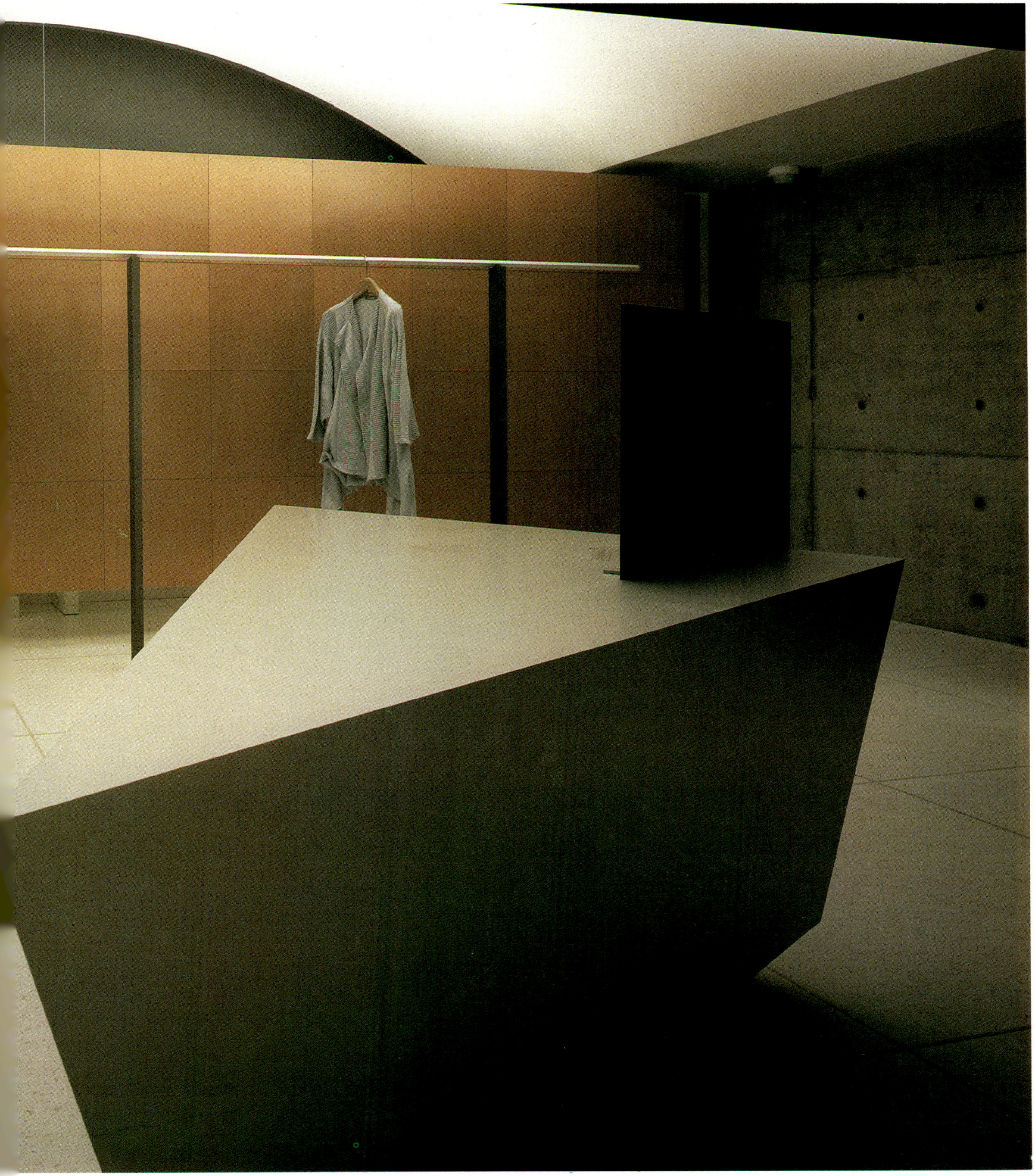

RAHIKAINEN FURS
HELSINKI, FINLAND

Designed by Leo Design

Like so many other European cities, Helsinki was taken over in the 1970s by the pure white, neutral store interior, especially for upmarket, expensive products. Fortunately, these timid, recessive interiors are now on the wane, and a richer style that relies on a complex use of materials and a sensitivity to spatial possibilities can be glimpsed. As one critic has observed, the only danger is that the interiors may now 'exceed the standard of the products they are supposed to complement and support'.

Tua Rahikainen is seemingly unworried by such a possibility. When she commissioned young designer Leo Mitrunen to redesign her fur store, she wanted to achieve some of the style and finish found in Tokyo's new shops. Mitrunen's notion was to create a 'natural Finnish landscape' as a setting for the furs.

A curving path of small black stones (reminiscent of Japanese garden design) leads the visitor through the store. Mitrunen likens the meandering path to a dry riverbed dotted with miniature pebbles. It serves a function in leading the customers naturally through the store, ensuring that they see all the products on display. The path is set in a floor of grey Finnish granite, and the walls are a rich, dense marble. The hard surfaces offer a direct contrast to the soft furs. Mirrors are used extensively to encourage an illusion of space.

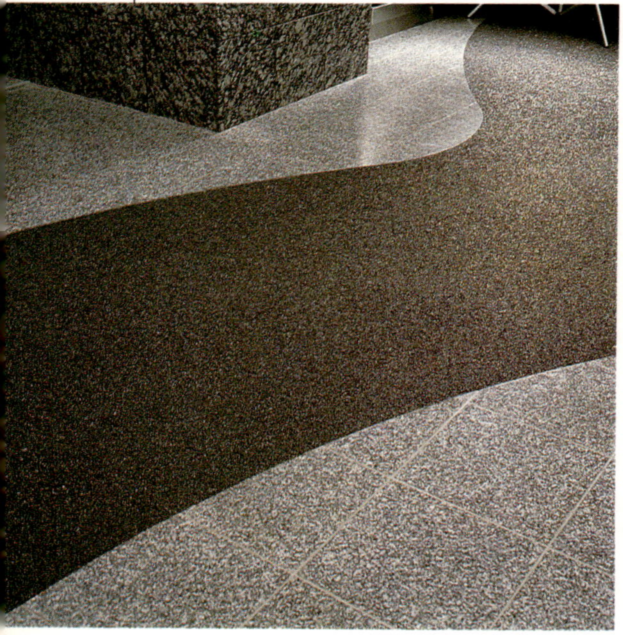

(left) The meandering stone path is set in a floor of grey Finnish granite.

(right) To create a sense of spaciousness, mirrors are fixed to the sides of the shelving units.

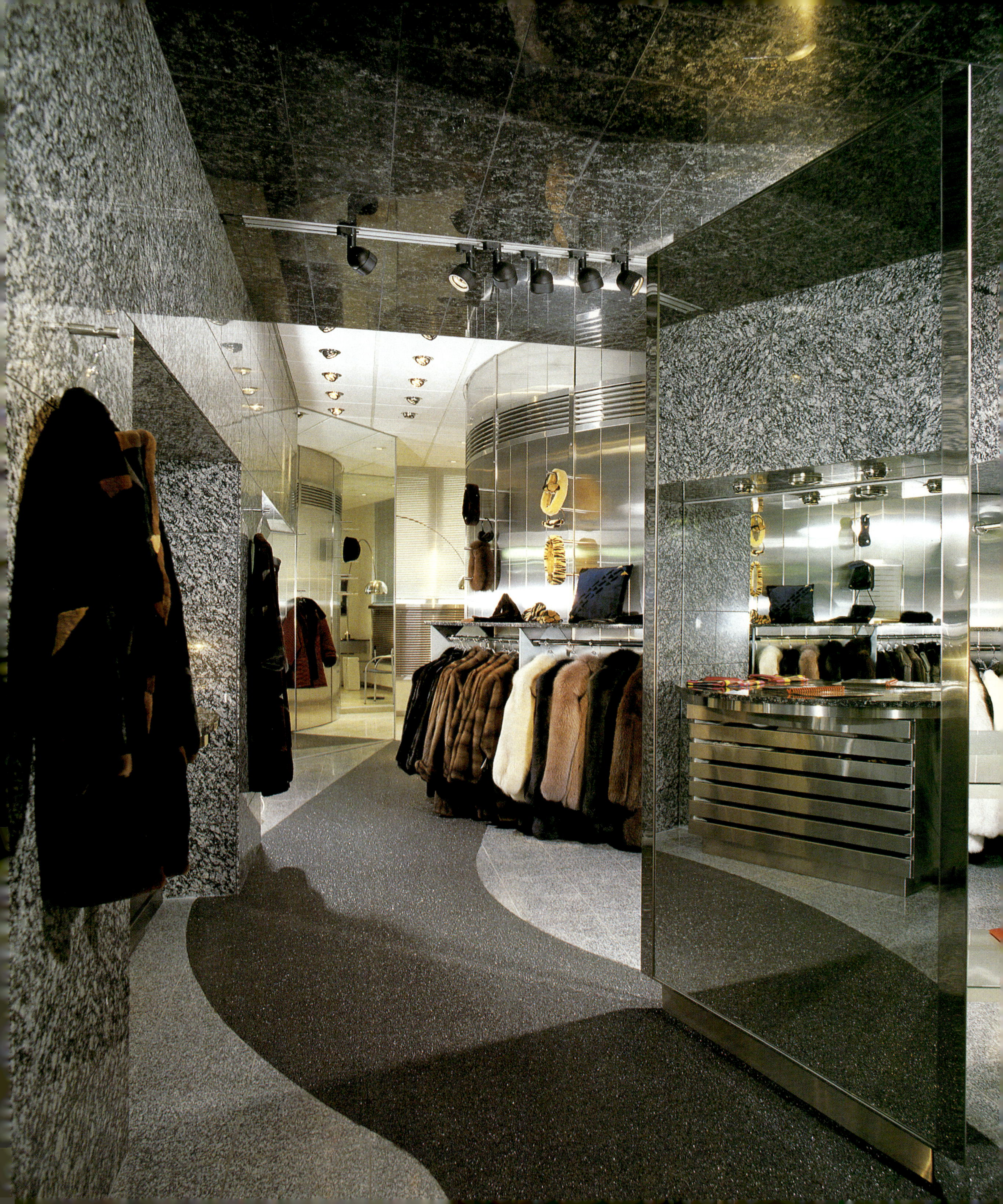

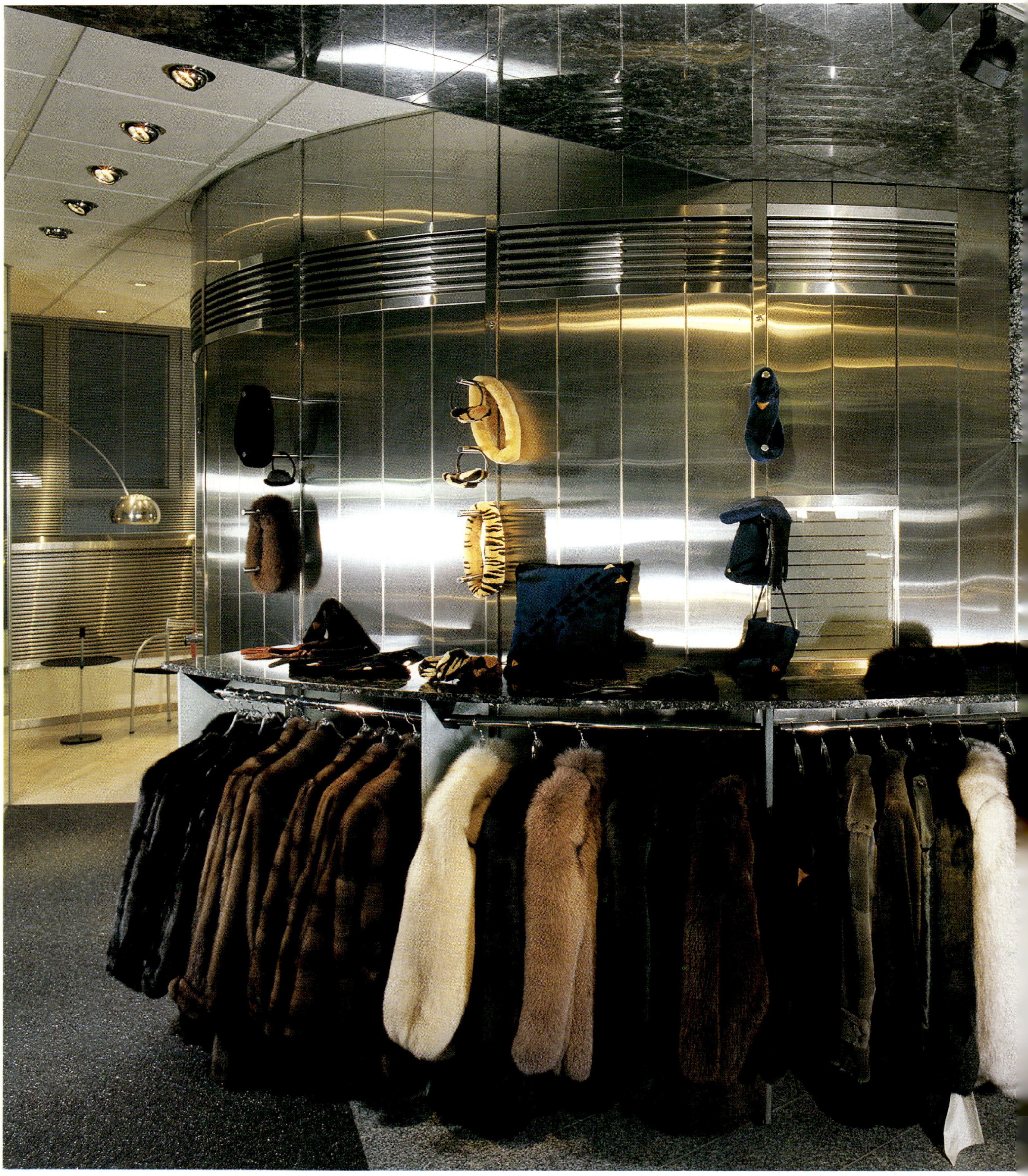

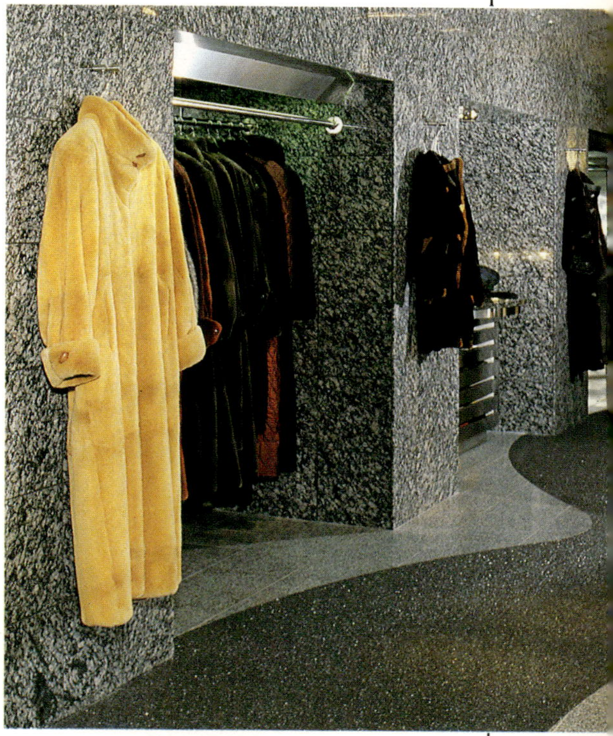

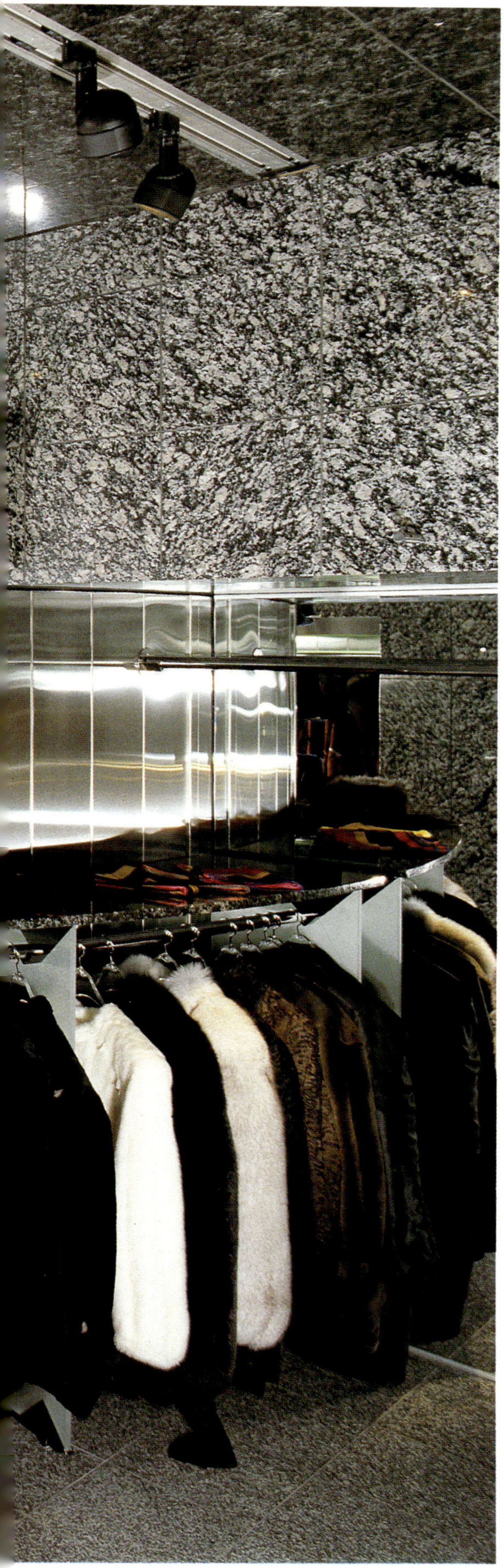

(above) Hard surfaces, such as the marble walls, serve to accentuate the softness of the furs themselves.

(left) A less than exclusive treatment for some of Rahikainen's expensive products: a large carousel packs them together.

W H SMITH
SOUTHAMPTON, UK

Designed by Peter Leonard Associates

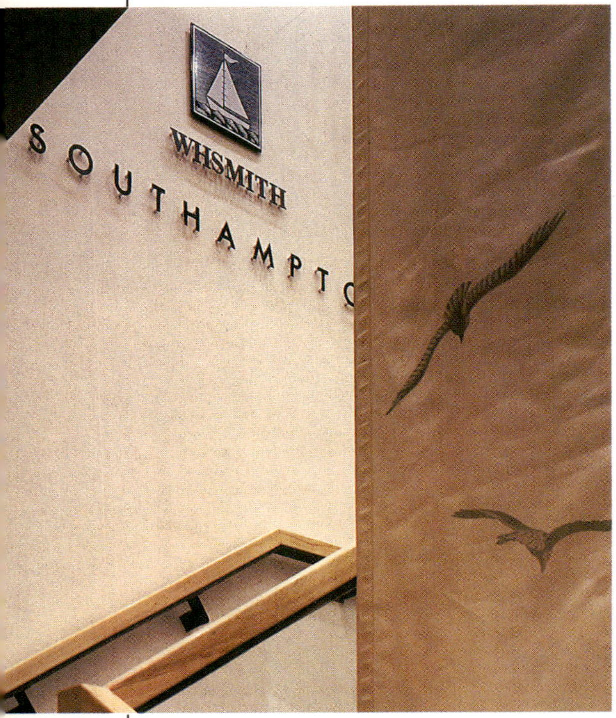

W H Smith took slightly longer than many of Britain's other high-street giants to update the image of their stores. Their orange and brown fascia has been familiar to the country's shoppers for years, signifying a place to buy greetings cards and sticky tape, pencil cases and newspapers – comfortable, convenient and, as many people would have agreed, not really the least bit exciting.

However, once W H Smith's management had decided to restyle their interiors they moved swiftly and imaginatively, opting for the relatively unknown practice of Peter Leonard Associates rather than one of the heavyweight retail design groups. The aim was to introduce a concept of 'leisure shopping', to encourage people to spend longer in the stores and to attract new and younger shoppers. At the same time, W H Smith were anxious not to alienate their established, loyal customers and therefore wanted to retain some familiar aspects of their previous image. Leonard's design was given the go-ahead, and it happened that the scheme was first implemented in the town of Southampton.

From street level, the new W H Smith image is immediately visible. The fascia logo has been restyled and now appears as bright white lettering on a background of very dark brown. Almost full-height glazing and an absence of store risers mean that much of the ground floor is visible from the street too, with only three free-standing metal display panels to block the passer-by's view inside. These display panels are components in a kit of parts devised by Leonard, and they reappear throughout the shop in free-standing form or fixed to floor and ceiling. Their purpose is to create clearly distinguishable areas for each department. To help

(above) The designers' aim is that each branch should somehow be personalized: in the Southampton branch, a sailing-ship logo and banners painted with seagulls proclaims the town's maritime associations.

(right) A clean, bright treatment contrasts with the client's previous uninspired colour scheme of orange, brown and more brown.

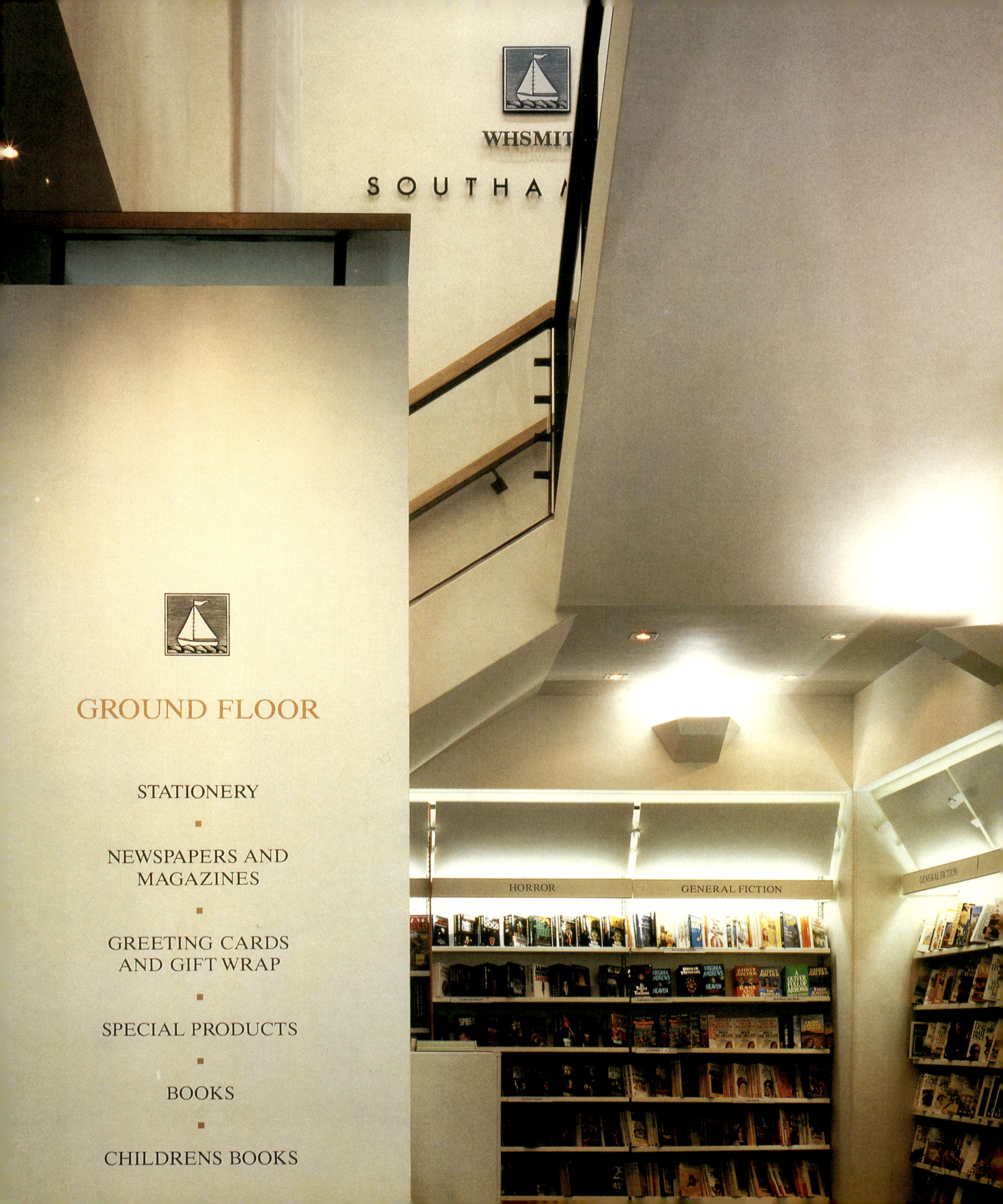
WHSMIT
SOUTHA
GROUND FLOOR
STATIONERY
NEWSPAPERS AND MAGAZINES
GREETING CARDS AND GIFT WRAP
SPECIAL PRODUCTS
BOOKS
CHILDRENS BOOKS
HORROR
GENERAL FICTION
GENERAL FICTION

them do so, they carry graphics or photographs on Foamex card.

Graphics of a more permanent nature appear on angled frieze panels which run above the perimeter wall units. More traditional in approach, they have been screen-printed by Andrew Davidson and look more like old woodcuts. Each 'woodcut' logo is in a different shade according to the department that it represents. This colour-coding recurs on the aluminium extrusion moulding to the display units.

Because the Southampton project was a model to be repeated in all of W H Smith's branches, Leonard Associates have decided to add a 'personalized' touch for each store. In the case of the Southampton store this is a sailing ship logo and three banners painted with seagulls to acknowledge the city's maritime links. Such personalization may provide a more general solution to the problem of uniformity among multiple retailers in many different towns.

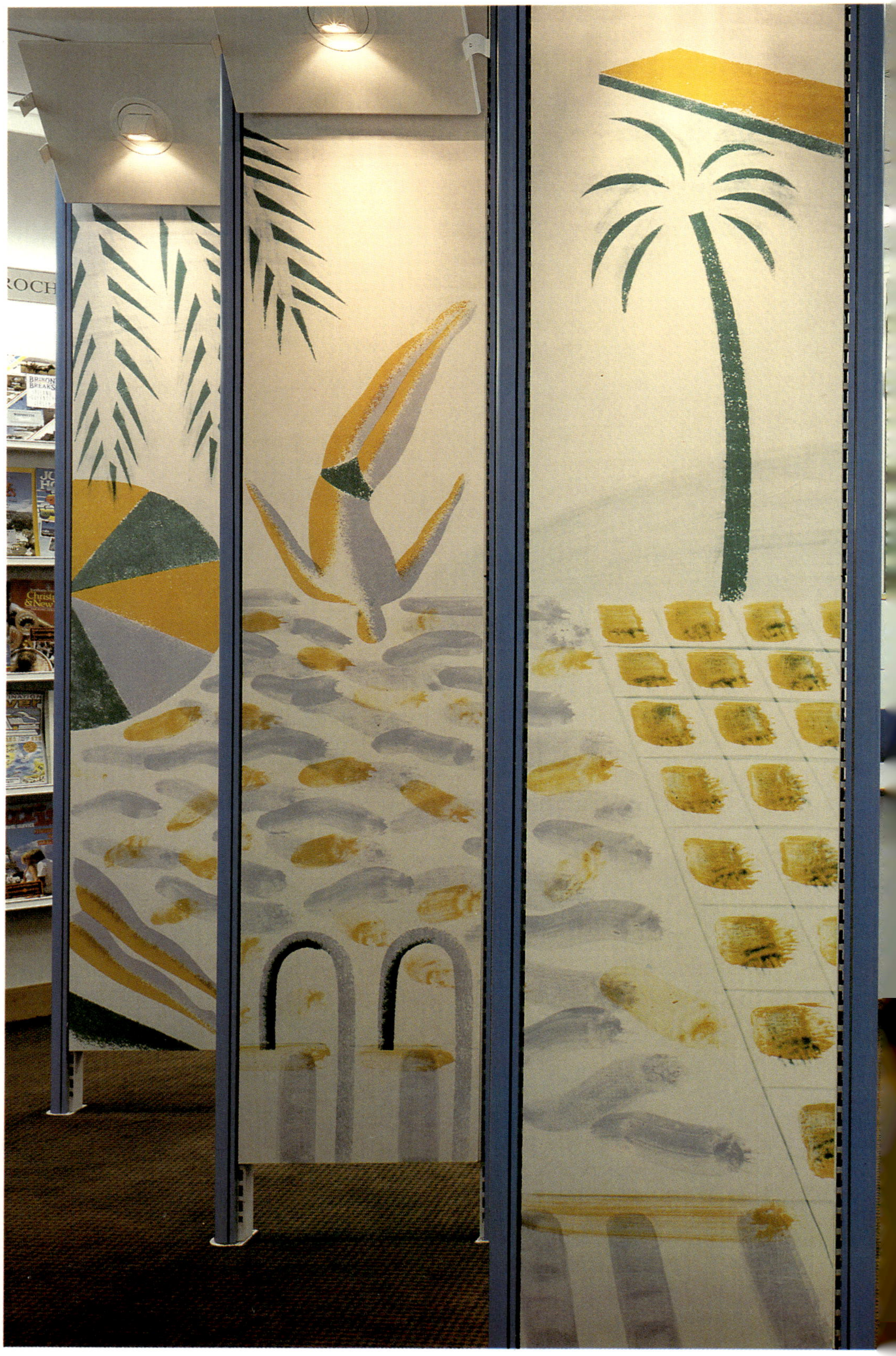

Downlighters focus on the graphics panels and display boards which provide customers with easy-to-understand information about the different departments and types of merchandise.

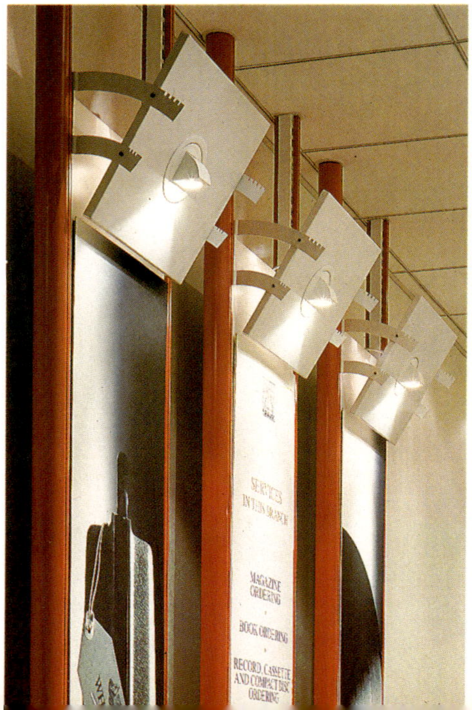

(left) Colours, as well as graphics, are used to identify the different sections within the shop: for the travel department, for example, graphics and panels are predominantly blue.

(below) Display panels, fixed to floor and ceiling, are a key element in the new design. The graphics can be changed.

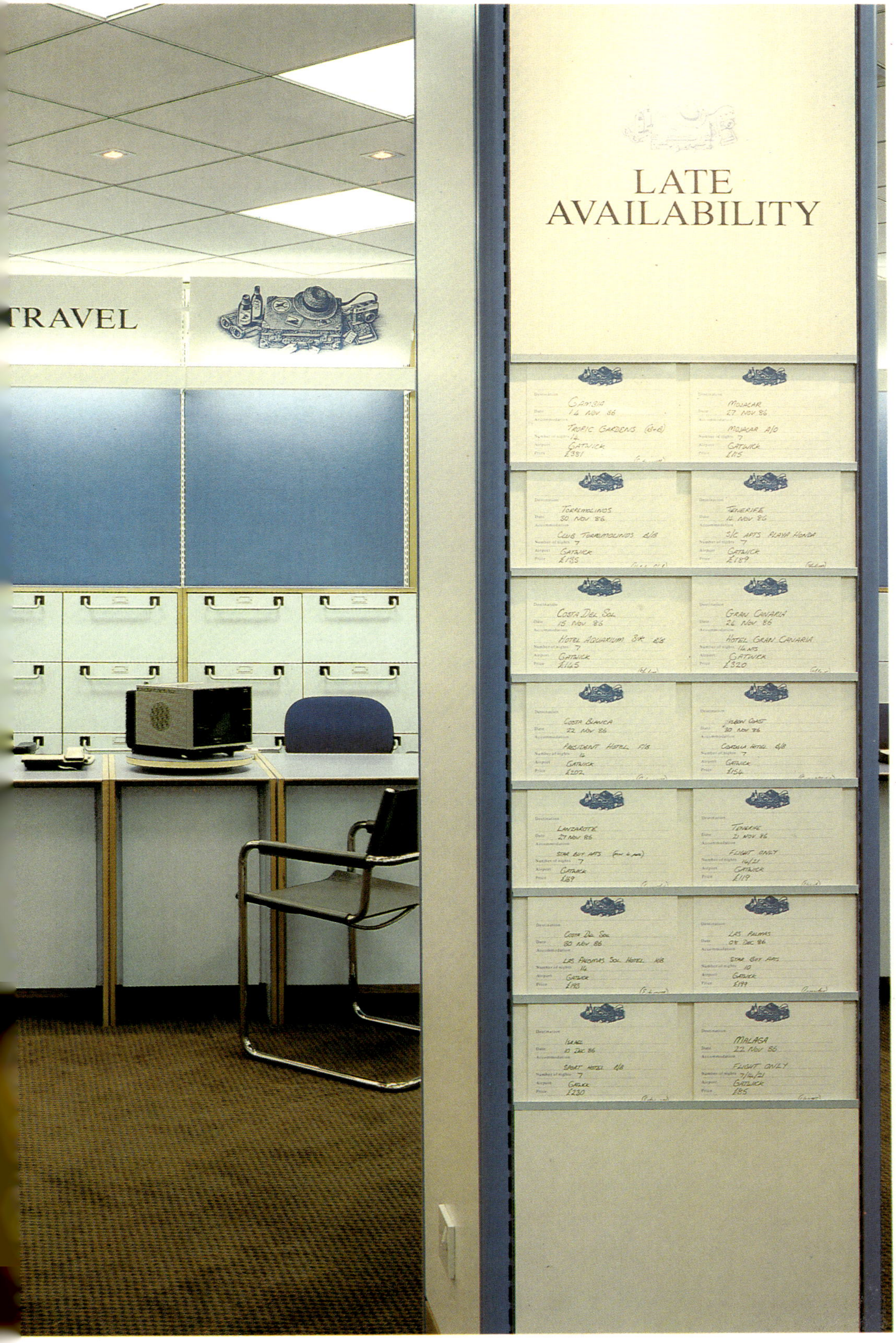

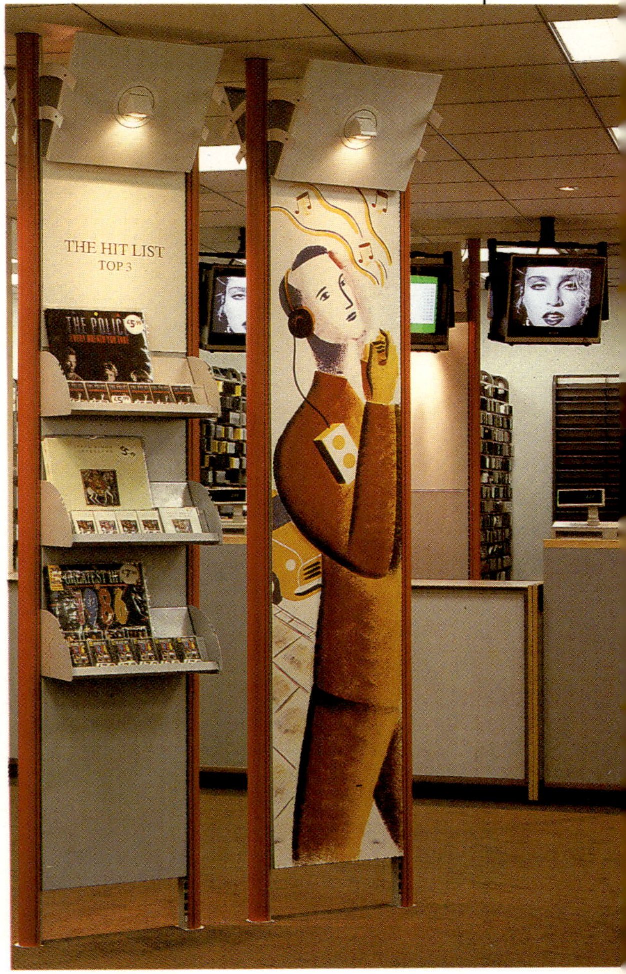

EIGHT STAR DIAMOND
TOKYO, JAPAN

Designed by Masaki Morita

Ideally, the design of a showroom should reflect and enhance the product, rather than providing a neutral backdrop for it; and when the product is diamonds, there is plenty of scope for the imagination.

Masaki Morita's design for the Eight Star Diamond showroom in Tokyo includes an entrance lobby, office, showroom and reception room, all within a compact 1,356 square foot (126 square metre) space.

Through the glass doors, the visitors' first sight of the interior is of a blue pyramid, like a solidified shaft of light from the ceiling to the Travertine floor. Passing through they enter the main showroom, off which are a small office and, through open arches, a reception room. Furniture is beautiful but minimal – one sees simply a green marble table, a solitary chair upholstered in suede.

The showroom, with its green terrazzo floor and white walls, is equally bare, save for black display cases and a mysterious upturned cone table, made of steel, on which sits a water-filled glass sphere. This is the *tour de force*: by placing a diamond under the sphere and directing a laser beam on to it, the refracted light from the gem is magnified, throwing a spectrum of colours on to the walls and ceiling.

Such effects are not all that expensive – the overall budget was 150,000 dollars – but they are typical of Morita's work. In Japan he has earned the nickname of 'Masaka', meaning 'incredible' or, more ironically, 'Is he for real?', and he has the reputation of being a philosopher and dreamer. A reputation borne out by the almost mythical qualities of this showroom design.

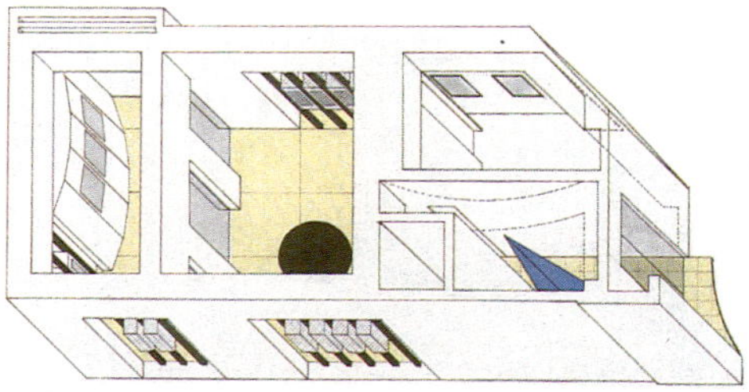

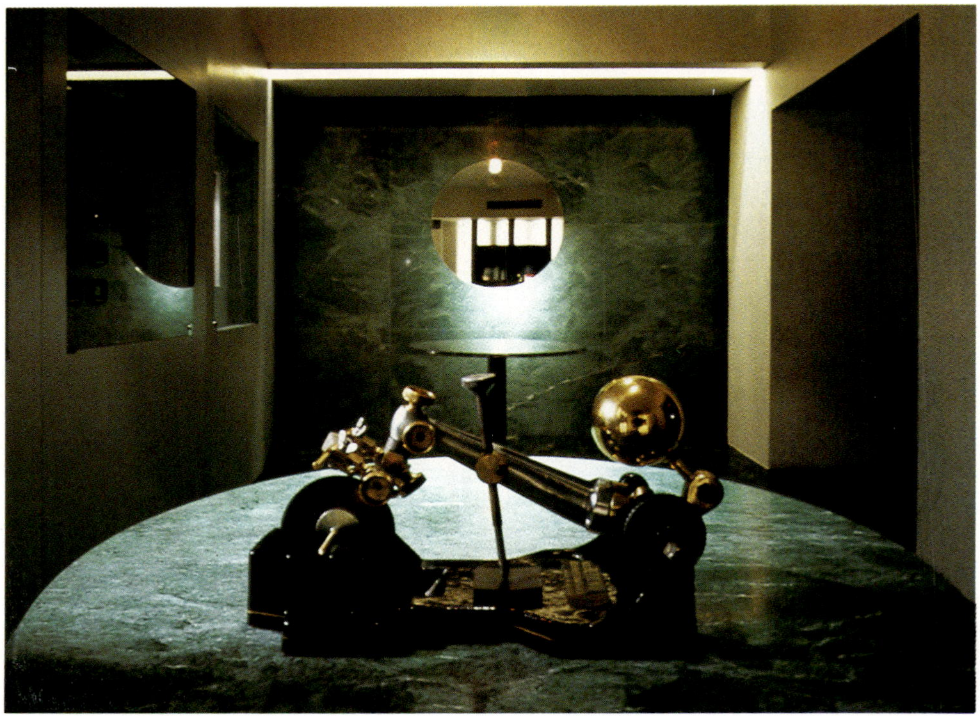

(above) In a 1,356 square foot (126 square metre) space, Morita has managed to include a narrow entrance lobby as well as the main showroom area.

(right) Deep inside the showroom, green terrazzo gives an atmosphere of mystery: here, too, the designer has played games with light by directing a laser beam on to a diamond.

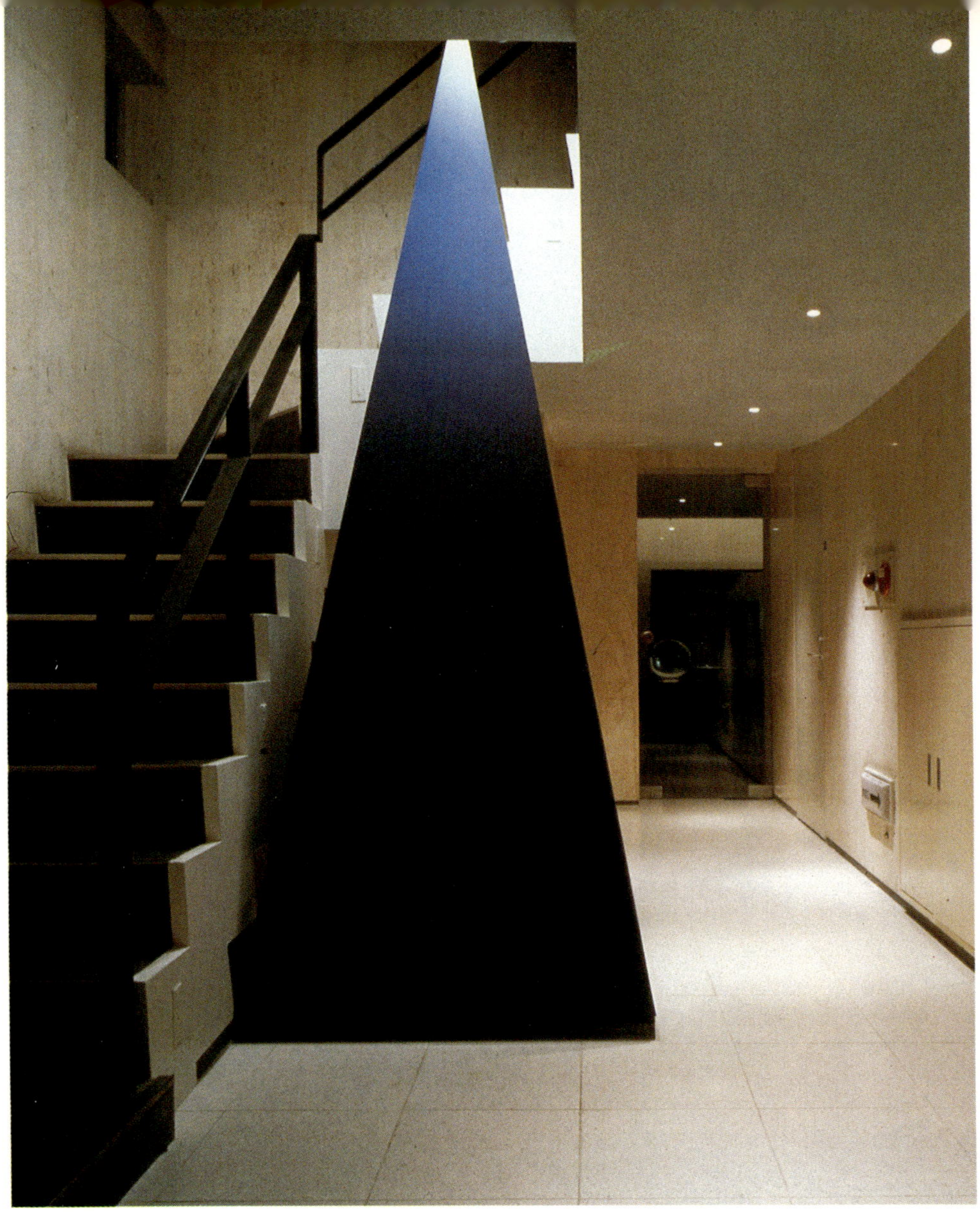

(left) A blue pyramid, rather like a solidified shaft of light, is the first thing visitors see as they enter the showroom.

(below) An inverted cone shape, the table is the focus and centrepiece of the showroom.

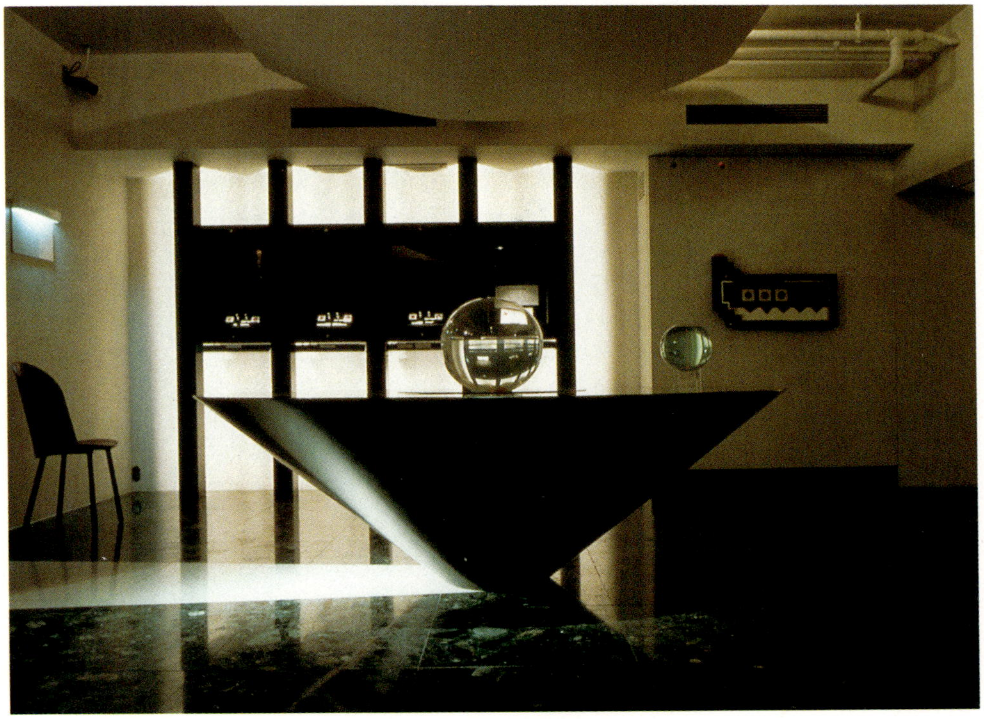

DOMAIN
CHESTNUT MILL, MASSACHUSETTS, USA
Designed by Schwartz/Silver Architects

One of the first considerations before Schwartz/Silver when they began designing an interior for Domain – a new chain of stores selling European furniture in the USA – was to what extent it should complement the merchandise, not compete with it.

What they have done is to create a large-scale, very architectural backdrop for the chairs, rugs, lamps and glassware on sale, and in doing so have provided a modern, abstract environment. From the shopping mall, customers enter the store through three pivoting doors which have been hand-treated to resemble large painted canvases. Inside, striking shapes and colours are juxtaposed to contrast with the softer lines of the furniture, much of which is traditional in style. Most noticeable at Domain is the way in which everything appears to be not quite complete – walls tilt and are unfinished at their edges, ductwork is left visible in places and partitions are asymmetrical. This, explain the designers, is to give the effect of a theatrical set, to create a sense of illusion.

Architecturally, Domain is made up of sweeping lines. Of these, the most striking is the tilted wall of yellow fresco secco plaster which runs the whole length of the store and which, at uneven intervals, contains the entrances to a series of display rooms or 'caves', like something out of an Eastern bazaar. Throughout the space, there are floor-to-ceiling steel and silk panels which can be moved on track for flexibility of display.

Materials are mostly natural so that they are sympathetic to the wood, leather and linen of the merchandise: the floor, for example, is black marble terrazzo, and skirtings are wood. Colours, too, are subtle: predominantly soft yellow with turquoise and grey.

What the owners of Domain wanted from Schwartz/Silver was an interior that would tell their customers that here was something special. The result is a clever balance between a cool, spacious showroom where everything can be seen clearly and a series of treasure troves where something unusual or surprising can be found.

(below) Customers enter Domain from a shopping mall via three large hand-painted pivoting doors.

(below right) Accessories on sale can be glimpsed in nooks and niches within the wall of yellow secco plaster. The effect is rather like a treasure trove or bazaar.

(right) Isometric projection.

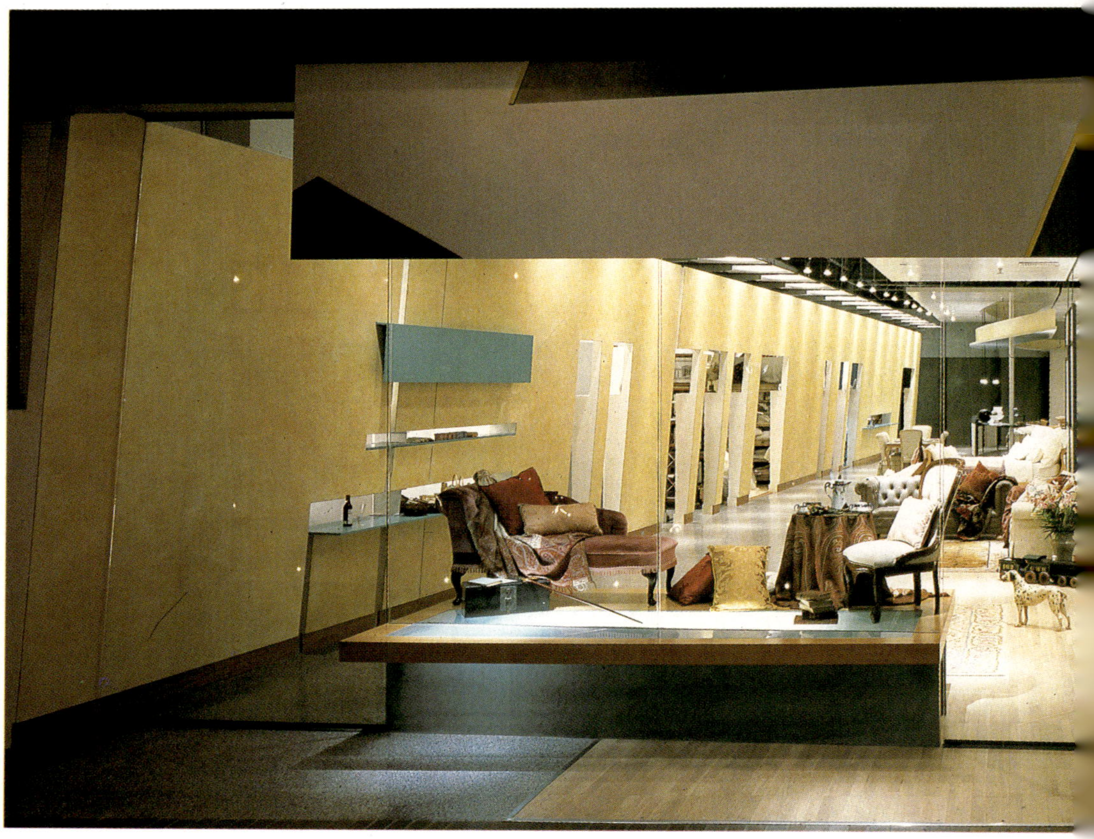

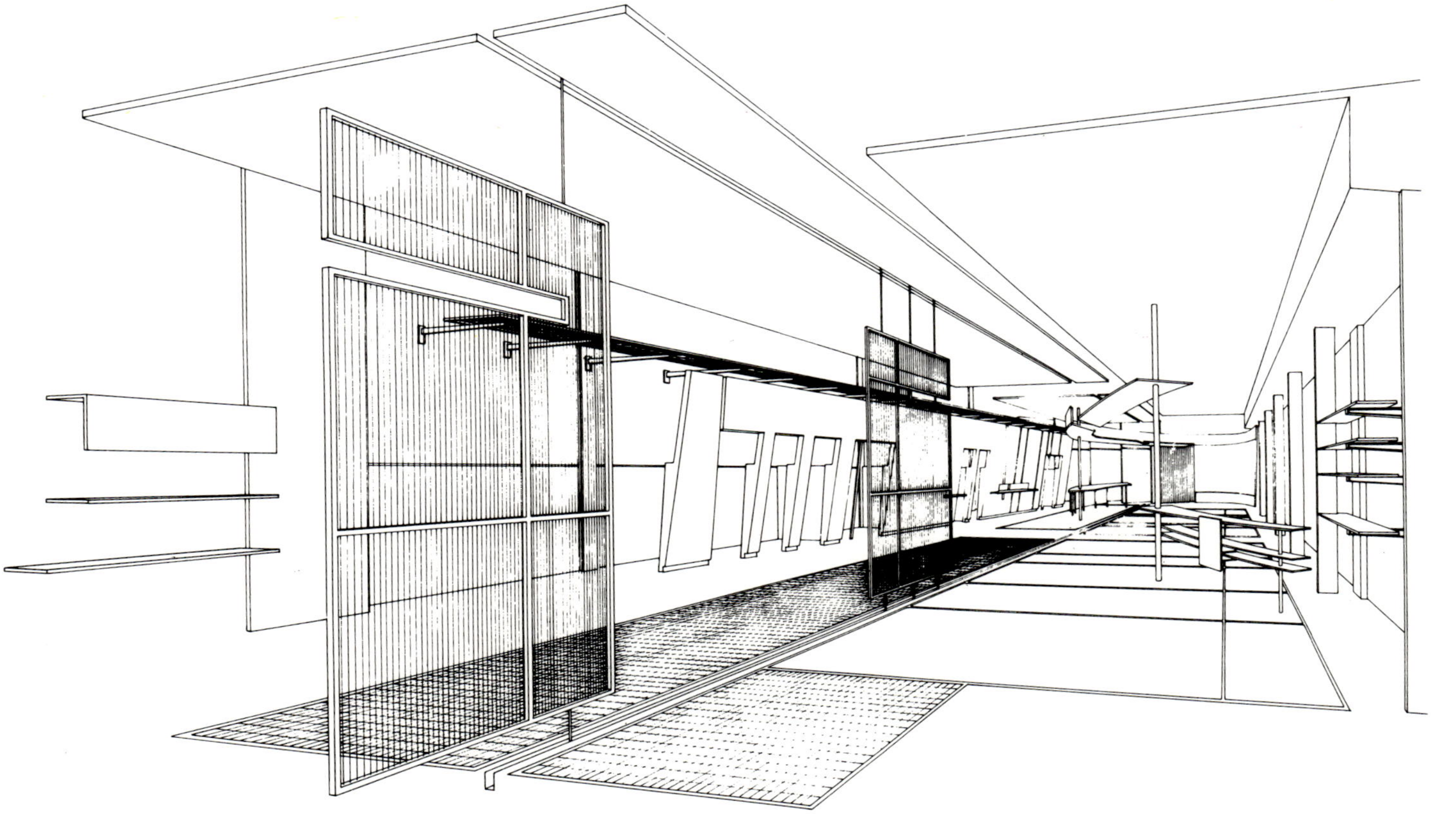

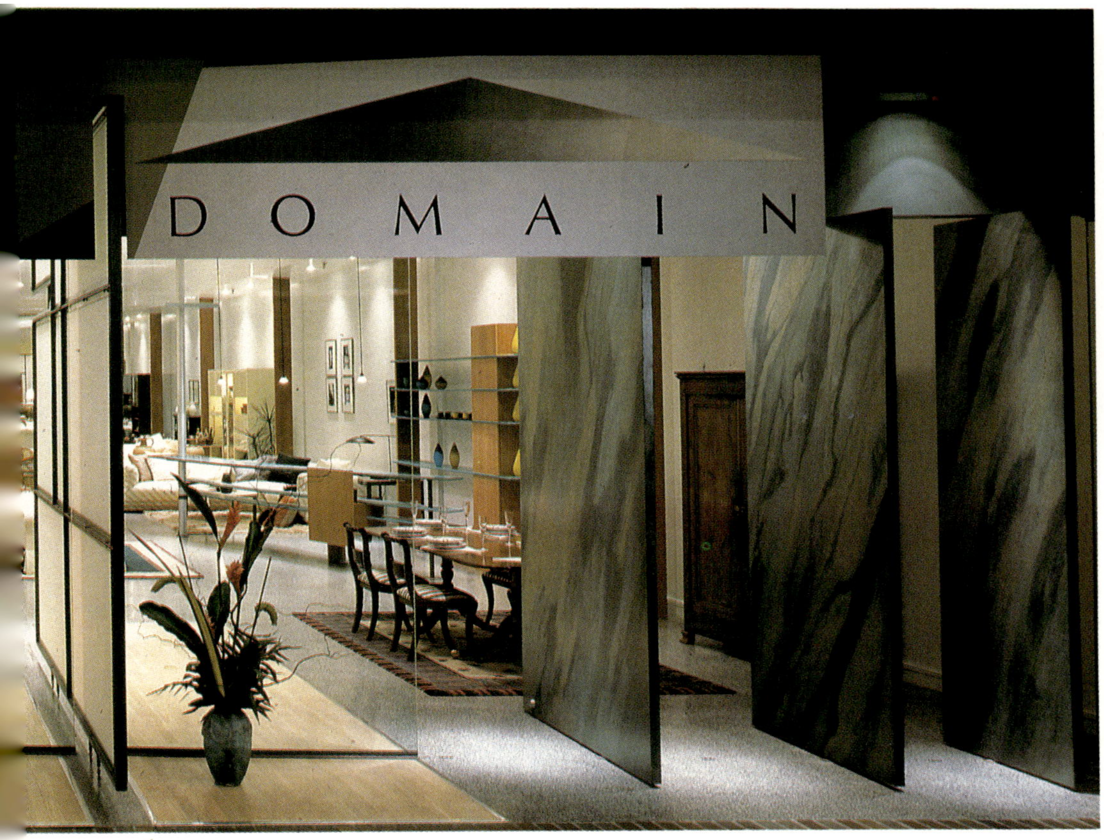
DOMAIN

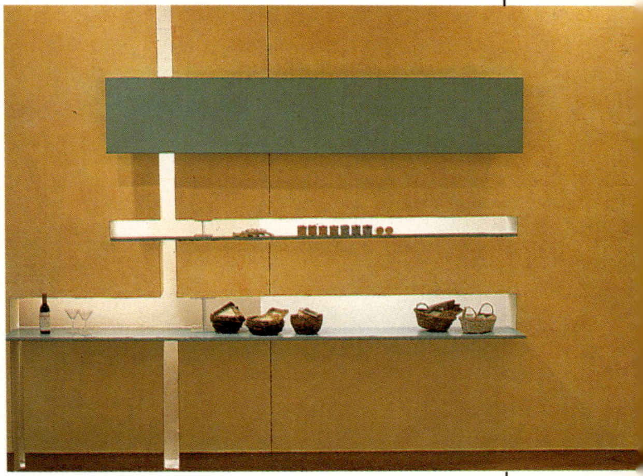

ESPRIT DE CORP
DÜSSELDORF, COLOGNE, BERLIN, MELBOURNE

Designed by Sottsass Associati

No designer has had a bigger influence in the 1980s than Ettore Sottsass. Although well-known to cognoscenti for years for his work for Olivetti and other Italian manufacturers, his creation of Memphis in 1981 catapulted him into the centre of the design world. With a mixed band of designers, Memphis set out to challenge, and in some ways destroy, the conventions of modern design. Decoration, clashing patterns, artificial materials and, above all, the banal were celebrated. With his bassett-hound eyes brooding over his offspring, Sottsass became *the* guru of design.

At about the same time that Sottsass was marching to the forefront of the design world, two San Francisco-based designers from the generation of the 1960s were building a giant fashion empire. Doug and Susie Tompkins started Esprit de Corp, generally known as Esprit, in 1968 on their kitchen table. Growth was slow and steady until their first mail-order catalogue in 1980 which stunned the fashion world with its defiance of convention: no professional models were used, since Doug and Susie preferred ordinary people; outfits seemed to obey no rules, but were mixed-and-matched. By 1986, Esprit were nearly a one-billion-dollar company, larger than the better-known Benetton.

The parallel success stories of Sottsass and Esprit made them perfectly suited to each other, particularly given the Tompkins' belief in the importance of environment for their commercial image as well as the general corporate culture. When Esprit decided to open both stores and showrooms in Germany, they turned to Sottsass Associati.

Esprit's brief to Sottsass might have been a recipe for disaster: the designers were given *carte blanche* to create stores without equal; the budget was unspecified; and no direction as to the market was given (in an age when store design is dominated by market research). Although all the work Sottsass have done for Esprit is breathtaking (and the success of the German venture led to commissions in Australia and Denmark), neither the stores nor the showrooms are mere exercises in bravura or self-indulgence. They work, both on the practical level of selling the clothes effectively, and, equally important, in terms of promoting a grand image of Esprit.

Certain elements are common to all the projects. Like Esprit's clothes, textures and patterns are apparently mixed in an almost wild fashion (though all have, of course, been carefully controlled by the designers). Materials are a combination of the traditional and natural, and the highly synthetic. Functional elements – such as display units, cash tills and changing-rooms – are movable, flexible assemblies that enable regular variations as Esprit's fashions change.

At the heart of Sottsass Associati's designs for Esprit is a playful use of colours, textures and shapes.

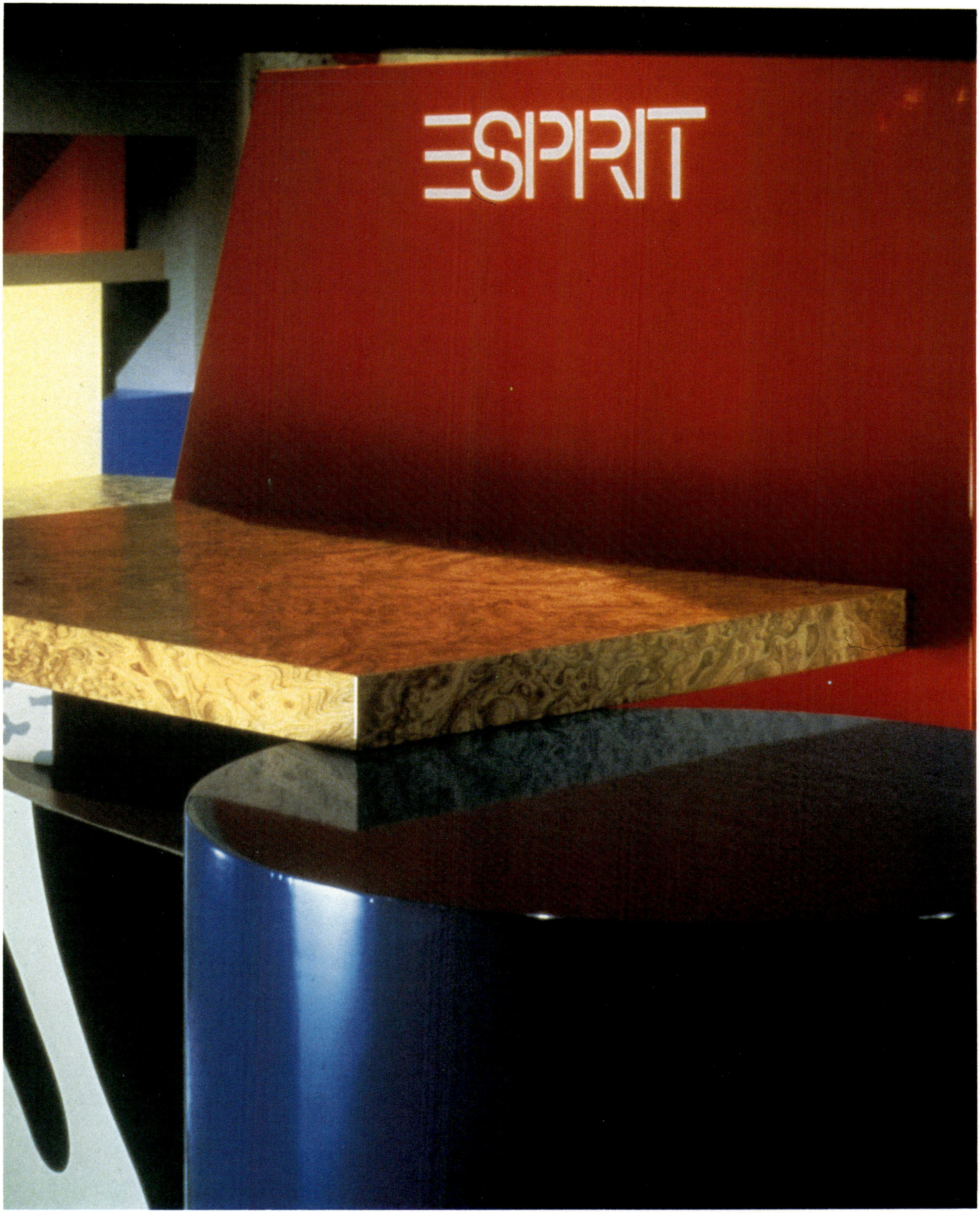
ESPRIT

ESPRIT DE CORP
DÜSSELDORF, WEST GERMANY

Designed by Sottsass Associati

Esprit Germany is headquartered in Düsseldorf, where Sottsass took a large, anonymous industrial building and transformed it into a showroom, design studio and administrative office. From the outside, small hints of the inside are given: a marble pergola near the entrance and a monumental entrance porch have been added. Inside the entrance, visitors are confronted with a riot of colour and pattern. An amoeba-patterned carpet leads to the reception desk, while walls of nougat-like terrazzo create a central mezzanine. Visitors are asked to wait on a circular raised platform, dubbed the 'hot tube'.

The mezzanine, with a conference area on top, is reached by a yellow glass tile-clad bridge; the mezzanine itself is ringed by walls of blue glass tiles that oddly evoke the image of a swimming-pool. But the showroom has a practical function: to sell clothes. The selling is done using a variety of architectural elements: clothes are stored in metal roller-shuttered 'garages' on wheels with space for an entire collection; prospective buyers sit round a table under a 'pergola', facing a movable wall on which the salesperson displays the collection.

Since everything is on wheels, it is simple for Esprit to shift all the elements out of the way for a special event such as the launch of a collection, or to group a number of 'garages' and walls together to sell to a large team of buyers from a department store. In these 15,000 square feet (1394 square metres), everything is mutable.

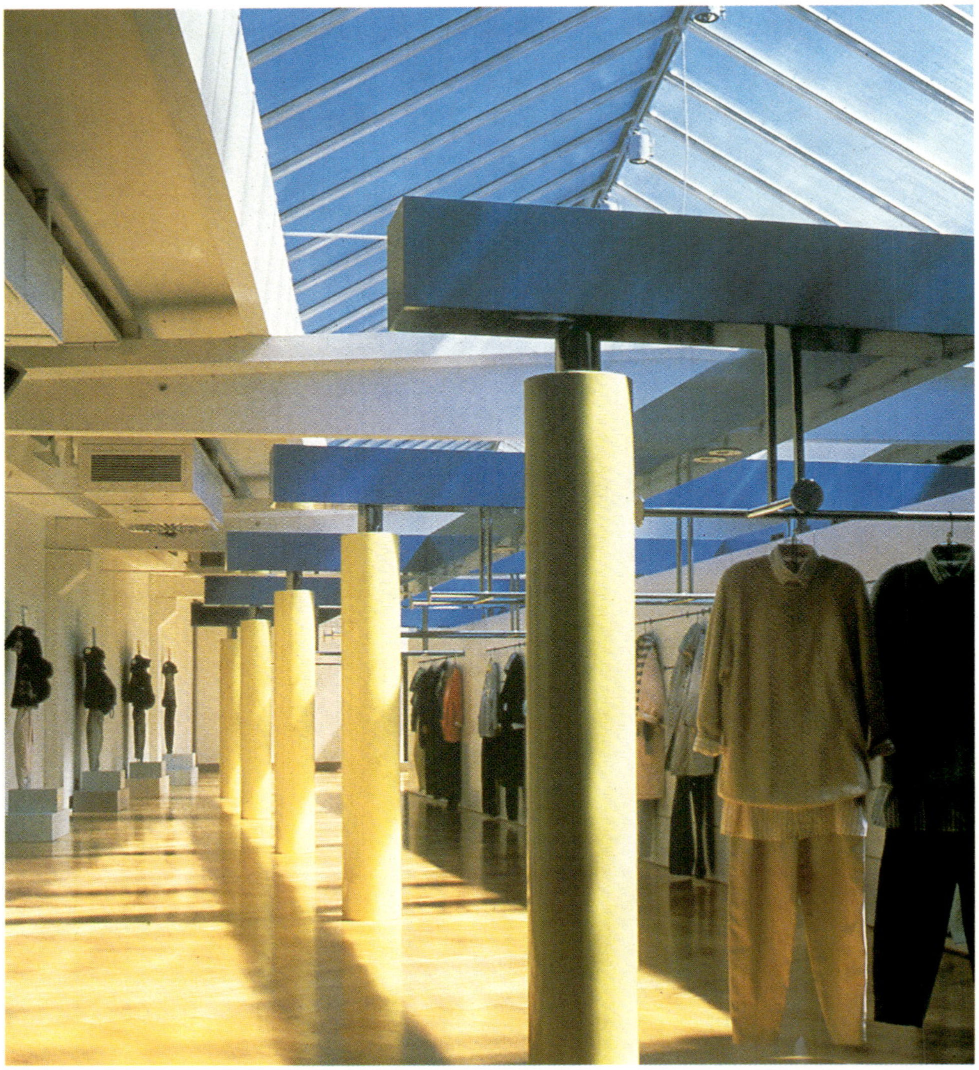

(above) The regular march of a post and lintel display system organizes the sky-lit showroom space.

(right) Different stained woods create pattern on the floor, and help define internal areas.

(below) Movable walls and 'pergola' ceilings form enclosed spaces in which the salespeople can make their pitch.

(below right) Walls of blue glass tiles in the mezzanine oddly evoke the image of a swimming-pool.

(right) Nougat-like terrazzo clads the stairs to the 'swimming-pool' meeting area.

(far right) Cartoon cutout shapes animate the showroom.

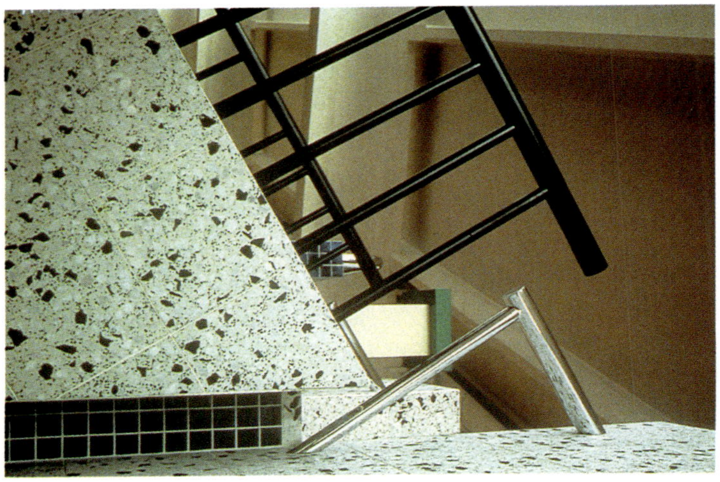

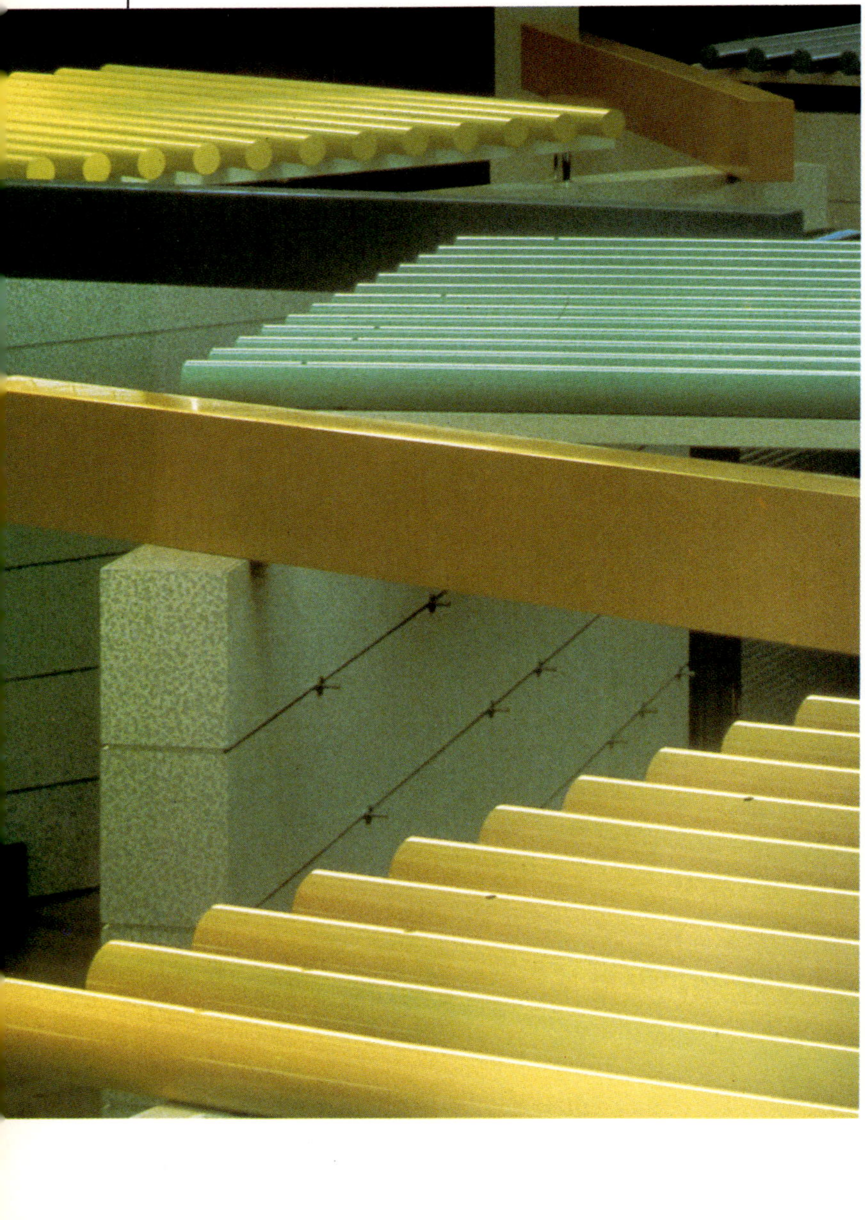

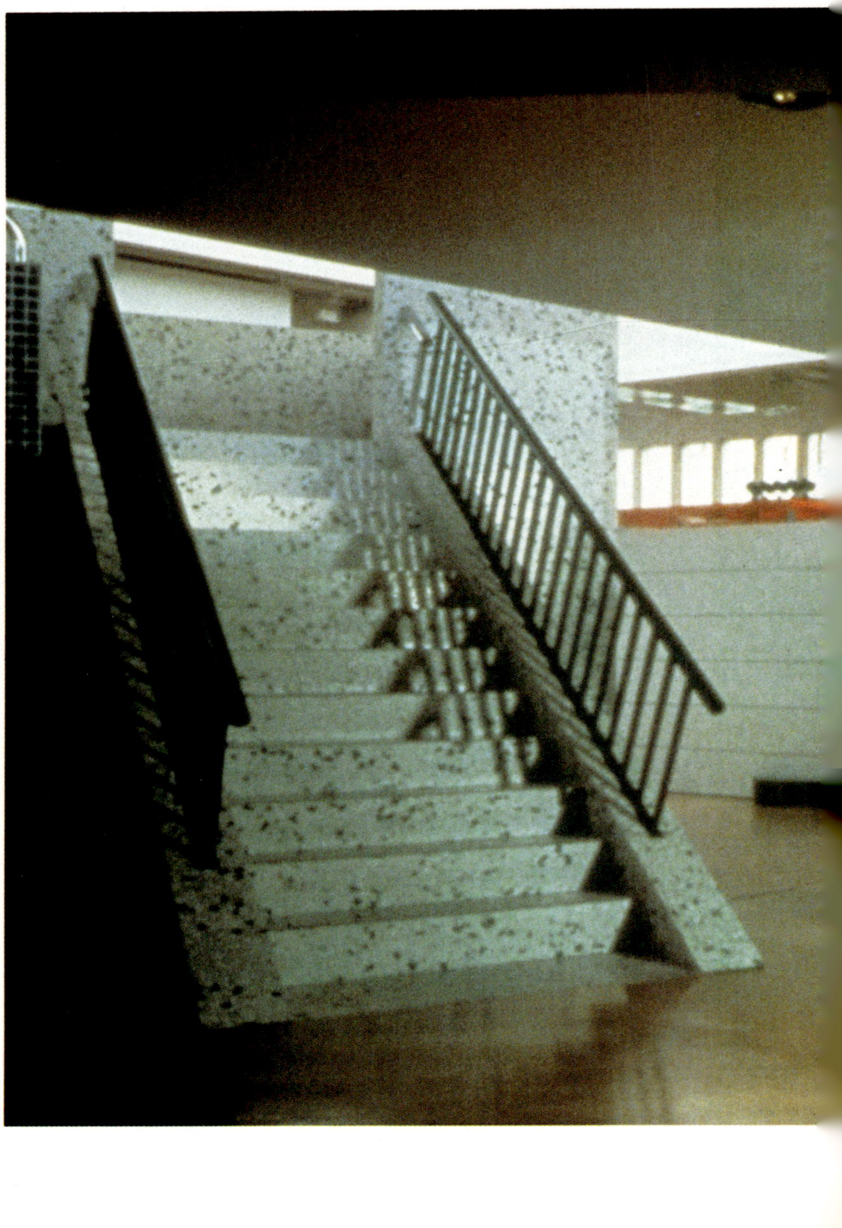

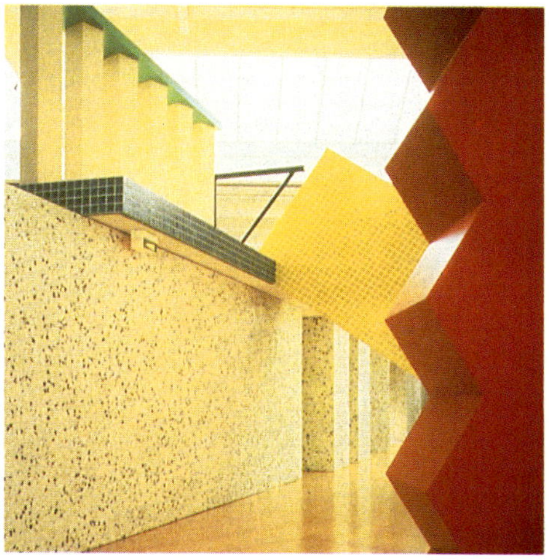

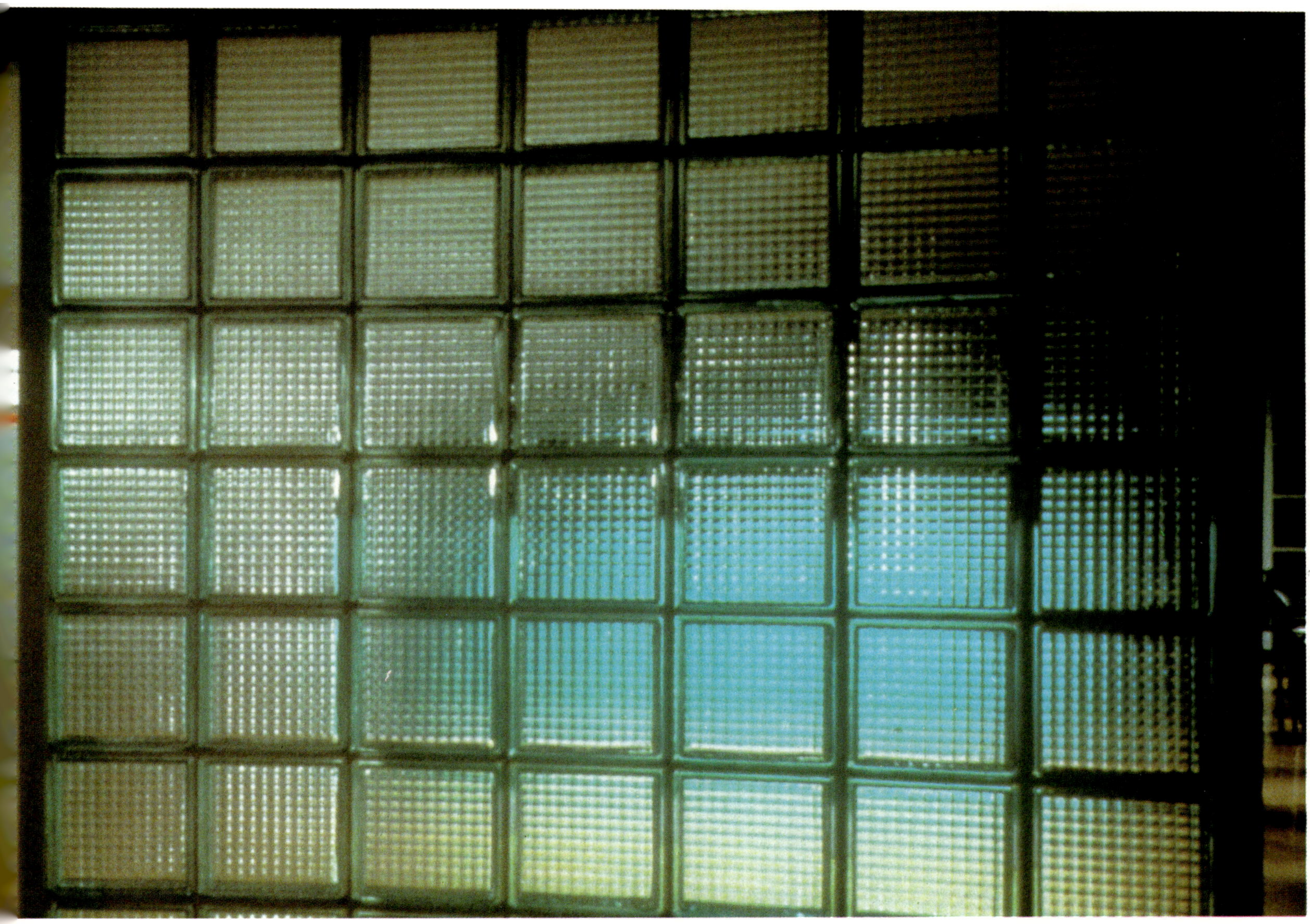

ESPRIT DE CORP
COLOGNE, WEST GERMANY

Designed by Sottsass Associati

Cologne was conceived as Esprit's first 'flagship' store in Germany, and suitably is the most spectacular of the designs. The 10,000 square foot (929 square metre) store was completely stripped by the designers to create a complex and at first sight disorientating series of spaces. The internal shell of the building was clad in a black-and-white speckled terrazzo, and within this Sottsass created a three-storey extravaganza of retail design.

The store is entered over a bridge that offers vistas both to the floor above and to the one below. To the right of the entrance stands a pair of specially constructed elevators, with cabs glazed with one-inch-thick plate glass (reminiscent of British high-tech architect Norman Foster). Marble architraves frame the elevator doors. At the back of the store is a surprise: a gem of a pink hand-finished stairwell. The stairwell's soft delicacy is achieved by a covering of Marmorino, a fine marble powder that was hand-applied by two Venetian craftsmen who were personally brought to Cologne by Sottsass' partner Aldo Cibic.

Like the Düsseldorf showroom, the Cologne store uses a range of movable elements for displaying clothes. Cash-desks are clad in colourful plastic laminates, a jigsaw of L-shaped lamination pieces acts as a display for shoes, modular clothes islands contain hanging racks, shelves and a mirror (these islands can be reconfigured with changing collections). Even the changing-rooms are inventive: they are laminate-clad 'beach cabanas'.

(right) An entrance bridge slices through the three-storey space.

(below left) The simple geometries of a colourful cash-desk which sits in a sea of speckled terrazzo.

(below right) Store spaces are open and easy to comprehend. At the back is the lure of the pink Marmorino staircase.

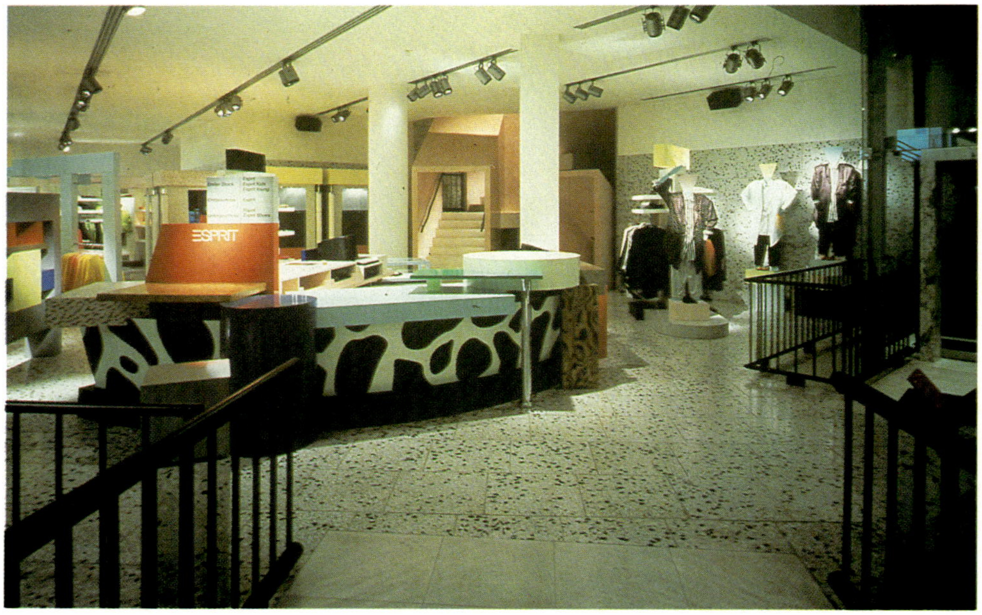

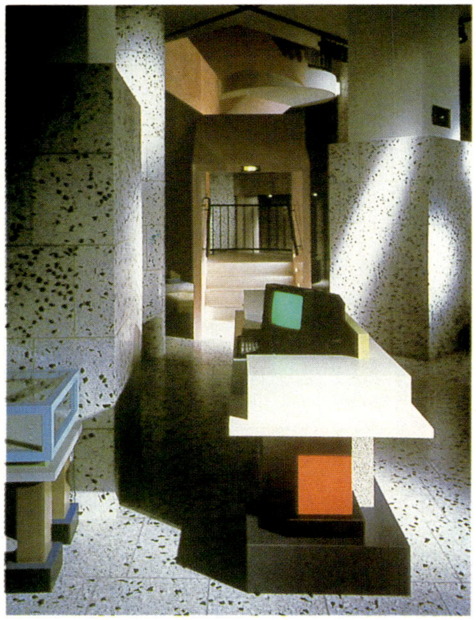

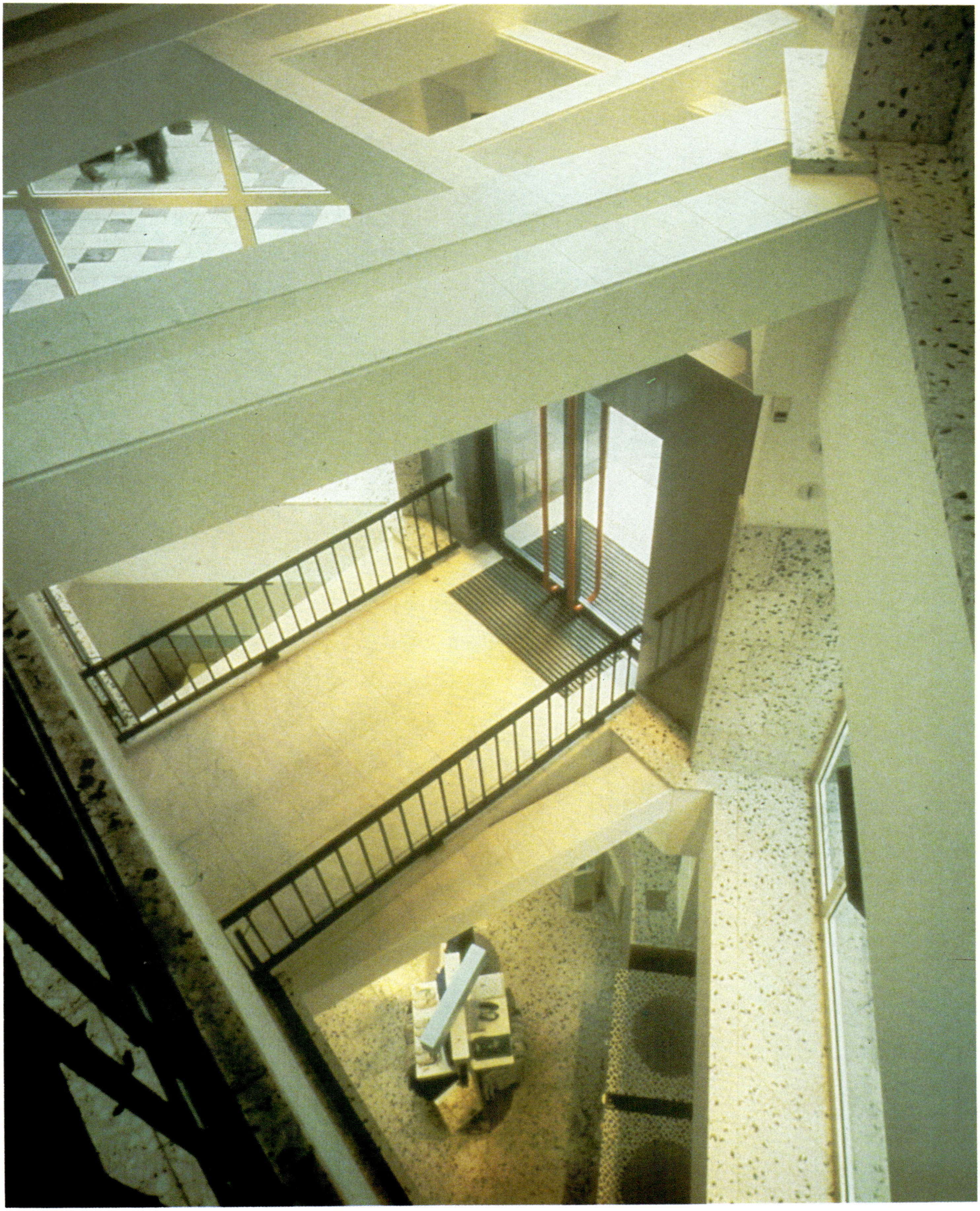

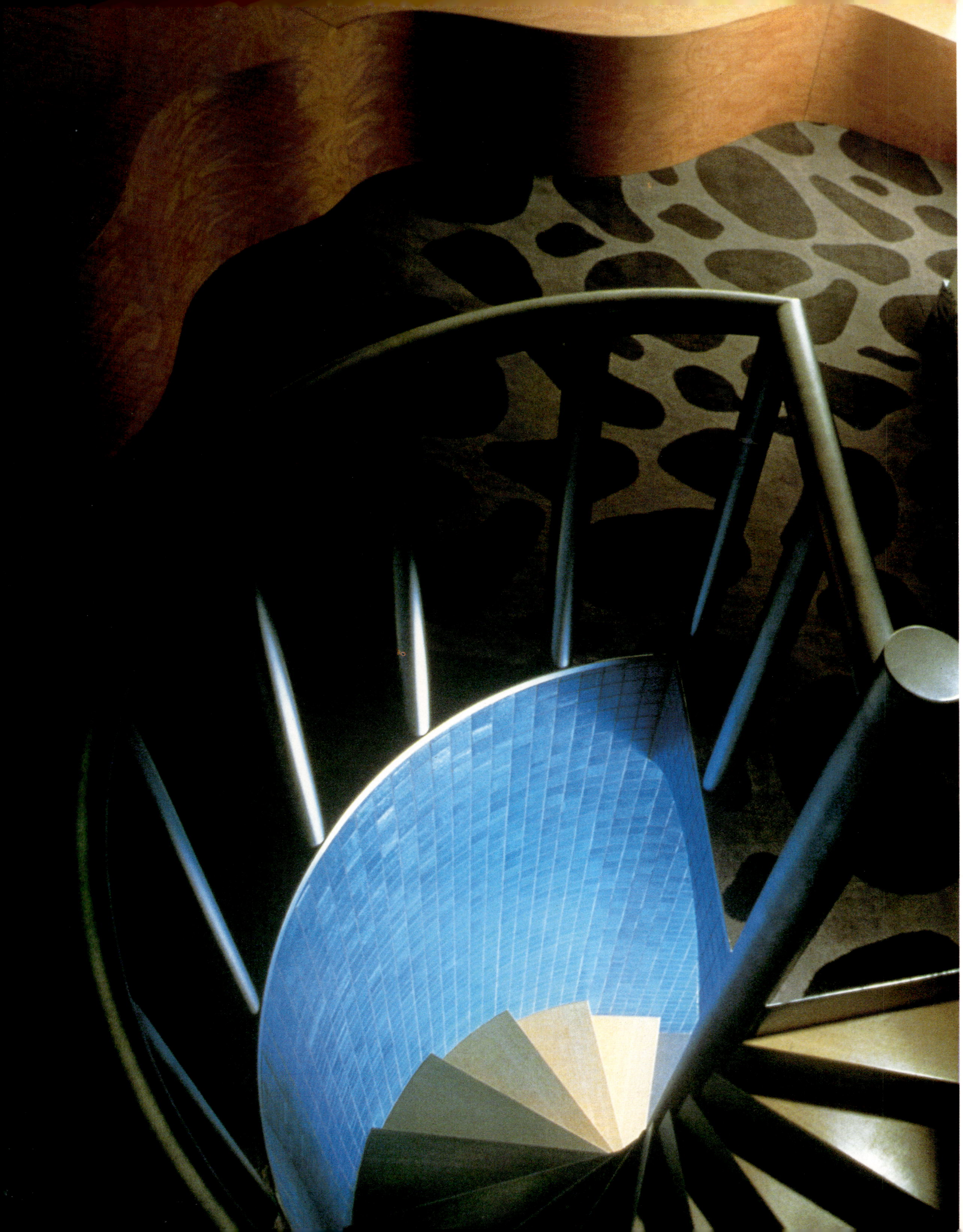

(left) Inventive clashes of pattern and texture in a spiral staircase at the back of the store: blue ceramic tiles, 'cowhide' carpet, and wood-grain laminate.

(below) Even the well for the elevators' hydraulic rams has been enlivened by the use of colour and texture.

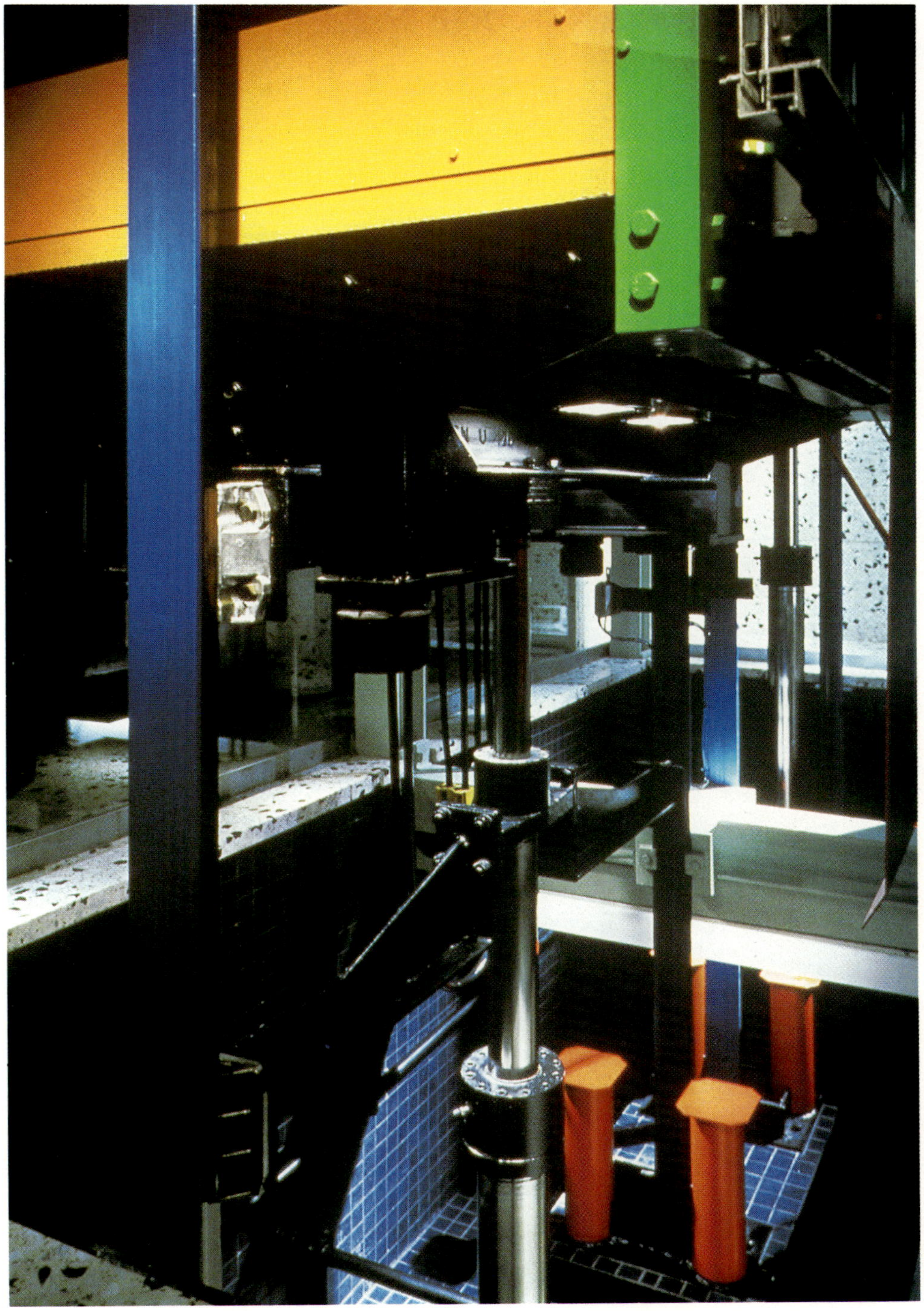

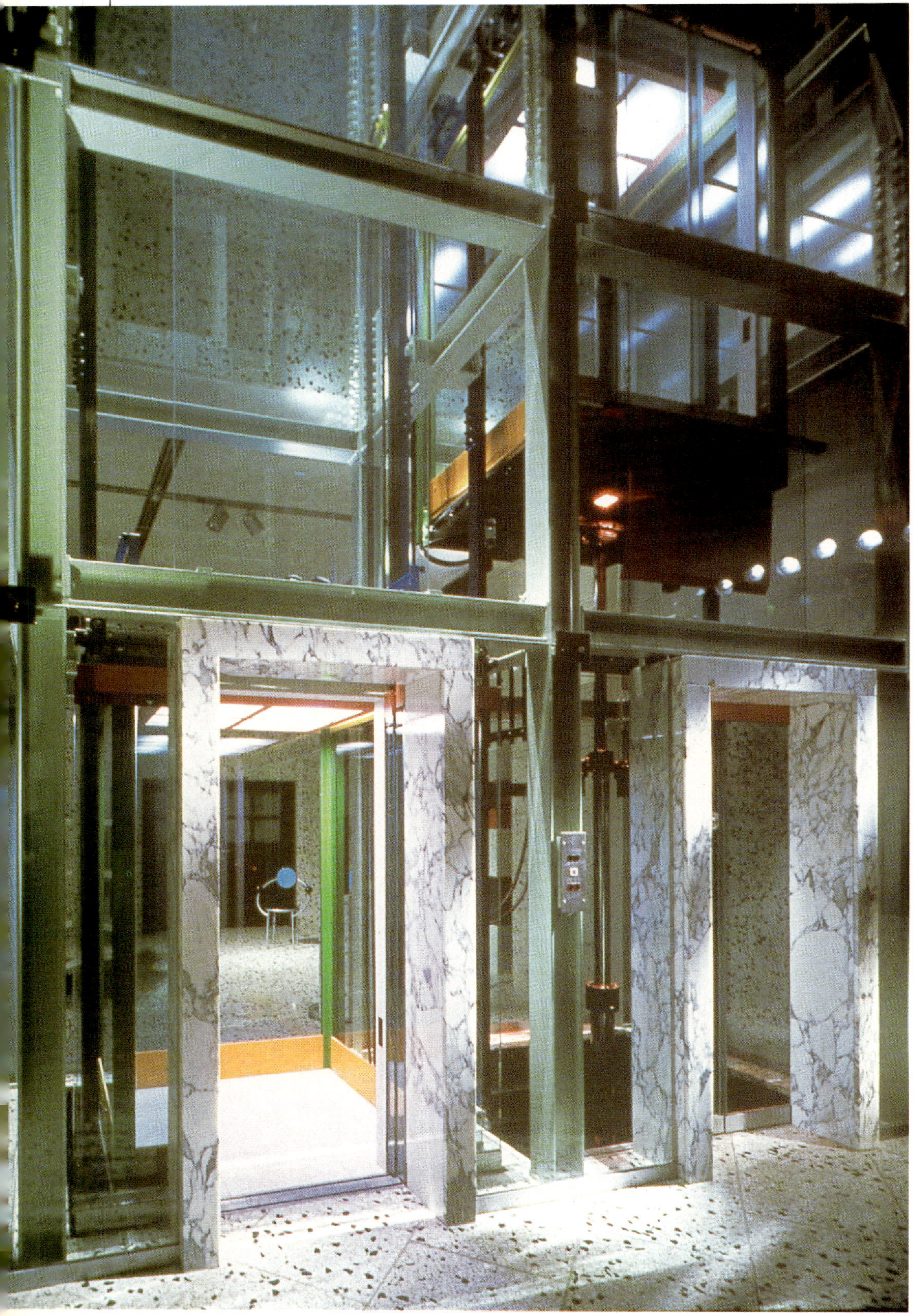

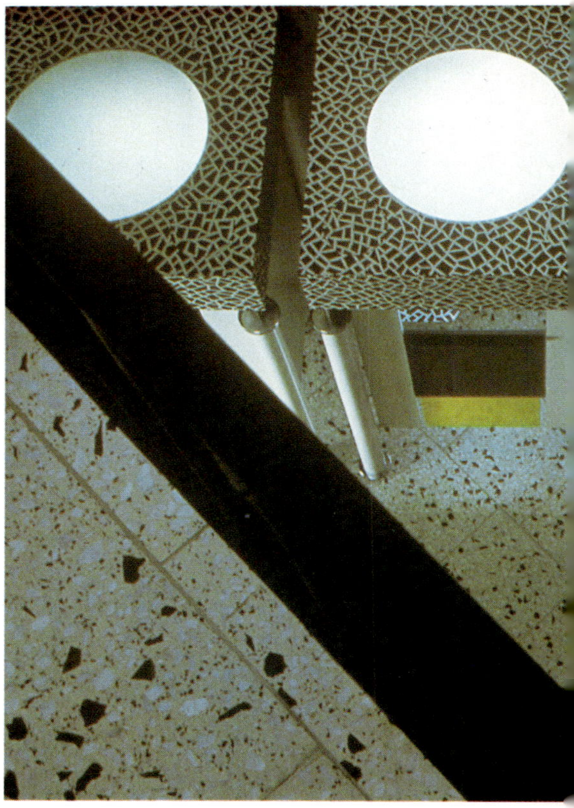

(far left) High-tech glazed elevators are lent a sense of fun through the use of colour.

(left) Modular clothes islands contain hanging racks, shelves and a mirror.

(below left) Seen from above, the laminate-clad 'beach cabanas' that serve as changing-rooms.

(below) A meeting room with slightly zoomorphic Memphis chairs and a table that jauntily punctures the glazed partition.

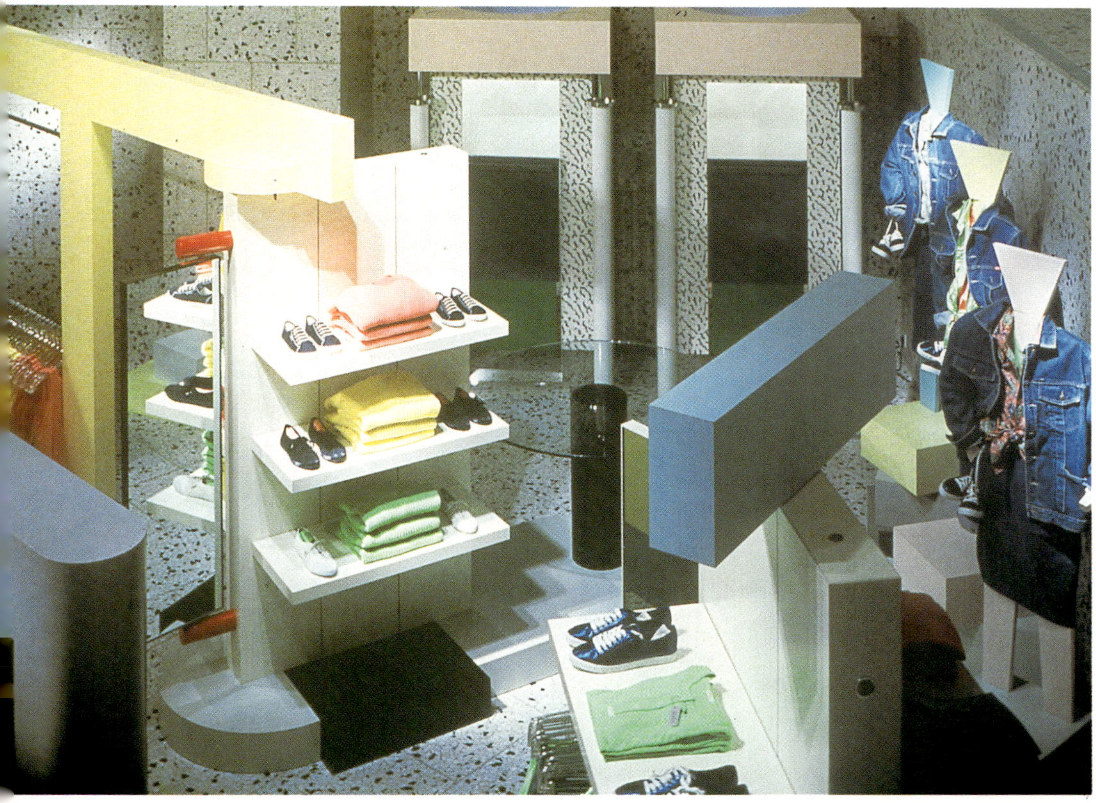

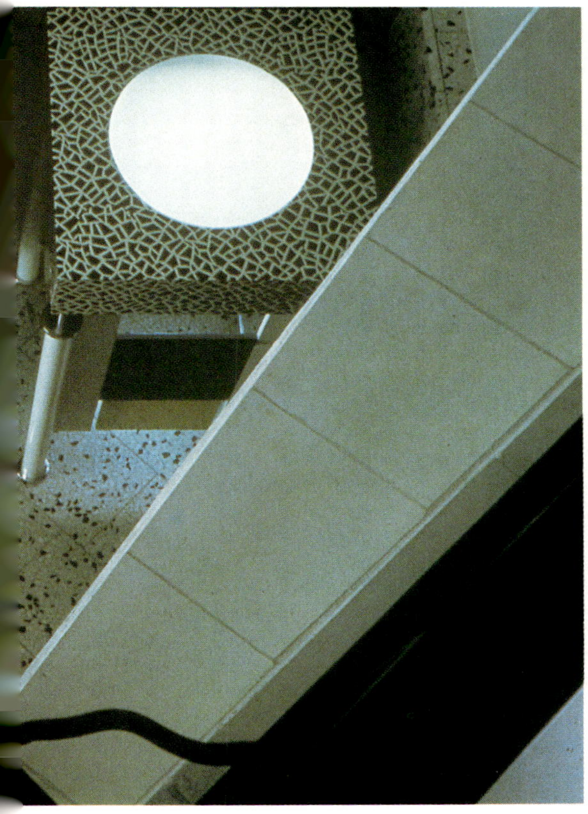

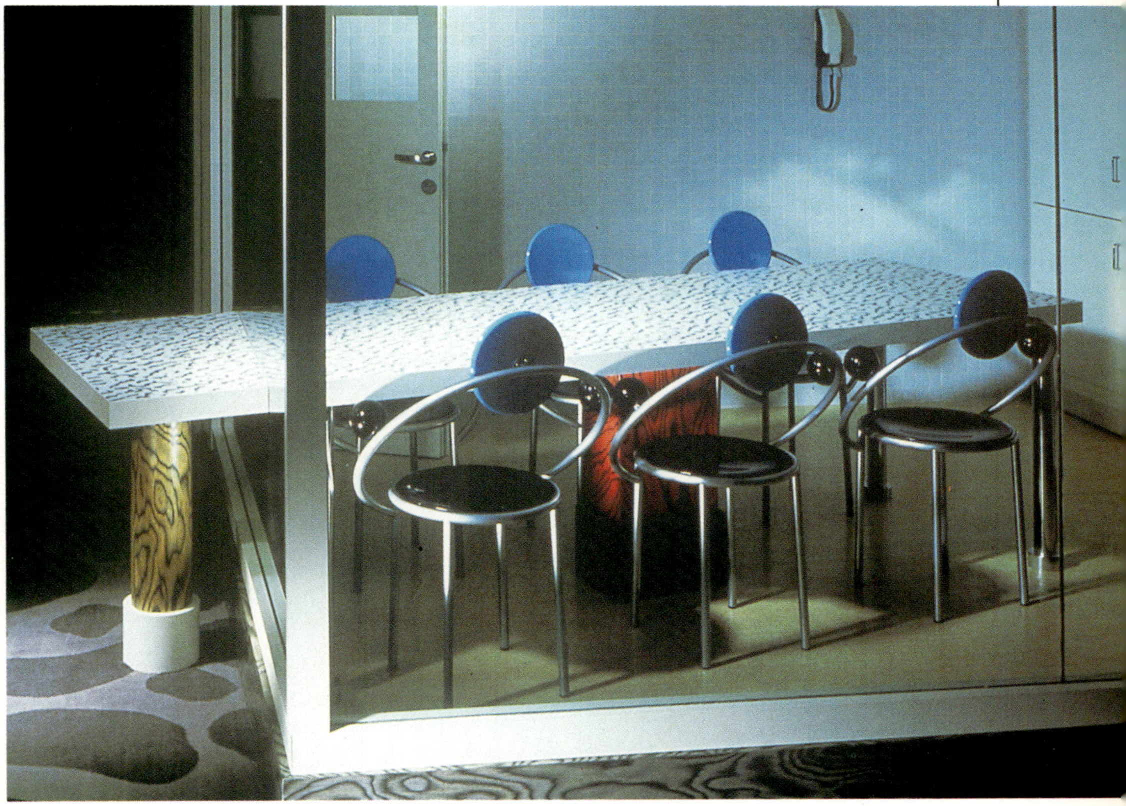

ESPRIT DE CORP
WEST BERLIN, WEST GERMANY

Designed by Sottsass Associati

The grandeur of both the Düsseldorf showroom and the Cologne store is not repeated in the Berlin showroom, which is far smaller. Berlin is also unusual in this series of projects, because the space near the Kurfürstendamm (West Berlin's principal shopping street) has some true architectural character of its own. Elaborate, old wooden doors, ceiling mouldings and wooden architraves all lend the showroom an air of elegance which the other Sottsass designs positively shun.

But Sottsass Associati (in association with Gerard Taylor) have spun their web here as well. Outside the entrance, a bright red mat greets visitors, and a dado of white, grey and black decorative laminate hints that behind the baroque doors might be something unusual. Inside, each room is a set piece, with an artful arrangement of elements used for display. Typical is the room where the selling table is. With its integral computer where the salesperson can check stock, place the order and draw up the invoice for the client, and its bird's eye maple top, it rests on a carpet that could best be described as having a 'spotted cow' design, against the backdrop of one of the movable display walls.

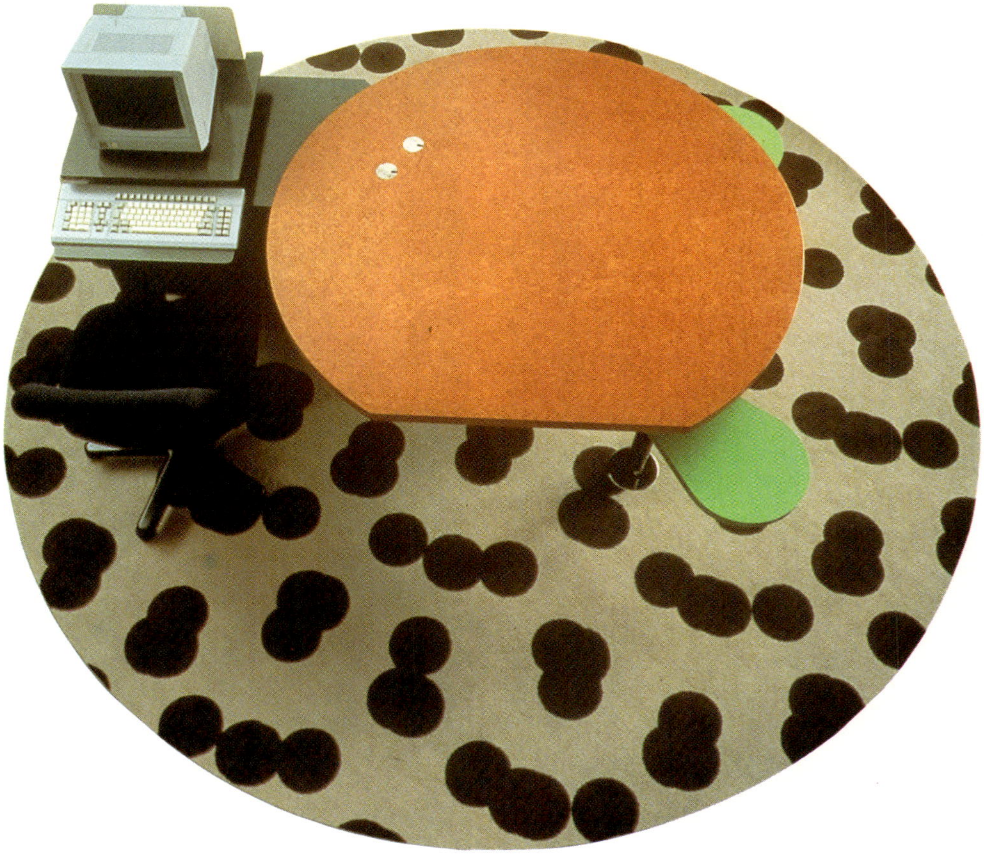

The selling table with its integral computer rests on a circular, extravagantly patterned carpet.

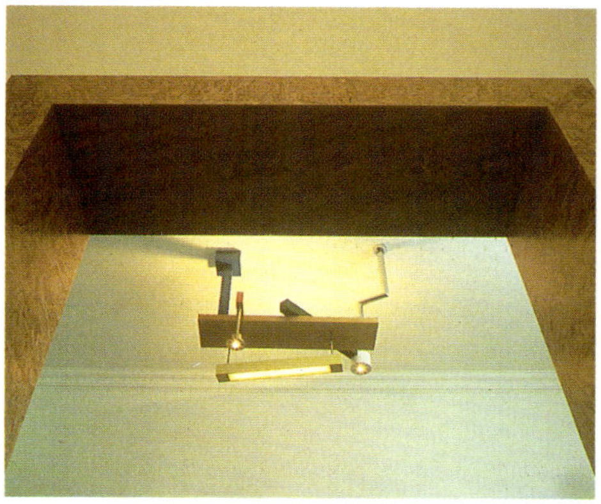

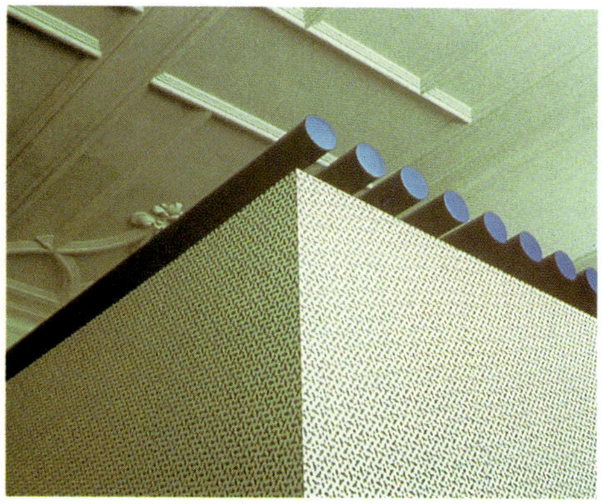

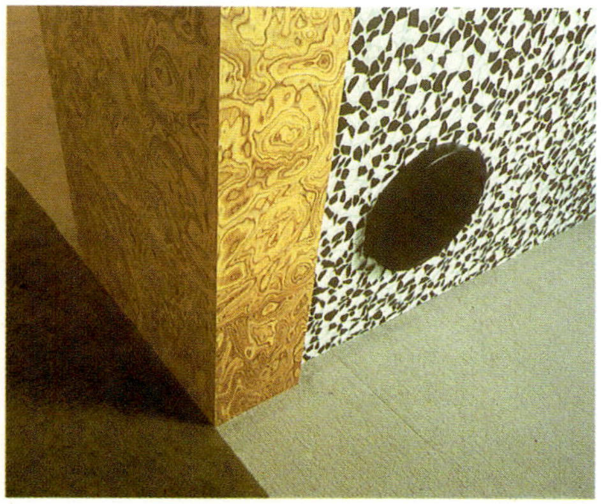

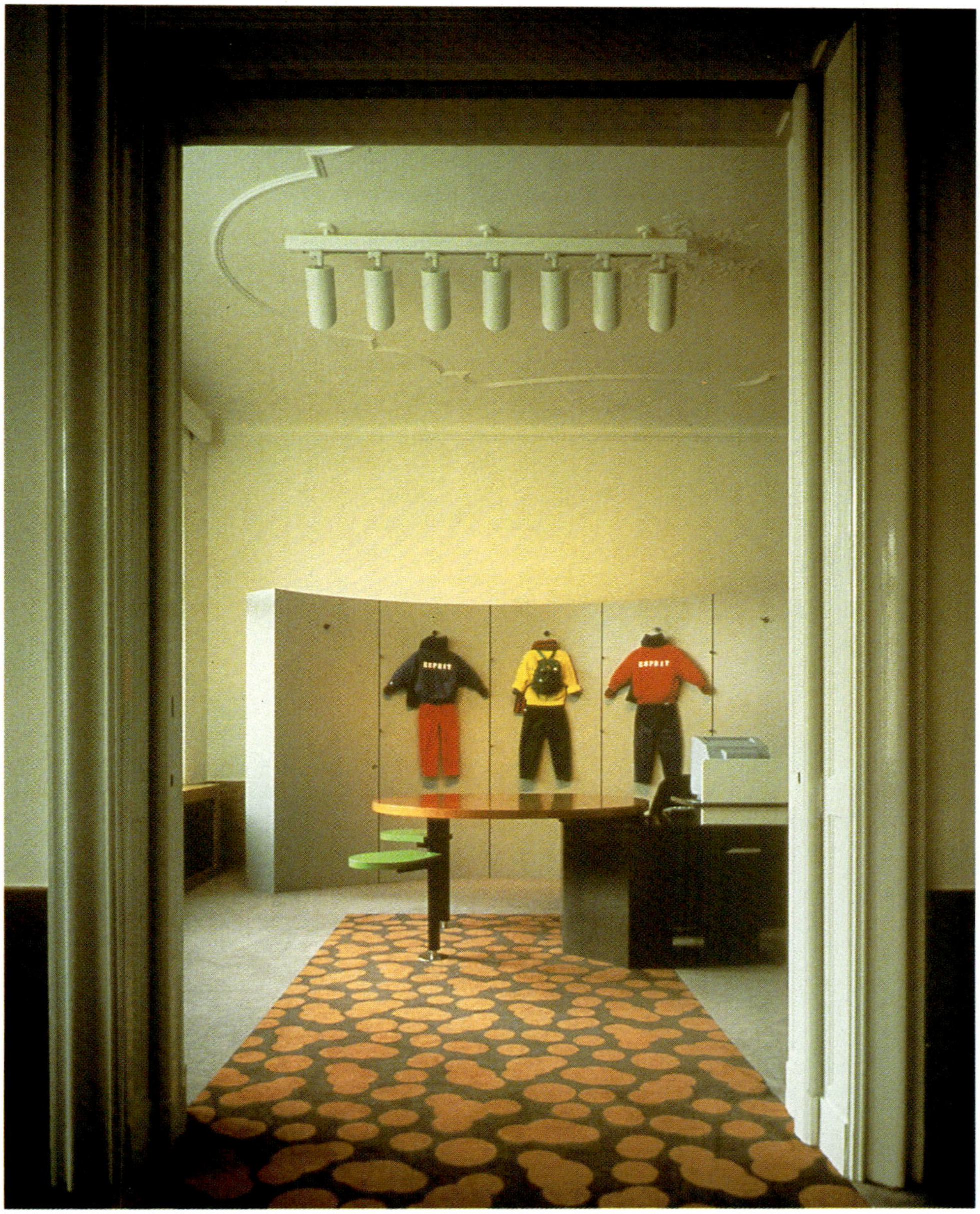

(above left) A characteristic Memphis-style lighting fixture is glimpsed through the wood-like laminate door surround.

(above right) Original architectural features such as ceiling mouldings have been maintained in the Berlin branch.

(above) Typically, textures and patterns are juxtaposed throughout.

(left) A carpet with a classically Memphis-style print leads the way into one of the display rooms.

ESPRIT DE CORP
MELBOURNE, AUSTRALIA

Designed by Sottsass Associati

At the same time that Sottsass were developing the German designs, they initiated a number of stores and showrooms in Australia (in collaboration with Gerard Taylor and Daniel Weil). The ideas are fairly similar to those of the German stores, but the Australian projects seem to be infused with a special sense of whimsy and lightness. This may partly be because the budgets did not run to the German extravagances: more is made of the play of shape and form, and less of the juxtaposition of (sometimes expensive) materials.

The characteristic terrazzo recurs in the Melbourne store, used on the floor, some walls and as a skirting. The architrave is an amalgam of wavy yellow 'columns' and wood-grain-effect metallic beam that extends beyond the bounds of the door. Perhaps the most successful element of the Melbourne store is the Mondrian-like appearance of the cash tills: basic geometric shapes, skilfully massed, with a sure use of contrasting colours.

These stores and showrooms created by Sottsass Associati are brilliant works of design, appealing to both cognoscenti and public, who delight in the playful use of colours, textures, patterns and materials as well as in the spatial bravura of the grander schemes like Cologne. What is particularly interesting about the work is the designers' acknowledgment of the true reasons for, and their justification of, such extravagant design: for all the hype, Esprit is selling clothes that are now arguably little different from a number of their competitors', but when it comes to environment, nobody – but nobody – can touch Esprit.

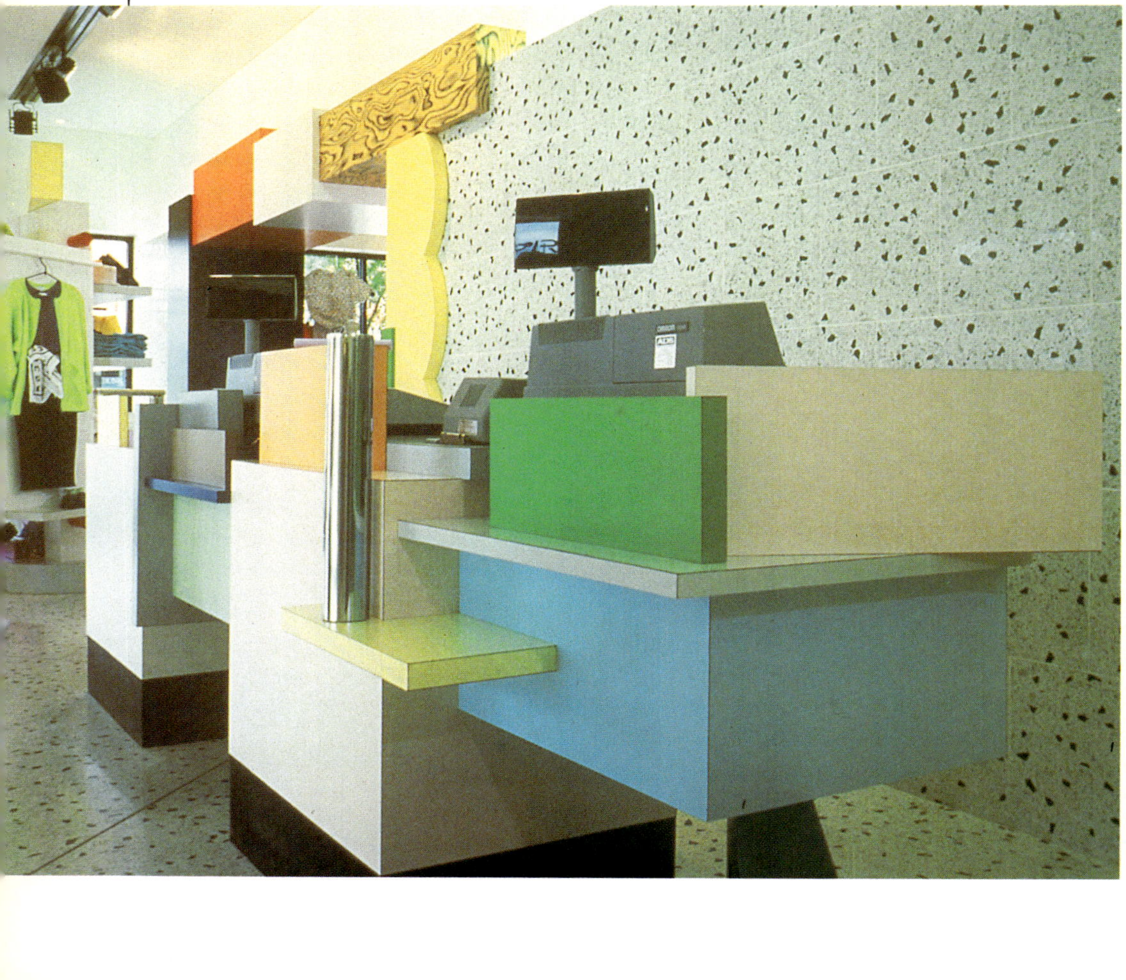

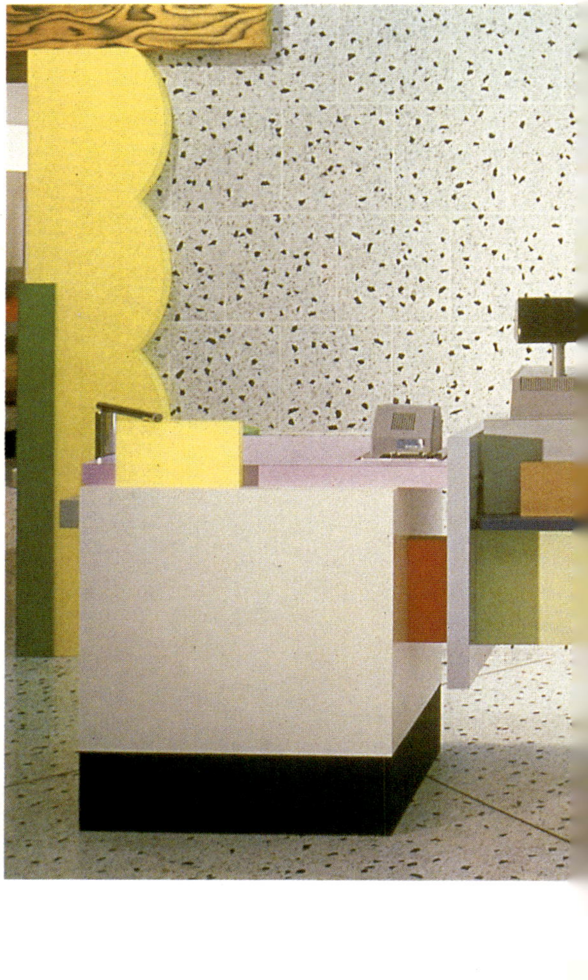

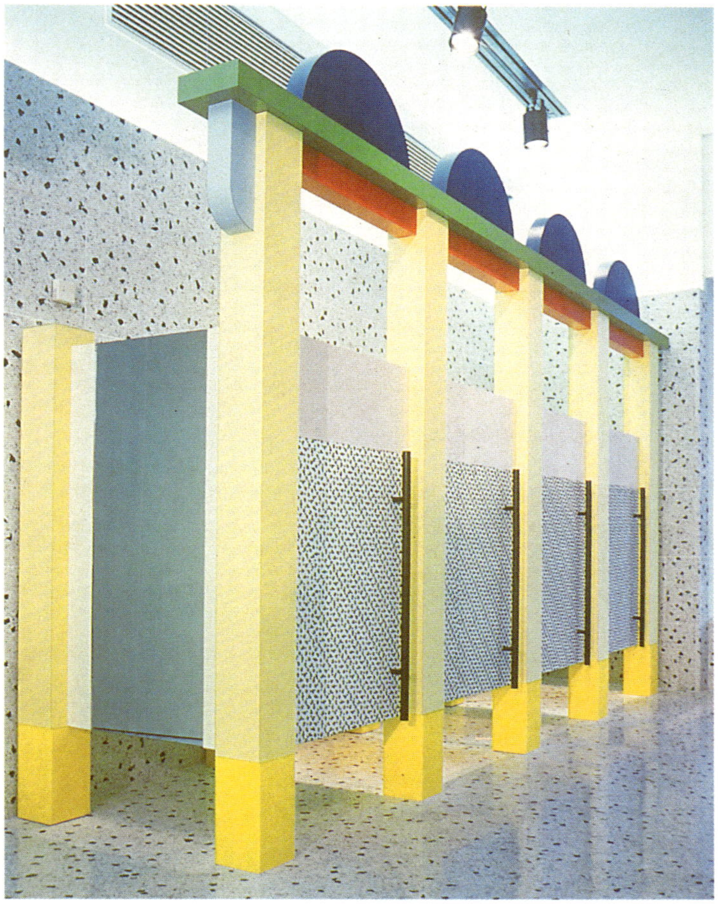

(below) A more 'tropical', jazzy image seemed appropriate for the Australian Esprit.

(left) Changing-rooms, mostly in bright blues and yellows, introduce a note of humour and whimsy.

(below, far left) Made up of basic geometric shapes, the cash-desks, in bright primary colours, have an almost Mondrian-like appearance.

(below left) Cash-desks contrast strong colours and shapes, while the architrave mixes wavy yellow columns and wood-grain effects.

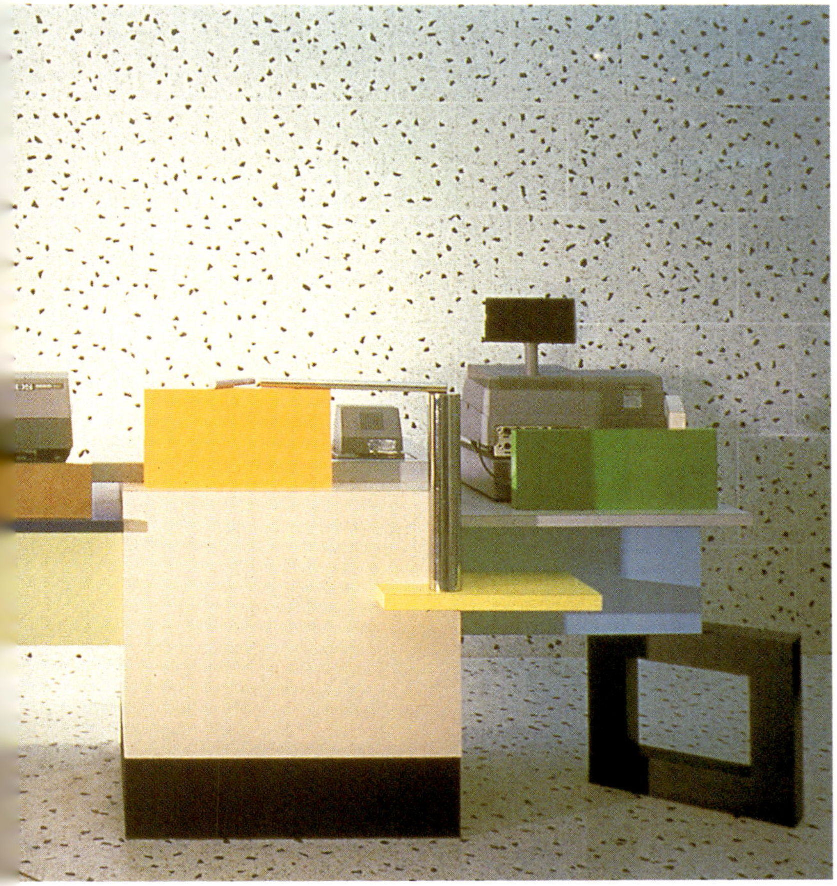

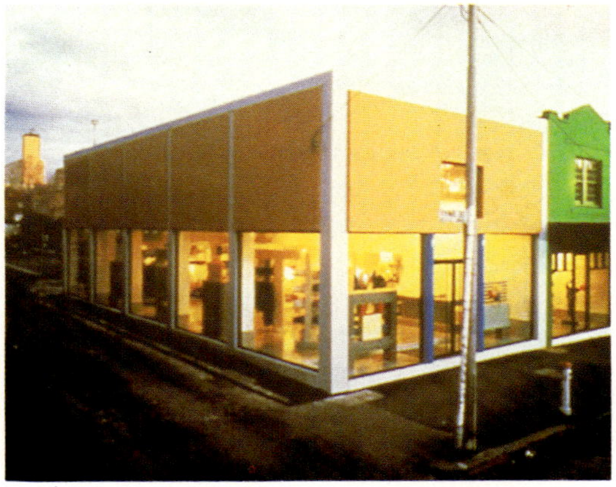

FORMICA CORPORATION SHOWROOM

CHICAGO, ILLINOIS, USA

Designed by Tigerman Fugman McCurry

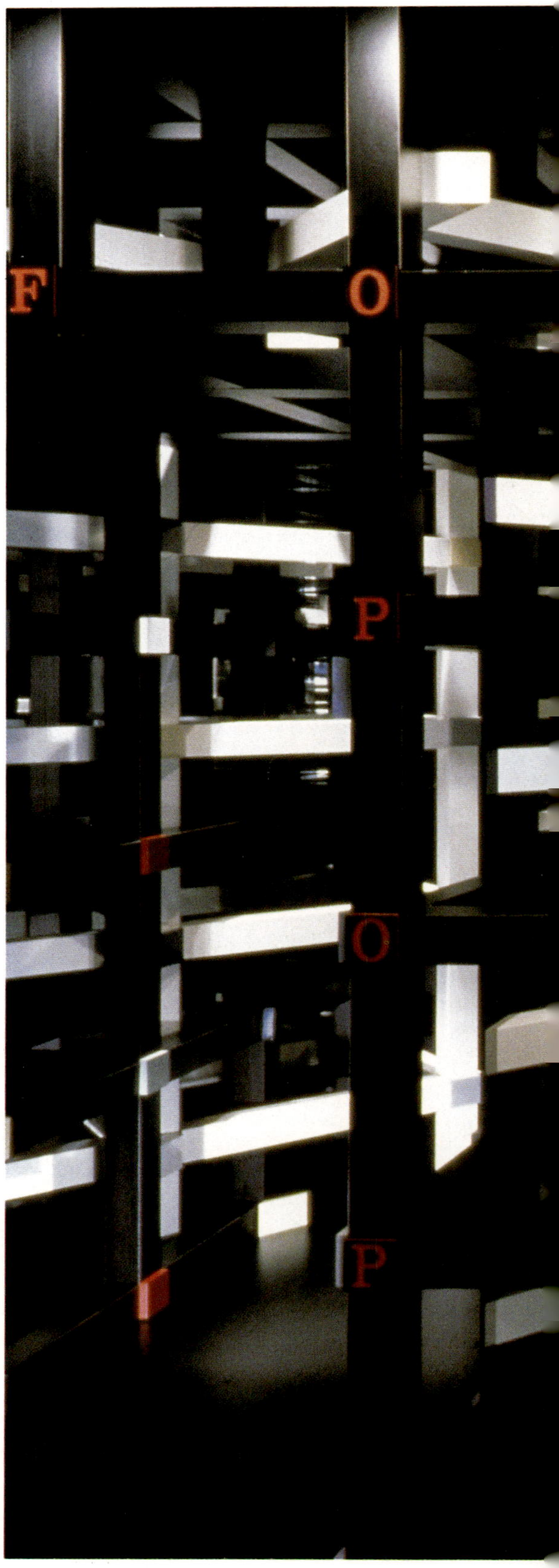

Showrooms were once utilitarian spaces in which manufacturers could show off their wares. But in the world of products aimed at architects and designers, showrooms have been transformed into the principal battleground for rival manufacturers. Nowhere is this skirmishing more evident than in the cavernous Merchandise Mart in Chicago. Here, hundreds of showrooms jostle for attention along endless anonymous corridors in the building that for long held the distinction of being the world's largest in terms of floor space.

When Tigerman Fugman McCurry tackled the problem of a new showroom for Formica in the Merchandise Mart, they faced a seemingly intractable set of problems: a tiny space (less than 538 square feet/50 square metres) and a product range of hundreds of items. Stanley Tigerman's own explanation of the solution is filled with obfuscating complications: 'The purpose of the project is simply to demonstrate that this product does not require things extrinsic to itself in order to verify, indeed to justify its existence.'

Whatever this means, the result is an intricate double grid of Formica sections, based on the geometry of the Merchandise Mart itself, which in turn has a geometry determined by Chicago's grid and the bend of the river on which the Mart sits (the orthogonal grid is black, the diagonal grid white). The resulting grids have been carved away to provide a path through the showroom. At grid junctions, 450 samples of Formica laminate are set like jewels which can be inspected and touched. Hidden in the centre of this labyrinth is Tigerman's 'object of desire', a totem containing product brochures.

There are additional nuances to this clever geometric game. The black grid is sized at 1 foot 8 inches (50 centimetres), apparently the length of the Biblical cubit, and the 2 foot 4 inches (71 centimetres) length of the white grid's beams has been derived from the Pythagorean theorem. The entire complex assembly was built at Formica's Cincinnati factory using carpenter's clips, and then reassembled in Chicago.

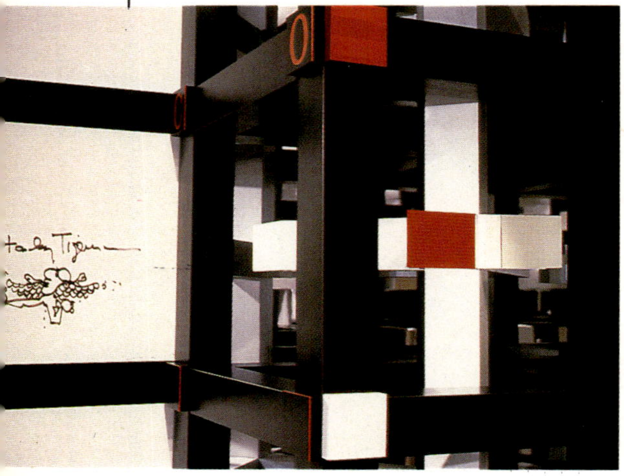

(right) Like a labyrinth, the showroom invites visitors to go inside and explore.

(left) In the manner of painters, Stanley Tigerman has signed his work with a flourish.

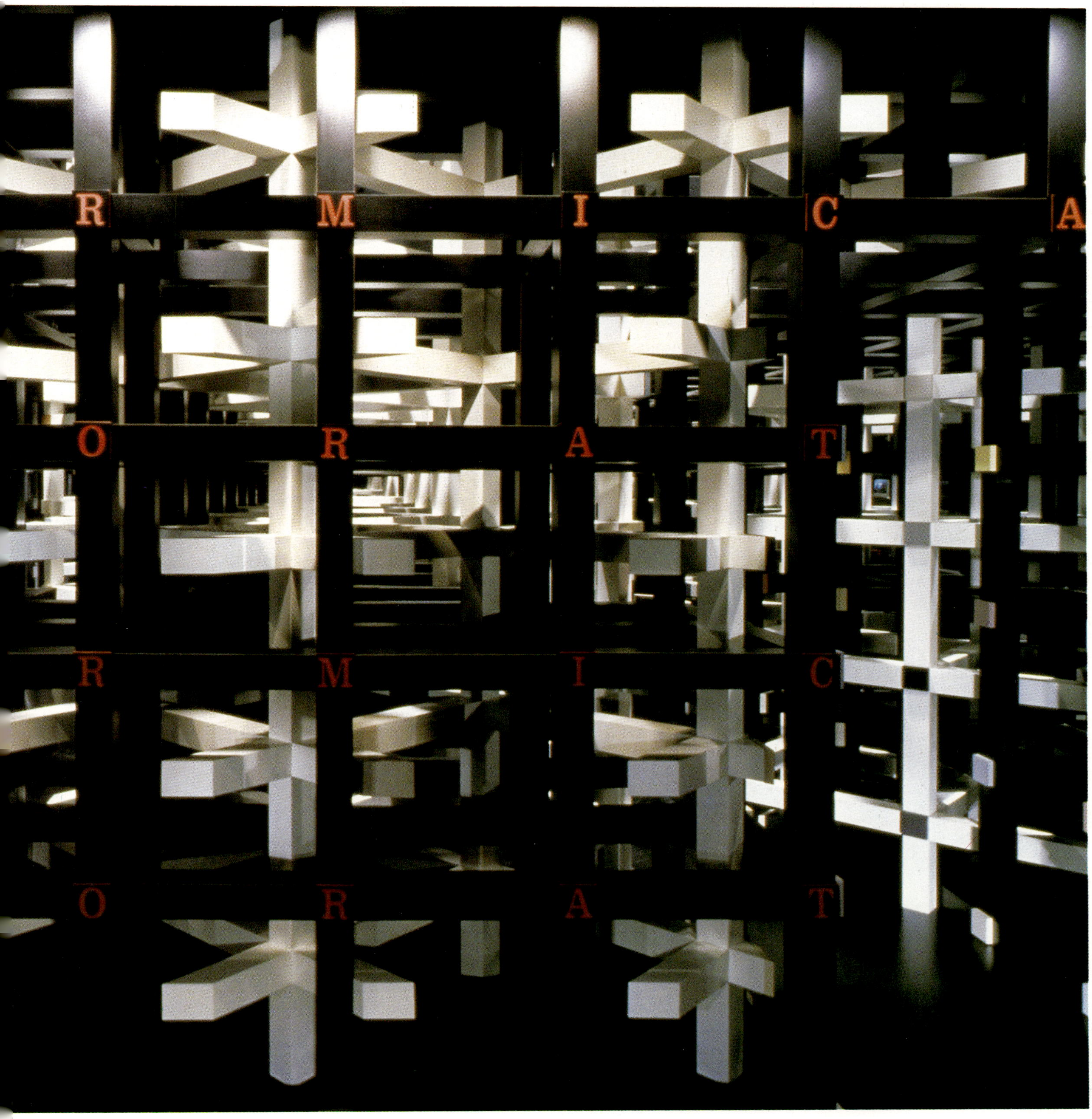
R M I C A
O R A T
R M I C
O R A T

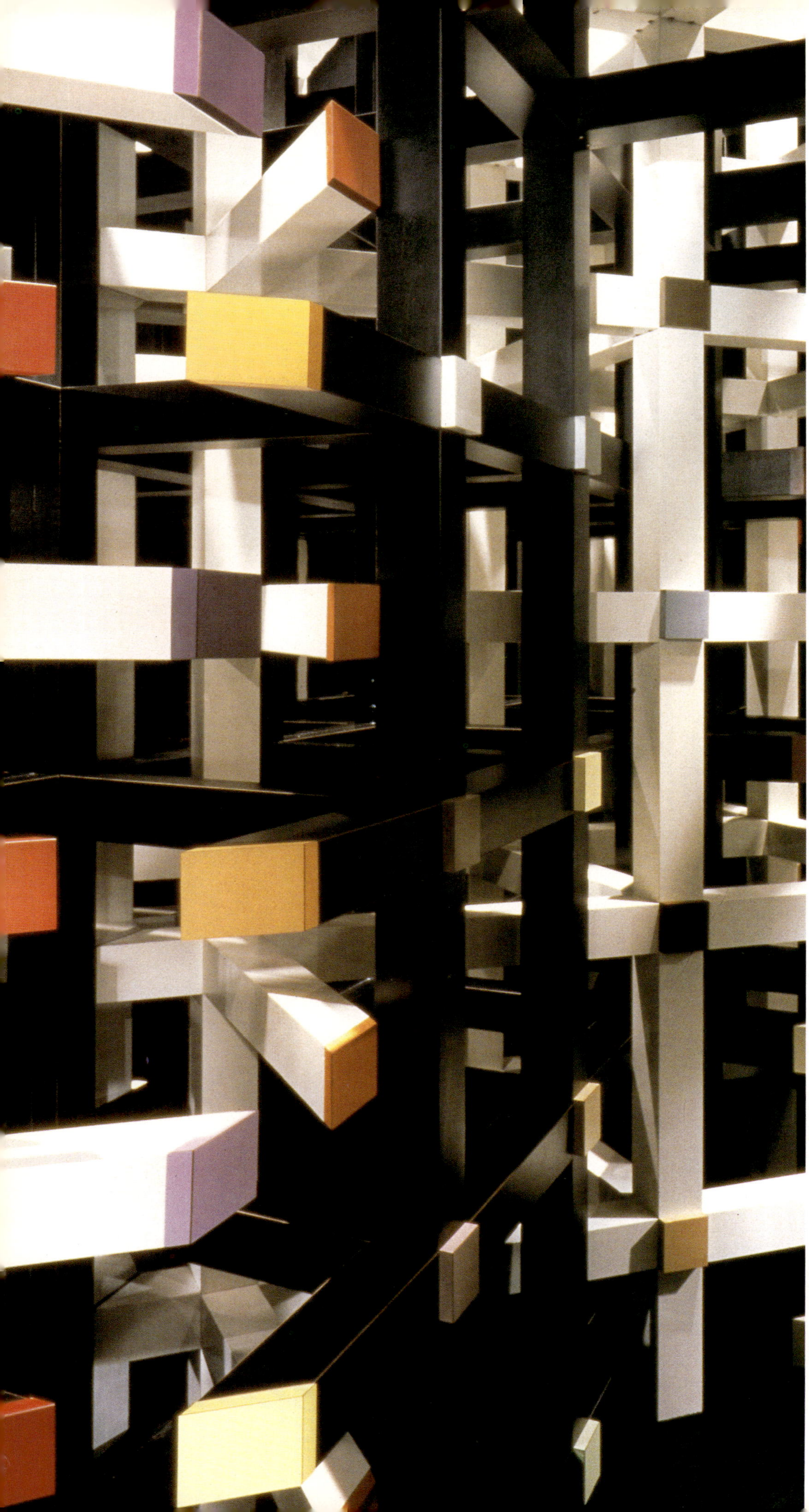

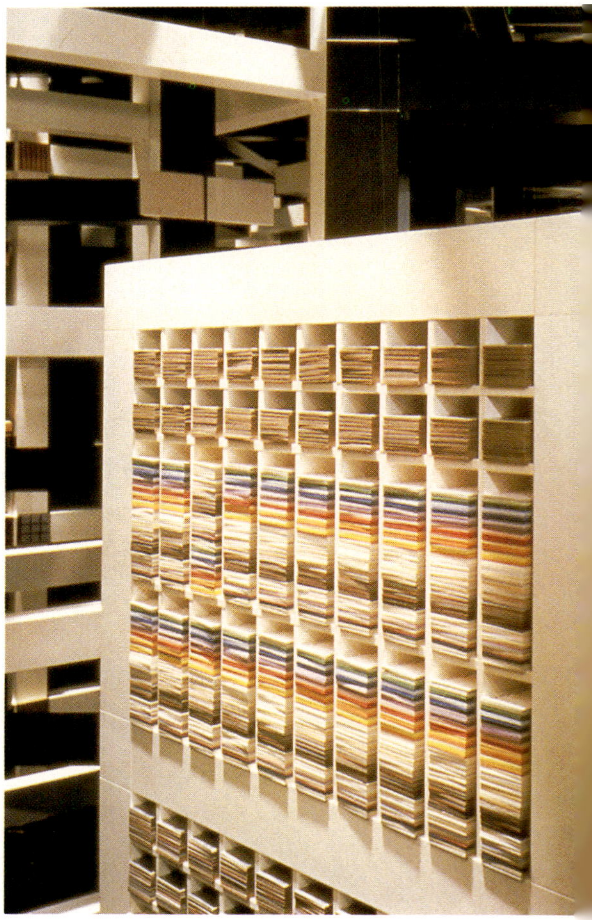

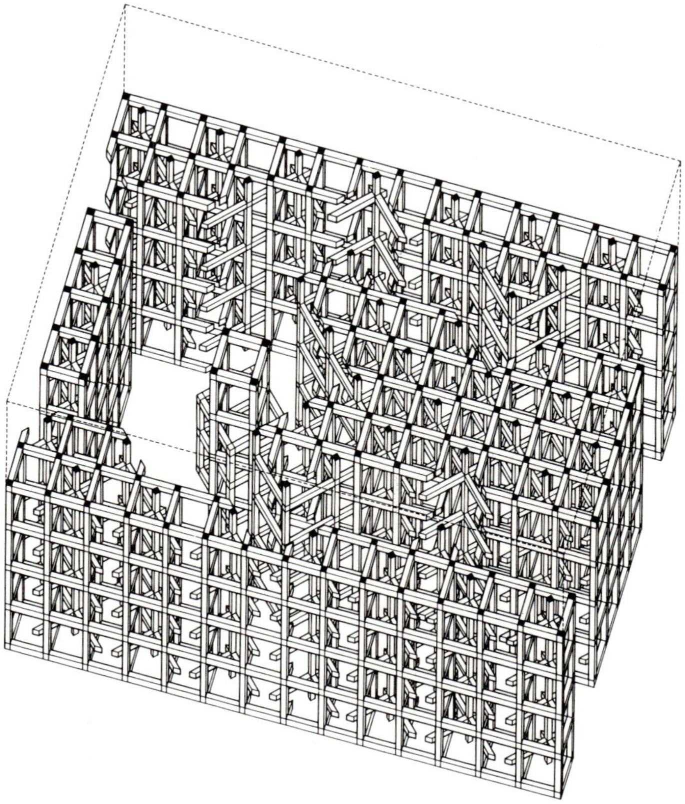

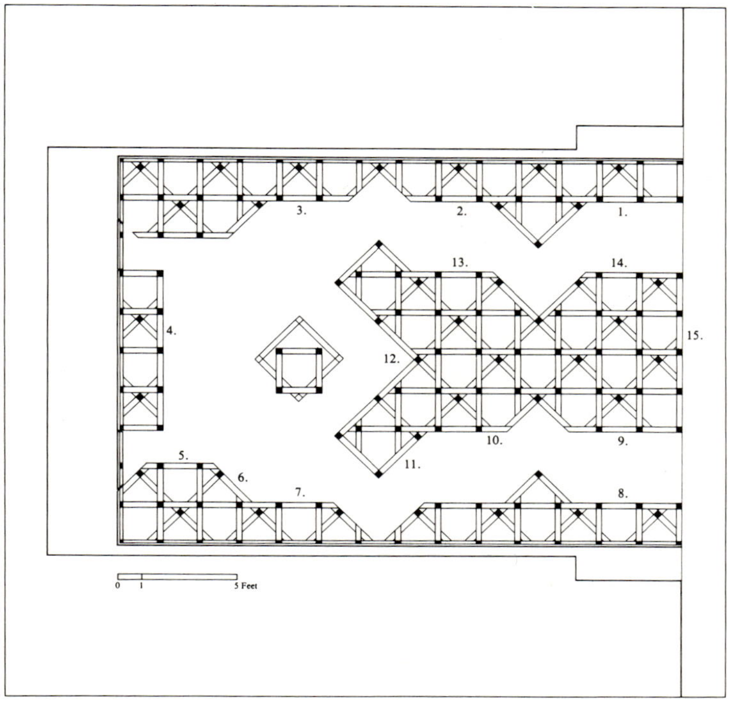

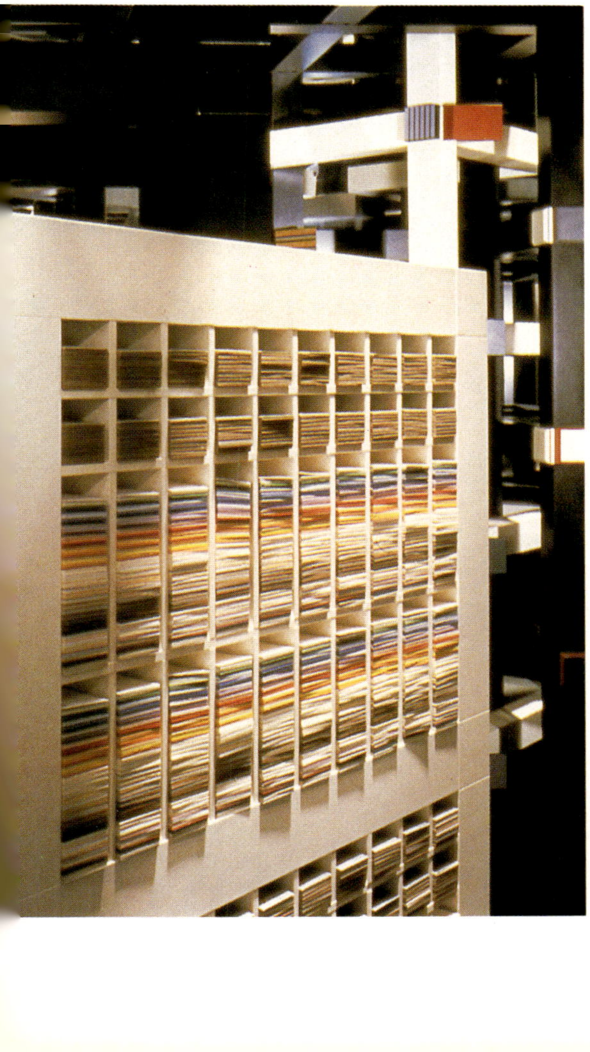

(above) Floor plan.

(above left) Axonometric projection.

(far left) Colourful samples of Formica are set, jewel-like, in the complex structure of the showroom.

(left) Tigerman has designed a totem containing product brochures, which stands at the centre of the grid.

YAMATO
TOKYO, JAPAN

Designed by Masanori Umeda

The influence of Memphis has been one of the strongest and most pervasive in recent design history. Not only has it spawned endless imitations, particularly in furniture design, but it has also made it 'respectable' for designers to adopt a light-hearted, irreverent approach. In Japanese, the nearest term might be *iki*, or sexy flamboyance. It is this that can be seen in the Yamato kimono store by Masanori Umeda, a designer who has a long association with Italy and, in particular, with Memphis.

Kimonos are, of course, associated with Japanese tradition, but the brief for the store was to present them in a way that would appeal to a younger audience. Thus the design includes many traditional elements, which are interpreted in a contemporary style. Inset into the coffered ceiling, for example, is a light-box in a figure of eight (the symbol for infinity), to suggest the lasting success of the store. Similarly the bold motifs decorating the screens – the crescent moon, birds, rain and lightning – are traditional Japanese forms.

Along with other screens of etched glass and natural wood, these provide the scenery for movable stages on which the costumes, the kimonos, are displayed. Even the lighting is theatrical, with white and coloured spotlights focused on the clothes.

As with all Memphis-inspired designs, there is something here that borders on the kitsch, but there is also just enough of the traditional – restraint, harmony, quality – to prevent its becoming so.

(below) The design is undeniably contemporary in approach, but in fact the motifs chosen – lightning and rain, for example – are traditionally used in Japanese design.

(right) Stages with screens of latticed wood or etched glass provide dramatic settings for the kimonos.

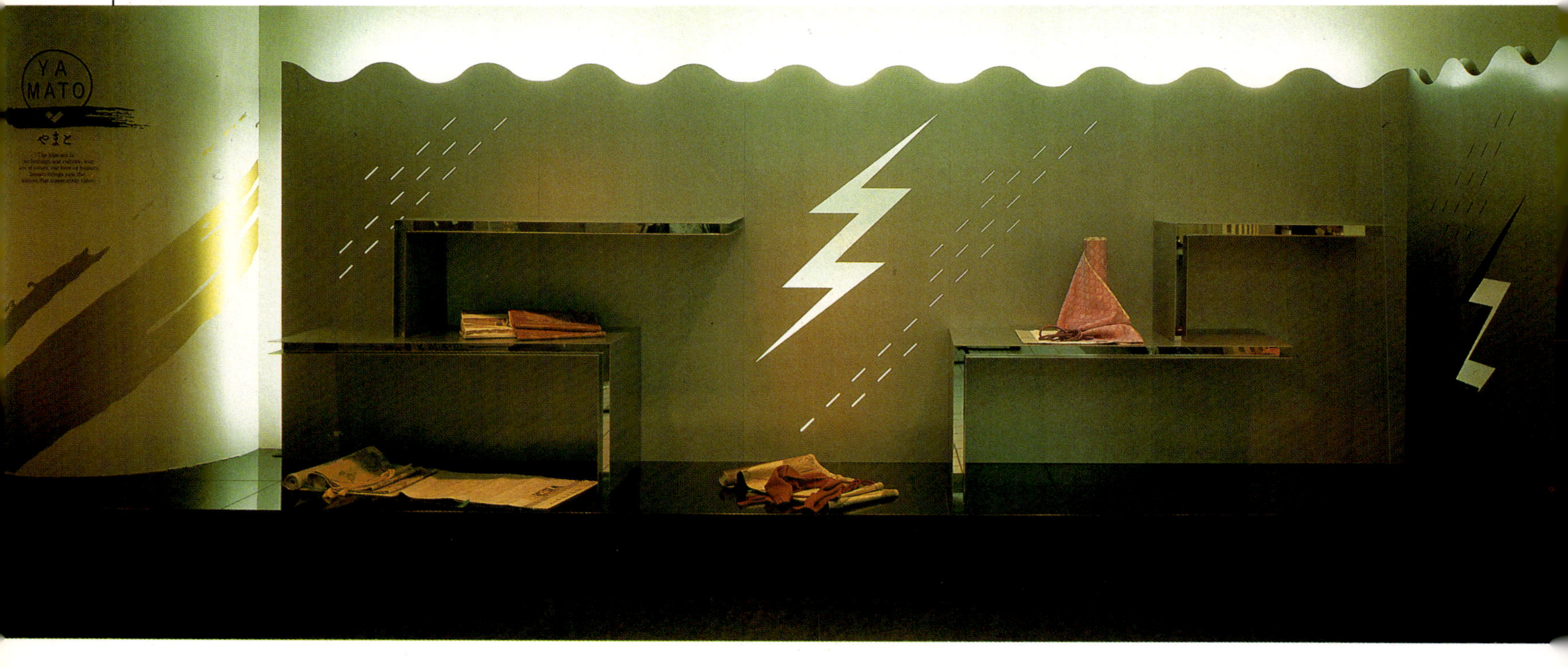

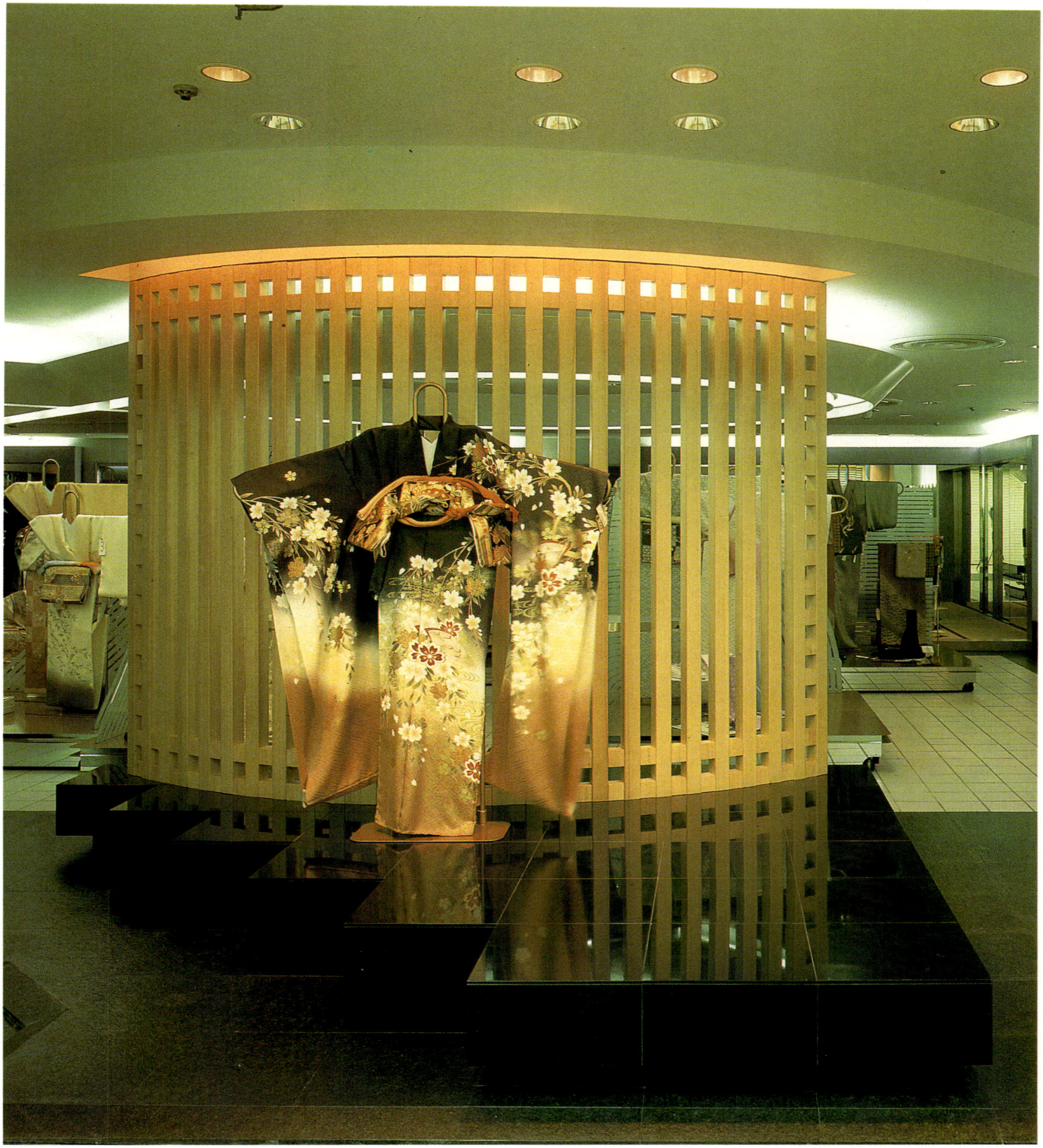

(right) A light-box shaped like a sweeping figure of eight makes the coffered ceiling a focus of attention.

(below) Umeda's unusual and humorous treatment stays on the right side of kitsch, and, it is hoped, will attract new and younger customers.

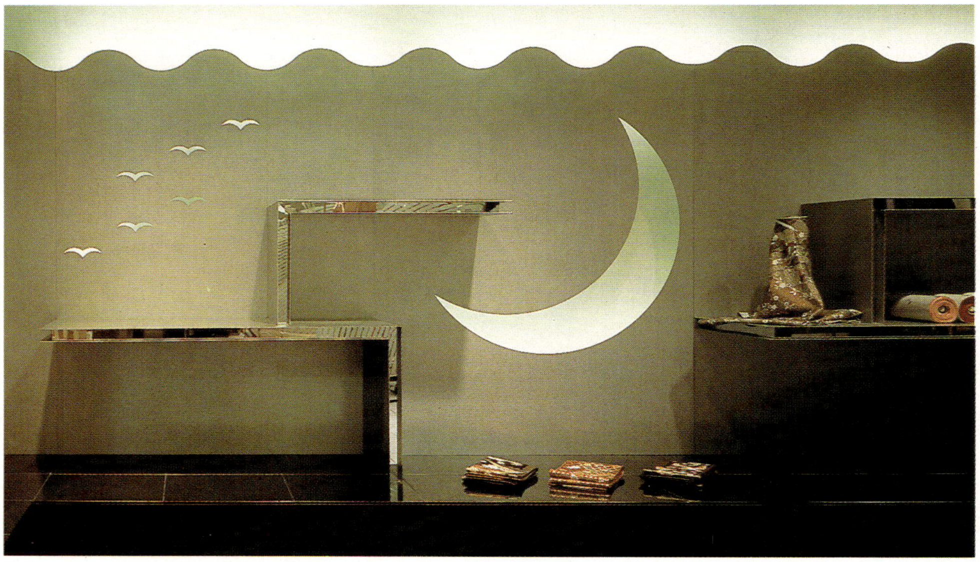

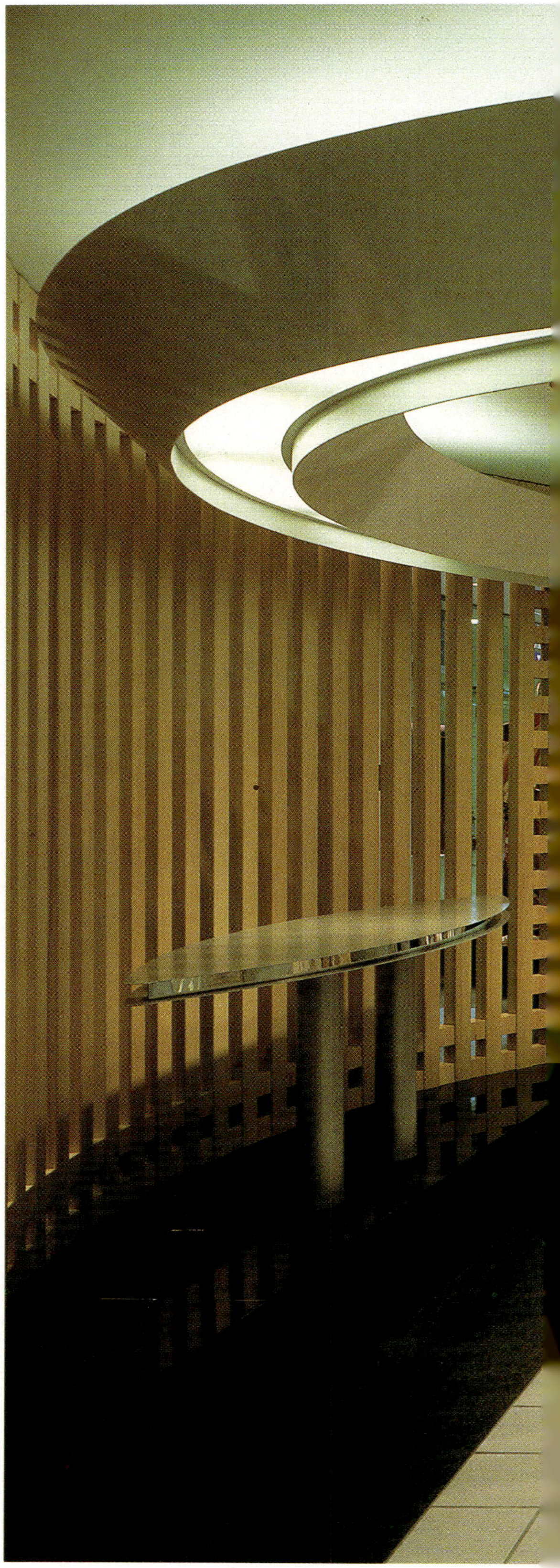

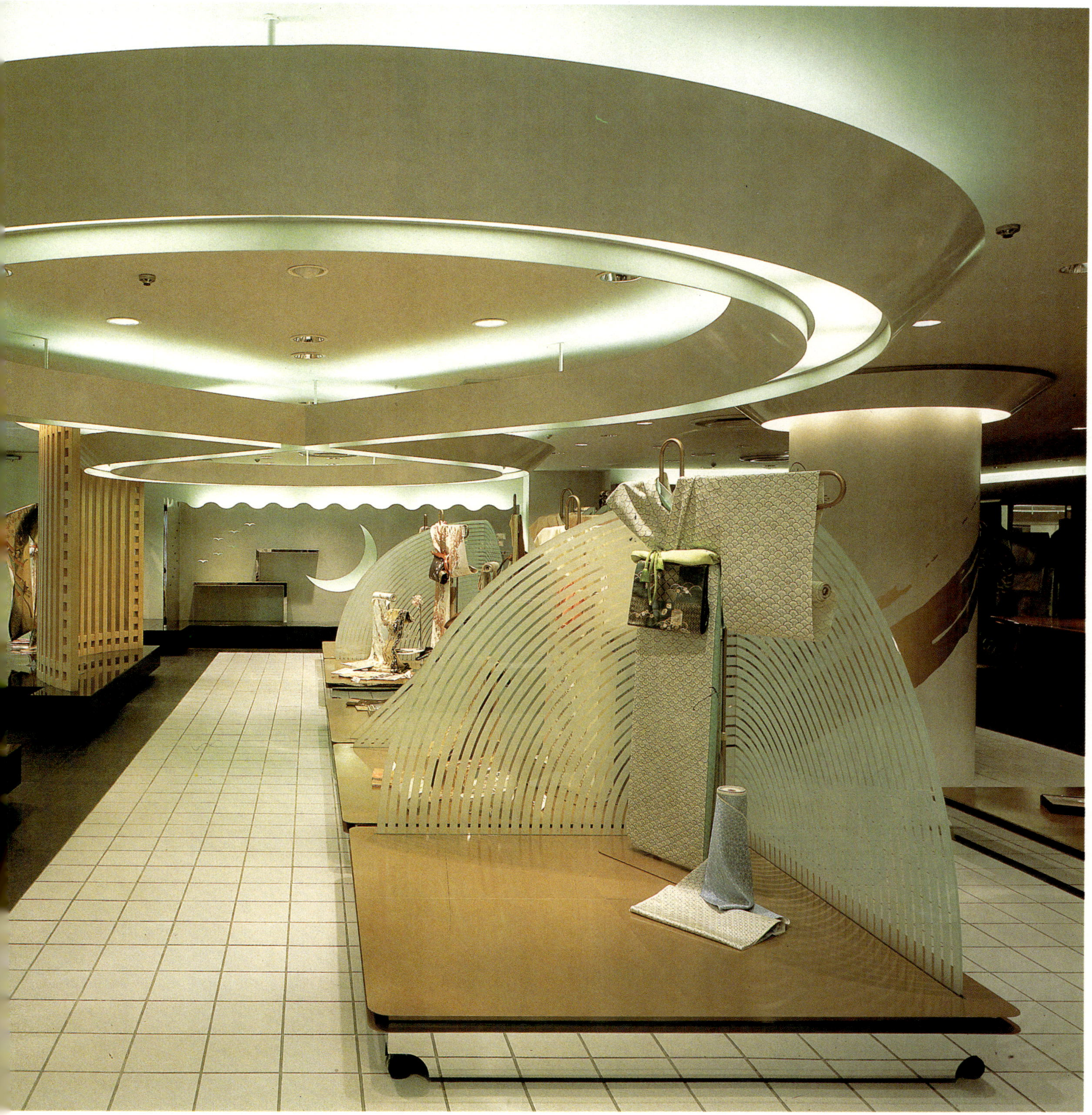

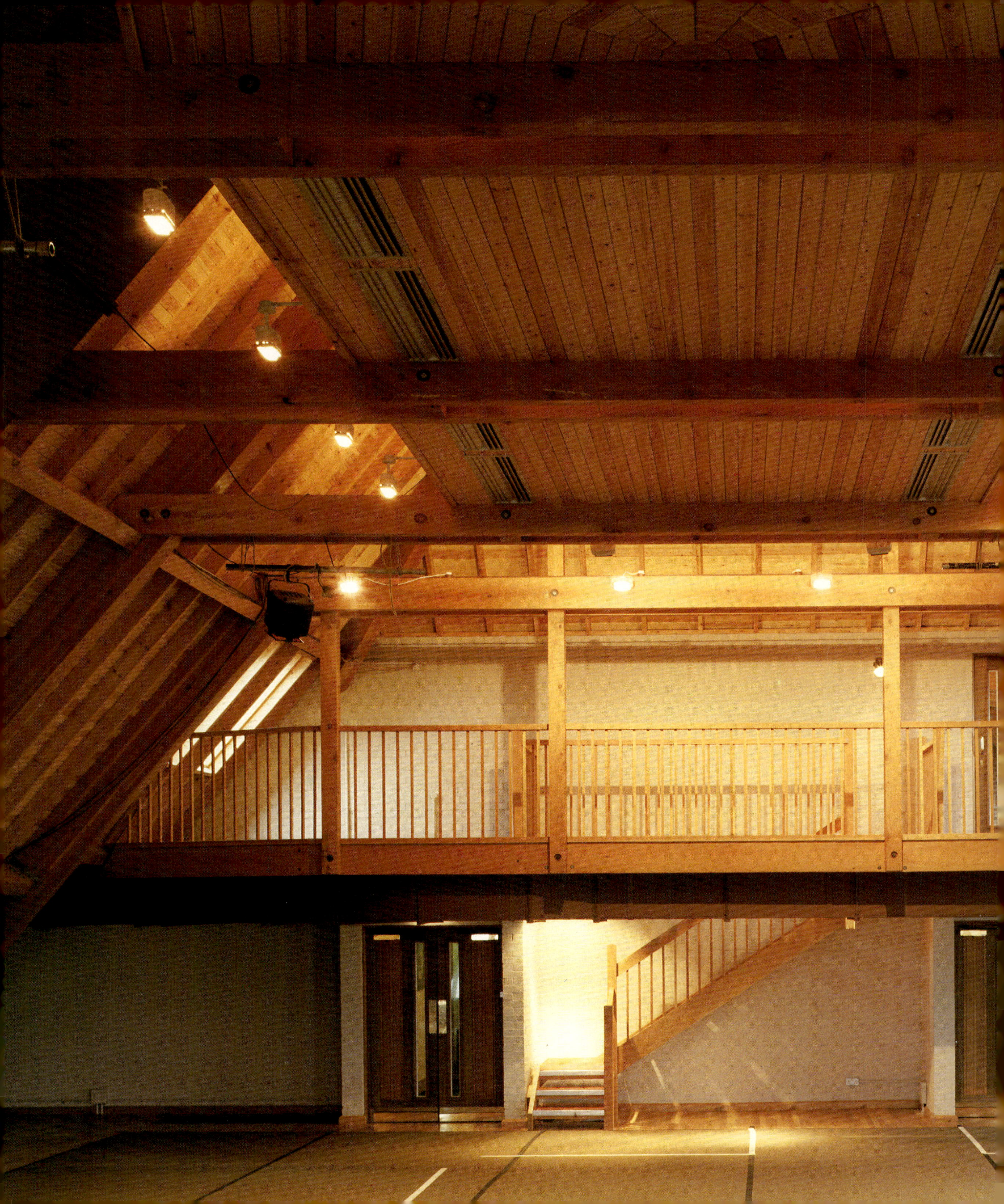

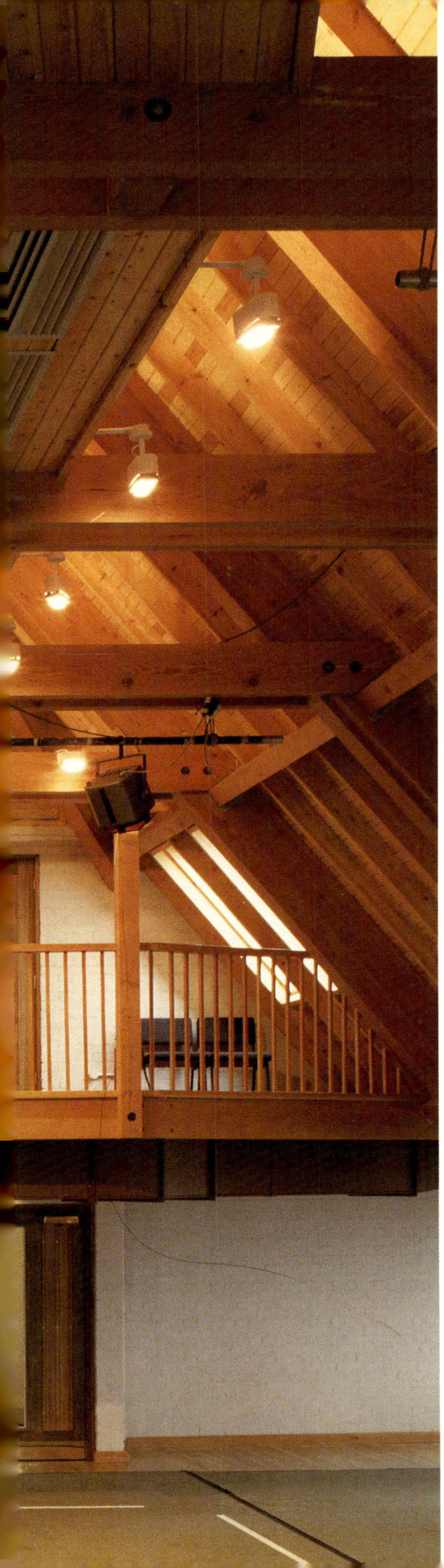

CULTURAL AND SPORTS BUILDINGS

Centerbrook Architects, Williams College Museum of Art, Williamstown, Massachusetts, USA

de Blacam and Meagher Trinity College, Dublin, Eire

Faulkner Browns The Waves, Blackburn, UK

Leers, Weinzapfel Associates, Architects, Inc. and Chan & Krieger Architects Photographic Resource Center, Boston, Massachusetts, USA

Diane Lewis and Peter Mickle Kent Gallery, New York City, USA

Maki Associates Spiral, Tokyo, Japan

James Stewart Polshek and Partners Carnegie Hall, New York City, USA

Michael Reardon & Associates Swan Theatre, Stratford-on-Avon, UK

Basil Smith Freud, London, UK

Laminated Douglas fir beams lend a warm glow to the rehearsal area of the Swan Theatre, Stratford-on-Avon, designed by Michael Reardon & Associates.

WILLIAMS COLLEGE MUSEUM OF ART
WILLIAMSTOWN, MASSACHUSETTS, USA

Designed by Centerbrook Architects, Robert L. Harper and Charles W. Moore

Charles Moore, a consultant to Centerbrook Architects, has established a reputation for delighting in difficult building programmes. With a wide range of collaborators, Moore has over the years built an extraordinary range of projects, from the seminal to the whimsical: Sea Ranch, Kresge College, the Piazza d'Italia in New Orleans, the same city's World's Fair Wonderwall and the Hood Museum at Dartmouth College, among many others. His latest work, a small museum for Williams College, exhibits many characteristics of his design.

Before the recent project, Williams' museum was housed in a series of handsome rooms in an 1846 building which originally served as the college library. Centerbrook Architects were asked to design a building that had a complex set of requirements: it would be used by visitors, art history students, artists, faculty and administrators, each group with its own needs and requirements for access and security. The site, too, posed its own challenges: a too-small, level triangular plot adjacent to a 33 foot (10 metre) drop down a steep hillside.

Centerbrook's solution was to build an atrium on the level ground south of the existing museum building, which acts as the key transitional space (what Moore likes to call 'an in-between space') for all building users. Galleries are on the top floor, and, with museum offices, on the entry floor; on the lower level are a lecture room, slide-room and faculty offices. Below this are studio spaces which can be entered independently.

In terms of the interior, the atrium is the most interesting part of the scheme. A grand staircase meanders up to the gallery levels from the entrance, and a bridge soars across the atrium. The stairs link the three levels of the

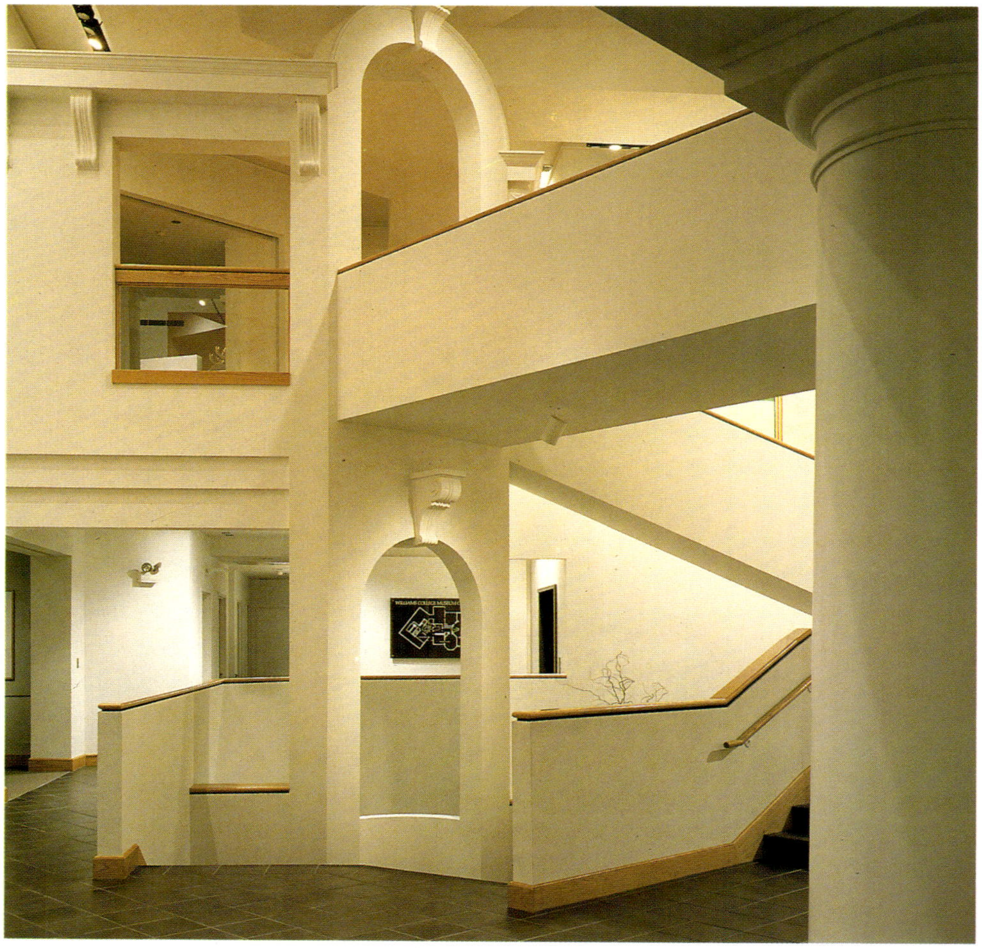

(left) In the atrium which links the new building to the old, a grand staircase meanders up to the gallery levels.

(right) A long axis that runs the length of the building, including across the atrium bridge, provides the gallery rooms with a clear organization.

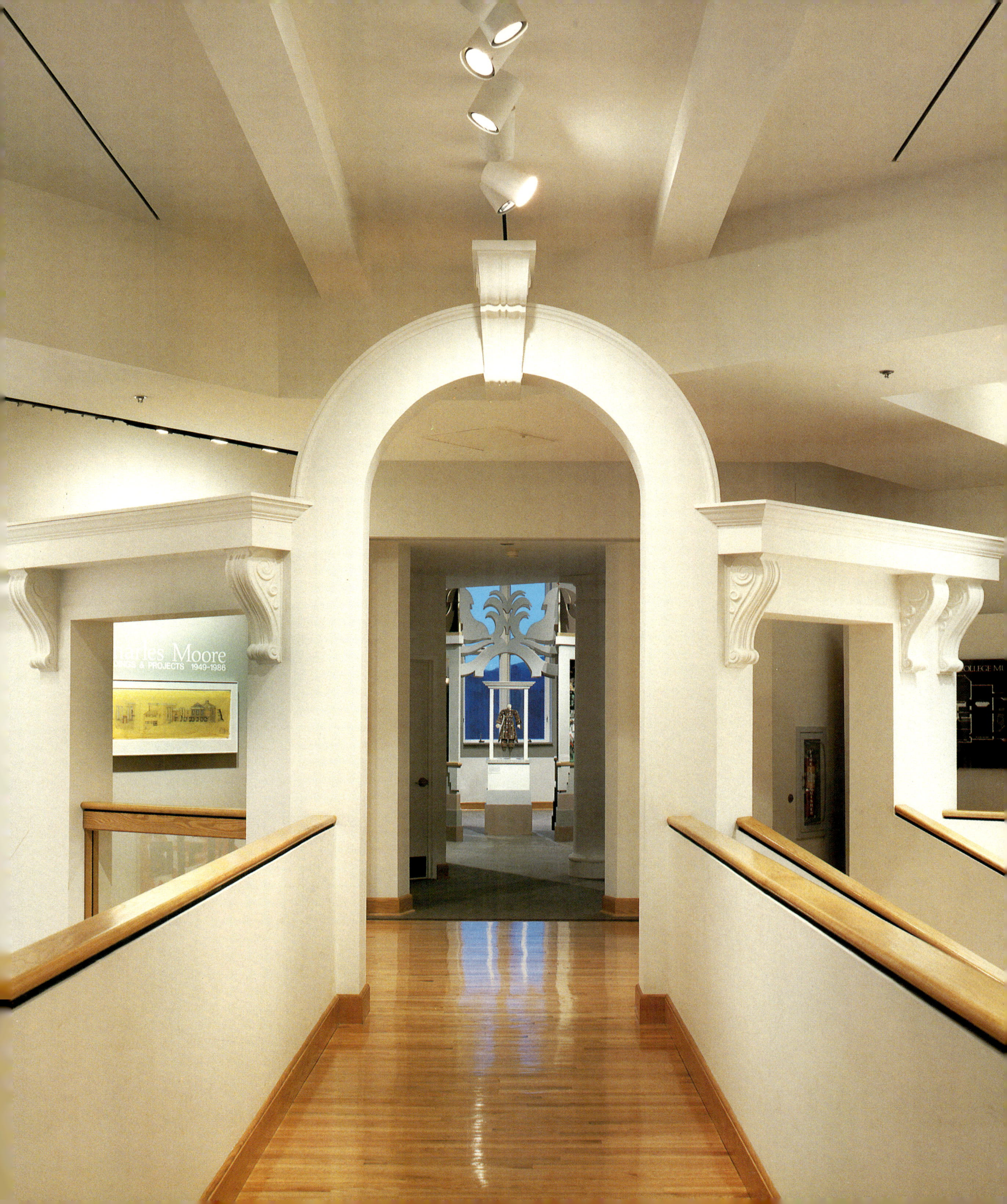
Moore
PROJECTS 1949-1986

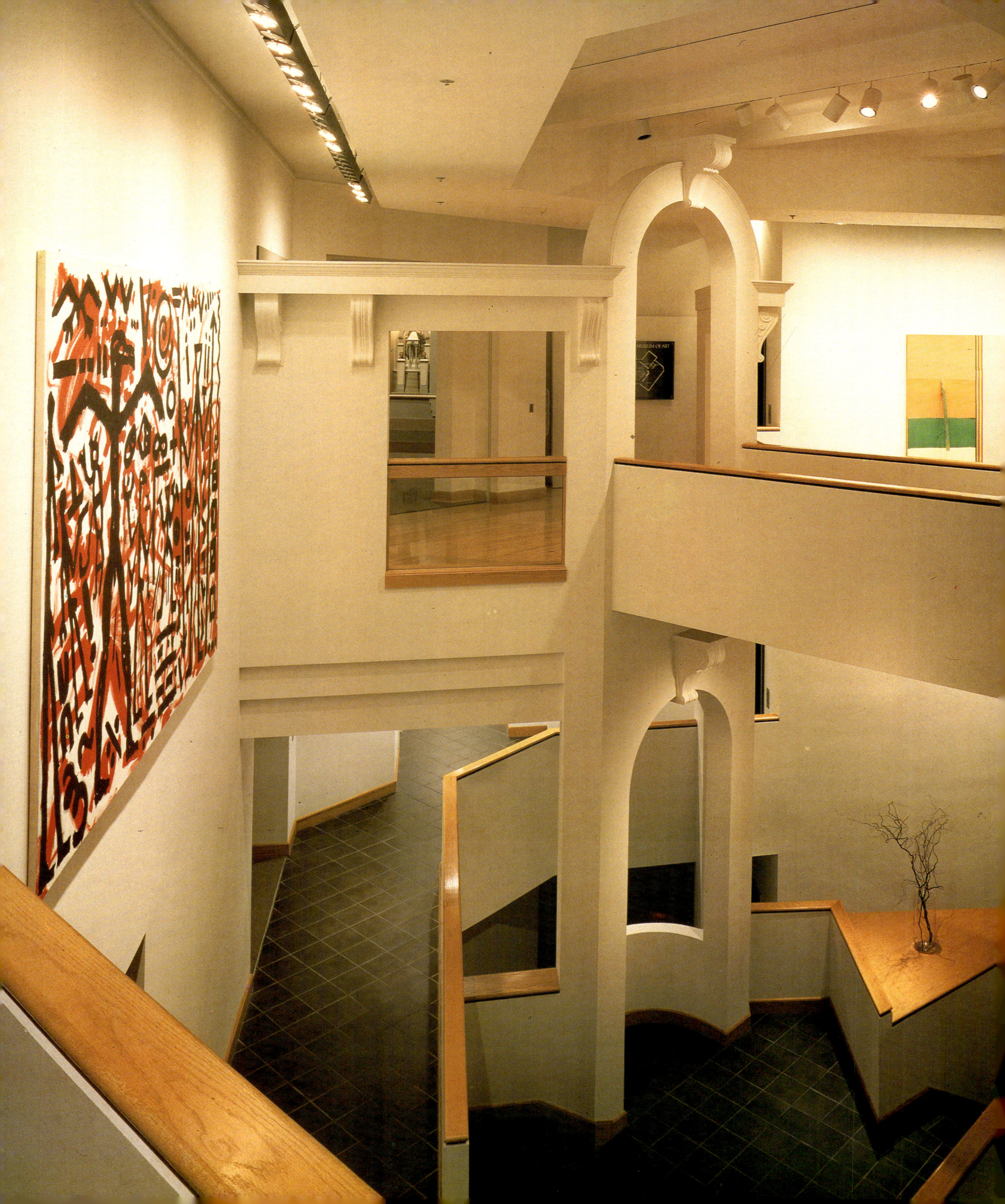
MUSEUM OF ART

building, while their generous shape offers spots and landings in which to pause and look across at the bridge and other gallery visitors, or to peer into revealed areas on other levels.

The architectural exuberance of the atrium is in deliberate contrast with the more simple and calm spaces of the galleries, classrooms and slide-room. The gallery spaces borrow their character from the original building. The rooms are organized around a long axis that runs the full length of the building, including the span of the atrium bridge.

The interior is filled with details that recall the 1846 building. Rustication, brickwork, string courses, cornices and pitched roofs all appear at odd junctures in the new building, always with mannerist hints to convince the visitor of the novelty of the design.

(left) The bridge, spanning the atrium, adds an element of drama to the space.

(below) Doric columns, exposed brickwork and jutting classical scrolls recall the details of the 1846 building.

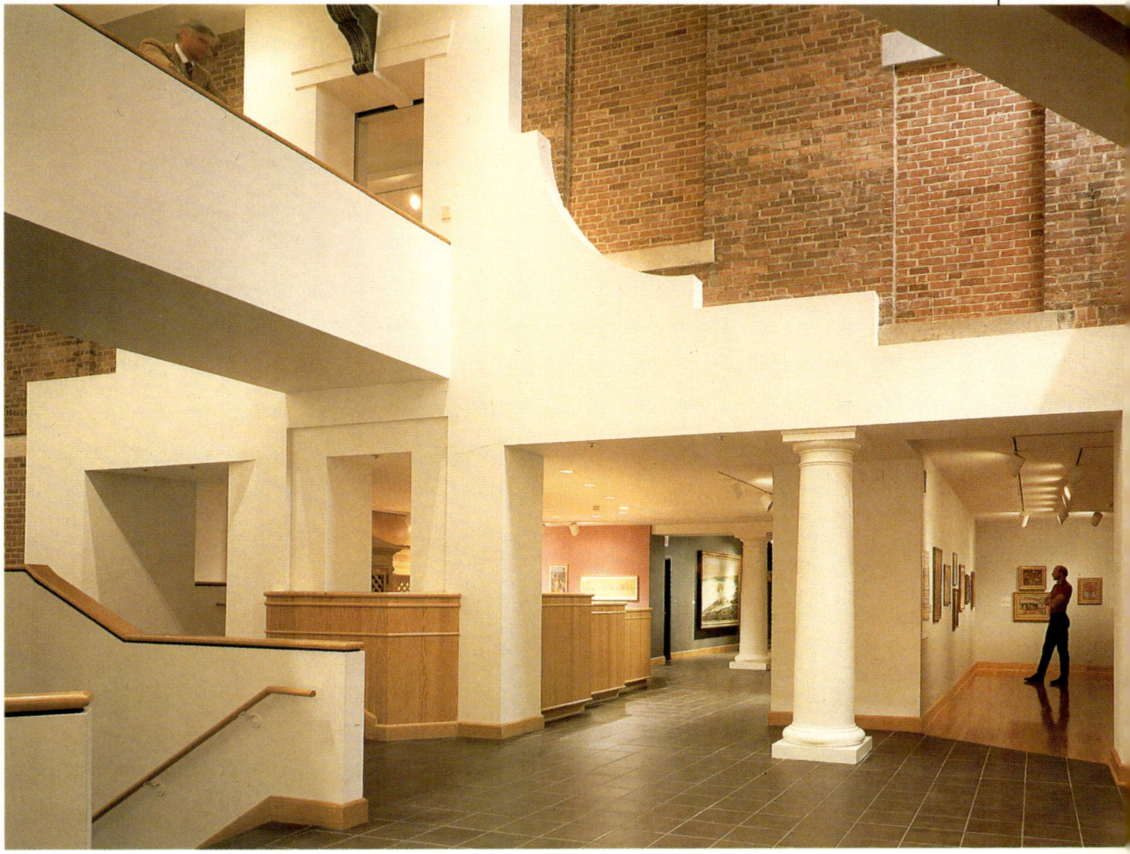

TRINITY COLLEGE
DUBLIN, EIRE

Designed by de Blacam and Meagher

When Dublin-based architects de Blacam and Meagher won the competition to design a theatre for the four hundredth anniversary of Trinity College, Dublin, they were asked at the same time to consider ways of improving the university's rather neglected eighteenth-century dining hall and adjoining catering areas. Shortly afterwards, however, appropriately on Friday the 13th, a fire reduced much of this complex to a charred ruin. The fire presented de Blacam and Meagher – together with a large team of specialist craftsmen, contractors, college staff and other experts – with two clear tasks: to restore the eighteenth-century parts of the building to their original simple elegance, and also to take into account the demands placed on the buildings by the practical realities of modern university life.

Much of the work is restoration, which had to undo both the fire damage and the ill-advised changes of the last hundred years. Meticulously designed furniture and fittings were used throughout the scheme: for example, the English oak chairs in the dining hall went through six prototype versions before the design was agreed.

But not all the work at Trinity has been restoration. One of the most striking of the designers' contributions to Trinity's dining complex is a modern extension: a 20 foot by 12 foot (6.2 metre by 3.6 metre) re-creation in medium-density fibreboard and mirrors of Viennese architect Adolf Loos' turn-of-the-century Kartner bar. Another is their atrium, a space of beautifully detailed beechwood balustrades and shutters; this has been designed as a meeting place and as a focal point for student life. Here, a series of enclosed rooms round a double-height exhibition space caters for some forty or so student societies.

Finally, the buttery and food hall are at basement level. Maintaining the classical idea of plainer, direct detailing for the lower levels, these areas have been restored with strong, simple materials: quarry tiles, unpolished Kilkenny marble and scrubbed oak.

Throughout the project, architects and craftsmen had to restore Trinity's dining hall without the help of any official records, which were lost in the fire. A few colour photographs in a tourist brochure became a vital guide. Nevertheless, even the briefest glance at their work today shows just how much de Blacam and Meagher achieved.

(right) de Blacam and Meagher's work on the fire-damaged eighteenth-century building involved both meticulous restoration and the design of new elements to take account of modern university life.

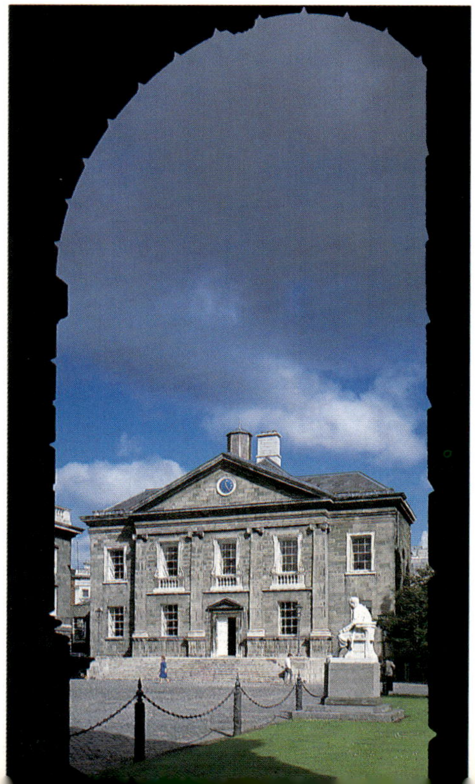

(right) The atrium, detailed with beechwood balustrades and shutters, provides a double-height exhibition space and enclosed rooms for the meetings of the numerous student societies.

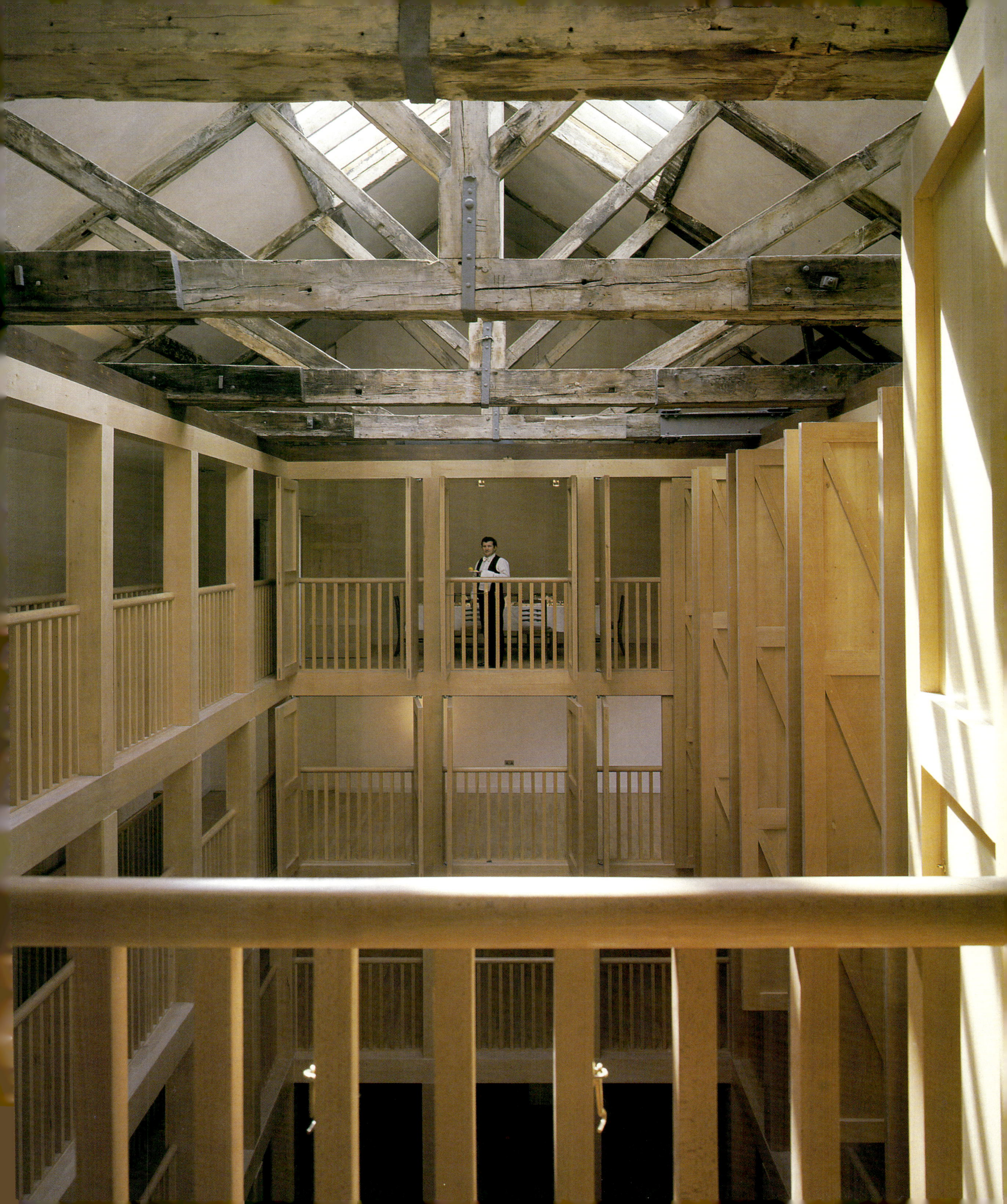

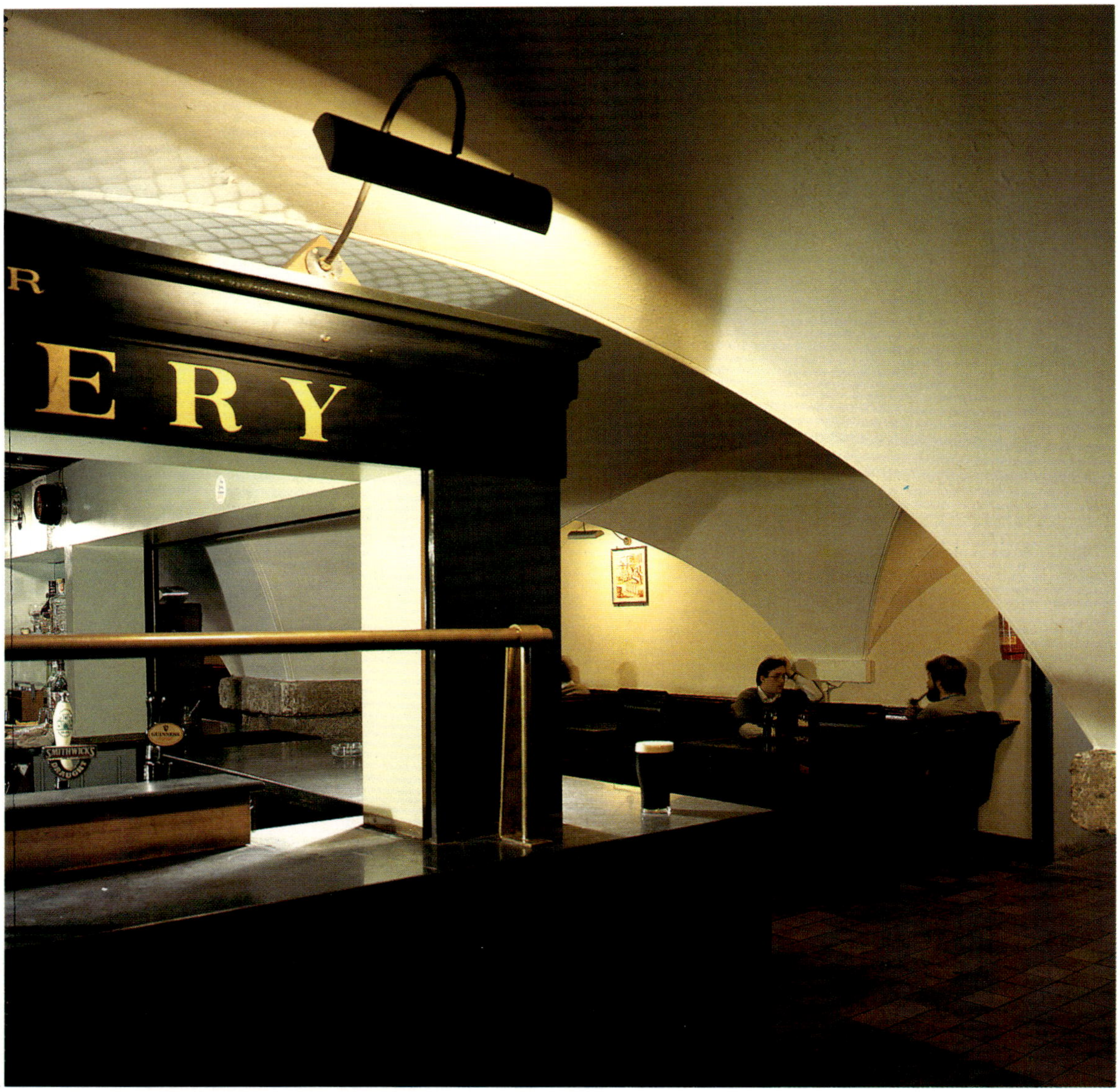
R
ERY

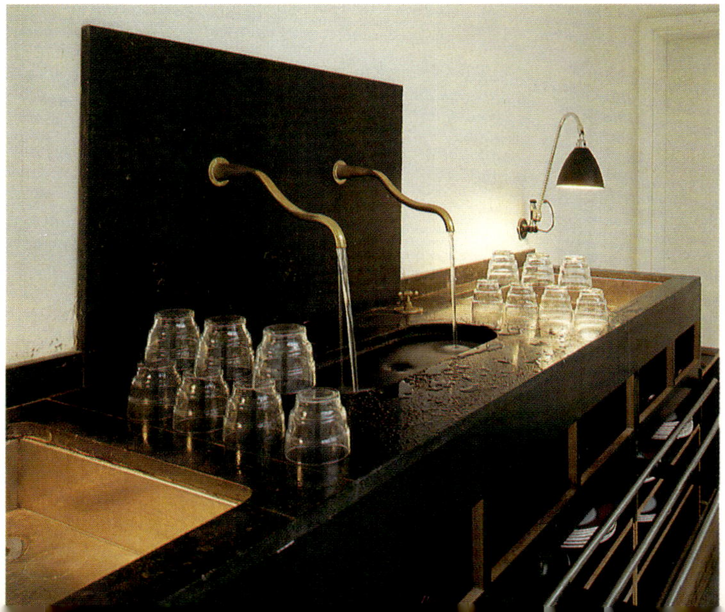

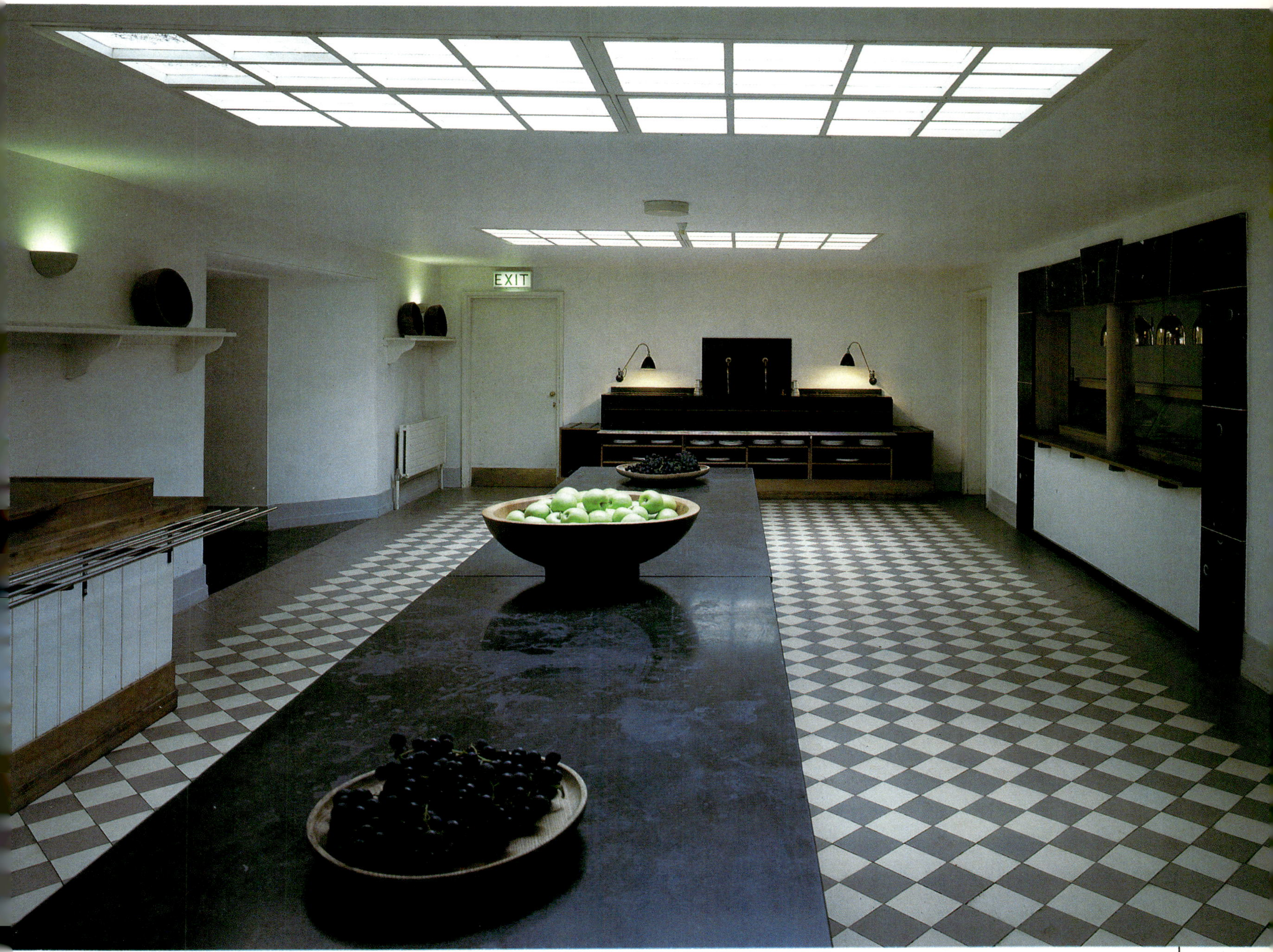

(above) Classical simplicity creates a visually powerful yet functional food hall.

(above left) The basement-level buttery has a plain, direct design with simple materials: quarry tiles, unpolished Kilkenny marble and scrubbed oak.

(left) The designers did not neglect the more mundane areas of the design. Brass plumbing fittings and marble tops in the food hall are convincing attempts to recapture the eighteenth-century aesthetic.

THE WAVES
BLACKBURN, UK

Designed by Faulkner Browns

The Waves at Blackburn, completed by architects Faulkner Browns in June 1986, shows that public baths have come a very long way since the days of chlorinated oblongs in tiled surrounds. In fact, this 'leisure lagoon', as it is called, goes a significant step beyond even the wave-machines, kidney-shaped pools and copious planting of recent years.

The designers' brief was for a building whose style and quality of construction would make a positive contribution to a formerly derelict site in the centre of the town. From outside, the building takes its tone from its surroundings; its pinkish Bath stone blocks and paving stones fit in well with the nearby Victorian technical college, library and dance hall. Also visible from the exterior – and giving a hint of the surreal leisure environment inside – is a dramatic pink water chute which jets out at a high level from a stair tower and then curves over the paved approach area to re-enter via a wavy glazed wall.

Once inside, visitors are met by a view from an open balcony of the pool itself. Then, past the payment desk, they go down to the changing-rooms, which are alongside the pool, to the café, to the 'beach', or to the promenade decks with their seating and metal table umbrellas (low-energy compact fluorescent fittings give uplight and downlight from the hub of the umbrella stand). Interestingly, there are no barriers between wet and dry areas, though a change of floor surface from rubber to non-slip mosaic tiles is intended to avoid confusion.

Visually, the rectilinear shape of the main pool, and the lines of the roof trusses and the stainless-steel wires that support the flume (a 197 foot/60 metre long translucent chute), contrast with the predominant curves of the flume, the table umbrellas and the wavy wall. As for lighting, columns with uplighters, underwater lights and backlighting to plants, as well as the small fluorescents on the umbrella stands, all add up to an environment that is exciting and inviting. Certainly, with all the different facilities it offers, The Waves lives up to this promise: as well as the flume, there are geysers which reach within a metre of the ceiling, a waterfall spilling from a moat around a twenty-seater spa pool, and, finally, a system of hydraulic rams operated by microprocessor controls to create twenty-four different wave patterns. This is clearly a place for fun, though

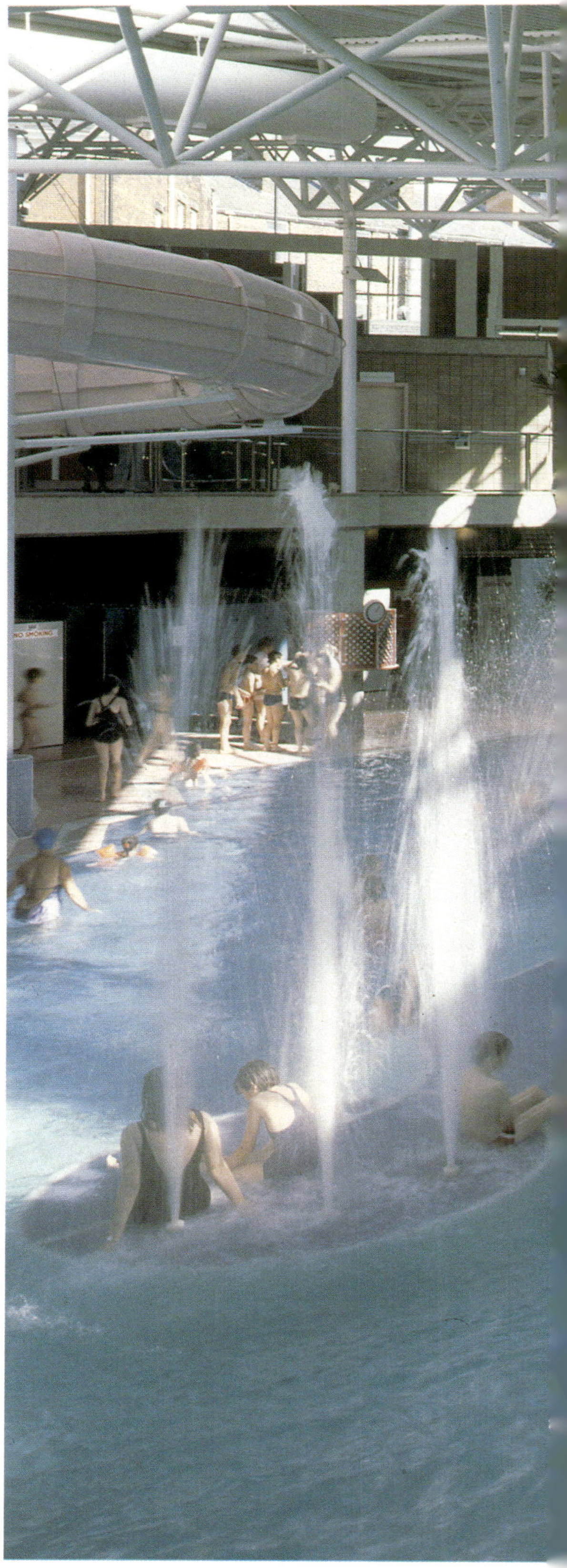

A water wonderland under the steel roof structure: the designers have tried to re-create the seaside with bright colours and palm trees.

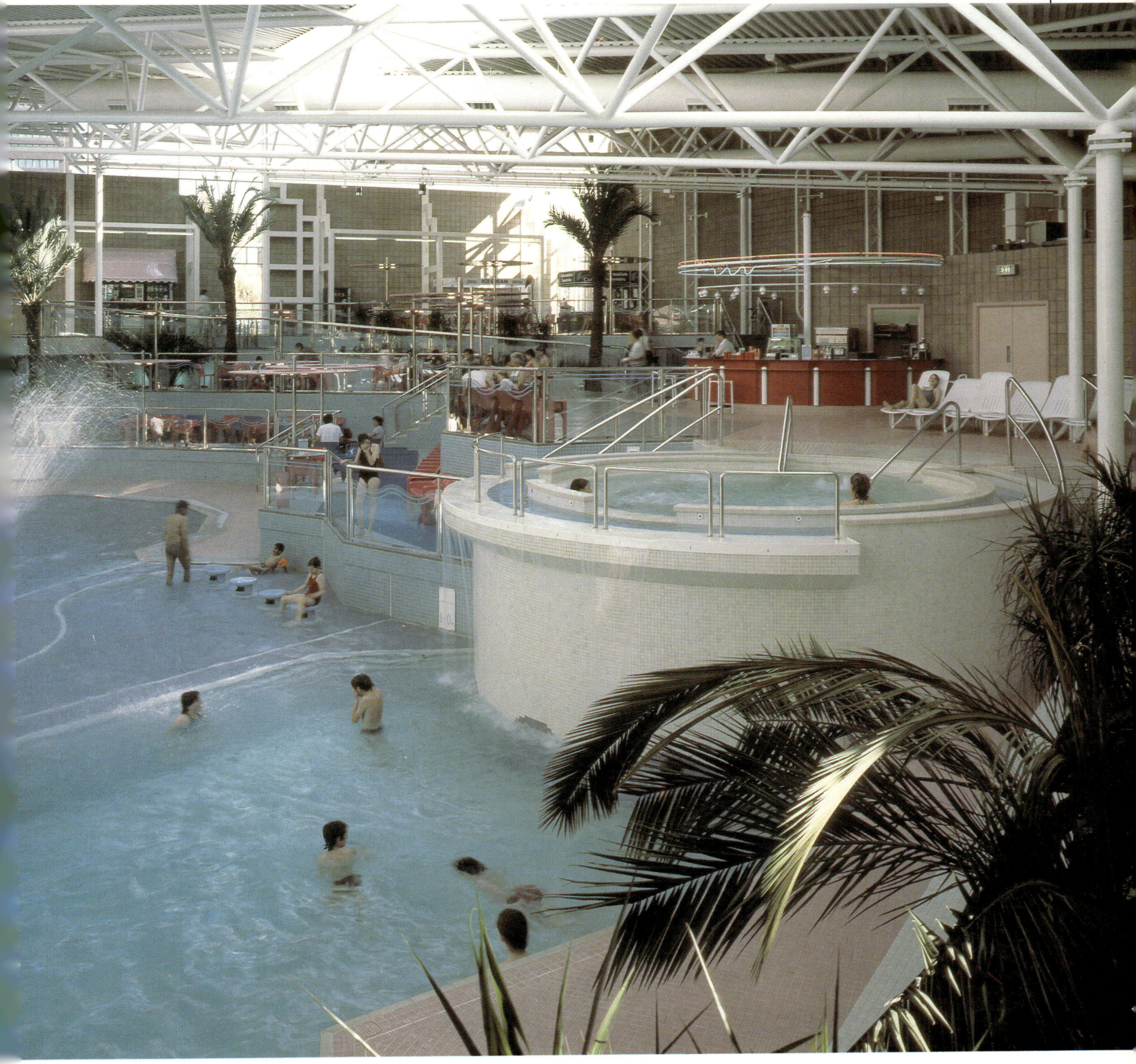

serious swimmers may lament the lack of good old-fashioned lane swimming.

The colours chosen by the architects emphasize this overall feeling of fantasy: the building's white steel structure is softened by the pinks and blues of the tiles, the table umbrellas, the flume, and the neon strips that announce the food bar. Finishes and fittings are of a very high standard: for example, the reception counter and the café tables are made in solid-grade plastic laminate; the mosaic tiling has a special non-slip finish; changing cubicles have high-impact, coloured glass.

With total building costs around the £2.15 million (3,600 million dollars) mark, and running costs estimated at something like £620,000 (a million dollars) a year, The Waves has received criticism from some quarters. There are those who question the spending of this amount of money on one single building; why not, they ask, spend less on individual public leisure buildings, but build more of them? But the fact remains that, architecturally, The Waves is an important contribution to Blackburn's townscape. Moreover, it has been welcomed enthusiastically by the town's residents; in fact the ambitious attendance target of one thousand visitors per day has been easily met.

(right) A twenty-seater spa pool sits next to the centre's 'dry' area café.

(far right) A dramatic pink water chute curves over the paved approach area.

(below right) Stainless-steel wires suspend the water chute from the main structure.

(below) Axonometric projection.

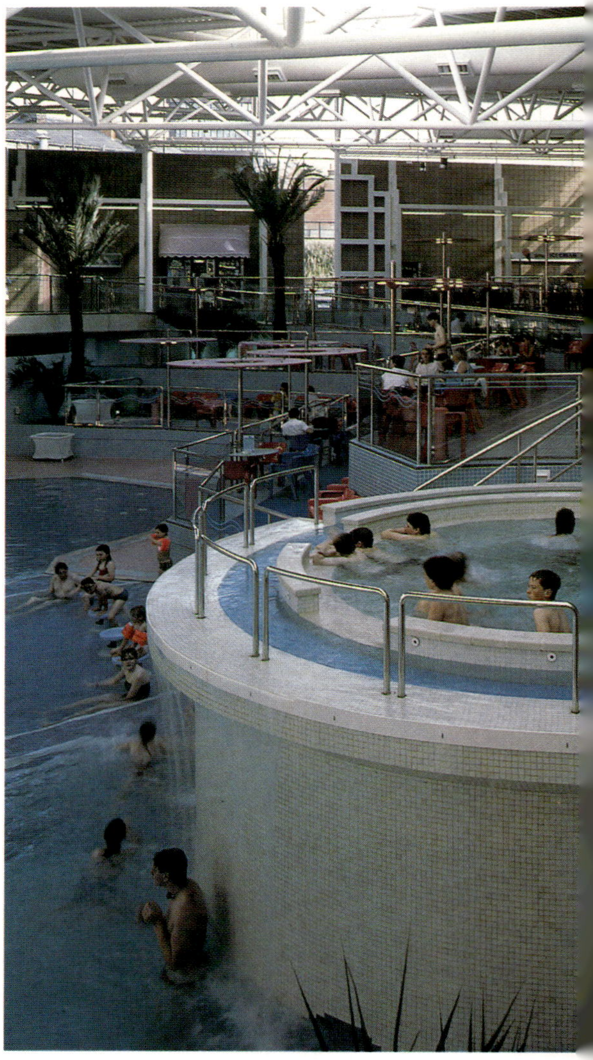

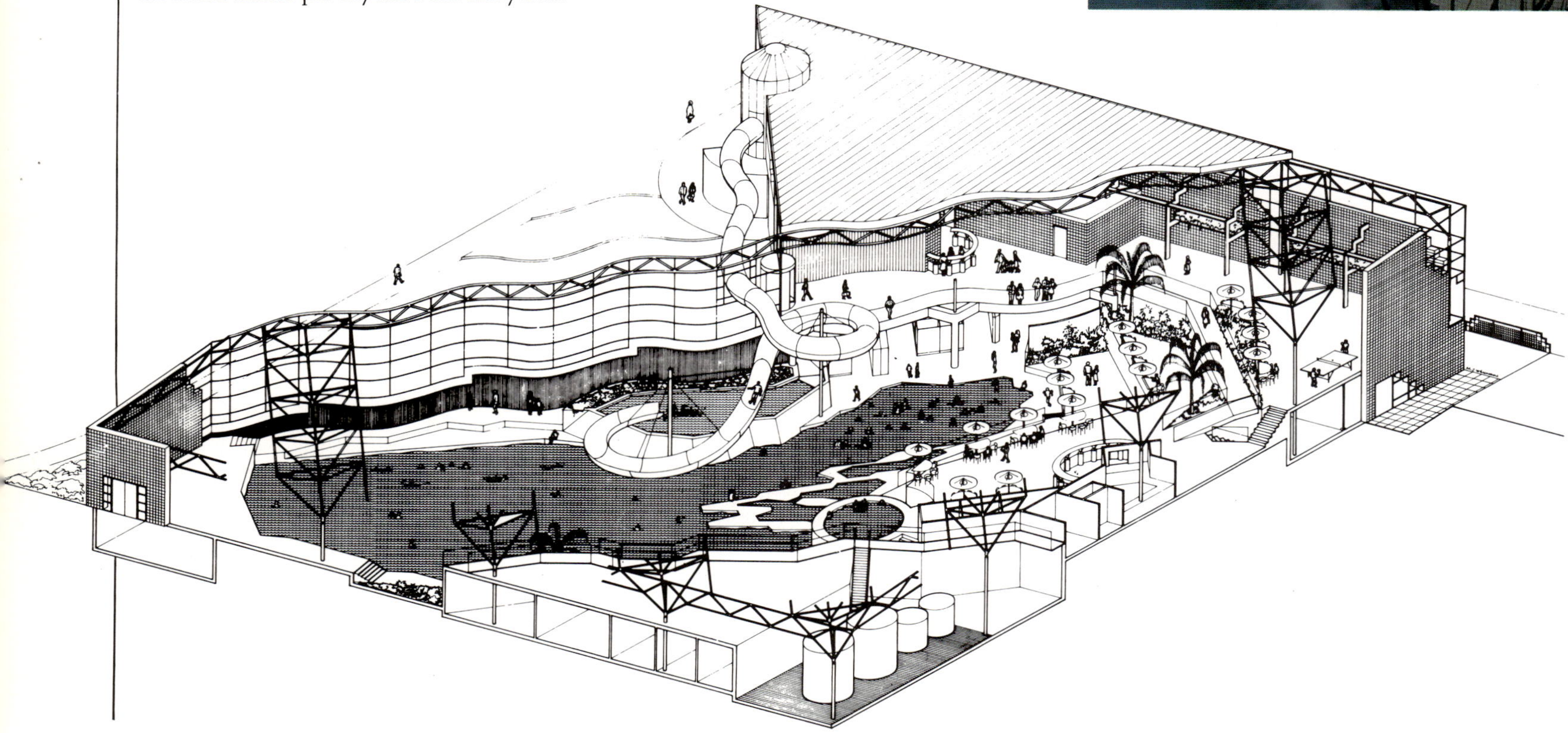

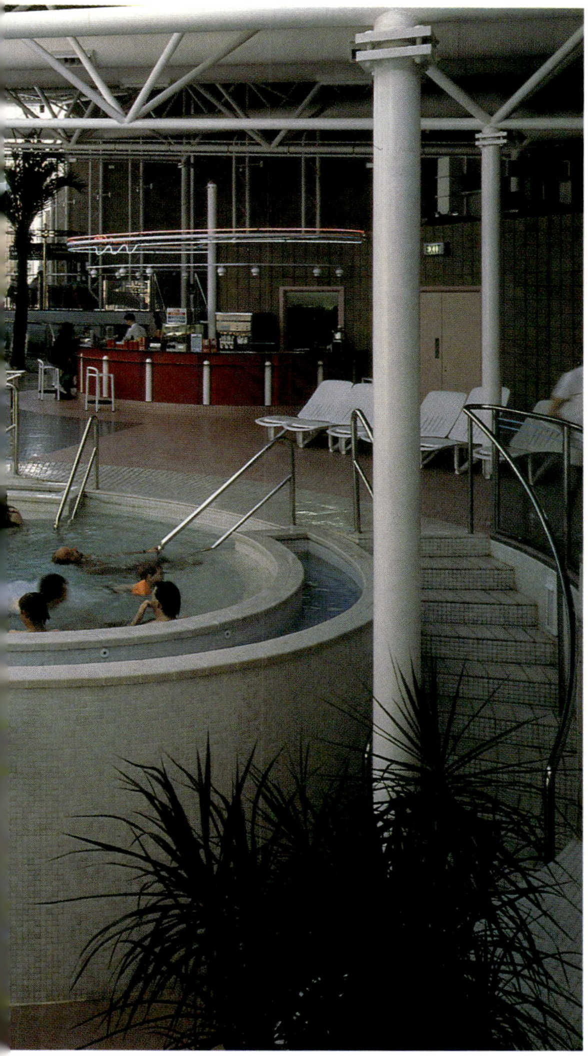

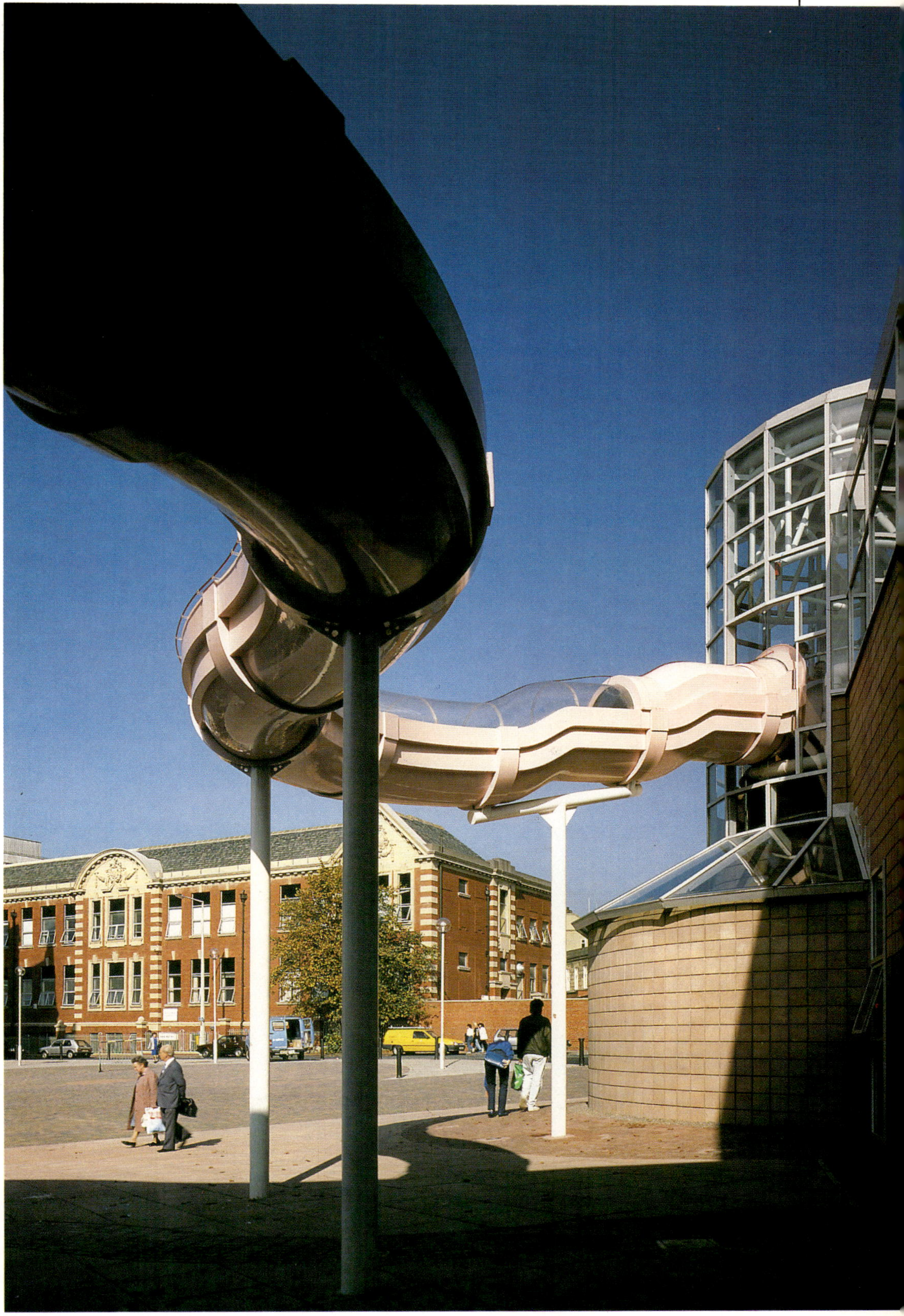

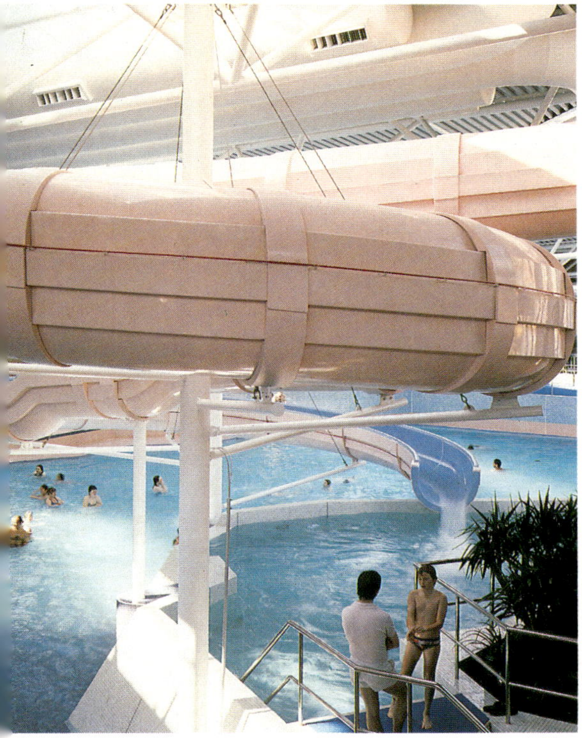

PHOTOGRAPHIC RESOURCE CENTER

BOSTON, MASSACHUSETTS

Designed by Leers, Weinzapfel Associates, Architects, Inc. and Chan & Krieger Architects

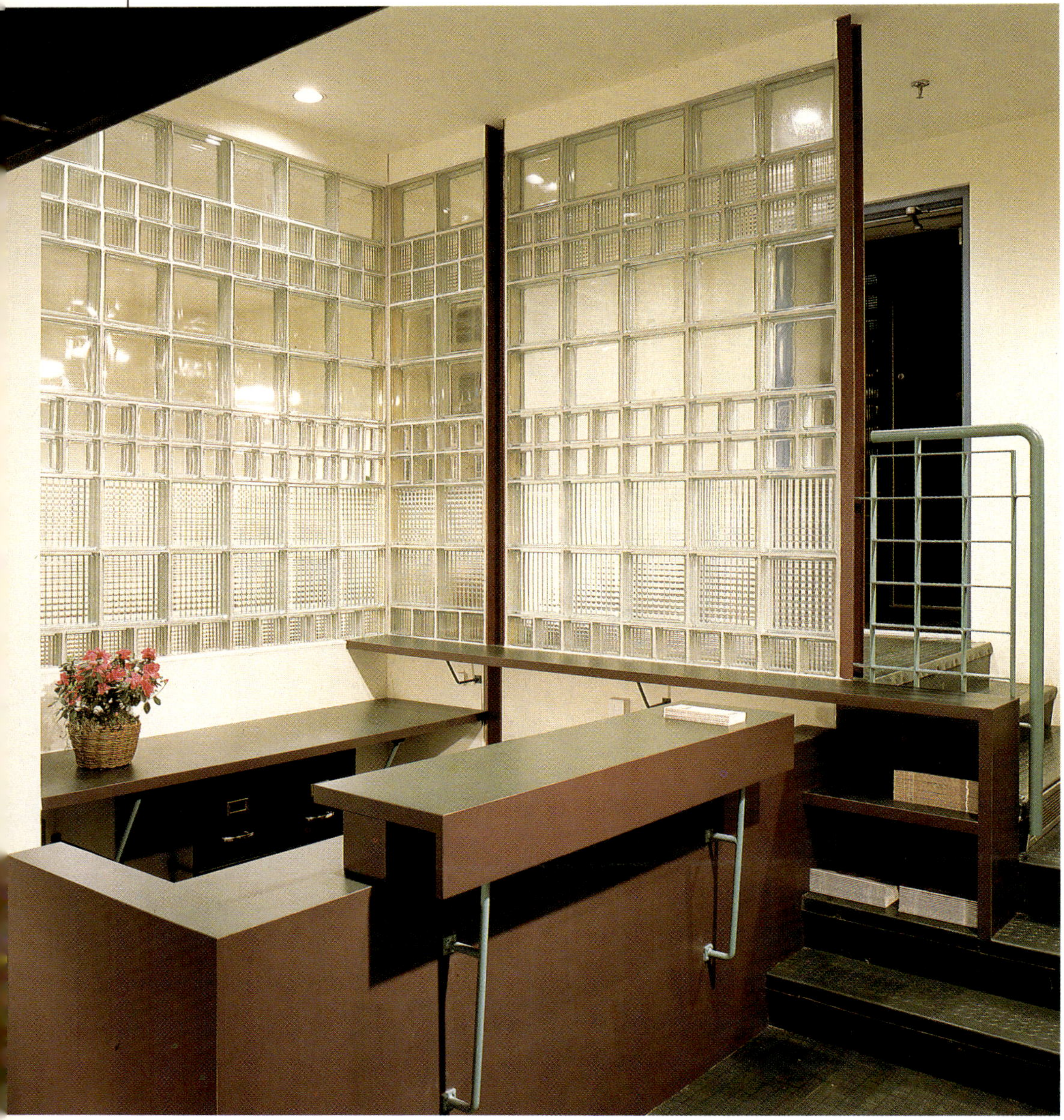

Founded in the mid-1970s, the Photographic Resource Center is a non-profit-making organization offering a variety of exhibitions and lectures as well as library and reference facilities for the photographic arts. For ten years, the centre operated from volunteers' homes or from a back room lent to them by Boston University – so when the lower level of one of the university's major lecture halls became availiable on a permanent basis, they wanted an inviting interior that would give them a coherent, established image.

An entrance of glass blocks and steel greets visitors, who then progress to a reception area and from there to a small, informal gallery. Inside, glass blocks have again been used to allow light from outside to penetrate into what would otherwise be a rather dark and gloomy space. The reception area and the small gallery next to it are made up of several areas of different size and shape, unified by the use throughout of the glass blocks, painted steel and plaster detailing.

In contrast, the larger main gallery and the library adjacent to it are regular and simple in shape. Such straightforward treatment works especially well in the gallery where photographs can be exhibited to maximum effect. The display boards here and in the smaller gallery are illuminated by Lightolier spotlights on tracks. Other rooms at the centre are used for storage, offices, a darkroom and a design studio.

(left) In the reception area, exposed steel frames, rubber-studded flooring and the glass blocks used throughout create a predominantly industrial look.

Materials used at the centre have a predominantly industrial look: wire mesh for the ceilings, exposed structural steel frames for walls, and rubber flooring. Most effective, however, are the translucent glass blocks which bring to mind camera lenses and the photographic process – and so make this an appropriate place in which to celebrate the photographic arts.

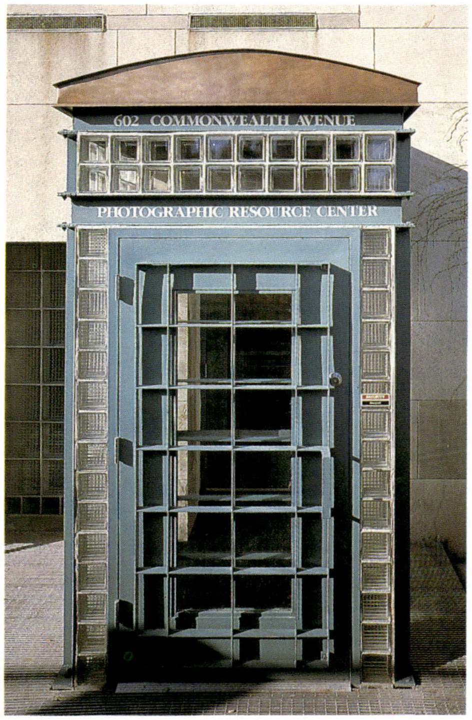

(left) The entrance of glass blocks and steel sets the consistent aesthetic of the design.

(below) Glass blocks have been used to allow light from outside to penetrate the basement level.

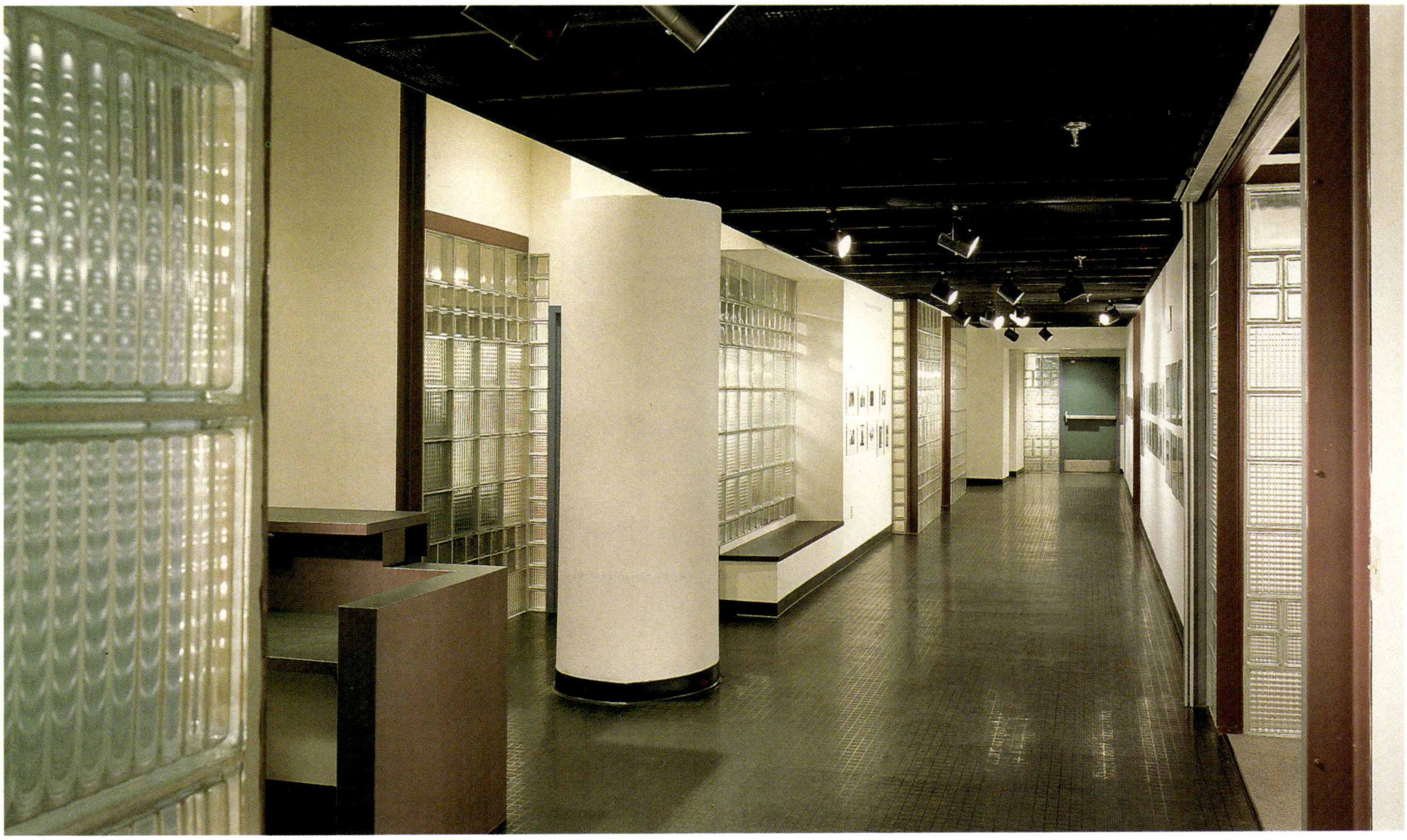

KENT GALLERY

NEW YORK CITY, USA

Designed by Diane Lewis and Peter Mickle

There has been a tradition in recent years for art galleries to be cool, neutral spaces where the art can dominate, the architecture recede. This contrived neutrality has been a response to the needs of modern art, which looks misplaced in the plush, fabric-lined galleries where collectors seek Old Masters. The Kent Gallery is clearly part of this modern tradition, but the designers have exploited small details to produce an interior that rises above the ordinary.

The 4,800 square foot (446 square metre) gallery is on the third floor of a 1929 gallery and office building on the corner of Madison Avenue and 57th Street. In addition to the display spaces, there are research, conservation, storage, shipping and office areas; communications are aided by an extensive network of personal computers. The designers conceived the gallery so that the qualities of the exhibition spaces are maintained throughout the work areas, and, in theory, exhibitions can be installed anywhere in the entire premises.

Spaces in the gallery are separated by 8-inch thick partitions, constructed of ¾-inch

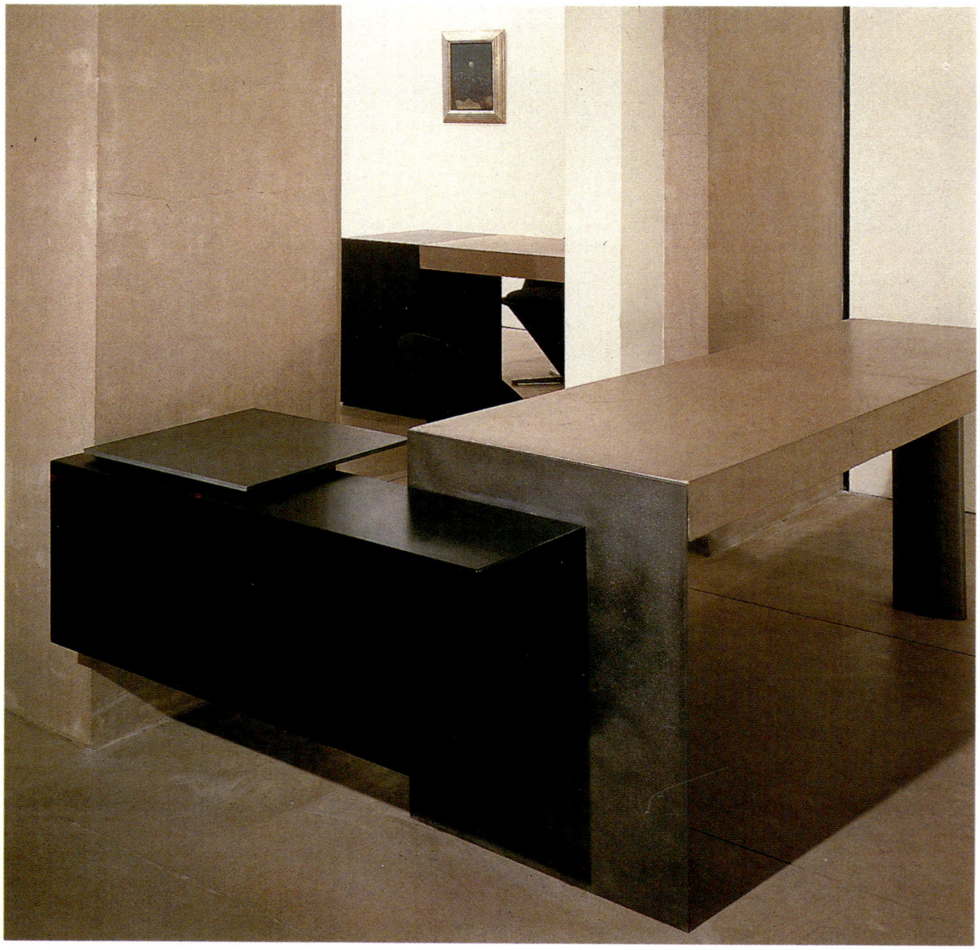

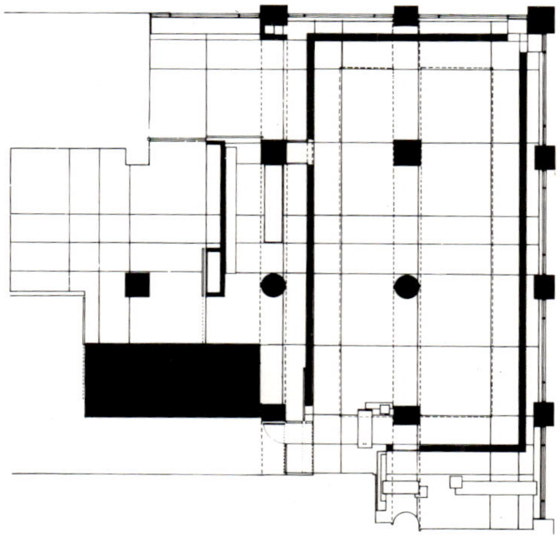

(above) Floor plan.

(left) The reception desk, of structural steel and precast terrazzo, continues the design's aesthetic.

(right) Detail is all in the minimalist design of the gallery. Saw-cut joints in the floor follow the grid of the plan.

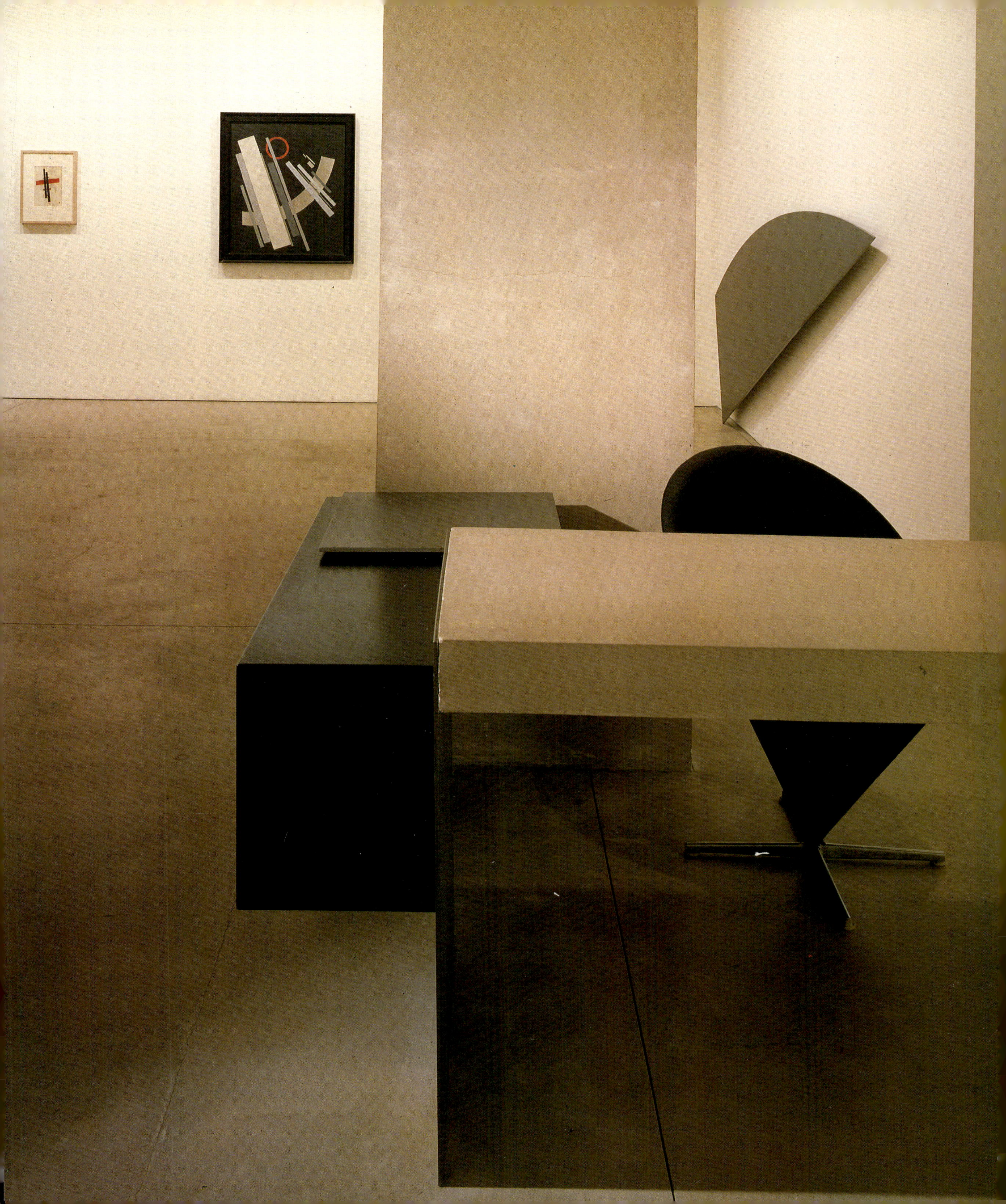

(below) Structural steel frames hold sheets of highly tempered glass in the doors. The steel is 'torched' and sealed with a clear lacquer.

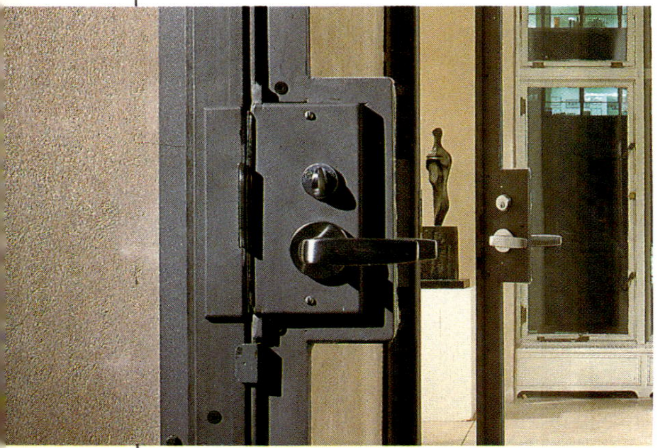

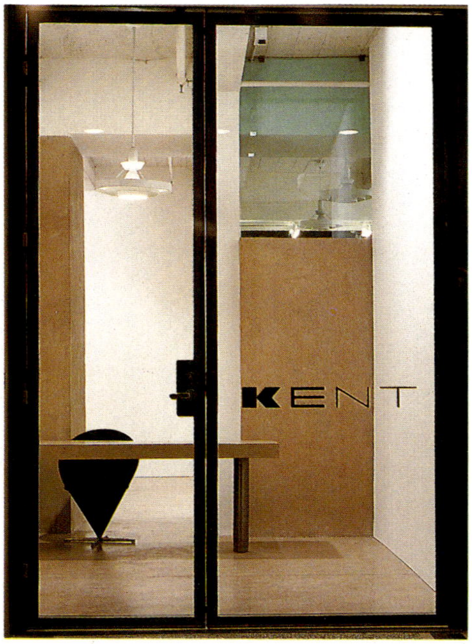

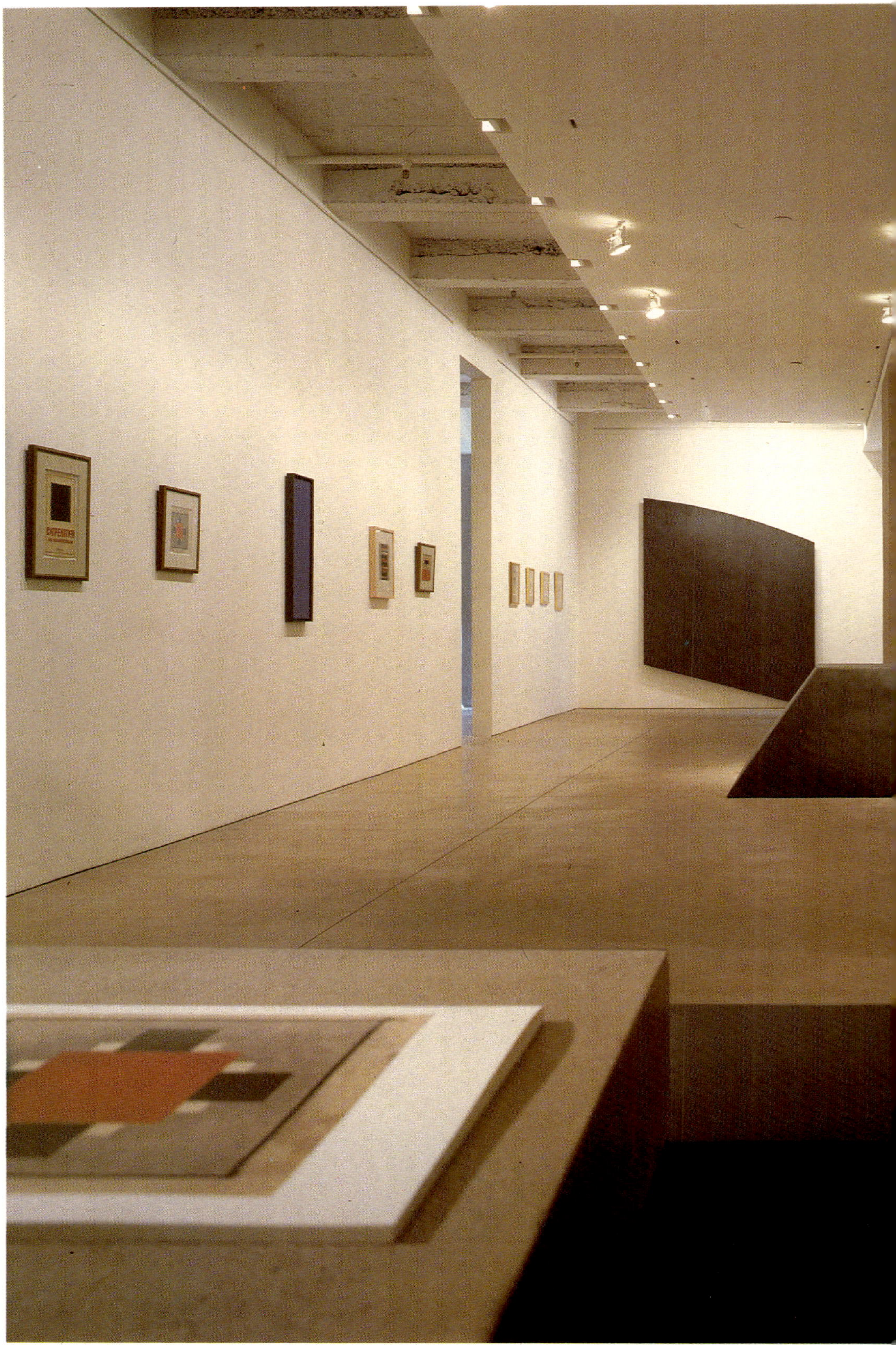

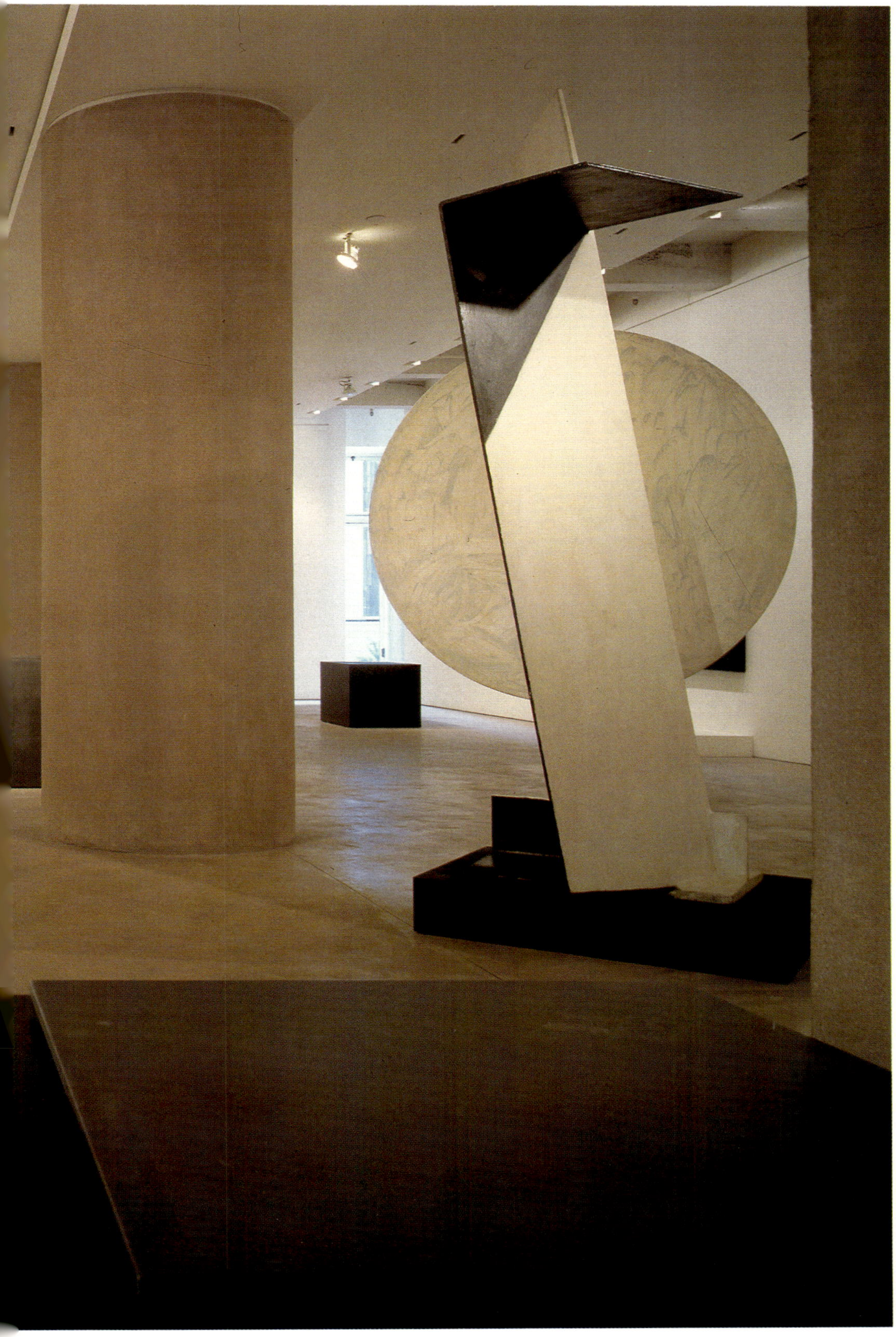

plywood nailed to both sides of 6-inch wood studs, with a finish layer of 5/8-inch gypsum board at areas where paintings are to be hung. At corners, inside and outside, and at the base of the panels, there is an 8-inch frame of three-coat plaster, flush with the face of the gypsum board, and separated from the gypsum board by a 1/16-inch hairline joint. The tops of the partitions are also of three-coat plaster, separated from the gypsum board by an extruded, brushed stainless-steel, 3-inch deep picture-hanging track. All partitions are revealed above the floor by 3/8 inch.

The same care has been lavished on the soffits and ceilings, which are also constructed of three-coat plaster. Indentations for lighting fixtures (which are 250 watt quartz lamps) are spaced at 4 foot 7 inch (1.4 metre) intervals round the perimeter, at the intersection of the sloping planes and the vertical returns to the structural slab.

The existing building columns have been stripped to the steel, refireproofed and reconfigured, and then finished with a 1-inch thick coat of hand-trowelled, ground and polished terrazzo, composed of white cement, silica, quartz and a small quantity of very fine black granite aggregate. The floor is in an identical terrazzo, 2 inches thick, with saw-cut joints following the grid of the gallery's plan.

The carefully composed restraint of the main elements of the gallery is mitigated slightly elsewhere. Cabinets convey a rougher aesthetic, constructed of structural steel and pre-cast terrazzo. Doors, too, continue this rougher look, with frames of structural steel holding the sheets of high-tempered glass. The structural steel has been 'torched' and sealed with a clear lacquer. But these deliberately rough elements only serve to stress the refinement and immaculate detail of the design.

(left) Three-coat plaster is used for partitions, soffits and ceiling. Structural columns are finished with hand-trowelled, ground and polished terrazzo.

SPIRAL
TOKYO, JAPAN

Designed by Maki Associates

Maki Associates' work for the Wacoal Corporation is design on the grand scale. The project, appropriately called Spiral, is a new building to house cultural activities, including a contemporary art gallery and a theatre as well as a café and restaurant. Part of the client's brief was that its design and function should reflect the characteristics of the modern Tokyo – collaged, multi-purpose and cosmopolitan.

Certainly it is more Western-influenced than many Japanese projects, so it is not surprising to learn that Fumihiko Maki studied in the USA, at Cranbrook and Harvard. Characteristically Japanese, however, is the considered use of light, both natural and artificial, to give each area a distinct character. The entrance hall, for example, is an imposing, luxurious space with marble steps and specially designed carpets by Kei Miyazaki that have a textured trompe-l'œil effect. Marble columns both di-

(below left) The Esplanade gallery is stark, with large areas of glazing and white walls.

(below) The imposing entrance hall has marble steps and a trompe-l'œil carpet designed by Kei Miyazaki, leading to the spiral ramp that gives the building its name.

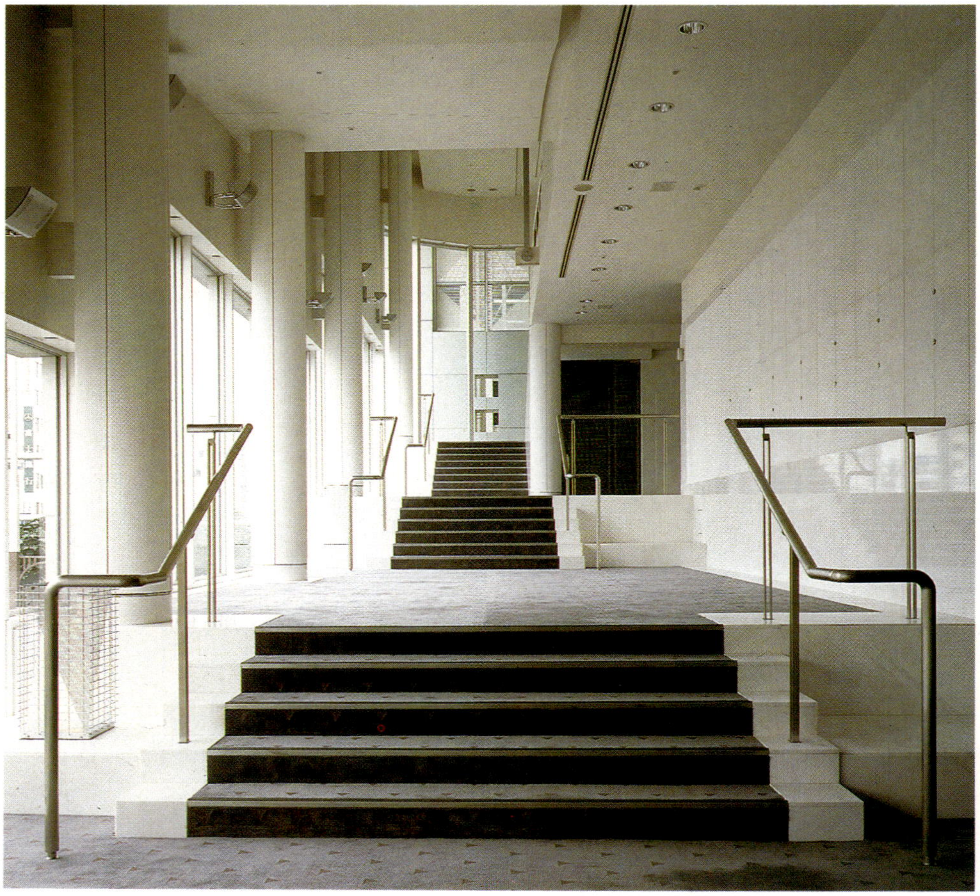

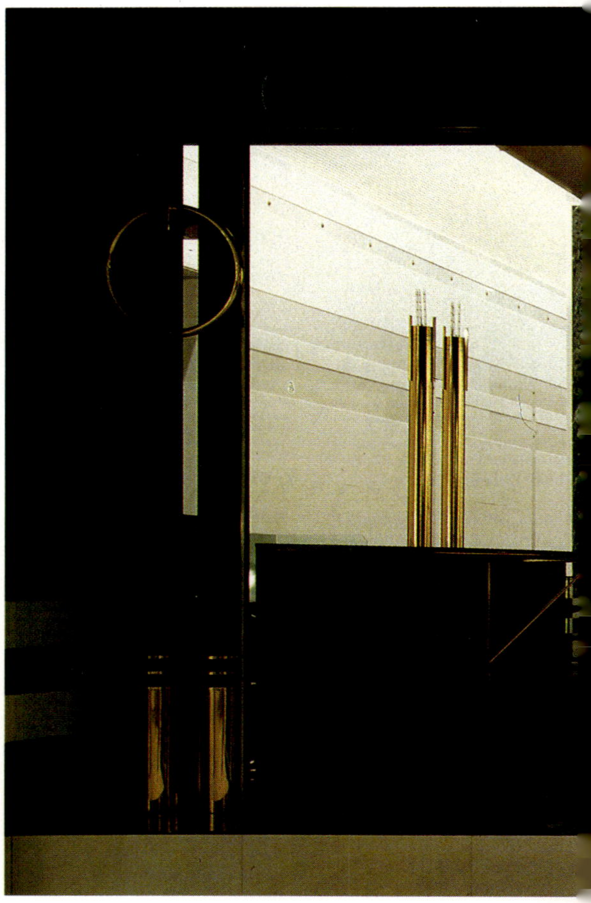

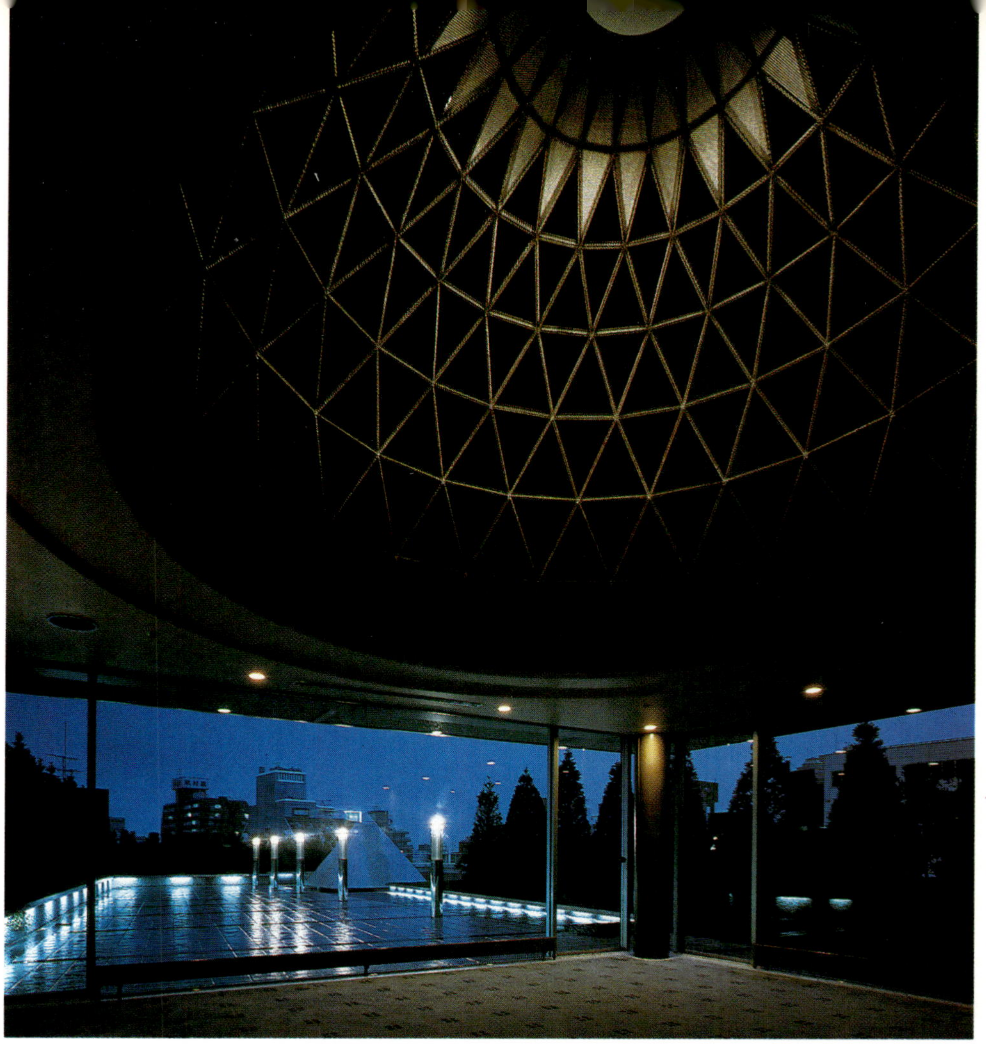

vide the cafeteria, with its custom-made gold lighting poles, and lead the eye down to the warm, top-lit atrium.

In contrast, the Esplanade gallery is stark, with large areas of glazing and white walls so that there are no distractions from the pictures. Yet it is saved from being cold and bland by stepped levels and columns, and an elegant steel handrail.

In the restaurant, there is yet another change of mood. Here again there is a mixture of natural light (coming in through the glazed screens overlooking the city) and artificial light. A domed ceiling of punched metal finished in gold and silver conceals indirect lighting above, creating a relaxed, opulent atmosphere.

(left) A domed ceiling of punched metal finished in gold and silver dominates the restaurant.

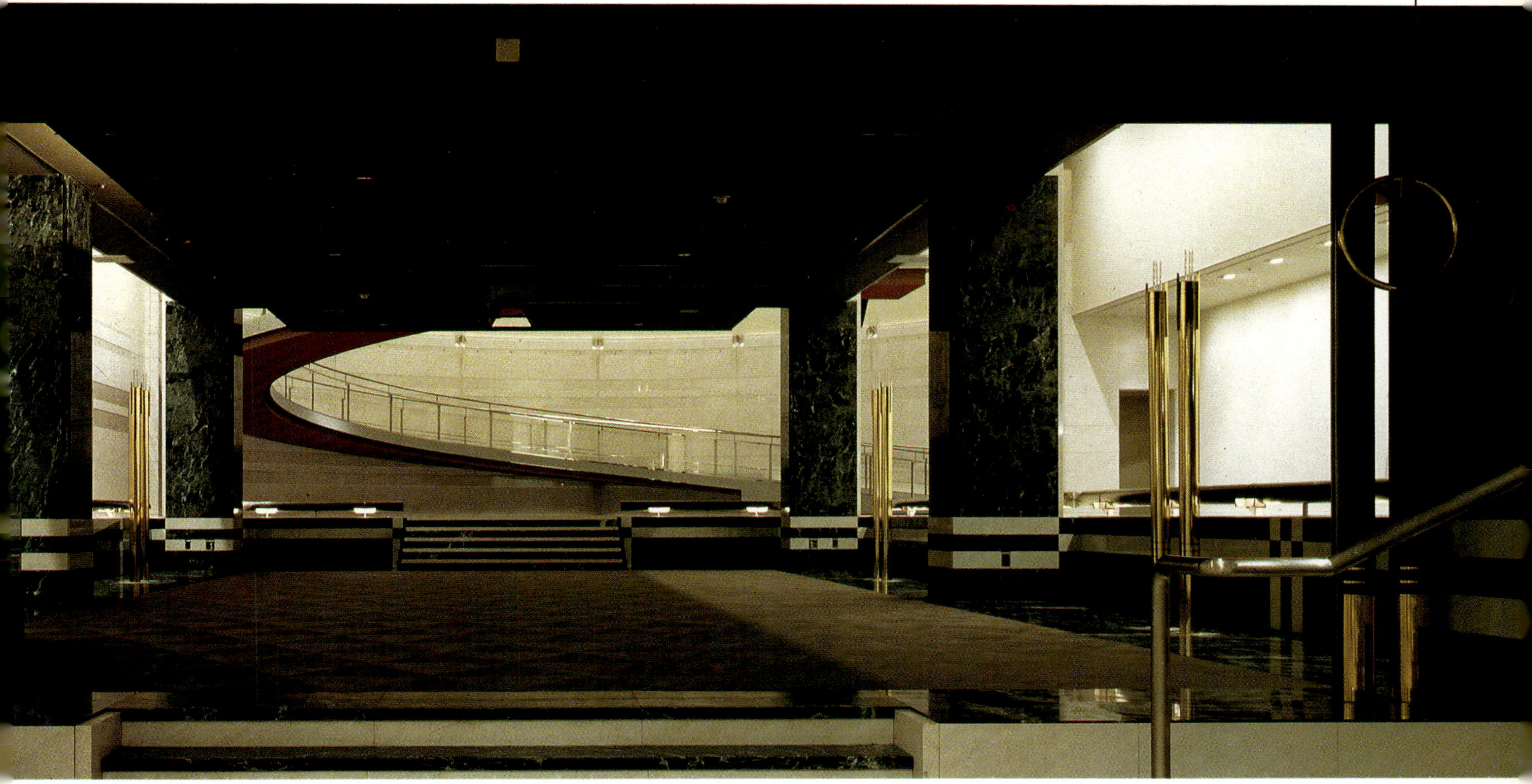

CARNEGIE HALL
NEW YORK CITY, USA

Designed by James Stewart Polshek and Partners

Since its 1891 opening, Carnegie Hall has earned a reputation as the most famous concert auditorium in the world. But thoughtless renovation and neglect over the years had sadly ravaged the acoustically superb hall. In addition, Carnegie Hall lacked many of the facilities required both by modern symphony orchestras and the audiences that patronize its concerts. In 1978, the trustees of the Carnegie Hall Corporation, the non-profit-making organization that operates the hall, engaged James Stewart Polshek and Partners to prepare a master plan to restore and preserve Carnegie Hall in the light of these problems.

The designers devised a complex plan, with work ranging from emergency stabilization of deteriorated structural and ornamental elements (all concert-goers have heard and felt the subway trains rumbling underneath the hall), to major reconfigurations of lobby and backstage areas. The master plan provided packages of work which could be undertaken as money and time became available and which would result in a structurally and fiscally sound Carnegie Hall. The total cost of the extensive refurbishment – including the interior elements of the design project – was 30 million dollars.

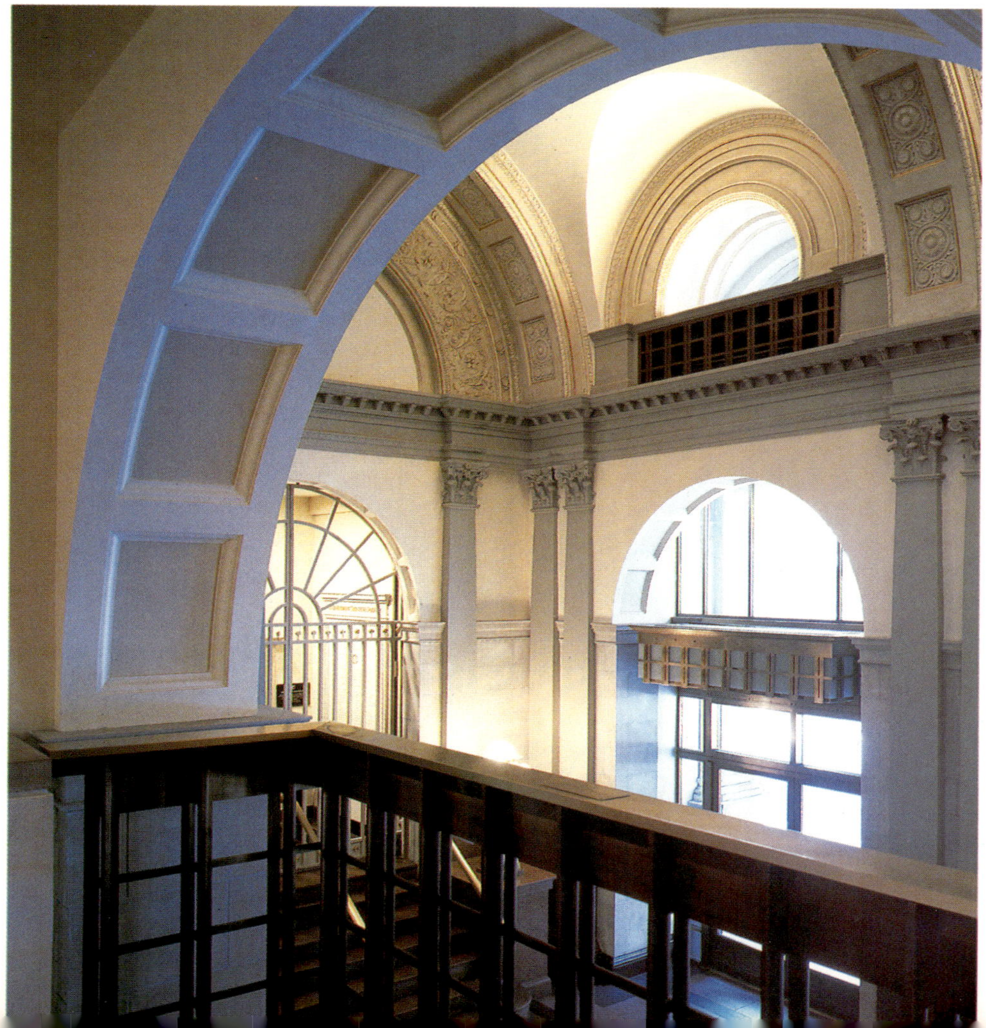

Time, in fact, was a serious constraint on the project. Much of the design had to be carefully planned to be executed within the three-month 'dark' periods between concert seasons.

The first package of work, completed in 1982, was the restoration of a separate entrance to the recital hall, as well as renovation of the studio lobby, providing improved access and egress, and an entrance for disabled visitors to the recital hall. Over the next three years, major works were done on the main concert hall's services: new mechanical equipment, new electrical services and distribution and the complete replacement of the plumbing were all arranged. In this time, the designers also embarked on the major task of the exterior restoration of the hall.

In 1986 the designers turned to most of the 'visible' work of their project. Much of their restoration involved removing additions from earlier unsympathetic renovations and the restoration of missing structural and ornamental elements. New house, concert and theatrical lighting was also installed, as were video and audio recording and broadcast

(left) Lobby spaces were renovated, removing earlier unsympathetic renovations and restoring missing structural and ornamental elements.

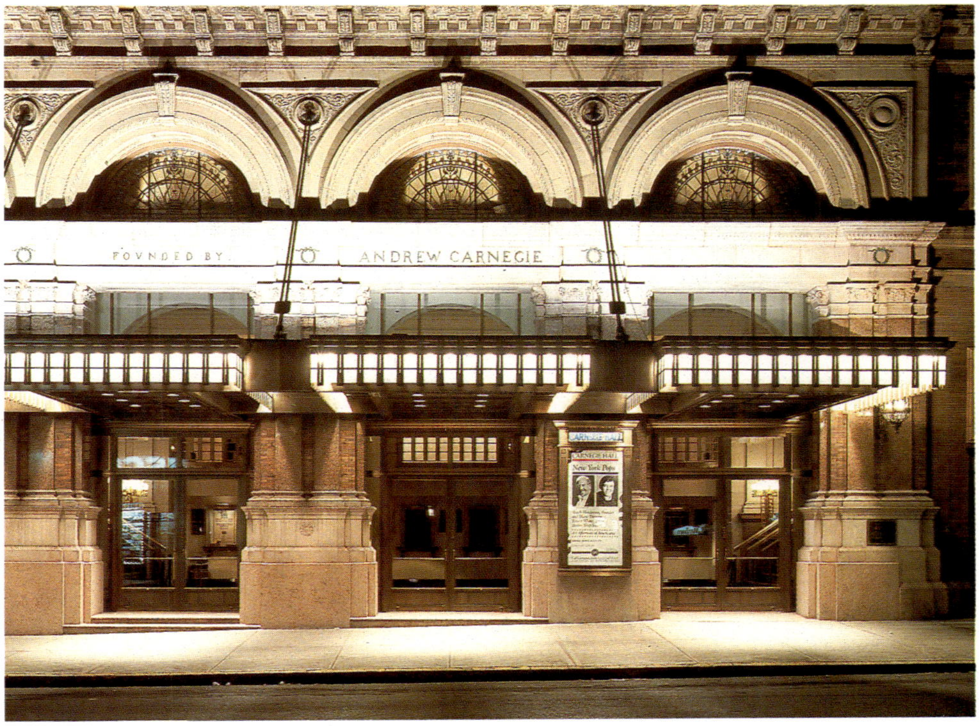

facilities. Backstage and lobby spaces were renovated, as were lavatories and dressing areas, which were at the same time enlarged, and, a reflection of changing times, security was improved.

In all aspects of the project, perhaps the best accolade the designers could have is recognition of the seamless nature of the renovation and restoration: to those unfamiliar with the 'old' Carnegie Hall, it looks as though nothing has been done.

(left) Clutter at the entrance, accumulated over the years, has been stripped away, leaving the elegant simplicity of the original design.

(below) The skill of the renovation makes unwitting observers think that nothing has changed. But behind the carefully restored surface, Carnegie Hall now has a full complement of modern performance facilities.

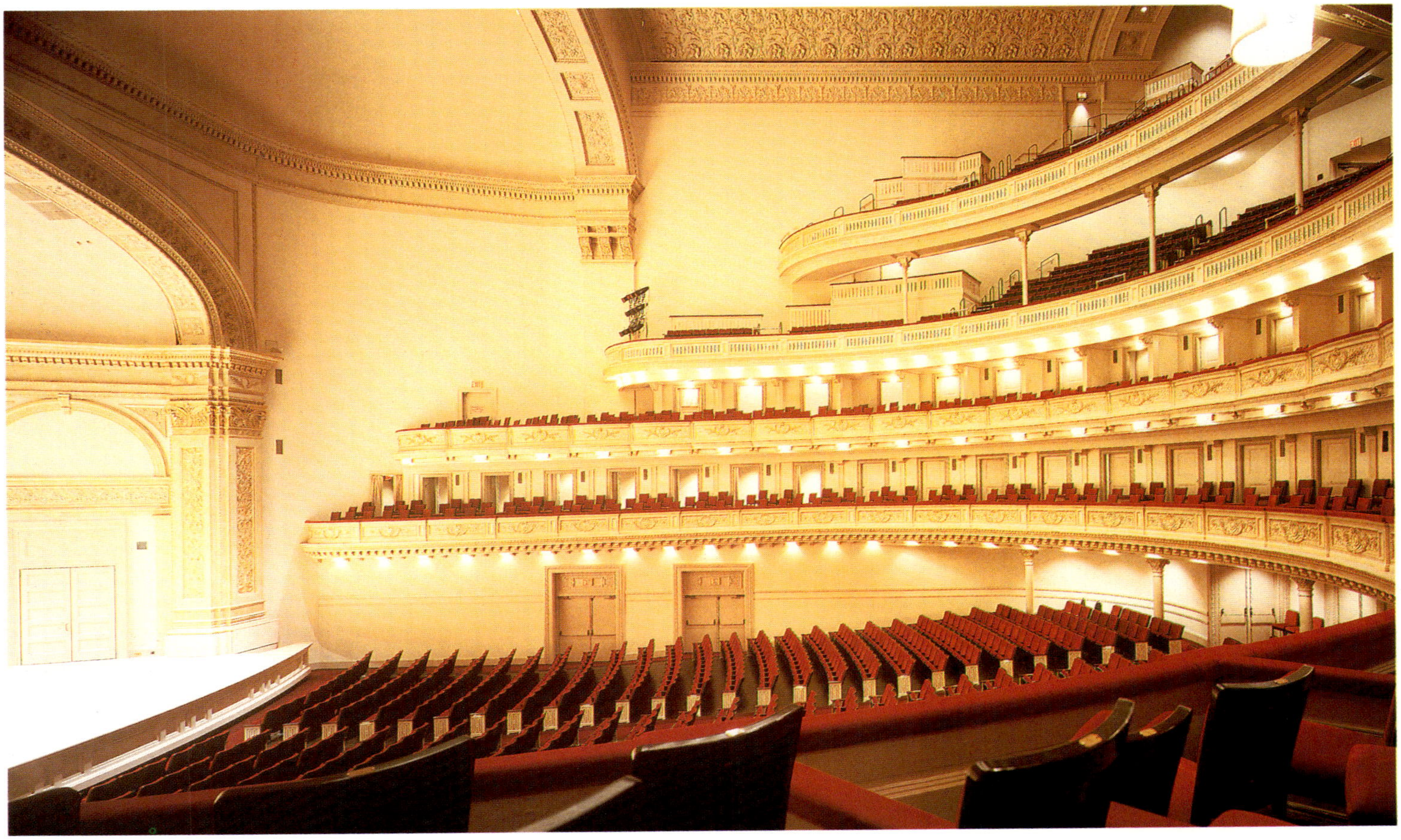

SWAN THEATRE
STRATFORD-ON-AVON

Designed by Michael Reardon & Associates

In 1978, architects Michael Reardon & Associates were asked to look into the feasibility of restoring the original Shakespeare Memorial Theatre, which had been severely damaged by fire in the 1920s, and which had been used since then only as a sort of conference-cum-rehearsal space. However, lack of funds put a stop to the project and only a donation from an anonymous benefactor finally allowed work to start on the Swan in January 1985. It opened sixteen months later with a production of *The Two Noble Kinsmen* by Shakespeare and Fletcher.

The refreshing thing about the Swan (particularly within the context of olde worlde Stratford) is that it is no direct reconstruction of F.W. Unsworth's gothic-style theatre, nor is it a pastiche of a Jacobean theatre. Instead it is, according to Michael Reardon, a building that has been produced – like the plays it hosts – fresh for a new generation.

Most noticeable and most effective is the use of timber in the auditorium: the three tiers of galleries that surround the simple trapped stage are all, like the columns, in a light-coloured Douglas fir, giving a warm and natural effect against the exposed, wire-brushed brick of the walls.

Seating an audience of only 461 (about a third of the main Shakespeare Theatre), the Swan is small and intimate. But the seating is comfortably spaced and sufficiently well-stepped to allow every spectator a clear view (and no one is more than 33 feet / 10 metres from the stage). Moreover, a small shelf, constructed just inside and below the gallery balustrades, permits front-row audiences to lean forward for an even better view.

Above the stage is the musicians' gallery. The stage itself has no fly tower, but it does have lighting bridges to support winches if suspension or 'flight' is called for by the plot. Additional lighting comes from discreet light tracks with spotlights positioned below some of the spectator galleries.

Immediately above the auditorium and directly below the Swan's new tall pitched roof is the rehearsal room. The laminated timber beams that are used in the auditorium work just as successfully here; the floor is wooden too, and several gothic windows give restful views over the Warwickshire landscape.

The rehearsal room is directly below the tall pitched roof. Gothic windows suffuse the space with a glow of natural light.

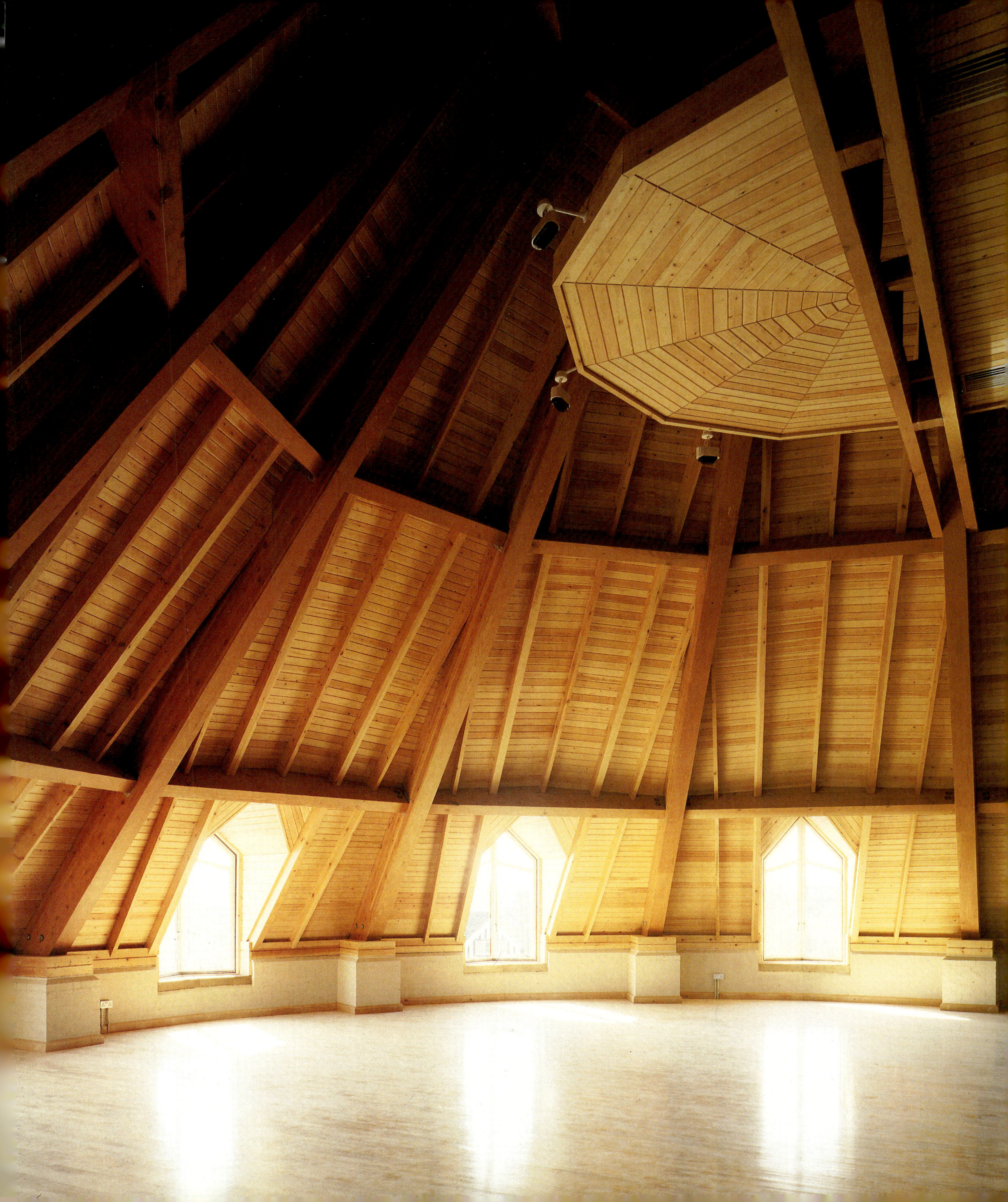

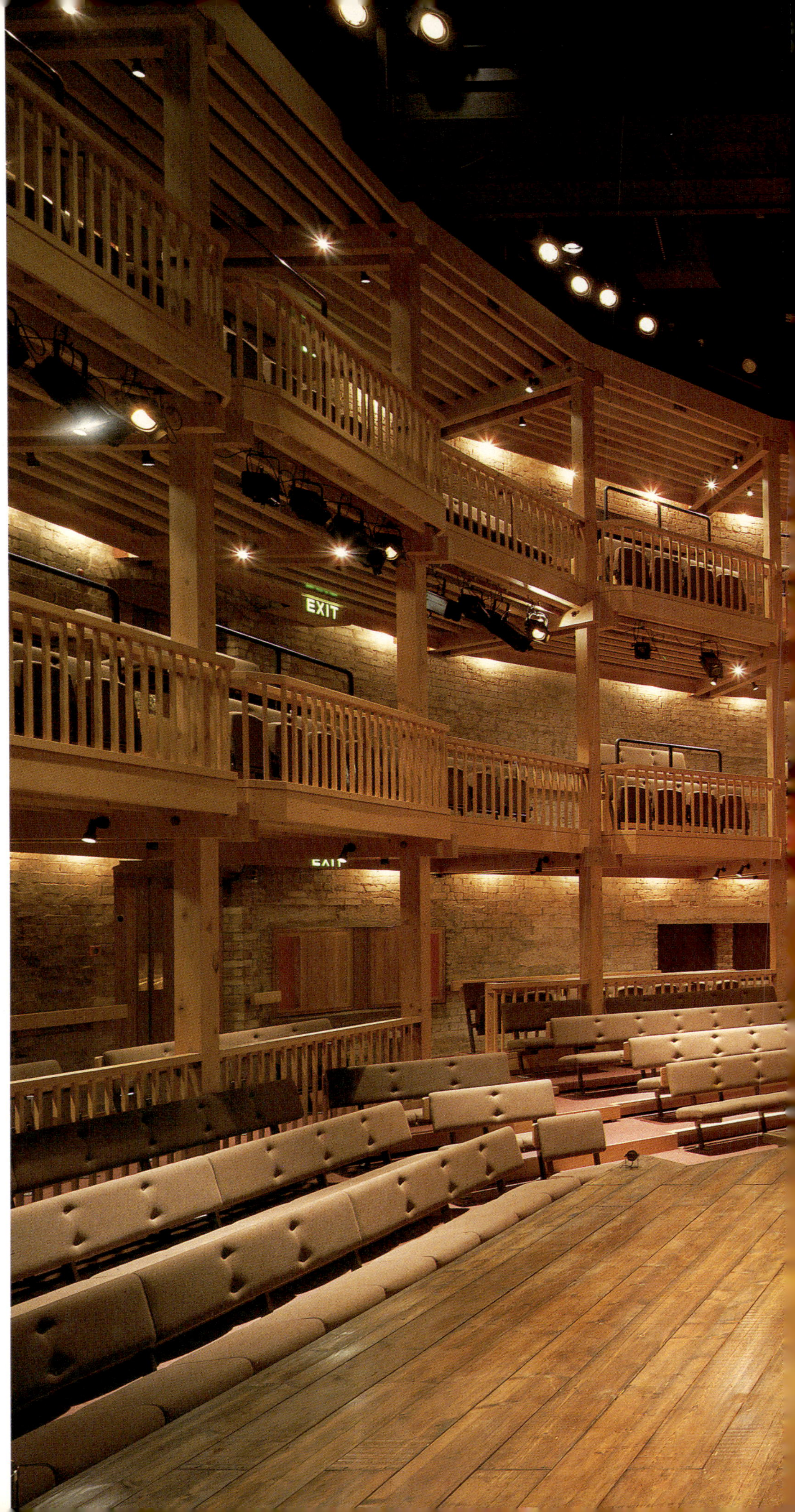

Three tiers of galleries surround the simple trapped stage. The light-coloured Douglas fir gives the theatre a warm, natural atmosphere.

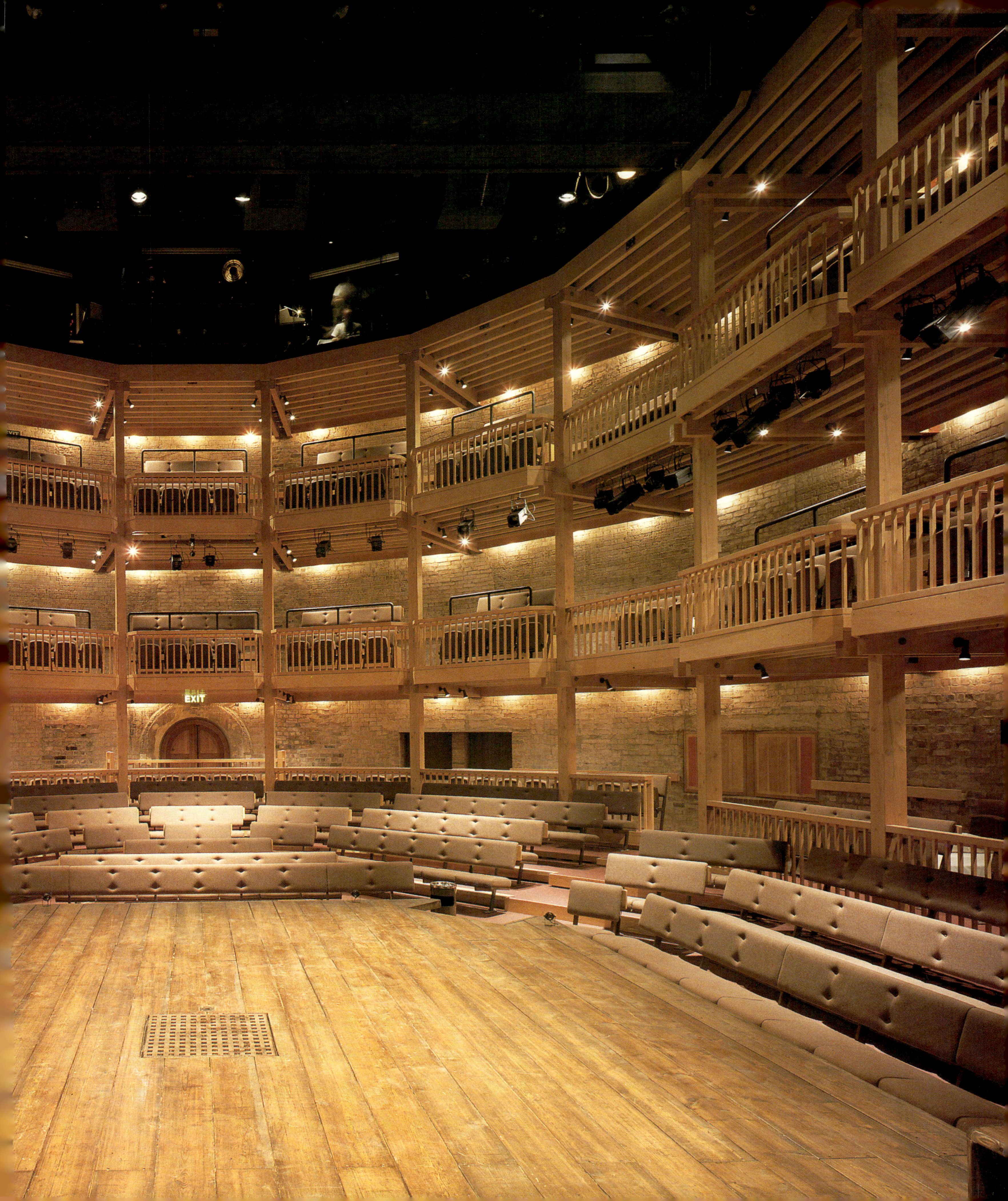
EXIT

FREUD
LONDON, UK

Designed by Basil Smith

Most interiors fit into neat categories: store, restaurant, office, hotel. But Freud is an odd mixture, both furniture store and café-bar. On the ground floor is a store that is rather odd itself, selling a strange collection of Charles Rennie Mackintosh chairs and tables, electric fans from India, and a few pieces of furniture by young English designer Jasper Startup. Downstairs in the basement is the café, which rapidly became one of the trendiest hang-outs in London, due in no small part to its rough, minimalist appearance.

Freud's Shaftesbury Avenue site originally housed a tiny Italian coffee-bar, and the first step in the project was to strip away what was left. Fortunately, behind the polystyrene tiles were a number of interesting elements, notably some cast-iron columns and a skylight. Designer Basil Smith, who had never built a project before Freud, squeezed the most out of every detail in the scheme. Materials are treated almost lovingly, with clever juxtapositions of different-coloured slates against cement, stone and steel. Steel panels in the store have acquired the patina of age after being immersed in salt water and then varnished. A sand, cement and Unibond mix is used for the not-quite-smooth cement walls. Shelves are of the same mixture.

For the basement café it was necessary to dig down nearly one metre into the foundations to achieve the desired height of the room. A York stone sill runs around the edge of the café and serves as a bench (black Bakelite telephones, one to a table, rest on this surface). All of the café furniture (mostly in metal) was designed by Smith and Startup, and, needless to say, is for sale in the store above.

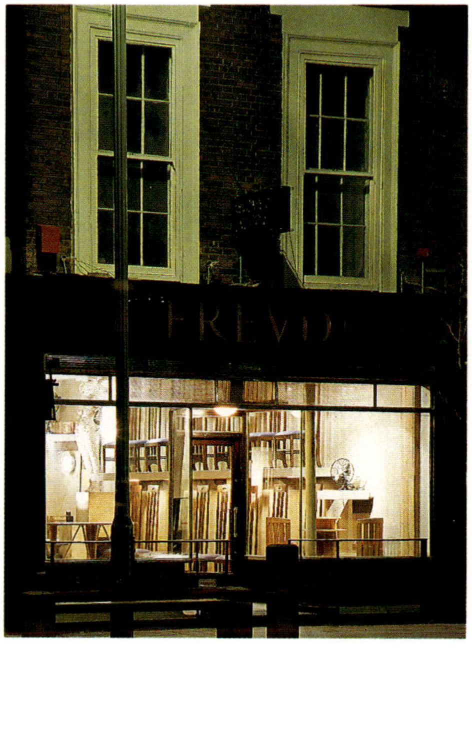

(right) Freud was previously an Italian coffee-bar; its odd combination of Mackintosh furniture and Indian electric fans can be glimpsed from the outside.

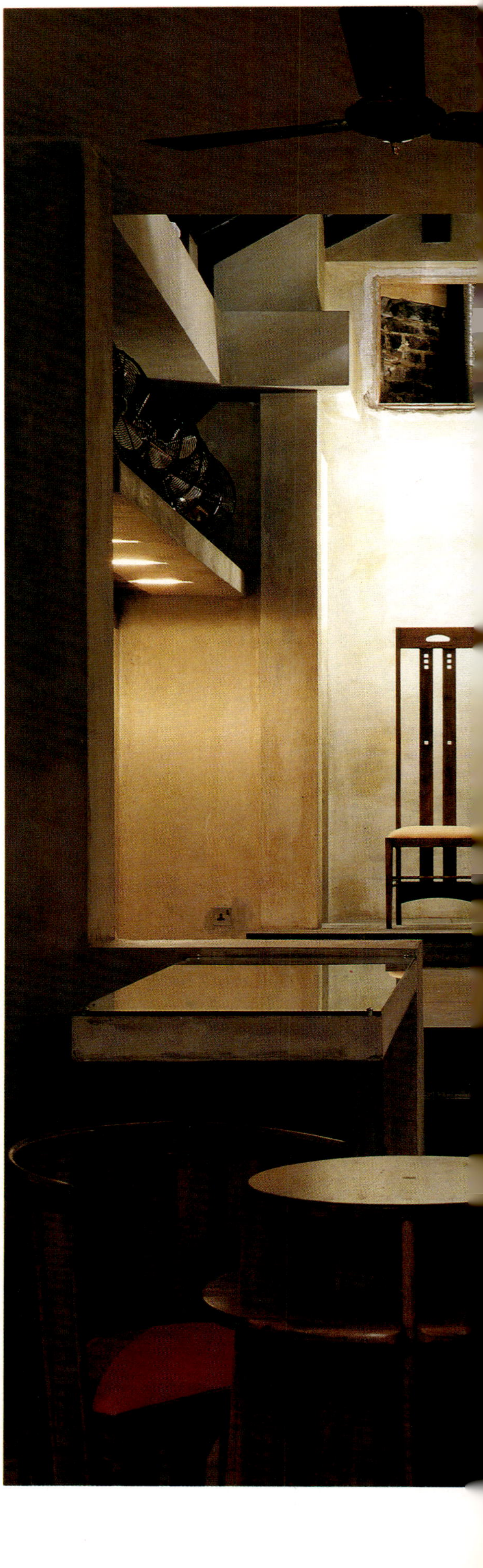

(far right) The non-structural caryatid, by artist Tim Southall, mimics the iron columns. The not-quite-smooth walls are made with a sand, cement and Unibond mix.

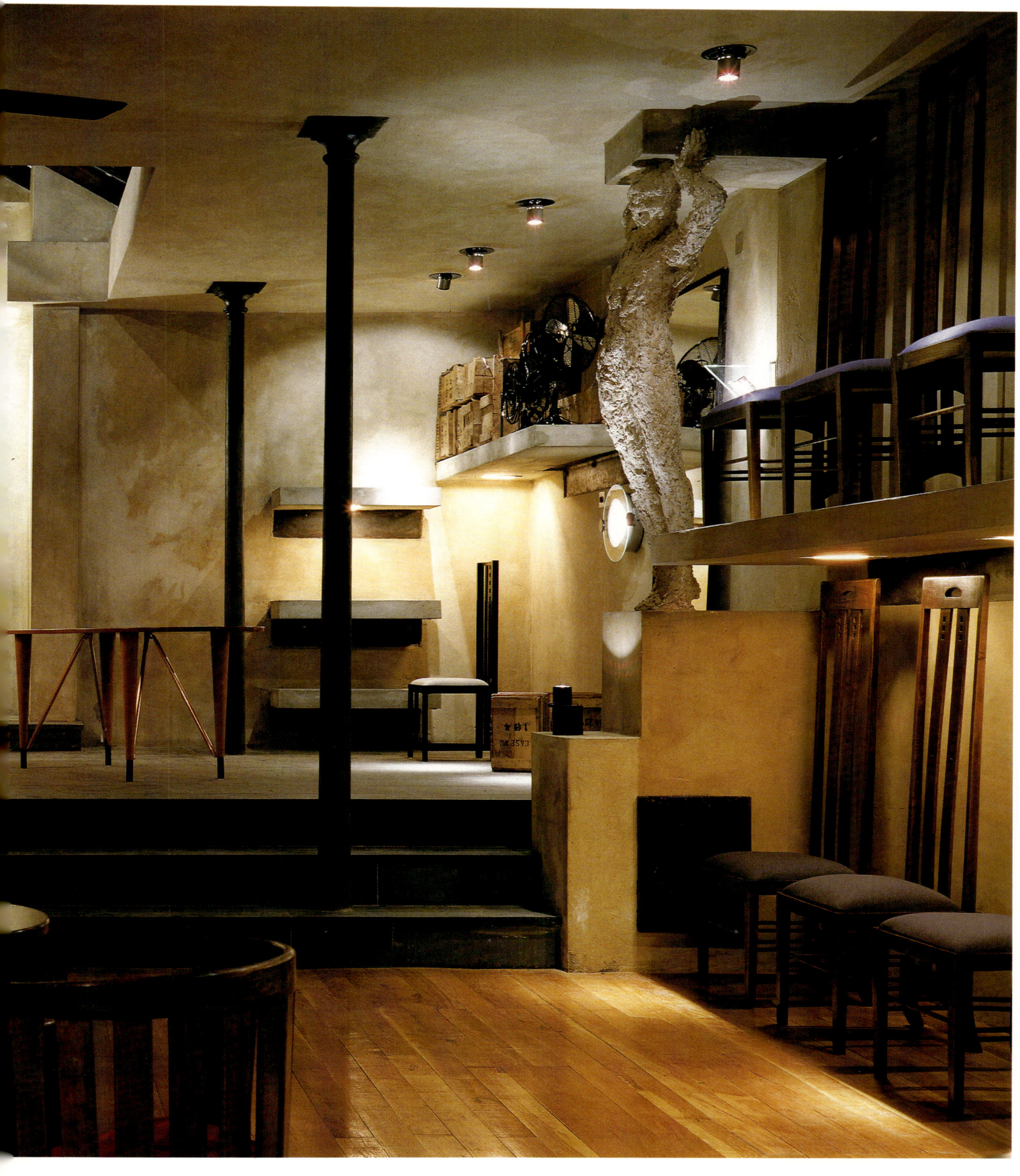

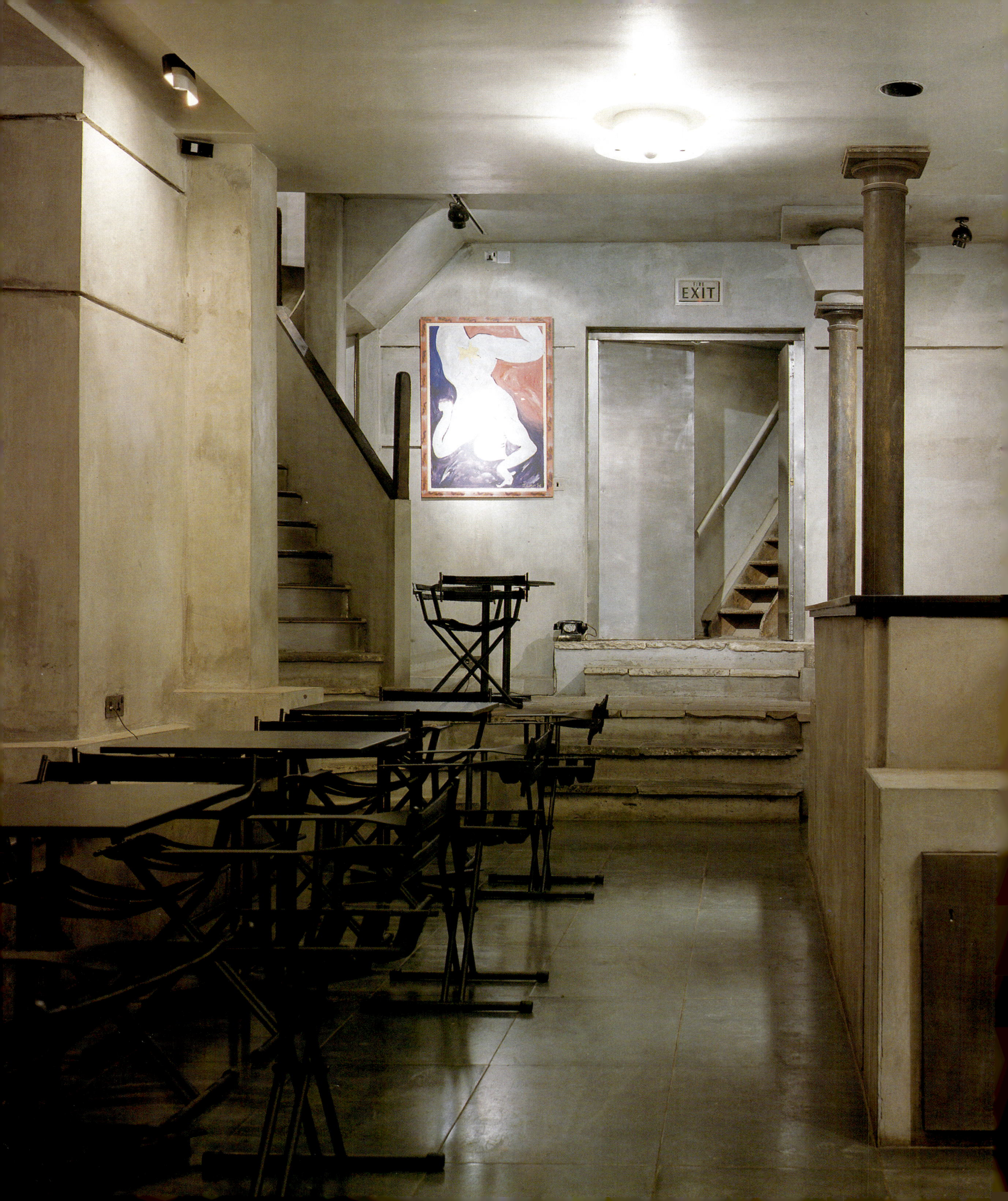
FIRE
EXIT

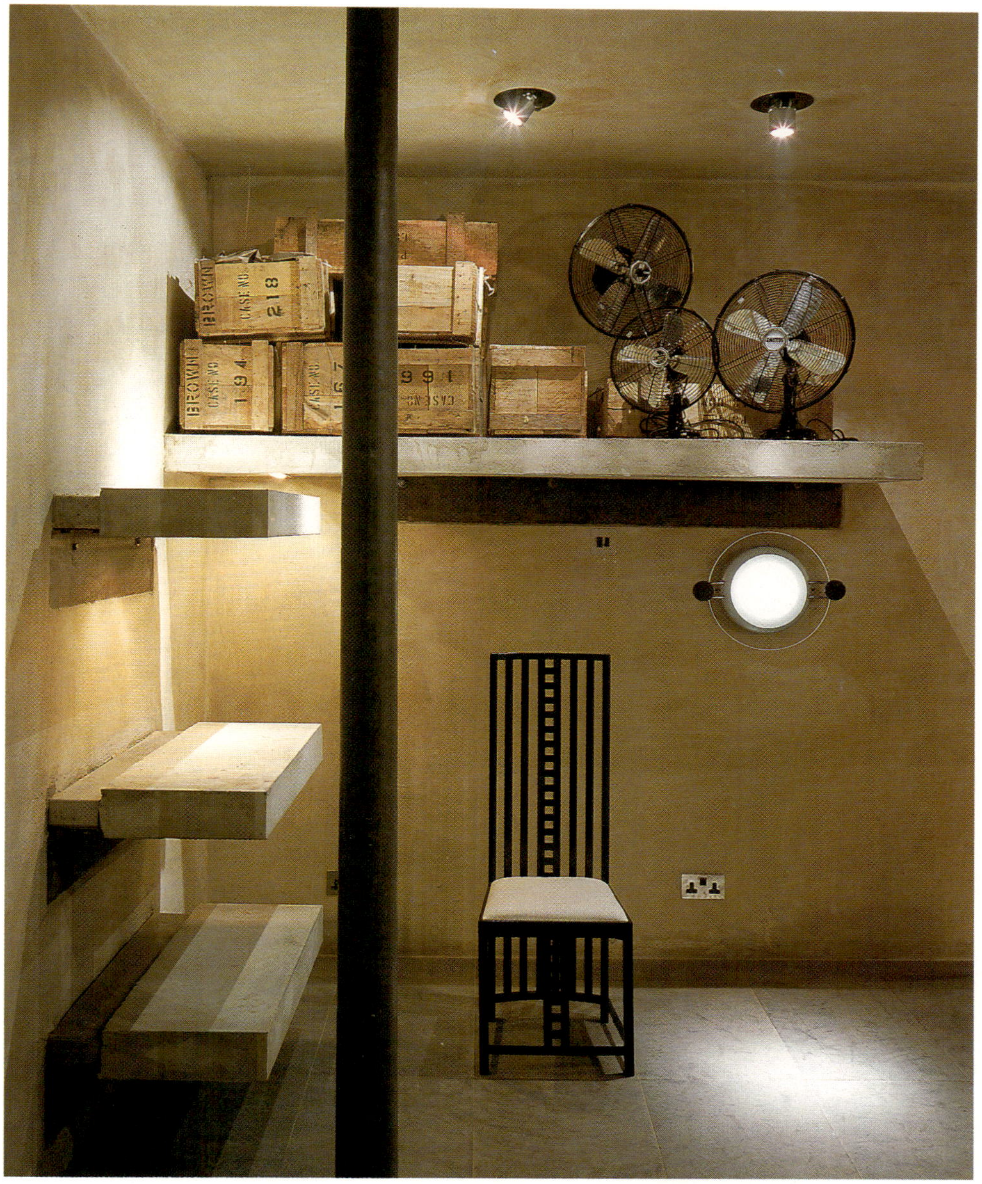

The details are the most successful aspect of Freud. One of the cast-iron columns is topped by a new capital of a ball and inverted pyramid – derived from Borromini, according to Smith. Harshly etched into the cement walls of the café is a picture rail; the rough York stone floors provide a contrast to the sharp-edged lines elsewhere. Most curious of all in this mixture of modern minimalism and erudite architectural reference is the store's caryatid, made by artist Tim Southall, mimicking the supporting role of the iron columns. The caryatid is not, in fact, structural, but then nothing is as it seems at Freud.

(above) Cantilevered shelves for display are of the same sand, cement and Unibond mix as the walls.

(left) In the downstairs café, rough York stone is used for floors and for a sill, which serves as a bench.

BIOGRAPHIES OF DESIGNERS

NOTE: Numbers in brackets following entries refer to page numbers.

WILLIAM ADAMS is an architect with his own practice based in Santa Monica, California. He is also an Associate Professor at Architecture Pomona, California. (10–13)

EMILIO AMBASZ studied at Princeton University where he received a Master's degree in architecture. He served as Curator of Design at New York's Museum of Modern Art from 1970 to 1976. Ambasz's many architectural projects include the Museum of Folk Art in New York City and the Houston Center Plaza. He also holds a number of industrial and mechanical design patents and is the chief design consultant for the Cummins Engine Company. (14–17)

RON ARAD studied at the Jerusalem Academy of Art between 1971 and 1973. He later moved to London and studied at the Architectural Association until 1979. Following two years in architectural practice, he founded his own London-based company, One Off, in 1981. One Off is best known for its designs of furniture. Recent exhibitions include 'Rare Horns, Endangered Forms' in Milan, and 'Subject Matter' in London. (18–19)

KEN ARMSTRONG trained at the Architectural Association in London and later worked for both Richard Rogers and Norman Foster. He founded Armstrong Chipperfield Associates in 1984 and has since established his own practice in London. (138–9)

BENTLEY LAROSA SALASKY is a New York-based architectural practice. (146–7)

LARRY CHAN and ALEX KRIEGER are principals in Chan. Krieger. Levi Architects with offices in Cambridge, Massachusetts and Chevy Chase, Maryland. (230–1)

SHI YU CHEN is president of Creative Intelligence Associates. Previously he worked as consultant to World Co. Ltd, as research and development director of Alpha Cubic Co. Ltd, as president of Alpha Cubic International Inc., and as chief director of Kansai Super Studio. (54–9)

DAVID CHIPPERFIELD trained at the Architectural Association in London and later worked for Richard Rogers Partnership and Foster Associates. In 1984, he founded Armstrong Chipperfield Associates and later established his own practice, Chipperfield Associates. (140–1)

NIGEL COATES studied architecture at Nottingham University and at the Architectural Association, where he has been teaching since 1976. With Doug Branson, he formed Branson Coates Architecture in 1985. Coates was a founding member of NATO (Narrative Architecture Today). He also designs his own range of furniture, which is manufactured in Japan by Rockstone. (54–9)

DEGW is a London-based architectural practice specializing in office developments and design issues involving the workplace. Founded by Francis Duffy, Peter Eley, Luigi Giffone and John Worthington, DEGW now has offices in Milan, Glasgow and Mexico City, in addition to their London base. (8–9, 20–3)

DE BLACAM and MEAGHER is a Dublin-based architectural practice. (222–5)

MAX and KARL DUDLER are German architects, with offices in Berlin, Frankfurt and Zurich, who have completed numerous projects in many cities of West Germany and Switzerland. (60–1, 144–5)

JOSEPH PAUL D'URSO is one of America's leading designers, having been responsible for numerous showrooms, restaurants and private home and office schemes, including stores for Esprit in Los Angeles and the 1 Club in Hong Kong. (146–7)

FAULKNER BROWNS is an architectural and design practice based in Newcastle upon Tyne, which has established an innovative reputation in the design of sports and recreation centres. (226–9)

FITCH & CO. is one of Europe's largest design companies, with divisions active in retail, product, graphic, leisure and office design. (148–53)

NORMAN FOSTER is one of the world's leading architects, well known for his highly refined, 'high-tech' approach to design. Among his best-known projects are the headquarters of the Hongkong and Shanghai Banking Corporation, the Sainsbury Centre for the Visual Arts, the headquarters of Willis Faber Dumas and the Renault Distribution Centre. Since 1969 he has worked independently as Foster Associates. (154–7)

GRAHAME FOWLER studied at West Sussex College of Art & Design and at the Royal College of Art before establishing Timney-Fowler, which is best known for its fashion and furniture fabrics. (128–9)

DANI FREIXES is an architect based in Barcelona, having trained at Barcelona's Higher College of Technology. He works in partnership with Vincente Miranda. (62–5)

FRANK GEHRY is one of the world's leading architects, having established his reputation with – among others – the design of his own house in Santa Monica. His unique assemblage of *objets trouvées* and twisted geometries, and his distinct sense of architectural humour led to a series of projects that have included Los Angeles' Temporary Contemporary Museum of Art, the Cabrillo Marine Museum, Loyola School of Law and numerous private houses. (52–3, 66–9)

MILTON GLASER studied at Cooper Union from 1948 to 1952. With Seymour Chwast, he founded Push Pin Studios in 1954. In 1968, with editor Clay Felker, he launched *New York Magazine*, and was president and design director until 1977. Among his numerous magazine designs are *The Village Voice*, *Cue*, *L'Express* and *Paris Match*. His output now includes interiors as well as a constant stream of graphic design. (70–1)

VITTORIO GREGOTTI has been one of Italy's leading architects since the 1950s. He founded the Milan-based Gregotti Associati in 1974 with partners Augusto Cagnardi and Pierluigi Cerri to work in architecture, urban planning and graphic design. (158–61)

TOM GRONDONA is an architect based in San Diego, who often explores the dividing line between architecture and art. (72–7)

ROBERT L. HARPER has been a partner of Centerbrook Architects since 1975. He has been teaching for twelve years as a visiting critic at the Rhode Island School of Design and Yale University. He and Centerbrook have received several awards, including an AIA honour award for Jones Laboratory at Cold Spring Harbor and a Massachusetts Governors Design Award for the Williams College project. (218–21)

TRIX and ROBERT HAUSSMANN are architects based in Zurich, and have practised together since 1967. Robert Haussmann studied in Zurich and Amsterdam and has taught at the Swiss Institute of Technology and at the Stuttgart Academy of Art. Trix Haussmann studied at the Swiss Institute of Technology, graduating in 1963. (78–81)

BIOGRAPHIES

COOP HIMMELBLAU is a Vienna-based group, founded in 1968 by Wolf Prix and H. Swiczinsky. Past projects include the Reiss Bar and the Angel Bar in Vienna, and shoe stores for Humanic. Their book, which explains their design philosophy, is entitled *Architecture is Now*. (24–7, 142–3)

STEVEN HOLL studied architecture at the University of Washington and at the Architectural Association in London. In 1970 he studied in Rome and worked for Astra Zarina. From 1972 to 1975 he worked for various San Francisco firms including Lawrence Halprin Landscape Architects, before moving to New York City to establish his own practice. Since 1981 he has been Associate Professor of Architecture at Columbia University. (136–7, 162–5)

NAOKI IIJIMA graduated from Musashino Art College in 1972. He joined Superpotato Design Studio in 1976 and established his own practice, Naoki Iijima Design Studio, in 1985. (82–3, 166–7)

TOYO ITO studied architecture at Tokyo University. Between 1965 and 1969 he worked with Kiyonori Kikutake and Associates, and in 1971 founded URBOT, which became Toyo Ito & Associates eight years later. The practice was awarded the Japan Architects Association's Annual Award in 1984, and was given the Japan Institute of Architects Award. (84–7)

EVA JIRICNA was born and educated in Czechoslovakia. She settled in England in 1968 and worked with Louis de Soissons, Norman Foster and Richard Rogers before founding her own practice with Kathy Kerr. They have worked on a number of domestic and commercial interiors in London, notably Way-In at Harrods. (88–91)

SETSUO KITAOKA, born in 1946, has his own design practice in Tokyo. In addition to designing interiors, he is an active furniture and lighting designer. (168–71)

YASUO KONDO graduated from the interior design department of Tokyo University of Art and Design in 1972. He joined Masahiro Miwa Environmental and, in 1977, moved to Kuramata Design. Kondo founded his own practice in 1981. (172–5)

SHIRO KURAMATA, born in Tokyo in 1934, studied at Tokyo College of Art and at the Kuwasawa Institute of Design. He founded his own practice in 1976. In addition to interiors, he is an active furniture designer. Kuramata Design was awarded the Mainichi Industrial Design Prize in 1972, and the Japan Cultural Design Prize in 1981. (176–9)

LEERS, WEINZAPFEL ASSOCIATES, ARCHITECTS, INC. was founded in 1970 in Boston, Massachusetts, and is headed by Andrea Leers and Jane Weinzapfel. Leers is a critic in architectural design at Yale University Graduate School of Architecture. Weinzapfel has taught at the Massachusetts Institute of Technology. (230–1)

LEO DESIGN is headed by Leo Mitrunen, who was born in Canada and studied architecture in Halifax, Nova Scotia. He worked in Costa Rica and Vienna before moving to Helsinki where he established the practice in 1985. (28–9, 180–3)

PETER LEONARD studied at Kingston Polytechnic and the Royal College of Art. He founded his own practice, Peter Leonard Associates, in 1983. Leonard specializes in retail design, but has also completed a number of office projects and has established a furniture company, Soho Design. (184–7)

DIANE LEWIS studied architecture at Cooper Union. She won the Rome Prize in Architecture, American Academy in Rome, 1976–77, and went on to work in the offices of Richard Meier and I. M. Pei & Partners. She has been Associate Professor of Architecture at Cooper Union since 1982, and established her practice with Peter Mickle in 1983. (232–5)

MARK MACK was born in 1949 in Judenburg, Austria, and studied in Graz and Vienna. Following his 1973 graduation from the Academy of Fine Arts, Vienna, he moved to New York and worked with Emilio Ambasz.

He later moved to the San Francisco area where he formed a partnership with Andrew Batey in 1978, and then in 1984 his own practice. (30–1)

FUMIHIKO MAKI is one of Japan's leading architects. Born in Tokyo in 1928, he studied at the University of Tokyo, Cranbrook Academy of Art and at Harvard University's Graduate School of Design. He worked for Skidmore, Owings & Merrill and Josep Lluis Sert in the United States before returning to Japan to establish his own practice. Among his major works are the 1968 Kumagaya campus at Risho University, the 1972 Kato School, the Tokyo Kuragaike Memorial Center in 1974 and the library at Keio University in 1981. (236–7)

McDONOUGH NOURI RAINEY is a New York-based architectural practice. (92–7)

PETER MICKLE studied architecture at Columbia University. Before joining Diane Lewis to establish their architectural practice in 1983, he worked with Araldo Cossutta & Associates and Skidmore, Owings and Merrill. (232–5)

VINCENTE MIRANDA is an architect based in Barcelona, having trained at Barcelona's Higher College of Technology. He works in partnership with Dani Freixes. (62–5)

LEO MITRUNEN was born in Canada and studied architecture in Halifax, Nova Scotia. He worked in Costa Rica and Vienna, before moving to Helsinki where he established his own practice in 1985. (28–9, 180–3)

CHARLES W. MOORE is a consultant to Connecticut-based Centerbrook Architects, and a partner in the California firm of Moore Ruble Yudell. He is in private practice in Austin, Texas. Moore is head of the architectural programme at the University of Texas, Austin. He has won many major architectural awards. (218–21)

MASAKI MORITA was born in 1950. He graduated from the Kuwasawa Design Institute in 1975. In addition to designing interiors, he is an active furniture designer. Recent work includes a number of projects for the French furniture company Tribu. (188–9)

MORPHOSIS is a Los Angeles-based architectural practice, headed by Thom Mayne and Michael Rotondi. Mayne studied at the University of Southern California and at Harvard University's Graduate School of Design. Rotondi studied at the Southern California Institute of Architecture. (98–103)

GABRIEL ORDEIG is an architect based in Barcelona, having trained at London's Architectural Association. (104–7)

JAMES STEWART POLSHEK and PARTNERS was founded in 1963. The major projects of this New York-based architectural practice include the Riverside Convention Center, Rochester, New York, 500 Park Tower, New York City, and Stroh River Place, Detroit, Michigan. (238–9)

MICHAEL REARDON is an English architect who specializes in the repair and adaptation of historic buildings. Reardon is architect for two cathedrals, was responsible for the Riverside Studios in Hammersmith, London and works regularly for the National Trust. (216–17, 240–3)

RICHARD ROGERS PARTNERSHIP is one of the leading exponents of the 'high-tech' style of architecture today. Richard Rogers and his partners shot to fame with their competition-winning project for the Centre Pompidou, the 'Beaubourg', built with Italian architect Renzo Piano. In addition to the Lloyd's building, recent projects include PA Technology, Princeton, New Jersey and Inmos, Newport, Wales. (32–7)

DENIS SANTACHIARA was born in Italy in 1951. He is a self-taught designer, and began working in the car industry designing car bodies in Modena. He participated in the 1983 Milan Triennale with his Dream House project. Since then he has produced numerous designs for furniture as well as interiors that blur the distinctions between art and design. (108–11)

SCHWARTZ/SILVER was founded by Warren Schwartz and Robert Silver in Boston in 1980, but the pair had worked together since 1974. Among Schwartz/Silver's projects are the student centre for Emerson College and a $15 million renovation of the Colonnade Hotel, Boston. (190–1)

SKIDMORE, OWINGS & MERRILL, founded in 1936, is the world's largest architectural and design practice. Its reputation was secured largely in the 1950s and 1960s when SOM established the American corporate style with a series of skyscraper office towers in Chicago, New York, Boston, San Francisco and most other cities of North America. Numerous large- and small-scale projects include offices, banks, hotels, airports, hospitals, commercial and industrial buildings. (38–9, 112–15)

BASIL SMITH, born in 1961, is a London-based architect. He was a runner-up in the 1985 Venice Biennale and joint winner of the 1985 Royal Institution of British Architects student award. (244–7)

ETTORE SOTTSASS Jr was born in Austria in 1917. He studied at the Milan Politecnico, and opened a design office in Milan in 1947. Since 1957 he has done design work for Olivetti, but is also active in fields as various as ceramics, jewellery, decorations, lithographs and drawing. In 1980 he established Sottsass Associati, and has designed many pieces of furniture for Memphis, which he was instrumental in creating. (192–207)

PHILIPPE STARCK was born in Paris in 1949 and works as a product, furniture and interior designer. His interiors include private apartments for President Mitterrand at the Elysée Palace, and the Café Costes in Paris. His furniture is made in Italy and Spain by a number of companies including Driade and Disform. (116–19)

STUDIOS San Francisco and Washington DC is a national architectural practice headed by Erik Sueberkrop, principal in charge, Martin Yardley, Darryl Roberson, Gene Rac and Phillip Olson. Among their projects have been numerous works for Apple Computer, a headquarters in Santa Clara, California for 3Com Corporation and headquarters for Morgan Olmstead Kennedy & Gardner in Los Angeles. (40–3)

SUPERPOTATO DESIGN STUDIO was founded by Takashi Sugimoto in 1974. The practice has won a number of design awards, including the Japan Interior Design Committee Award in 1984.(120–3)

SHIN TAKAMATSU graduated from the school of architecture of Kyoto University in 1971. He worked at Kiyosi Kawasaki until 1975, and completed a doctorate at Kyoto University in 1980, following which he founded his own practice in Kyoto.(124–7)

STANLEY TIGERMAN was born in 1930, and studied architecture at Yale University. He was one of the organizers of the 'Chicago Seven' group of architects and is now a principal in Tigerman Fugman McCurry in Chicago. Tigerman has won numerous architectural and design awards and has exhibited his work widely, in the States and abroad.(208–11)

TILTON+LEWIS is a Chicago-based design firm, founded in 1973. Specializing in interior office planning, Tilton+Lewis have completed projects for IBM, Manufacturers Hanover Trust and the United Bank of Illinois.(44–7)

SUE TIMNEY studied at Edinburgh University and the Royal College of Art, before establishing Timney-Fowler, which is best known for its fashion and furniture fabrics.(128–9)

SVEIN TØNSAGER is a Danish architect with his own practice based in Århus, Denmark.(130–3)

SHIGERU UCHIDA graduated from Kuwazawa Design School in 1966, and four years later established his own practice. In 1981 he founded Studio 80 with Toru Nishioka and Ikuyo Mitsuhashi. In the same year Uchida won the Japan Interior Designers Association Award. In 1982, he opened his own furniture showroom, Chairs.(134–5)

MASANORI UMEDA graduated from the Kuwasawa Design Institute in 1962. From 1966 to 1969, he worked in the Castiglioni studios in Milan. Umeda won the Braun Prize in Germany in 1968, and was design consultant for Olivetti between 1970 and 1979. He founded his own practice in Tokyo in 1979. Umeda has also worked with the Memphis group.(212–15)

LELLA and MASSIMO VIGNELLI studied in Venice, Italy, and in 1960 established the Massimo and Lella Vignelli Office of Design and Architecture in Milan, working with graphics, products, furniture and interiors. In 1965 they founded Unimark International Corporation, and, in 1971, Vignelli Associates, with an office in New York and associate offices in Paris and Milan. (*frontispiece*, 48–51)

PRODUCT SUPPLIERS

The list below gives addresses worldwide of the suppliers of mass-manufactured products featured in the book.

Abet Laminati, Viale Industria 21, 12041 Bra (CN), Italy. *Outlets:* UK: Abet Ltd, Nicholas House, Riverfront, Enfield, Middlesex.

Ahrend, Groe BV, Postbus 70, 1000AB Amsterdam, Singels 130, Holland. *Outlets:* UK: Humber Contract Interiors, 43 Berners Street, London W1.

Alias SRL, Via Respighi 2, 20122 Milan, Italy. *Outlets:* UK: Artemide GB Ltd, 17–19 Neal Street, London WC2H 9PU. USA: ICF, 305 East 63rd Street, New York, NY 10021.

Atelier International Inc., 595 Madison Avenue, New York, NY 10022, USA. *Outlets:* Italy: Cassina SPA, PO Box 102, 20036 Meda, Milan.

Bieffeplast SPA, Via Pelosa 78, 35030 Caselle di Selvazzano, Padova, Italy. *Outlets:* USA: Gullans International Inc., 227 West 17th Street, New York, NY 10011.

Driade SPA, Via Padana Inferiore 12, 29012 Fossadello di Caorso, Piacenza, Italy.

Erco Leuchten GMBH, PO Box 2460, 5880 Lüdenscheid, West Germany. *Outlets:* UK: Erco Lighting Ltd, 38 Dover Street, London W1X 3RB.

Flos SPA, Via Moretto 58, 25121 Brescia, Italy. *Outlets:* UK: Flos Ltd, Heath Hall, Heath, Wakefield, WA 5SL. USA: Atelier International, 235 Express, Plainview, New York.

Formica, Suite 1519, 1501 Broadway, New York, NY 10036, USA. *Outlets:* UK: Formica Ltd, Shearwater House, 21 The Green, Richmond, Surrey TW9 1PJ.

Freud, 198 Shaftesbury Avenue, London WC2, UK.

Fritz Hansens eft, Depotvej 1, DK-3450 Allerod, Denmark. *Outlets:* USA: Rudd International Corporation, 1025 Thomas Jefferson Street NW, Washington, DC 20007. UK: Scott Howard Furniture, 32 Broadwick Street, London W1V 1FG.

Herman Miller Inc., 8500 Byron Road, Zeeland, Michigan 49464, USA. *Outlets:* UK: Herman Miller Ltd, Lower Bristol Road, Bath BA2 3ER.

Kartell SPA, Viale delle Industrie 1, 20082, Noviglio, Milan, Italy. *Outlets:* UK: Ideas for Living, Lin Pac Mouldings, 5 Kensington High Street, London W8 5NP. USA: Kartell USA, PO Box 1000, Easley, SC 29640.

Knoll International, The Knoll Building, 655 Madison Avenue, New York, NY 10021, USA.

Lightolier Inc., 346 Claremont Avenue, Jersey City, New Jersey 07305. *Outlets:* U.K.: Concord Lighting Ltd, 241 City Road, London EC1V 1JD.

Marcatre, Via Sant'Andrea 3, 20020 Misinto, Milan, Italy. *Outlets:* UK: Marcatre, 179–99 Shaftesbury Avenue, London WC2H 8AR. USA: Atelier International, 595 Madison Avenue, New York, NY 10022.

Memphis SRL, Via Olivetti 7, 20010 Pregnana Milanese, Milan, Italy. *Outlets:* UK: Artemide GB Ltd, 17–19 Neal Street, London WC2H 9PU. USA: Memphis Milano, International Design Center, Center One, Space 525, 30 Thomson Avenue, LIC, New York, NY 11101.

OMK Design, Stephen Building, Stephen Street, London W1, UK.

One-Off, 56 Neal Street, London WC2, UK.

Steelcase, 1120 36th Street SE, Grand Rapids, Michigan 49501, USA.

Sunar Hauserman, 5711 Grant Avenue, Cleveland, Ohio 44105, USA. *Outlets:* UK: Sunar Ltd, 41–43 Chalton Street, London NW1 1JE.

Tecno SPA, Via Bigli 22, 20121 Milan, Italy. *Outlets:* UK: Tecno (UK) Ltd, 19 New Bond Street, London W1.

Vitra International AG, 15 Henri Petri Strasse, Postfach 257, CH-4010, Basel, Switzerland.

Ward Bennett, 515 Madison Avenue, New York, NY 10022, USA.

Zeus, 8 Via Vigevano, 20144 Milan, Italy.

ACKNOWLEDGMENTS

The Publishers wish to thank Peter Popham and Ray Porfilio for their help in the research of Japanese and American projects respectively; the designers and architects featured for their co-operation; and the photographers whose pictures are reproduced here. All photographs in this book are copyright, and none should be reproduced without the prior permission of the Publishers. The following credits are given with thanks to the photographers whose images have been used (page numbers are given in brackets): Aldo Ballo (192–207); © Tom Bonner 1986 (100–1); copyright Richard Bryant (8–9, 20–3, 32–7, 88–91, 154–7, 184–7); Mario Carrieri (50–1); Lluis Casals (62–5); Peter Cook (148–53, 222–5); Mitsumasa Fujitsuka (84–7); © Eduardo Firpi (104–7); Alfred Hablötzel, Wil (78–81); Edward V. Hames (54–9); Hiroyuki Hirai (172–9); © Wolfgang Hoyt/Esto Photographics Inc. (112–15); Ernst Kallesøe (130–3); copyright © 1987 Karant & Associates, Inc. (44–7, 208–11); Masanori Kato (128–9); Toshiharu Kitajima (236–7); Hiroshi Kobysahi (126); © Waltraud Krase (60–1); photographs © Nathaniel Lieberman (92–7. except below, page 97); Hitsuo Manno (124–5, 127); Paavo Martikainen (28–9, 180–3); © Peter Mauss/Esto Photographics Inc. (70–1); Shiochi Muto (18–19); T. Nacása & Partners (188–9, page 135, right); Cervin Robinson (238–9); Steve Rosenthal (190–1, 218–21); Yoshio Shiratori (82–3, 120–3, 134–5, except right, page 135, 168–71, 212–21); Tim Street-Porter (10–13, 30–1, 52–3, 66–9, 98–9, 102–3); Yoshio Takase (116–19); Masao Ueda (below, page 97); Luca Vignelli (frontispiece, 48–9); copyright © Paul Warchol (14–17, 136–7, 146–7, 162–5, 40–3); Nick Wheeler (38–9); Miro Zagnoli (108–11); Zoom-Yoshio Shiratori (120–3); Gerald Zugmann (24–7, 142–3).